University of the Philippines

The First 75 Years

(1908-1983)

A DIAMOND JUBILEE PUBLICATION

Oscar M. Alfonso
Editor

Leslie E. Bauzon Napoleon J. Casambre
Rosario Mendoza Cortes Bernardita Reyes Churchill
Jose N. Endriga Silvino V. Epistola Oscar L. Evangelista
Milagros C. Guerrero Guillermo R. Lazaro
Bonifacio S. Salamanca Donata V. Taylo
Contributors

Raul R. Ingles
Executive Editor

University of the Philippines Press
Quezon City, 1985

International Standard Book Number
(ISBN) : 971-105-018-8

First Printing: June 1985

Printed in the Philippines by the
University of the Philippines Press,
Diliman, Quezon City

University of the Philippines

THE FIRST 75 YEARS

" This is the University—an institution
greater than any single truth. Not the embodiment
of one truth, but an invitation to find
truth's manifold face in history. . . ."

—Edgardo J. Angara

Preface

The writing of history, whether that of a nation or an institution, is a laborious task. The burden eases somewhat when the historian has a strong affinity with his subject such that he is endowed with the insight to pick out the significant facts and make of them a coherent and vibrant narrative as close as possible to the truth. But the burden increases in the effort to be impartial, the closer the historian to his subject both in time and place.

A panel of eleven, all drawn from the ranks of the faculty of the University of the Philippines, eight of them professionally identified with and three close to the discipline of history, undertook the writing of *The First 75 Years*. Each was assigned to cover a historical phase, corresponding for convenience of reference to the term of each University president, from the first to the latest, from Murray Bartlett to Edgardo J. Angara. The result is this book, historically the first of this magnitude to come out of salutary collaboration among several of the faculty of the UP Department of History (nine including the editor).

For coherence, the panel agreed upon preset guidelines. The development of the University of the Philippines as a Filipino university was made each writer's overall and principal concern: "development" to include growth in terms of enrolment, number and quality of faculty (including faculty development), academic programs, graduates and buildings; and "Filipino university" being taken to mean the Filipinization of the UP's presidency, the Board of Regents and the faculties, but also and more importantly of its philosophy and orientation including curricular programs. In sum, how the UP grew in size and stature in filling the nation's needs. And how, in the process, movements and commovements for faculty participation in decision-making, for unit autonomy and for greater student say became a concomitant of growth.

But the story would also be that of UP making its way in the world of scholarship, as a continuing concern from administration to administration.

The focus would be on the administration of each president, not on the presidents themselves *per se*, though something on each president as a person, or as a scholar, would be apt. So also something on the essence of each presidential leadership, and on the major or peculiar problems that confronted it. And how did the President's performance measure up against the enounced goals?

Several of this book's writers may appear to have concentrated overmuch on the presidents themselves. But this seems unavoidable. The fact is that the history of the University of the Philippines exemplifies in many cases how one man alone can make such a great difference in the direction of events or the production of results. Without necessarily falling latter-day prey to the late unlamented great man theory of history ("History is but the biography of great men"), our writers essay to show how this or that President made the difference. Hence, the protracted discussion of issues or controversies in some chapters, unabridged for that reason and because the issue or controversy involved some important principle for the University or its constituents. In this the editors deferred to the writers' sense of proportion, while leaving them entirely to their own judgment of persons and events in every case without editorial intervention.

All these, in no more than 50-60 typewritten pages per chapter, double-spaced, because of which, obviously, no chapter is or could be a full-blown history of the administration covered by it. The extended treatment of each president's administration in all its aspects, including his biography in detail, awaits the interested student of history with proclivity both to research and a particular president. Notably not much in evidence here, for example, because needing much further work and deserving of fuller coverage in order to do them justice beyond the capacity of this book, lengthy as it already is, are the individual achievements of numerous alumni, including many of the faculty. Prof. Justina S. Ocampo of the UP Department of History has fortunately done much in that regard. Her work when expanded and then published, perhaps soon and hopefully by the UP Alumni Association, would be an important companion volume to this one.

This book comes off the press in June 1985, two years after the UP Diamond Jubilee it is supposed to commemorate. The lesson is that when you have more than three supposed to be collaborating, one or even two could "gum up" the work. Thus, it turned out to be seemingly interminable waiting, particularly for the other nine writers, who did their part of the work splendidly on time and therefore had much reason to fret over the delay. The delay is a proper charge laid at the door of the Editor, whose function and responsibility it was as Director of the UP History Project to choose dependable as well as capable writers for the project. It is illustration anew of how the history of the University is filled with trial and agony as well as frustration with resources that never seem to measure up to the needs of an institution committed to academic excellence.

This work comes into being with the funding provided by both the Presidential Commission on the 1983 Diamond Jubilee of the University of the Philippines headed by Prime Minister Cesar E.A. Virata and from the University because of President Angara, whose unwavering support ensured the completion of the project.

Dr. Leslie E. Bauzon's authorship of two chapters, not just one, distinguishes his participation in this project. Not only did he have to rush the updating of the last chapter of this book within a very short time, bringing the text up to early June 1985, he also volunteered to do the index for free, finishing it within practically a few hours only.

Dr. Bauzon shares the largest measure of appreciation with his fellow authors, to whom this book owes its substantive merits: Professors Napoleon J. Casambre, Bernardita R. Churchill, Rosario M. Cortes, Jose N. Endriga, Silvino V. Epistola, Oscar L. Evangelista, Milagros C. Guerrero, Guillermo R. Lazaro, Bonifacio S. Salamanca, and Donata V. Taylo.

The book owes a great deal to Executive Editor Raul R. Ingles for his vast expertise and experience, a whole lot more for his carrying his load with alacrity and aplomb, but most of all for his abiding love for UP. Whatever faults in policy decisions there may have been, and in the final editing, are all the Editor's.

Mrs. Edwina K. Arroyo so graciously volunteered to do the art design of the book and its cover without remuneration, with felicitous results in the execution of the design despite being harried by time constraints.

Only the fullest and most active cooperation of Dr. Benjamin V. Lozare, Director of the U.P. Press and his staff and workers saw this book off the press in the shortest time possible. Also hereby acknowledged is the work done by the Main Library Staff, coordinated by Ms. Candida Sarmiento, in the compilation of the impressive historical data contained in the Appendices.

It was a laborious task accomplished not without tears, and to all who have made it possible—who stayed with us through the glimmering hours and the wasted months—let the birth of this book be cause for jubilation and a testament that our Alma Mater will surely endure with our common faith and persistence.

OSCAR M. ALFONSO
Editor

Executive House, U.P. Campus
Quezon City, Philippines
June 12, 1985

Contents

The First 75 Years

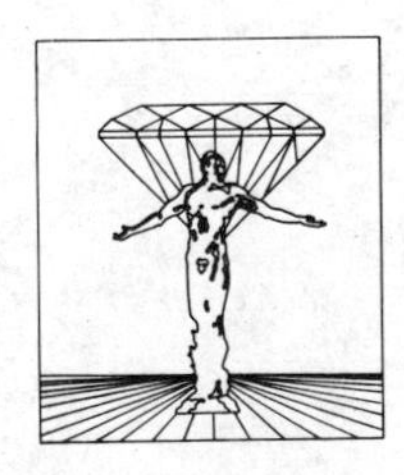

A Diamond Jubilee Publication
University of the Philippines

I

Bartlett as First President (1911-1915)

Laying the Foundation of the University

by Donata V. Taylo

Bartlett as First President

Higher Education within the First Decade of American Rule

THE beginning of higher or tertiary education in the Philippines under American rule may be traced to the decision of school authorities in 1904 to authorize the Philippine Normal School to offer "extrasecondary instruction" to students who did not intend to pursue a teaching career. In this connection the annual report (1907-1908) of David P. Barrows, Director of Education, said:

> [There was] . . . no other public school in the city of Manila [that] was affording such instruction, courses in preparation for different professions. [Thus, courses of these kind] have been opened from time to time. These include a course in preparation for medicine, a course in preparation for appointment as magistrate or for entrance to a law school, a course in preparation for admission to an engineering school, a secondary course in agriculture, a course in domestic science, and a course in preparation for nursing.[1] *

Emergent Needs for Professional Training

That there were existing needs for subjects other than those intended for students who would go into teaching was substantiated by the following information, also submitted by the aforementioned official source:

> . . . Of 334 secondary students enrolled July 23, 1908 only 60 are taking the course in teaching, 75 are preparing for medicine, 33 for law, 33 for engineering, 18 are taking the agricultural course, 17 domestic science, 41 are preparing for nursing, while 67 are taking the regular course in literature, science and industry.
>
> Other professions are appealing more strongly to students . . . than the profession of teaching . . .[2]

But as early as 1904, when instruction in the arts and sciences was started in the Philippine Normal School, David P. Barrows, then Super-

*Footnote references are compiled in the NOTES section at the end of this book.

intendent of Schools, was already articulating views in favor of the establishment of a university to meet the increasing demands for instruction in the higher levels of learning.

Barrows' annual report to the Secretary of Public Instruction of that year expressed concern over the "considerable number of young men, graduates of Spanish colleges in the Philippines, . . . of professional schools, who [were] desirous of taking up professional studies in medicine, law, engineering, or applied sciences." Although convinced that there was lack of funds, he suggested that lectures and seminars in the professional subjects be organized "to commence June 1905."

The establishment of a university, according to Barrows, would encourage and inspire the Filipino people in a very considerable degree. "It would," he emphasized, "moreover provide for the continuance of the system of public instruction beyond the primary and intermediate grades and the high schools to undergraduate and professional courses."[3]

Meantime, the first batch of graduates from the public high schools was being expected, as many of them were apparently set to proceed to college. The passage of Act No. 1870 was, therefore, in the order of things as it was meant to fill a very important need. To this effect *Bulletin No. 1* of the UP announced: "The University of the Philippines is thus the logical outgrowth and culmination of efforts made during the past ten years to establish a complete system of education for the Philippine Islands."[4]

Founding of the University

The Philippine Commission in its annual report of 1907 included a recommendation from W. Morgan Shuster, the Secretary of Public Instruction, for the establishment of a university in the Philippines to be located in Manila. Shuster himself drafted and submitted to the Philippine Commission in February 1908 what came to be known as the "Philippine University" bill or Commission Bill No. 33, "An Act for the purpose of founding a University of the Philippine Islands, giving it corporate existence, providing a board of regents, defining the board's responsibilities and duties, providing higher and professional instruction and for other purposes."

The First Philippine Legislature (as the two houses – the Philippine Commission and the First Philippine Assembly – were referred to in the *Journal of the Philippine Commission*) deliberated on and discussed the bill as one of the items in the agenda of its first (3 February 1908–21 May 1908) and special sessions (22 May 1908–19 June 1908). It finally became a law on June 18, 1908, subsequently enrolled and printed as Act No. 1870.[5]

Matters pertinent to the "Philippine University" and the Act proposing its establishment apparently made good newspaper copy.[6] Pronouncements by highly placed officials, as the one by Leon Ma. Guerrero, the Chairman of the Committee on Public Instruction, representative from Manila and formerly in the faculty of the Universidad Literaria, did not go unnoticed.[7]

Provisions of the University Charter

Section 1 of Act No. 1870 authorized the Governor General to establish the University of the Philippines "within the powers and limitations . . . specified," in the "city of Manila, or at a point he may deem most convenient."

The mission of the University and the general principle that would govern its admission policy were provided for in the next two sections. The Act stipulated that the University of the Philippines was to give "advanced instruction in literature, philosophy, the sciences and arts, and to give professional and technical training" to every qualified student irrespective "of age, sex, nationality, religious belief, or political affiliation."

Section 4 provided for the creation of the Board of Regents to serve as the highest governing body of the University. It also indicated the composition of the Board, to be as follows: "the Secretary of Public Instruction, the Director of Education, the Chairman of the Committee of Public Instruction of the Philippine Assembly, the president of the University, and five additional members to be appointed by the Governor General, by and with the advice and consent of the Philippine Commission."

According to the amendment introduced by Act 2024,[8] the composition of the Board increased with the inclusion of the Secretary of Interior and a member of the Supreme Court. This was upon the recommendation of the Board itself. It was of the view that the inclusion of the Secretary of Interior was necessary since his office supervised the scientific and research work of the government, which work would in fact be eventually turned over to the university. On the other hand, it was believed that the presence of a member of the Supreme Court in the Board would not only give dignity to the body but also provide it with a ready source of counsel and valuable advice. Besides it was an accepted practice in the United States to have a member of the judicial body in the boards of the state universities.

Section 4 also specified that the president of the University was to be elected and his compensation fixed by the Board of Regents. The designation of the president as "ex-officio chairman of the board" was likewise provided for, but Act 2024 reassigned the position to the Secretary of Public Instruction.

Aside from its general powers of administration and corporate powers, the Board of Regents had authority with regard to (1) the receipt and appropriation of "such sums as may be provided by law for the support of the university"; (2) the establishment of the colleges indicated in the Act (this was amended by Act 2024) as well as those that might be created by legislative fiat; (3) the conferment of honorary degrees; (4) the establishment of chairs; (5) the appointment of the faculty members and officers of the administration "on recommendation of the president of the university"; (6) the approval of the courses of study and rules of discipline drawn up by the University Council; and others.

The University Council

The creation of the University Council was provided for in Section 9, according to which the Council would be composed of "the president of the university and of all instructors in the university from the rank of assistant professor." The powers of the Council, accordingly, were enumerated, and these included the power to "prescribe the courses of study and rules of discipline . . . ," "fix the requirements for admission to any college of the university as well as for graduation and the receiving of a degree," and "recommend students or others to be recipients of degrees."

Concerning the faculty, Section 10 provided that "the body of instructors of each college shall constitute its faculty. . ." Its "presiding officer," as the dean is referred to according to the original provision, is to be "elected by the faculty to which he belongs." As amended by Act 2024 the provision says that the dean "shall be elected . . . from the members of such faculty by the board of regents on nomination by the president of the university."

Other important provisions having to do with the faculty pertain to the prohibition against practices involving religion as criterion for appointment and their exemption from the civil service examination as requisite to appointment.

The Board of Regents

The Charter designated the Board of Regents as the highest governing body of the University. It was originally composed of nine members – four government officials or ex-officio regents and five appointive members. Act 2024 increased the membership to eleven. To the previously designated list of ex-officio Regents, namely, the Secretary of Public Instruction, the President of the University, the Director of Education and the Chairman of the Committee on Public Instruction in the Philippine Assembly, were added the Secretary of Interior and a member of the Supreme Court.

The appointive members were recommended by the Governor General subject to the approval of the Philippine Commission; these were to serve for varying lengths of time. On October 12, 1908, except for one member, the Board was constituted. Trinidad Pardo de Tavera, Rafael Palma, Jose Rosales, and Enrique Mendiola were named Regents for a tenure of five, four, three, and two years, respectively.

Since the post of University President was still vacant, the position of ex-officio Chairman of the Board was assumed by then Secretary of Public Instruction, Vice-Governor Newton W. Gilbert. Like his predecessor, Morgan Shuster, Gilbert came to be prominently associated with the early years of the University. As Chairman of the Board, he convened that body for the first time on 6 March 1909 with the following as members: Dr. David P. Barrows, Director of Education; Honorable Leon Guerrero, Chairman of the Committee on Public Instruction of the Philippine Assembly; Commissioner Rafael Palma, Honorable Enrique Mendiola, Honorable T. H. Pardo de Tavera, and Honorable Jose Rosales.

The operationalization of the UP Charter thus began. The first Board meetings were devoted to discussions relative to the first colleges named in the Act. A committee of ways and means was created.

Searching for a Suitable Site

According to the UP Charter, the Governor General was to establish the University "in the city of Manila or at a point he might deem most convenient." At the executive session of the Philippine Commission of October 7, 1908, the matter was discussed in connection with the plan to establish an "educational center" in Manila. Earlier, Commissioner Benito Legarda offered 100,000 square meters of land in the district of Sta. Mesa for the University. Another place even more prominently mentioned was the Exposition grounds in Ermita. This was government property, where the Philippine General Hospital, the Philippine Medical School building and some other government buildings had already been erected.

But the decision reached at that meeting favored neither of the two places. The Legarda offer was not even discussed. Instead, it was agreed to reserve the Exposition grounds for "public purposes" and that immediate provision should be made to secure a proper educational center in the city of Manila. Another resolution at the same meeting said that "the tract of Insular property lying back of the present city hall in the City of Manila should be reserved as a site of the Philippine Normal School and for such other public educational purposes as may be decided upon by competent authority."[9]

But perhaps because that "tract of Insular property" was not big enough to provide room also for the University, negotiations for the purchase of a 10-hectare lot in due time were undertaken. The *Manila Times* of April 12, 1910 reported this transaction as "the biggest real estate deal in Manila since the American occupation," involving the sum of ₱206,000.

Located between Calle Isaac Peral and Padre Faura, "it extends westward to the bay as far as Calle San Antonio (now Maria Y. Orosa). On the north it is bounded by the Manila Protestant Cathedral and the Columbian Club, while its Southern limit is defined by the Jesuit observatory, the Exposition Grounds and the newly built Philippine General Hospital." The first building to be erected was finished in 1913: the University Hall, renamed later in honor of Rafael Palma.

Commenting in 1911 on this newly acquired place for the University, the annual report of the Philippine Commission suggested that "the anticipated rapid growth of the university [would] make it undesirable to continue to occupy the site." This was not the last time that the "appropriateness" of the university site from the standpoint of the expected expansion of the university was seriously considered. It was not until 1948, however, when the move to the Diliman campus was finally effected.[10]

THE ACADEMIC UNITS WHICH COMPRISED THE NEW UNIVERSITY

PURSUANT to Section b (5) of the Charter, the Board of Regents immediately took steps to establish the first academic units of the University. *Bulletin No. 1* (actually the first catalogue issued by the University of the Philippines which was meant for the schoolyear 1910-1911, with announcements for 1911-1912) stated that as of 1911, the University of the Philippines included the following colleges and schools:

- College of Liberal Arts
- College of Medicine and Surgery
- College of Law
- College of Veterinary Medicine
- College of Agriculture
- College of Engineering
- School of Fine Arts

The following historical sketches of each one of these academic units, arranged in the order of their founding, describe briefly their early years of existence.

College of Medicine

The College of Medicine of the University of the Philippines had its beginnings in the Philippine Medical School established by a special act, Act No. 1415, on December 1, 1905 giving due course to the resolution passed at the second annual meeting of the Philippine Islands Medical Association.

At that meeting it was demonstrated that there was "the great need of supplying physicians to the people of the Islands." Statistics then presented showed that there was only one doctor "to each 21,209 people," or "to each 430 square miles of territory."[11] The College of Medicine formally opened on December 10, 1907. Three years later, almost to the date (December 8, 1910), the control and management of the Philippine Medical School passed to the Board of Regents, with its name changed to "College of Medicine and Surgery."

Subsequent laws provided for other matters pertinent to the Philippine Medical School. Act 1682 indicated the manner by which scholarships in the college might be obtained. It also provided that the graduates of the college were to be exempted from the required examination before practice. By virtue of Act 1651, other medical schools in the country were placed under the college's supervision on matters that had to do with curriculum, textbooks, laboratory work, methods of instruction, student work and examination. Another law, Act 1688, provided a ₱250,000 outlay for the construction of a building of strong materials to house the college.

Meant to provide the best that there was to assure top-rate instruction in medicine, the proposed building would have the most modern classrooms and laboratory facilities to accommodate some 200 students. It was to be located on Calle Herran, near the already existing building of the Bureau of Science and just some 400 meters from where the proposed government hospital would be built.

Yet another milestone in the early years of existence of the college was marked when on July 1, 1910, it moved to the newly built medical school building. Soon after, a ₱780,000 budget was approved for the construction of the modern hospital.

College of Agriculture

At its very first meeting on March 6, 1909, the Board of Regents by unanimous vote established the College of Agriculture. The problem of finding a suitable place for the agricultural college was solved when a piece of land near Los Baños in "La Laguna," which had been previously acquired by the Bureau of Education for an agricultural school, was transferred to the University. Thus the College of Agriculture opened on June 14, 1910 in Los Baños, some 50 kilometers from Manila, with an initial enrolment of 50 students under very unfavorable circumstances.[12]

Led by Dr. Edward Bingham Copeland as Dean and Superintendent of the College, the faculty and the students began the awesome task of carving out from the inhospitable tropical forest the 72 hectares that was to become the world-famous campus of the University of the Philippines at Los Baños. Dean Copeland's enthusiasm was matched by the warm response and resolute determination of the students whose number by then had grown to 55.

Together, the Dean, the students and their professors bravely tried to cope with numerous initial problems: securing accommodation for both the academic and non-academic personnel, obtaining water and electricity, providing food, and making the place accessible to the "outside."

The houses of the faculty and tents loaned by the Bureau of Education served as classrooms in the beginning, even while permanent buildings to meet administrative and academic needs were still under construction. The first buildings of reinforced concrete were constructed by January 1911: the administration and academic building, a laboratory building, a stable and bodega, a silk-culture house and a plant propagation house. The mountain streams were harnessed for irrigation and electricity. An "excellent macadamized road" was constructed, a move which ended the college's isolation from the outside world.

One of the student pioneers, Jose Zamora, looked back nostalgically to those early days of the College, beaming with joy and pride at having been there, when and where "the happenings" took place. He recalled the transfer of the whole college: students, professors and paraphernalia, from Camp Elridge to a "better place" with the help of a carabao-drawn cart, which proved unable to negotiate the impassable muddy mountain trails without human help. Zamora also recalled the "mongo con leche" concoction which was nothing more than mongo boiled in bulk over which milk was poured, eaten with steaming, newly cooked rice.[13]

In "no time," however, nature was "under control." Soon "the rest is history" aptly described the case of the College of Agriculture. Some two decades later, Joseph Ralston Hayden, writing on the development of the Filipino nation in general and of some institutions in the Philippines, the College of Agriculture in particular, noted:

> . . . Situated on the lower slopes of forest-covered Mt. Makiling, overlooking lovely Laguna de Bay, adorned with tropical trees and carefully tended vegetation, its campus is one of the most beautiful under the American flag. As is appropriate of an overwhelmingly agricultural country, the College of Agriculture is the strongest of the major units of the university.[14]

School of Fine Arts

The School of Fine Arts was the first to be established of the several units set up in 1909. It was temporarily housed in a rented place on Calle San Sebastian (the present R. Hidalgo), Quiapo. Rafael Enriquez of the well-known Escuela de Bellas Artes or Centro de Bellas Artes headed a staff of nine members, all well known figures in the field, like Dean Enriquez himself. Concerning this last point, an account on the University of 1911 says:

> It will be a surprise to most persons in Manila to learn that the majority of the instructors of the School of Fine Arts have not only resided and studied in Europe, but are medalists of exhibitions in Paris and Madrid. The dingy building in Calle San Sebastian holds many surprises for those who do not know about the work done in it.[15]

Apparently due to the interest in the arts nourished and kept alive before by the still-famous school of Dean Enriquez, the School of Fine Arts was unable to accommodate the rather big number of students seeking admission to its courses. A further increase in enrolment by the schoolyear 1910-1911 brought the total number of registered students to 703.

College of Veterinary Medicine

The name of Dean C. Worcester is usually associated with the College of Veterinary Medicine, particularly in connection with the steps taken toward its early establishment. A former member of the Philippine Commission and later Secretary of the Interior, Worcester, who was also a zoologist, strongly recommended to the authorities that a school for veterinary medical purposes be established in the country.

Thus, the annual report of the Secretary of Public Instruction for 1910 announced that the Vet-Med buildings for the animal hospital, schoolroom, and laboratories would be constructed near the animal quarantine station in Pandacan. By 1910 these buildings were supposed to have been constructed but Dean Lope M. Yutuc, incumbent Dean in 1958, recalled that when classes started in June 1910 the college had no buildings as yet. Classes were held wherever space was available in the medical compound and in the premises of the Normal School.[16]

Although the arrangement inconvenienced both professors and students, there really was no problem of accommodation because the enrolment was very small. Planned for a college to serve some forty students, only ten registered in the first year of its operation, and of these only four appeared when classes finally began. It was immediately apparent that the primary problem would be how to attract students to the Vet-Med course.[17]

Forestry Course

One of the three undergraduate courses offered when the College of Agriculture opened for the schoolyear 1910-1911 was a four-year course in forestry. To qualify for admission, the student-applicant was required to have finished at least the intermediate course in the public schools.

The first two years of the curriculum was no different from the curriculum in agriculture. In the third year which served as a transition period, the students took mathematics, physiography, soils and climatology, law and procedure of forestry, forest botany and ecology, among other subjects.

"Vacation" time was reserved for forest mensuration and camp life in the public forest in Mt. Makiling. For purposes of practicum in lumbering, a summer vacation spent right in the heart of a lumbering concession was arranged with the Cadwallader-Gibson Lumber Company in Bataan. In their fourth year, the forestry students took courses in wood technology, forest engineering, silviculture and forest management.

College of Liberal Arts

The catalogue, 1910-1911, carried a list of the already existing colleges at the time showing to what extent the University had developed since its creation. At the top of that list, which was arranged neither alphabetically nor chronologically, stood the College of Liberal Arts as though in anticipation of the role that it was to assume vis-a-vis the other units of the University. Eventually, the professional schools came to depend on the College of Liberal Arts for the preparatory courses required of their students. On the other hand many of the units created very soon after (such as the School of Pharmacy) or later (like the College of Education) were started as "mere" units of the College. It might be said, therefore, that the College of Liberal Arts served the purpose of a "nursery" both for the prospective students of the professional schools and the academic units established later as separate colleges.

The College of Liberal Arts had its beginnings in the so-called Insular schools of the Philippine Normal School. As early as 1904, the Philippine Normal School occasionally had to provide courses alien to its original purpose "because no other public school in the city of Manila could provide instruction for the courses preparatory to the different professions."

In the first semester of 1909-1910, there were 218 secondary students enrolled in the Normal School for such preparatory courses (preparatory to medicine, "for appointment as a magistrate," "for entrance into law," "for admission to an engineering school," and others). The following December, these students "were separated from the regular students of the Normal school and organized into a distinct insular school within the Bureau of Education" that "became known by common usage, though without legal designation, as the Academy and Junior College of Liberal Arts." This took over the four-year high school courses and two-year collegiate course. College level courses were given in such areas as logic, psychology, English, chemistry, history, "growth of law," to mention a few. The degrees of Bachelor of Arts and Bachelor of Science, as authorized by law, were granted upon completion of certain requirements.[18]

On June 3, 1910, by virtue of a decision by the Board of Regents, the College of Philosophy, Science, and Letters of the UP was established, and this took over the studentry of the Academy and Junior College. On January 30, 1911, the college was renamed College of Liberal Arts. The first Dean was George Wm. Beattie who held that position in an acting capacity for the schoolyear 1910-1911.

Dr. Lawrence E. Griffin, Beattie's successor, left this description of the College:

> . . . There were two sections in the college: the Junior College, giving two years of work leading to the degree of Bachelor of Arts, and the Senior College with three years of work leading to the degree of Master of Arts. Graduation from the Junior College corresponds to the German Gymnasium or the French Lycee, while the degree of the Senior College is exactly on the same basis as the Master's degree in American universities. The work of the Junior College is so arranged as to enable such of its students, as desired to prepare for the professional course. For example, for preparatory courses in two years, each for engineering, law and medicine are offered.[19]

The College of Liberal Arts, like most of the other newly established units of the University of the Philippines, had classes but no rooms for them. The College of Liberal Arts together with the College of Engineering held "some of their recitations in a dwelling house at 100 Isaac Peral, and for laboratories used those of the Normal School and of the College of Medicine."[20]

In June 1911, a course in Pharmacy was offered for the first time in the College of Liberal Arts. The course attracted quite a number of registrants. A three-year course, the program of studies led to the degree of Graduate in Pharmacy. The addition of a fourth year satisfied the requirements for the degree of Pharmaceutical Chemistry. That course was believed to be equal to the best and even superior by far to most pharmacy courses in most schools in the United States.

College of Engineering

The College of Engineering was established on June 3, 1910 simultaneously with the College of Liberal Arts. At once it had to wrestle with the problem of low enrolment, although it was apparent that the need for engineers in the Philippines would increase in the face of American plans for an improved and expanded public works system. In any case, "it [was] the aim of the University to require thorough preparation and high standards of scholarship, in all of the professional schools, rather than to secure a large number of students."[21]

The College of Engineering opened on June 12, 1910 with course offerings for the first year of the program in civil engineering. The Board of Regents decided on June 31, 1911, to require all engineering students to take a two-year preparatory course in the College of Liberal Arts.

Dr. Lawrence E. Griffin, Dean of the College of Liberal Arts, served concurrently as Dean of the College of Engineering until William Joseph Colbert was appointed Acting Dean and served in that capacity from June 1910 to June 1911.

College of Law

In appointing Cayetano Arellano as Chief Justice of the Supreme Court almost at the beginning of American rule, the Americans acknowledged that they would have to involve the Filipinos in the government (foreshadowing the adoption of the policy of Filipinization, written into law with the promulgation of the "Instruction to the Second Philippine Commission"). Arellano's appointment was practically an open admission that no American in the Philippines was qualified for this demanding and exalted position. This could only be filled by someone schooled in Philippine law. Cayetano Arellano was schooled in the system introduced by the former regime like other Filipinos who went into the legal profession. With the change of administration, it was now imperative that a law school be organized to give instruction "according to the American plan."[22]

In 1910, an embryonic school of law (a one-room affair) was started to give instruction in law in English. Classes were held amidst the very modest circumstances of the old Manila High School (renamed later as the Araullo High School) in Intramuros under the auspices of the education department of the YMCA. Fifty students enrolled but only 35 completed the term. These were the very same students who would, along with their professors, become part of the UP College of Law in the following year.

By virtue of a decision of the Board of Regents on January 12, 1911, the College of Law, one of the last academic units to be created before the first president of the University was finally chosen, was established. Justice Sherman Moreland of the Supreme Court and George A. Malcolm were appointed Dean and Secretary, respectively

The aim of the College of Law, according to *Catalogue 1911-1912* was:

> . . . to furnish facilities for legal training in English, covering all the fundamental law subjects necessary for the practice of law in the Philippine Islands. Competent instructors, including leading members of the bar and judiciary, compose the faculty. Thorough and practical instruction is given.[23]

From the very start, admission requirements to the College of Law were very stringent. At first the applicants were "merely" expected to be at least 18 years old and qualified according to the University rules on admission, but more requirements were added in the succeeding years. The same *Catalogue 1911-1912* indicated that by 1912, "a certificate showing the completion of one year of study in the preparatory law course in the College of Liberal Arts" of the University, or its equivalent, would also be required. There was, nevertheless, a proportionate increase in the number of applicants for admission to the College of Law despite additional requirements.

In 1911, out of so many hopeful aspirants, only 118 were finally admitted to the first-year class. The second-year group was composed of 29 students from the older law schools and some special students. The group of 1911 would go down in the history of the College of Law as the one with the most number of name figures. Many of them would make and leave their mark in their chosen field as law practitioners *(abogados de campanilla),* or as high government officials with distinctive records, as Dean or as professors of Law or of political science and others.[24] As a group they set a pattern and started a tradition that would leave "no choice" for those coming after them but to emulate or equal, if not to surpass, their accomplishments.

APPOINTMENT OF THE FIRST UNIVERSITY PRESIDENT

THE University Act provided for the election of the president of the UP by the Board of Regents. Although the Board was finally constituted as early as October 12, 1908, it did not choose the first appointee to the UP presidency until June 1911. The more immediate task of setting up the colleges was its main preoccupation during the first two years after the enactment of the Charter of the University.

Desirable Qualities

Whatever reasons might be advanced to explain the delay in appointing the President of the University, lack of interest in the post whether within or without the University itself could not have been one of them.

The editorial of the *Manila Times* of December 13, 1910 viewed the UP presidency in the light of prospects that the university "might some day become the intellectual center in this part of the orient . . . ." At that time when the University of the Philippines could be "the most effective agent" in the Filipinization movement,[25] the question of who should be the president of the UP naturally took on great significance. The editorial noted the "widespread demand from the native press" for the appointment of a Filipino to the post. However, the *Manila Times* posed a diametrically opposing view.

On the other hand the *College Folio*, in its second issue (December, 1910) which was edited by Victoriano Yamzon, expressed the UP students' view that "the President of the University of the Philippines must be a scholar and need not be a money petitioner," "a man of sterling qualities – with a penetrative and far-reaching intellect, with broad learning, of an impartial judgment, and an attitude of mind, neither so ultra conservative as to keep any department stationary nor so radical as to plunge any into disorder and confusion," "one so experienced that he can build up the various colleges into a real university capable of taking rank with the famous educational institutions of the world."

The same editorial also asked in all seriousness: "Is there a Filipino equipped to hold this office of first President? " Answering its own question, it declared, "We think not, but if there is, produce him and we will welcome him. If there is not, let the Filipino sentimentalists keep still. Are there any Americans with qualifications to be found in the Philippines? If there are, let us have one of them. If there are not, let us go beyond the Islands."

There is no mistaking the view of the *College Folio* that citizenship or race should have no place or room in the final choice of the UP President. But the editorial did not end there. It expressed in no uncertain terms what would happen if "a man unfit for the office" were appointed instead of "the best man" – "a scholarly, strong, practical, pure, wide awake, sensible, honest and reliable educator."

The Philippine Commission in its annual report for 1910 also touched on the UP presidency in this manner: "The great need now is the guiding hand of a man of high character and large educational experience as president of the University. The Board of Regents earnestly recommends that provisions be made whereby such man may be secured."

Bartlett Appointed

On March .6, 1911, Murray Bartlett who had earlier been offered the UP presidency accepted the position. But the formal announcement by the Board of Regents was made only on June 1, 1911, when that appointment also took effect.

Bartlett had been a member of the Board of Regents since July 1909, and at the time of his appointment was serving in the capacity of acting secretary. To his position he brought his two degrees from Harvard – a

Bachelor of Arts and a Master of Arts, earned one after the other in 1892 and 1893. His third degree was in theology obtained in 1896 from the General Theological Seminary in New York. In 1908, the University of Rochester conferred upon him the degree of Doctor of Divinity. His record of service in his previous assignments before coming to the Philippines to become Dean of the Cathedral of St. John on Calle Isaac Peral in Manila showed his active participation in various educational and civic projects.[26] Evidently a good follower, no less than an inspiring leader, Bartlett was thus characterized by Bishop C. H. Brent, his superior in the Episcopalian religious community:

> Few men have come to the Philippine Islands without the expectation and purpose of bettering their efforts and advancing their personal interest; still fewer have come from a greater to a lesser position.
>
> Dr. Bartlett is one of the few. As he comes from the greater to the lesser from a sense of duty and in the spirit of self-donation, so now that he is called from the lesser to the greater we know that it is under the same sense of obligation.
>
> A man who has once shown absolute indifference to the emoluments of office can always be trusted to act unselfishly. Moreover it is only the men who are a loss to the position relinquished who are a gain to the position laying its claim upon them.[27]

Inaugural Address

Murray Bartlett was sworn in as the first President of the University of the Philippines on December 20, 1911 in well-attended ceremonies held at what was still the almost bare campus in Padre Faura. But that campus, Bartlett himself said "[spoke] of hope rather than achievement, of promise rather than fulfillment." He perceived the University of the Philippines, as it were, as a university still on the threshold of a very important but tremendous undertaking. It had been there, it is true, for about the last two years but so much still remained to be clarified or defined. Immediately wanting was a definitive view of the role that the university must assume or play. As the first occupant of the presidency of the University, Bartlett had the task of conceptualizing that role according to the *spirit,* if not also the *word,* of the law that created the university.

In his inaugural address[28], the newly installed President unfolded what he called his "vision" of the university as a "University for the Filipino," on the basis of which he spelled out the policies that were to guide his administration.

Bartlett firmly avowed that the University of the Philippines must be "for the Filipino" as he stressed that it was to be "supported by the people's money" with a charter having been framed by the people's representatives and "its hope based upon the confidence and sympathy of the people." Proceeding from the most important Charter provisions in sections 2 and 3, Bartlett expressed the certainty that the scope and area of concern of the University was the "whole field of intellectual activity," where the "guiding spirit" for both the faculty and the students would be "Truth, unfettered by social, political, and sectarian limitations," and whose portals would be open to everyone regardless of age, sex, nationality, religious belief or political affiliation. In other words, the University of the Philippines "for the Filipino," as Bartlett affirmed, would be *no* different from other universities. It would be a "real" or "true" university, that is to say "a university that measures up to world standards."

Thus, in Bartlett's view, the University of the Philippines must aim to be an "abode of scholarship" like the older universities, and must seek to be an efficient training ground for men "who [would] be the leaders of their people," in the manner of the "new universities of the New East – India, China and Japan." Research must be an important component of the life of the university. "If scientific truth is to be efficiently applied to practical conditions and needs," Bartlett stated, "there must be first of all the possibility of the search of truth for its own sake. Research without application is an expensive luxury, but application without research is folly."

Summing up on this point, Bartlett noted: "Efficiency, then, founded upon scholarship should be our aim, but even this is not enough." As a prominent pillar of the highly respected Episcopalian church, Bartlett was strongly inclined toward a university that would seek to develop the total man – his whole self, both the material and the non-material aspects. He expressed his commitment to this view in the following words:

> . . . The first necessity of the university is not to graduate skilled engineers, agriculturists, or physicians, nor is it even to produce efficient scholars; first of all it must turn out men and women, and manhood and womanhood are built upon one foundation – the development of character.
>
> The atmosphere of this place must be filled with those great ideals that throughout the pages of history have been the cause of the true greatness of men and nations. The real wealth of a country is not to be found in its material resources, but in the strength and courage of its manhood and the purity of its womanhood. The university must be a training school for the development of character. Our *alma mater* is not to breed aristocrats, but unselfish workers for the common good. There must be taught here, throughout the years to come, the sublime moral value of work – that the honor due any profession is to be judged alone by the measure of its services to the people, whether it be law or agriculture, medicine, or veterinary science.

Further supporting his contention with words taken from the inaugural address of the president of the University of Minnesota, he defined his concept of "efficiency" in terms of the University. He advocated it as the "watchword in developing the university for the Filipinos—efficiency, founded upon scholarship and inspired by character."

A University for the Filipino

In what may well have been his concluding message as first president of the university, he reaffirmed the same "vision" of a University of the Philippines for the Filipino.

> It is my conviction that if we have before us this ideal, our university will measure up to world standards, thereby carrying out the manifest provision of our charter, but it must never be forgotten that this is and shall always be a university of the Philippines. It has been truly said that there can be no greatness without nationality. The world-centers of knowledge are essentially national. With students from all parts of the world, Berlin is essentially German and Oxford essentially English. This university should not be a reproduction of the American university. If it is to blossom into real fruit, it must grow in Philippine soil, it must not be transplanted from foreign shores. It can serve the world best by serving best the Filipino.

Having identified the hallmarks of the "University for the Filipino," Bartlett also delved into the useful and relevant ways through which the university can be truly "for the Filipino." He cited what he called "the practical function" that the university could exercise in the implementation or concretization of certain projects, such as those pertaining to government and industry. He expressed the view that in both of these, the university could provide the leadership and manpower if not also the proper attitudes.

Of the UP and particularly of the Filipinization movement, Bartlett said, "The surest and quickest way of bringing about the Filipinization of government is through the university, where skilled and efficient public servants will be trained for the various bureaus."

By providing courses and instruction in the fields or areas immediately concerned with the problems and needs of the Filipino, the University, in the opinion of Bartlett, could truly be "for the Filipino." He called attention to the two-year post-graduate course in medicine and the five-year course in veterinary medicine. Bartlett stressed that only the properly and adequately trained Filipino could fully comprehend and empathize with the problems of health and disease in the country that were peculiar, if not endemic, to the Philippines.

As to the relationship of the University with other institutions of learning such as those schools in the lower levels of the public school system and those that were privately owned and administered, Bartlett stated that the University if it must be "for the Filipino" could and should not assume the ivory-tower stance, or attempt to isolate itself and be removed from all the rest. All Philippine schools including the University itself have a common goal and that is to provide for the education of the Filipinos.

Bartlett's concern for a faculty staff that would minister to the instructional needs of the "University for the Filipino" was manifest when he said that no task could be more immediate and important "than that of laying the foundation in this university for a permanent faculty of Filipino scholars." Obviously believing that it would take a Filipino faculty to bring about the realization of a "University for the Filipino," Bartlett reassuringly concluded: "The world's standard of excellence and the spirit of nationality may be effectively combined by having taught in these halls all the learning of the world by Filipinos."

Thus, the first President of the University of the Philippines, Murray Bartlett, squarely set before him – if not also for those who were to come after him – the concept of a university imbued with the finest traditions of the great universities of the world, borrowing from them only what could be re-fashioned to meet the needs of the Filipino studentry. The University of the Philippines was meant to be a "University for the Filipino," a university in the finest tradition of the great universities of the world.

Reaction from the Press

Especially noteworthy was the report on the event by the widely circulated *Manila Times.* Its issue of December 21, 1911 carried a full coverage of the inaugural ceremonies and a lengthy editorial on the Bartlett speech.[29]

The *Manila Times* considered the address "admirable in many ways but chiefly . . . in its wise insistence on the truth that the methods and customs of other countries however well-suited to those lands, should not for that reason be adopted to the Philippines." It expressed relief in "the assurance that Philippine conditions and Philippine needs [would] have first and constant attention." The editorial further commended the inaugural message in the following terms:

> For this is a University of the Philippines and for the Filipinos. The Board of Regents, the president and faculty have it in trust to develop the institutions to the point at which it may not only serve but be served by Filipinos themselves. "If it is to blossom into fruit," said Bartlett, "it must grow in Philippine soil, it must not be transplanted from foreign shores. It can serve the goals best by serving best the Filipino." If clearness of vision, high ideals, and a determination to follow only what is best and truest amount for anything, then President Bartlett and with him the University set forth together well-equipped.

A Pioneer's Work

"You are undertaking greater and more lasting responsibilities than most men have the privilege of accepting." On these words Vice-Governor Newton W. Gilbert prefaced the investiture rites highlighting the inaugural ceremonies for the first President of the University of the Philippines, over which Gilbert presided as Secretary of Public Instruction.

As the first President of the University of the Philippines, Bartlett assumed a task without parallel in Philippine history. The Philippines had no stored experiences from the past that came close to administering a university. And in light of what he himself said, that the University of the Philippines was to be "for the Filipino," the problems of administration for him acquired greater proportion and complexity.

There was practically nothing in the Philippines from which Bartlett could possibly have drawn to help him in administering the University. Neither the University of Sto. Tomas, as secularized and renamed Universidad de Filipinas by the Moret Decree of 1870, nor the Universidad Literaria de Filipinas that was created by the Malolos Republic, had anything useful to offer to the first president of a newly established university that was meant to serve as a university for the Filipinos. He was truly on his own, as his inaugural address would show; he knew what lay ahead of him and he was prepared to act accordingly. As the editorial of the *Manila Times* had put it: "If clearness of vision, high ideals, and a determination to follow only what is best and truest count for anything, then President Bartlett and with him the University set forth together well-equipped."

Bartlett assumed the presidency of the University of the Philippines on June 1, 1911 and remained in office until the commencement exercises of the schoolyear 1914-1915. He served as President Emeritus from April 1, 1915 to July 1, 1915. Between the later part of 1912 and most of 1913 he was on official leave, visiting institutions of higher learning abroad.[30]

Organizational Tasks

In his first months in office, Bartlett expectedly addressed himself to the more immediate administrative and academic needs of the University. The organization of the University Council was one of these. In accordance with the Charter, the University Council was organized as the highest academic body, composed of faculty members from the rank of Assistant Professor or higher with the President as presiding officer. This took place at its meeting on June 18, 1911 in the Amphitheater, College of Medicine and Surgery. The Council assumed the duties and powers it was assigned to undertake and exercise, pertaining to the courses of study and rules of discipline, rules of admission to the different colleges, graduation, as well as the granting of honorary degrees.

To expedite the discharge of its duties and functions, the Council constituted the Executive Committee made up of the president, the deans of the degree-granting colleges and the registrar of the university. In his first annual report, Bartlett described how the Executive Committee had "served as an excellent adviser to the president on University matters; that [it] considered matters in advance after which it made recommendations." It also acted on cases of discipline referred to it by the deans. The Executive Committee decided to meet regularly every month; for this purpose the second and fourth Mondays of every month were set aside.

Bartlett happily noted how the University Council fulfilled yet another important function of bringing the various faculties "into personal relations" thereby fostering "a real interest in the University *as a whole* and not merely in *one of a group* of colleges" (underscoring supplied).[31]

For administrative purposes, a system of centralized control was established under the office of the President. Bartlett said that this was along his efforts to be "in direct touch with every department of the university." There was a division of records that "duplicated" and kept the research papers of the various colleges after these were reported to him. An important official in the setup was the Registrar who served as the disbursing officer of the whole university and supervised the disbursing officers of the different colleges. The head of the accounting division as well as the property officer of the central property division were also under the Registrar.

In the words of the annual report of the Philippine Commission to the Secretary of War, in 1912, the Bartlett administration in its first year of actual operation "[had] been mainly one of organization and of laying the foundation of the institution on the broad lines which [were] necessary if it [was] to fulfill its purpose."[32]

When Bartlett assumed the stewardship of the University in June 1911, the UP was made up of seven colleges – Medicine, Agriculture, Veterinary Medicine, Fine Arts, Liberal Arts, Engineering and Law, which were widely dispersed in location. The College of Agriculture was in Los Baños, the School of Fine Arts somewhere in Calle San Sebastian (the present R. Hidalgo) in Quiapo, the College of Medicine on Calle Herran, the College of Veterinary Medicine in Pandacan, the College of Law in Isaac Peral (now United Nations Avenue), the College of Liberal Arts in various government buildings in Ermita. Only the College of Engineering was located on the Padre Faura campus. Neither were there physical plants for permanent use of these colleges. Only the College of Medicine was housed in its own newly constructed building in the medical compound in Ermita. The rest were either housed in some government building or holding classes in private residences rented for the purpose. The Padre Faura campus was still to be built and developed, although the purchase of the lot intended for that campus had already been consummated. That "almost bare campus" was in more ways than one like the UP that Bartlett took over. Much, much more remained to be done.

Bartlett identified the two main tasks that the University should undertake: to be a university in the finest traditions of the older universities and to be a "university for the Filipino."

Efforts toward Stabilization

With regard to the first objective, the University of the Philippines grew slowly in the four years of the Bartlett administration. In addition to the units that were already established, only the department of Education was created within the College of Liberal Arts and the department of Dentistry was established in 1915 as a part of the College of Medicine and Surgery.

It appeared though that actually, the UP was concentrating quite a bit more on the further development and stabilization of the already existing colleges, which was all that the limited resources available could allow. It was only in response to the pressing problem of training and hiring teachers for the secondary schools and for the UP as well that the new department of education was created, and to the need for graduates in dentistry that the unit for the purpose was organized.

Toward the improvement and expansion of the academic offerings of the University, some important changes were undertaken in the already existing degree courses. Some needed programs were also introduced. Thus, in the College of Engineering, in response to a clamor, a four-year course in Civil Engineering was instituted to replace the existing five-year course, with the proviso that admission to the program would be limited to high school graduates who have earned additional units in solid geometry: a requirement over and above the two-year pre-Engineering course taken at the College of Liberal Arts. This was followed by the institution of new degree courses in mechanical, electrical, and mining engineering. In 1915, the College instituted a degree program of studies leading to the Master of Science in Civil Engineering.

In the College of Medicine and Surgery, the position of Assistant Dean was created. This was an indication of the expanding activities of the College, if not its stability and efficiency as noted in the first annual report of Bartlett in 1912. After only five years of existence, it graduated nine new doctors all of whom found placement in the "hospital and scientific services of the government" (at a time when appointments to government posts, as against those of private establishments, were considered premium appointments).

In 1913, applicants for admission to the College of Medicine were required to take a one-year preparatory course in the College of Liberal Arts. Meanwhile the Philippine General Hospital, one of several government entities that worked closely with the College of Medicine, was placed under the Dean of the College. The dean was designated "Chief of the PGH, division of the Bureau of Health."

More New Programs

A project close to the heart of Bartlett was launched in 1914, when the Graduate School of Tropical Medicine and Public Health was set up within the College of Medicine. Intended for graduates with the medical degree, there were actually two course offerings from which they could choose: a one-year course leading to the degree of Doctor of Tropical Medicine and a two-year course leading to the degree of Doctor of Public Health. Students were required to do course work and undertake research on a subject approved by the head of the appropriate department.

Evidently, the progress chalked up by the College of Medicine even before 1913 was so impressive even by foreign standards that it was admitted to the Association of American Medical Schools in 1913. As a matter of fact, in the ranking of that prestigious group, the UP College of Medicine was in the "Class A" category.[33]

The College of Law was not far behind in the almost University-wide effort toward expansion and improvement of academic offerings. Established on January 12, 1911 or only six months before Bartlett assumed the UP Presidency, it was, by the schoolyear 1912-1913, already offering all of the prescribed courses in the four-year degree program. Also in that second year of its existence, according to the results of the study of the Committee on the College of Law, steps were initiated to bring about a permanent faculty and provide instruction outside the "evening hours" to accommodate the increasing number of students who could be on full-time for their studies. The services of eminent specialists who were in the government as well as members of the Manila Bar were sought. While the four-year course tailored to meet the needs of students who were full-time employees was allowed to continue, a course for three years was designed for those who could be full-time students.

A two-year preparatory course administered by the College of Liberal Arts was required by 1913 of every applicant to the Law degree program, a practice common to law schools abroad. Still another requirement, which was to be fulfilled in the senior year, was the writing of a thesis on "a subject upon which the law is unsettled, disputed or in a formative condition."

Bartlett was all praises for this added requirement of the College of Law, a requirement that was yet to be introduced in the law schools abroad. He believed that the thesis requirement redounded to the advantage of the student "whose interest in his legal studies is increased at the same time that his initiative is drawn and developed."[34]

By 1913, the Master of Laws degree program was instituted. Also in the same year, the College produced its first batch of graduates. The roster of that graduating class would today read like a "Who's Who."

Before the end of Bartlett's presidency, the College of Law had distinguished itself as one of the most efficient units of the University. This distinction was ascribed to two factors: the appointment of a permanent dean, George A. Malcolm, "who gave all his attention to teaching and to the work in connection with his office" and "the enlargement of the permanent faculty."[35]

Peak Enrolment at Agricultural College

The College of Agriculture by the time of Bartlett had outstripped (particularly its student population) the limits of the existing physical capabilities of the college and of the fiscal resources of the University. It proved to be a major cause for worry for the University President not only because of the extremely limited annual appropriations made available for the operation of the University but also because of administrative problems.

The distance between Los Baños and Manila simply defied all efforts to maximize the use of the still-limited laboratory facilities of the University by students taking different courses yet required to take the same subjects. There were, by force of circumstances, two sets of facilities when perhaps only one set would have sufficed. This was only one among many problems of administration. Bartlett's proposal to shift at least a part of the burden of providing instruction in agriculture to the elementary schools, did not get the support and encouragement from the directors of both the Bureau of Agriculture and the Bureau of Education as well as the Dean of the UP College of Agriculture. This problem remained unsolved till the end of the Bartlett era.

Preparatory Courses

Developments in the College of Liberal Arts were of a different nature. In the main the College was preoccupied by the undergraduate degree programs in medicine, engineering and law. Otherwise its attention was directed toward the need to revise the Bachelor of Arts program, a legacy from the Spanish period. This two-year course was believed to be inferior to similar A.B. programs in American colleges and universities. The proponents for its revision suggested that its graduates be given the Associate in Arts (A.A.) degree and that the Bachelor's degree be reserved for those who had completed four years of study. But the proposals were never implemented during Bartlett's presidency because the Board of Regents viewed the matter differently.[36]

Another degree offered by the College of Liberal Arts was that of Master of Arts which was granted to graduates of the two-year A.B. degree program upon completion of three more years of study.

The School of Fine Arts was meanwhile getting more and more students although, noticeably, the number of its graduates did not match the increasing enrolment. One explanation for this was that a good number among them were only interested in the skills they could acquire by enrolling in the Fine Arts courses rather than getting the degree. Also, as noted by Bartlett in his first annual report, many of the students were actually cross-enrollees from other schools. Perhaps the large enrolment was also due to the evening classes meant for those who were "engaged during the day in the various trades."

More Vet-Med Students Needed

In the College of Veterinary Medicine, the problem of a very small enrolment continued despite all efforts to whip up interest in the Vet-Med course. The curriculum was revised into a five-year course that took effect in the schoolyear 1911-1912. Meantime, an information campaign directed at prospective students pointed to the opportunities and advantages awaiting the Vet-Med graduates. Among the opportunities cited, service to the community, at one extreme, and pecuniary returns, at the other, were emphasized.

Although enrolment in the College increased in succeeding schoolyears, since it opened in 1909, many more students were needed to maximize the use of the facilities and other resources. The degree program itself compared favorably with some of the best in the world. The first graduates demonstrated the high level of their professional competence when they registered 100 per cent passing score in the board exams. President Bartlett did not miss the chance "to plug" for the Vet-Med course in his inaugural speech. After saying that the Veterinary Medicine program in the University "was more thorough than the one given in America," he said that "in the great work of stamping out animal epidemics the government needs Filipinos to teach people lessons which taught by strangers are hard to understand."[37] An earlier move to get more students into the program came in the form of government scholarships provided for by Act 2040.

By the second year of its operation, the College moved to another place in San Lazaro upon the recommendation of one of its first Filipino faculty members, Victor Buencamino.

Graduate Program

The first catalogue of the UP featured a very modest announcement under the title of "Opportunities for Graduate Study." The University had much to offer to the prospective graduate student though not yet at the Ph.D. level. The Executive Committee of the University Council, which supervised graduate work, decided to accept "candidates for that degree only in those subjects where the staff of instructors is unquestionably qualified to recommend such a degree and where the facilities of investigation are adequate."[38]

Otherwise, the UP offered exceptional opportunities for masteral studies in the areas of Chemistry, Botany, Tropical Medicine and Zoology. A wealth of research materials and very adequate laboratory and library facilities were available to graduate students pursuing graduate studies who, upon graduation, had all the opportunities for advancement and employment.

In the schoolyear 1911-12 seven students, six of whom were Americans, were registered for graduate work, with majors in zoology (3), Chemistry (1) and History (1).

The catalogue for 1912-13 carried a detailed description of the degrees of Master of Arts and Master of Science. Students whose major subject was one of those usually recognized as "the humanities" were conferred the former title while the latter was reserved for those whose thesis was "scientific or technical." The same catalogue indicated the general conditions for the granting of the master's degrees. Usually required were course work, a reading and speaking knowledge of French and German, and the writing of a thesis.[39]

Concerning the requirements for admission to the degrees of Doctor of Tropical Medicine and of Public Health, the same catalogue for 1912-13 supplied in addition some details on the very favorable study and research conditions in these two programs. Qualified for admission to the program were graduates of the UP College of Medicine as well as those from other schools "granting a degree of Doctor of Medicine or its equivalent, which are recognized by the authorities of the University of the Philippines." Finally in 1914 the two graduate medical courses were offered. Enrolment for the two successive years 1914 and 1915 were 22 and 56, respectively, with the second year showing an increase of 34 students.

The announcement in the fourth bulletin of the University on further opportunities for graduate study was an invitation for people interested in history to make use of "the best collection of Filipiniana in existence." In addition, it took note of "records of the first missionary efforts in Asia," records "in the convents of the religious orders," found in Government Archives. Thus, the announcement confidently concluded that "nowhere also will the students find such opportunities in the primary sources for studying the beginnings and progress of European and American influence in the Far East, a subject of increasing interest since the modernization of the Orient."

BASIC ACTIVITIES LAUNCHED OR STRENGTHENED DURING BARTLETT'S TERM

THE value and importance of research and scientific investigation in the life of the University was emphasized in ways other than the institution of graduate studies. Bartlett affirmed the importance of research in no uncertain terms as this had particular bearing on the discharge of the role of the University in the community.

Research and Scientific Inquiry

Bartlett pointed out the intimate relation between teaching and research. He believed that research was an all-important component of effective teaching, and in the teaching of the Filipinos it was all the more necessary. Convinced that it was the spirit of initiative in the Filipino students "which needed more development," Bartlett thought that this can be awakened with exposure to the research undertaken by their teachers. Finally, with regard to the development of a Filipino faculty, Bartlett held that research opportunities made available to the faculty "would serve to attract good faculty material because working for the University would afford them the means and the time for original investigation in their chosen lines of work."

But scientific investigation need not involve only graduate students according to Bartlett. The development of research interest and capabilities of the undergraduate students should also be taken into account, for on their level research was equally important and necessary. Thus in many undergraduate degree programs, to complete some kind of research work was one of the important requirements.

The College of Agriculture, for instance, required its students "to prepare a thesis on some original problem of practical agriculture." In the College of Law, as already noted, one of the requirements in the senior year called for the writing of a thesis on a "subject upon which the law is unsettled, disputed or in a formative condition."

Towards a coordinated and organized scientific investigation, the Bureau of Science and the Department of Zoology of the UP conducted a "joint marine biological survey during the vacation months" of the schoolyear 1911-1912. While the project mainly involved teachers in the field, there were also student participants. The place finally chosen in 1912 to be the site of the marine station was "Porto Galera," Mindoro where "the opportunities for studying tropical marine life were unexcelled."[40]

Links with Government Agencies

It is noteworthy that in the interest of promoting research, the University worked in cooperation with other government institutions, notably the Bureau of Science. Bartlett foresaw the need for an arrangement of this nature whereby the UP and its counterpart can maximize the results of their efforts through combined cooperative endeavor, with the University providing the expertise and its counterpart providing the facilities and other resources. To the Bureau of Science, the University was also indebted for the publication of the reports of its faculty members in the *Journal of Science.* In the meantime it was proposed that a report on the research "of the faculty of the College of Liberal Arts upon original matters connected with literature, history and economic conditions" be made available. This finally materialized with the inclusion of a section in the university catalogue of a list of individual faculty research accomplishments.

It is probably also significant, in connection with research in the University, that the Secretary of Interior was appointed to the Board of Regents by virtue of the first amendment (Act 2024) of the Charter. His office supervised the scientific and research work of the government that was eventually turned over to the University. Also significant was the designation of the division of records, one of the first offices of administration to be established, to keep "the research of the various colleges."

Admission of Students

Any consideration of the efforts of the University during Bartlett's time toward excellence, as the UP was pledged to do, would be incomplete without an accounting of its admissions policy. The quality of the admitted students ultimately counted a good deal in the pursuit of excellence.

Bulletin No, 1 spelled out the admissions policy of the University for the schoolyear 1910-1911. Changes and revisions adopted later were entered in subsequent catalogues. What appeared to be the most outstanding feature of the admissions policy in those very early years was the entrance examination required "as evidence that the applicants for admission [have] satisfactorily pursued the subjects required for admission" although certificates may be presented to the University "as equivalent for all or any part of their subjects."

The subject matter of the entrance examination covered broad areas of English, History, Mathematics, Economics, Latin and Spanish, Physics, Zoology, Botany, and even what was called "Commercial Geography." A total of 14 or 18 units of the listed entrance subjects was required, depending on what the student was applying for. The extent to which the student applicants must prepare for the examinations might be gleaned from the details given about each subject.[41] Where laboratory exercises were supposed to have been conducted, the candidate was required to present at the time of the examination "a notebook containing the student's own record of his laboratory experiments . . ." duly certified by the teacher.

In sum, the policy of admission of the University was quite strict, with the examinations serving the purpose of effectively screening the applicants. The examinations were tough and trying, thereby assuring the University that only those who were "college material" were admitted. Scholastic delinquency was treated just as strictly if not more severely, perhaps proceeding from the assumption that the privilege of admission to the University was in itself a contract between the student and the University, with the latter having the right to withdraw the privilege where there were enough grounds for doing so.

A case in point was the "rule" governing law students, as announced in *Bulletin No. 2* of the University which reads as follows: ". . . The faculty will not hesitate to drop a student from the rolls at any one time during the year when satisfied that he is neglecting his studies, is not conforming to the requirements of the college, or is not fitted for the profession of law."

Emphasis on the Filipino

Toward a "University for the Filipinos," Bartlett envisioned a University that would take its place alongside the great universities of the world at the same time that it carried out its role as the "University for the Filipino" or a university committed to the service of the Filipinos. He perceived no incompatibility, only congruence, between the twin roles – one in the world of the academe, the other in the Philippine community to which the UP belonged.

The University, according to Bartlett, "can serve the world best by serving best the Filipino." Thus he expressed the hope of seeing a UP that was deeply concerned with and always responsive to every need and problem of the Filipinos, and pursuing its work not removed from but in relation to the life beyond the "walls of the academe."

To Bartlett, even the Filipinization program should find in the UP a means toward its implementation and fulfilment. Therefore, for the reason alone that the UP was "for the Filipino," if for no other, Bartlett addressed his administration equally to the development of a Filipino faculty. As he stressed in his inaugural speech: "There is no task more immediate and important . . . than that of laying the foundation in this university for a permanent faculty of Filipino scholars." . . . "The world's standard of excellence and the spirit of nationality may be effectively combined by having taught [in the UP] all the learning of the world by Filipinos."

The Bartlett proposal was timely and practical as it was wise. Carried out properly, it would not only have achieved the goal Bartlett had in mind but would have also helped in solving the problem of faculty recruitment as well as other problems arising therefrom.

Usually the faculty were recruited either through the Bureau of Insular Affairs that took care of locating teachers in the United States[42] or through recruitment of some government personnel. But problems arose from these practices. One consequence was the fast turnover of teachers. Only a few remained for some length of time with the faculty.

And in at least one instance the recruitment from a government office caused a mini sort of "brain drain." This was what happened in the Bureau of Science from which so many resigned to accept full-time, high-paying teaching positions in the University. Which is just as well because, after all, those transferees had the qualifications needed by their new positions in the UP; except that even among them there were many who did not stay permanently. Quite a number stayed on just long enough to "qualify" for a recommendation for a teaching post back in the United States. Experience demonstrated in not a few instances that their University connection was a credential that served them in good stead.[43]

The use of the University as a "stepping stone" to some other job should not have been allowed in the first place. Transients that those short-term faculty members really were, it is doubtful if they taught with dedication. But was their lack of commitment, if not of loyalty to the University, if it were the case, more or less to be expected? [44]

Building Up the Faculty

The plan to develop a permanent Filipino faculty went off to a good start even before Bartlett's inauguration. In his inaugural address, he reports the outcome of his "lobby" for the passage of a bill which would provide fellowships for deserving "Filipino members of the teaching staff of the University." Bartlett also reported that "members of departments have been instructed to watch for promising students and to encourage them to remain in the University as assistants and instructors."

The first scholars under the fellowship program left for the United States in 1912. Several slots were available but only two were selected by the President "in consultation with the Deans and with the approval of the Board of Regents." These scholarships however did not mean additional or extra appropriation for the University.

The pace and progress of the program for the development of a Filipino faculty was reflected in the roster of faculty members included in the annually issued University catalogues.[45] By December 1926 when there were 6,464 students, there was an "instructing force" composed of "44 Americans and foreigners and 419 Filipinos."[46] This was significant for it meant that after about a decade and a half, only 10 per cent of the faculty was still American. Necessarily the increase in the number of Filipino faculty members was almost imperceptible during the Bartlett period. Among them were many with degrees from the University of Santo Tomas, Ateneo de Manila and schools abroad.

Toward Relevant Curricula

Meantime, in many other ways, Bartlett translated his concept of the University for the Filipino. Certain courses that to him were necessary and relevant to the efforts of the University to involve itself with the community outside its confines were given utmost attention. For several years, until the course was instituted, the graduate course on Tropical Medicine and Public Health preoccupied Bartlett. So did the problem of very small enrolment in the Veterinary Medicine course, because he felt that the Philippines was in need of its graduates.

For the first year of his administration, Bartlett reported on the measures taken "to bring the University to the people": obstetrical services were given free in the city of Manila particularly through the free clinics of the Philippine General Hospital, and stock judging contests were among the activities of Los Baños. Bartlett further suggested that the University "by all means continue this effort to make the College at Los Baños a real teaching center of practical agriculture."[47]

The need "to furnish the high schools with thoroughly competent and trained Filipino teachers. . ." was another opportunity, according to Bartlett, for the University to bring itself closer to the people.

Start of Athletic Program

When the University Council decided at its very first meeting to create several committees to enable it to discharge its responsibilities more efficiently, one of the committees established was that on University athletics which was assigned to carry out the athletic policies determined by the council and to report on the health of the student body. This committee, in other words, would look after the physical welfare of the students to balance what seemed at times to be too much emphasis placed on their intellectual growth.

Among the steps taken in that direction was the creation of an athletic board of control composed of three faculty members elected by the University Council and three student members chosen by the students of the various colleges. Its job was to supervise the activities having to do with the physical welfare of the students.

All the students, except those of the College of Law who were working students, were required to take what may be termed as the first "P.E." (Physical Education) subjects in the University, consisting of athletic exercises and "a series of contests in tennis, baseball, track and field events . . ." Expansion in the next years included the plan to appoint a competent instructor "to devote his whole time" to supervising the physical activities of the UP students, and to make available the "complete anthropometric records" of all students and the acquisition of an "apparatus for testing the strength of the different muscles of the body."

The plan was "for every student to be measured and tested at the start of each year and at the end of each semester" after which he is given advice "as to proper development in each case." The collected data, it was hoped, [would] enable [the UP] to turn out from the University young men who [were] thoroughly equipped physically as well as intellectually, to undertake the battle of life."[48]

Character Development

Bartlett saw the importance of developing another dimension in the growth and education of the student: his character. He touched on this point lengthily in his inaugural speech. It was not enough, he said, that a man is intellectually developed; he must likewise be developed or refined or chiseled off to smoothen his rough edges.[49]

As President of the University, Bartlett appeared to have seriously considered developing a sort of person-to-person relationship with all students which was not however realized due to constraints of time and "the great pressure of office work." Instead he gave "students of all departments . . . free access to his office at all times" and he addressed them at mass meetings whenever possible. Because there was lack of a commodious and convenient place for those meetings, Bartlett considered the possibility of meeting the need through the inclusion of such a place in the proposed "University Hall" where "all students may meet at regular intervals" and where he could meet them for "frequent and intimate talks about matters vital to the development of character and a healthy university life."

To assist the president in providing for the other needs of the students such as better living accommodations and finding ways of at least alleviating their problems, "a committee of young Filipino faculty members on student welfare" was formed. Bartlett expressed the hope that with the help and assistance of these young men "representing the various colleges who [were] imbued with a spirit of personal loyalty and enthusiasm for the purpose in view," activities of student life "may be organized along sound and helpful lines . . . that the moral tone of the student community may be safeguarded and maintained."[50]

Student Housing Problems

Since the student population of the University came from all over the country, whether enrolled in Manila or in Los Baños, the problem of living accommodations became a persistent one. The fiscal situation of the University gave little or no possibility at all to provide for their needs. In Los Baños, the students were allowed to put up their accommodations. Otherwise, the University was practically forced to depend on the private sector for a solution. In the absence of government supervision, however, the privately run dormitories left so much to be desired.

The seriousness of the problem was underscored in the report of the Philippine Commission to the Secretary of War in 1913 which observed:

> The conditions under which many of them live, in the absence of dormitories owned by the University, offers a serious problem, and it is probable that the university authorities will be obliged to take steps to exercise a rigid supervision in the matter. A physical examination made of a considerable number of students disclosed a somewhat alarming proportion affected with more or less serious organic troubles, though they are representatives of the best class of Filipinos.[51]

Apparently due to the findings concerning the state of health of the students in 1914, incoming students had to pass through a rigid medical examination. And although the results of the examination were not really alarming, it was decided that careful supervision of the students' health and physical development be a continuing practice in the university. Regular outdoor exercises, group games and other similar physical-building activities were planned for them.

Disciplinary Measures

High in the list of duties and responsibilities assigned to the University Council was one that pertained to student discipline, attesting to the importance attached to it and the need for this to be maintained or kept on an "even keel." Fortunately, at a time when the University had other more pressing problems, student discipline was not a cause for concern at all. There were in fact indications that the Filipino students were capable of doing "work of the same grade and fully as much" as their American counterparts.

Concerning this, Bartlett excerpted from the annual report of the Dean of the College of Liberal Arts for inclusion in his report in 1912 "an interesting . . . bit of testimony [to this effect] by one who [was] qualified by experience to speak:"

> The discipline of the College has been almost perfect. There is a slight disposition among the students to absent themselves from classes more than is necessary, but aside from this they furnish almost no reason for the exercise of disciplinary measures. No case of a serious nature has occurred. The students of the college have always shown themselves willing to cooperate with the faculty in every way which has been suggested. The question as to whether there is any difference in the ability of Filipino students compared with that of American students is almost constantly being suggested in some way. After four years of experience with Filipino students, I am still of the opinion which I formed during my first year, that there is no real difference between Filipino students and American. Our freshmen accomplished work of the same grade and fully as much of it as at the Universities of Minnesota and Missouri, and other smaller institutions with which I am acquainted maintaining a high standard of work.[52]

In any case, in 1914, a student council was organized to which body was referred matters pertaining to student discipline. The results produced were excellent as the recommendations of the council were carried out for all the disciplinary cases referred to it.[53]

Campus Publication

The students had a newspaper from as early as 1910. This was the *College Folio,* which was actually a literary magazine published by the students of the College of Liberal Arts. Its editorial for the second issue expressed its two-fold objective: to serve as vehicle for "the expression of their thoughts in literary form and in correct English" and to play the role of "recorder of the past and present national traditions and customs."

The *College Folio* was almost, if not wholly, a student enterprise. The editors and business managers were elected by the students with the approval of the Dean. The contributors to the paper were mostly students. It was also supported by money that came from or were raised by the students.

Although for and by the students, the *College Folio* actively participated in the discussion of important issues, such as the appointment of the first President of the University. The *Folio* served as an effective channel for voicing student opinion on matters directly or indirectly affecting them. It was also a sounding board, as it were, for the authorities of the University.

The *College Folio* looked different from what people today would expect of a literary magazine. The *Folio* had the size of a tourist brochure but not the usually attractive cover of one. On the top of the front page, below the name *College Folio* appeared a quotation from Carlyle that read thus: "Literary men are a perpetual priesthood." The next line carried the volume and number of the issue separated at the middle by the date of publication. Below this, to about half of the page, the names of the members of editorial staff were listed. The second issue dated December 1910 listed the following:

Victoriano Yamzon* .... Editor-in-Chief

Dolores Asuncion* ....)
Maximo M. Kalaw* ....) Assistant Editors
George B. Vargas*................)
Mateo Tecson** ....)

Eusebio Lopez* .... Business Manager

Wilfredo de Leon*.................)
Adolfo Scheerer* ....) Assistant Managers

*College of Philosophy, Science and Letters
**College of Education

The rest of the page was devoted to the editorial and some notes on where to send articles meant for publication, where to inquire about advertising prices, and the rate of subscription at one peso for the school-year or 30 centavos a copy.

Alumni Association Founded

The Alumni Association of the University of the Philippines (UPAA) came into being in 1913. Dean George A. Malcolm conceived of the idea that found immediate and enthusiastic support from Jorge Vargas, Alexander Reyes and Victoriano Yamzon, all graduates of the University. As an organization it was meant to foster the university spirit and maintain strong ties of friendship among the graduates. Its constitution, adopted in April 1913, called for the election of a president, a vice-president, a secretary-treasurer, and a board of directors composed of one delegate from each college.

The UPAA has gone a long way since then. Today it is represented in the Board of Regents, the highest governing body of the University, by the President of the Association. The organization can also point to the pre-war UP Press as one of the projects that to a certain extent was realized through its efforts.[54]

LAYING DOWN A SECURE FOUNDATION DESPITE MEAGER RESOURCES

FROM the very start, the UP was beset with what came to be the perennial problem of limited appropriations. In fact, this was one of the major reasons why the establishment of the UP was delayed. David P. Barrows, who proposed in 1904 that a university be put up, knew only too well that the problem of funds could be used as a very strong argument against the whole idea. His proposal, therefore, was presented complete with suggestion on how, in spite of the problem of funds, the University might still begin to exist.

The "Philippine University" bill of 1908, though a reflection of the importance attached to the institution and the recognition of the place of the University in the life of the country, did not provide the University with a budgetary allocation commensurate to the scale of the tasks that the University was expected to accomplish. No less than the Secretary of Public Instruction in 1909 noted with the apparent feeling of relief that in spite of the "most meager" appropriations "a beginning [in the University] nonetheless has been made."[55]

Not Enough Funds

All throughout the Bartlett period, the amount appropriated for the University remained small with very meager increases from one fiscal year to another. On occasions when the Philippine Legislature failed to pass the budget, the University had to make do with the same allocation as in the previous year although it had expanded and its needs had correspondingly grown. On top of this, the University was perpetually at the mercy of the Governor and the Philippine Legislature who "held the money bag." The appropriation for 1912 was ₱575,000; in 1914, ₱625,000.[56]

The Philippine Commission Report for 1913 happily noted the "satisfactory" financial situation of the University though "the work that might be done [was] far beyond its resources."[57]

Considering the meagerness of budgetary allocations, the scholarships for the development of the Filipino faculty that began in 1912 were adversely affected. The development of a Filipino faculty required a huge outlay that should have been either provided for separately from the UP budget or scrapped altogether as a project.

Bartlett was left to his own devices to make do with funds appropriated for the University. Thus he sought to relieve the University of expenses for items "not strictly within the scope of its purposes" such as the maintenance of 100 free beds in the Philippine General Hospital for the College of Medicine. As it were, because of those free beds, the College of Medicine had been allocated "an appropriation entirely out of proportion" to its number of students.[58]

Bartlett likewise proposed a continuing annual appropriation of ₱750,000 for four years instead of the existing practice of yearly appropriations.

Meantime, the University had to wait for additional or separate appropriations for urgent projects on account of the huge amounts involved. It could not provide funds for modest projects let alone for the construction of buildings that at the very least would cost ₱250,000. Consequently, the construction of the proposed buildings proceeded rather slowly. The first edifice on the Padre Faura Campus was not finished until 1913. The University Hall (as it was then called, later renamed Palma Hall) housed "the general offices" and the classrooms of the Colleges of Liberal Arts, Engineering, and Law.

Dreams of Greatness

To what extent the problem of funds caused the University of the Philippines to lose the chance to become "a great educational center for all" in the Far East can only be speculated about. But serious thought was definitely devoted to the possibility of giving the University a "wide usefulness not only in the Philippines but in the Orient as well."

Even before Bartlett's term the idea was given more than passing notice, as the editorial of the *Manila Times* on December 12, 1910 would attest. The very title of the editorial posed the question: "Why not a great oriental University? " The editorial replied, with the newly established UP in mind: "It would be possible to create here a great institution based upon high western ideals and yet be fitted to its larger environment." After citing what the UP can offer, it concluded with this statement: "We have already the beginnings of what may be a great institution worthy of the help and encouragement of all who are interested in making Manila the intellectual center of the Orient."

The increase in enrolment of foreign students, particularly those from Asia, made it necessary for a policy to be formulated and adopted. The influx was so heavy that ultimately foreign students were required to pay an admission fee equivalent to "the actual cost of their instruction" because the University, as it were, was finding it difficult to provide education even for the Filipinos themselves.[59] Whether the imposition dampened the enthusiasm for seeking education in the UP or created a barrier for the less financially capable should be worthwhile looking into. The fact was that the hope and dream of making "Manila the intellectual center of the Orient" did not materialize. The fee requirement could very well have been one of the reasons, no matter how indirect a bearing this might have had on the whittling down of foreign student enrolment.

The problem of limited resources likewise had a negative repercussion on the problem of administering the College of Agriculture. Bartlett at one time appeared to have reversed himself on his pet idea of a "University for the Filipino." Because Los Baños had become so big as to put a heavy strain on the University budget, Bartlett seriously considered limiting the enrolment there. He also expressed doubts whether the administration of the agricultural college properly belonged to the University of the Philippines.

Both ideas were in effect a retreat from what Bartlett promised to do as President of the University. More students in agriculture could have meant more Filipinos who were capable of putting to good use the agricultural resources of the Philippines while administration over Los Baños could have meant a better agricultural school for the country.

Personnel on the Move

Despite limited funds, however, the faculty of the University of the Philippines in those early years appear to have been well-paid, this being one reason why many government offices lost some of their men to the University. But perhaps the reason for the high salaries was to induce people to stay longer in the faculty. As it happened, however, the opposite resulted.

A fast turnover of personnel both in the academic as well as in the administrative sectors characterized the University in its early years. This meant lack of continuity or disruption of programs in the case of the former and lack of dedication on the part of the latter.

Another problem, almost exclusively true of Los Baños, was its great distance from the rest of the University. While the suggestion of Bartlett that the UP be relieved of administering Los Baños placed him in an embarrassing position in light of his idea of a University for the Filipino, he was right. The College of Agriculture did pose a very serious administrative problem, considering the remoteness of its location. The idea of autonomous UP units engaged the thinking of some people as shown in the manner the problem of Los Baños was handled. Eventually indeed, it acquired autonomous status, an arrangement adopted for some other units as well.

An Attempt at Appraisal

As the first President of the University, Murray Bartlett was fortunate in that he was not saddled with having to reckon with precedents nor with problems inherited from previous administrations. However, he had problems enough. As the first President of the University, Bartlett had no precedents to guide him.

Prof. Leopoldo Y. Yabes thought it important that Bartlett (like another American president of the UP) "did not have the proper background and outlook to lead a Filipino university." Prof. Yabes conceded that the foundation of the University was laid down during those early years but he said that the beginnings of the University "as a university in the true sense of the word" could be traced only from the time of the Palma presidency.[60] This was also tantamount to saying that the Bartlett administration had not accomplished much; the university had to wait for some time before it could hold its own.

Given the facts surrounding the first assumption of the UP presidency, however, perhaps the Bartlett era should be judged not on the basis of what it failed to do but on what it seriously hoped to achieve.

At any rate, two "issues" raised against the Bartlett administration were the two-year Bachelor of Arts course and the American/foreign orientation of the curricular or academic offerings of the university.[61] It appears that critics in both instances took issue with Bartlett over his "failure" to exercise "academic leadership" because the University's prospects depended "on the initiative of the President." They even suspected that the phrase "for the Filipino" in Bartlett's concept of the University meant that higher education in the Philippines should be modified or revised to the level of competence of the Filipino student, that it should be cut "to the size of the Filipino." The two-year A.B. course of the University, two years less than its American counterpart, was believed to be a perfect example of such "highly suspicious" efforts.

As discussed elsewhere in this account of the first years of the University, the two-year A.B. degree was a continuing source of discussion in the College of Liberal Arts. Perhaps it was this fact that led the University authorities to include documents pertinent to the course in the first catalogue issued. Unfortunately, the negative views appear to be due not only to ignorance about that particular A.B. program in comparison with the course in American schools, but also due to the lack of appreciation of the fact that the Philippines had moved from one system of education to another, with the two systems being quite different in many aspects.

The first years under American rule were necessarily transition years, when even academic courses in some cases partook of both systems at the same time. Therefore, any evaluation of certain changes will have to take into account what was there during the period of transition and what finally emerged. In the case of the A.B. program of the University, the change from the "old" to the new A.B. took some time and was not finally effected till almost the next decade.

Was the A.B. course in the University similar to the A.B. courses in American universities? Was it really inferior as suggested by the length of time required to get the degree?

Criticisms of the A.B. Course

The original A.B. course in the University was a legacy from the Spanish system of education which took after the Lycee of France. Secondary education in the French system meant "a complete course in general education taken at a very early stage which terminated with a bachelor's degree." After which "only the specialized courses of the University and of the great technical schools" remained. "The French scheme of secondary study, therefore, cover(ed) the work of the American high school with about two years of the courses" of American colleges.[62] In other words, the bachelor's degree from the French Lycee was acquired at about the same age and stage of development that a student in an American school completed his sophomore year in the college.

On the other hand, the high school graduate in America went to Junior College for courses that served as transition courses from high school to college. This was for two years after which he went to the third and fourth years for the specialized course that earned for him the A.B. degree.

Thus the holder of the "junior certificate" in California, the "associate in Chicago" and the "bachelor" from the French Lycee completed their course and entered the specialized courses "at about the same age."[63]

In the Philippines during the Spanish period, the leading private schools conferred the bachelor's degree. The Ateneo de Manila and San Beda required nine years for primary and secondary study while San Juan de Letran and Liceo de Manila required only eight years. Under the American government, these schools sought authority to continue the granting of degrees while some of them increased the required period of study to 13 years.[64]

Even as these developed, the University provided for admission requirements that practically allowed only graduates with as much preparation acquired from those private colleges. And in cases where the certificate submitted proved unsatisfactory, the applicant for admission had no choice but to take and pass the very tough admissions tests in order to qualify.[65]

The aforementioned facts were apparently taken into account when the Board of Regents had to render a decision on the petition for changes in the existing A.B. courses. Bartlett's annual report (1912) noted the contention that "although (the) degree (was) undoubtedly the equivalent to the corresponding Spanish degree and very much higher in standard to the degree of Bachelor of Arts as hitherto known in these islands, it (represented) only half of the work of the Bachelor of Arts degree in the American University."

The points raised were well taken but the Board deferred action on the matter. At the same time it indicated that Bartlett "as soon as convenient, should seek the advice of presidents of American Universities regarding this important matter."[66]

Bachelor's Degree Defended

In the same annual report, Bartlett articulated the other factors or reasons that favored the deferment of action on the proposed changes. Adverting to the decision of the Board, he said:

> . . . The chief consideration was that the term Bachelor of Arts has a distinctive meaning in the Philippine Islands as it has in the United States . . . It was felt [also] that the abolition of this title by the University [in favor of "Associate in Arts," similar to the practice in Chicago] would therefore cause a great deal of confusion . . .[67]

Bartlett wholeheartedly agreed with the opinion of the Board. He expressed himself strongly in favor of the "old" A.B. degree which was consistent with his view that the University is "for the Filipino." Therefore, "qualifications for degrees in the University of the Philippines should be governed by the needs and conditions existing here."

That the "present degree of Bachelor of Arts was admirably adapted for our own needs" was, according to Bartlett:

> . . . strongly confirmed by an official decision of the imperial authorities of public instruction in Germany . . . to the effect that students in the preparatory medical course in the College of Liberal Arts who obtain the degree of Bachelor of Arts will be admitted to the universities of Germany without further requirements as candidates for the degree of Doctor of Medicine.[68]

"This important decision," Bartlett concluded, *puts a recognized standard of value upon our bachelor's degree,* which undoubtedly (would) be given weight in our negotiations with the authorities of American Universities." (Underscoring supplied.)

The foregoing makes explicit the stand taken by President Bartlett on the issue of the "old" A.B. If academic leadership dictates involvement rather than aloofness in the discussion of all issues affecting the university, "being in the fray" rather than "sitting on the fence," then Bartlett may be said to have shown academic leadership. He was not a firebrand of sorts who would call everyone's attention to what he was saying, but he was fully aware of the issues which surfaced from time to time specially as these pertained to his own overall view of what the University of the Philippines should be.

Palpable American Presence

The American/foreign orientation of the curricular offerings of the University may not be valid ground for criticizing Bartlett who just continued what had been started before he assumed the presidency. One has only to situate the establishment of the University historically to have an idea of how it happened to acquire American or foreign orientation.

The models on which the administrators patterned their plans and programs were American or foreign-oriented because they themselves were, by culture and training, Americans or foreigners. The point that perhaps is more relevant to consider in connection with Bartlett is the fact that he had, as a matter of principle, pledged to mould the University into one "for the Filipino." But this was something easier said than done.

A case in point was the plan to institute graduate courses in Tropical Medicine as there was obvious need for this in the Philippines. However, it took about three years (in 1914) for the program to be implemented. It had an initial enrolment of over 20 students which more than doubled the following year but fell by half in the third year. Then the number of enrollees started to dwindle progressively until the program was abolished in the early 1920s.

With respect to the graduate offering in history that appeared in the Catalogue for 1913, which promised opportunities "for studying the beginnings and progress of European and American influence in the Far East," it should be pointed out that 1913 was yet so many decades removed from the time history would be pursued not only "for its own sake" but also for "one's own country's history's sake." And this was the case in the Philippines as elsewhere.

There seems to be no reason to doubt that the Bartlett administration was single-minded in its declared purpose to realize a university for the Filipinos. Seeming deviations from that plan as in the case of Los Baños, were only and actually improvisations in response to the needs of the moment and times and were apparently not meant to be permanent.

Calm and Uneventful Years

Bartlett's term was really very short if one were to consider the man-sized job he took on, that of laying the foundations of the University. In comparison with other presidential terms, except perhaps the two succeeding ones, the Bartlett period was, therefore, seemingly uneventful and perhaps unexciting. There was nothing like the usually volatile student front of our times. In the case of the faculty, except for the usually anticipated yet unwelcome resignations that caused the rapid turnover of academic personnel, they really posed no serious problem.

The Board of Regents appeared to be no cause for worry either. Even the apparent fear expressed at the beginning of the Bartlett period that it might not be given the opportunity to be "an active body" did not develop into a real issue between the President and the Board.[69] But apart from the prevailing cultural idiosyncracies and/or mores of those times, credit for what perhaps appeared to be cordial and harmonious relations between Bartlett and the Board, the faculty, and the studentry should be accorded to all sides, with the President deserving more of it. He devised ways whereby he would not be out of touch with the Board, the faculty and students. As many meetings with each group as deemed necessary were called to keep channels of communication open and working at all times.[70]

The UP today has come a long way from the University that housed its first academic units in temporary, rented or borrowed accommodations; that ministered to a student population of a few hundreds; and that was staffed by a faculty with just a handful of Filipino members. Yet no matter how long ago that was, there is much of what the University is today that dates back to those very early years. In "one sense," however, in the view of the *Manila Times* editorial that appeared the day after the inauguration of the first UP President, the "life of the University of the Philippines. . . [began] . . . only with the inauguration of [Bartlett]". This, of course, rightly stressed the fact that it was only then that the "role and mission" of the University of the Philippines was actually defined.

The reactions to Bartlett's inaugural message were expressions of elation and confidence in the future of the University, convinced as those people were that the first president of the UP had a clear-cut view of the task before him. If Bartlett also sounded optimistic and confident that he would succeed in concretizing the concepts that he had propounded, his optimism and confidence were tempered by an equally firm grasp of the realities surrounding him at the time. This is evident in the passage of that same speech where Bartlett said:

> We fully realize that the great work before us cannot be done in a hurry. We realize that there are public improvements of great importance that may have the first claim upon the resources of the government. It may be that I have been called here simply to dream the dream; that it may be left for others to make the dream a reality. Should that be my lot I shall be content, so long as my vision be clear and just, my purpose brave and true.

Achievements in Retrospect

An objective appraisal of the Bartlett period would show, nevertheless, that far from just "dream [ing]" or leaving "[it] for the other [administrations] to make the dream [for the university] a reality," some significant strides were made toward achieving the twin goals identified in the Bartlett speech: a University "for the Filipino," and one in the finest traditions of the older universities.

To the already existing colleges: that of Medicine, Agriculture, Veterinary Medicine, Fine Arts, Liberal Arts, Engineering, Law and the department of Pharmacy in the College of Liberal Arts – were added two new sub-units: the department of Education in the College of Liberal Arts and the department of Dentistry in the College of Medicine and Surgery. In just a few years, these two new units became fully operational as independent colleges.

Curricular changes and revisions aimed for more realistic course offerings along with the adoption of more stringent admission requirements. Also important in this connection were the masteral programs offered by several colleges for those who wanted to go beyond the baccalaureate degree.

Research and scientific investigation that very often is taken to be synonymous with a university's existence found a very solicitous patron in Bartlett and more than ample room for growth and expansion in the University of the Philippines.

Enrolment in the University gradually increased from the 67 students which started out during the foundation year in 1908 to a total of 2,075 at the end of Bartlett's term in 1915. The yearly figures are listed hereunder:

STUDENTS ENROLLED IN THE UNIVERSITY

Academic Year	*Total Enrolment*
1908-1909	67
1909-1910	832
1910-1911	1,213
1911-1912	1,400
1912-1913	1,398
1913-1914	1,502
1914-1915	2,075

Student welfare and interest was accorded equal, if not more than its share of the, attention and concern of the University authorities. Already very much a part of University life were the *College Folio,* the student newspaper, and the Student Council. Both served as training grounds for budding talents and leaders in the making.

Bartlett's pet project, the Filipino faculty development program, went off to a good start with the passage of a law that provided for government scholarships for deserving and promising young Filipinos who had set their sights on making a career of teaching in the university.

Also during the Bartlett period, the UP Alumni Association was created thereby institutionalizing the substance and meaning of all that the University stands for: as *alma mater* to its growing legion of graduates.

The operationalization of the two major concepts of Bartlett was definitely underway but the other ideas could not be planned for that early, let alone concretized. Many of them were equally deserving of consideration; as the one which called for a university that, in the words of Bartlett, "[did] not stand alone" but rather one that closely coordinated its work with other private "institutions of higher and professional learning," with the lower levels of the public school system, and with government agencies with concerns or interests similar to those of the University.

Today, about 70 years since the Bartlett administration, we find the UP a member of several consortia of educational institutions that have pooled their resources in pursuit of their common goals, a partner in programs closely coordinated with the public schools such as the off-campus practice teaching requirement of the UP College of Education, and as a counterpart in mutually beneficial arrangements where the professional expertise of the faculty is shared and exchanged for the use of the highly sophisticated facilities of certain government agencies. One such "partnership" is with PAGASA, the government's weather bureau.

Solid Foundation

In short, despite the constraints posed by many problems, particularly lack of funds, if not also the background and expertise required of the first president of the UP who was an American, success was realized even in a limited way in putting up the first and real beginnings of the University, as envisioned by Bartlett – a University "for the Filipino" and one in the finest traditions of the older universities. The tangible and discernible manifestations of these were in themselves auspicious and significant, only exceeded in importance by the general and specific principles upon which they were based.

Both the principles and the results of attempts to concretize them were the achievements of the Bartlett administration. They constituted the foundation, upon which the University in the years to come would be built and developed. Upon these "modest" accomplishments firmly rested what could be the rightful claim of the Bartlett administration to a place in the history of the University of the Philippines.

II

Villamor's Filipino Perspective (1915-1920)

The University's Tenacious Growth to Adolescence

by Napoleon J. Casambre

Villamor's Filipino Perspective

WHEN, on November 21, 1914, President Murray Bartlett officially announced his resignation from the University presidency at the University Council meeting,[1]* the question of who would succeed him became an interesting guessing game within and outside the University. Members of the University constituency began to speculate as to who would be their next president. The metropolitan newspapers also picked up the issue, and the *Manila Times* published some of the names of the probable candidates: Jose Escaler who, himself, was a member of the Board of Regents; Commissioner Trinidad H. Pardo de Tavera; Director of Education Frank L. Crone, also a member of the Board of Regents; Dean George A. Malcolm of the College of Law; and a certain Mr. Batchilder.[2]

Each of these candidates was assessed, and while all of them appeared to be qualified for the position, they had certain handicaps that would lessen the prospects of their appointment. Regent Escaler was reported to have "the disadvantage of being young. . . and more inclined to accept a judicial position than the U.P. presidency." Commissioner Tavera had been out of the country for too long and, therefore, would not be knowledgeable of local developments, aside from the fact that he "seemed to be hostile to Filipino aspirations."[3] Dean Malcolm, Director Crone and Mr. Batchilder were Americans and this put them at a disadvantage. For by this time, there was a growing sentiment among the Filipino members of the Board of Regents and political leaders that a compatriot should be appointed to the University presidency, in line with the objective of establishing a "University for the Filipinos" and of Governor General Francis B. Harrison's policy of "Filipinizing" government offices. It was reported in the newspaper *Democracia* that even out-going President Bartlett himself favored a Filipino for his successor.[4]

MOST QUALIFIED CANDIDATE FOR THE PRESIDENCY

MEANWHILE, the name of Judge Ignacio Villamor was being prominently mentioned as the next university president. On the basis of his qualifications, he appeared to be the strongest candidate. At age 52, he had the advantage of maturity and experience. He had a long and varied record in the government service, having been a provincial fiscal,

*Footnote references are compiled in the NOTES section at the end of this book.

Judge of the Court of First Instance, Attorney-General and Secretary of the Executive Department. Moreover, he was an experienced educator, having founded two colleges where he taught at the same time. On top of that, he was no stranger to the University since he was a lecturer on a special subject in the College of Law and at the same time a member of the Board of Regents.[5] As a member of the University's governing body, he knew at a higher level the developments in the University. However, like the other candidates, he also had his own handicap as pointed out by those who probably were against him. His critics argued that he could not make a good university president because he lacked executive ability. He manifested this weakness when, as Secretary of the Executive Department, he could not deal effectively with the local government officials who were under his supervision and control.[6]

That Judge Villamor's candidacy was being considered seriously can be gleaned from the exchange of secret cablegrams between the two most important Filipino political leaders at that time – Sergio Osmeña, Sr., the Speaker of the Philippine Assembly, and Manuel L. Quezon, the Filipino Resident Commissioner to the United States Congress. The two political leaders were very much interested in, and concerned about, the matter and on the basis of available evidence, it can be safely said that their thoughts and wishes were taken into consideration by the Board of Regents when they elected the second president of the University. In a cablegram to Commissioner Quezon dated January 30, 1915, and marked "Strictly Confidential," Speaker Osmeña indicated his support for Judge Villamor's candidacy. In part he said: "Villamor considered highly qualified scholar. . . combining Philippine experience with modern university ideals. His success as judge dealing with American jurisprudence shows remarkable fitness. . ."[7]

Commissioner Quezon replied by cablegram also marked "Strictly Confidential." In his reply, he pointed out the difficulties of having Villamor appointed to the university presidency. For one thing, Vice-Governor Henderson Martin, who was the Secretary of Public Instruction and ex-officio Chairman of the Board of Regents, would not favor his appointment because he lacked executive ability.[8] Besides, the Vice Governor would consent to a Filipino appointee only if Rafael Palma, who was a member of the Philippine Commission and the Board of Regents, was recommended. Concluding his reply, Commissioner Quezon stated the criteria which he perceived to be a good basis for the selection of the University president. "I see objection about an American president," he said, "but we should be careful to select one who besides capacity believes in nationalism and would not bring incompetent professors . . ." And he added: "Teachers should not be allowed to discuss politics . . ."[9]

A few days later, Speaker Osmeña again cabled Commissioner Quezon acknowledging the latter's earlier message. He stated that he also believed in the teaching of nationalism by Filipinos and that the university president should be a Filipino for two reasons: first, the time had come to carry out the Filipinization policy in the Philippine schools; and second, transformation through the educational system should "respect natural culture and conditions and men like Arellano, Palma, Villamor, Kalaw represent progress of the present combined with new ideals."[10]

On May 20, 1915, it was reported in the *Manila Times* that Vice Governor Martin had made the announcement that the new university president would be named at a meeting of the Board of Regents in Manila. By this time, there was already a widespread rumor that Judge Villamor would be chosen. In fact, it was also reported in the *Manila Times* that the good Judge had made a trip to Baguio "to accept the U.P. presidency which was offered to him by the Acting Governor General (Vice-Governor Martin)." Four days later, the Board of Regents met in an executive session in the office of Commissioner Palma to select the new University President. With Vice-Governor Martin presiding, most of the members of the Board were present except Archbishop Jeremias Jacob Harty and Supreme Court Justice E. Finley Johnson. The nominating committee composed of Commissioner Palma, Archbishop Harty, and Atty. Escaler presented the name of Judge Villamor to the body. In making the nomination, the Committee submitted its report to the Board, which said in part:

> The special committee to which the nomination of the President for the University of the Philippines has been referred, begs leave to report as follows:
>
> It is the sense of the Committee that in considering the qualifications of the man to be selected it should be borne in mind, first of all, the fact that the University of the Philippines is meant to prepare the Philippine youth to face actual conditions and problems of its country. It is therefore of paramount importance that such a man be thoroughly familiar with those conditions and problems – of course, he must be also a scholar of high attainment and a man of good executive ability, and whose character and reputation are above reproach. Such a man must not only add prestige to this institution of learning and command the respect of the heads of the several departments and colleges and of the American and foreign community as well but he must furthermore accomplish the object for which the institution was founded.
>
> Your Committee has carefully weighed the qualifications of the persons who are available for the position and, after mature and careful deliberation of the matter, has agreed to recommend Honorable Ignacio Villamor for the post of President of the University of the Philippines. Judge Villamor is a citizen of the P.I. and holds the following degrees from the U.S.T.: Bachelor of Arts, Master of Arts and Master of Laws. He has occupied respon-

sible positions in the Government, on account of which he has had unusual opportunities to know the conditions and problems of the country. First in the bench, later as Attorney General and now as Executive Secretary, Judge Villamor has been in touch with every branch of the Government, but more important still with every part of the country and patriotism has been amply demonstrated in every one of these positions.[11]

Regent Winfred Thaxter Dennison nominated Jacob Gould Schurman, President of Cornell University. At the same time, he presented a motion that in case Schurman was not acceptable to the Board, a special committee be formed "to study available material of experienced university administrators in the United States and report a recommendation." The motion was voted down and so the Board proceeded to consider the nominees. Regent Dennison voted for his candidate, but all the others favored Judge Villamor. Thus, the question of the University presidency was finally resolved. Judge Villamor became the second president of the University, the first Filipino to hold that position. This was a significant step taken by the Board of Regents to build the University into a Filipino University.

JUDGE VILLAMOR TAKES OVER AS UNIVERSITY PRESIDENT

AS soon as the news of his appointment broke into the newspapers, President Villamor received numerous congratulatory messages. Speaker Osmeña sent this simple message: "Hearty Congratulations! "[12] Governor General Harrison, who was on leave from his office, cabled his Secretary, Ferguson, the following message: "Please convey to Judge Villamor my sincere congratulations upon his appointment as President of the University."[13] General Frank McIntyre, the head of the Bureau of Insular Affairs, which was the agency in charge of the colonial administration of the Philippines, also wired his congratulatory wishes. "Let me congratulate you on your election as President of the University of the Philippines," he said, and went on: "Your selection for this position is an honor which will be increased by the knowledge of the fact that you deserved the honor. With best wishes to you personally and for continued success in your office. . ."[14]

Of great significance, perhaps, was the letter he received from Regent Dennison, who, in effect, opposed his candidacy by nominating a fellow American, Jacob Gould Schurman. In his letter, the Regent promised to support the newly appointed president:

Permit me to assure you of my hearty support in your administration of the great office which you have been honored. As you know, I have always felt that the educational needs of the P.I. required the selection of a man of extended, practical experience in the management of a great modern University of the Philippines, and therefore I voted for President Jacob Gould Schurman. This opinion of mine, however, has never diminished my high regard for you, and will never interfere with my cordial assistance in your work. . . .[15]

While the general reaction to President Villamor's selection was one of jubilation, it was reported, however, by the *Manila Daily Bulletin* that many of the students of the University were disappointed because the Board of Regents used nationality as the sole criterion in the selection of the university president. They thought it would have been better had the Board disregarded that consideration and instead chosen a man with "a strong hand" to run the university and bring it "to a footing similar to that of the universities of Europe and America." The press report further stated that since the selection had been made the students could not but rejoice to have as their head one of the most efficeint Filipinos to administer the affairs of the University.[16]

Perhaps, the reaction of the University faculties can be gleaned from some of the events that transpired at the meeting of the University council held at the University Hall on July 31, 1915, the last meeting attended by President Bartlett. With Dean William E. Musgrave of the College of Medicine and Surgery presiding, the Council members passed unanimously a congratulatory resolution which stated:

Whereas, The Regents of the University of the Philippines have elected as the second President of this institution the Honorable Ignacio Villamor, and

Whereas, Judge Villamor not only brings to University the ripened experience of an extended and distinguished career in the public service together with the resulting general confidence in his integrity and administrative ability among his wide and representative acquaintanceship throughout these Islands, but as well life-long devotion to the cause of Philippine higher education and a notable record of conspicuous achievements in its behalf, thus inspiring confidence in his administration and appreciably enhancing the prospects of the institution which looks to him for guidance, therefore be it,

Resolved, That the University Council, cordially welcome its new head, congratulate him most sincerely upon his accession to a post so important in the advancement of the country, and assure him of its fullest cooperation.[17]

To welcome the new President, the Council approved the appointment of a committee of nine, each member representing one of the nine schools and colleges that constituted the University of the Philippines.[18] Appointed to the committee by Dean Musgrave, the presiding officer, were the following professors: Professor Sixto de los Angeles, College of Medicine and Surgery; Assistant Professor Felix Hocson, School of Pharmacy; Professor Ernest B. Conant, College of Law; Assistant Professor Francisco Benitez, School of Education; Associate Professor Louis F. Snow, College of Liberal Arts; Professor Horace G. Deming, College of Agriculture; Assistant Professor Victor Buencamino, College of Veterinary Science; Dean Clarence G. Wrentmore, College of Engineering; and Dean Rafael Enriquez, School of Fine Arts.[19]

The Committee presented the Council's congratulatory resolution to the newly appointed President. After he was introduced to the Council by the presenting officer, President Villamor assumed the chair and made this address:

> I have always considered the office of the President of the University as one of the most difficult and responsible positions in the public service. This consideration becomes more impressive to me on this occasion, because the presence of so many learned men in the different branches of human knowledge, requires on my part such qualifications that I fear I do not possess.
>
> A president of a university, indeed is placed in a unique position, due to the multitudinous relations which he has to maintain. He has to deal with the Government, with the Board of Regents, with different faculties and with the public at large.
>
> Now referring to his relations with the different Faculties, it seems that a close relation should exist between one another, as interchange of ideas and sentiments tends to create not only good personal association, but also earnest cooperation which is essential to the accomplishment of results beneficial to the University.
>
> The President and the Faculties have the same purpose to attain, and this purpose is the progress of the University. I know from my personal experiences how difficult are the duties of the Faculties, but it would not be amiss to remember that the teaching profession is the noblest work in which man can engage, for to teach means to make men, elevate society, and in its ultimate result, to advance civilization.
>
> The members of this Council, too, are aware of the difficulties with which the President of the University is confronted. So I expect that the cooperation and advice of the Faculties will help me in the solution of university problems. On my part, I wish to state that everything possible will be done to promote the happiness of the professors, so that they will find university life agreeable.
>
> I highly appreciate the affectionate demonstration of welcome that the Council has just rendered to me. It does not only show courtesy and delicate sentiments on your part, but also constitutes a powerful stimulus for me to advance the work that I am called upon to perform.[20]

INAUGURAL RITES FOR PRESIDENT VILLAMOR

TWO weeks later, President Villamor was formally installed into office in an impressive and solemn ceremony. The inaugural rites were held at the Philippine Normal School Auditorium on its new location at Taft Avenue. In attendance was a large audience consisting mostly of university students and faculty members and high-ranking government officials. Governor General Harrison noted the significance of the occasion in his welcome address. He pointed out that the University had just passed its first period of development and, therefore, was about to enter the second and even greater stage of its development.[21] Commissioner Quezon introduced President Villamor and in his speech he voiced his ideas on what he believed to be one of the paramount duties of the President of the University. He declared:

> We want our girls and our boys to be taught that they are Filipinos, that the Philippines is their country and the only country that God has given them; that they must keep it for themselves and for their children; and that they must live for it and die for it if necessary. This is the thought that I want strongly to impress upon the President of the University who is about to be formally inaugurated. He is a Filipino himself, and had given, on every occasion in the past evidences of his sincere and earnest patriotism.[22]

Quezon further expressed the belief that President Villamor was chosen for the exalted position "not merely because of his well-recognized competency to conduct this institution, but because he is expected to instill in the hearts of his students a very strong spirit of Philippine patriotism both by his example and by his teachings."[23] Vice-Governor Martin, Chairman of the Board of Regents, inducted President Villamor into office, after which the latter gave his inaugural address.

At the outset, President Villamor expressed to the Board of Regents his high appreciation for having appointed him to the exalted position. As head of the institution, he considered it a great privilege "to be associated with men of learning and character" as were those in the faculties and to have his name connected with the highest educational institution in the country.[24]

Later in his address, he dwelt on the mission of the University as envisioned in the legislative act establishing it and as he perceived it himself. "For us," he declared, "the University of the Philippines, designed as it is to meet the needs of this country, should aim, firstly, to extend the field of scientific knowledge, essential to the development of the natural resources of the country; and secondly, to mold character, by promoting among the students the sense of justice and responsibility, honor and dignity, good fellowship and self-help, perseverance in their work, compliance with their duties, and love of the Alma Mater. *Her ideal should be efficiency founded upon science and inspired by character.*"[25] He underscored the fact that since the University was being supported financially by the government, it must, therefore, serve the interests of the Filipino people by contributing to the fullest measure to the preservation of their life, their rights and their nationality.

He made this mission the goal of his administration and he pledged to carry it out. But, for him to succeed, he would need the following: the keen mentality and great adaptability of the students, the efficiency of instructors and the material endowment of the institution, plus the advice and support of the Board of Regents.

Before closing his speech, President Villamor identified some of the pressing needs of the University. He was more or less cognizant of these matters since he was a member of the governing body of the University and part-time faculty member before his elevation to the presidency. There was the need to establish in the university "a permanent faculty of Filipino scholars." Moreover, he said:

> The University should have an annual endowment sufficient not only to ensure its existence but also to provide for its development. A building for the laboratory of engineering, a gymnasium for physical training, and a central auditorium are insistent needs of the University. We need to erect *Rizal Hall* for the classrooms and laboratories of zoology, botany and physics and for the museum and library of these departments. I mention Rizal Hall as the construction of this building has already been authorized by the legislature; its plans and specifications having been prepared and approved by the Board of Regents. We need to enlarge our lands for the experiments of the College of Agriculture. We should also organize new departments and courses as the needs of the University may warrant.[26]

These were the things he proposed to accomplish during his administration. After his predecessor's tenure which were the "foundation years," the time had come for him to develop and expand the University. President Villamor was very much aware of that role and he played it dutifully during his incumbency.

GROWTH OF THE UNIVERSITY UNDER PRESIDENT VILLAMOR

THE University continued to grow and expand under President Villamor. When he assumed office June 1915, the University consisted of seven "departments" or units, namely: College of Medicine and Surgery, College of Agriculture, College of Liberal Arts, College of Engineering, College of Veterinary Science, College of Law, and School of Fine Arts. Out of some of these older units were created new ones which later would become separate schools or colleges of the University.

Expansion of Academic Units

The first of these additional units established during Villamor's presidency was the School of Education. It came about when the Department of Education in the College of Liberal Arts was organized into a school on June 22, 1915, upon the recommendation of the President of the University and the Director of Education, who was an ex-officio member of the Board of Regents.[27] The aim of the School was to prepare well-qualified teachers for the public high schools. Admission to the school required the completion of a preparatory course in education or its equivalent as determined by the education committee. After finishing this course, the candidate was recommended by the committee to receive a high school teacher's certificate. Another year of further study as approved by the committee would entitle the student to the degree of Bachelor of Science in Education.

Still a constituent part of the College of Liberal Arts, the school was placed under the direction of a committee composed of the dean of the College as chairman, the school director, and the chiefs or acting chiefs of the departments of English, mathematics, history, physics, botany, zoology, and education.[28] Prof. Francisco Benitez, who was sent to the United States as a university fellow to take further studies in the field of education, became its first director.

Also established in the College of Liberal Arts that same year was the University Chorus, the forerunner of the Conservatory of Music. The plan to organize it was made when the Acting Dean of the College of Liberal Arts proposed at the University Council meeting of July 31, 1915, to create a University Chorus which would offer music education in the University.[29]

To study further the matter, the council formed a three-man committee consisting of Reinhart Parker Cowles, the Acting Dean of the College of Liberal Arts, Prof. Ernest B. Conant, and Prof. Conrado Benitez. The Committee rendered its report to the University Council in its meeting of October 17, 1915, and among other things, it recommended the creation of the University Chorus in the College of Liberal Arts to be supervised by a "Committee on Courses on Music" formed by the Dean of the College of Liberal Arts, a musical director, and one other member of the University Council appointed by the President of the University.[30]

When it was finally organized, Prof. Guy Harrison became its first musical director. It was opened to all the students of the University who could pass the qualifying examination. These students would earn College of Liberal Arts credits only and no one among them would be allowed to take more than four units of music courses for the degree.

In 1915, the Board of Regents authorized the creation of the School of Dentistry in the College of Medicine and Surgery. Admission to the School required graduation of the applicant from an accredited high school or an equivalent education. The school offered two distinct academic programs: one a three-year course leading to a degree of dental surgery and the other a four-year course leading to the degree of dental medicine.[31] Understandably, only a few students were attracted to the four-year course.

Owing to increased student enrolment and the availability of funds, some of the newer units that had been attached to the older ones separated and became independent schools or colleges of the University. The School of Forestry, for instance, became independent from the College of Agriculture when it organized itself in 1916.[32] In that same year, the Third Philippine Legislature passed Act No. 2623 setting aside funds "for the establishment and maintenance of a Conservatory of Music."[33] Hence, the University Chorus was removed from the College of Liberal Arts and transformed into the Conservatory of Music. Its course of study was "designed to educate pupils who desire to make a serious study of music with a view to a professional career in some branches of art." It formally opened its classes in September 1916, in a rented building located at 963 Calle R. Hidalgo, with Prof. Wallace W. George as its first Dean. Two distinct courses were offered to the students under the supervision of a musical director: one was a special course on general music instruction and the other was a regular course leading to a diploma or degree.

To provide classes for practice teaching for students in the School of Education, the University High School was established in July 1916.[34] However, its graduates could also enter the University since it followed the course of study prescribed for public secondary schools. Those students wanting to be admitted to the school were required to present a certificate of completion of the intermediate course from an accredited intermediate school and to pay a fee of ₱25 a year. In spite of the matriculation fee and the existence of a free high school in the city of Manila, many students from the city enrolled in the University High School.

In 1918, two new colleges of the University were established, one of which was the College of Education. The Board of Regents at its meeting of March 8, 1918, authorized the organization of the School of Education in the College of Liberal Arts into a separate College of Education.[35] The Board's decision was prompted by the significant increase in the number of students enrolling in the education course and by the Board's desire to give to the teaching profession the importance which it really deserved. Director Benitez became its first dean. Also organized was the Junior College in Cebu City with an allocation of ₱50,000 set aside by the Philippine Legislature. It opened classes with 20 students and four instructors.[36]

Building Up of Facilities and Services

At the same time that new schools and colleges were organized to form the larger University, new facilities were added to the older units to provide better and more effective instruction to their students. The School of Fine Arts started to develop a museum of artistic reproductions where models of statues, busts, bas-reliefs, paintings in water color and in oil by famous painters, were deposited and exhibited.[37] These reproductions were intended to serve as guides to the fine arts students and to the artists in the Philippines. The School also installed a "reducing machine," the first and only one of its kind in the country at that time, for the class in engraving. It was a necessary piece of equipment in the study of the art of engraving as it permitted work of the highest degree of precision. In the College of Medicine and Surgery, a Pharmacy Laboratory was established above the dispensary of the Philippine General Hospital. A students' group known as the Pharmaceutical Students' Association encouraged the establishment of the laboratory.[38]

By virtue of Act No. 2730 of the Philippine Legislature, an Experimental Research Station was organized in the College of Agriculture. President Villamor, underscoring the importance of this facility in his *Seventh Annual Report,* said: "Great was the need for this experiment station in that College, in as much as it helps the carrying out of investigations of a high order, reporting the results thereof to the agricultural community by means of journals and scientific pamphlets."

In the College of Law, Dean Bocobo spearheaded the creation of a Legal Clinic which would serve not only the interests of the law students but also the general public, specially those belonging to the poor families. In his memorandum to President Villamor, the Law Dean cited five benefits that could be derived from the establishment of the Clinic, namely: (1) actual practice of the law by the students; (2) moral education; (3) more speedy administration of justice; (4) additional material for study by the Law Faculty; and (5) reputation to be gained by the University of the Philippines in the United States.[39]

While it was primarily established to enhance the study and practice of law by the students and the faculty, the Legal Clinic was also used as an instrument to render direct service to the people. On one occasion, President Villamor offered the services of the Legal Clinic to the rural credit workers of the Bureau of Agriculture so that they would be able to help the poor farmers in the countryside fight the evil practice of usury to which they had been subjected for so long.[40]

Curricular Changes and Developments

The establishment of new units involved a corresponding increase in the number of academic course offerings which formed part of the growth and expansion of the University under President Villamor's administration. In some instances, though, it was the institution of new courses of study that led to the organization of more schools and colleges. For a new course of study to be instituted, the procedure was (as in President Bartlett's time) for any of the standing committees of the Board of Regents to make the proposal which was then sent to the University Council for discussion and for writing up in final form; then it was returned to the Board for approval after which it could already be offered in the college concerned.

The procedure was followed when the curriculum of the newly organized School of Education was established. The Board's Standing Committee on Liberal Arts recommended the course of study at the meeting of the Board on July 15, 1915.[41] It was discussed and put into final form by the University Council at its meeting on July 31, 1915, after which it was sent back to the Board for final approval and for offering.[42]

The institution of new curricula took place not only in the newly organized units of the University but also in the older ones. In the College of Engineering, new courses of study for mining, mechanical, and electrical engineering were adopted in addition to civil engineering. The recommendation to institute these new course offerings originated from the Board of Regents' Standing Committee on Engineering. It was discussed at the meeting of the University Council on July 31, 1915. The dean of the College of Engineering outlined the proposed curricula, and after an extended discussion, the Council voted "to refer the curricula to a committee of three for final consideration and report." The Committee submitted its report at a meeting of the University Council on October 17, 1915, and, among other things, it recommended "the adoption of the course of study as presented to the Council by the Dean of the College of Engineering."[43] Each of the new curricula as finally approved by the Board of Regents was of the same length as that of the civil engineering course and would lead to the corresponding degrees of Bachelor of Science at the completion of four years and a Master of Science at the end of five years.

New courses of study were also introduced in the other schools and colleges of the University. In the College of Liberal Arts, the period from 1915 to the close of the academic year 1917, witnessed the introduction of new curricular offerings in Commerce, Biology, and Library Science. A two-year preparatory course leading to the Bachelor of Arts degree was required of the student before entrance into any of the three courses of study. Upon completion of the fourth-year schedule, the student was awarded the corresponding Bachelor of Science degree.[44] Likewise, in the College of Medicine and Surgery, courses of study in Nursing and Pharmacy were established.

The Philippine General Hospital Training School for Nurses was given supervision over the offering of the Nursing curriculum which was a three-year schedule.[45] The Pharmacy curriculum was also of the same length leading to the degree of Bachelor in Pharmacy. One more year of study would entitle the student to the degree of Bachelor of Science in Pharmacy.[46]

In the College of Forestry, a new degree course was offered to students who possessed the following qualifications: (1) graduates of Philippine high schools, (2) had completed the ranger's course in the School of Forestry, (3) proficient in the use of English and Spanish, (4) had accomplished two years of successful field service in the Bureau of Forestry; or had training equivalent to these four requirements. After completing two years of satisfactory work in residence in the School of Forestry, the students would earn the degree of Bachelor of Science in Forestry.[47] This new course was aimed at preparing personnel for the higher grades of administrative work in the Bureau of Forestry.

Along with the establishment of new courses of study, there were other curricular changes and developments that occurred in the University under President Villamor. In the College of Liberal Arts, the two-year Bachelor of Arts Curriculum was enlarged and expanded to four years. The change was made partly to place the Bachelor of Arts degree on the level of the Bachelor of Science degree and the Bachelor of Arts degree of the professional colleges which were of four years study, and partly to bring the University's Bachelor of Arts equal to its corresponding American degree since at this time several Filipino students were going to the United States to continue their studies.[48] Included in the new four-year Bachelor of Arts curriculum were the required courses in the first two years and the 42 units of "major" study. New courses in Sociology, Economics and Political Science were instituted in the College of Liberal Arts as they were needed in the Commerce curriculum.

Sometimes, however, it was the presence of an instructor specialized in a particular field of study, and also the demand for a certain type of university training and preparation, that led to the introduction of new academic subjects.

With the institution of more courses, there was the necessity of realigning departments of instruction as well as organizing new ones. This resulted in the creation of the Department of Sociology and Economics under Prof. Conrado Benitez and the Department of Political Science with Dean George Malcolm of the College of Law as chief. In the latter department, five subjects were offered, namely: Political Science 1 – Principles in Political Science; Political Science 2 – Constitutional History; Political Science 3 – American Government; Political Science 4 – Philippine Government and Politics; and Political Science 5 – Oriental Governments. Later, these courses became the core of a four-year Bachelor of Science in Government curriculum which was offered for the first time in the school year 1918-1919.[49]

In that same year, a novel curriculum was introduced, making it possible for a student to finish two undergraduate degrees in five years. This was the combined five-year course of study in Law and Government. In this curriculum, the student would have to earn all the units (110) required for the Bachelor of Laws degree and, in addition, 31 units in the College of Liberal Arts, but the College of Law would not excuse him from any subject.[50] The Liberal Arts subjects required in the curriculum were as follows: Political Science 6 – European Government; Political Science 7 – Political Parties; Political Science 8 – Municipal Government; Political Science 9 – Theory and Practice of Legislation; Political Science 11 – Diplomacy; Economics 2 – Economic Development of the Philippines; Economics 10 – Public Finance; Sociology 2 – Social Ethics; History 6 – Oriental History or Anthropology 1 – General Anthropology; English 4 – English Literature, and a Thesis course.[51]

At the College of Agriculture in Los Baños, a proposal was made to give an award to an alumnus of the school who had achieved distinction in the field of agricultural education. Thus the Dean of the College of Agriculture presented a resolution in the University Council which partly stated: "Resolved: That the faculty of the College of Agriculture, on the suggestion of the President of the University, recommends to the University Council, that it authorizes the granting of a diploma to state that the recipient is recognized by the University of the Philippines as a 'Master Farmer'; this diploma to be conferred only on the vote of the University Council in the same manner that candidates are recommended for degrees. . . ."[52] Those eligible to receive this post-graduate diploma of distinction should be holders of the degree of Bachelor of Arts or Bachelor of Agriculture, or its equivalent formal education, and had distinguished themselves in the practice of agriculture. The honor of being the first "Master Farmer" was subsequently given to Jose Zamora of Tarlac province. His name was presented by Dean Copeland for having "distinguished himself by activity in local agricultural education and by developing a method for the profitable production of upland rice."[53]

German Course Dispensed With

An opportunity to revise the curriculum of the College of Agriculture came when the Board of Regents, at the meeting of March 5, 1917, passed a resolution eliminating the teaching of the German language in the first two years of the College curriculum and at the same time proposing a revision in the admission requirements of the College. The resolution as presented at the meeting of the University Council of March 10, 1917 read as follows:

"Resolved; That it is the sense of the Board of Regents that the course of study in the College of Agriculture should be so modified as to exclude from the 1st and 2nd years the teaching of German and that more agricultural subjects be taught thereof, and be it further.

"Resolved, That the University Council be requested to amend the entrance requirements of said College with the end in view of raising the standard of admission, eliminating such courses as are equivalent in the high school."[54]

The Council considered the resolution which generated "one of the most exciting discussions" in the body. On the issue of entrance requirements, it was pointed out that students who wanted to pursue the degree of Doctor of Dental Surgery in the College of Medicine must fulfill the admission requirements demanded of students who would work for the degree of Doctor of Medicine. The Board of Regents' position relative to admission requirements in the College of Agriculture was upheld, although it was believed that such a subject need not be a Board matter. Dean Copeland of the College of Agriculture and several of his colleagues in the Council thought it was practically impossible to settle the question of German, without at the same time considering the question of admission requirements and the subjects to be substituted in lieu of German.[55] The others thought that the problem of teaching German and the question of admission requirements were not inseparable; rather they were two different and separate issues. In a move to resolve the question, Dr. Louis Franklin Snow, Chief of the English Department, introduced a resolution asking the University Council to uphold the action of the Board of Regents pertaining to the admission requirements for the College of Agriculture.[56] The decision on the matter, however, was postponed until the next meeting of the body.

The "German Language issue" arose at the time when the First World War was taking place in Europe. This was after 1914, about the time when anti-German feeling was being overtly manifested in many American universities by consigning German textbooks and other forms of material to the flames. As will be shown later in this chapter, the University was in some ways affected by the war since the Philippines was then under the colonial rule of the United States.

When the University Council met on March 17, 1917, the question of German was again discussed for final consideration. Dean Malcolm proposed a resolution which was later amended and approved by the Council, expressed as follows: "Resolved, That the Council sustains the resolution of the Board of Regents dated March 5, 1917, and that the subject of German be eliminated from the first and second years of the six year course in the College of Agriculture."[57] The Council then proceeded to discuss the question involving "the manner and extent of substituting other courses in the place of German." It was at this point that the Dean of the College of

Engineering made the request that the body be advised in a general way as to the wishes and intention of the Board of Regents concerning the proposed policy of making changes in the curriculum in the College of Agriculture.

Dean Copeland, on behalf of his faculty, proposed that the following subjects be substituted for German in the six-year course: Agricultural Economics, Shop Work (wood and iron), Stock Judging, and Farm Accounting. Some members of the Council noted the arbitrariness of the procedure of effecting immediately the substitution of courses and requiring additional entrance requirements. They considered it unfair to the Filipino people in general and to those students in particular who had already made plans to attend the College the following year. They averred that "such an abrupt change was not in conformity to university procedure in the United States and other countries of the world."[58] After a lengthy discussion, both for and against the substitution of courses and the time such action should be made effective, the following resolution was proposed:

> "Resolved, In order to raise the entrance requirements of the College of Agriculture, that as a prerequisite for entrance two years of High School work be required, effective April 1, 1918, and that in the six-year course there be substituted for "German" the subjects of Economics, Shop Work, Field Work and Accounting, and in place of Mathematics there be substituted a modern language requirement."[59]

The Council approved the resolution by a vote of 30 in favor and 26 against. In another resolution, an attempt was made to require four years of high school work or its equivalent for admission to the College of Agriculture starting with the academic year 1919-1920. However, this was not adopted by the Council mainly upon the advice of Dean Copeland. The Dean noted that if the requirement would be adopted that year, his college would have only about 30 students admitted to the first year; yet it could accommodate 500 students. Besides, many members of the Council believed it would be "wise to move slowly in the matter, try out the proposed changes gradually – and in 1918, 1919, and 1920, introduce such additional requirements as the Council might deem proper."[60]

Realignment and Adaptation

Some major changes in the existing curriculum of the School of Pharmacy under the College of Medicine and Surgery were also introduced. At the request of its chief, the Department of Pharmacy and Materia Medica was reorganized in order to institute a course in Elementary Chemistry. This subject was deemed necessary for the students enrolled in the department so that they might understand better the succeeding courses. Also, the course in Pharmacy involving 34 hours was reduced to 17 hours to give way to the new subject in Chemistry. A further change was made in the curriculum when some subjects were transferred from one semester to another to benefit the students. The course on Materia Medica was transferred from the second year to third year. Likewise Pharmacy 4 (Galenical Preparations) and Pharmaceutical Chemistry (Inorganic and Organic Preparations) were to be offered in the first and second semesters of the second year respectively.[61] In adopting these changes, the Council laid down the policy that future changes of this nature should be left entirely to the discretion of the faculty of the school or college concerned.

In the College of Medicine and Surgery, radical changes were made both in the curriculum and in the organization of the departments of instruction. At the time new four-year degree courses were being instituted in the College of Liberal Arts, the medical faculty, with the approval of the University Council, made a two-year pre-medical course a requirement for admission into the college. The aim was to raise the academic standards of the College to the level of the "Class A" colleges in the United States. Consequently, the medical curriculum was completely revised with the subjects properly arranged and distributed into a five-year schedule. The college itself was reorganized into 13 departments of instruction, namely Anatomy, Physiology and Physiological Chemistry; Pathology and Bacteriology; Parasitology; Pharmacology-Materia Medica and General Therapeutics; Medicine; Surgery; Obstetrics and Gynecology; Pediatrics; Eye, Ear, Nose and Throat; Legal Medicine; Medical Economics; History of Medicine and Medical Ethics; and Hygiene.[62] The new medical curriculum took effect in the academic year 1919-1920 and applied only to students who entered the following year. However, all the students who had satisfactorily completed and passed the examination in the fourth year based on the old course of study had to take the fifth year subjects in the new curriculum with some modifications.[63] Early in 1920, the title of department chiefs was changed to "heads of departments."

It should be noted that in making the necessary curricular changes – the adoption of new courses of study and the revisions and/or modifications of existing ones – those responsible for doing it were, to a certain extent, inspired or influenced by outside ideas and developments, especially from the United States. This was somewhat natural and inevitable, since the University, like the public elementary and secondary school system, was organized under the auspices of the American colonial regime. However, these foreign curricular influences were not merely copied; rather they were modified and integrated into what was being developed in the University, so that the end product was not a mere copy from abroad but had the mark of being Philippine made.

As mentioned earlier, there was the growth and expansion of the University as a result of the establishment of the new units and the institution of more courses offerings. While the vision and the initiative to accomplish these things came from the President and the Board of Regents, the burden of further building up the University was shared by the different faculties.

RECRUITMENT AND DEVELOPMENT OF THE FACULTY

BY the time President Villamor assumed his office in June 1915, the University faculty had already developed its core and was on its way to increasing its number. It was composed of a few Filipinos and many foreigners, mostly Americans.

The heads of the faculties – the deans and directors of the different units – were all foreigners: Dr. W.E. Musgrave, College of Medicine and Surgery; Dr. Edwin B. Copeland, College of Agriculture; Dr. R.P. Cowles, College of Liberal Arts; Prof. Clarence G. Wrentmore, College of Engineering; Dr. William H. Boynton, College of Veterinary Science; Prof. George A. Malcolm, College of Law; Prof. Rafael Enriquez, School of Fine Arts; and Prof. Andrew Grover Du Mez, School of Pharmacy.[64]

Likewise, the great majority of the rank and file of the teaching staff, specially those of the higher academic ranks, were Americans. Many of them had joined the University during its founding years with the hope that they would be able to contribute their knowledge and skills in the building of the University as the highest institution of learning in the country. Some of them brought honor and prestige to the University by being in the faculty, while others were honored by the institution by having that connection.

Like their foreign colleagues, the few Filipino faculty members were not graduates of the University. However, they were recruited because they possessed the necessary credentials, having graduated from prestigious foreign universities.

Owing to expanded academic course offerings and increased enrolment, the university faculty during the Villamor years grew in number. In the academic year 1914-1915, there were 143 faculty members; the following year, the figure jumped to 156, or an increase of more than nine per cent. The number progressively increased until the fifth and the last year of President Villamor's administration, as shown in the table below:

TABLE I

Academic Year	Number of Faculty Members
1914-1915	143
1915-1916	156
1916-1917	167
1917-1918	204
1918-1919	245
1919-1920	274

Source: Paul Monroe (et al.), *A Survey of the Educational System of the Philippine Islands.* Manila, Bureau of Printing, p. 616.

Fewer Americans and More Filipinos

The character and composition of the teaching staff changed patently as it increased in number. The number of American faculty members gradually declined as many of them left the service to retire or move on to better academic opportunities in the United States or elsewhere, while a few returned to the government positions which they formerly held. Replacements were made, but not many Americans could be hired. It was difficult to recruit them from abroad and neither could they be convinced of the opportunities for academic enhancement here. Thus, Filipino instructors were appointed to fill the vacant positions as well as the newly created ones. Their number increased considerably, so that by the close of President Villamor's term, they outnumbered the Americans by three to one.

Equally significant was the fact that many of these Filipinos had attained the professorial rank – assistant professor to full professor. Those who had started as instructors in Bartlett's time were now in the professorial level, and some of them were serving as regents or heads of units in the University. The ones who became members of the Board of Regents were Dr. Fernando Calderon of the College of Medicine and Surgery, representing the faculty, and Prof. Bienvenido M. Gonzalez of the College of Agriculture, representing the alumni.[65] In later years, the latter would become president of the University.

Those who became deans and directors of schools and colleges were the following: Dr. Fernando Calderon, College of Medicine and Surgery; Jorge Bocobo, College of Law; Conrado Benitez, College of Liberal Arts; Francisco Benitez, College of Education; Mariano V. del Rosario, School of Pharmacy; and Domingo J. Sandoval, School of Dentistry.[66] Thus the Filipinization of the University faculty, which began during the "founding years," was carried out at a greater pace during President Villamor's incumbency. Moreover, the Filipino faculty members grew not only in number but also in importance since some of them became leaders of the faculties of some of the University units.

Scientists from Government Bureaus as Teachers

As it was in Bartlett's time, the usual method of faculty recruitment was to hire qualified personnel of some technical agencies of the government such as the Bureau of Science, Bureau of Health, the Philippine Library, and the Justice Department. The president of the University had leeway to recruit under liberal or favorable terms and issue appointment into the faculty for full-time or part-time service. In some instances, the University entered into an agreement with a particular government office whereby some of the latter's personnel would serve as instructors in a particular unit of the University. This was the case of the Bureau of Forestry; some of its personnel became members of the teaching staff of the School of Forestry. Such an arrangement was a fine example of the close working relationship between the government and the University. It should be noted, however, that most, if not all, of the students of the School of Forestry were government pensionados or scholars. After finishing their studies they had to render service for a certain number of years with the Bureau of Forestry to reciprocate the government's benefaction in providing for their schooling.

Graduates Appointed to the Faculty

As more members of the teaching staff were needed in the classroom, the University began to appoint many of its graduates into the faculty. The practice started during the "foundation years," but more and more graduates were recruited in President Villamor's time. Precisely because of these faculty appointments, there developed a large body of instructors and teaching assistants during this period. In the academic year 1915-1916, in a faculty of 156, there were 51 instructors and 49 assistants;[67] in 1919-1920, instructors and assistants numbered 71 and 60 respectively in a teaching staff of 247.[68]

The large number of junior faculty members was partly due to the difficulty of hiring candidates with advanced degrees and teaching experience, and partly due to fiscal economy. It was more economical to employ instructors and assistants than faculty members of the professorial rank. However, the composition of the faculty was not a happy one. While the University was able to save a little, the quality of instruction suffered. Besides, in-breeding began to develop, since many of the members of the teaching staff were graduates of the University.

Fortunately, several of these low-ranked faculty members were sent abroad for advanced studies, and in later years became well-known professorial figures in the University. Aside from acquiring better training to enhance their teaching capacity, these faculty scholars came back with new ideas, insights and perspectives on matters relating to the institution.

As members of the University teaching staff, they performed certain academic duties and functions. One of these was taking part in the development of the curricula of the various schools and colleges, although only those who had attained membership in the University Council were the ones involved in this academic activity. Teaching, however, was one academic function which every faculty member was expected to carry out with zeal and dedication. During the Villamor administration, this primary function was performed not only steadily but with some progress and advancement.[69]

Distinguished Professors

Around the personality of some faculty members began to grow "professorial legends." In the College of Medicine and Surgery, it was Dean Paul Casper Freer and Musgrave, then Dr. Edward S. Ruth and Dr. Philip Kingsworth Gilman; among the Filipinos, Dr. Fernando Calderon and Dr. Arturo Garcia–the former was the perennial vice-dean whose booming voice was heard in the College of Medicine and Surgery and the Philippine General Hospital, and the latter was beginning to be identified as the "aristocrat of the dissecting table." In the College of Law, there were founder Dean George Malcolm and Jorge C. Bocobo, who would succeed Malcolm to the deanship. In the College of Liberal Arts, there were Dr. Lawrence Edmonds Griffin, the Benitez brothers and Leandro H. Fernandez, the history professor whose main interest in teaching centered around the origins and growth of Philippine nationalism.[70]

Extension and Research Services

Aside from teaching, many instructors also rendered direct service to society. Those who were from the College of Medicine and Surgery, for example, performed all the technical work of the Philippine General Hospital, trained the nurses, attended to the public dispensary, and inspected the hospitals for infectious and contagious diseases. Those who were connected with the College of Veterinary Science cooperated with the Bureau of Health, specially in the sanitary police activities. In the same manner, it helped the police department and the Bureau of Agriculture in enforcing quarantine rules and examining animals infected with contagious diseases. Those from the College of Law, besides their regular work of training lawyers, had a summer course for justices of the peace and police officers.[71]

Moreover, the faculty members of the University devoted themselves to research. They investigated and studied important questions, not only for the advancement of knowledge, but also for the benefit of society at large. Some of the results of their research works were presented in conferences, such as the Third Agricultural Congress held in the city of Manila in 1917.[72] The nature and range of the subjects covered in the faculty researches during the time of President Villamor can be gleaned from his annual reports.

In his report covering the academic year 1916-1917, four pages were devoted to the listing of faculty researches; in the 1917-1918 report, these increased to six pages. These scholarly works and studies contributed, not only to the advancement of knowledge, but also to the prestige of the University. Thus, in a very real sense, the University was beginning to be recognized as a "community of scholars."

In one of the earlier annual reports, a title listed – "The Present Criminality in the Philippines" – was contributed by President Villamor himself. That he had a much deeper interest in research and its promotion as a university function can be seen in his recommendation to establish a university publication:

> After having considered the matter very carefully, I am of the opinion that the University should issue a publication to stimulate the faculties to undertake work involving scientific investigation and at the same time publish the textbooks which our professors may write from time to time. It is thought that an appropriation of ₱5,000.00 annually would be sufficient to start this work. If we consider the work of the student body and what it means in the development of the sciences, and with further consideration that the money originally invested in this publication will be returned in the form of subscriptions and sales of the books, I believe that it is worthwhile for us to undertake this venture even at the risk of having to suffer some losses during the first few years, losses which may be easily made up by the material benefits which this work will confer upon the general public. It is, therefore, earnestly recommended that the scheme herein proposed be adopted as a means of enhancing and fostering the progress of this institution.[73]

Other incentives to stimulate scholarly studies among the members of the instructional staff were considered, such as the reduction in teaching load and the granting of adequate resources. It was then generally recognized that by making research an important function of the members of the faculty, the University would be able to carry on its mission of transmitting knowledge as well as expanding it.

Salary Scale

In 1916, the Philippine Legislature passed a law limiting the annual salaries for the various grades of the teaching staff of the University as follows:

President of the University	₱10,000
Deans who are at the same time professors, not to exceed	6,600
Full Professors	6,000
Associate Professors	4,500
Assistant Professors	3,600
Instructors not to exceed	
a) Instructors in Laboratories	2,200
b) Instructors in general	2,000
Assistant Instructors not to exceed	
a) Instructors in Laboratories	1,200
b) Instructors in general	960
Graduate Assistants	360

The salary scale[74] shows a substantial difference in the salary of a full professor serving as a dean of a unit and the salary of a full professor without a deanship. There was also an appreciable difference in the salary of the laboratory instructor compared with that of an ordinary instructor. It was then a university policy that faculty members with official duties aside from teaching be given extra pay or honorarium.

Promotional Appointments and Fellowships

As part of the reward system of the University, promotions were given to deserving faculty members. Those who were of lower academic ranks could expect to rise to the higher ranks as almost everyone did in later years. There were faculty members who in "due course" were able to attain full professorship and became heads of units – and "due course" here meant about ten years.[75]

During the Villamor years there were no specific criteria for promotions in the University. The standards found in higher institutions abroad seemed to be the basis, like advanced academic degrees, teaching experience, and research. Since possession of a graduate degree was necessary to ascend the academic ranks, many instructors who had only the Bachelor's degree were encouraged, if not compelled, to pursue graduate studies at the University or abroad.

Several of those who attended foreign universities, specially in the United States, were given university fellowships as it was the practice in those years. The faculty grantee continued to receive his salary while studying abroad, while all his expenses relating to his studies were paid for by the University.[76] In return for the scholarship, he had to come back and serve the University. Partly due to these fellowships, the university faculty was further developed and its efficiency maintained during the time of President Villamor. As it happened, American and Filipino instructors with the same qualifications were promoted at the same time. In some cases Filipinos replaced Americans as faculty members and as academic administrators.

Disciplinary Measures

The efficiency of the faculty was maintained and preserved not only by the fellowship system, but also by weeding out the undesirables from the University. Members of the teaching staff who were found to be "incompetent" or "remiss of their academic duties" were dismissed from the service. One such case involved Prof. Charles Banks of the College of Agriculture. The Dean of his College charged him on four counts, the most serious of which was the "unsatisfactory character" of his work in economic entomology and his "failure to teach and make research concerning insect pests attacking cultivated crops. . . ."[77] The Board of Regents investigated the matter and having found the American professor remiss of his duties, dismissed him from the service.[78]

Sometimes the criticisms were levelled not just against a faculty member but against a course offered in the University. This occurred when an American military doctor, enrolled as a graduate student in the School of Tropical Medicine, criticized a course, alleging that the methods were not adequate, the experimentation was off, and in general found fault with the instruction.[79] The case was investigated by a faculty committee and the result was that the criticisms were found to be unfair and untruthful. The student was punished by denying him further enrolment in the school.[80]

STUDENT ENROLMENT AND ACTIVITIES

AS mentioned earlier, the teaching staff of the University grew in number, partly because of the expanded course offerings and partly because of increased student enrolment. There was indeed a steady growth of the student population of the University during the five years of the presidency of Villamor.

Enrolment Figures: 1915-1920

Within the first academic year of President Villamor's term in 1915-1916, the total number of students enrolled was listed at 2,401. The enrolment increased every year, so that in his last academic year, 1919-1920, there were 3,409 students registered in the University. The annual increase in the student enrolment during that five-year period is shown in the table below:

TABLE NO. II

Year	Number of Students
1915-1916	2,401
1916-1917	2,975
1917-1918	3,289
1918-1919	3,312
1919-1920	3,409

Source: Paul Monroe (et al.), *A Survey of the Educational System of the Philippine Islands.* Manila, Bureau of Printing, p. 616.

The table shows an average increase of about 10.35 per cent in student enrolment during the five-year period. The figures also show that the highest increase occurred in the academic year 1916-1917. Compared with the previous academic year, there was an increase of 574 students, or 24 per cent. Of the 2,975 students in that academic year, 2,471 were males and 504 were females. Based on nationality, there were 2,215 Filipino students, 36 Americans, 9 Chinese, 4 Spaniards, 3 Japanese, 3 Thais, 2 from Guam, 1 German, 1 Swede, and 1 from Singapore.[81]

The Filipino students came from different parts of the country. By the logic of geography, many of them came from the city of Manila and neighboring areas. Several students, however, came from such distant provinces as Ilocos Norte and Isabela in the North and Agusan and Zamboanga in the South.[82] This meant, in effect, that the University had become a national institution with the different regions sharing in the benefits offered.

Table III shows the student enrolment in the different schools and colleges of the University for the same five-year period.

TABLE III

College or School	1915-1916	1916-1917	1917-1918	1918-1919	1919-1920
Junior College of the University	---	---	---	20	29
College of Liberal Arts	429	520	377	517	573
College of Education	---	---	238	285	310
College of Medicine & Surgery	162	172	205	152	149
School of Pharmacy	74	64	83	105	123
Graduate School of Tropical Medicine and Public Health	57	29	34	17	21
School of Dentistry	10	15	22	24	25
College of Agriculture	444	431	564	363	444
College of Veterinary Science	30	35	90	92	73
College of Engineering	47	74	108	144	146
College of Law	212	234	251	210	186
Total	1,465	1,574	1,972	1,929	2,077
Less Duplicates	50	---	24	24	32
Net Total	1,415	1,574	1,948	1,905	2,045
School of Fine Arts	986	842	699	525	497
School of Forestry	---	45	45	50	42
Conservatory of Music	---	138	208	187	211
School of Nursing	---	376	315	364	226
University High School	---	---	74	281	388
Grand Total	2,401	2,975	3,289	3,312	3,409

Source: Paul Monroe (et. al), *A Survey of the Educational System of the Philippine Islands.* Manila, Bureau of Printing, 1925, pp. 615-616.

From the figures in this table, the following observations can be made: first, as mentioned earlier, there was a consistent increase in the student enrolment in the entire University during President Villamor's term; second, some of the units, specially the new ones, such as the College of Education, School of Pharmacy, and the School of Dentistry registered a steady increase in their student population; third, other units experienced fluctuations in student registration; fourth, the enrolment in the School of Fine Arts declined, whereas in the College of Engineering, the enrolment steadily increased.

The reason for the decline in the student registration in the School of Fine Arts was largely due to more strict entrance requirements. On the other hand,the steady increase in the number of engineering students was due to the growing popularity of the engineering courses because of the need for skilled manpower for the material development of the country.

Table III also records a diminishing number of students in the College of Law. While it is true that the College gained an increase in enrolment in 1916-1917 over that of the previous year, it had the smallest number of students among the four colleges that had more than 200 enrollees. The figures are 520 for the College of Liberal Arts, 431 for the College of Agriculture, 280 for the College of Medicine amd Surgery, and 234 for the College of Law.

Commenting on this decline of student enrolment in the College of Law, President Villamor said:

> This decrease might be considered as an indication of a change in the general tendency on the part of the students to give the legal studies a preference to any other courses given in the university. Such decrease in the number of students in the College of Law makes it more notable when we take into consideration the unusual increase registered in other colleges. This seemed to be the result of the influence that public opinion has exerted on the minds of our youth as regards the election of professional courses in the University. In recent years, public opinion had openly denounced the customary liking of our students to pursue legal studies, and now we see that our youth, giving heed to these wise and timely counsels of public opinion take up other professions.[83]

Graduate Students

What is not well reflected in Table III is the number of graduate students enrolled in the University. The only graduate students included in the Table were those studying in the Graduate School of Tropical Medicine and Public Health, which was then the only identifiable graduate unit of the University.

Those working for a Master of Laws degree, Master of Science in Engineering, Master of Arts and Master of Science were probably listed in the students' registry of the unit that was offering the graduate program.

As it was in Bartlett's time, there was no single Graduate School that took charge of graduate studies in the University. The academic body that directed and supervised graduate offerings and related matters, except those offered by the Graduate School of Tropical Medicine and Public Health, was the Executive Committee of the University Council under the chairmanship of the President of the University.

There are no available data on graduate enrolment from 1915-1920 but it is safe to assume that the number of graduate students increased during that period. The basis of this assumption is that the graduate degree was a prerequisite to faculty appointment, or for promotions if one was already in the teaching staff. Some of those who graduated with masteral degrees and joined the faculty were: Amando Clemente (M.S. '17), Jose J. Mirasol (M.S. '17), Encarnacion Alzona (M.A. '18), Francisco Quisumbing y Arguelles (M.S. '18), Leopoldo Uichanco (M.S. '18), Ramona S. Tirona (M.A. '19), Francisco O. Santos (M.S. '19), Nicolas Zafra (M.A. '20), Maria M. Valdez (M.A. '20), Gerardo O. Ocfemia, and Mariano C. Medalla.[84]

With many of these graduates directly going into the faculty, it seemed as though the graduate studies of the University were geared toward the training and preparation of those who would be members of the teaching staff. In this manner, the University itself contributed to the Filipinization of its instructional staff.

Despite the steady increase in student enrolment, the lack of accommodation was no problem at all during the Villamor years. The different units of the University were prepared to accept more students and to "house" a consistently expanding amount of academic work. About this time, Dean Copeland made the announcement that his college at Los Baños could accommodate 500 students, and this was true for the College of Medicine and Surgery and the College of Liberal Arts, though in lesser numbers. The only unit of the University which turned down many student applicants for lack of accommodation was the School of Education under the College of Liberal Arts. It was compelled to do this in the academic year 1916-1917, its second year of existence, because it was faced with an extraordinarily heavy registration of new students.[85]

Drop-Outs and Delinquents

The real problem that confronted the University during the period relative to expanded student enrolment was academic delinquency. A considerable number of students dropped out from the University without finishing their studies. This was particularly true among the members of the freshman classes. It was noted that the average rate of scholastic delinquency was 35 per cent. In the academic year 1916-1917, when the highest increase in student enrolment occurred during President Villamor's term, 39.36 per cent of the first year students quit their studies.[86] Of that group, 25.43 per cent left college before the final examination.[87]

Of those who left the University, some transferred to other colleges, others were forced to leave for financial reasons, some found jobs, and still others were compelled by their instructors either to quit or to repeat the course, because they failed to fulfill the requirements of the University.

The reasons for failure were noted down as follows: students lacked natural ability, Manila offered many attractions to the students and therefore many of them did not spend as much time as they should in their school work, language deficiency, wrong choice of course, and fundamental differences in the method of teaching used in the University and that used in the secondary schools.[88]

The University faculties and administrative officials were alarmed at the high rate of scholastic delinquency. To solve or minimize the problem, President Villamor, himself, made the following recommendations: that secondary schools should change their teaching methods so that their graduates might be better prepared to study in the University; that the instructors in the University should look after their students, encourage them and teach them new methods of study; and that students should also realize the difficulties in their first year in the University.

The President also made a recommendation to solve the problem of students who lacked the "natural ability for the professions." In part it stated:

> . . . in addition to the barrio schools, and to the primary schools in every municipality, every province should have not only an intermediate school as they now have, but also one agricultural school, one industrial school and one commercial school where those students who are not endowed with natural ability for the professions may pursue a practical course of study for two or three years. Instead of a high school in every province there should be only one high school for every two or three provinces, and a general average of 80 per cent should be required for entrance into these high schools. In this way, by increasing the number of vocational schools and decreasing the number of high schools as well as enforcing higher scholastic requirements for admission into them, we shall have four advantages of equal importance:
>
> 1. Those who intend to enter the high schools will study more diligently to meet the requirements of admission into the high schools.
>
> 2. Those who are unable to enter the high schools will be encouraged to enter the vocational schools or agriculture, industry, and commerce.
>
> 3. The high schools will be fewer in number and will, therefore, have stronger faculties and better equipment.
>
> 4. The graduates of these high schools who desire to continue their studies in the University will be better qualified, because they are better selected to pursue professional studies in the University.[89]

That life in the University was a difficult and trying one, specially to a first-year student, can be seen in the following essay written by Encarnacion J. Gonzaga, a student, entitled "A Student's View of University Life."

> Life in the University is a continuous struggle for existence. From the very day we step within its halls to matriculate until we finish our respective courses, we meet nothing but diversified problems to solve. To some, these problems may offer easy solutions, but to many, it must be confessed, they do not. Trace the history of a student during his University life, and you will find my statement justified.
>
> In his first year, he finds everything so different from his high school life that he feels as if he were entering into an unknown world. Stranger to the place, he finds unfamiliar faces. Unacquainted with the rules, he hesitates to do anything. Unused to hard lessons, he usually gets lower grades than he expects, and, disappointed, he would only end by leaving his studies and going home were there not a stronger power in him to compel him to continue – his will. He is aware of the fact that he can never rest in peace. Troubles, cares, worries, and disappointments – these are his constant companions, his most faithful attendants. From the very beginning of his University life until the end, daily problems arise, and daily, too, has to battle against them. In his hour of weakness, how many times has he thought of picking up his pen in order to write home to parents and friends to ask for their comfort! How many times has he gone to bed with a heart heavy and oppressed, and how many times has he been heard sighing and exclaiming, "Ah, how hard it is to study."[90]

Number of Graduates

Despite the difficulties and hardships in studying, many of the students who survived their senior year were able to graduate from the University. The number of graduates during the administration of President Villamor steadily increased as the table shows:

TABLE IV

Year	Number of Graduates
1915-1916	306
1916-1917	337
1917-1918	380
1918-1919	532
1919-1920	572

Source: Paul Monroe (et al.), *A Survey of the Educational System of the Philippine Islands.* Manila, Bureau of Printing, p. 616

The table shows that the highest increase in the number of graduates during the five-year period occurred in the school year 1918-1919. In that year, there were 532 graduates compared to 380 of the preceding year, a difference of 152, or an increase of 28.57 per cent. The average rate of increase during those years was 16.71 per cent – quite significant at the time when the increase in student enrolment in the University averaged 10.35 per cent.

To get a good idea of how the students regarded their Alma Mater and the kind of education and training they were acquiring, the following comments are cited:

From Gabriel A. Bernardo, who in later years became the University Librarian: "I consider the U.P. as an institution of men and women who will endeavor to make 'Free and United Philippines' a reality, a center from which will radiate all over the Orient, the true and enlightened spirit of Democracy."[91]

From Jose O. Cabalquinto, a prize-winning student in history: "The real product of the U.P. is an intelligent and faithful citizen who is determined to put all his powers at the service of his country and mankind."[92]

From Jose R. Sucre, a native of Calibo, Capiz: "The very atmosphere we breathe in the U.P. is the atmosphere of social science. We are trained so that we may become efficient to serve society."[93]

From Nicolas Zafra, who in later years served as head of the Department of History: "The U.P. has acquired the enviable reputation for thorough and superior instruction. It remains for it to show by the quality and worth it develops in the youth whom it nurtures within its halls that it stands, not only for thorough and superior instruction, but also for high and noble ideals."[94]

Incentives toward Excellence

Although the University had just passed its organizational years, it was beginning to acquire the reputation of being the greatest center of learning in the country. It was attracting the "cream" of the high school graduates of the land every year, not only because of its "thorough and superior instruction," but also because of the incentives it gave to the students for study. For example, there were scholarships to be enjoyed by those who were qualified. Honor graduates, such as valedictorians and salutatorians from accredited high schools were admitted into the University free of tuition fees.

Aside from the scholarships made available by the Philippine Legislature and some other government agencies, there were other grants donated by generous and civic-minded individuals. In 1916-1917, Governor General Francis B. Harrison established a scholarship in the College of Engineering for the good and needy students, and the first awardees were Hilarion Henares and Roman Ilagan. In that same year, Mariano Limjap donated a scholarship to the College of Veterinary Science to be awarded to a student of that

College for five years. In the College of Medicine and Surgery, Dr. Ariston Bautista, Chief of the Department of Clinical Medicine, gave a liberal donation to support the study of a graduate of the College in the United States specializing in nervous and mental illness. The President of the University considered this generous act as "a manifestation of the praiseworthy spirit pervading the University."[95]

The best students were not only given scholarships, but also were made members of an honor society known as the "Rizal Center" even without their knowledge. It was a form of recognition of great value as its members included student scholars as well as alumni who in their university days were also honor students. With "Honesty and Social Service" as its motto, the society had as one of its functions to honor worthy faculty members and individuals outside the University who had contributed to the progress and welfare of the country. In 1916-1917, the society honored Prof. Austin Craig who was about to retire from the University with a reception and dance. It also rendered another program in honor of Manuel L. Quezon, President of the first Philippine Senate. The success of these activities impressed President Villamor so much that he allowed the organization to "conduct hereafter any movement tending to promote university spirit among the student body."[96]

Extra-Curricular Opportunities

The University under President Villamor saw the existence of all kinds of student organizations. Some of them could trace their beginnings from the "founding years" of the University; the others, however, were just newly established. Like the "Rizal Center" which was intercollegiate in nature, the University Dramatic Club, which was organized in 1916, had members coming from the different schools and colleges of the University. With Prof. George St. Claire of the English Department as Director, it made President Villamor an honorary member. It presented plays inside and outside the University to the delight and satisfaction of its audience. In its fourth year, it became "the most popular and progressive organization in the University."[97]

The popularity of the University Dramatic Club spread throughout the country. Aside from entertaining people, it also functioned as some sort of a philanthropic group donating part of its earnings to some needy organizations like *The Philippinensian,* the University Woman's Club, the Philippine Orphanage, the American Red Cross, the *Varsity News,* and the *Philippine Journal of Education.* It gave training in Pronunciation, Enunciation, Accentuation, and Interpretation of Dramatic Role to students from the different colleges of the University. By sponsoring contests in drama writing, it discovered several budding playwrights among the students.

The club presented good plays realistically portraying Filipino life with a view to encouraging further Filipino drama in English. Three plays of this kind were shown by the Club namely: "The Twelfth Commandment," "The Recruiter" and "Thy Neighbors' Creed" – all written by Professor St. Claire.

An entirely different university organization was the Students' Cooperative Association. It was a truly student-oriented type of society with the following objectives: to encourage self-help among the students through cooperation; to raise funds for the general welfare of the students; and to help students find work for their support.[98]

Aside from the intercollegiate organizations, there were also the collegiate groupings, which were similarly engaged in making life in the University "so pleasant and so vigorous." All the schools and colleges had more than one student organization and their memberships were confined to the students of each unit. There was always a student council in a school or college, plus one or more organizations. Some of them were already existing when President Villamor assumed office; others were formed during his incumbency.

In the college of Medicine and Surgery, the oldest unit of the University, there were about five of these organizations, namely: Medical Students' Association, Students' Pharmaceutical Association, the CoMaS (College of Medicine and Surgery) Glee Club, Medical Students' Association String Circle and the Women's Medico-Pharmaceutical-Dental Association. The College of Agriculture at Los Baños had the greatest number, for aside from the Student Body Organization, there were the Batangas Agriculturist and Forester Association, Pangasinan Club, La Union Club, the Visayas Planters and the Cagayan Valley Junior Planters–Associations based on the province where the members came from.

Although these organizations were established in the different units of the University, they, however, had a common objective in promoting the general welfare of their members and their respective colleges. This was accomplished through various means: sponsoring college programs and convocations whereby the students of the college came to know each other better and also their instructors, acting as information disseminators as to what was happening in the University, serving as channels through which the needs and interests of the students were made known to the college authorities, putting up publications wherein the works of faculty and students were published, and serving as discussion groups on subjects of mutual interest to the students and the teaching staff.

Of the organizations primarily interested in discussions, the most popular was the Law Forum in the College of Law. It sponsored public lectures by prominent figures during the academic year on topics which were of great interest to the law students and the faculty. In the academic year 1915-1916, the lectures delivered were the following: "The Jones Bill" by Resident

Commissioner Manuel L. Quezon; "Paper on Mabini" by Commissioner Rafael Palma; "The Effects on Hereditary Tendencies on Criminology" by President Villamor; and "How to Draw a Bill" by Judge Stuart of the Philippine Code Committee.[99]

Equally active in sponsoring similar activities was the Student Council of the College of Law. The Council sponsored annual oratorical contests and debates in the University – two events which were eagerly awaited by the University constituencies and the general public during the academic year. These contests did not only develop the forensic skills of the students, but also drew to the campus important American and Filipino personalities to act as presiding officers or as members of the board of judges.

In the Fourth Annual Oratorical Contest held on December 15, 1915, presided over by President Villamor, the following high public officials acted as judges: Newton Gilbert, former Vice-Governor and Secretary of Public Instruction; Judge Mariano Cui, President of the Public Utility Commission, Lt. Col. Henry M. Morrow, Judge Advocate of the Military Court; Felix Roxas, President of the Municipal Board of Manila; and Felimon Perez, Delegate to the Philippine Assembly.[100] In the fourth Annual Debate held on January 29, 1916, with prominent lawyer Jose Escaler presiding, the members of the Board of Judges were: Judge George R. Harvey, James Ross, Carlos Sobral, Delegate Miguel Romualdez and Felipe Buencamino, Jr.[101]

Campus Festivities

There were other cultural and extra-curricular activities held in the University during the administration of President Villamor. In the academic year 1916-1917, exhibits were shown by some of the older units of the University such as the College of Medicine and Surgery, College of Agriculture, College of Veterinary Science, and the School of Fine Arts. The School had a reason to celebrate, for it received a medal and a diploma at the Panama-Pacific International Exposition, thus bringing honor to the University.

Despite the distance of Los Baños from Manila, there was a large group of "interested visitors" from the city who went to view the exhibits of the College of Agriculture. It included high government officials, businessmen and even farmers.

Besides holding an exhibition, the College of Medicine and Surgery also celebrated its tenth annual anniversary. A play entitled "The Mirror" was shown to the public. It was specially written for the occasion by one of the faculty members of the College and had for its plot a realistic portrayal of life in the University.

In late March of the same year, the Conservatory of Music which was just a year old, held its first recital, and like other events that happened in the University that year, it elicited favorable comment from the newspapers and from the general public. Not to be outdone, the College of Liberal Arts celebrated its Liberal Arts Day. There was the usual fanfare, but what made the occasion memorable was the huge bonfire put up by the students in the evening. This was to show their gratitude to the Filipino Legislators for having alloted "great sums of money" for the University that year. A resolution of thanks and gratitude to the Philippine Legislature was introduced and approved by popular acclamation. Witnessing this event, President Villamor expressed his great joy and satisfaction over what the students had done.

But the biggest celebration during the year, or perhaps since the founding of the University, was the first observance of University Day on December 15, 1917. As reported in the press, it "drew the biggest crowd that has ever been gathered at the spacious campus of the U.P. on Calle Padre Faura."[102] The festivities included a band concert, a military parade, a dramatic presentation, and an oratorical contest.

Emphasizing the significance of the event in his speech, President Villamor stated:

> Of all the events recorded in the University heretofore, there is none, I am sure which is so inspiring and significant as the University Day. These thousands of students, these young men and young women, from every nook and corner of the archipelago, and gathered in our campus today inspired by the same sentiments of nationality and cherishing the common ideals of the country are, in my opinion the most convincing proof that the University of the Philippines is not only the crowning institution of our educational system, but it is also the institution which embodies the greatest purpose of the Filipino nationality.[103]

It was a big affair and the thousands of eager spectators who attended the festivities left the University campus with vivid impressions of the highest institution of learning in the country.

Athletic Competitions

These various festivities were not the only ones that attracted the crowds of visitors to the University campus; there were also the different sports and athletic competitions engaged in by the students. These were held during the academic year as part of their extra-curricular activities.

As it was in President Bartlett's time, the Board of Athletic Control took charge of the planning and directing of all athletic affairs in the University. However, during the administration of President Villamor, the membership of the Board was expanded to include one student representative from each of the units of the University. It also adopted a Constitution and a set of By-Laws to govern student athletic activities.

Under the able leadership of Prof. Ernest Bancroft Conant, President of the Board of Athletic Control, and Prof. George M. Cassidy, the Physical

Director and ex-officio member of the Board, a greater interest in and love for sports developed in the University during the presidency of Villamor than in the preceding years. In all lines of sports and athletics, there was expansion and greater systematization.[104]

The schools and colleges were encouraged to form and maintain their sports teams. Intercollegiate athletic competitions were held during the schoolyear, resulting in the development of the physical well-being of the students as well as fostering in them the "college spirit."

The University participated in inter-university sports contests; therefore, it had to maintain varsity teams in basketball, indoor baseball, tennis, track and field, and baseball. In all these sports, the University emerged with an enviable record.

In baseball, the varsity team won four championships, and as many trophies, namely: the Baguio Open Carnival Baseball Championship, the Independent Baseball League Championship, the Philippine Intercollegiate Baseball Championship, and the Carnival Open Championship. These victories made the varsity baseball team the best amateur baseball team in the country in 1916.[105]

The successes of the varsity teams could be attributed partly to their good training and discipline, and partly to the strong varsity cheering squad. Organized only that year, it really contributed immensely to the victories of the varsity teams. With these outstanding achievements in sports, the Univeristy was not only on its way to becoming the greatest center of learning, but also the training ground of the best athletes then.

Military Training

In addition to sports and athletics for physical development of the students, a military training program was carried out. It was in this period of the history of the University – the Villamor years – that the program was first established. The College of Liberal Arts started it by conducting military drills among its male students in spite of the fact that the university campus at Padre Faura was not yet ready for that kind of activity.

In the academic year 1916-1917, the boys of some other units also began to undergo military training, though it was not yet adopted as compulsory. On June 26, 1917, however, the Board of Athletic Control presented to the University Council a resolution making military training compulsory for all male students in the University, except those who were physically unfit to do so. In part the resolution stated:

> *Resolved,* That military training is a useful and desirable training for all male students of the University of the Philippines; and further resolved,

> that military training should be made compulsory for all male students, unless physically unfit, or those excused for some other valid reason by those in charge of military training at the University, in the College of Liberal Arts, Medicine and Surgery, Agriculture, Law, Engineering, and Veterinary Science.[106]

The resolution was approved as amended by the University Council in its meeting of September 7, 1918.[107] In that academic year, therefore, every male student entering the University who was physically fit had to undergo military training twice a week for one hour each during the first two years of residence.

Also, those boys who had already matriculated in the University before the opening of the academic year 1917-1918 were required to undergo military instruction for a period of two years unless exempted by the proper authorities. President Villamor fully recognized the importance of military training in the University when in his speech during the first University Day celebration, he said in part:

> . . . these hundreds of young people who have taken part in this parade as brave and well disciplined soldiers, show once more that the University of the Philippines trains not only scientists and professional men, capable of directing the material and moral progress of our country but it also inspires the youth with the ideal that the Philippines is the only country which God has given us, and that it is our duty to preserve it for ourselves, for our children and that we should devote our lives to her, and if necessary also die for her.[108]

Protests and Demonstrations

Other developments during President Villamor's administration made this chapter in the history of the University eventful and exciting. There were stirrings of student unrest as reflected in the signing of petitions and sending them to the university authorities and also the holding of protest marches and demonstrations to dramatize their grievances.

On one occasion, students protested against a Manila police captain and his men for arresting Victoriano Yamzon during the celebration of the first University Day. The former thought that the latter was part of the unruly crowd witnessing the military parade that day. However, it was a case of mistaken identity, for the victim of arrest was no less than a university instructor and a member of the Committee on University Day Celebration.[109]

On another occasion, a group of first-year students who were formerly high school valedictorians and salutatorians and were enjoying entrance scholarships in the University submitted a petition to the Board of Regents, requesting that their scholarships be extended beyond their freshman year.

Their petition was prompted by the statement issued by the Secretary of the University that the kind of scholarship they were enjoying was good only for one year.[110]

PRESIDENT VILLAMOR CRITICIZED AND VINDICATED

PERHAPS the most dramatic and most vehement student protest during those years happened when an editorial attacking the President of the University appeared in the *Manila Times* issue of July 17, 1918. Entitled "Wanted, A University President" and signed by Manuel Xeres Burgos, Jr., one of the staff members of the publication, the editorial said:

> It is no longer a secret to anybody that President Villamor has been pronounced by nearly all working under him (students and professors) as a marked failure in the University.
>
> The University has proved too big a job for him. He lacks those personal characteristics and qualities which fit a man for a position of the importance and responsibility attached to the post of a university president.
>
> Moreover, his mental preparation, his training and experience, have not been broad enough to enable him to possess that vision which a man in his position should have or to take in at a glance the vast and vital problems which are ever present in the operation and management of a university that is worth the name.
>
> President Villamor's lack of character – and by this is meant not lack of morality, but lack of courage, – is proverbial among all who have had official contact with him. The lack of this quality which is so essential in any executive officer caused him to fail in the position of chief of the executive bureau as is not generally known; but it cannot be denied that when he took over that bureau it was considered as being of at least or equal importance with any of the executive departments then existing; but it was not long after he had taken it over that a good many of the most important functions therefore were performed by the executive secretary to the governor-general, who under the terms of the law, was his immediate subordinate.[111]

It was alleged in some of the newspapers that the then Senate President Quezon "inspired" the writing of the editorial. [112] Quezon was quick to deny this, and in a statement he issued to the press, he said, "I never authorized the publication of Mr. Burgos' editorial, nor was I consulted on the matter at any time. Mr. Burgos has no connection whatsoever with the editorial staff of the paper, his connection being solely with the business department".[113]

Quezon also wrote the editor of the *Manila Times,* Mr. Thibault, making the same denial and at the same time pointing out that the matter had caused him "embarrassment and therefore something should be done to set the people right on this matter." In this letter, he said:

The truth is that, my official position, my part in the nomination of Judge Villamor to the presidency of the institution, my place in the confidential counsels of the Philippine government, forbid my even entertaining such views, much less sanctioning their expression by any man so close to me as Mr. Burgos has been. This fact has placed me in a very embarrassing position and I am appealing to you to suggest such means of putting the public right on the matter.[114]

To protest against the unwarranted press attack on their president, the students led by Carlos P. Romulo and Jose Romero held a mass meeting inside the University campus and passed the following resolution condemning the editorial:

Whereas, the *Manila Times* in its issue of Wednesday July 17th 1918, made certain references in its editorial page to the President of the University – – – references derogatory to the honor of the University as well as to that of its head;

Whereas, the statements in question are utterly unfounded and unjustifiable, and constitute a direct negation of the facts as they exist;

Whereas, the article referred to, contained statements purporting to express the opinion of the student body of the University, Manuel Xeres Burgos, Jr., arrogating to himself the right of voicing the sentiments, thus investing himself with the power of a self-appointed spokesman; Now therefore,

Be it resolved by the student body of the University of the Philippines, that far from lacking in that spirit of respect, reverence and affection towards their President, which the article intimates we hold ourselves privileged to have been under the benign, democratic, progressive and salutary administration of the the President; that we express, as we do hereby express, our unrequired condemnation of the spirit of destructive criticism that runs throughout the article; that we indignantly repel the suggestion that we have even countenanced opinions of the sort suggested by the article, and

Be it further resolved, that a copy of this resolution be sent to the Manila Press for publication and to the President of the University for his information.[115]

From the University campus, the group marched toward the vicinity of Sta. Cruz Bridge on the Pasig River where the editorial offices of the *Manila Times* were located. Another demonstration was held in front of the building and Mr. Thibault, the *Manila Times,* editor, finding the students angry and vengeful, apologized and retracted his paper's unfounded criticisms against President Villamor and the University.[116]

The members of the University teaching staff also vehemently condemned the editorial. Their condemnation was embodied in a resolution they passed which said:

> The Faculties of the different colleges and schools of the University of the Philippines wish to make the following statement in connection with an editorial of the *Manila Times* on July 17, 1918, signed by Mr. Manuel Xeres Burgos, Jr., concerning President Villamor:
>
> Mr. Burgos has never been given authority whatsoever to speak for the University faculty. Hence, the editorial mentioned expresses merely the personal opinion of Mr. Burgos but not the attitude of the teaching staff of the University. We emphatically deny the statement that President Villamor has ceased to be a leader that commands the love and respect of his subordinates and that the work of the different faculties is being hampered and interfered with by the above. The members of the university faculty love and respect their president. His administration has been a distinguished success and under his able guidance the university had greatly progressed.
>
> We hereby disavow said editorial which misrepresents the sentiments of the faculty of the University of the Philippines.[117]

The *Varsity News,* the official organ of the University, in a ringing editorial entitled "We Are Behind You" came in defense of President Villamor. Printed under the caption "Speaking for Ourselves," it expressed this stand:

> For the good name of our institution which is at present at stake more than anything else, we come forward in defense of Honorable Ignacio Villamor, president of our University of the Philippines, who received a severe blow from a hissing red hot ingot in the form of an editorial published in Wednesday's issue of the *Manila Times* under the caption "Wanted a University President."[118]

Likewise, the public joined in defense of President Villamor. In a letter to the editor of the *Cablenews-American,* a concerned Filipino raised a rhetorical question: "If Mr. Villamor is and was always a failure, why was he made Judge, Attorney General, Solicitor General, Executive Secretary, and University of the Philippines President?"[119] In a written statement, Maximo M. Kalaw, then Professor of Political Science in the University, defended not only his President, but also the very idea that the head of the institution should be a Filipino. He said:

> The Philippine University is a state institution supported by the money of the Filipino people at a most critical stage of their history when they are asked to prepare for complete nationhood. The mission of the University, therefore, as a state institution is to help prepare the Philippines for independence, to prepare young men and women to become responsible leaders of the future Republic, to orientate the intellectual development of the islands along the lines best adapted to their history, their traditions, and their nationalist creeds, to help create, in short, a true Filipino nation. That mission cannot be properly fulfilled unless there be at the head of the institution a Filipino imbued with the Filipino life and ideals. No American or foreigner can give that inspiration and can assume that role better than a

> Filipino. By this we do not mean that the University should be entirely conducted by Filipinos. Let the best scientists, mathematicians, professors of English literature be imported from abroad, but the policy-determining factor should be Filipino.[120]

Equally vigorous in their protest against the editorial were the majority of the newspapers at that time. The *Consolidacion Nacional,* and *La Nacion* as well as *El Ideal* and others were unanimous in their opinion that the criticisms were uncalled for and that it was "too raw."

The *Independent* branded the editorial "a glaring instance of the most unjustified and vicious editorial scribbling in the whole history of journalism in the Philippine Islands . . . . "[121] *The Cablenews-American* branded it as "a brutal stab."[122]

Not to be outdone in expressing their sympathy and support of the University President were the students and faculty of the Liceo de Manila, of which President Villamor himself was a co-founder. They marched toward the University campus and saw the President in his office. They handed to him a resolution in token of the students' recognition of his efficient work in the University.[123]

Though the criticisms were scurrilous and unfounded, President Villamor deemed it wise not to issue a statement to refute them. Perhaps, he did not want to dignify his critic by answering him. He knew too well that the charges were the same old ones leveled against him when his name was being considered for the university presidency. Instead of being upset and infuriated, he characteristically remained calm and unperturbed. He continued to discharge his duties and functions as University President until the end of his term with honor and dignity.

PROBLEMS OF UNIVERSITY ADMINISTRATION AND FINANCES

THE First World War was taking place at the time when the military training program was inaugurated in the University. The country was then a colony of the United States and therefore could not remain unaffected by the war. There was a call for war preparedness among the Filipinos and the best means to carry it out was to adopt a program of military training for male students in the colleges and universities. The establishment of compulsory military training in the University in 1917 was most likely brought about by war conditions then.

Repercussions of World War I

Even before the United States entered the war in May 1917, some developments in the University were directly related to the outbreak of the war in Europe. There was the decision on the part of the American authorities to terminate the employment of German citizens in the University. To carry it out, Acting Governor General Martin requested the Office of the University President to furnish him a list of university employees who were neither Americans nor Filipinos. In response to that request, a list was submitted to him which included the names of Otto J. Scheerer, Assistant Professor of German, and Henry Levy, Instructor in Engraving, the former being a German citizen and the latter a Frenchman.[124] Professor Scheerer was not only disallowed to continue teaching in the University, but was also to be deported from the country.[125]

Moreover, the Board of Regents decided to eliminate the teaching of the German language in the first two years of the College of Agriculture curriculum. When this "German language issue" confronted the other units of the University, President Villamor issued a memorandum indicating his desire that the teaching of German be continued in the interest of the University and those of the students enrolled in the course.[126] At that time, there were about 160 freshmen and sophomore students taking the course and most of them were in the preparatory medical course.

Because of the war, too, all German textbooks being used in the University were reviewed to eliminate those which might be used for German propaganda. As a result, a number of pages referring to modern German history were cut out from a certain reader, leaving only literary matters approved by former Dean Cowles. One volume was removed from the shelves of the Library of the College of Liberal Arts upon the suggestion of the chief of the German Department. Also, the German Club of the College was abolished.[127]

All these were negative responses of the University to the war conditions; in a positive way, it encouraged its faculties, employees and students to volunteer in the Philippine National Guard. President Villamor himself sounded the call on September 13, 1918, when he issued a circular which stated in part:

> It should be borne in mind that the showing to be made by this organization will be the best brief that we can put forth of the Filipino people's sense of responsibilities. Nothing short of our utmost efforts is needed to interest our teaching staff, employees and students, to join the National Guard. . . .
>
> The University of the Philippines is in a better position to furnish the most splendid supply of men to the National Guard than any other Government Department. The example has been set by our sister American universities. I would like to see the members of the teaching staff, employees, and students, just short of disorganizing our activities, join the National Guard.[128]

The response of the different sectors of the University was "spontaneous", especially on the part of the students. To prepare them for enlistment in the National Guard, the whole student body of the School of Dentistry petitioned their school officials to offer summer courses. More significantly, the entire student body of the College of Agriculture volunteered into the service for the following reasons: love of country, love of Alma Mater, and obedience to President Villamor's memorandum.[129] Together with the many other volunteers from other schools and colleges, they formed the University's contribution to the Philippine National Guard.

Since their studies would inevitably be disrupted, the Executive Committee of the University Council made special provisions for them: all were to be granted leaves of absence for the period of the emergency, their matriculation fees and deposits already paid by them were to be put on "reserve" until their return to the University, and those who were to graduate that year (April 14, 1918) would be allowed to receive their degrees provided that they were not failing in their courses as of January 7, 1918.[130]

Taking note of the University's contribution to the Philippine National Guard, President Villamor said:

> The University has not been unmindful of the needs of the Philippine National Guard for men with high academic qualifications. It has given the National Guard all help possible and the spontaneous response of professors and students alike to the call once more gives credit to the way the University fosters public spirit. . . .[131]

Transfer of the College of Veterinary Science

Another incident in the University which became an issue was the transfer of the College of Veterinary Science from its original site in Calle Tayuman, Manila to Los Baños where the College of Agriculture was and still is located. At this time, President Villamor was on leave from his position and Regent Escaler took over as President Protempore. Before the Board of Regents decided to make the transfer, a special committee was created to study the matter.

A report which included the arguments for and against the relocation was submitted to the Committee and on the basis of this report, the Board of Regents approved the transfer effective the academic year 1919-1920.[132] But the relocation could hardly be carried out due to the strong opposition of the students, some faculty members and high government officials. Four professors of the College tendered their resignation and refused to teach in Los Baños.

To resolve the controversy, it was decided to effect the transfer gradually; only first and second-year classes would be held in Los Baños while the third, fourth and fifth-year classes would remain in Manila. The resigning professors withdrew their resignations and agreed to teach the students in Manila.[133] The relocation of the College resulted in some of the students transferring to the College of Medicine and Surgery, while a few others left for the United States to pursue their studies.

Financial Difficulties

After a leave of absence of a little over five months (December 28, 1918 to June 14, 1919), President Villamor resumed his duties and functions as head of the University. This was his last year as University President, but it seemed as though he had not done enough in the past four years. For the University was still beset with certain problems which he, as chief administrator, had to solve. Difficulties in the transfer of the College of Veterinary Science to Los Baños had to be coped with.

But more pressing was the problem of finances which had been a major concern since the "founding years." Much time and effort were spent in lobbying for funds provided through the Philippine Legislature, and whatever amount was subsequently approved seemed not quite enough to bolster the University's development and expansion program.

While the growth and expansion of the institution was noticeable in the increase in the number of academic units, student enrolment and the number of faculty members and graduates, the appropriations from the Legislature did not allow for the construction of more buildings to house instructional and research activities.

There was hardly any change in the physical makeup of the University. Only one permanent structure was visible at the Padre Faura campus – the University Hall. Rizal Hall which was started in 1918 had not yet been finished primarily due to the difficulty of securing the needed funds for its completion.

In the academic year 1919-1920, the problem of finances was more serious than in the previous years. For aside from the old problem of being almost completely dependent on the appropriations of the Philippine Legislature, the budget was hardly adequate to meet the growing expenditures of the various units of the University. To make available funds suffice, some adjustments had to be made in the allocations of the different schools and colleges. Appropriations for some of them had to be cut while others already in dire straits were given more.

Dean Baker of the College of Agriculture, anticipating the reduction of the finances of the College, wrote a memorandum to President Villamor, which partly said:

> . . . the College of Agriculture is still an extremely underdeveloped college. Agricultural experts from abroad visiting the College say that "we do not have here a proper College of Agriculture."

> The reduction of the estimates of 1919 will worsen the situation. There is a need for physics laboratory, equipment for the Shops and Library. Laboratories are overcrowded and in temporary quarters.[134]

Dean Baker also wrote a memorandum to the Board of Regents requesting that his College and the Experimental Station be allocated ₱332,880 and ₱88,830 respectively for the schoolyear 1919-1920. To justify the request, he gave the following reasons:

> 1. To bring the teaching force to a reasonable basis in accordance with the present curriculum of the College.
>
> 2. To provide sufficient housing to the present classes of the College.
>
> 3. To provide sufficient supplies and equipment for regular operation of classes through the schoolyear, preventing further entire or partial dropping of classes for lack of supplies and equipment, as has commonly occurred in the past.
>
> 4. To provide for the proper support of the experimental station project in such a manner as shall protect the initial outlay and carry forward the work in reasonably efficient manner.[135]

The austere budget granted to the University for the academic year 1919-1920 was a reflection of the poor state of the finances of the Philippine Government at that time. There was very little money in the central treasury partly because of the business recession and the Philippine National Bank scandal that took place that year.[136] Due to the bank scandal and the failure of some of the government corporations, so much money was lost that the Philippine Legislature had to adopt fiscal restraint in the allocation of funds among the different agencies and departments of the government, including the University.

To solve the problem of finances, President Villamor and his Executive Committee brought forth the idea of establishing a permanent fund for the University which should come from a certain percentage of the property tax of the land. The idea was premised on the fact that the people who are in a position to support university education are the ones who have permanent sources of income.

Since the plan could only be realized through government action, the Executive Committee passed a resolution to this effect and presented copies of it to the Governor General, the Council of State which then actually prepared the government budget, and the Philippine Legislature. Dean Jorge C. Bocobo of the College of Law prepared the resolution which read as follows:

> *Whereas,* a permanent fund is necessary for the purpose of laying down far-sighted, intelligent and business-like plans for the development of

the University of the Philippines so that the institution may at all times adequately meet the ever growing demands of the country for properly-trained graduates, and in order that the University may steadily extend its activities calculated directly to serve the people;

Whereas, such a permanent fund would place the University on a more independent basis, and would allow the university authorities more freedom in shaping the policies and managing the affairs of the University, which freedom, according to the experience of other universities would be conducive to the greater usefulness and rapid growth of the University;

Whereas, a permanent fund automatically accruing from the public taxes would intensify the sense of direct responsibilities to the people of the P.I., and would foster greater interest of the people in the University;

Whereas, the idea of a permanent university fund from the public taxes has been found successful and beneficial in many state universities, such as the great Universities of Wisconsin, Michigan, Minnesota, and Illinois; now therefore, be it

Resolved by the Executive Committee of the University Council, University of the Philippines, that the Governor General and the Council of State be asked and are hereby asked to recommend the passage of, and the Philippine Legislature be requested and is hereby requested immediately, permanent fund for the partial support of the University of the Philippine Islands.[137]

Evidently, the request was not approved at that time as it was going to be taken up again in later years. Nevertheless, the first serious efforts to establish a permanent fund for the University were made during the administration of President Villamor.

Benton's Fleeting Performance (1921-1923)

The Second and Last American at the Helm of the Filipino University

by Leslie E. Bauzon

Benton's Fleeting Performance

GUY Potter Benton assumed the presidency of the University of the Philippines when the institution was going into its thirteenth year of existence. The University was then well into its second decade of service to the Filipino people.

Historically, the period of the twenties in Philippine history marked the end of the process of "taming the Philippine frontier,"[1]* when the forests that once covered the country's interior portions literally disappeared, and the cleared areas were transformed into agricultural settlements rendered productive by migrant settlers or laborers coming from heavily populated regions like the Ilocos provinces, the Tagalog provinces, and the central and western Visayan provinces of Cebu, Iloilo and Antique.

Colonial Orientation

In the preceding century, Spanish, and then American, colonial policy encouraged the development of a cash crop economy in the Islands. Thus, the country was transformed from that which merely depended on agricultural subsistence to that which was export oriented, producing cash crops like sugar, tobacco, copra and abaca for the world market. Under American rule, the production of these cash crops expanded tremendously especially after the elimination of all quota restrictions with the passage of the Underwood-Simmons Act by the United States Congress in 1912.

However, as exports boomed and more lands opened up for the commercialized production of cash crops, the profits derived from the economic bonanza hardly filtered down to the agricultural laboring population. The people in the frontier did not benefit from the windfall. Their real purchasing power did not increase. Tenancy conditions deteriorated instead. There was a corresponding rise in agrarian unrest, as evidenced by the proliferation of mass peasant movements and by the outbreak of disturbances in the countryside.[2] Meanwhile, the country became increasingly dependent upon the American market for the exportation of Philippine cash crops.[3]

---

*Footnote references are compiled in the NOTES section at the end of this book.

Politically, there was talk of Philippine independence in electoral platforms both in Manila and in Washington. The granting of political emancipation was preconditioned on the attainment of political maturity by the Filipinos. The United States colonial administration in the beginning aimed at shifting the balance of power from oligarchical rule to grassroots democracy.[4] However, as the decade of the twenties came, this objective was still far from being realized. The situation in fact turned out the opposite of what the American regime intended. The Filipino socioeconomic elite became more firmly entrenched in native society through their control of local politics, reinforced by the political institutions which the Americans brought with them to the Philippines in their efforts to enlarge the sphere of democracy.[5]

Glimpses of Democracy

The consequences though of introducing democratic practices and institutions were that the same were manipulated by the Filipino elite for their advantage, aided by strict suffrage qualifications imposed by the United States colonizers for participation in the colonial political process.

Members of the Filipino elite took advantage of the issue of Philippine independence to project their respective political careers. The most prominent of these Filipino colonial leaders was Manuel L. Quezon, who showed an all-consuming desire to become the first Filipino governor-general.[6] He spoke of Philippine independence when it was convenient to gain electoral support. In reality, he favored a longer political tutelage by the United States not only because of his manifest desire to become the first Filipino governor-general of the Islands but also because of vested economic interests. He was the spokesman of the sugar bloc, which wanted the prolongation of American rule because of the benefits that such an arrangement brought to the sugarcane planters and landowners.[7]

In brief, the period of the twenties was a critical era in the history of the Filipino people. Agriculturally, the Philippine frontier had been opened up for pioneer settlement. Socially, the Filipino peasant was growing desperate due to the failure of the colonial authorities to arrest the deterioration of tenancy conditions. Economically, the Philippines was well on its way to becoming a classic colonial economy by producing raw materials to export to the American market. And politically, the democratic institutions and practices introduced by the United States appeared to benefit only the members of the upper strata of the Filipino population. This was the situation overall as the University found itself struggling to establish its footing on firmer ground.

UP in Perspective

When Guy Potter Benton became the president of the University of the Philippines, the institution had seen the coming and going of two bonafide presidents, namely Murray Bartlett and Ignacio Villamor, and two acting presidents, namely Jose Escaler and Alejandro M. Albert, all in the span of a little over a dozen years.

By 1921, the University had the following units in operation: Junior College, College of Liberal Arts, College of Education, College of Medicine, School of Pharmacy, School of Dentistry, College of Agriculture, College of Law, School of Fine Arts, School of Forestry, and Conservatory of Music.[8] Total enrolment had grown from 304 in schoolyear 1910-1911,[9] when the University was still without a fixed academic leader and administrator, to 4,693[10] in schoolyear 1921-1922, when Benton had just been appointed president of the University.

In 1909, a year after the enactment of the University Act which gave birth to what was destined to become the premier institution of higher learning in the Philippines, there were only three units in actual operation, namely the College of Medicine and Surgery, the School of Fine Arts, and the College of Agriculture.[11] As seen in the listing above of units in operation by 1921, the number of colleges and schools within the University had quadrupled from three in 1909 to thirteen in 1921. This growth in the number of units, not to mention the growth in enrolment, can only be described as phenomenal. Most of the units were of course established during the early years of the University.

However, if one realizes that the University was thirteen years old in 1921, and that by that same year, the number of units in the University had grown from three in 1909 to thirteen, one can conclude that the University established a unit at an average rate of one per year. This was attained despite severe budgetary constraints under which the University operated during its infancy.

Early Efforts toward Fulfillment

It was remarkable that the University expanded the way it did during the years under review. That was the only way it could accomplish its mission of contributing toward the educational uplift of the Filipino masses, and thereby justify its existence and its use of the appellation of a "university."

It may be apropos at this point to state that the establishment and the maintenance of the University as a public institution supported by the money of the taxpayers fitted in perfectly with the American concept that education was to be used as a means not only for purely academic training but also for citizenship training specially on the rudiments of democratic living.

In other words, the University was conceived and envisioned to play a crucial role toward the democratization of Philippine society and toward the inculcation of nationalistic pride in the hearts of Filipinos. The "democratizing" role, while laudable, would turn out to be a very difficult and enormous challenge to meet, considering the fundamental imbalances in the distribution of political and economic power in Philippine society.

On the other hand, the "nationalizing" role, while also laudable, would turn out to be a far easier task to fulfill, as proven by the fact that the graduates of the University during the colonial regime of the United States would place themselves in the forefront of the efforts to effect the restoration of Philippine political independence by the Americans, and then much later on, following the withdrawal of United States sovereignty over the Philippines, the students and the graduates of the University would be the most outspoken critics of neocolonial policies pursued by the former colonial master.

Background of Benton

Guy Potter Benton was born in Kenton, Ohio, USA on May 6, 1865, the same month and year when the last Confederate forces surrendered to the Union Army, thus ending the drama and the tragedy that was the United States Civil War.

His father was a Methodist pastor. The son started his undergraduate career in the fall of 1882 at Ohio Wesleyan University, a coeducational Methodist institution of higher learning located in Delaware, Ohio. However, he transferred to another coeducational Methodist college, Baker University, which is situated in Baldwin City, Kansas. It was from this latter institution that he received his bachelor of arts degree in 1885.

He was apparently a precocious student, as he finished his baccalaureate degree, transferring from one school to another at that, in the span of three years. Upon the completion of his A.B. degree, he returned to Ohio Wesleyan University in 1885, this time as a graduate student. The following year, 1886, at the young age of 21, he received his M.A. degree in history and sociology. Benton pursued further studies in history and sociology at the College of Wooster, a coeducational Presbyterian institution in Wooster, Ohio, and at the University of Berlin in Germany. After his advanced studies at Wooster and at Berlin, he embarked on his career in education.

He started out as a country schoolteacher, evidently engaging in the teaching profession while doing further studies at Ohio Wesleyan and at Wooster. In 1890, he became the superintendent of city schools in Fort

Scott, Kansas. He served in this capacity for five years, until 1895. Then he received a higher appointment as assistant state superintendent of public instruction in Kansas, a position he held for a year from 1895 to 1896. Benton rendered deeper service to Kansas and to his nation when Baker University, where he finished his A.B. degree, appointed him professor of history and sociology in 1896. He remained with the Baker faculty until 1899, when higher responsibilities fell on his shoulders. That year, he became the president of Upper Iowa University, a private, coeducational institution of higher learning located in Fayette, Iowa. From then on, it was a career involving the holding of one college presidency after another.

Presidential Record of 20 Years

After serving for three years as president of Upper Iowa University, where he succeeded in obtaining one of the first unconditional gifts by Andrew Carnegie, the American steel magnate and philanthropist, to a college, Benton proceeded in 1902 to Miami University, a state-supported institution located in Oxford, Ohio. He served as president of Miami University for nearly a decade from 1902 to 1911. In 1910, Boston University in Massachussetts elected him with a salary advance to its presidency but Benton declined the offer, preferring to stay on at Miami. Benton made a lasting imprint in Miami, for he was instrumental in enabling that institution to take great strides toward Miami's transformation from an obscure landgrant college to a major national university in the United States, with outstanding departments and faculty members.

In 1911, the University of Vermont, one of the oldest state-supported institutions in the entire country, tapped him for its presidency. He was in Burlington, Vermont, for eight years, from 1911 to 1919. During his incumbency as president of this university which was founded in 1791, Vermont became one of the 15 universities in the United States which the War Department rated as "distinguished," thereby empowering its head, namely Benton, to make appointments involving Vermont graduates to regular commissions in the United States Army. His appointees were subject only to a demonstration of satisfactory physical condition.

During his tenure as president of Miami University and as president of the University of Vermont, he was active in the National Association of State Universities, serving as the Association's secretary from 1910 to 1916, and as its president from 1916 to 1917. When the United States entered the First World War, Benton felt compelled to be with the boys at the war front, although even before going to Europe, he was in effect already involved in the war effort when the United States government named him in early 1917 as a member from New England of the educational commission of the council of national defense. When he joined the war, Benton was the first American college president to do so.

Wartime Services as an Educator

Benton was with the American Expeditionary Forces from 1917 to 1919. First he was detailed as general secretary of the Young Men's Christian Association (YMCA) in Paris, France. He served concurrently as director of welfare work of the YMCA. Later, he became the chief organizing secretary for the YMCA with membership on the staff of Brig. Gen. William R. Sample, commander-in-chief of the "advance section" of the American Expeditionary Forces. Benton eventually received appointment as the chief secretary of the 8th Region, American Expeditionary Forces, and in January 1919, he was appointed member of the United States Army Educational Corps and chief educational director, American Army of Occupation, with headquarters in Coblenz, Germany.

As chief educational director of the American Army of Occupation, he exercised control over all educational matters from Germany all the way to France and Luxembourg. He took charge of everything from elementary education to university curricular offerings, benefiting more than 35,000 American fighting men in the European theater. This educational enterprise under his jurisdiction was the largest ever organized in the world for unified management. Because of his outstanding contributions to the war effort in the education sector, the United States government awarded Benton in 1919 the Distinguished Service Medal.

Upon his return to the United States in June 1919 soon after the termination of the First World War, he entered private business. He became Chairman of the Advisory Council of the Associated Educators of America. This is a group which specialized in the application of the motion picture to education and industry.[12] However, in August 1920, he decided to accept the invitation from the United States government for him to re-enter army educational work by being a consultant to the commanding general of the American forces in the Philippines. By October 1920, he was on his way to Manila from San Francisco to take up his new post in the Education and Recreation Office, Headquarters, Philippine Department, United States Army.[13]

UNIVERSITY CONSTITUENCY AWAITS APPOINTMENT OF NEW PRESIDENT

THE presidency of the University of the Philippines, for all intents and purposes, fell vacant when Ignacio Villamor, its first Filipino occupant, received positive indications as early as the beginning of 1919 that he was headed for appointment as an associate justice of the Supreme Court of the Philippines. At that time, Villamor could no longer attend fully to his duties as the chief executive of the University, necessitating the designation of Regent Jose Escaler as President Protempore. In that capacity, the good Regent ran the affairs of the University for the entire academic year of 1919-1920. By the end of that academic year, Villamor formally resigned on account of his expected "promotion" to the highest court of the land.

The University Council took official cognizance of Villamor's resignation during that body's regular meeting on July 7, 1920. And so for the entire academic year of 1920-1921, Alejandro M. Albert, Undersecretary of Public Instruction, acted as the University's interim president.[14] The Executive Committee of the University assisted the interim president in administering matters involving academic instruction.[15]

Searching at Leisure

Meanwhile, a mechanism for the selection of a "permanent" University president took effect. This mechanism took the form of a committee tasked with the responsibility of recommending to the Board of Regents someone who could be appointed president of the University as soon as a suitable candidate could be found. Apparently, though, the Board of Regents took its own leisurely pace in appointing a new chief executive. In fact, the body had to be "nagged" into performing its appointing power. For example, in the beginning of 1921, more than half a year since the resignation of Villamor, the Board had not yet acted on the matter, thereby prompting the committee created to select the new president to issue a petition for the appointment of the head of the University even prior to the holding of the commencement program for 1921. Even the University Council made known its impatience at the way the matter was kept dragging.[16]

Despite efforts for the early resolution of the issue, and despite the apparent "inaction" of the Board of Regents, the said body actually commissioned late in 1920 a man by the name of W. W. Marquardt to search quietly for someone in the United States suitable for the position. A member of the Board of Regents under President Ignacio Villamor, Marquardt was primarily responsible for Filipino *pensionado* scholars in American institutions of higher learning, helping them adjust properly in the social and educational milieu of the United States, and then seeing to it that the *pensionados* went back home to serve after successful studies abroad. Now he had the additional chore of looking around for prospective appointees to the University's presidency.[17]

Few Prospects Identified

Marquardt surveyed a field composed of distinguished candidates. The most prominently mentioned as early as October 1920 were Paul Monroe,

John Dewey, and Francis Shepherdson. A fourth, George A. Malcolm, was also considered.

The abovenamed candidates were highly respected. Paul Monroe was a recognized authority in the field of education. He was connected with the School of Education of Columbia University, and was to leave an indelible imprint in Philippine educational history when he headed a team which surveyed Philippine education, publishing its report in 1925.[18]

John Dewey, also of Columbia University, was an American philosopher and educator who led a philosophical movement called *pragmatism* and whose philosophy, *instrumentalism,* advocates the use of intelligence in overcoming any form of obstacle, instead of relying simply on habitual action and thought. As an educator, Dewey stressed innovative learning methods, as opposed to rote memory, which are related to the interests of students and to problems faced by society.[19]

Francis Shepherdson, meanwhile, was a professional historian who once taught at the University of Chicago. He was serving as registrar of the University of Illinois at the time his name was mentioned in connection with the presidency of the University. Shepherdson was no stranger to the Philippines since the Department of Education sponsored a trip by him to the Islands once for a series of lectures.[20]

As for Malcolm, he was familiar to his fellow Americans in the Philippines as well as to the Filipinos. He was a lecturer in the College of Law of the University, later becoming its Dean, and eventually appointed Associate Justice of the Supreme Court.[21]

The field of candidates was however not limited to the aforementioned scholars. Lawrence E. Gurney, a faculty member of the Department of Mathematics of the University, and John W. Osborn, the Assistant Director of Education in the colonial government, were likewise considered.[22]

None of the above obtained the presidency of the University though, either because the salary to induce the best of them was too high for the University to meet, or because they were probably not regarded by the Board of Regents as being of "presidential timber." The prevalent belief was that Paul Monroe or John Dewey could be lured to accept the position only on the basis of a firm commitment by the University to pay them at least US $20,000 per annum. There was even talk of an offer having been made to Woodrow Wilson to become the president of the University at a salary of US $100,000 yearly.[23] However, the amounts mentioned were obviously way beyond the capacity of the University to pay so that in the end, the University had to settle with less renowned prospects but who nevertheless had impressive academic credentials.

Fate or Propitious Circumstance?

The name of Guy Potter Benton came into the picture in November

1920. Marquardt wired the University that two American university presidents had contacted him to recommend Benton. The two presidents were those of the University of California and Miami University (Ohio).[24] The *Philippines Herald* of October 14, 1920 earlier ran a story about Benton's expected arrival in Manila as an educational consultant of the American defense forces in the Philippines.[25]

Obviously, Benton did not know, when he was on his way to the Philippines as an educational adviser and soon after his arrival in the country, that his name would be submitted to Marquardt for consideration by the Board of Regents for the presidency of the University. One of the men with whom he maintained close and regular correspondence throughout his stay in the Philippines was R.M. Hughes, his successor at the helm of Miami University. As noted above, Hughes was one of those who nominated Benton to Marquardt, who then cabled the name of Benton to Manila.

Thus, when Benton arrived in Manila, he became the object of undue attention by Philippine colonial and University authorities. Hughes wrote to him, in a letter dated November 10, 1920, that his name had been submitted to the University. In his reply to Hughes dated December 9, 1920, Benton has this to say:

> Your reference to the University of the Philippines explains somewhat all the activities that are just now in progress here. Of course I need not tell you that I am not a candidate for this or any other University presidency. I am not unmindful of the opportunities afforded and I do not care to say that no circumstances could arise which might not be offered. The newspapers have had a good deal to say on the subject lately, but they have had no encouragement from me. Indeed I have never so much as mentioned the subject to newspaper representatives. The regents of the University, however, are giving me a dinner tonight and something may develop which may give me a different view. I am extremely anxious to make the next twenty years of my life count for the utmost to humanity and I do not care to say that I would refuse any challenge that might come to me for larger accomplishment.[26]

It is quite clear from the above quotation that Benton was surprised to learn of his being considered for the presidency of the University. While he initially reacted by saying that he was not a candidate for the presidency of any institution of higher learning, and while he did not seek the position, it is equally clear that he had an open mind toward the matter. Apparently Benton maintained a "wait and see" attitude because he did not flatly reject the overtures of the University, particularly the members of the Board of Regents. In keeping his options open, Benton was specifically concerned with his desire to be of service to "humanity" and to have the opportunity for "larger accomplishment."[27] However, Benton was not necessarily thinking of the Philippines when he stated that he was leaving all possibilities to present themselves for him to consider.

Two Options Unfold

Based on the records available, Ohio University in Athens likewise proffered its presidency to Benton. This proffer was confirmed by Benton in another letter to Hughes dated January 4, 1921.[28] It appears though that the offer for the UP presidency was presented to Benton ahead of the Ohio offer. The University appeared to have persisted in obtaining the services of Benton; that in effect, the Board of Regents had decided, once the offer was made to him, that he was the man needed by the institution.

How did Benton himself view the situation wherein he was faced with two offers: one from the University and the other from Ohio University? In his January 4, 1921 letter to Hughes is this passage:

> Late the same week that the cablegram [received by Benton on 20 December 1920] came from Mr. Foster, proffering the Presidency of Ohio University, I received a call from a Committee of the Board of Regents of the University of the Philippines, who offered me the Presidency of that institution. I must confess that this makes strong appeal to me, for somewhere in the Orient there must be developed a great educational institution that will bear the same relation to the United States in the Far East that the German Universities bore to our country on the other side of the world prior to the War [i.e., the First World War].[29]

While he seemed enthusiastic about the prospect of being able to render service to humanity on this side of the Pacific Ocean, Benton still vacillated over what decision to make. This vacillation is reflected in his statement toward the end of the same letter to Hughes: "I do not know, however, whether the next ten years of my life, which should be the very best, ought to be spent in the Philippines. I wish I had you and Mr. Tobey and some other good friends here to advise me."[30]

The reason for the vacillation was probably because Benton was counting on getting the Ohio University presidency. His succeeding letters to Hughes noted that he expected to get additional details about the offer and that the cablegram he claimed to have received would be followed up by a lengthier communication containing the concrete particulars of the terms of the appointment proposed by Ohio University.

Ultimately No Other Choice

In another letter to Hughes, dated February 24, 1921, he confessed that "Nothing more had been heard . . . . from Ohio University since I last wrote you [on 4 January 1921]."[31] Meanwhile, Benton wrote, "The Board of Regents of the University of the Philippines are still urging the opportunity offered by that institution, and I am trying to give their suggestions careful consideration."[32] He said he had not made up his mind for the simple reason that he and the Board of Regents had not fully agreed yet on the terms of his appointment. According to Benton, the University offered at first a salary of US$10,000. This was later increased to $15,000 with a furnished house and an automobile.

Actually, there was another reason for Benton's hesitation in accepting the University presidency. He wrote: "Mrs. Benton feels that the climate here does not agree with her and the girls think that their larger opportunity is in the States. I shall not feel that I ought to go contrary to their judgment unless the opportunity here impresses me as one so stupendous that I should disregard every other consideration."[33]

That the Ohio University offer was his first choice becomes clear in his March 1, 1921 letter to Hughes. In this letter, he wrote:

> All that you have to say about Ohio University interests me very much, but I am beginning to think that they must have found someone else. When the pressure became very strong from the Board of Regents of the University of the Philippines for an answer, I cabled Mr. Foster on February 9th as follows: 'Please cable whether Ohio still wants me as another University demands an immediate answer.' To this no reply has come and this I can only interpret as meaning that they have not thought enough of my candidacy to comply with my request for a reply.
>
> Let me confess that I am somewhat disappointed because I had begun to think of the possibility of return of Ohio to wind up my professional career there during the next fifteen or twenty years. The desire is emphasized by the letters received from you and Mr. Tobey this morning.[34]

The University, for its part, increased its offer to "US$18,000 a year, with an automobile and traveling expenses, on a ten-year contract."[35] Despite this increase in the offer, Benton still seemed "reluctant" to accept it, mainly because of Mrs. Benton's objections on the ground that the climate in the Philippines did not suit her and because of the hope that he himself nurtured about being able to return to his native state of Ohio. But then toward the end of his letter, Benton went on to say:

> Of course I am not unmindful that all this may be providential for certainly there is a great opportunity for service afforded in the challenge made by the University of the Philippines. The money consideration looks big but I think I should not consider that for a moment when set against the privilege of making my life count for the utmost, even at a much smaller compensation. I am only anxious to know where my duty lies and it has begun to look as though it might be in these islands.[36]

From the above discussion and passages, it is evident that Benton, when faced with the pressure of making a decision between the University of the Philippines and Ohio University, decided in favor of the latter. However, when Ohio University failed to follow up its offer, precisely because it found somebody else, Benton then tried to compensate for his disappointment over his non-appointment to the Ohio post by falling back on the offer of the University of the Philippines.

It may be pointed out that Benton formally declined the University presidency on February 4, 1921, but the Board of Regents made "an urgent appeal for reconsideration."[37] Benton, however, heeded this appeal only after it became manifest to him that the presidency of Ohio University was not his for the taking. He did acknowledge the failure of Ohio University to make good its offer as a factor in making up his mind eventually to accept the presidency of the University. In this connection, he said: "Perhaps the fact that I have failed to receive any further word from Mr. Foster concerning Ohio University may have emphasized the importance to me of the present opportunity."[38] While not discounting the role of "self-interest" in his action, he hoped that in the final analysis, it was his animation by "high ideals" that led him to favorably reconsider his earlier decision to decline the University presidency.[39]

Terms of Appointment

By March 3, 1921, the *Manila Times* could report to its readers that Benton had been offered the presidency at ₱30,000 per annum, or $15,000 in American currency in addition to which he was offered an allowance of ₱3,000 for housing.[40] The offer was formalized on March 7, 1921 after a special Board of Regents meeting that day wherein he was officially elected as the third president of the University.[41] The full text of the official communication to Benton by the Board of Regents, signed by Alejandro M. Albert as chairman, follows:

> This is a formal notification that the Regents have today elected you President of the University of the Philippines and, in behalf of the Board, I hereby tender to you this position of large responsibility and great opportunity.
>
> From various conferences with you the Board understands that you hold the conviction that this work of establishing our newly created National University on permanent foundations will require the earnest efforts of an undisturbed administration through at least ten years, you also feel it will be impossible to determine with satisfaction to yourself, whether you can assume such a responsibility for so long a term until you have had the opportunity during some months, to study the problems of the University from an inside point of view.
>
> The Regents are in full accord with your views and therefore offer you a contract for one year from April fourth, 1921, at a salary of thirty thou-

> sand pesos with three thousand pesos additional in lieu of a president's house, – payable in twelve equal monthly installments on the last secular day of each month, – with automobile, within the Islands.
>
> In the event relations prove mutually satisfactory after one year of such connection, this contract will be made permanent for a ten-year period. By due notice of either party to this tentative agreement, on April 1st, 1922, that continuation of these relationships is not desired you will be released from any further obligations to the University, and if such initiative originates from the Board of Regents you will be paid an additional year's salary on the terms herein named exclusive of house rent and other perquisites.

Benton was apparently satisfied with the terms of the offer. On March 8, 1921, he formally accepted the presidency of the University through a letter addressed to Chairman Albert. At the same time, he officially sent his resignation as educational consultant to the Headquarters Philippine Department, Education and Recreation Office, United States Army.[42]

In his own words, Benton had this to say concerning the terms of his election by the Board of Regents as president of the University of the Philippines:

> The present arrangement, which gives me the privilege of a year to study the problems from the inside with the privilege of honorable retirement at the end of that time if I feel disinclined to remain, with assurances of an additional year's salary in the event the Regents take the initiative in terminating their relationship, seemed so eminently fair that I felt impelled to accept the challenge of what promises to be a splendid opportunity for human service.
>
> The salary is, of course, attractive. Thirty thousand pesos is equivalent, approximately, to Fifteen thousand dollars and with the three thousand pesos additional in lieu of a furnished house with automobile and servicc guaranteed, means a compensation equivalent to about $18,000. This may seem exorbitant to you as it does to me. *However, I have been so long in altruistic work without giving much heed to the remuneration therefor that I felt the time had come when I must insist upon safeguarding Mrs. Benton and myself against the anxieties of old age by selling my services for their full potential worth.* I trust, however, that the thought of service to mankind is the dominating motive in my mind.[43]

Still, Benton continued to feel dejected over his non-selection as president of Ohio University. In another letter to Hughes, written several days after his election to, and his acceptance of, the presidency of the University, he remarked: "It is something of a disappointment, I confess, to abandon the dream I had allowed myself to entertain of returning to Ohio."[44]

Facing Up to the Challenge

At any rate, once he decided to accept the presidency of the University, Benton reconciled himself to the idea that he had a duty to perform in the Philippines and that he was dedicating himself to it. He said:

> It promises such an opportunity for service it is possible I shall be glad to stay for ten years.[45]

It seems that he wanted to make every moment of his remaining years as fruitful as possible in terms of service to mankind that he desired to make sure that wherever he settled down for a job, that was where he could realize his fullest potential and leave an indelible imprint for the benefit of humanity. As he wrote:

> Questions of independence and political movements, however, make the situation uncertain. I feel that the next twenty years of my life should be the best and I must take no chances in tying myself up in an institution where I can not realize on my hopes of service to mankind.[46]

In his acceptance letter, addressed to Chairman Albert, Benton expressed his feelings in this manner:

> Permit me to say, however, that I am dedicating my abilities and experience for whatever they may be worth, without reservation, to the high task committed to me in full expectation that with the unqualified support promised by your leading statesment (sic) and the Regents these relationships will continue through an indefinite future.[47]

The two immediately preceding quotations from two separate letters written by Benton reveal an inner conflict and ferment despite his remark that his acceptance of the presidency was "without reservation." Of course there was an escape clause for both parties in the contract they entered into. By mutual agreement, Benton would be given the chance to study the internal situation in the University for a year, giving the presidency a try during that period, and should he find the job to his liking, and should the Board of Regents find Benton's performance satisfactory, then the contract would become binding for ten years until 1931.

Reassessment of the Situation

To the credit of Benton, he never sought the presidency of the University of the Philippines. When he came over to the country in the last quarter of 1920, it was without thought of ever becoming the head of the national university of the Filipino people. It would be more accurate to say that the presidency sought him. The evidence shows that by the time Benton arrived in Manila with his family in November 1920, his name, without his knowledge, had been submitted to the Board of Regents, which was then undertaking the search for a permanent university head as a result of the resignation of Ignacio Villamor.

The Board of Regents first formally offered the presidency to Benton during the week of December 20, 1920. On February 4, 1921, he declined the position in a formal communication to the proffering agency. However the University renewed the offer and asked Benton to reconsider his decision. Then on March 7, 1921, the Board of Regents officially elected him to the presidency. The following day, March 8, 1921, Benton signified in writing his acceptance of the task of leading the 13-year-old institution of higher learning.

His election to the presidency, however, was not made without a note of dissent and adverse publicity, despite the generally cordial reception accorded him before and after his designation as president.

Initial Doubts and Fears

An alumnus of the University who was a practicing attorney and legal counsellor, Victoriano Yamzon, addressed an appeal to Manuel L. Quezon asking the latter to use his "good offices in bringing about a postponement of action on the recommendation of the [selection] committee, the members of which are inclined to favor the appointment of Dr. Benton."[48] Yamzon based his petition simply on what he read in an article published in the *Philippines Herald* on March 5, 1921. The article was written by a faculty member of the University, Austin Craig. Craig belonged to the Department of History. According to Yamzon, echoing Craig, Benton was "not the man we want for the University."[49] He claimed that "the great majority of the graduates of the University favor the appointment of Justice Malcolm of the Supreme Court of the Philippine Islands."

Quezon, while feeling "sorry" that Yamzon's letter came to his attention much later after the Board of Regents had made its decision on the matter, dismissed the petition and pointedly declared that "this matter falls exclusively under the jurisdiction of the Board of Regents." Not to be swayed by innuendoes and negative remarks made by people out to discredit Benton, Quezon candidly told Yamzon his personal feelings in these terms:

> I have had several conversations with Dr. Benton regarding the University, and I feel that we may count upon Dr. Benton doing his best in building up that institution and, what is better, all recent developments lead me to believe that he will be a success.[50]

In the article by Craig referred to by Yamzon, Benton was the object of vicious and scurrilous attacks. He was described as a Protestant clergyman in a Catholic country, with Craig downgrading further the academic experience of Benton including his presidential stints in "fourth-rate" institutions.[51]

Brighter Aspects Appreciated

However, Benton ignored these comments publicly; that is, he did not deem it proper to reply to them. In a letter to his bosom friend, R.M. Hughes, Benton said:

> Of course, I paid no attention to these comments for some of them were conglomerate collections of half truths and you know a half truth is oftenmore (sic) dangerous than an absolute falsehood. There were other glaring mis-statements probably due to ignorance or hasty conclusions. The disparagement of Miami University and the University of Vermont as institutions "not up to standard" gave me greater offense than some of the strictures made against me as an individual. I was inclined to tell them how the Institutions I had served stood in the world of education at home but I finally concluded it wise to adhere to my well established policy of dignified silence and I, therefore, refused to make any reply to these untruthful and unwarranted attacks. Once more I am convinced that this was the wisest course to pursue for a great majority of the Alumni and Faculty and the leading people of these Islands whose opinion counts have received my election with enthusiastic expressions of satisfaction and they have given me their assurances of cordial support in the great task that confronts me.[52]

Nevertheless, the adverse publicity generated by the strong criticisms voiced by Craig in the *Philippines Herald* was balanced by favorable accounts about Benton in the other Manila dailies. For example, the March 3, 1921 issue of the *Manila Times* carried a story about his impending appointment by the Board of Regents. And on March 8, 1921, the same paper not only carried the announcement concerning his election to the presidency of the University, but also ran a full account of his life and academic background. In other words, because the position in question is one with utmost prestige and honor, it is natural that whoever occupies it would get the attention from the press it fully deserves, regardless of whether the accounts printed are positive or negative in tone.

When Benton assumed the presidency of the University on April 4, 1921, he had definite ideas and visions about what he would like the institution to be. He drew from his rich and long experience as an academic administrator in universities in the United States. His public pronouncements of course gave valuable insights into his educational philosophy and goals, but his letters were even more important in revealing his innermost thoughts. Benton candidly put down his views and feelings in these letters.[53]

Visions of a Great University

His vision was related to how he would like to spend the next ten to twenty years of his life. As alluded to earlier, he would like to be of utmost service to humanity wherever he was assigned. Thus, even when he was still under consideration for the presidency, he always spoke in terms of where he could leave the most indelible imprint in the life of all humanity. Therefore, upon his accession to the position of president and chief executive of the University, Benton had decided that the Philippines was the place where he could leave his mark.

His overriding ambition was to transform the University of the Philippines into the greatest institution for higher learning in the Asian region. This was to be the "crowning feature" of his life "dedicated to the service of mankind."[54] In his view, the University was established not just for the purpose of serving the Filipino nation, but also for the purpose of the "promotion of civilization among the teeming millions on the Asiatic shores nearby."[55]

As a great educational institution, then, the University was viewed by Benton as a vehicle for the training of young men and women in Asia to become responsible and efficient citizens who shall bring progress and enlightenment to their respective peoples. On the observance of "University Day" on December 12, 1922, Benton exhorted the constituents of the University to "engage, with high resolve, to make the University of the Philippines the mightiest possible instrumentality for the advancement of civilization in these Islands, in the Far East and throughout the entire world."[56]

Liberalism, Relevance and Nationalism

Benton dwelt on the same theme in an article he was expressly asked to write for the April 4, 1921 issue of *The Varsity,* then the official student newspaper in the University. It will be recalled that Benton assumed his position in the University on this day. In his words, it was the task of the University "to promote efficient citizenship of the highest type in the world-wide brotherhood of man."[57] While Benton did say that the University should not in effect be parochial in its outlook, and that the University should orient its educational mission not just to the people of the Philippines but also to the nations of Asia and of the whole world,.he did recognize that the University "belongs to the people of these Islands."[58] In this regard, he said:

> The University of the Philippines is at once the tangible encouragement and the inspiring hope of youthhood and citizenry in all these Islands from the Celebes sea to the Batanes Islands and from the Strait of San Bernardino to Palawan.[59]

He went on to say that while the Filipino nation adhered to the Christian faith, he stated, in the true spirit of liberality and tolerance, that all faiths and creeds should be protected and allowed to flourish in the confines of the University "without molestation or discouragement."[59] Benton therefore envisioned the University as an institution where "narrow-minded sectarianism" would have no place and where everybody was "guaranteed the right to think and act as their own conscience dictate(s)."[60]

As an educational institution supported by public funds, the University, according to Benton, should not be content sitting on top of the academic ivory tower, unattuned to the realities of society. The University, in Benton's view, was not simply a place where one solely studied "abstruse philosophies" or where one promoted "impractical scholarship."[61] Rather, he envisioned the University to be one where the street literally *ran through* the campus and "out upon highways that reach to the doorsteps of the remotest and humblest citizens."[62] The University should also be the training ground for men and women who will go into industry, commerce, agriculture, education and the professions.[63]

And because the University derived its financial sinews from the taxpayers, Benton considered the University to be the seedbed of democracy in the Philippines. In true American fashion, he regarded public education as the handmaiden of progress toward implanting democratic roots in native Filipino soil. Again, in his own words, Benton said the University "must afford incentives for the pursuit of the highest ideals of citizenship that does not run to the extreme of superficial aristocracy on the one hand or to that of object (*sic*) penury on the other hand. The golden mean between the two extremes must be found in quality of privilege through plain living and high thinking."[64]

Specific Objectives of the UP

Benton had the occasion to elaborate on his conceptions of what the University should be during the presentation of his inaugural address when he was publicly and ceremonially installed into office on December 16, 1921. In his speech entitled "Objectives of the Tax-Supported University in the Philippine Islands," Benton stated in concrete terms what the objectives of the University would be under his administration. He divided the objectives of the University into four, which he noted were the same as those pursued by state universities in the United States: (1) service to students; (2) service to elementary and secondary schools and other colleges and universities; (3) service to the State in its various activities – agricultural, educational, manufacturing, industrial, commercial, and social; and (4) service to the cause of education at large.[65]

Under each major objective, Benton gave specific proposals to best actualize the vision he had for the University. In connection with service to students, he visualized preparation for responsible citizenship as the chief mission of the tax-supported university. However, the University should not open its doors to just anybody wishing to enter its academic groves. It must ensure institutional efficiency in the conduct of extensive training for the students through the adoption of "the sound educational policy of restricting our student body to an enrollment that will assure every student the expert teaching service essential to academic training of the highest quality."[66] This policy of limiting enrollment could best be achieved by a selective process so that "we may guarantee value received to the country in a manhood and womanhood of the most serviceable type."[67]

The limitation of the enrollment of the University through the selective process, according to Benton, should be accompanied by a corresponding reduction and streamlining of existing courses. Benton observed that faculty specialists were creating courses left and right, with "so many alternatives. . . offered to immature students entering college today that they are confused by the choice of studies . . . presented to them on the threshold of their undergraduate life."[68] The idea then was to abolish the courses which were unnecessary and retain only those that would promote the most elevated ideals of the University.

Benton likewise proposed the limitation of the number of faculty members, removing those whom he called "immature instructors," and retaining only those with maximum ability even if they constituted a small number. To make undergraduate instruction relevant to the needs of Filipino society, Benton batted for a combined cultural and vocational curricular program in the University. By this he meant the "middle ground between ancient and modern educational policies by bringing undergraduate curricula down to irreducible minimums which will ensure the enlargement of life essential to citizenship with the added preparation necessary for advanced study in the several professions."[69] Under this scheme, the University would give two degrees to each graduate after a span of six years in the institution. One degree would be vocational in nature while the other degree would be a regular bachelor's degree.

Indispensable Components

Furthermore, in keeping with his vision of a first-class university, Benton cautioned against unnecessary and uncontrolled expansion by the University. Benton remarked that he would not hesitate to recommend the curtailment of colleges and departments which "seem less necessary to the public welfare."[70] Without mentioning which colleges and departments were unnecessary, he cited the College of Medicine, the College of Agriculture, the College of Education, and the Department of Commerce as "indispensable components of the University system."[71]

However, he followed his enumeration of these indispensable units by saying that the Philippine colonial legislature should not "neglect the adequate support of our College of Liberal Arts, the heart-center of all University life; or our College of Law to guarantee a necessary supply of high-grade lawyers so that the public may not be victimized by pettifogging charlatans; or the College of Engineering so essential to the training of experts for public works; or the College of Veterinary Science for cooperation with farmers in conserving our valuable live-stock; or the Forest School to guarantee the conservation of one of our best natural resources."[72] For a well-rounded education, Benton likewise mentioned art, music, and drama, for their role in the cultural development of the Filipinos.

Toward Financial Stability

To ensure that the University would have the necessary means to sustain itself, and thus accomplish the objectives discussed above, Benton emphasized the need for adequate appropriations, reinforced by the income derived from a mill-tax levy of one-half of one percent on all the taxable real estate in the country. Benton hoped that the revenue derived from the mill-tax levy would put the University on a sound financial basis permanently, particularly if such revenue was supplemented by the allocation of some portions of the public domain which could be held in trust by the University for, say, half a century.[73]

Actually, even before Benton assumed the presidency of the University formally, and during the time the Board of Regents held talks with him prior to his official election as President of the University, Benton had already expressed concern over the need for placing the finances of the institution on a permanent basis. This can be seen in the formal letter of invitation sent by Alejandro M. Albert, Chairman of the Board of Regents, to Benton on March 7, 1921. In this letter, Albert alluded to the numerous meetings the Board had had with Benton, during which the latter expressed his desire to work for the establishment of permanent foundations for the University, an effort by Benton which would require a term of at least ten years.[74]

As for the objective of the University in rendering service to the State, Benton pointed out that the University was meant not only to serve the students "but also for the promotion of the general welfare."[75] In line with this objective, the University should aim to collaborate with various agencies of the State in discovering and developing the natural resources of the country. For such collaboration, Benton advocated the balancing of instruction with research, so that the two could go hand in hand, without one outdistancing the other. This would ensure that the work of the University would be well-rounded.

In Benton's view, the "best University instruction comes from the professor fresh from his investigations in the laboratory, and the research scientist finds the best confirmation of his conclusions by their application with his students in the classroom or lecture hall. The University teacher, without the research habit, is dead on his feet, and the scientific investigator who does not teach, is usually an impractical theorist."[76]

A Model to be Emulated

With regard to the objective of providing service to other educational institutions, the University should become a "standardizing factor" by limiting its student enrollment so that it could be served more efficiently by a competent teaching body. Being a public institution for higher education, it should be the obligation of the University to serve as a training ground in the tertiary level for pupils produced by the public elementary and secondary institutions in the country. This would "guarantee the eternal salvation of civilization throughout this great Archipelago."[77]

As a tax-supported educational system, the University should also exercise leadership over private and denominational schools by maintaining high standards which could be emulated by those in the private and church-affiliated sectors. This would ensure the improvement of the educational atmosphere in the entire country, thus benefiting the whole population.[78]

In connection with his idea that the University should also be of service to education at large, Benton stated that the University should perform its duty as an educational institution not just for the benefit of the Filipino people but also for the benefit of the entire humankind. In his words: "There are no State or National boundaries in education. The Republic of Letters, in its legitimate activities, reaches out to the ends of the earth and takes in all the races of mankind."[79]

The foregoing, then, were the hopes and visions of Benton as to the objectives of the University he was to lead and what he would have liked the institution to become had his health remained unimpaired. Unfortunately, Benton had to cut short his ten-year term as President in late 1923 when his illness compelled him to resign from his position. It was a case of sleeping sickness resulting in fatal neurological impairment.

At any rate, even if he had to resign from the presidency, he was in the University long enough to institute certain measures, and to take part in some of the events that would have great impact on the life of the institution.

FROM PROMISE TO PERFORMANCE: THE PRESIDENTIAL RECORD

THE obvious question to ask at this point is, just how successful was Benton in accomplishing the objectives discussed in the preceding section, which he indicated in his April 4, 1921 article in *The Varsity* and in his inaugural address, and which incidentally passed the critical examination of Manuel L. Quezon? [80] In fact Quezon gave his own constructive suggestions on how to make the speech more appropriate for delivery to a Filipino audience, before it was finalized and given on December 16, 1921.[81] More particularly, how successful was the University under the presidency of Benton in putting itself on a sound and permanent financial foundation?

Within the first month of Benton's accession to the presidency of the University, on April 23, 1921 he made a formal proposal and special recommendation, among others, to the Board of Regents for the establishment of permanent University support based on a mill-tax levy. This particular recommendation of Benton was consistent with his ideas and thoughts about putting the University on a sound foundation which he held even prior to his formal election by the Board of Regents on March 7, 1921. Soon after his accession to his new office, Benton embarked with apparent enthusiasm on a course which he strongly felt would lead to the realization of his prime objective of firmly securing the finances of the University so it would not become dependent upon the vagaries of legislative capriciousness.

Underlying Principles

Benton's proposal for a mill-tax levy was in reality a part of the four fundamental principles which he was to enunciate before the Board of Regents on August 22, 1921. These four principles were considered by Benton "as prerequisite to the establishment of a firm foundation for the University of the Philippines and the erection thereon of a proper institutional superstructure."[82] These principles were (a) the revision of the Charter law of the University, (b) the selection of a final location for the physical plant of the University, (c) the passage of a mill-tax levy for permanent University financial support, and (d) the granting of public lands to serve as a secure source for a permanent University endowment.[83]

Each of these principles interlocked with one another. They could not be separated from each other, and the fulfillment of each was indispensable for the realization of the larger objective of firming up the University's financial foundations and the related objective of reorganizing the institutional structures of the school for greater efficiency in the delivery of vital educational services.

The crucial point with regard to the fundamental principle of revising the University Charter is contained in Section 18 of the proposed revisions. This particular section states: "The Legislature may provide means for the permanent support of the University of the Philippines and the Governor General, subject to the approval of the Council of State, shall designate public lands for the endowment of the University."[84] This proposed amendment was submitted by Benton, with the approval of the Board of Regents, after the original proposed amendment did not receive a favorable response from Governor General Leonard Wood. The original proposed amendment apparently contained a more explicit statement about the mill-tax levy and the allocation of public lands as sources of permanent income for the University.

The proposed amendment of the Charter, as acted upon by the Board of Regents, was referred to the Committee on Reorganization which the body created, upon the recommendation of Benton, to take a closer look at the structures and programs of the University to ensure that they were efficiently working and were attuned with the overall objectives of the administration. This same committee then proposed a revision addressed to the Philippine Legislature. The revision which was submitted for consideration by the lawmaking body was the one that contained clear reference to the mill-tax levy and the allocation of public lands for permanent University financial support. This proposed revision went straight to the Philippine Legislature without being coursed through the Office of the Governor General, which was simply furnished a copy.

Governor Wood nevertheless indicated his support for the University's proposal. In a letter from Wood to Quezon, the former said: "I believed that, as I have stated, that provision for the University should be made in part by a mill tax and in part by setting aside public lands whose constantly increasing value will tend ultimately, to meet the expenses and upkeep of the University."[85]

The progress of the revision of the Charter of the University was definitely tied to, and contingent upon, the progress of the proposal to impose a mill-tax levy for the support of the University. The same is true with regard to the determination of a final location for the University campus, as well as the allocation of portions of the public domain so that the income derived from the land grant(s) will contribute toward the maintenance of the existence of the University as a first-class educational institution. At the level of the Board of Regents, the above fundamental principles received full approval.[86]

Background on the Mill-Tax Levy

Because of the crucial nature of the mill-tax levy proposal, and because of the great importance attached to it by Benton and his supporters in the University, it may be worth looking into its rise and fall. Based on the evidence, the idea of a permanent source of income for the University was not really original with Benton. The political leadership of the country was apparently cognizant of the felt need to put the University on a sound basis even before Benton came to the Philippines. In October 1920, for instance, Governor General Francis Burton Harrison stated in his 8th message to the Philippine National Assembly:

> The University of the Philippines has now developed to a point where it is worthy of more self-government and more opportunity for self-development; I recommend to you a reform of the Charter of the institution, giving control of the University to the faculty, as is customary in the great universities of England and continental Europe, thereby insuring to the faculty that absolute freedom of thought and of speech, which is essential to a true attainment of its proper place in the intellectual life of this country; *to this end I also request you to provide a plan for the permanent endowment of the University.*"[87]

Within the University, as early as February 1920, long before Benton set foot on Philippine soil, Dean Jorge C. Bocobo had drafted a plan for a permanent endowment for the University. Bocobo's plan recommended the enactment by the Philippine National Assembly of a law that would allocate a portion of the public taxes for the permanent support of the University.

The Executive Committee of the University adopted Bocobo's plan on February 20, 1920. This same committee noted Harrison's advice on October 23, 1920. Under the acting presidency of Alejandro M. Albert, Chairman of the Board of Regents, the University undertook and completed a study aimed ultimately at proposing specific revisions in the University Charter, and at securing the passage of a law for the purpose of guaranteeing an adequate and a stable source of funds for the maintenance of the University.[88]

Therefore, when Benton came to the University and assumed its presidency, talks about a permanent endowment for the institution were very much in the air. The Board of Regents undoubtedly mentioned the idea of a permanent support for the University to Benton during the times when negotiations were still under way between the Board and Benton for the presidency. Benton himself realized that the establishment of a permanent endowment fund for the University would be his top item in the agenda upon his accession to the presidency. It must have been on this basis that he asked for an undisturbed term of ten years so he could pursue the matter until it was realized. All the other plans and programs of Benton for the University apparently hinged on the successful adoption of the mill-tax levy proposal.

Benton immediately discussed the revision of the Charter with Governor General William Cameron Forbes and with Leonard Wood in the summer of 1921. Both colonial leaders approved the same, including the proposed establishment of a central business management for the University.[89] Apparently, the University transmitted the proposed revised Charter to the Speaker of the House and to the President of the Senate for their consideration. Of the proposed revised Charter, the only section which met with the disapproval of Forbes and Wood was that which provided for a mill-tax levy, but which was later on substituted by the University with a proposed amendment making that section less specific and giving it a more flexible and broad character. This amended version gave the Philippine National Assembly the power to provide at its discretion and pleasure a plan for the permanent support of the University. Furthermore, the amended version authorized the Governor General to allocate portions of the public domain for the endowment of the University. The latter was in accordance with the suggestion of no less than Wood himself.[90]

Special Committee Proposed

In addition, the University by resolution of the Board of Regents, proposed the creation of a committee to be composed of the President of the University, one member of the Lower House to be designated by the Speaker, one member of the Senate to be named by the Senate President, one member of the Board of Regents to be chosen by the Board, and one member of the University faculty to be appointed by the President. This committee would be tasked with the formulation of an appropriate plan for permanent support of the University. The plans so formulated by this committee would then be presented, through the Governor General, to the National Assembly for its consideration and approval.[91]

As already alluded to earlier, Wood himself endorsed the proposal favorably to Senate President Manuel L. Quezon, along with the creation of a special committee to draft the plan for the permanent support of the University.[92] Quezon, for his part, gave his attention to the matters mentioned above, and informed Benton that he had "substituted for the House bill the fifty-million-peso plan submitted by the University" and that the matter would be presented to the Legislature at its 1922 session.[93] This was Quezon's response to Benton's letter of February 8, 1922, wherein Benton sought to enlist the personal and immediate support of the Senate President for the proposed permanent support of the University.

In this letter to Quezon, Benton recognized the impossibility of the passage of the bill introduced by Representative Eulogio Benitez of the Lower House embodying the mill-tax levy in the form of an additional one-half of one percent tax to be imposed on all real property and improvements in all Philippine municipalities, including the cities of Manila and Baguio[94] or the fifty-million-peso plan that Quezon referred to above.[95] Therefore, Benton, in the same communication to Quezon, suggested an alternative measure which would provide the amount of three million pesos annually for a period of two years[96] and the creation of an ad hoc committee, as mentioned previously, which would devise a plan for the permanent support of the University.

Benton hoped this plan would be ready for the consideration and approval of the Philippine National Assembly in 1923 or in 1924 so it could take effect on January 1, 1925. The substitute measure proposed by Benton to Quezon would then enable the University to meet its increasing and anticipated needs over the next two years, during which time the University would develop "a program for permanency that will relieve us from uncertainty of annual appropriations which you and all other friends of the University think necessary."[97]

Osmeña's ₱50-million Plan

As for the nine-year development program of the University which required the appropriation of ₱50 million, the same was really the counter offer made by Sergio Osmeña, Speaker of the Lower House, in lieu of the mill-tax levy proposal of the University. Osmeña personally discussed his suggestion with Benton and Deans Francisco Benitez and Maximo M. Kalaw. This sum was to be incorporated in a bill to be introduced by Osmeña to the National Assembly.[98] The University proved amenable to the counter proposal of the Speaker of the House.

Under the ₱50-million development scheme envisioned by Benton within the context of the Osmeña suggestion, the University would embark on a "construction binge" to have separate physical plants for the College of Education, the College of Liberal Arts, the College of Law, the Conservatory of Music, and the School of Fine Arts. The balance of the money would be used for Benton's "faculty recognition" program by sending faculty members abroad for doctoral work, by increasing their salaries, and by recruiting additional faculty to handle the increasing student population.[99]

The ₱50 million became a "mere" ₱18 million though, by the time Osmeña's suggestion – as embodied in a bill presented to the Fifth Philippine Legislature upon recommendation of the deans and the President of the University – went through the legislative mill.[100] In effect, the mill-tax levy proposal, while passing the Board of Regents, did not make it in the Legislature. When the mill-tax levy proposal reached the colonial lawmaking body, it was substituted by the Lower House with a bill containing the Osmeña suggestion of a nine-year University development program requiring the appropriation of ₱50 million[101] for the construction of academic buildings, for the improvement of classrooms and research facilities, and for the "faculty recognition" program of Benton.

What the Legislature approved therefore in February 1922 was a substitute bill appropriating ₱18 million for the support of the University over a period of nine years. While the amount appropriated by the Legislature – the Senate and the Lower House – was very much less than the ₱50 million contemplated originally, the Board of Regents, the President, and the deans of the different colleges were still elated and gratified at the outcome of their legislative battle. Under this measure, the ₱18 million would be used within nine years "for improvements in the various colleges, the extension of laboratory and research work, the expansion of buildings and other improvements which may be necessary as the institution grows."[102]

Governor General's Veto

However, when the said bill reached the hands of the Governor General after its approval by both chambers of the Philippine National Assembly in February 1922, it met a stonewall in the form of a veto. Gov. Gen. Leonard Wood vetoed the ₱18-million bill, except one section containing the provision for an additional amount of ₱816,000 for the University.

The veto came perhaps because what the Legislature approved was not the mill-tax levy proposal and the allocation of public lands proposal for which Wood had expressed support in a letter he sent to Quezon on February 8, 1922. As finally passed by the Legislature, the bill Wood vetoed was an *appropriation bill,* and this Wood could not approve because of the prevailing economic difficulties of the colonial government.

The veto message of Wood read in part as follows:

> I appreciate and am fully in sympathy with importance of the extension of university work in the Philippine Islands and will be glad to cooperate to the fullest extent consistent with the public interests in the worthy efforts of the president of the university to extend university education and place it on a sound basis, but I do not feel that I can properly approve all the items of this appropriation bill, as the present financial condition of the government and the outlook for the immediate future do not warrant the assumption of an obligation of this magnitude, imposing, as it does, upon the government heavy outlays for nine years.
>
> I am informed by the Attorney-General, and his opinion is concurred in by the Secretary of Justice, that this Bill is, according to the meaning of the organic act known as the Jones Bill (Act of Congress approved August 20, 1916) an appropriation bill and that the Governor-General under provisions of said law may disapprove any item or items of appropriation in the said bill (H.B. No. 1334) except the appropriation of the sum ₱816,000 available for expenditure January 1, 1923. This item alone I approve. All other items involving appropriation in this bill are disapproved.[103]

Despite Wood's disapproval of the ₱18-million appropriation measure, the Governor General stated that he would be willing to approve any suitable bill containing concrete proposals for *raising* the increased outlays needed for University support. It was Wood's idea that there should be a definite source of income so the University would not just be dependent on periodic legislative appropriations.

Special Board Constituted

Toward this end, Wood in 1922 recommended in his message to the Sixth Philippine Legislature the mill-tax levy for permanent University support. This recommendation was actually the product of the deliberations made by a special Board which the Governor General himself created on April 4, 1922. This Board was empowered to devise a policy for permanent and dependable University support, and it was composed of the Secretary of Public Instruction, the President of the University, the Director of Education, Regent Rafael Palma, Regent Jose Escaler, Dean Fernando Calderon, and Dean Francisco Benitez.[104]

This Board reported to the Governor General on August 18, 1922, two recommendations: that there should be a mill-tax levy of three-tenths of one per cent annually on the taxable realty of the Philippines for the permanent support of the University, and there should be an allocation of not less than 400,000 but not more than 500,000 hectares of public lands distributed throughout the country for the establishment of the permanent endowment of the University. The second recommendation was tied to the encouragement of agricultural vocation in cooperation with the College of Agriculture of the University.[105]

The Governor General accepted the Board's recommendations in toto and recommended the approval of the report without change in his message to the Sixth Philippine Legislature. As he promised, the recommendations were embodied in bills for the mill-tax levy and for the allocation of public lands for the permanent support of the University. These bills were transmitted by the Office of the Governor General to the Philippine National Assembly on December 3, 1922. The bills were drafted by another special body created by the Governor General, a committee chaired by the Vice Governor General, with Benton, Director of Education Luther B. Bewley, Regent Rafael Palma, Regent Jose Escaler, Dean Fernando Calderon, and Dean Francisco Benitez, as members.[106]

Funding Bills Lost in Political Maze

In the end, the abovementioned bills got nowhere in the Philippine colonial legislature. Thus the Benton program of firming up the foundations of the University as a precondition to the attainment of greatness in stature as an educational institution was caught in the middle of two political forces: a Republican-controlled colonial regime that apparently was not wholehearted in committing public funds to the University on a long-term and not on a piecemeal basis, and a Filipino-dominated colonial assembly led by Quezon and Osmeña.

Benton's being an American citizen probably led to the frustration of many of his own programs for the development of the University into a greater institution. There is no denying the fact that the man meant well when he embarked on his bold and ambitious course to "reestablish" the University of the Philippines. However, with the pursuit of Filipinization in the twenties, the presence of an American citizen at the helm of what Benton himself described as the national university of the Filipino people must have rubbed some Filipino leaders the wrong way. Benton thus found himself in the crossfire of Filipinism and anti-Filipinism controversies.[107]

While there may have been some Filipinos in particular who were genuinely nationalistic, and who had the true national aspirations of the Filipino people at heart, the same could not be said of the Filipino leaders who stood out at that time. Revisionist historiography on the Philippines within the past decade or so has turned up evidence showing that Quezon and Osmeña had feet of clay.[108] They compromised legitimate Filipino aspirations and needs for their consuming personal ambitions to remain politically prominent in native society. Quezon was specifically consumed by his overwhelming desire to become the first Filipino Governor General of the Philippines. Therefore, he and the other members of the Filipino elite class could not be true supporters and sympathizers of the University's cause, because the University's cause was to prepare its students for responsible and democratic citizenship.

Involvement of Oligarchs

The University was viewed to be the handmaiden for allowing democratic institutions and practices to take deep roots in the Philippines. It would exercise a strong influence in bringing about a shift in the balance of power from oligarchical rule to representative government and popular sovereignty. Such a shift in the balance of power was farthest from the minds of members of the elite class like Quezon and Osmeña, who had been co-opted into the American colonial order[109] and who favored the retention of the status quo in so far as the Filipino social structure was concerned.

It would appear then that the two most powerful Filipinos at that time did not care, together with the rest of those belonging to the landed gentry situated with them in the colonial legislative body, to bring about the promotion of the educational welfare of the Filipino people. This view is in fact reinforced by the finding of a scholar, Frank Jenista, Jr., who made a study of the legislative record of the Philippine National Assembly during the period 1907 to 1913. In this study, Jenista found out that the Assembly had a near-zero record as far as social welfare legislation was concerned. However, when it came to promoting the interests and welfare of its wealthy members, the Assembly was quick to move, as when it passed a resolution soon after it was convened in 1907 increasing the allowances and remuneration of its members.[110] Quezon and Osmeña evidently maneuvered to substitute the mill-tax levy proposal and the allocation of public lands proposal of the University with their own proposal for a ₱50-million appropriation, knowing fully well that this would be vetoed by the Governor General because the bill containing it would be classified as an appropriation bill, and because the colonial government simply did not have the money to make available the huge outlays for the University. The University's request for a permanent income was therefore tossed back and forth between the executive branch and the legislative branch, preventing the University from carrying out its far-reaching development program for lack of adequate funding, and clearly demonstrating how vulnerable the University was to political influences and manipulations despite its autonomous character.

Year in and year out, then during Benton's time, the finances of the University remained at essentially the same level, and always subject to legislative appropriation annually. Benton never succeeded in getting the funds he wanted, the promises of support from the colonial authorities notwithstanding. Despite the severe budgetary constraints within which he operated, one finds it difficult to agree with the evaluation that the University did not progress under Benton. In fact, in spite of everything, Benton did accomplish a number of major changes designed to reorganize the University.

University Reorganization

Quite important institutional developments occurred within the three years that Benton occupied the presidential seat. These developments occurred within the framework of the reorganization of the University undertaken by him.

In line with Benton's stipulation, prior to his formal election on March 7 as the president of the University, that he be given a one-year period to familiarize himself with conditions in the University, the President's Intramural Committee on University Survey was constituted on May 12, 1921, just a little over a month after he assumed office. This committee was composed of Jorge C. Bocobo as Chairman, and Lawrence E. Gurney, Conrado Benitez, H. Windsor Wade and Inocencio Elayda, as members, all of whom were teachers in the University. It was the responsibility of this committee to undertake a full survey of every facet of the University's operations, with particular emphasis on what the University had done, what it may do, and what it should do. This committee reported to the President on December 21, 1921.[111]

Basically, the committee recommended the continued occupation by the University of its location in Manila, the granting of uniform pay to its personnel, the designation of a business manager to take care of the University's business affairs, the reorganization of the faculty, the establishment of a permanent endowment for the University's support via a mill-tax levy, the institution of a program of academic exchange and cooperation with universities in the United States, and the adoption of a blueprint for physical expansion, which would include the construction of dormitories for students.[112] A review committee of the University Council apparently did essentially the same thing as the said committee and this completed its work on December 4, 1922.[113]

Several days prior to the creation of the President's Intramural Committee on University Survey, on April 23, 1921, Benton recommended and the Board of Regents approved, the formation of a Committee on Reorganization. The task of the committee was to consider and report on plans for the betterment of the University. Regent Rafael Palma headed this committee, with fellow Regents Escaler, Bewley and Alejandro de Guzman as members, along with Benton.[114] This committee functioned as a permanent committee to which matters involving specifically the reorganization of the University were referred for further study. Based on its careful study of matters referred to it, the committee would then make appropriate recommendations to the Board for its consideration and action.

Beneficial Changes Instituted

Based on the recommendations made by this Reorganization Committee, a number of changes and policies were instituted and adopted by the University, with the proper approval of the Board of Regents. It might be pertinent to point out at this time that this committee played an active role in the proposed revision of the Charter law of the University so as to secure a permanent support for the institution. For example, this committee drafted and presented to the Philippine Legislature a proposed revision of the Charter law of the University.[115]

One important change which the University adopted as a result of the recommendations of the Reorganization Committee benefited the academic personnel. Prior to this time, members of the faculty of the University were treated like ordinary bureaucratic personnel. They were required to stay in their respective offices during office hours. However, with the modification of the rules, as recommended by the Reorganization Committee, the situation became very flexible for them, as they were no longer under obligation to spend their hours in their respective departmental offices. They were simply held accountable for results, and the University no longer minded where and how they spent their hours – whether in the libraries, in the laboratories, in their homes, or in other places – provided they performed and delivered results. The Board received and approved this recommendation on February 15, 1922.[116]

Another important recommendation acted upon favorably by the Board of Regents during that same meeting was the expansion of library activities through the establishment of an autonomous Department of Library Science. Such a unit was made independent of any particular college. It was related to the entire University, and it stood on equal terms with the other departments of the University.[117]

Regents Receptive to Reforms

The February 15, 1922 meeting of the Board of Regents may be regarded as a landmark in the history of the University, for on this day, the University experienced several other changes designed to transform itself into a greater and more efficient educational institution. Jamias erred in saying the recommendations were submitted to the Board on this date for consideration at its March meeting.[118] Actually, the Board received and acted on the said recommendations on this same day.

The University acquired centralized control over all publications within itself. Under this new arrangement, all allotments for printing and binding were subjected to centralized control. Moreover, all publications were integrated into a single monthly publication. The only paper that received exemption from integration into the planned University monthly was the student organ.[119]

With regard to the proposed establishment of exchange professorships with educational institutions in the United States, the Board of Regents favorably acted on the matter. This was in lieu of the system of sabbatical leave, which the University was still unable to finance at that time. Under the exchange professorship program, the salaries of University professors going abroad would be paid by the universities to which they would be attached, while those coming from American universities would have their salaries paid by their home institutions, with the University paying only the difference in salary schedules and providing compensation "for prolonged absence from home."[120] The faculty members who were slated to go abroad under this newly established system of exchange professorships included Maximo M. Kalaw, Artemas L. Day, Austin Craig, H. Otley Beyer and Randall A. Rowley. Those going to the United States would have the opportunity to work on their respective doctoral programs.[121]

In addition to the above changes, there were others that the Board of Regents approved on February 15, 1922. It was during this time that the Junior College of Liberal Arts in Cebu was given a new name. By action of the Board, its name was changed to the Junior College at Cebu, with Jose J. Mirasol, a Ph.D. from the University of Illinois, designated by the Board as its dean.[122] The Board likewise approved Benton's request for leave of absence at stated times to enable him to participate in educational conferences as well as to scout around for prospective members of the instructional staff of the University. The Reorganization Committee recommended the approval of this request, but Benton himself withdrew it because of the fact that he could actually go on leave of absence anytime a need would arise.[123]

Innovative Developments

One change which Jamias failed to discuss clearly and adequately was the separation of the Department of Mathematics from Physics, although he did mention the relief of Lawrence E. Gurney as acting head of the Department of Mathematics and his replacement by Vidal A. Tan in that post. Gurney remained head of the Department of Physics. The change in personnel was designed for greater faculty efficiency.[124] The Board action of separating Mathematics from Physics was no doubt due to the growth of mathematics as a discipline, thus meriting an independent structural status from the discipline of Physics.[125] The separation of the two disciplines and departments was in accordance with a recommendation made by the Reorganization Committee.

The Board also favorably acted on the recommended equalization of departmental and professorial service in order to guarantee "a just and equitable division of individual loads."[126] There was indeed a felt need for an equitable arrangement with regard to teaching loads. In the past, some faculty members carried a greater load than the others, to the detriment of those who were heavily loaded. The result of the previous system was to demoralize the faculty members affected and to reduce their scholarly and teaching effectiveness. Hence, the equalization scheme, which was to be worked out by the deans and the professors, was meant to correct an imbalance in the division of teaching duties.

In Benton's inaugural address, one of the objectives he discussed was the institution of a combined six-year course covering both vocational and professional training. The Reorganization Committee took up this matter during its deliberations and recommended its approval by the Board of Regents. Predictably, the Board acted favorably on the matter, adding the condition though that "no student shall be granted more than one degree by the same college during one academic year."[127]

Surprisingly, Jamias treated this important curricular change lightly in his chapter entitled, "Reorganization for a Greater University." Benton in fact considered his combined six-year course proposal as "revolutionary," meant to upgrade the standards of the University as well as to ensure that the University would produce graduates with disciplined minds and with practical abilities.[128] One can say therefore that the approval of this proposal by the Board of Regents was a real accomplishment of Benton toward the realization of his objectives for the University.

The Agricultural Station in Los Baños, overlooked by Jamias in his historical account, was established at this time. Suitable land had been bought by the University for this Station with the funds used for the purchase appropriated by the Philippine National Assembly. The University established this facility near the College of Agriculture and it was expected to provide complementary services to the said college.[129]

Faculty Fellowships

As an incentive to the members of the faculty who had given outstanding performances in their respective areas of concentration and expertise, the Board of Regents (likewise upon recommendation by the Reorganization Committee) established Preferential Faculty Fellowships. Again, one can relate this measure to passages contained in the inaugural address of Benton. In that address, he favored the reduction of the size of the faculty in order to maximize efficiency and to safeguard the quality of instruction in the University.

For example, in one part of his inaugural address, Benton says, "It is not so important that we have *large* Faculties as it is that we have the *best* Faculties of properly trained men and women that can be assembled from the Philippines, America, Europe and the ends of the earth."[130] Therefore, to ensure that the members of the faculty who had stood out in their fields of specialization were amply recognized for their academic labors and achievements, the Preferential Faculty Fellowships program came into being. The Board also approved the granting of transportation privileges to deans on the merits of each case.

Programs and Proposals Rejected

Prior to Benton's time, a Department of Journalism existed in the University. However the Board of Regents, upon recommendation of the Reorganization Committee, abolished the same department as a matter of economy. In the words of Benton, the abolition of the Department of Journalism effected "a saving of approximately ₱10,000 and now utilized in other departments where added funds were sorely needed."[131] One can only speculate, in the absence of hard evidence, as to the real reason for the abolition of the Department of Journalism. It may be that the course program offered by the department did not attract a sufficient number of students to warrant its continued existence. Moreover, it may be that there were not enough instructors competent to handle the courses in journalism. Whatever the case may be, Benton must have looked at the department as a "white elephant" and was strongly persuaded that its abolition was for the best financial interest of the University.

A number of recommendations of Benton presented to the Board of Regents were not acted upon or were referred back to him for appropriate action or further study. These matters equally impinged on the administrative structure and on the capacity of the University to efficiently manage its operations. One of these had to do with the appointment of a Business Director. Benton felt that such a position was needed. The appointee to the proposed position would have the task of collecting and disbursing all funds of the University. He would also be responsible for purchasing and distributing supplies, for taking care of and maintaining every property of the University, for the hiring and firing of laborers, and for overall overseeing of the business affairs of the University.[132]

The Board of Regents, however, on recommendation of the Reorganization Committee, deferred action on the matter. Jamias states in his work that the Business Director was to be appointed effective July 1, 1922,[133] implying that this particular recommendation was eventually approved after its deferment by the Board on February 15, 1922. However, in the "Outline of Institutional Policies and Accomplishments During the Present Administration from the Fourth of April 1921," there is no reference whatsoever to its ever having been acted upon by the Board of Regents. This "Outline" covers virtually the entire period of Benton's presidency, at least until the early weeks or months of 1923. At any rate, that Benton ever made the recommendation is consistent with his concern for efficiency in the manner the University discharged its functions and its duties.

Another matter deferred by the Board had something to do with requisitions for furniture and supplies. Benton proposed that a general fund be established for this purpose, instead of the usual practice of appropriating specific amounts to each college in the University. This particular proposal of Benton was consistent with his recommendation for the centralization of control over publications in the University. The general fund would have been under the control of the administration. However, upon recommendation of the Reorganization Committee, the Board postponed consideration of this matter.[134] The evidence shows that it was never taken up again under Benton.

Related to the above recommendation was Benton's proposal for the establishment of a central storehouse in the University. The existing college storehouses would then be dispensed with, as the central storehouse would serve as a substitute for all of them. The idea of having a central storehouse, to replace the college storehouses, was to avoid duplication in the requisition of supplies needed by the University and its various components. Such a central storehouse would effect economy in the operations of the University, and would contribute to greater institutional efficiency.[135]

The Board of Regents, though, postponed action on the matter, again on recommendation of the Reorganization Committee, for the simple reason that the University did not have ample funds to build an edifice that could serve as central storehouse.[136] Likewise, the Board deferred action on the proposed construction of a University Union or Commons which would provide inexpensive but good food to the constituents of the University, particularly the students.

Compact Staffing Pattern

Benton's concern for efficiency and the streamlining of the performance of the institution he headed likewise led him to recommend the cutting down to size of what he perceived to be an over-staffed University bureaucracy. He wanted to reduce the number of clerical and administrative personnel. From his viewpoint, it was better to have a small but efficient and properly compensated clerical staff than to have an oversized but inefficient and poorly paid clerical and administrative complement. This recommendation is in fact something that was congruent with some of the ideas he ventilated in his inaugural address, such as the curtailment of student enrolment through a selective process, the elimination of unnecessary courses, the reduction of the teaching staff, and the combination of curricular offerings.[137]

The Board of Regents, instead of approving or disapproving Benton's proposal on the reduction of the clerical and administrative personnel, merely referred the matter back to him for any readjustment deemed fit and necessary by the University, under his presidential supervision and control.[138] In effect, the Board told Benton that as the person tasked with the responsibility of exercising overall direction of the business affairs of the University, he could do anything with the bureaucracy to enable it to keep up with the accepted norms of efficient institutional performance.

New Buildings Rise

Benton, on his own, presented certain matters to the Board of Regents even before the constitution of the Reorganization Committee. These recommendations were made within the first month of his assumption of the presidency of the University. In fact, he made the recommendations during his very first meeting with the Board in his official capacity as the head of the institution. One such recommendation made on April 23, 1921 pertained to the completion of buildings within the original campus in Manila which were then under construction. Perhaps because he was still having his "honeymoon" with the Board, the latter obliged him by approving the transfer of funds for unfinished construction projects in the University. Because of this Board action, Rizal Hall was completed in time for the opening of the second semester of academic year 1921-1922. Other buildings, started before Benton assumed the presidency, were finished within his term.[139] With regard to Benton's recommendation that temporary buildings be erected on permanent foundations, the Board decided to defer action on the matter. For the record though, some members of the Board voiced opposition to the erection of non-permanent structures.[140]

A Few Setbacks

Also during the first meeting of Benton with the Board of Regents on April 23, 1921, the President proposed the upgrading of University standards and the maintenance thereof by imposing on the instructional staff of the

University the requirement that they give their whole service only to the institution and to none other.[141] This recommendation was in keeping with his own idea that whoever joins the University should unselfishly and unstintedly spend all his time for its benefit and advancement. Total devotion and dedication by the instructors and professors would then improve and sustain the high quality of instruction offered by the University.

However, because of financial constraints, and pending the establishment of a permanent and stable source of income for the University, the Board postponed action on this particular proposal. The Board must have felt that to ensure the total devotion and dedication of the teaching faculty, its members should be given incentive grants so as to motivate them into performing up to par, and even excelling in their respective fields for that matter. Thus, the Board waited until better financial conditions were attained by the University.

The same financial constraints were cited by the Board of Regents in failing to take favorable action on Benton's recommendation for a University Press.[142] Benton believed that such a facility was needed in order to take care of all the printing requirements of the University, such as the printing of forms for official records and transactions, the publication of the student organ as well as the planned University monthly, and the scholarly journals essential to academic life.

During the April 23, 1921 meeting of the Board of Regents, Maximo M. Kalaw received confirmation of his appointment as Dean of the College of Liberal Arts.[143]

Aid from Rockefeller Foundation

In the early months of his administration, Benton moved and acted toward establishing cordial and cooperative relationships with the Rockefeller Foundation, an American philanthropic agency founded by the oil magnate of the late 19th century, John D. Rockefeller. Senate President Manuel L. Quezon apparently played an active role in the efforts to enlist the support and assistance of said foundation in the realization of the development program of the University, specially in gearing itself for greater efficiency. On August 30, 1921, for example, Quezon while in New York, dispatched a cable to Manila instructing Benton to ask Dr. Victor Heiser for his help in linking up the University with the Rockefeller Foundation, particularly in establishing a School of Hygiene in the University. Subsequently, on September 1, 1921, Benton wrote a letter to Dr. Heiser in compliance with Quezon's instruction. This was followed by a series of meetings between Benton and Heiser, together with a certain Dr. Welch of the Rockefeller Foundation, in October 1921. No less than the Governor General of the Philippines, Leonard Wood, endorsed the efforts to link up with the

Foundation; Wood wrote letters soliciting the cooperation of the funding agency.

On October 22, 1921, Wood, Quezon, Osmeña, Benton, the director of the Bureau of Health, the director of the Bureau of Science, and the dean of the College of Medicine of the University, signed a joint application for the cooperation of the Rockefeller Foundation in the improvement of the delivery of public health services and of medical education in the country. To this joint application by some of the most influential people in Philippine colonial society at that time, the Rockefeller Foundation responded favorably by underwriting the appointment of Dr. W.S. Carter, a prominent American physician and a well-known figure in medical education in the United States, as associate dean of the College of Medicine and Surgery of the University. In addition, the Foundation provided financial support to make it possible for Miss Alice Fitzgerald, a New Yorker, to come to the Philippines and assume direction and responsibility over the training of Filipino nurses and to prepare Filipino women to serve as public health officers.

Moreover, J. M. Tiedemann, an engineer and a statistician of the Rockefeller Foundation, arrived in the Philippines to undertake a study and to experiment on methods of eradicating malaria in the province of Laguna. For its part, the University provided free housing to Tiedemann within the College of Agriculture campus in Los Baños.

Public Health and Farm Services

In August 1922, the University, the Bureau of Health, and the Rockefeller Foundation established a training school for nurses. This may well have been the precursor of the present College of Nursing of the University. Meanwhile, the Rockefeller Foundation established and supported four fellowships for Filipino scholars to go to the United States for further studies in medicine, nursing, and public health. The recipients were Wilfrido de Leon, assistant professor of Pathology and Bacteriology; Emilio Bulatao, assistant professor of Physiology; Paciencia Cornista, graduate nurse; and Socorro Salamanca from the Public Welfare Board. To coordinate and supervise all the joint efforts toward the betterment of the public health service and medical education in the insular colony, the Rockefeller Foundation made a grant which led to the appointment of Dr. C. N. Leach as general supervisor.[144]

In other spheres of University life, Benton proposed the creation of the Agricultural Extension Service in Los Baños. This proposal received the support and endorsement of the dean of the College of Agriculture. Realizing its worthiness, the Board of Regents approved the proposal on October 8, 1921. Following a long search, Benton recommended, and the Board approved on June 2, 1922, the designation of Inocencio Elayda, a professor in the College of Agriculture, as director of the Agricultural Extension Service. Elayda inaugurated the extension service of the University on November 30, 1922 with the organization of the Farmers' Association of Laguna Province.[145]

The establishment of the Agricultural Extension Service was a concrete achievement of Benton, and it reflected his desire to make the University relevant to the needs of the Filipino people. Cognizant of the importance of agriculture as the backbone of the Philippine economy, Benton wanted to draw from the expertise of the College of Agriculture in order to render assistance to Filipino farmers not only in Laguna, where the College of Agriculture was situated, but across the archipelago.

Founding of Cadet Corps

Benton also achieved something in the field of military training for Filipino citizens. He organized the University Cadet Corps on June 1, 1922. This was the origin of the Reserve Officers Training Corps (ROTC) now known as the Department of Citizens Military Training.

Actually, Benton first proposed to the Board of Regents the establishment of a systematic military training program in the University on November 4, 1921, the day the Board granted its approval to the proposal. On November 8, 1921 Benton requested the Governor General, Leonard Wood, to ask the War Department of the United States to detail at the University an officer of the United States Army who would serve as Commandant of the University Cadet Corps to be organized, and to serve as a professor of military science and tactics. Wood complied with the request by dispatching a cable on November 9 to the Secretary of War in Washington, D.C. The War Department responded six weeks later by cabling its appointment of Capt. Chester A. Davis as commandant and as professor of military science and tactics.

When the University Cadet Corps was formally set up on July 1, 1922, Davis assumed his post, and he was assisted by Captain Emmanuel Baja of the Philippine Constabulary, two lieutenants in the United States Army, and a number of non-commissioned officers from the United States Army. The University Cadet Corps was composed of a thousand students, enjoying regimental strength and status. This University regiment of cadets received 1,000 Springfield rifles from the United States Army. The rifles were valued at ₱70,000 with the University putting up a bond on them. Subsequently, the University constructed a modern cadet armory inside the campus costing ₱10,000.[146]

The bright side of this episode under Benton was that many of the members of the University Cadet Corps, particularly during the Second World War, fought and died valiantly against the enemy in defending the Philippines from a foreign aggressor. They rendered a real service to the Filipino people, making the supreme sacrifice in order to see their country freed from the hegemonial ambitions of an expansionistic Asian nation. The gloomy side was that the University Cadet Corps became identified with reactionary military elements especially after the Second World War and in more recent times would be blamed for the weakening of democratic institutions and practices in the Philippines.

Student Dormitories Needed

Two other actions of Benton deserve mention in this chapter. One had something to do with a recommendation made by him to the Board of Regents on April 14, 1922. This was on the creation of a committee, composed of faculty members, which would study the problem of student housing and subsistence in the University. Mandated to come out with its findings and a report by February 1, 1923, its recommendations would serve as the basis for taking whatever action was necessary on the question of constructing a University Union or Commons and a complex of dormitories and dining halls inside the campus, so that the University would acquire the atmosphere of a residential institution with adequate facilities for a wholesome life away from home for the students. This committee was composed of Regino R. Ylanan as chairman, and with Ramona Tirona and Chester A. Davis as members.[147]

In general, the Committee found living conditions for students wretched and deplorable, and called attention to the "urgent necessity" to build adequate housing and dining quarters within the campus. Unfortunately, the lack of funds hampered the realization of Benton's dream to establish a "dormitory atmosphere" in the University. According to Jamias, the failure to attain this objective proved to be "one of the deepest-cutting disappointments that was inflicted upon Dr. Benton."[148] This may have been so, but Benton should at least be credited for bringing into the University the idea of a residential campus. Perhaps his administration was not the time for the concrete realization of this goal. Eventually, when the University would transfer to its present location in Quezon City, Benton's hopes would see the light of day. The same was true with the establishment of dormitories and dining facilities in the branch of the University in Los Baños.

Faculty Benefits

For all the shortness of Benton's term as President of the University, he had contributed significantly to the advancement of the welfare of the faculty. As noted earlier, he was successful in having Civil Service rules modified to allow faculty members to be held accountable for results rather than for them to spend all their waking hours in the University even when not inside the classroom. Moreover, he had succeeded in having the Board of Regents approve the establishment of Preferential Faculty Fellowships in recognition of the scholarly ability of outstanding members of the teaching staff of the University.

Benton likewise instituted, for the first time in the history of the University, the system of sabbatical leave. He presented this recommendation to the Board of Regents on October 18, 1922, more than a year after he assumed the presidency of the University in early April 1921. His proposal was for the granting of a leave of absence with pay to faculty members with professorial rank provided they had rendered seven years of uninterrupted service to the University. The leave may be used either for advanced study in the United States, or to reinvigorate one's self while engaged in undisturbed research and writing. The sabbatical leave may be stretched to two years, in which case the faculty member concerned would receive half pay for the whole period, rather than the full pay granted for a one-year sabbatical leave.

Sabbatical Leave Instituted

The Board of Regents approved Benton's recommendation, albeit with the proviso that the body would have the right to look into the merits of each application for sabbatical leave, and to decide whether or not the funds of the University could sustain each application.[149]

Benton could therefore be credited with the institutionalization of sabbatical leave in the University. Every faculty member of professorial rank should feel grateful to him for this benefit. Indeed, the sabbatical leave is something that every faculty member looks forward to as a kind of reward – a well-deserved one at that – after years of continuous service to the University. The sabbatical leave in fact is no longer regarded by the faculty as a privilege to be dispensed by the University as it wishes to a chosen few. It is claimed by every faculty member as a right to be enjoyed to avoid being "burned out" or going stale, after having served continuously for seven years in a professorial rank.

COPING WITH PECULIAR PROBLEMS HARASSING THE PRESIDENCY

EVERY president of any educational institution, no matter how well-intentioned, sooner or later finds himself being criticized by diverse groups within his constituency. The situation of an administrator is that of being caught between two extremes. He may be damned if he does, damned if he does not. It would in fact be impossible for him to please everybody. A decision he makes may be pleasing to an individual or to a group, yet that same decision becomes the source of displeasure or discomfiture for another individual or group not so favored. At any rate, while every now and then he would be praised, he would also be indicted at times. This was the state into which Benton got himself when he became the president of the University. A particularly interesting and vexing case he faced during his term was that involving Austin Craig, the head of the Department of History of the University.

Craig in the Role of Nemesis

Even prior to Benton's formal election to the presidency of the University by the Board of Regents on March 7, 1921, Craig waged an almost single-handed campaign to dissuade the Board from electing Benton. In particular, Craig wrote a strong letter in the March 5, 1921 edition of the *Philippines Herald* questioning the personal and professional credentials of the would-be President. Craig also denounced the financial terms offered by the University to lure Benton into accepting the position proffered to him. Furthermore, Craig belittled the experience of Benton as president of a number of American universities prior to his coming to the Philippines, saying that the institutions Benton served were "fourth-rate" or Podunk-type colleges.

Craig severely criticized the Board of Regents for choosing Benton, saying in effect that the Board committed a grievous error in electing the latter, an ordained Methodist minister, to head an educational institution located in a country which is predominantly Roman Catholic in religious upbringing and orientation. This published letter of Craig would be used, among others, against its author more than a year later when the case involving him would preoccupy the attention of everybody for several weeks.

The Craig case, as it came to be known, would have repercussions far beyond the dismissal of a regular faculty member of the University. An offshoot of the case would be the investigation of an incumbent president by the Board of Visitors of the University. Such an investigation was unprecedented. Nothing quite like it happened before Benton's presidency, during the terms of the first two duly elected University presidents, namely Murray Bartlett and Ignacio Villamor. The investigation of Benton by a body higher than the Board of Regents was not only unprecedented but unparalleled. Nothing quite like it could be found in the history of the University since then. True, charges were made against a president of the University sometime after the Second World War by an interested person. However, no investigation was ever conducted, either by the Board of Regents or by the Board of Visitors.

It is also true that the Board of Regents conducted an investigation during the incumbency of another University president. However, the object of the investigation was not the president personally, but the events within the campus which were beyond the control of anyone at any rate, because they were related to the national issues gripping the country at the time. Therefore, the investigation of Benton was indeed unique and extraordinary in the annals of the institution.

Tracing the Course of Discontent

Jamias in his history of the University gives February 15, 1922 as the beginning of the Craig case. This was the day Benton unveiled his plan for the reorganization of the University. The plan involved granting sabbatical leaves to four faculty members of the University, including Austin Craig, to give them the opportunity to pursue their doctorates in American universities.[150] Jamias likewise cites the efforts of Benton to have the administration acquire centralized control over all publications in the University as a contributory factor to the emergence of the Craig case.[151]

Actually, the Craig case appeared to antedate Benton, or at least the events which led to the dismissal of Craig occurred even before Benton assumed the presidency. It would seem that Craig had acquired a reputation for being a "character" of sorts. Luther B. Bewley, director of the Bureau of Education, described him to Benton as a "crabid [sic] old bachelor,"[152] who became the "self-appointed censor of the educational and political leaders both American and Filipino" in the colony.[153] As the self-appointed "censor," Craig attained "notoriety" for his outspoken and critical attitude toward the American colonizers in particular. When Benton arrived in Manila, Craig was already unpopular among the members of the American community and among the "best thinking" Filipinos.[154]

Immediately upon Benton's installation in office in April 1921, and this is where this account differs significantly from that of Jamias, the former Secretary of Instruction and then Acting Governor General Charles E. Yeater filed formal charges against Craig before the Board of Regents. Yeater charged Craig with (a) grave dereliction of duty and irresponsibility, and (b) gross misconduct inimical to the common good of the public. The issue served as a fiery welcome and a challenge to the new president. He came upon a situation when the anti-Craig sentiments among the top officialdom in the colony happened to be reaching the point of intolerance just at the start of Benton's administration. Therefore, contrary to the account of Jamias, Benton did not trigger nor cause the affair to come about. Benton merely inherited the "Craig Problem."[155]

At any rate, when Yeater filed his formal charges against Craig, Benton strongly opposed giving due course to the same "on the ground that they belonged to a previous administration."[156] Other members of the Board of Regents apparently wanted to have the charges heard. However, Benton appealed to these Board members until he succeeded in having the Yeater charges shelved. This success could have been partly due to the Board's own sense of fairness and decency.

A Lull That Led to Reassessment

Following the "tabling" of the Yeater charges, the Craig controversy simmered down for the rest of 1921 and into the early months of 1922. For his part, during his first year in office, Benton tried to display statesmanship by trying to get along with Craig, deliberately avoiding putting himself in a situation of discord with the latter.

Meanwhile, Benton, in accordance with his own vision and hope to transform the University into a great institution of higher learning, and in pursuance of his objective to upgrade University instructional standards, proceeded to take a closer look at the academic standing and performance of the faculty of the University.

He discovered that some of the professors were inadequately trained and did not have the proper academic background to qualify them for inclusion in the faculty roster, despite the fact that many of them had taught in the University since its inception. In Benton's own words, these professors "could hardly hold high school positions at home (i.e., in the United States)."[157] One of these untrained and unqualified professors happened to be Austin Craig, who in fact rose from the ranks to become the head of the University's Department of History by the time Benton assumed the presidency. The others were Randall A. Rowley, head of the Department of Geology, Artemas L. Day of the Department of Zoology, and H. Otley Beyer of the Department of Anthropology and Ethnology.

Benton cited the fact that Harvard University turned down the application of a graduate of the University simply because that graduate studied under Craig, who it turned out earned his bachelor's degree from an obscure American institution called Pacific University in Forest Grove, Oregon. (And yet Craig himself had attacked Benton for having served as president of "little known" American institutions!) To top it all, Craig had not earned a single graduate unit whatsoever. Moreover, according to Benton, other American institutions, notably the University of Illinois, had notified the University categorically that *pensionados* and fellows from the University would not be accepted on the ground that their work had been done in departments headed by faculty members who could not show proof of having undertaken training beyond the baccalaureate level.

Remedy to a Tricky Situation

Concerned that the graduates of the University wishing to go to the United States for further studies were not getting proper recognition and accreditation from American institutions, and wishing to do something about the problem, Benton thought he could take the first step toward improving the situation by recommending to the Board of Regents that the abovementioned professors be given the fullest opportunity to pursue advanced graduate studies in accredited American universities.

Benton gave due credit to the long years of service rendered by these faculty members. His desire was to see them develop professionally in their respective areas of specialization. Hence, he offered to give them sabbatical leaves during which they could undertake doctoral work in the United States. It will be recalled that Benton was then in the process of institutionalizing sabbatical leave. Accordingly, he asked the Board that his recommendation on sabbatical leaves for these professors be approved. The Board gave its support and so, in February 1922, arrangements were made by the University to send Rowley, Day, Craig, and Beyer to the United States for further studies.

Rowley refused to take his sabbatical leave. He declined to go to the United States to pursue a Ph.D. in geology, reasoning out that he did not need the degree and that nobody could teach him anything else since his knowledge of the field was just as much as, if not more than, any Ph.D. in his discipline. Instead, Rowley opted to resign from the University and was subsequently given his retirement allowance.

The three others, meanwhile, indicated acceptance of Benton's policy. Day, Craig, and Beyer manifested in Febraury 1922, as soon as Benton obtained Board approval of his recommendation, that the arrangement would afford them a splendid opportunity to advance their professional careers and keep up with the latest trends in their respective disciplines. Subsequently, Day proceeded to the University of California in Berkeley for his Ph.D. program in zoology. Beyer, who really had made a name for himself at that time as the "Father of Philippine Prehistory," was promised by Harvard University that upon the mere presentation of his dissertation, he would be conferred the Ph.D. degree, and accordingly made plans to leave for that institution.

Craig Hedges and Retracts

As for Craig, when the new academic year started in June 1922, he changed his mind and gave all kinds of excuses for not wanting to leave for the United States. One excuse he gave was that he had to be around to advise three masteral students in history. Another was that he did not wish to be a burden financially to the University. A third reason was that he preferred to study at the University of Tokyo, the only place, according to him, where one wishing to gain expertise in Asian history could go to for competent training. And a fourth reason he offered was that if he did go to the United States, particularly to the University of Illinois, he may be compelled to take a specialization other than Asian history and this change may be detrimental to him as well as to the University. He related this to the possibility of Benton's resigning from the presidency unexpectedly and then his successor reversing the policy pursued by the former. Craig felt that such changes may jeopardize his career.[158]

The Board of Regents was however resolute about sending Craig to the United States, based on the arrangement made as early as February 1922. Craig responded by heaping abusive language on the Board, literally imputing improper motives of coercion to individual members of the body. It was at this unpropitious time that the Governor General of the Philippines, Leonard Wood, endorsed charges against Craig to the Board of Regents for "willful failure to pay just debts."[159] These debts consisted of the following: (a) an indebtedness of ₱882.66 to the Philippine Education Company, Inc.; (b) an indebtedness of ₱2,184.06 to the Whipple S. Hall and Company, Inc.; and (c) an indebtedness of ₱500 to the McCullough Printing Company.[160]

The whole affair reached the point where the Board had no other alternative but to take disciplinary measures. Since Craig clearly showed evidence of non-compliance with a duly approved resolution of the Board of Regents, the latter felt compelled to create a committee to act on the formal charges against the former. This committee investigated the charges against Craig and eventually came up with its findings, as follows:

1. Willful failure to pay just debts involving various amounts to the Philippine Education Company, Inc.; the Whipple S. Hall and Company, Inc.; and the McCullough Printing Company.

2. Attributing improper motives to the Board of Regents and non-compliance with the resolution of the Board sending him to the United States for doctoral work.

3. Unwarranted attack upon a fellow professor in a letter he published in the 17 August 1922 issue of the *Philippines Herald*.

4. Activities discrediting the University and its officers of administration, such as (a) causing friction between the Bureau of Science and the University through various articles he published in the press; (b) gross misconduct inimical to the public welfare, based on the charges preferred by Acting Governor General Yeater on 6 July 1921; (c) attacking unfairly the person of Alejandro Albert, Chairman of the Board of Regents, on 19 May 1920, during a faculty gathering at the Philippine Columbian Association; (d) imputing to the Board of Regents improper motives of coercion in connection with his application for accrued leave of absence on 28 August 1922; (e) attacking the Board of Regents in the 5 March 1921 issue of the *Philippines Herald* for choosing Guy Pot-

ter Benton; and (f) misrepresentation of facts in connection with the election of Dean Fischer for membership in the Board.[161]

Answers to Accusations

The Board gave Craig the chance to defend himself, although on a very short notice, since the charges were formulated on September 4, 1922, communicated to Craig on September 5, and had to be answered noon of September 7, 1922.[162] Craig gave a point by point reply, with exception of the charges on the non-payment of debts, which were explicit in themselves.

On the charge of imputing improper motives to the Board of Regents in connection with his non-compliance to go abroad, Craig argued in terms of "safeguarding his rights" because he did not want to go through the trouble and expense of undergoing another doctoral program when he claimed that he was on the verge of getting his doctorate in Asian history from Tokyo University.[163] As for his alleged attack on a colleague in the faculty, Craig replied that the faculty member in question, Leland H. Tracey of the Department of Sociology, libelled the entire Filipino people by saying that the Filipinos belonged to a puerile culture with the people incapable of attaining progress. Therefore, said Craig, such a slur on an entire race had to be answered only in terms of a strong language.[164]

As for the charge that he brought dishonor to the University by his activities, he clarified that when he used the word "coercion" he meant it in terms of its English meaning of "compulsion" and not in terms of its Philippine-Spanish legal meaning of "coercion" or "force." On his remarks concerning Alejandro M. Albert, he insisted that there was nothing personal in them. (Craig said that Albert was not competent to handle a freshman course in the University.) With regard to his alleged attempts to drive a wedge between the University and the Bureau of Science, he claimed that he was in fact in favor of a merger between the two bodies in order to improve the latter in particular, and finally, in connection with Arthur Fischer's election as a Regent, he remarked that he was simply stating the facts as he knew them.[165]

Dismissal from the Service

How did the Board of Regents dispose of the charges upon receiving Craig's reply? The Board acted by (a) dismissing the charges on Craig's non-payment of debts; (b) sustaining the charge involving Craig's non-compliance with the Board's resolution for him to go to the United States to pursue his doctorate in history; (c) finding out that Craig's article attacking Tracey constituted a "repetition of a mis-statement of fact, and therefore would not be considered as coming within fair comment and criticism;"[166] and (d) sustaining all counts under Charge 4. Accordingly, the Board ordered, during its meeting on September 11, 1922, the separation of Craig from the service of the University effective September 15, 1922. Craig elevated his case to the House of Representatives of the Sixth Philippine Legislature[167] but that body apparently failed to take any action on the matter.

Jamias overlooked the fact that Benton tried very hard to prevent the formal separation of Craig from the service of the University based on the charges preferred by the Board of Regents. Benton actually requested the Board to refer to him the charges against Craig, and for him, as President of the University, to be empowered to take appropriate action on the matter. However, the Board refused to accede to the request. Benton then asked that Craig be placed on a probationary status. Regent Rafael Palma quickly branded Craig's being on probation, if ever it was granted by the Board, as "high comedy," with Palma insisting that so long as Craig was with the University, the institution would never be at peace.[168] With Benton's failure in his bid to intercede, he was carried along by the prevailing sentiment and voted along with the other members of the Board for the dismissal of Craig. There was only one Regent who voted against dismissal and this was the alumni representative, Conrado Benitez. However, he himself considered Craig guilty. His dissenting vote was more against the penalty as too heavy.[169]

Craig's dismissal generated a lot of protest both in the campus and in the colonial press. Within the University in particular, mass actions were staged by the students, specially on September 14, 1922, demanding that the Board reconsider its decision, and demanding that Craig be given back his status and rights as a full professor in the University. Even the alumni of the University got themselves excited one way or another about the Craig case. A few of the alumni asked for the resignation of the appointive members of the Board of Regents, such as Rafael Palma, Jose Escaler, Fernando Calderon, and Benton, as President of the University. In the colonial press, coverage and editorial comment came from such publications as *La Nacion, El Comercio, El Mercantil,* the *Manila Times* and others.[170]

In the face of all this, the Board stayed firm in its decision, with the majority of the constituents of the University expressing their support for and confidence in Benton.

Craig's Shadow Persists

Privately, Benton felt relieved that Craig was no longer around, although he was sure that the latter would "attempt to hinder the progress of the University whenever possible,"[171] regardless of where he was. Benton thought of Craig as a "demagogic American" who did not truly love the Filipinos, but who did not hesitate to exploit the "supersensitiveness" of the people by masquerading as their "true friend" and agitating them against the Americans.[172] He also thought of Craig as a "hypocrite" in professing to be zealously upholding Roman Catholicism in the Philippines when he was in fact a "preacher's kid," his father being an ordained Congregational clergyman and one-time president of Antioch College in Yellow Springs, Ohio. Craig happened to be a high degree Mason, too.[173]

The dismissal of Craig really never receded from the consciousness of the constituents of the University. This means that the episode remained very much in the minds of the students, the faculty members, and the general public. Despite the expressions of confidence by some sectors in the ability and in the good faith of Benton as the chief administrator of the University, the Craig case appeared to have fueled more criticism against Benton and his high post, and provided additional ammunition to the critics of his administration. While Benton could claim in one letter to his bosom friend Hughes that he had the support of all high-minded Filipinos, his detractors never rested, and they must have made him wary and anxious. In fact, as the Craig controversy intensified in August up to September 1922, by Benton's own admission, "numerous intimations of irregularities in reference to contracts and charges of favoritism have become current."[174]

To his credit, it was Benton himself who invited the investigation of his administration by the Board of Visitors of the University. It was his letter to Governor General Wood on November 4, 1922 that set the investigation by the Board of Visitors into motion. In that letter, Benton asked Wood to convene the said body to scrutinize his administration and his way of handling the affairs of the University, as well as to look into "institutional conditions in general."[175] It was the desire of Benton to make a clean breast of everything, and stressed that he had "no desire to conceal the policies of the operations of this institution from the public."[176] He wanted to set the record straight, and to ensure that all the rumors concerning the alleged anomalies in the University would be laid to rest permanently, so that the progress of the University would not be retarded.[177]

Investigation by Board of Visitors

Wood immediately complied with the request of Benton. He convened the Board of Visitors on November 7, 1922. In accordance with the Charter of the University, the Board was composed of the Governor General, the President of the Senate, and the Speaker of the House of Representatives. These were Leonard Wood, Manuel L. Quezon, and Manuel A. Roxas, respectively.

A number of formal letter-complaints reached the Board of Visitors for its consideration. One letter was written by Randall A. Rowley, who it will be recalled, resigned from the University on July 1, 1922 instead of accepting Benton's offer for him to go the United States for further studies.

Rowley, in his letter to the Board of Visitors dated November 6, 1922, submitted a copy of a questionnaire which he earlier published in the August 26, 1922 edition of the *Philippines Herald* and in the August 26, 1922 issue of *The Independent*, and asked the Board of Visitors to direct Benton to answer the questions contained therein. Since the appearance of the questionnaire in the two newspapers mentioned above, Benton chose to remain silent, or to put it in his usual words, assume "dignified silence."

Rowley's questionnaire contained twelve queries, six of which focused on the financial arrangements offered by the Board of Regents to Benton to entice him to accept the University's presidency. In these questions dealing with Benton's monetary privileges, Rowley was essentially asking the former to explain the justification for the expenditure by the University of what appeared to be an unduly large sum going to just one man. In fairness to Benton, at this point it has to be stated that he did not seek the presidency of the University; that he did not ask for the amount the Board decided to pay him; and that it was the Board of Regents that fixed the financial condition attached to the offer given to Benton. It was hardly proper, therefore, for Rowley to demand an explanation from Benton when in fact he should be directing the questions, at least on the remuneration issue, to the Board of Regents.

The other questions found in Rowley's questionnaire dealt with (a) whether or not the President of the University was immune from criticism; (b) whether or not it was good "sportsmanship" for Benton to ask his subordinates in the University to go abroad for advanced degrees when he himself did not have one. (Benton had an M.A. from Ohio Wesleyan University and three honorary doctorates: D.D., L.H.D., and L.L.D.); (c) whether or not Benton had succeeded in fulfilling his promise to make the University a "distinctively Philippine institution" (Benton was just into his second year; Rowley therefore was not giving the President a chance to fulfill whatever promise he had made); (d) whether or not Benton was justified to refuse consideration of any promotion or salary increase to Filipinos because of budgetary constraints while allowing the importation of American teachers at salaries higher than those given to Filipinos; (e) whether or not Benton could itemize his achievements within his first year in office; and (f) whether or not he really believed in academic freedom in the University.[178]

Complaints against UP President

Austin Craig took advantage of the Board of Visitors' inquiry into Benton's administration as an occasion to air his own charges and grievances both against Benton and the Board of Regents. In his letter to the Board of Visitors dated November 7, 1922, Craig criticized Benton as a "weak" and a "vacillating" administrator. His specific charges were (a) that the Board of Regents was more concerned with its own dignity than with the real welfare of the University; (b) that the University administration violated the Charter law of the institution in allowing the Board of Regents to act on special instances rather than confine itself to general principles and larger policies; and (c) that the Board of Regents was too secretive, like meeting behind closed doors and refusing free access to the records of its proceedings.[179]

Asked by the Board of Visitors meanwhile to comment in writing about the discriminatory salary law governing the University, Jorge C. Bocobo stressed the advisability of amending Act No. 2787, the law governing the payment of salaries within the University. Bocobo noted that Act No. 2787 authorized the University authorities to contract the services of experts from the United States and foreign countries, but gave no authority to the Board of Regents to contract the services of experts available locally, whether Filipino, American or foreign resident. The recommendation of Bocobo, therefore, was for the Board of Visitors to make representations with the Philippine Legislature for the amendment of Act No. 2787 to provide for the authority of the Board of Regents to hire local people and to delete the portion "from the United States or foreign countries."[180]

Others came forward to ventilate their complaints and charges against the Benton administration. Among them were Vicente Hilario, Gaudencio Garcia, and Conrado Benitez. In written briefs filed with the Board of Visitors, Hilario invited the body's attention to such "irregularities" or "deplorable tendencies" in the University as (a) the appointment of an educational agent who superseded the President of the University; (b) the occurrence of "a serious anomaly" in the School of Forestry in Los Baños; (c) the occurrence of "three grave anomalies" in the College of Liberal Arts; (d) the "scandalous case" of a Filipino Ph.D. candidate at the University of Chicago who was subjected "to a most humiliating treatment by certain of his University superiors;"[181] (e) the occurrence of an "anomaly" in the College of Agriculture in Los Baños; and (f) the discriminatory policy of appointments in the University.[182]

The complaint of Gaudencio Garcia focused on the "scandalous case" of a Filipino Ph.D. candidate, Jose K. Santos, at the University of Chicago, who was allegedly humiliated by Benton. This complaint was occasioned by the publication in the November 9, 1922 issue of *El Debate* and in the November 10, 1922 edition of the *Philippines Herald* of the letters of Benton and Henry Pratt Judson, President of the University of Chicago, to one another. It appears that upon unanimous instruction of the Executive Committee of the University,[183] Benton wrote a letter to Judson protesting what looked like "special concessions" given to Jose K. Santos to make it easy for him to obtain his Ph.D. in Botany from the University of Chicago. Benton's letter reads in part:

It is incredible to us that a young man with such a poor undergraduate record as that of Mr. Santos . . . could have received the recognition thus far given him in the University of Chicago. It is more incredible to us that there can be hope of his getting the degree of Doctor of Philosophy at the time foretold by him.

The letter of Mr. Santos gives evidence of having been dictated, if not written by someone else. We prefer not to believe that the Head of the Department of Botany in the University of Chicago, could have sanctioned the ridiculous statement that Mr. Santos has 'got acquainted practically with all the flora of the North Eastern part of the United States as well as part of the Central flora.'

We have greatly appreciated the many courtesies shown to Filipino students in the University of Chicago and we are planning to send more of our pensionados to your institution. I believe, you will agree, under the circumstances, however, that it is wise for Mr. Santos to follow the instructions of the Head of our Department of Botany and transfer to John [s] Hopkins University.[184]

Judson replied trenchantly to this letter from Benton. Said Judson:

Of course the transfer of Mr. Santos to another institution is a matter in which the University of Chicago is not concerned. The authorities will take such steps as they think proper. The suggestion that Oriental students in this place receive exceptional help in the way of making it easy for them needs no discussion on my part. Frankly it is too preposterous for comment. The young man has done exceptionally good work with us. He has been in continued residence with us through the four quarters in the year which, of course, lessens the time in which he may obtain a degree.[185]

Despite Benton's official efforts to effect the transfer of Santos from Chicago to Johns Hopkins in Baltimore, Maryland, Santos stayed put at the University of Chicago and proceeded to complete successfully all the requirements for his Ph.D. in Botany.[186]

Apropos the above exchange of letters between Benton and Judson, Gaudencio Garcia complained before the Board of Visitors (a) that there was indiscretion on the part of Benton in letter writing; (b) that there was negligence or misconduct on the part of Benton and the other authorities of the University in the choosing and designation of University fellows and *pensionados;* and (c) that there was an attempt to make a false, if not a malicious, assertion.[187] In effect, claimed Garcia, the letter of Benton to Judson reflected badly on the University and its administration, because the said letter was "self-accusatory" in nature and revealed flaws in the governance of the institution.

From one's vantage point today, Benton actually erred in writing to the University of Chicago concerning the performance of Jose K. Santos. Benton was in effect belittling the academic record of Santos in the said institution, and unfairly suggesting that Santos obtained good grades purely on the basis of "easy treatment" by his professors because he was an Asian, instead of giving due recognition to his scholastic abilities. What Benton should have done was to commend Santos for doing extremely well academically in a tough school like the University of Chicago.

More Charges Specified

A prominent faculty member of the University, Conrado Benitez, pinpointed to the Board of Visitors specific causes of dissatisfaction with the Benton administration: (a) discrimination against the faculty of the Spanish Department; (b) the inauguration of the President before the expiration of the one-year probation period as stipulated in the contract; (c) the dismissal of Austin Craig; (d) the appointment of Lawrence Smith despite the availability of local experts and the violation of the policy involving extraordinary contracts; (e) discrimination against Filipino Ph.D. holders; (f) efforts to block the graduation of Jose K. Santos from the University of Chicago; (g) discrimination against Filipinos holding masteral degrees through their non-promotion to professorial rank, as in the case of Nicolas Zafra, Maria Valdez, and Andrea Mariano; (h) the attempted separation from the service of the University of three history instructors without just cause; (i) the attempted dropping of an instructor in French and his replacement with an imported American Ph.D. holder at the cost of ₱8,000 per annum; (j) the dismissal of E. Natividad; (k) discrimination against H. Otley Beyer; and (1) discrimination against Filipino deans in the University.[188]

Benton was not without his defenders. One American member of the faculty, Henry A. Townsend, a professor of philosophy and psychology, wrote a letter to the Board of Visitors in defense of Benton. Townsend described Benton as "by far the ablest President we have ever had."[189] He went on to say that "Dr. Benton is the first man who has ever brought to this office a wealth of experience gained abroad."[190] Townsend called upon all the sectors of the University to unite in going back to the work of transforming the University into the greatest institution of higher learning in the country.

Board Exonerates Benton

For its part, the Board of Visitors conducted public hearings on all the charges and complaints brought before it against Benton and other University authorities. After receiving all the testimonies and the evidence, the

Board of Visitors released its statement to the press on the outcome of its investigation. This brief statement is worth quoting in its entirety:

> The Board of Visitors is of the opinion that no evidence has been presented to justify the claim that there has been any organized attempt to denationalize the University; that, as stated by the Filipino Deans themselves, there has been no deliberate or systematic discrimination against Filipinos; that there is no evidence indicating that the Board of Regents has failed to exercise proper care and discrimination in the matter of appointments, promotions and salaries; that the Board of Regents has acted strictly within its legal powers and for the best interests of the University; that the President of the University is actuated by a sincere desire to maintain and elevate the standards of the University and to so conduct the University as to turn out good citizens; that there is no evidence of prejudice against Filipinos on the part of the President of the University; and that the action taken in the Craig case was purely within the jurisdiction of the Board of Regents and the Board of Visitors is without authority to intervene in this matter.
>
> The above conclusions are based upon the examination of such charges and evidence as the Board of Visitors feels come properly within its purview, and other charges and communications that have been submitted are being considered with reference to their falling within the jurisdiction of the Board of Visitors, and if it is found that they do so fall further opportunity will be given for an additional hearing.[191]

This statement was issued by Leonard Wood, Manuel L. Quezon and Manuel A. Roxas who constituted the Board of Visitors. The investigating panel virtually exonerated Benton of any wrongdoing and gave him a vote of confidence.

NOTEWORTHY GOALS ABLY ACCOMPLISHED DESPITE UNEXPECTED RETIREMENT

UNFORTUNATELY, despite Benton's remaining in good standing in the eyes of the highest government officials in the Philippines at that time, Benton could not obtain the funds necessary to carry out his development plans for the University. He frequently made personal representations with the officials of the colonial administration, both American and Filipino, for increased budgetary appropriations for the University, but to no avail.[192] Thus, the University continued to suffer from inadequate funding support[193] in spite of rising enrolment figures. From an enrolment of 4,693[194] for academic year 1921-1922, the number rose to 4,839[195] for academic year 1922-1923. This rise in enrolment was of course reflected in the rise of the number of graduates of the University. Thus in 1921, a total of 517 students earned their degrees from the University.[196] In 1922, the number of graduates rose to 617.[197]

However, even with such increase in enrolment, the budget of the University remained constant. Because it could not get adequate funding, the University could not obtain nor even retain the best teaching personnel. There was specifically noticeable reduction in the number of American personnel. Moreover, the University was beginning to reap the ill effects of inbreeding, or the practice of hiring its own graduates to become faculty members. Because of inbreeding, the University risked being afflicted with intellectual ossification, a situation detrimental to the role of the University as a marketplace of diverse ideas and creativity. Moreover the University's financial condition was aggravated by the ban on faculty promotions,[198] which naturally lowered the morale of the teaching force. In a personal note, Benton appealed to Quezon to prevent the adoption of any proviso in the appropriation bill for 1924 that would prohibit salary increase for the faculty members of the University.[199]

Frustration and Exhaustion

Benton undoubtedly worked hard to achieve his objectives as President of the University. However, by the time he went into his third year as chief executive of the institution, he was not only a deeply frustrated man for failure to obtain the necessary financial support for his development and reorganization plans for the University, but he was also a man worn out by the stress and strain of running the University. In March 1923, he fell seriously ill, so that he had to stay in Baguio for several weeks for purposes of convalescence.[200] By Benton's own account, he suffered a "complete nervous break"[201] thus forcing him to slow down his pace of activities. As the year 1923 progressed, his health deteriorated, with his illness eventually diagnosed in a Minneapolis hospital as sleeping sickness.[202] Benton was to have gone on leave of absence in late 1923, but because of the rapid decline of his physical well-being, he felt compelled to resign on October 10, 1923. He returned to the United States with his family immediately thereafter. Benton struggled to regain his health but it was a losing battle. He passed on to the ages on June 28, 1927.

The Board of Regents generously released him from his ten-year contract to serve the University, and voted to give in advance his salary for one year from October 1, 1923.[203] At the same time, the Board gave due recognition to his accomplishments, despite the severe constraints he had to labor under, during his term. In a resolution passed by the Board of Regents on October 8, 1923, the Board recognized Benton's achievements in (a) mapping out a comprehensive program for the long-range development of the University into a top-rate institution of higher learning with an international status; (b) conferring prestige upon the University because of his personal achievements in the world of scholarship; (c) fostering the unity of the different regional units with the main Manila campus of the University; (d) endeavoring to enhance the instructional standards of the University through his program of sending *pensionados* to universities abroad for higher education; (e) promoting camaraderie and harmony among all the constituents of the University; and (f) inaugurating the Friday convocations for the purpose of serving as a forum for the expression of concern for national issues.[204]

Accomplishments Recapitulated

The University under Benton experienced growth and progress despite the frustrating lack of financial support from the government. The failure of Benton to realize his objective of obtaining a percentage land tax (mill-tax levy) as a basis for establishing a permanent source of income for the University, and obtaining an allocation of 500,000 hectares of public land for the University, need not diminish the credit that he richly deserves for his solid accomplishments during his brief but eventful years at the helm of the institution. While the mill-tax levy and the allocation of public lands were not ideas original with him, Benton nevertheless showed remarkable foresight in making those twin objectives the cornerstones for his long-range development plans toward establishing the University on a sound financial condition.

During the Benton presidency, the University witnessed the completion of Rizal Hall among other academic buildings. The University also experienced a rise in standards because of Benton's policy of making the academic staff accountable for results rather than for the actual time they spent in their respective offices. In terms of organizational changes, the University saw the creation of the School of Hygiene, a nursing training school, an agricultural extension service, systematic military training through the University Cadet Corps, the Department of Library Science, separate departments of Mathematics and Physics, and an agricultural station.

In terms of benefits to the faculty, Benton initiated and secured the approval of faculty fellowships to enable faculty members to go abroad for advanced training; the establishment of exchange professorships with American institutions of higher learning; the equitable distribution of individual teaching loads, the extension of transportation privilege to college deans, the establishment of preferential faculty fellowships in recognition of the achievements of outstanding professors, and the establishment of the system of sabbatical leave.

In the area of curricular change, Benton implemented the combined six-year course for the professional and vocational education of students enrolled in the University. This, together with the others already mentioned, contributed toward bringing the University closer to its aim of becoming the premier educational institution of the land.

A comparison of Benton's performance with his promise would bring out the fact that he did fairly well, given his limitations and given the obstacles he encountered along the way. The Benton years were indeed dynamic years for the University, and the developments during that time have had a far-reaching impact on the future course of the institution. Benton was a visionary whose feet were firmly planted on the ground. Had he lived longer to finish his full term of ten years, there is no telling what he could have accomplished more for the University and its constituents. His greatest legacy to us was perhaps his commitment to the idea of planning for the long-term development of the University, instead of just doing things on an ad hoc basis. Taking the longer view would assure the maximization of the University's civilizing influence on Filipino society, and would ensure that the institution would survive the vicissitudes of time.

IV

Palma's Momentous Decade (1923-1933)

The University in an Era of Political Imperatives and Economic Disequilibrium

by Bernardita Reyes Churchill

Palma's Momentous Decade

RAFAEL Palma formally assumed the Presidency of the University of the Philippines on July 18, 1925, after having served as acting President for nearly two years. "I never accepted a post with more fear and trepidations and with very little confidence in my capacity as I did that of the Presidency of the University," Palma wrote in his autobiography.[1] * Such honesty and humility personified the character of Rafael Palma even as he could look back to a distinguished career as revolutionary journalist, political figure, public servant, statesman, scholar, and man of letters, highly respected in the national community.[2]

Palma was cognizant of the grave responsibilities and tremendous demands placed on a university president – "He no longer is to rest content with being a scholar, but must also show an administrative genius. No one can rival him in being accountable to a great variety of constituents; to wit, the Legislature, the Chief Executive, the Board of Regents, the Faculty, the Alumni, and the students."[3] So he refused the position of permanent president of the University for more than a year. His reluctance to accept the position was due to his feeling that he did not have the necessary academic qualifications and what he really wanted was to resume his law practice. He finally relented when Speaker Manuel Roxas appealed to his patriotism, alleging that Governor General Leonard Wood might not find any other Filipino acceptable and thus might insist on appointing an American. Palma was not without experience in educational matters, however, having served with the Board of Regents since the founding of the University in 1908. On several occasions, he had also served as acting Secretary of Public Instruction in the absence of the American Vice-Governor who held that position.[4]

FROM ACTING TO PERMANENT PRESIDENT BY UNIVERSAL ACCLAIM

PALMA was sworn to the Presidency of the University by Vice-Governor Eugene A. Gilmore, who was also chairman of the Board of Regents, in "picturesque" ceremonies at the Philippine Normal School Auditorium, attended by high government officials, diplomatic and university representatives, faculty, alumni, and students. The sentiment of

---

*Footnote references are compiled in the NOTES section at the end of this book.

the academic community was best expressed by Prof. J.R. Higgins (of Los Baños) who said, "Seldom do we witness a University President so widely approved by the Faculty, Student Body, and the general public, as President Palma today."[5]

In recommending Palma to the position of permanent president of the University, the Board of Regents selection committee took into consideration his "character and unstained reputation," his knowledge of public affairs, and "his acquaintance with men and conditions in the Philippines," all vitally needed in the leadership of the University. He was also the choice of the faculty.[6] Palma by then had had more than a year of experience as acting President, having taken over from President Guy Potter Benton in October 1923.[7]

Inaugural Address

Palma's inaugural address mirrored his lofty vision of the role of the University not only in the development of the individual, but also in the growth of the Filipino nation. The University was created, he said, not only "to provide advanced instruction in literature, philosophy, the sciences, and arts, and to give professional and technical training," but more than that, to serve as "a manifestation of the efforts of our people to become a nation." What he wanted the University to produce for the emerging Filipino nation were "men of broad culture and open mentality," possessed of "a solid basic culture in the higher studies" and with "developed strong habits of mental discipline." This could be acquired through the liberal education the University should provide. "The liberal education insures a broader outlook on God, man, and events; skills the student to react properly to the prompting of truth and to the world; develops in him acumen and quickness of mind, so that in the course of time he is able to learn thoroughly the particular practices of a certain professional or technical activity, because they are nothing more or less than the specific utilization of general cultural attainment." Thus the University would do well in placing stress on the "diffusion of liberal studies and in insisting that the majority of its students pursue the cultural courses, if its aim would be that of sending forth scholarly men, truly great by reason of their broad outlook on life, their tested openness of mind, and the vast range of their accomplishments."[8]

Palma was proud of the University he had come to preside over. Only 17 years old (in 1925), it consisted of eight faculties – Liberal Arts, Education, Engineering, Law, Medicine, all in the Manila campus; and Agriculture, Veterinary Science, and Forestry at Los Baños. In addition, there were the two non-collegiate institutions of Fine Arts and Music, and the Junior College in Cebu.

But the University had to grow. It should rightfully be the country's greatest institution of learning, and as the University of the Filipino people, it should satisfy "the people's longing to enjoy the richest privileges of modern education." To develop the University to the limit of its potential excellence, Palma listed down its great need of many things: "increased personnel, enlarged equipment, and above all, more plants and buildings."[9]

Review of the University's Operations

Palma's presidency had the benefit of an external review of the University's various colleges and schools, as well as its administration. In 1925, the Monroe Educational Survey Commission conducted an extensive survey, the first ever made since the founding of the University in 1908.[10] Many of the Commission's findings and recommendations, especially those touching on university administration and financial support, coincided with President Palma's views on reorganization to insure the University's growth.[11]

The Commission noted that the chief cause of what was unsatisfactory was "too rapid and too extensive expansion" of the University. "When an institution has grown so rapidly as has the University of the Philippines, it is almost inevitable that the growth would be accompanied by elements of weakness in organization and administration." And yet support necessary for efficient administration had not kept up with expansion. After the business depression which hit the country in 1919 and the years immediately following, appropriations for the University had not increased. Obviously reliance upon public support had not sufficed to run the University efficiently and new sources of greatly increased revenue were needed.

The remedy proposed was for the University "to concentrate upon the fundamental things which are essential to develop a really great university." Thus it should limit the number of its students by some selective process, while it should also eliminate all unnecessary courses and activities. The Commission advised that "the desire for bigness on the part of University officials must play a smaller part in its administration."[12]

To maintain the highest scholarship standards expected of an institution like the University of the Philippines, the Commission recommended that scholastic and intelligence tests be adopted for purposes of selection in the College of Liberal Arts. This would reduce numbers to a point more nearly in consonance with resources available for efficient instruction, while reducing the number of failures, especially in the freshman class.[13] The Board of Regents in 1928 limited enrolment by prescribing admission of students through an entrance examination consisting of a series of ranking (not qualifying) examinations.[14]

The Commission also referred to political interference in the affairs of the University in matters of appropriations, appointments and promotions of faculty and administrative staff. This had tended to stifle the freedom of action of the University President and had affected the qualitative growth of the University. "Higher education," it went on to note, "is an activity which can be carried on effectively only in an environment of detachment and independence reasonably far removed from considerations of expediency and policy (such as governed political affairs). To discharge its functions of training youth and of investigating and extending the realms of knowledge, the members of its teaching staff and of its administrating and governing boards should not be in too close contact with those who are directly and immediately concerned with the administration of the affairs of State and who must also inevitably yield to a considerable extent to temporary considerations of expediency and policy."[15]

Composition of the Governing Board

This most serious defect, the Commission Report went on, could be removed only by entrusting the immediate administration of the University to a governing board whose members had no direct or active concern with the affairs of State and whose primary interests were educational. A reform in the composition of the Board of Regents was thus needed. The Commission recommended that the two legislative members should be dropped from the Board of Regents and that the only ex-officio members should be the Secretary of Public Instruction, the Director of Education, and the President of the University. The Board of Regents would thus become a definitely non-political body, with a real measure of administrative autonomy.[16]

Palma had been cognizant of the need to keep the University beyond political interference and to this end had recommended to the Legislature the adoption of a measure to reorganize the Board of Regents. In January 1924, Act No. 3197 was presented to the Legislature for the purpose of removing from the Board of Regents any member who was in any way connected with the political machinery of Government and restoring to the Board its former powers regarding appointments to the faculty and fixing their salaries.[17]

The measure became law in December 1924, but it only removed the Secretary of the Interior, and in his place an alumni representative was elected. The Board of Regents was thus composed of the following: the Secretary of Public Instruction as ex-officio Chairman; the Chairman of the Senate Committee on Public Instruction; the Chairman of the House Committee on Public Instruction; the UP President; the Director of Education; a faculty representative (elected by the University Council); two alumni representatives (elected by the Alumni Association); and three members appointed by the Governor General with the advice and consent of the Philippine Senate.[18]

Palma continued to seek the amendment of the University Charter to remove the administration of the University from the direct influence of the

Legislature. He repeatedly recommended reducing the size of the Board of Regents by eliminating those members whose actuations might be influenced by political exigencies, such as members of the Legislature and the faculty representative, while he expressed the need to broaden the powers of the University President in the interest of efficiency. (In this respect, he also recommended making the University President the ex-officio Chairman of the Board of Regents.) But his recommendations were not acted upon. With regard to the faculty regent, this position was finally abolished by the Legislature in 1933 on its own accord without consulting Palma, and the unilateral action seemed to have been taken because of Palma's involvement in the controversy over the Hare-Hawes-Cutting Act.[19] It appears, nevertheless, that Palma maintained good relations with the Board of Regents, which was generally supportive of his policies and recommendations.

Organizational Structure

The success of the University as a real institution of higher learning depended in large measure on the way the University was organized.

The Commission found the University's administrative structure seriously defective and recommended remedial measures. For instance, the University Council should be composed of the President, the Secretary of the University, deans, heads and acting heads of departments, directors of schools, and full professors. (This would reduce the membership of the Council considerably, but would require an amendment of the University Charter, and it appears that this recommendation was not implemented.) A General Office should be established for clerical and stenographic service, as well as an Office of the Registrar, with that official to take charge of the General Office.[20]

On May 28, 1926, Palma appointed Prof. Vidal A. Tan (Mathematics) to take charge of the registration of students. This was the first step taken toward separating the duties of the University Secretary and the Registrar.[21] In the following year, Dr. Leandro H. Fernandez (History) was appointed first Registrar-in-Charge, upon reorganization of the Office of the Secretary separating registration and other related academic duties from the business office.[22]

A growing University, the Commission Report noted, needs increased physical facilities – buildings for classrooms and laboratories, faculty offices, and student housing. Almost from the start of his presidency (even as acting president in 1923), Palma attended to what he considered the urgent need of the University for more buildings and equipment for its growing population. In 1923 there were only two real buildings on the campus in Manila – bounded by Taft avenue, Padre Faura, Florida (now Maria Orosa street) and Isaac Peral (now United Nations Avenue). These buildings were Rizal Hall and University Hall, twin buildings housing the general administration and the Colleges of Law, Liberal Arts, and Education, the last two being the largest units in the University. A number of small buildings nearby housed the College of Engineering and some of the other departments. On Herran street stood the College of Medicine, within the grounds of the Philippine General Hospital.

There was considerable congestion all around, and also considerable confusion, especially in view of the rapid growth in enrolment of the University. (See Annex A for Table on the Growth of the University.) Faculty offices were also sadly lacking or inadequate. Between 8:30 and 11:30 in the morning, there were few rooms not in use. Because of the hot and humid climate, there was no classroom work until mid-afternoon, and so much of the instruction had to be carried on during the late afternoon and evening.[23]

The University library, such as it was, was pitifully inadequate. Not only was there no library building, but the main collection of books, about 12,000 volumes, was housed in a building constructed for chemical laboratory purposes and placed upon stacks of poor-quality wooden construction vulnerable to fire and destructive insects. The capacity of the main reading room was 180 in a University of 3,500 students.[24]

Special Building Fund

To carry out methodically a plan for building construction and improvements, Palma realized that the University must generate its own funding and not depend on legislative appropriations. On May 3, 1924, Palma submitted to the Legislature a plan for financing the expansion program of the University by exclusively designating the matriculation fees collected for buildings and permanent improvements. (This amount was not to be counted as part of the yearly appropriations from the Legislature.) The plan was approved in November 1924, and thus began the construction of lateral buildings to increase the number of rooms for classes and laboratories and to provide offices for the faculty. Palma believed that the expansion of the physical facilities of the University would allow for admission of more students and maintenance of a high standard of education in the University.[25]

Between 1923 and 1932, when this special building fund was available to the University, the Manila and Los Baños campuses saw the construction of much-needed buildings while the University expanded its academic programs. Landscaping of the campus was also undertaken.

In 1923-1924, Palma's first year as Acting President, wooden buildings were constructed for the practice teaching of the College of Education (this was the University High School building), as well as other buildings for the Colleges of Medicine, Liberal Arts, and Engineering, and that for Agriculture in Los Baños.[26]

During the school year 1924-1925, Palma built a swimming pool (reportedly the largest in the Philippines at that time) and a grandstand, the Faculty Hall, the Amphitheater for Surgery in the College of Medicine, the Boiler's building for the College of Engineering, and the General Luna Hall (annex to the temporary gym) to house the Department of Military Science.[27]

The building program was continued until 1932 when the funds for the project were no longer available and the University budget was reduced considerably by the Legislature. By that time, however, the major projects had already been completed. The quadrangle of the College of Liberal Arts (Rizal Hall) was completed by 1926, along with the College of Medicine annex on Herran street and the Central Building of the College of Engineering. The building for the University Library, set back from Padre Faura street between the University Hall and Rizal Hall, was started in 1928 and completed in 1931. To fill its stacks, the University adopted the policy of devoting all library fees to the purchase of books. The Conservatory of Music building (Ignacio Villamor Hall) was built on the corner of Taft avenue and Padre Faura. Palma had hoped to build the School of Fine Arts on the corner of Taft and Isaac Peral, and a modern little theater between these two schools, to be used for convocations and graduations. But he was unable to accomplish this because of a lack of funds.

Playground facilities were provided for on J. Zamora street, in Pandacan. Here Palma started to build the Armory, Gymnasium, and Auditorium, and access to this facility, located some three kilometers from the main campus, was to be made possible by commuter bus.

To provide medical facilities for the students, a medical clinic was opened in May 1929, supervised by Dr. Alberto Tupas. This provisional hospital was opened on Calle Florida fronting the Engineering building. The UP Infirmary was completed in June 1931.

In Los Baños, an armory, gymnasium, auditorium, and infirmary were meanwhile built. Additional buildings were also constructed for the Department of Rural Education, the College of Veterinary Science, the School of Forestry, and the Rural High School.[28]

Palma was proud of the growth of the University through new structures which meant better facilities for instruction and was not particularly appreciative of those who were critical of his building policy criticizing it as misdirecting efforts onto the "apparent grandeur of the institution and not on the fundamental issue, that of making men." He felt, however, that his "ambitious building program" was necessary to create a modern university at par with any in the world. He justified this activity by pointing to increased enrolment in the University, while he also felt happy in the appreciation shown by the faculty for greater space and expanded facilities for teaching and working.[29]

Palma was not thoroughly satisfied with the improvements he introduced in the University landscape. For instance, he did not like to see the Little Theater and the Faculty Hall being used for classes as a means of coping with the shortage of classrooms. Several laboratory courses could not be given properly because of lack of space. Language classes were altogether too large, with sometimes as many as 60 to 80 students to a class. Classes in the afternoon session continued till 9 o'clock in the evening. Registration was still congested and chaotic because of the lack of space. The University still did not have a social hall, and there were no study rooms and mess halls for students. Faculty and staff were still crowded in small rooms. And even the Commencement Exercises had to be held on a provisional platform. Palma felt frustrated in being hampered by legislative stringency as to funding.[30]

BUILDING A UNIVERSITY SENSITIVE TO THE NEEDS OF THE TIMES

THE University must move with the times, Palma declared, "to carry out fully its mission in this country and thus aid in solving our national problems." "It is our bounden duty," he continued, "to help the State in the solution of its manifold problems," especially in a country "still in the springside of life, as is the Philippines." Thus "the University should be willing and ready at all times to answer all questions to unveil the past, to counsel the present, and to predict the future."[31]

Programs were initiated by the Legislature and the University relevant to the social and political growth of the country. In 1925 a School of Surveying was attached to the College of Engineering. In 1927 the School of Sanitation and Public Health (later the School of Hygiene and Public Health) was established as a joint enterprise of the Bureau of Health and the University. It was envisioned to benefit the health services of the country. Appointed to run the school were Dr. Fernando Calderon and Dr. Hilario Lara. In 1929, a Graduate School of Public Health Nursing was instituted.[32] On February 14, 1929, the Board of Regents created the School of Business Administration because "commercial education needs to be fostered more as an instrumentality to awaken our people to the proper place of trade and commerce in the prosperity of our country."[33]

Realignment of Academic Programs

The Department of Agricultural Education was established in the second semester of academic year 1928-1929, for the maintenance of agricultural education courses. Palma hailed the move "timely" as it would enable the University to turn out much needed teachers in the various agricultural schools under the Bureau of Education.[34] Soon after, a Rural High School was opened as a teaching laboratory for the Department of Agricultural Education. This was a type of vocational high school intended to correlate the instruction given in high school to the basic industry of the country, *i.e.*, agriculture.[35]

A branch of the College of Liberal Arts in Vigan – the Northern Luzon Junior College, authorized in 1921 – actually began classes in June 1930 to serve students in that area. There were attempts by the Legislature to establish other branches, in Iloilo, Pangasinan, Albay, and Laoag, but these were vetoed by Governor General Leonard Wood, who felt that the University should concentrate more on running efficiently the units already operating.[36]

On the other hand, there were academic units that were closed or came under some criticism. The School of Dentistry was closed in June 1932 due to decreasing enrolment. However a *Philippines Herald* editorial (July 2, 1932) attributed the decrease in enrolment not to any lack of interest in the dental profession but to the "unsavory and unhealthy atmosphere in the school created by a pervading spirit of active antagonism among the faculty members, a condition which the president did not have the courage to nip in the bud and which he finally remedied, when it had become intolerable, by uprooting an entire school." The School was reopened in 1933 upon the initiative of Quezon, then in the midst of his controversy with Palma over the Hare-Hawes-Cutting Act.[37]

The Monroe Commission condemned the existence of the College of Veterinary Science as a separate institution, saying it was the "wildest form of extravagance," and had recommended its transformation into a department of veterinary science in the College of Agriculture. The College, in 1924-1925, had an enrolment of 34 students and a teaching staff of eight – or a ratio of one instructor to every four students. Palma had made the same recommendation as that proposed by the Commission, but this was not approved by the Board of Regents. The College was retained, and in July 1933 it was relocated from Los Baños to Pandacan.[38]

The Conservatory of Music also came under some criticism about the time when the University was looking into economy measures in view of the reduction of its appropriations from the Legislature. The Conservatory of Music was not of collegiate standing and "not being essential to the state university (it) can be closed without much harm to the cultural life and development of the country." In order to economize, it was pointed out, the University should close its least essential departments.[39]

Revitalizing Relations with Alumni

Palma was impatient with the University's dependence on the Legislature – he disliked "bothering the Legislature with a constant petition for funds." He contended that "a University of the people and for the people must not subsist wholly on the aid granted it by the government, but also rely on the munificence of the public in general." He thus enjoined the alumni to be among "the first donors of gifts, of pecuniary aid, and other concrete help to their Alma Mater." To him the University "is a worthy object of private munificence because it fulfills its mission without discrimination and because the blessings it radiates reach all the people and go far beyond the present generation."[40]

Palma spared no effort to make the Alumni Association an "effective instrument for cooperation" to meet the needs of the University for financial and material support. The Alumni Association was brought to life once Palma proposed that an initiation fee of six pesos be collected from each graduate for the operational expenses of the association. Through alumni contributions, an Alumni Hall was built on the University campus. The Association also invested its funds in the University Printing Press, established in 1930, to help publish the works of University professors. A University Day-Alumni Homecoming Reunion was held every year from 1924, a step toward developing interest and enthusiasm among alumni in the affairs of the University. Palma always invited alumni to the President's Reception in honor of the graduating class in a further effort to cultivate the loyalty of that group.[41]

The support of the University, however, should really be the people's chief concern, for the "civilization of a people is best gauged by the amount of aid they give to their university." The development and advancement of the sciences furnish the key to the prosperity and well-being of the country. Thus "the wisest and most utilitarian investment is the outlay for higher education," and it should be generous, for if by reason of a lack of means, the products turned out by the University should in any way suffer in quality, not alone the University, but society itself will have to put up with the dead-wood of middling and indifferent leaders.[42] Palma was clearly aware of the acute need of the University for sufficient funds to carry on its activities, and these words were obviously intended for the Legislature, the major source of finance for the University.

Financial Resources and Management

The University would never realize its opportunities to advance education in the country unless it had more adequate support. It depended chiefly upon legislative appropriations which had been uncertain – these had been generous in prosperous times but parsimonious in times of economic depression. Fifteen per cent of its income came from sources other than legislative appropriation, chiefly from fees charged from students, rentals, and sale of produce. If the University must plan properly for the future, it was to be assured of the major part of its annual income and of an annual increase of income. In 1922, the Board of Regents recommended that a mill-tax levy of three and one-half tenths of one per cent be laid annually on the real property of the country for the support of the University, and that public lands be allocated to form the basis of a permanent university endowment. What the University needed was a plan for a dependable and permanent method of support.[43]

It was not until February 1930 that the Legislature passed Act No. 3008 – the Land Grant Bill – endowing the University with portions of lands of the public domain for additional support and maintenance. The University had asked for a land grant of 200,000 hectares, but got 10,000 instead. "Too insignificant," Palma intoned, while expressing the opinion that the legislation was "more of a disappointment than a gratification."[44]

To properly utilize the funds of the University, Palma introduced a plan for stabilizing its finances through standardization of teaching positions. Palma had promised the Legislature that if it approved his building program, he would not ask for an increase in the University's appropriations for ten years. According to his standardization scheme, each department, depending on its size and importance, was given a certain number of faculty positions, with properly graded ranks. In other words, each department was given a fixed budget, with little room for expansion for the next five years. Faculty members occupying the lower rungs of the academic ladder could aspire to promotions as fast as vacancies in the upper ranks permitted, so long as their promotions were warranted by such criteria as research work, important publications or manuscripts evidencing high scholarship, teaching ability and seniority in the service. Under this plan, no faculty member was taken in unless warranted in the departmental schedule and by the needs of the unit concerned.

The plan resulted in some savings for the University and avoided overloading at the top. Palma was quite pleased with the success of the system, and he was glad that the plan proved convenient when he had to refuse the insistent demands of "aggressive" heads of departments who wanted to hire extra personnel unnecessarily.[45]

The second step in the stabilization of finances was an increase in the tuition fees of the students. Palma recommended to the Board of Regents the gradual increase in matriculation fees, and the institution of various other fees for services rendered by the University. So a library fee was set at ₱2.50, a medical fee at ₱5.00; an athletic fee at ₱1.50, the *Philippine Collegian* fee at ₱1.00, and the Student Council fee at ₱1.50. In this manner, Palma succeeded in increasing the income of the University and was able to carry on the various activities of the University without soliciting additional funds from the Legislature as he had promised.[46]

Depleted Budget during the Depression

Starting in 1932, the University came upon hard times. The Depression was first felt in the country in 1931 and the Legislature had to pass measures for economy to meet the financial crisis. The already insufficient funds appropriated by the Legislature for the University were slashed by 27 per cent in 1932, a move that Palma and the University constituents deplored. The budget cut remained for several years and it had serious consequences for the University.[47] Permanent improvements could not be undertaken and fellowships to send faculty members to train abroad were stopped. New personnel to fill up vacant positions could no longer be hired. Promotions were likewise stopped.[48]

To meet the contingency, Palma offered to reduce his salary from ₱18,000 to ₱12,000 per annum. The reduction was in fact carried out in 1933. He promised not to decrease the number in the teaching staff but there would necessarily have to be a curtailing of some services in the University.[49] However there would have to be a reduction of 10-15 per cent of the salary of UP faculty and 5-10 per cent reduction of secretarial and clerical salaries.

As a result of the reduction of the UP budget, the Board of Regents authorized an increase in tuition fees in several units, effective in June 1933. This move did not go well with the students and the public. Students in the College of Education, one of the schools affected, thought the increase "inopportune and exorbitant" and engaged in a peaceful demonstration against it on June 5, 1933. They appealed to the Board of Regents and 90 per cent of students enrolled refused to pay their fees pending reconsideration of the matter by the Board. Editorials were written attacking the increase and lamenting the fact that the University would now become "an exclusive school for the rich." To placate the students and alumni, various university officials offered recommendations to either reduce the tuition increase by 50 per cent or to allow the payment of tuition in two installments.[50]

Palma defended the tuition increase as a good idea because it would make the University less dependent on the government for support, while he regretted the fact that the tuition hike coincided with the Depression. "We are liberal in time of plenty, but now we need the money," Palma explained. The Board of Regents refused the petition to reduce the increase and to allow payment in installments, but it did extend the period of payment of fees until July 31st.[51]

There was no question of the need for the University to increase its income that year. For despite higher tuition fees, the University's income fell by ₱60,000 due to poor enrolment.[52]

A PRESIDENT EARNESTLY INVOLVED IN STUDENT ACTIVITIES AND YOUTHFUL ENTHUSIASM

DESPITE such unpopular issues as tuition fee hikes, Palma devoted considerable attention to the welfare of students. His policy was to grant them as much autonomy as possible in the management of their affairs and in the exercise of student rights consistent with University interests.

Student Council Revived

Thus the inactive University Student Council was revived and its first meeting was held on September 27, 1924. In explaining the rationale for reactivating the Student Council, Palma told the student leaders of his "earnest desire to invest (them) with the rare privilege of controlling (their) own affairs and interests," and "to place within (their) reach all the instrumentalities that may be necessary in order to carry out the purposes of this organization." Through participation in the Student Council, Palma explained that the students would be afforded an opportunity "for practical training in the discharge of the duties and responsibilities of active citizenship."

Privileges, however, implied certain responsibilities. He reminded the student leaders:

> In drafting your own constitution and by-laws, you should always bear in mind that the purposes of this organization are primarily to take charge of your affairs and to help the University officials in the promotion and administration of your interests. You should, likewise, remember that this institution supported as it is by the State is governed by law, and should not, therefore, include in your constitution and by-laws any provision contrary to the University Charter or to established rules and regulations of the University. Although we are constituting a government for yourself and by yourself, you should take care in observing the fundamental or organic law of the institution.[53]

The Board of Regents authorized funding for the Council by charging each student a fee of ₱1.50. Palma was pleased with the university spirit generated by the activities of the Student Council, which launched such commendable projects as the establishment of a post office in the University and the awarding of scholarships and medals to outstanding students. Student resourcefulness was further manifested in such activities as the staging of dramatic plays not only on the University campus but also as a feature of the Philippine Carnival.[54]

University Dramatic Troupe

During the years 1926, 1927, and 1928, gala performances were given at the Manila Grand Opera House, the proceeds of which were donated to the University for campus beautification. The University Dramatic Troupe performed successfully in Baguio in the summer of 1929, inspired by Palma to raise funds for their club. Palma himself went with them to Baguio, organizing picnics and excursions and joining the students in hiking and climbing mountains, much to their delight. Palma was particularly proud of such activities as the historical pageant presented in the Philippine Carnival of 1926, the Agricultural Pageant in 1929, the Living Pictures (historical tableau vivant) in 1930, and the "Bagong Katipunan" in 1931.[55] Such performances netted the University a sizeable income for campus beautification.

A campaign for a University Press fund was launched for the establishment of a press in the University, an idea originated by Palma. The Student Council, under the chairmanship of Francisco Imperial, solicited money for this project and flyers were sent to important political figures, including Manuel Quezon.[56]

To foster better university spirit, class organizations for junior and senior classes were established. These made for a community of interests among students of the different colleges.[57]

Collegian Fee Authorized

The *Philippine Collegian,* the organ of the student body, had in the past been a source of irritation to the administration because it was never run on a stable financial basis. It depended on voluntary contributions from students which handicapped the regular work of publication. In 1925, the Board of Regents sanctioned the collection of a fee of ₱1.00 from every student every semester and with its finances stabilized, the *Collegian* came out more regularly.

The University maintained no dormitories, not even for women students. Most of the students boarded in Intramuros. To look into the adequacy of dormitory facilities for the students (also a concern of the Monroe Commission), Palma appointed, from time to time, faculty committees to make a survey of dormitories and boarding houses around the University. A list of approved dormitories and boarding houses was made available for the guidance of students. Certain uniform rules were also introduced for these dormitories to safeguard the moral well-being and health of the students, especially in view of the observation that among students in the College of Medicine there was a "gradual weakening of their physical conditions and of their alertness in mental perception," probably attributable to unfavorable living conditions. Because of the priority given to buildings for teaching purposes, the University could not undertake the building of dormitories for its students.[59]

Physical and Social Development

Palma also fostered student athletics for both sexes in the University. He built a swimming pool and a women's gymnasium and bathroom.[60] He encouraged inter-university student contests such as those held with the establishment of the N.C.A.A. and the "Big Three" for the promotion of athletic games and the advancement of physical culture among the students.[61]

Another measure for the welfare of students was the creation of a student loan fund in 1927, to enable students with limited financial means to continue their studies in the University. The fund came from interest accrued by the deposit fees paid by students to cover loss of apparatus, supplies, books, etc. This fund was formerly used by the University as additional income for general expenses, but Palma diverted it for the use of the students.[62]

An employment agency was started by the Dean of Men so that self-supporting students in the University might have the means to continue their studies. The Monroe Commission had noted that one-third of the students of the College of Liberal Arts were either partly or fully working their way through college and had suggested the establishment of this facility for UP students.[63]

To develop closer contact between students and professors outside of class hours in a way not simply limited to helping students matriculate and arrange their schedules, faculty counsellors were appointed to help the Dean of Women or Men to look after students who might feel discouraged or forsaken in their studies. And to afford contact among students of the different colleges, regular weekly convocations (held on Tuesdays) became a tradition in the University. During these forums, Palma often spoke to the students to encourage them in their pursuit of excellence or to congratulate them on their achievements. For instance, Palma was particularly pleased with the UP Debating Team, coached by Prof. Carlos P. Romulo of the English Department, which went on a tour of the United States (1928-1929) and won all their debates there.The team was composed of Teodoro Evangelista, Jacinto Borja, Pedro Camus, and Deogracias Puyat, all of the College of Law.[64]

Motivating the Youth

Palma felt an affectionate affinity with the University youth, and some of his beautiful prose was directed at them. He particularly sought to instill in them the lofty ideal of love of country. "The first thing a young man or woman should study," he said, "the first question that he should ask himself is, 'What is my country? ' Without a knowledge of his country, its history, its government, its institutions, what shall it profit a man to be educated?" Education, he told them, "furnishes the instrumentalities through which a person, by becoming useful to himself, may do better work for the prosperity and aggrandizement of his country."[65]

He also infused the hearts of the young with the spirit of aggressiveness and independence of mind, enjoining them "to find the truth above the conventionalism and the cowardice of our forbears, and endeavor to be better morally and less hypocritical." For according to him, "we need new ideas and new conceptions which can better respond to the needs of the day, to the new conscience which has been produced by the industrial progress and the economic wonders of our age." He encouraged them toward constructive criticism and originality for only in that way can humanity and wisdom progress.[66]

Ever the progressive thinker, Palma reminded his contemporaries that "we cannot educate the youth of today under the tenets and doctrines bequeathed to us by our ancestors." Educating the youth demands "a change in principle and methods in the same way that science and industry have sought new by-paths." He declared, "The world of our forefathers is no longer the world of today. To feed our youth with the aggregate of the theories and beliefs which have already lost their usefulness with the march of ages, would be to commit a gross mistake."[67]

He understood the "spirit of restlessness and revolt of youth against aged norms of conduct and action," and justified it by saying that "youth will always endeavor to avail itself of the privileges of this age of machinery and social revolt, regardless of the consequences." It would indeed be tyrannical to require them to chain themselves to the dogmas of the past. The young people should be allowed to express their opinions on important issues and their elders should be tolerant and considerate of the attitudes and opinions of the youth.

> Youth must be trusted. Their heart is sound, their vision is not blurred by selfish passion, their blood beats with high idealism; and no sordid interest has polluted their soul. They look to this university for enlightenment and power. Let us give them light and truth, not partisanship and error that when their time comes to perform their duties as citizens, they might in turn impart light and strength to their fellow citizens for the guaranty of the permanence of free institutions in this land of ours.[68]

Advent of Modern Ideas

Sometimes Palma seemed to be a man in a hurry to strip the Filipino mind of the narrow and conservative attitude, the fanaticism and obscurantism in the mould of the past era, especially when he spoke on religion and morality. He seemed almost always to be challenging the youth "to open our windows and see the world without," "to drink deep of the wisdom of the world," "to enrich the mind with the ideas of the present." The University should provide the venue for these activities. Hence he said:

> I am interested in this University's becoming the source of a new light which shall radiate new teaching more in accord, in flesh and blood, with the realities of life. Filipinos should not live in a world of abstractions, but in the atmosphere of this age in which destiny has placed them. This is the only way to achieve lasting and beneficial progress and prosperity for our country.[69]

One writer described him thus: "Palma attuned himself to the thoughts of the new generation. He was understanding, guiding rather than imposing, a wise old man who had a shy and slightly envious sympathy for the enthusiasm and agnosticism of youth."[70]

CENTRAL ROLE FOR THE FACULTY IN UNIVERSITY AFFAIRS

THE University can only be as good as its faculty. One of Palma's main policies was devoted to the well-being and contentment of the faculty, even as he demanded from them nothing but the highest standards of morality and academic competence.[71] "The meaning of a modern state University," he reminded them, "also takes in the idea that the services of those who are in the employ of the University should not be measured by a lower standard than that which the state measures the service it requires of other public servants in the courteous and considerate treatment of the public, in the simplicity of administrative routine, in the pithiness of communications, in the order and regularity of every step in a given procedure, and in the sincere and wholehearted willingness to work without being a clock-watcher when circumstances so demand." In other words, he demanded of his faculty a conscientious devotion to public service.[72]

An Intellectual Perspective

A faculty that is thoroughly trained and adequately equipped with all the means for proper teaching is absolutely necessary for the success of the University. So Palma counted upon the "unstinted cooperation and loyalty of a faculty that is not only duly prepared for its grave tasks, but is also imbued with the highest ideals, prompted by the ambition to make study and the research habit their primary aims in life, and moved by a love of country which sways each member to dedicate to the fatherland and the youth of the country the treasures of the mind and the will."

"We should wish our teachers in this University," he declared, "would be not mere hirelings pressed into service for the salaries that are given them and the lessons that they give, but faithful trustees or high priests of the science that they have pledged to espouse, of practicality, and of spirit of self-effacement and devoted service to the nation and to the world."[73]

More than teaching, "the promotion of intellectual life. . . is part of our solemn obligation to the country. It is not enough for us to teach, to cultivate scholarship; it is necessary to encourage and advance the intellectual life of the country in a way that would not only show to the public achievements of higher education, establish friendly contacts among university men and women but would also furnish the people the necessary guidance and information on all living problems with which it is confronted." Such, he reminded them, are the stern demands of scholarship.[74]

Palma often spoke to his faculty of "the doctrine of individual freedom" in education. "The best education can do in our times is to train the individual for freedom in order that he may make good use of it and not misuse it. Training for freedom requires a constant and methodical practice of the will, in order to control bad instincts and stimulate good ones. There is need of creating moral restraints *within,* and not *without,* the individual, by developing properly in his conscience precise notions of good and evil and leaving him to his own responsibility." Thus the teacher is not supposed to dogmatize. "He has no longer the right to impose on his pupils his own theories or personal beliefs. He is expected to stimulate free discussion of the subject he teaches, leaving his students the choice of the system of thought which best satisfies their reason."[75]

With the purpose of promoting faculty contentment, a definite policy was adopted in relation to the duties and privileges of the faculty, such as their activities outside the University and the matter of vacation leave. In connection with the first point, outside teaching was allowed faculty members holding the rank of instructor or below since their salary was not enough "to maintain a decent living."[76] As regards the second point, a distinction was made between laboratory professors and lecture professors. The first were given accrued leave and the second were given short vacations on Christmas and long vacations during the end of semesters. The teaching load was set to a minimum of 15 hours a week.[77]

Fellowships and Research Grants

Palma was quite pleased with his faculty and their dedication to service and academic competence. He encouraged faculty development through fellowships awarded to outstanding and promising professors who were sent to undertake graduate studies in the United States and Europe. The first exchange professor, Dean Maximo M. Kalaw of the College of Liberal Arts, was sent to the University of Michigan to reciprocate that University's designation of Prof. J. Ralston Hayden as Exchange Professor at UP.[78] To encourage faculty members of the College of Agriculture to remain in the University, rather than join sugar centrals which offered higher compensation, he continued the policy of building faculty houses in Los Baños.[79]

Palma also promoted research and scientific production among his faculty. The Board of Regents established an annual research fund of ₱10,000, taken from the general administration fund, for the publication of worthy scientific work produced by the faculty.[80] The results of faculty research were published in the *Journal of Science, The Social Science Review, Pure and Applied Science Bulletin,* and *The Agriculturist.*

Speaking of the importance of research in the life of the University, Palma said:

> . . . the State University must live with the people, with their thoughts, necessities, and problems, and it does not, and cannot, fully discharge its obligations to the public that supports it, if it simply imparts knowledge of the past, if it does not enrich the stock of human knowledge, expand its frontiers, give color and life to its teaching, by providing means for the right kind of research.[81]

Besides, research would arouse "otherwise indolent minds accustomed to the daily routine of classroom and laboratory work."[82]

Filipinization as a Factor

Realizing that the University was still a young institution, Palma favored the policy of inviting eminent men to its faculties "regardless of land or race so as to serve as the polestar of mental and moral inspiration to its students."[83] Yet he did not overlook the desirability of Filipinizing the faculty as competent Filipino scholars became available.[84] By 1925, only one-eighth of the teaching staff of the University was American; the rest were Filipinos and were mostly graduates of the University. Indicative of the training and experience of the faculty was the fact that 82 per cent of the teaching staff was below 40 years old. The comparative youth plus the in-breeding of the teaching staff, noted the Monroe Commission, was no doubt the explanation of its relative sterility in scholarly productivity.[85]

While cognizant of the University's dependence on foreign experts to train Filipinos, Palma nevertheless hoped that the development of graduate studies would eventually "free the University from the thralldom of foreign intelligentsia in the solution of governmental problems." He acknowledged that the engagement of experts who are not familiar, generally speaking, with local conditions has always been a costly experiment and it would seem that the only way to solve the present shortage of high technical personnel is for the University to develop and turn out "specialists who will apply the high principles of science to practical problems."[86] The University should therefore conduct original investigations "in accord with our temperament, our character, and our environment," so that foreign specialists need not be brought into the country "to study our own problems for us."[87]

The problem of Filipinization of the faculty, however, was not entirely up to Palma to pursue. American teachers, particularly English instructors, were contracted for service as a matter of general policy. While everyone, including Filipinos, recognized the need, perhaps, of continuing to employ American teachers, it probably did not escape anyone's attention that sometimes awkward situations were brought on by indiscriminate comments made by American teachers which the Filipinos, ever sensitive to racial slurs, found offensive. Besides, American "contract" professors received bigger salaries than their Filipino colleagues and the frequent turnover in personnel, particularly in the English Department and the College of Agriculture in Los Baños, was disruptive of the system.[88] During Palma's time, the University was twice provoked by what it considered unsavory comments made by American professors.

Disenchanted Americans

In 1929, Jessie Downing Artamanoff, temporary assistant professor of English, became the subject of controversy when an article she had published in the United States was re-published in the *Philippines Herald.* The article, entitled "Filipino Girls Bribe their Way Thru School, Alleges American Teacher," spoke disparagingly of Filipino girl students, criticized the methods of teaching English in Philippine schools, and openly questioned the honesty of Filipinos, with some references to Philippine politics and alleged graft and corruption. Backed by the Chairman of the English Department, Robert J. Conklin, Artamanoff initially refused demands from the faculty and students for her resignation, claiming her statements had been given meaning she never intended them to have. Faced with a Board of Regents decision on her immediate separation, Artamanoff resigned on August 10, 1929.[89] Many saw the Artamanoff incident as the signal for the Filipinization of the English Department.[90]

The following year, in 1930, the English Department was once again the focus of attention. In a University Convocation held on September 30, 1930, Tom Inglis Moore, Associate Professor of English, made the statement that 90 per cent of University students cheated! But, he clarified, "they do it not maliciously but because they simply do not realize what such dishonesty means. They have no adult sense of responsibility. Yet efficient work is impossible when dishonesty is as prevalent. They must learn the significance of their conduct."

"Filipino students are mentally childish," Moore went on. "The childishness that persists in the mind of the great majority of students . . . is the charming childishness of blissful ignorance, not meaning what they do most of the time."

The entire University was greatly exercised over what it considered Moore's gratuitous statement, which had harmed the good name of the institution. And coming in the wake of the Hoover appointment of Nicholas Roosevelt as Vice-Governor, a move which the Filipino leaders opposed vehemently (for Roosevelt had been an acrimonious critic of the Filipino people),[91] Moore's statements aroused the indignation of some members of the Legislature, who threatened to reduce the appropriations of the University and conduct a formal investigation. Carlos P. Romulo, editor of the *Tribune,* and part-time associate professor at the University, wrote a strongly worded editorial against Moore. Moore was asked to explain and substantiate his charges, and unable to present specific cases of cheating as alleged, the Board of Regents decreed his immediate separation from the University.[92]

A POLITICAL ISSUE PENETRATES AND DOMINATES THE CAMPUS

IN January of 1933 an event of momentous significance affected the affairs of the University, as it affected the country in general. The campaign for independence had culminated in the passage of the Hare-Hawes-Cutting Act, secured by the OsRox (Osmeña-Roxas) Mission. Quezon, who had been ill and remained in Manila while the Mission worked in Washington, declared the independence bill unsatisfactory and wholly unacceptable, for "it neither grants us freedom nor safeguards our economic interests." As the bill went through its final stages in the United States Congress, opposition mounted, and Quezon became increasingly persistent in his denunciations.[93] The stage was thus set for a bitter political struggle, with the nation divided between the "Pros" who would accept the independence law, and the "Antis" who would reject it completely. At stake, of course, was really Quezon's leadership vis-a-vis Osmeña and Roxas.

Support for Hare-Hawes-Cutting Act

The University became a lively forum for the discussion of the independence law, with students, faculty, and administration officials openly expressing their views for or against the measure. President Palma himself came out categorically in favor of accepting the law. And so did Dean Maximo M. Kalaw (of Liberal Arts), a member of the OsRox Mission who returned ahead of the delegation, and who conducted a lively debate on the issue with Dean Jorge Bocobo (of Law), an Anti from the start and a Quezon partisan.

Palma made his first statement in favor of the independence bill late in December 1932, when the bill was going through its final stages in Washington. He subsequently issued another statement deploring the "absence of a perfect understanding among our leaders and a decided lack of harmony as to what exactly we want and what means are necessary to achieve our ends." The Mission, he said, in securing the approval of the bill, had acted in keeping with their instructions from the Legislature. "Let us give (the Mission) our support, for we believe in its sincerity, ability, and patriotism." When the bill was vetoed by President Hoover in January 1933, Palma openly expressed regret at such action, and when the veto was overriden, Palma, along with Deans Maximo Kalaw and Francisco Benitez, and Regents Vidal Tan and Jose Zamora, cabled their congratulations to the Mission for their success in having the measure go through despite efforts of some quarters to have it disapproved.[94]

Quezon Manifests Displeasure

Quezon had not looked with favor on the University's involvement in the controversy over the Hare-Hawes-Cutting Act. He considered it improper for the University to take part in political affairs. In fact when Quezon heard that the University Student Council and some faculty members of the College of Liberal Arts were planning to celebrate the passing of the bill, with Palma's permission, he called up Palma, and in a "choleric tone" (as Palma remembered it) told him that he thought "it was neither proper nor fair that any such demonstration should be instigated by professors." He finally told Palma that if the idea of those like him and certain professors who were in favor of the bill was to force the Legislature to take action, he had no objection to submitting the bill at once to the Legislature and the result would be the defeat of the bill.

The January 18 demonstration did take place, but no faculty member addressed the gathering, the speakers being students who discussed the provisions of the law. Quezon explained that he did not have any objection to students gathering and discussing the bill, although he believed that with the proximity of examinations, they should spend their time preparing for those tests. He considered it inopportune for the professors of the institution to devote their time staging discussions on the law when they should be attending to the preparation of their students for their final exams. Quezon was objecting to what he called "professorial influence," although he suggested that the University could hold a series of convocations in which speakers favoring and opposing the bill could be heard by the students, without the faculty initiating such activities. In fact he offered to address the University at one such occasion.[95]

Palma Disagrees with Quezon's Stand

Palma was alarmed by Quezon's gestures and interference in University activities. He also disagreed with the many remarks Quezon had been making condemning the law in the "most excruciating terms," when Quezon in fact had been in favor of the fundamental provisions of the bill. Declaring the bill was the best that could be obtained by the Mission under the circumstances,

Palma lamented "the inconsistency of our plan of action and the lack of fixity in our national endeavors."

Answering critics that national dignity, self-respect, and pride would not be sacrificed if the bill were accepted, he stated that it was "more dignified to accept [the law] with all its consequences as a priceless gift that Providence can bestow upon our people, above all considerations of an economic or materialistic character, than to beg and bargain for our independence."[96]

Addressing himself to Quezon's reasons for opposing the Hare-Hawes-Cutting Act, Palma admitted that "of course, if we read the bill with the glasses of suspicion, we would see danger in every paragraph." Quezon's logic, he said, was weak and inconsistent. He then proceeded to accuse Quezon of dividing and not uniting his people on the momentous issue of independence. Quezon, he charged, had failed to consult with the various elements of the Filipino people on the pending measure in order to obtain their true reaction. Instead, he had imposed his individual opinion, severely criticizing the US Congress and the Mission without knowing the true circumstances. These were by far the strongest words spoken by Palma on the controversy, and they were specifically directed at Quezon.[97]

Quezon Upset by Rising Opposition

Quezon had wanted discussions of the Hare-Hawes-Cutting Act played down until the OsRox Mission had returned to Manila and was furious at some members of the Legislature who were campaigning to influence the Filipino decision on the act. He warned that the Legislature, where clearly he had a majority on his side, might be provoked into taking a negative action on the Act before the return of the Mission if the campaign for acceptance did not stop.

But he was most upset by the attention being paid the issue by the University. Students in the main ranged themselves on the side of the OsRox Mission and the Hare-Hawes-Cutting Act, and Palma gave them permission to discuss the subject in campus convocations in the name of academic freedom. Quezon had no objection to academic freedom, but he did not want discussion of the independence Act specially by UP professors and student leaders led by Wenceslao Vinzons, Arturo Tolentino, and Carmen Planas.[98]

Kalaw and Bocobo in Earnest Debate

Also the press debate between Dean Maximo M. Kalaw and Dean Jorge Bocobo was being given front-page importance in the papers. The opening shot was fired on January 26, 1933 and continued through February.[99] Kalaw and Bocobo carried on their debates informally all throughout the period of the controversy over the independence law. Rumors had it that both of them entertained such strong and ardent convictions regarding the Hare-Hawes-Cutting Law that when the two met, they chose not to greet each other![100]

The Kalaw-Bocobo debate was criticized by A.V.H. Hartendorp, *Philippine Magazine* editor, who disapproved of a "scholar employing his talents as a political propagandist and pamphleteer." He went on to point out that had both men always spoken with entire truthfulness instead of writing for political effect as party henchmen, they could at this time have spoken with much more authority, the one as a political scientist and the other as a legalist. Worst of all, he deplored the fact that the entire University had become a center of political agitation, with the students outvying their professors, and the President himself taking part in this agitation.[101]

The *Philippines Herald,* recognized as a pro-Quezon newspaper, also criticized Palma for having stepped out "from his university cloister" and indulged in politics with his criticisms of the Quezon leadership. The *Herald* described Palma's criticisms as misleading and premature.[102]

Legislature Rebuffs Palma

Palma got a foretaste of how Quezon and his partisans in the Legislature would deal with their critics when the Legislature, during its special session in January, defeated measures desired by Palma. One of them was a bill that would have allowed the University to use tuition fees for university expenses (in view of decreased appropriations). Another measure abolished the position of Faculty Regent. Palma in fact favored the abolition of the position and had recommended it years back. but this time he was not consulted on the matter.[103] The timing of the action was clearly intended to annoy him. Quezon in approving the bill explained that the abolition of the faculty representative was done because "invariably the electioneering on the part of the various candidates has created disturbances within the University and has served to split the professional staff."[104]

Palma hinted at the possibility of resigning his post because of the fear that the Legislature's antagonism toward him was impairing his usefulness to the University. At the same time, he came out again against the opponents of the independence act. "The time has come for the country to change its leadership," he announced. "We need new direction and new guidance."[105] Clearly it was Quezon's leadership he was alluding to.

Upon being informed that Palma intended to resign, Quezon stated that he did not see why Palma should resign because they disagreed on the Hare-Hawes-Cutting Act. "Our points of view on this matter have nothing to do with the presidency of the state university. As far as I am concerned, irrespective of our present controversy, I am for him as the head of our state university, and he can always count on my support."[106]

On its part, the University Council passed a resolution expressing wholehearted support of Palma.[107]

Quezon Vexed with Palma's Persistence

Quezon was clearly quite displeased with Palma's outspoken criticism. He was particularly incensed by Palma's call for a change of political leadership in the country, Palma having also branded Quezon an inconsequential political leader, insincere, and having taken his current stand for political reasons. Coming from the President of the University, Quezon considered this a serious matter, for in that position Palma exercised a strong influence on professors and students. What followed was a public exchange of views between Quezon and Palma.

In a letter addressed to Palma on February 8, 1933, Quezon cancelled his scheduled speech at the University and advised Palma that the University should be free from politics. He also criticized Palma's partisan discussion of the Hare-Hawes-Cutting Act, stating that he had no desire to accentuate the "deplorable state of affairs" in the institution where the debate on the law was being made to appear as a Quezon-Palma issue. Up to this time Quezon had refrained from answering Palma's attacks, except for one occasion. This was when, after Palma had published his first statement, Quezon expressed surprise in the course of a speech before the Commission of Independence that in his position as President of the University, Palma had advocated publicly the acceptance of a law the official text of which he had no occasion to read. Quezon thought it was irresponsible of Palma to have done so.[108]

Political Implications Denied

In his reply to Quezon's letter, Palma pointed out that the discussion on the law within the University had been purely academic, with no partisanship or personalities injected into it. The normal operations of the University's functions, therefore, had neither been stopped nor hurt on account of the controversies on the Act. In explaining the action he had taken in openly commenting on the bill and criticizing those opposed to it, he pointed out that he was prompted to do so by the unusual activity of one of the Deans of the University who had come out openly for the rejection of the bill before and after its approval by Congress. The Dean referred to was Jorge Bocobo, who had participated at a public meeting on the bill at the Manila Grand Opera House on December 22, 1932. He was also constrained to speak out, Palma explained, because of the apparent antagonism of several public figures in the Legislature against the bill on account of its economic provisions.

Explaining that he had not gone into personalities, but rather had discussed mental attitudes and intellectual positions, he avowed that he did not have Quezon exactly in mind in most of his statements, but rather those persons who voiced their opinions and gave vent to their arguments in the newspapers.

Palma confirmed that he had been thinking of resigning his position because of the recent action taken by the Legislature on bills affecting the University. "I would not wish to be in the way of the University to receive the full support of the Legislature, and I am willing to step aside for the good of the University," he said. "Politics in the University does not exist, contrary to the prevailing opinion outside," Palma emphasized. He had spoken as he did, he explained, because it was the duty and the privilege of every Filipino to express his opinion on the crucial matter of the ultimate freedom of his country. [109]

Palma had given as the reason for his intention to resign the fact that the Legislature did not act on the Quirino amendment to the Appropriation Act affecting the University. In a letter to Palma on February 10, Quezon explained that the Senate did pass the amendment but the House Committee on Appropriations refused to take it up and recommend favorable action to the House. This only showed, he went on to say, "how wrong are those who believe that the Legislature simply registers the will of any one individual." Then as if to reprimand Palma, he said that "if you think that in order to continue as President of the University, the Legislature should be obliged to do whatever you ask it to do, you are bound to be disappointed. I am sure the Legislature is desirous to cooperate with you, and more than anyone else, you have in me one who is but too anxious to give you all the support your administration needs for the good of the University. But I want you to understand that this cooperation will never be on the assumption that the Legislature will renounce its legislative powers with reference to the University and place such powers in the hands of the University President." [110]

Clash of Irreconcilable Views

Palma reacted strongly to Quezon's charge that he had lobbied for bills affecting the University and that he had wished the legislature to renounce its legislative powers in order to please him. What followed was vigorous censuring from both sides, with both figures bringing up past records. When Quezon alluded to Palma's authorship of the Senate resolution offering cooperation to Governor Wood, Palma bitterly attacked Quezon's policies and attitude during the Wood regime, including his having provoked the Conley case (in 1923) because he had personal prejudices against Wood. He also criticized the usual methods employed in the campaign for independence. He recalled that "once in Washington. . . we begin to request and to beg from one side to another, give a banquet to this and offer a drink to that to interest him in our cause. For this the Americans have often charged us Filipinos with asking for independence but not really wanting it." Palma charged that Quezon's tactics were effective in winning votes and the applause of the galleries but "not for the building of a nation."

"We need less eloquence and more action in the solution of the multiple problems of the new situation," he said, and moreover "we may not have either independence or sugar."[111]

Quezon was greatly irked by Palma's "invectives." Palma, he complained, "seemed to relish dipping his pen in gall and making me the victim of his effusions." He declared, "It looks . . . as if President Palma does not view [my going to the US on a mission] with approval, because once he has said that we should accept the law, it behooves one and all to abide by his opinion and do as he says. Indeed, his dictum has behind it the authority of a dogma expounded by a university president, and it must neither be questioned nor discussed."[112]

Quezon was obviously beginning to lose his patience with Palma's broadsides. In a personal and confidential letter to Palma, he warned that while he was desirous of protecting the dignity of the position of President of the University who must not be dragged "into the mire of partisan squabbles," he might not be able to keep his silence if Palma continued "to take the field of politics with impunity and direct [his] broadsides against [Quezon] from the holy chair of a University President, with disregard of the law and Civil Service regulations."

"If you want to engage in a political fight with me, throw your hat into the political ring as a politician, but don't keep on wearing the cap and gown of a scholar," Quezon challenged Palma.[113]

Neither Polemics nor Partisanship

Palma explained that he had not attacked Quezon personally, nor did he wish to engage in polemics. "My only purpose," he said, was to exercise "the right of every citizen in a free country to express his own views on national problems." Philippine independence was a non-partisan question for all Filipinos were interested in its proper solution. He alluded to Quezon, he explained, because "I consider him the one responsible for the political derangement in which we find ourselves and for the deep cleavage existing among the Filipinos during this hour . . . when the need is for us to present a solid and united front." His criticisms were really directed at Quezon as a public man, and his political conceptions and ways.[114]

The Palma-Quezon controversy was temporarily suspended when Quezon, in mid-February, left for another mission to the United States, amidst appeals for union and harmony.

The OsRox Mission and Quezon's Mixed Mission returned to Manila in June 1933, and the controversy over the independence law intensified. Both

Quezon and OsRox partisans tried to influence public opinion to their respective sides. A heated public debate on the acceptance or rejection of the Hare-Hawes-Cutting Act led to a challenge to Quezon's leadership.

Quezon Denounced through Manifestoes

The most virulent opposition came from the League for the Acceptance of the Hare-Hawes-Cutting Act, a non-political civic body organized in March 1933 under the initiative of Maximo M. Kalaw for the purpose of "eradicating evils in the present system of government." On June 4, the League issued a manifesto, drafted by Benigno Aquino, Sr., Rafael Palma, and Kalaw, denouncing the current one-party system as dictatorial and urging the restoration of a two-party government. The manifesto also declared that the independence act was only a "means to an end," to establish a really democratic form of government in the Philippines.[115]

On July 2, a "violent partisan manifesto" was again issued by the League, from the office of President Palma, denouncing Quezon's "arbitrary acts and whims" which had been responsible for all the "internecine quarrels in our country." Taking advantage of the popularity he enjoyed and the confidence the people had in him, Quezon had "endeavored to establish himself as a sort of despot and master of destinies of the people," considering himself "omnipotent and sure to impose his will over the Legislature and the people." The League invited all citizens who sympathized with its ideals "to accept the struggle to the finish so that our people may be freed from a leadership without orientation, a leadership that is at once pernicious and irresponsible."[116]

The *PhilippinesHerald* held that the manifesto against Quezon's leadership was inspired "by pure hatred" calculated to sway the people's passion. It also decried the involvement of University officials like Palma and Kalaw in this "document of personal attack" against Quezon.[117]

SENATE PRESIDENT ASSERTS HIS POLITICAL LEADERSHIP

AMONG the studentry, "antis" and "pros" vied with each other in discussing the merits and demerits of the independence law. Convocations continued to be held in the University, with political leaders invited to address the student body to discuss such matters as academic freedom, the work of the OsRox Mission, and the acceptance or rejection of the independence law.[118]

The student paper, the *Collegian,* also devoted considerable space to the controversy. A group called the Anti-H-H-C Student Federation protested in a resolution on July 22, 1933 against the use of the paper as an organ of the Pro-H-H-C group who were apparently publishing only articles favoring the bill. Palma dismissed the complaint against the editor-in-chief, explaining that there existed no regulations prohibiting said editor from taking any definite stand on any question. "The University as an institution is devoted to encouraging students to take interest in public affairs and express frankly and fearlessly their opinion on any questions," he announced in a memorandum. The *Collegian* may thus print articles of a political nature as long as it kept away from partisan politics.[119]

Quezon's Three-Day Speech

When the Legislature convened in July 1933, Quezon determined to put his leadership to the test. On July 20, he submitted another one of his many resignations as President of the Senate and the Nacionalista Party, and in a three-day speech, he outlined his stand on the bill and his differences with the Mission. He attacked those who had challenged his leadership and had publicly declared that the people should demand his resignation, while he also denounced those who favored the unconditional acceptance of the Act. As a sidelight on the main theme of his speech, Quezon indulged in some thrusts at UP officials, specially at President Palma and Dean Kalaw whom he accused of "partisan leanings and personal prejudice."[120]

In his defense Palma denied he had ever attacked Quezon's leadership, and once again he insisted on his right and privilege as a Filipino and as president of the State University "to discuss divine as well as human questions of the day," such as the question of independence.[121]

Asked about his rumored resignation, Palma stated that he would not resign as President of the University "as long as I am not kicked out." Pointing out that he really intended to resign last year, he explained that he decided to "stick it out" when he heard that Quezon was interested in his resignation.[122]

On his part, Dean Kalaw took exception to the charge of partisanship and explained that it was his privilege as a professor to join in the discussion of national issues. Besides, he said, "If my activities in connection with the Act are improper, may I humbly ask 'How about Dean Bocobo's?' Surely academic freedom may be enjoyed by 'antis' and 'pros' alike!"[123]

A Political Triumph

The reorganization of the Legislature resulted with Quezon in complete control of both houses: his resignations were rejected; Roxas was ousted as Speaker and replaced by Quintin Paredes; Osmeña was ousted as President Protempore of the Senate and Vice-President of the Nacionalista Party.[124]

There were unmistakable signs that Palma had incurred the wrath of the Legislature under the command of Quezon. His support of the Hare-Hawes-Cutting Act and the OsRox Mission was qualified as a partisan move by Quezon, who seemed to have overlooked the activities of the Dean of the College of Law. The Legislature paid considerable attention to the budget of the University in that session and Palma was constantly referred to in both houses, and occasionally in the Quezon mouthpiece, the *Philippines Herald.* He was threatened with an investigation of his administration of the University (but this never took place) and his building program was attacked as extravagant.[125] Contrary to previous practice, he was made to appear for the first time before the Committee on Appropriations of the House (the Legislative Committee used to come to Palma's office to discuss appropriations), where he was made to explain how he had managed the financial affairs of the University, asking him to describe in detail the number of positions, salaries of personnel, income, and expenditures, which he never had to do before.[126]

Squeezing the UP Budget

Palma considered the UP budget of primary importance in view of the reduced appropriations and falling income of the University over a period of years. So he had hoped for a bigger outlay for 1934. The *Philippines Herald* immediately pitched in and allowed that the only salvation open to the University was the radical reorganization of its activities: it must purge itself of "the stale and the ossified in the faculty"; it must dissociate itself from low-standard schools and departments, for instance, the Conservatory of Music; its administration should not be unnecessarily distracted from academic to political interests. Increased appropriations would not do, as the University had become the "luxury item in our educational system."[127]

The discussions on the UP budget were deadlocked several times as some members of the House Appropriations Committee sought to introduce new regulations intended to put the financial administration of the University under tighter legislative control. Representative Juan Luna (Mindoro) proposed a new method of alloting funds for the University, consisting mainly in providing for an itemized, instead of a lump sum, allotment. The actual system of setting aside an appropriation for the University in lump sum was contrary to and destructive of the budgetary system, he explained. The practice was actually an encroachment on the right of the Legislature to determine the detailed expenses of all bureaus and branches of the insular government. "We want to know exactly how the University proposes to spend yearly insular aid the government extends to that institution," he said.[128]

Luna also drafted a bill seeking to amend the University Charter– the bill would take away control of all funds of the University from its authorities and would turn these over to the Insular Treasury which would retain absolute control of the disposal of all money for the maintenance and operation of the University. It would also fix the rates of matriculation, tuition, and other fees in the University. [129]

Drastic Reductions Carried Out

There was very little question that the members of the Committee would trim the UP budget every way they could. They wanted a general reduction of the scale of salaries of deans and professors by 10 to 15 per cent and a reduction of the item of the University for contribution and gratuities (from ₱30,000 to ₱10,000; this allotment was spent mostly for *pensionados*). They also wanted the annual aid of ₱25,000 for the Conservatory of Music withdrawn and the school placed on a self-supporting basis. Palma offered to have his salary slashed to keep faculty salaries intact, and so it was reduced from ₱18,000 to ₱14,000. The UP budget was slashed by ₱183,000, considerably less than the amount desired by the House Committee. [130]

Naturally protests came from University quarters who were dissatisfied with the treatment of the UP budget at the hands of the Legislature. Dean Kalaw attacked the Luna measure transferring control of UP finances from the Board of Regents to the Legislature, claiming the system would lead to political wire-pulling in the University. "The Legislature might as well abolish the Board of Regents if the proposed plan goes through," exclaimed Regent Jose Zamora. The Board of Regents drafted a resolution, penned by Regent Carlos P. Romulo, petitioning the Legislature not to act on the Luna plan requiring itemization of appropriations. And the UP Alumni Association, through its president, Jorge Vargas, presented a petition to Quezon protesting against the budget slash and itemization. Palma, who over a month earlier had categorically stated that he would not resign, was reportedly planning to do so rather than see the University suffer through a cut in its budget. [131]

"There seems to be a deliberate attempt on the part of some members of the Legislature to punish the University of the Philippines for the acts of a few of its officials," editorialized the *Philippines Herald* on August 12. Many members of the Legislature were obviously not particularly fond of Palma because of his activities which had not been "in consonance with his academic role in our national life." But why should the University be sacrificed "to the revengeful moods" of men whom Palma had antagonized? Why place it at the mercy of politics? The University, it declared, should be saved from the corruption of national politics by making it an independent, self-supporting institution. In proposing an investigation of the University, the *Herald* charged that the Legislature wished to "assert its power as creator of the University by investigating (the) finances of the University." The Legislature, in its desire to exercise its authority "for the mere sake of exercising it," would inflict a two-fold harm if it embarked on this investigation: first, that of going over the head of the Board of Regents, and second, that of unjustly placing the University in serious doubt before the public. What it wanted, said the *Herald,* was to "get even" with its President. Quezon praised the House plan to probe UP finances, claiming that it would be a distinct service to the institution.[132]

Quezon Explains Intent

In an effort to explain what the Legislature was doing in relation to the University budget, Quezon wrote the UP Alumni Association, through Vargas, that he was opposed to an itemized budget for the University. "The intervention by the Legislature in the affairs of the University," he said, "shall be in character negative rather than affirmative." The Legislature, he explained, had the right to tell the University what it should not do, but the Board of Regents should have complete freedom and liberty to use the funds appropriated by the Legislature to serve the interests of the University within the restriction imposed by the Legislature. He also held that the Legislature had the right to determine maximum salaries for the officers of the University and to rule what colleges and schools should be made self-supporting, and to what extent such colleges and schools should be given financial aid from the government.[133]

In a further effort to discuss the protests against itemization of the University budget, Quezon asked the Secretary of Public Instruction, Vice-Governor John M. Holliday, to convene a meeting of the Board of Regents. At the meeting, held on August 24, Quezon told the Board of Regents that the Legislature had a perfect right to dictate how the University should spend its funds. Stating that the University exceeded its authority in closing the School of Dentistry a year ago without consulting the Legislature, he declared that the School would reopen in 1933. The appropriations for the Colleges of Law and Education should be reduced, he said, as there were already too many lawyers and teachers in proportion to the other professions and the needs of the country. He advocated that the University turn its attention more to the teaching of mining and industrial engineering. He also advised the discontinuance of the building program. And finally, he reminded the Board members that the University should make it known to the Legislature that it had savings when it asked for appropriations.[134]

On August 19, the House passed the budget bill and appropriated ₱42,238,194, less than the amount proposed by the Governor General. It reduced its own appropriation by ₱72,488 and reduced and itemized the appropriation for the University. Luna explained that the reduction of the appropriation would not hurt the University as only the building activity would be curtailed. The Senate passed the budget carrying a total of ₱42,475,439 and restored the lump sum appropriation for the University. Quezon insisted on the reduction of his salary from ₱16,000 to ₱14,000, which minus the 15 per cent economy reduction, amounted to ₱11,900, the salary of the Speaker being reduced to a similar amount.[135]

The row over the budget of the University–itemized or lump sum– ended with a Quezon compromise proposal presented to the conference Committee. The compromise set a lump sum for salaries, a lump sum for sundry expenses, and a lump sum for other expenditures, leaving it to the Board of Regents to itemize these amounts. The proposal also fixed a maximum for the salaries of the President, deans, directors, professors, and instructors of the University.[136] When the deadlock was broken in the Conference Committee, the University appropriation for 1934 was set at ₱1,018,067 the same as in 1933, but less than the outlay proposed by the Board of Regents. Palma's salary was further reduced to ₱12,000. There were other restrictions imposed – such as giving the Vigan branch ₱23,000 a year regardless of the opinion of the Board of Regents, and forcing the University President to assume the expenses for entertaining visitors from his own pocket. On the other hand, students in agriculture, veterinary medicine, and mechanical engineering were exempted from the payment of tuition fees. The matter of the tuition fees reversed Palma's earlier recommendation on this matter.[137]

PALMA BOWS OUT BOLSTERED IN SPIRIT BY WIDESPREAD SUPPORT

PALMA realized by this time that it would be very difficult to work with a hostile Legislature, especially in view of the power exercised by that body on the funding of the University. So he thought of finally leaving the University. One other incident probably contributed to his resolve to resign his post.

Controversy over the Collegian

On September 13, the Board of Regents reversed Palma's ruling on the *Collegian.*[138] Earlier, the editor of the paper, Arturo Tolentino, was warned by Dean Bocobo not to discuss the Hare-Hawes-Cutting Act in the paper, it being a partisan issue. Tolentino appealed to Palma, who ruled that the *Collegian* could discuss the act, but the Board of Regents reversed the ruling and decided in favor of Bocobo's stand. The Board invoked a 1912 ruling which declared that "no student paper or publication shall take any stand on any partisan or religious question which may be the subject of any controversy between political parties or religious sects." The Hare-Hawes-Cutting Act had become a partisan issue and the *Collegian,* being a university paper, not a metropolitan paper, could not discuss the law.

Regent Romulo, during the meeting, alluded to the University having been dragged into politics. He said: "Individually let us express our convictions openly and courageously. But let us not enmesh the University in our controversy. Let us leave the University aside. If we must express our opinion because we believe it is our patriotic duty to do so, let us express it without fear and without equivocation, but in thus expressing it, we must do it on our own responsibility, that is, let us step out of the university to save it from the antagonism that our own deeds may bring upon it."[139]

Palma must have felt directly alluded to by these remarks. He declared that there was nothing bad in politics. "We teach political science in the University and there is no reason why we should ban the students from practicing what they study. Of course we have not yet reached the stage in our development in this country where we can divorce principles from personalities."[140] Tolentino charged that the action of the Board prohibiting discussions of the law smacked of an abridgement of the right of speech. "Somehow the action is a reflection on the freedom of expression of the students, but the regents have the right to interpret their own rules." He promised to abide by the decision.[141]

A Matter of Gratuity

Within a few days after this incident, Palma decided to find out from the Board of Regents whether he fell under the gratuity law or not, and if the decision was in the affirmative, he thought he would ask that he be retired. He expressed the feeling that ten years was long enough in any public office and the University needed new blood. The Board ruled that voluntary resignation did not entitle one to gratuity. The Secretary of Justice, Quirico Abeto, whose opinion was sought, also ruled that Palma could not claim gratuity as President because the University had not been reorganized by the government. His salary was merely reduced under the provisions of the Appropriation Act of 1934. Besides, the University was an independent institution, governed by a charter, and so Palma was not an insular government employee subject to the gratuity law.[142]

A group of faculty members, which included the Dean of Women, Ursula Uichanco, Deans Francisco Benitez (Education), Fernando Calderon (Medicine), Maximo Kalaw, Bienvenido Gonzalez (Agriculture), Arthur Fischer (Forestry) and even Jorge Bocobo, initiated action to retain Palma one more year "because for him to leave at the end of the year means the breaking into pieces of the administration." A faculty resolution was presented to Palma by a committee composed of Fernando Calderon, Maximo

Kalaw, and Edward Hyde (Engineering), asking Palma to reconsider his decision to retire.[143]

The *Collegian* also asked Palma to reconsider his resignation – "the University needs Rafael Palma." Articulating on the reasons for Palma's decision to resign, it said:

> ... We cannot understand why political considerations should enter in this matter. It cannot be argued that because the President of an institution, which is itself non-partisan, differs in political opinion with the controlling party leaders in the Legislature, such President should leave his office as having lost the confidence of the Legislature. Neither can it be rationally said that if such President desists from resigning because he firmly believes that the institution still needs his services, that Legislature would have the license to embarrass the institution in a thousand ways just out of spite for its President.

Such unwarranted vindictiveness cannot be justified by any moral or legal reasons, the editorial continued. Certainly the Legislature or any of its leaders could not be capable of such "recriminatory tactics."[144]

Majority in the University Council

A special meeting of the University Council on November 4 adopted a resolution – the first part of the resolution expressed the appreciation of the faculty for Palma's services (and little opposition was encountered with this one); the second part asked Palma to continue as President (but this was strongly objected to). The resolution was sponsored by Melquiades Gamboa (Law) and was attacked by Dr. Antonio Sison (Medicine). Supporters of the resolution were stunned to find the vote in the University Council not unanimous – 40 for the resolution of retention; 32 against. Those opposed claimed they were caught unaware and if all those who were with them had been present, they claimed that the resolution would have been turned down.[145]

Palma's resignation was accepted by the Board of Regents on November 8 (the motion to accept Palma's resignation was made by Regent Romulo) and Dr. Fernando Calderon, senior dean, was appointed Acting President. The Board turned down Palma's application to retire under the gratuity law but voted him an honorarium of ₱16,000 in recognition of his long service (later reduced to ₱14,000) and ₱8,000 in accrued leave (later reduced to ₱7,000).[146]

The *Tribune* called the disallowance of gratuity to Palma an injustice and expressed regret that he had been singled out for discrimination. Stating that cases could be cited of professors of the University who had been retired under the gratuity law, it sarcastically pointed out that such professors had not consistently and openly advocated the acceptance of the Hare-Hawes-Cutting Act. "It is President Palma's misfortune that the sincerity of his advocacy of the law has antagonized those in control of the government" noted the *Tribune* editorial. "A sense of justice, which is higher than the law, has collapsed. The law is sovereign to perpetuate an injustice."[147]

Integrity in the Public Service

Editorial comments on Palma's resignation seemed sympathetic to the move taken by the UP President to leave the University so that the institution would not suffer the fury of the Legislature. They generally paid tribute to the courage and integrity and independence of mind displayed by Palma in all the years of his public service.[148] There was, however, one bitter editorial from *Mabuhay,* which pointed out that the resignation was the only honorable thing for Palma to have done since the Board of Regents had, in so many ways, shown its impatience with him for having injected politics into "the otherwise unpolluted portals of the highest institution of learning in the country." Palma had failed to give "inspiration" to the Filipino youth in their search for the truth and for knowledge. And yet, it said, Palma was not going to leave the University empty-handed, as the University had generously given him an honorarium.[149]

The *Philippines Herald,* while praising Palma for his administrative ability, insisted that the next president of the University must, first and above all, be an educator, "who must remain completely divorced from the political imbroglios of his day and whose attitude towards political affairs must be purely academic." Palma was chosen as UP President not because of distinguished scholarship, it said, but because he was a notable political figure. "It is his passion for such a (political) career that has made it impossible for him to remain aloof from the confusion of partisan politics; in short he has failed to adopt the purely academic attitude on the political issues of his day." Palma, by "losing his temper," was "irredeemably lost to the cause of higher education."

Lamenting the fact that the University campus had, for a time, resembled a political camp surcharged with partisan animosity, the *Herald* intoned that such a thing must never happen again. The University must recede into its place of pure study.

> A University will not prosper in the vortex of turmoils, but it can watch the turmoils from a detached vantage point for the study of human nature and human relations. The sense of academic freedom must never be sacrificed, or even risked, in the interminable clashes of mundane interests.[150]

An Act of Self-Sacrifice

Probably the most touching tribute to Palma was written by Librado D. Cayco (Bureau of Education), published in the *Tribune*. To him Palma's resignation acquired the symbolism of both a "surrender and a revolt."

> A surrender because with his resignation is a sacrifice of self and whatever dignity is attached to his office for the welfare of some six or seven thousand students, who, Mr. Palma fears, might be done harm in the form of reduced appropriations for their institution by unthinking and unscrupulous lawmakers (to whom he has become a *persona non grata*) should he prolong his connection with the state university; a revolt because that resignation is at bottom an expression of extreme dissatisfaction with, and withal a roaring challenge against, the existing order of things.

He took to task Palma's "conscienceless detractors," "organs of special interests" with their full-page editorials, and apologists for Quezon, who had railed against Palma. "To attempt to belittle the man whose character is more 'sound and strong and true' than the belittlers', and whose record of public service is one anyone can be proud of, is next to useless; one could do better perhaps by railing at granite or barking at the moon. For Rafael Palma is Rafael Palma while 'debunkers' are only 'debunkers'."[151]

Farewell Messages

On December 16, Palma gave a farewell address to the University Council explaining why he was leaving the University presidency. He said:

> Circumstances stronger than your will and mine have determined this decision, in which the very interest and welfare of the University itself is not all foreign. I am fully convinced that my resignation from the University at this time will bring a permanent good and forestall a great harm. It will certainly restore to the University that atmosphere of quiet and moral tranquility so necessary in carrying out its mission towards the youth of the land, and will prevent the University from being in the future an object of violent and repressive measures such as those which have threatened the institution this year.

Thus, because his presence had become "unbearable" to some men in power, there was no other alternative left but for him to quit the University. In this way, he would free the University from the "pernicious influence of partisan politics." He then reminded his audience that during his administration of the affairs of the University, his primary concern had been to keep the University away from political interference. "Not only did I not choose to play politics inside the University but [I] also tried in every instance to prevent its influence from the outside."[152]

Palma delivered his farewell address to the student body on December 19. In a speech at times verging on the emotional, Palma spoke with the "counsel of a kind father to his dear children whom he does not expect to see again." To the students, he advised that: first, they should be guided by certain fundamental principles and rules of conduct accepted and observed by the community in which they lived; second, they should take interest in observing and studying the social conditions of their country and of their times and have definite ideas or plans for the cure of any social evil they may find; and third, they should be sincere and courageous in expressing their ideas and convictions and be ready to suffer whatever consequence may come in the exercise of their rights. Touching on politics, Palma said: "I cannot understand why in a country like ours, public questions of national import cannot rightfully be subjects of public discussion by those belonging to the brotherhood of higher education. Nothing that pertains to politics is unclean. Politics in its truest sense is the consecration of the service of one individual to the good of the commonwealth."

Rationale of a Resolute Man

Once again explaining why he spoke out on the Hare-Hawes-Cutting Act, he said:

> . . . Every citizen, whatever may be his position or his affiliation, has the right to publicly express his opinion on how the government is managed or how it should be managed. To deny a citizen this right is both an abuse and a usurpation. Not only every citizen, however humble he may be, has the right to publicly express his opinion in connection with the management of public affairs but also in connection with other questions of national importance. The freedom of thought and of expression is the cornerstone of a democracy.
>
> . . . Our country needs examples of courage and civic spirit in order to check the abuses of power, to expose the whims and caprices of the rulers . . . We would be unworthy of freedom to which we aspire if we do not begin to develop independent individuals who know how to think for themselves instead of being the mere echo or shadow of others; if we would only be used to apply harsh words to the Americans and not to our countrymen when they abuse and trample upon the rights of the citizens. . . .[153]

It seemed appropriate that Palma would leave the best sentiments of his mind and heart to the University youth, who received his words at times with tearful emotion, at times with thundering applause. Palma himself waxed emotional, as he told his audience how much he would miss the familiar scenes he had seen for many years around the University – "the radiant faces of youth on the campus, the beam of hope and cheerfulness in their eyes, the spirit and enthusiasm of military parades, the noise and laughter in athletic competitions, the marching of feet in the corridors and halls when the students go to, and come from classrooms and laboratories." And then he wished the University well.[154]

Palma said goodbye to the University and his friends on December 29.[155]

Calderon as Acting President

Dr. Fernando Calderon assumed his duties as acting President on January 2, 1934. He appointed Dr. Arturo Garcia as acting Dean of the College of Medicine. In his inaugural address, Calderon laid down two policies: first, he would oppose tuition fee increases; and second, insofar as political activities were concerned, he wished the students would abstain from all political activity which might tend to endanger the University's welfare in general and the University budget in particular. He may not have specifically said so, but Calderon clearly wanted to steer away from the controversies that involved his predecessor. At the same time, in order to run the University with the limited funds at its disposal (the Board of Regents had approved a greatly reduced budget for 1934-1935), a serious inquiry of the University was initiated – of its finances, activities, enrolment, personnel, and curriculum – in the hope of effecting economies.[156]

The appropriation of the University had suffered a proportional reduction as a result of the economies effected in the government. But the reduction was also made because of the conviction that the institution was top-heavy – there were 6,000 students against 1,013 positions of faculty and administrative staff. It was considered top-heavy also in other ways. Many courses were being offered with inadequate number of students in attendance. Some schools and departments were also oversized. The University was also faulted for failing to make any re-adjustments in its operations, despite reduced outlay, except to increase the tuition fees, which, of course, placed the burden on the students.[157]

The revamp body, created by the Board of Regents, would among other things look into the possibility of making the University self-supporting, in order to minimize its dependence on the Legislature. Suggestions were made for the acquisition of mining claims, timber lands, or city lots as sources of income for the University.[158]

Caution on Political Involvement

Discussion on the Hare-Hawes-Cutting Act continued in the University for a while longer even after the departure of Palma. Both the *Collegian* and a new organization called "Young Philippines" continued their discourse on the independence act.[159] In an attempt to explain the charge of "intellectual repression in the University" in connection with the *Collegian* publication and a convocation sponsored by the "Young Philippines," Calderon, in very definite terms, declared his views on politics in the University.

The Board of Regents, he said, had laid down the rule, since August 23, 1912, that students should not engage in any pursuits that might tend to involve the University in political discussion and forbade student publications from publishing articles of a political nature. This ruling was clarified in another Board of Regents resolution in September 1933. In addition, the University Council had prohibited the *Collegian* from publishing any matter "likely to injure the good name of the University; to lower the morale of the students at the expense of another faction, the student body or the whole University; or to promote dissension among students, or between students and the faculty." He then reminded the "Young Philippines" that the University could not allow the weekly convocation to be converted into an instrument for political propaganda tending to divide the student body or turning the University into an arena for various political parties.

Calderon emphasized that his administration desired "to direct the affairs of the University along educational lines, free from partisan controversies, in order to cleanse the campus of the noxious atmosphere of partisanship." He was mindful, he said, "of the fact (which many seem to have forgotten, deliberately or otherwise) that the University . . . is supported by all the taxpayers of this country, who have a right to demand that it shall pursue its educational objectives without disturbance from the clamor of partisans. As a result of allowing partisan discussions to reign on the campus of the University, much of the time which should have been devoted by the students to their assigned duties has been frittered away in endless discussions that developed heat rather than light."[160]

Discussions on the Hare-Hawes-Cutting Act ceased after Quezon secured the Tydings-McDuffie Law in March 1934, and the independence issue was finally settled.

A LEGACY OF UNYIELDING CONVICTION AND ALLEGIANCE TO THE UNFETTERED MIND

RAFAEL Palma was President of the University for almost ten years, during which time his determination and single-mindedness of purpose were instrumental in making the University the premier university in the country. He had a lofty view of the mission of the University not only in the development of higher education but also in the development of the national community, and he directed the University to these ends.

A real university, as Palma envisioned it, should be committed to the ideal of "freedom of the mind" and so he insisted that the University should provide the atmosphere for academic freedom. The University must be protected from external interference which would inevitably stifle its spirit.

"The atmosphere of freedom in a university," he said, "conduces to the healthy growth of science and the determined search of the truth in God, man, and things."[161] He emphasized further: "The conservation, diffusion, and advancement of science and culture give the raison d'etre of every university. So that the supreme ends of science may be freely sought and the zeal for scrutiny and for truth-telling may be secured against all molestation and persecution, the University is in dire need . . . of that state of independence and freedom which will lift it above petty influence and mercenary ends."[162] For "unlike the institutions of religion and politics, the University is open-minded, willing to hear and discuss and improve. It encourages criticism, deprecates bigotry, and leads in clarity. In the last analysis, the university, as the best training camp for intelligent citizenship, becomes the basis of democracy, which it interprets in terms of individuals with awakened conscience, sharpened intellect, and exalted ideals; with healthy bodies, refined tastes, and strengthened will for the service of the nation."[163]

Essence of Academic Freedom

At the height of the controversy over the Hare-Hawes-Cutting Act, Palma delivered this address on academic freedom:

> The events of the past few months have clearly shown the imperative necessity of the principle that the University should be absolutely free and independent from politics. Like all instrumentalities of civilization, the University has duties and responsibilities towards the people. Its chief work is the search for truth and the advancement of knowledge, and these activities cannot be accomplished except in an atmosphere free from political subjection and dictation. These objectives are as essential to the development of man and society as the objectives of the government and the church. The state being the dispenser and arbitrator for all the other instrumentalities essential to the life of society should be the first one to see to it that politics does not interfere with the University.

Surely University professors had the right to air their views on important national issues for "academic freedom comprises not only the freedom of inquiry into, and exposition of, the field of study in the classroom but also that which puts in writing and speech, matters beyond the classroom." Thus:

> Our academic community is so precious that no sacrifice is too big to preserve it pure and inviolate. If each professor cannot feel safe to proclaim what he considers the truth, because of fear of persecution or displeasure of the men in power, then truth would not come out from his lips or will be totally disfigured. And when that time comes, the University would be nothing more than a mere political agency of men in power instead of becoming the citadel of learning, unafraid and forward-looking in its sacred duty to reveal the naked truth as it is in its service to the State.[164]

Palma took seriously the responsibility the University, as the State University, assumed toward nation-building, conscious of the pervasive influence education exerts over the future and destiny of a nation. Like previous presidents, Palma emphasized the University's nationalistic goals, but the most explicit description of the role of the University in nation-building occurred during his term as President of the University. In all his addresses, always in eloquent prose,[165] Palma never swayed from his view of the role the University must play in the meaningful development and growth of the nation, fulfilling "the dream and the vision of its founders and organizers . . . of making this institution a trysting place of civilized and civilizing elements in the Far East and of lifting to a high level the spirit and fact of Filipino nationality."[166]

"The existence of the University is so linked with the future of the nation that the institution should not rest content with turning out finished products. . . .A university is not a mere settlement of scholars; it should join intimately in the social life that surrounds it, so as to be able to understand fully the underlying meaning of its time." Thus the University would mould not only the character of each citizen, but also the national character.[167] The University, he explained, would supply the nation with "guidance, leadership, expert knowledge, trained skill, and personal service." It is the institution that would link the past and the future of a nation's history, for while it would be dedicated to the furtherance and increase of human knowledge, it would also conserve and invigorate the traditions of the nation.[168]

Filipinism and Nationalism

Since the University, in the ultimate analysis, was committed unremittingly to the Filipino people, Palma made Filipinism and nationality the cornerstone of his administration. This was not unexpected for Palma assumed the leadership of the University at a time of heightened nationalism. Palma had lived through the Revolution against Spain and the War with the United States, and he took over as acting President of the University in October 1923, shortly after the Cabinet Crisis which marked the open confrontation between Governor General Leonard Wood and the Filipino leaders led by Manuel Quezon and Manuel Roxas.

Leonard Wood's tenure as Governor General was a stormy period, marked by deadlock and political strife, with the Filipino leaders led by Quezon openly challenging the authority of the American representative in Manila. The contest was naturally hopelessly enmeshed in the consuming emotional issue of independence. There was conducted an active campaign for independence during this period, culminating in the passage of an independence law in 1934.

Under the circumstances, it was not surprising that Palma should issue the call for Filipinos to realize their capacity to run their affairs and affirm their right to independence through the instrumentality of higher education provided by the University. Thus he said:

> ... the essence and reality of Filipinism will be the combination of the best and the greatest in the Orient with the greatest and the best in the Occident of the Latin and the Anglo-Saxon.
>
> Such should be the national character which the University ought to mould. Our national character should be no blind adaption of exotic theories to local problems, but an eclectic selection and sifting of the best from the worst; not an attitude of jaunty unconcerns and rude contempt of time-honored tradition and of indiscriminate, unconditional adherence to what is new-fangled and novel, but an attitude of mental equipoise and activity which will enable the race to assimilate all that tends to make our people sturdy and secure against any enervating forces within and without the country.[169]

Palma's nationalism was "no chauvinistic policy for the country." Love of country, he advised, should be "rational, intelligent, and not merely sentimental." He emphasized the need to study preferentially our own things, not only for the sake of keeping intact our love for what is our own and of rousing and strengthening a feeling of patriotic pride, but also for the sake of encouraging original thinking and of asserting our individuality in the realm of mind. A University exists for the sake of science and knowledge, and so instead of chauvinism, he preferred a "cosmopolitanism" which, however, should not dazzle the institution "into an attitude of blindness to local things of great goodness and surpassing beauty, which are easily of equal value with similar things elsewhere in the world."[170]

He looked forward to the growth of the University and had no use for an attitude "hedging us away from all the rest of the world." He declared that a university which slumbers on the same unchanging curricula and the same time-honored methods of teaching is as dangerous and harmful as a university which constantly alters its rules and policies, which seems to drift by chance. Hence, as the leader of the University he resolved to stand for "a University that always moves forward, never backward; that looks ahead, never behind; that is to win distinction and respect by its foresight, not contumely and distrust by reason of its hindsight; that will grasp opportunity always by the forelock, and will never mumble vain might-have-beens."

He said that in the final analysis, our entire educational program should address itself to this clear-cut question: "Is this study, this method, this point of view, of unquestioned and positive benefit to the Filipino people?" Such was Palma's commitment as a Filipino.

Adherence to Virtue and Honor

Palma left the University an enduring legacy of his convictions, reflected in his deep sense of liberalism, an untarnished essence of love of country and a total commitment as a Filipino, a tradition of high civic virtue and honest public service few could match, and the highest standards of academic freedom. These have become cherished values in the University. Perhaps the words of Palma's daughter seem appropriate to express Palma's convictions: "All he wanted . . . was that . . . each member contribute to human achievement in his own unique way so that the world may be a little better than when he came in. If he had one obsessive dream, it was for the whole family of Filipinos – that they keep a tight grip on their virtues . . . as if he held a secret fear that his country will one day run out of virtues."[172]

It is well to remember Palma's vision of what the University of the Philippines should mean for those who have chosen to be a part of its tradition:

> Let us keep keen faith in this University. Let us put forth every effort to extend its usefulness to all points in the Philippines, even to the furthermost. Let us use every lawful means to make this University the worthy custodian of the best patrimony we have inherited from our forebears so that it will continue as the custodian of the best that we of the present and of the future will be able to learn and assimilate from other people for the benefit of our countrymen. Lastly, let us always strive to review and to administer the affairs of this University, not as a bureaucratic office, but as a Republic of Science and Letters "where the lonely scholar feels himself least lonely, most positively furthered, and most richly fed."[173]

V

Bocobo Fosters a Vibrant Nationalism (1934-1939)

Reassertion of Filipino Values as an Underlying Concept of Academic Life

by Bonifacio S. Salamanca

Bocobo Fosters a Vibrant Nationalism

ON September 1, 1934, Jorge C. Bocobo took his oath as fifth President of the University of the Philippines. Swearing him into office was Supreme Court Justice George A. Malcolm who had a hand in recruiting Bocobo to the faculty in the early years of the College of Law. Bocobo's ascent to the presidency was decided upon by the Board of Regents which chose him from among such "strong" contenders as Deans Conrado and Francisco Benitez, Bienvenido M. Gonzalez and Maximo Kalaw, Dr. Arturo Garcia, Dr. Vidal A. Tan and the Hon. Jorge B. Vargas,[1]* after an eight-month hiatus immediately following the "forced retirement of President Palma effective 31 December 1933, as a result of the Hare-Hawes-Cutting Act controversy. . . .[2] It was a fitting reward for his 23 years of continuous service to the university, the last 17 years of which he held the deanship of the College of Law. He was almost 48 when elected President.

Bocobo's elevation to the premier academic and administrative post in the University marked the first time an "insider" had made a vertical ascent, not a lateral entry, as UP president, thus setting a tradition which would not be broken until almost 30 years later when Carlos P. Romulo became president, followed by yet another "outsider," Salvador P. Lopez (1969-1975).[3] Bocobo was the first of two deans of the College of Law to become the university's president—Vicente G. Sinco (1958-1962) was the other one—and one of five legal luminaries among 14 presidents so far. Bocobo would also be the first UP President to be appointed Secretary of Public Instruction (or Education), thus becoming Chairman of the Board of Regents and with opportunity as such to observe at close range his immediate successor's performance. Bocobo, it turned out, would be the last non-alumnus to be catapulted to the UP presidency during its first 75 years; after him, only alumni, whether "insiders" or "outsiders," would be chosen president.

Foretaste of Being President

It can perhaps be said that, cumulatively, Bocobo was more prepared than his predecessors, or even his successors, for the presidency of the state

* Footnote references are compiled in the NOTES section found at the end of this book.

university. This stemmed not only from long and sustained service in the University but also from his having served as Acting President for almost ten months when President Palma went on a world tour in 1927. Of that not-too-brief stint, President Palma had approvingly written:

> The temporary administration of Dean Jorge Bocobo... was fruitful of many constructive measures, especially those touching student life. He has minimized the number of student dances... [and] encouraged more literary-musical programs; attempted to improve student living conditions in dormitories and other boarding houses, with particular reference to their diet and medical service; inculcated civic leadership in the student constituency; and in general promoted a saner orientation of the student life. He has also displayed interest in university administration, and his influence has extended to all spheres of university life. His suggestions concerning the future progress of the University are worthy of serious consideration.[4]

This was a fitting supplement and endorsement of an earlier appreciation of Bocobo's Acting Presidency by the University's Board of Regents a month before Palma's return. Indeed, although six more years were to pass before he became president in his own right, any discussion of the Bocobo stewardship of the university would be incomplete without looking back, where appropriate, to that temporary presidency.

But first, a glance at Bocobo's early life preparation for service and pre-presidency career.

Family Background

According to his daughter-biographer, Bocobo was born on October 19, 1886 to a "middle class" Ilocano family from Gerona, Tarlac, which owned lands "though not extensively." His father was a self-educated strict disciplinarian who would later become a *delegado de policia* under the Revolutionary Government and during the succeeding American regime would successively serve as municipal secretary, auxiliary justice of the peace and municipal president.[5] It is probably more accurate to say that Bocobo's parents belonged to the landowning provincial gentry, or aristocracy, that narrow base of political power at the local level, rather than to the "middle class."

Like most children of his time, Bocobo learned his ABC from his parents, particularly his mother, Rita T. Cleofas, also from Gerona. His formal schooling during the remaining years of Spanish rule had been mainly with a privately run school of about 50 pupils, attending the local public schools only irregularly or at intervals, because his father felt that they taught nothing there but religion.

With the coming of the Americans, again like many a provincial schoolboy, Bocobo initially studied under an American soldier and later under one or two of the Thomasites. In 1901-1903, he attended the public schools in Tarlac, Tarlac, including the provincial high school. Soon he moved to Manila, enrolling at the Teachers Normal Institute then on Padre Faura; it was while studying here that he was selected as one of the first 100 government *pensionados* to the United States.[6] Bocobo's precocity as a pupil, spotted a couple of years earlier by Dr. Frank R. White, Tarlac's first American division superintendent of schools, had reaped for Bocobo a singular distinction which was to be the turning point in his life. For it is not farfetched to assume that Bocobo would have rejoined the teaching staff of the Tarlac public schools, where he had also served as a "barrio teacher from 1901 to 1903," before proceeding to Manila.[7] As it were, because of his having been a *pensionado*—and with the first batch at that—he became a lawyer instead.

Start of an Illustrious Career

Returning to the Philippines in 1907 with an impressive academic and extra-curricular record at Indiana Law School, Bocobo found employment in the Law division of the now defunct Executive Bureau. Dr. White again helped him here. He remained in this job for the next four years, perhaps unhappy for the most part because his salary was not only much less what an American with comparable responsibilities and credentials received, but also because the government retained one-half of it, no doubt in payment for his state-subsidized studies in the United States. Perhaps, Bocobo was also beginning to feel the boredom of doing the same thing for four years.

It was, therefore, probably a welcome change for him to join the faculty of the newly organized UP College of Law as lecturer in 1911 under Dean George A. Malcolm. Appointed to full-time status as instructor a year later, he rose spectacularly to the rank of full professor within five years. That was in 1917, the same year he was also appointed dean of the College of Law, a position which he relinquished only when he was elected president of the University.[8]

A retired university professor, on the occasion of the Diamond Jubilee of the University, gave this flattering appraisal of Bocobo as College of Law dean: "Bocobo's stewardship of the College of Law from 1917 to 1934 is a brilliant era in the history of the College, more distinctive than his subsequent stewardship of the University of the Philippines (1934-1939). . . ."[9]

This, in spite of his reputation, specially among the law students, of being a "gloomy dean"—perhaps, because he preferred intellectual and cultural activities to dances and other frivolous diversions.[10]

In 1923, President Benton resigned as President of the University after two turbulent years. Bocobo was rumored to be interested in the position—and may very well have manifested his desire as such. But probably because he was too young for the job—he was only 37 then—the Board passed him over and chose the towering statesman Rafael Palma instead. But in 1927 up to 1928, he was given the opportunity to be at the helm of the University, thus enabling him to broaden his academic and administrative perspectives and enhance his stature. No doubt, this acting presidency helped convince the Board of Regents to select Bocobo on August 11, 1934 to succeed Palma.

CHARTING A COURSE FOR THE PRESIDENCY ILLUMINED BY NATIONALISM

THERE were, undoubtedly, other reasons why Bocobo was eventually chosen president after an almost eight-month search by the Board of Regents. Carlos P. Romulo, then one of the Alumni Regents and a fellow Tarlaqueño who would himself become UP President in 1962-1968, enumerated the reasons why he had nominated Bocobo;[11] we may assume that his colleagues in the Board of Regents agreed with him since the election procedure called for balloting to be "preceded by a full discussion of the merits and qualifications of the candidates."[12] Reason No. 2 probably clinched Bocobo's "unanimous" election.[13]

> President Bocobo is the only one among the candidates who has been honored, not only in the United States, but also in Europe for his scholarship. The University of Southern California has conferred upon him the honorary degree of Doctor of Laws, and the Learned Society in Spain, called Real Academia de Jurisprudencia y Legislacion, has elected him an honorary member in recognition of his mastery of the Spanish civil law.

Prof. Leopoldo Y. Yabes, in his controversial manuscript on the College of Law, has recorded the speculation, which may or may not have any basis, that Bocobo's having sided with Quezon's Group ("Antis") in the celebrated Hare-Hawes-Cutting Act controversy, "was believed to have had considerable weight in favor of his election."[14]

Notwithstanding any possible "political pull" which may have been exerted, the reactions to the Bocobo choice were generally very favorable, although some were guarded or cautious. The *Philippines Herald* issued an *extra* upon Bocobo's election and made an editorial comment, a portion of which reads:

> Let us rejoice that a man of his integrity has been chosen to direct the affairs of our highest center of learning. Let us be thankful that one so righteous will guide the views of our youth. The university of the state needs a man like him.... With the destinies of our higher education in his keeping, our common men can look forward to the University of the Philippines without a feeling of betrayal.[15]

Accolade for the New President

According to the *Philippine Collegian*, "... the news that Dean Bocobo has been chosen president of the State Institution spread like wildfire.... Everybody was happy. Cheers of Mabuhay! echoed and re-echoed among the magnificent buildings of the [University]. *Mabuhay si President Bocobo* was everywhere."[16] The *Collegian* said in its editorial:

> As he has served in the capacity of acting head of the University when ex-President Palma was abroad... much can be expected of the new President. His long stint in the University has made him aware of its many and difficult problems, and this should have pointed out to him the resources to draw from in meeting these problems....
>
> In the past, he has always been criticized as a "straight-laced" moralist and idealist whose head is high up in the clouds—and his ascendancy to the new post should be a splendid opportunity to show the broadest broadmindedness he can muster.
>
> The student body of the University expects of the new President an unparallelled broadmindedness.

It might be worth quoting a *Collegian* contributor at the time Bocobo was elected president, specially since what he thought of President Bocobo then was in sharp contrast to what he would write almost 50 years later. Then student Leopoldo Y. Yabes started by praising Bocobo as a great man for having the courage of his beliefs. "It is precisely his courage, his irrepressibleness of spirit," he continued, "that has made the new President of the University a much criticized, a much misunderstood man. It is this courage to do what he honestly believes that spurs him on to do things even in the teeth of disapproval." He concluded with the feeling that Bocobo's "rise to the presidency of this University is most fortunate for the youth of the land, in whose welfare he has always been interested."[17]

The *Tribune* was less effusive. After wishing him success as the new head of the University, it further editorialized: "His [Bocobo's] is the opportunity to serve his people greatly. It will be upon the fact of what that opportunity will do to him which will determine the greater fact of what he can do for the university constituency and for that larger constituency which is his own people."[18]

In more recent times, a well-known UP alumna who had taught with eminence as a faculty member of the Department of English and Comparative Literature, described the essence of the Bocobo Presidency: "The two distinct flavors of President Jorge Bocobo's administration were nationalism and morality."[19]

Promotion of Nationalism

One is not surprised that nationalism should be a hallmark of Bocobo's presidency. He was born and spent his early childhood during the most tempestuous period in our history, a generation of nationalism and revolution against Spain, and of war in defense of a new-born nation against America. It was impossible for Bocobo not to have been affected by the currents and emotions generated during the first decades of the twentieth century. His espousal of freedom for our people even as he was enjoying as a student the hospitality of America probably came naturally.[20] Thus, his oratorical piece in which he "fervently pleaded for Philippine independence," which won for him the second prize at an annual oratorical contest at Indiana University:[21]

> Here is a people who for thirty years have struggled for liberty. Here is a race who have shed blood, suffered desolation and national calamities in striving for the coveted prize of independence. Are you [i.e., the American people] going to end this struggle so as to make every drop of blood shed, every life sacrificed, every mother's heart broken, every friend's sigh, and every dying soldier's last wish all in vain and fruitless?

This was in 1907. On December 31 of the same year, during the literary-musical program at the Manila Grand Opera House in honor of Dr. Jose P. Rizal, our national hero, Bocobo delivered a passionate speech advocating Philippine independence and exhorting his countrymen to "prepare themselves economically" as a means toward that goal. It is said that Governor General James F. Smith, who was among the guests, was provoked and hurriedly left after Bocobo's speech, in spite of the fact that the program was only half-through. The following day, he wrote Bocobo's superior, Executive Secretary Frank Carpenter, "that if Bocobo wanted to agitate for independence," he was free to do so but not as a government employee.[22]

There would be many other occasions when Bocobo dwelt on Philippine nationalism, as the campaign for independence from America gathered momentum. The national leadership did not forget Bocobo's individual campaign for our freedom. So, he would be tapped as a technical adviser to three independence missions to the United States: the First Parliamentary Mission in 1919, then the Second Parliamentary Mission in 1922, and the Roxas Special Mission in 1923-1924.[23] During one of these when the mission ran out of funds, Bocobo even offered to serve without remuneration, provided his room and board were paid for.[24]

Vagaries of Independence

The first years of the 1930s turned out to be the moment of golden opportunity, as it were, in the Filipinos' campaign for independence from the United States. The Great Depression had created advocates of Philippine independence from among powerful and influential interest groups, where before there were hardly any except the noisy but cloutless idealists. Filipino nationalists suddenly were joined by American allies—but for the wrong motives and reasons.[25] The prospects of an independence law being enacted by the American government were bright, indeed.

Ironically, it was at this point that the Filipino leadership—the political and intellectual elite of the country—began to entertain serious doubts as to the wisdom of obtaining independence abruptly or too soon. They must have known or felt that after an otherwise benign, if not also benevolent, American regime for more than 30 years—or maybe because of such a regime[26]—the Filipinos had yet to be firmly welded into a nation; that what had been behind their visible display of unity in the past had been the issue of independence. But that issue would soon be a thing of the past—no longer would it be possible to rally the people behind the national leadership in the campaign for independence, because there would be no more campaigning to do.

Indeed, it can even be argued that the rhetoric of independence, which was once such a powerful catalyst for unity during the first 15 years of American colonial rule, had begun to lose its mystique and potency after 1916. In that year, through the Jones Law, the United States conceded to the Filipino nationalist leaders that it would grant Philippine independence upon the establishment of a "stable government" here. The magic of *independencia* would be revived during and after the tenure of Governor General Leonard Wood in the 1920s, if only to ensure that this stern American proconsul did not totally undo the gains of Philippine autonomy and to remind his successors that the Filipinos wanted to govern themselves with only a minimum dose of American "guidance."[27]

Of course, if American governors-general or presidents did not get the message, then the alternative was independence. But there was the feeling that the majority of the Filipinos seemed contented with the Jones Law dispensation, if not also the way the country was being governed even under Wood and his successors, specially since no less than General Emilio Aguinaldo had sided with Wood during the so-called "Cabinet Crisis."[28]

By the 1930s, therefore, it must have dawned upon the Filipino leaders that as a form of group loyalty, nationalism among the vast majority of our people was rather tenuous and there was a need, an urgent need, to generate a stronger bond of unity, to anchor Filipino nationalism on more solid foundations than a flickering "discipline" for independence campaigns. "The nation in the making," to use Prof. Peter W. Stanley's apt phrase,[29] should be a nation made before the formal assumption of independence.

But how?

The Filipino leadership, specially of Quezon and Roxas, saw in a Filipino code of ethics a possible hope. Roxas was ahead, time-wise, with the "Decalogue" of *Ang Bagong Katipunan* (1931);[30] Quezon had his Code of Citizenship of the Commonwealth of the Philippines, which became a required reading at all levels of the educational system starting the second semester of 1939-1940.[31]

There is only circumstantial evidence of Bocobo's role in the formulation of the Decalogue of *Ang Bagong Katipunan* based on his close association with Roxas, but in the case of the Quezonian Code, we are certain that he had a hand in formulating some of its 16 precepts, since he was a member of the committee Quezon had appointed to frame the ethical code.[32] It might even be suggested that the choice of "16 principles" was his, because upon Bocobo's election in August 1934, he had outlined a 16-point program for his presidency.[33]

Need for National Discipline

Bocobo's idea of nationalism while President of the University included not only love of country or patriotism and preservation of the cultural heritage, but also duty, discipline and sacrifice for the national welfare, the national security and happiness. At his inauguration in December 1934, he said it was the mission of the State University, for that matter of all universities in the Philippines, during the years of the Commonwealth and later, years that will indeed "try men's souls," to prepare or invest the youth with the "ardor of courage and abnegation" and to imbue the students "with a deepening sense of stewardship for the [Filipino] people."[34] He voiced similar sentiments in June 1936, before the first year of the Commonwealth of the Philippines was over: University education, he said, "must above all deepen the sense of consecration, intensify the love of country and harden the moral make-up of the citizens of tomorrow."[35]

At the same forum a year later, Bocobo again dwelt on the theme that the University, which is "supported by the taxes of the people," should increasingly foster love of country or patriotism, "a cementing and unifying principle."[36] He identified three attitudes of the mind as essential to the "proper cultivation of patriotism," these being:

1. Firm and sincere belief in "our country's high destiny," to sustain which we would need to remember the heroism of our heroes from Lapulapu to Diego Silang, Burgos to Del Pilar, Rizal and others, and to "ponder on our peaceful but courageous struggle for freedom during the last three decades";

2. Solid character, by which Bocobo meant with Dr. Rizal, that the lives of the youth "should be pure and spotless to be worthy sacrifices at the altar of our country"; and

3. Reverence for, fostering and preservation of, our "racial heritage," which includes "love of home and family, courtesy, respect for our elders, courage in the face of adversity, and the beauty of our folk songs and dances."

National unity and discipline, Bocobo regarded as prerequisites to nation-building and to the national welfare. His contention: "No long-term program, for economic development, of national defense, or social uplift, can be carried out, unless there is an all-pervading spirit of national solidarity and national discipline."[37]

Bocobo was obviously aware that the Filipino people of his day were sorely wanting in these desirable attributes. How to mold them, specially the youth destined to be the stewards of a future independent Philippines, was a tremendous task which could not be ignored. He looked beyond the country's horizon and was fascinated by "what the Germans of today [i.e., Hitler's time] call the heroic interpretation of life," which he wanted his countrymen to emulate. As a matter of fact he had openly "expressed admiration for Mussolini and Hitler while still a dean," claims Professor Yabes, who goes on to conclude that Bocobo's "nationalism was closer to the Mussolini-Hitler-Franco type than the liberal democratic type one finds in the liberal democracies."[38]

No "Fascistic" Implications

This bold assertion calls for an explanation and clarification, or at least qualification, specially since Bocobo, who served as justice of the Supreme Court under the Japanese Military Administration and the Japanese-sponsored Republic which followed it, was arrested by American military authorities in 1945, and thus the inference could very well be that other than his having "collaborated" with the Japanese, it was because of his alleged "fascistic" leanings.[39]

It is my view that what Bocobo admired was the national discipline and the upsurge of patriotic fervor and national pride that were very visible among the Italians, Germans and Spaniards under Mussolini, Hitler and Franco, respectively. I do not think such an admiration included the core, or content, of their totalitarian ideology; it is even more farfetched to assume that he desired its implantation here. But the discipline which these leaders were generating among their peoples—this Bocobo wanted very much for his own people, as they prepared to rendezvous with their destiny as an independent entity, again, as they traveled the semi-sovereign threshold of the Commonwealth to the dignity and status of a full sovereign.

As I have said elsewhere: "So the intent here was not really to borrow the fascistic ideology of Hitler, Mussolini, and Franco, but rather an admiration for the way these leaders were disciplining their people."[40] A strong sense of nationalism prevailing among our people in his time would have made Bocobo's admiration for the discipline under the totalitarian states unnecessary; but apparently, Bocobo and some of his colleagues in the nationalist movement realized that this was not the case, hence the need to "instill nationalism among our people."

This is not an *apologia* for Bocobo, just one individual's attempt at an understanding or explanation. And it is something that the evidence supports, or at least suggests: his thoroughly American education, for one. There is buried in the minutes of meetings of an earlier committee to study the possible transfer of the University to a new site, this information: during Bocobo's only appearance before that committee, he was presented with a proposal to transfer most of the Manila units to Los Baños, where it would then be possible for all male students in the first and second year courses to be placed "under military discipline for at least two years." Whoever provided the argument must have been familiar with Bocobo's nationalist preachings and penchant for discipline. Bocobo, who disliked the proposed transfer to Los Baños generally, emphatically replied that, with regard to discipline, such "should certainly not be military."[41]

Assertion of Courteous Behavior

Any discussion of discipline under the Bocobo presidency must necessarily include the cultivation of proper student decorum and behavior. For this purpose, he appointed a Committee on Courtesy, with Prof. Melquiades J. Gamboa of the College of Law as chairman. Rules on appropriate decorum within university premises and off campus were printed and "distributed to every student during registration."[42] There were courtesy appeals on as many topics as necessary. One of these was on:

CLASSROOM COURTESY

1. Boisterousness in the classroom while waiting for the professor disturbs other classes. How would you like your own class to be similarly bothered?

2. Talking, whispering or the like during the class impairs the work of the class, and is a discourtesy to the professor.

3. Placing your feet on the back of the seat in front of you molests the other students.

4. Please do not take the floor without the professor's permission. In addressing the professor, say "Professor," "Sir," or "Madam." The professor will tell you other forms of proper address. The shortened word "Prof." or "Ma'am" are not recommended.

5. At the end of the class hour, please let the professor and the ladies go out first.[43]

Another "courtesy appeal" reads:

COURTESY TO HIS EXCELLENCY,
THE PRESIDENT OF THE PHILIPPINES

When the President of the Philippines visits an office or establishment, all the persons in that office or establishment should rise and remain standing until he leaves or until he indicates that they may sit down. The same rule should be observed by all when he visits a classroom or laboratory in the University.

Professors were obliged to read these courtesy appeals in their classes, and to remind an erring student of lapses in his deportment or action. An otherwise cultured assistant professor of engineering who was rather casual with respect to this requirement was to suffer momentary humiliation and "resignation with reprimand" during the last academic year of Bocobo's presidency.[44]

Reverence for Cultural Heritage

Another facet of the nationalistic flavor of Bocobo's presidency was what we might call cultural nationalism. Point Six of his 16-point "new deal" for the university reads: "Conservation of Filipino customs and traditions, at the same time fully appreciating the universal heritage of culture."[45] He linked this activity more fully with nationalism in 1937 when he said, as earlier mentioned. that "patriotism demands that we revere, foster and preserve our national heritage," or national legacy, which "includes love of home and family. . . and [of] the beauty of our folk songs and dances."

His own desire to make a meaningful contribution to the formulation of a national code of ethics would lead him to "indicate what in [his] humble opinion should be some of the principal sources of such Filipino ethical system." To him these were "(1) Filipino proverbs; (2) the lives and writings of our national heroes; (3) Christian principles; and (4) the best customs observed from time immemorial."[46]

Bocobo created the atmosphere for the study of Philippine culture and history, in general, and undertook specific actions designed to attain his objectives. He himself collected proverbs and sayings from among the major languages of the country. He created in 1934 the President's Advisory Committee on Dances and Folk Songs composed of Francisco Santiago, H. Otley Beyer, Cecilio Lopez, Antonio Molina, Antonino Buenaventura, Ramon Tolentino, and Francisca Reyes Tolentino,[47] names that now adorn the dictionary of Philippine cultural biography.

Bocobo's daughter has written:

> He gave this committee his unstinted support in its work of collecting and recording songs, dances, music, costumes, musical instruments, and customs of the country. From 1934 to 1938 [practically the entire Bocobo era] three committee members [the Tolentinos and Buenaventura] went out each summer to the remotest provinces to gather their material directly from the old people who used to sing and dance in their youth.[48]

An upshot of such activities was the founding of the UP Folk Song and Dance Club in 1937 and of the UP Folk Song and Dance Trcupe. Folk dancing also became a feature of physical education at the University of the Philippines and a "professional course in Philippine folk dances" was instituted.[49]

Widening the Scope of Filipinism

Yet for all the laudable work of the Committee on Folk Dances and Folk Songs, it obviously was dealing with only a limited area of the arts—just the performing arts. Hence, Bocobo found it necessary to include a recommendation in the report by the Committee on Educational Policy, whose draft he prepared, that the commendable work by the Folk Songs and Dances Committee should be paralleled by an activity on "Filipino sculpture, painting, music, home decoration, and other native arts."[50]

Bocobo was even less pleased with the study of the Filipino cultural heritage. Thus, he wrote for the Committee on Educational Policy:

> Your Committee finds that the curricula of the University of the Philippines do not give sufficient importance to the Filipino cultural heritage. For example, Philippine history is given a small place in the scheme of studies, and our future citizens do not learn enough of the historic forces in our country to give them a proper appreciation of present-day issues and a clear vision of the future. . . . [Philippine] history should be given more time and place in the curriculum.
>
> Moreover, the writings of Filipino heroes and patriots and the addresses of leading men since the inauguration of the American regime are not being sufficiently taught. The same may be said of the writings of Filipino men of letters of the past. Neither is adequate importance attached to Filipino legends, proverbs, vernacular literature, and the like. Thorough knowledge of all this Filipino material is indispensable to a well-rounded culture.[51]

What could not be mobilized or generated through his carefully crafted speeches, Bocobo thought a Board of Regents committee could more easily accomplish, as part of the reorganization of the University, including revamp of the various curricula.

Bocobo's nationalism, which we may properly call Filipinism, may in our own day seem questionable because of his earnest encouragement, indeed full support of the Spanish language, something not unexpected since he was a member—one of the few Filipinos—of the *Real Academia de Jurisprudencia y Legislacion*. He reported that in 1935-1936 the University "continued the policy of encouraging the Spanish language. And as expected there was an increase in the enrollment in Spanish classes." It was also during that year that a *Sala de España* was opened in the main library with over a thousand volumes of Spanish works, ten Spanish paintings (reproductions), six pamphlets and over three hundred back issues of periodicals. Visiting Spanish lecturers also spoke before university audiences, which invariably included Bocobo.[52] Bocobo was intensely sincere and so dead serious in his advocacy of the Spanish language that when Editor Walter J. Robb of the American Chamber of Commerce *Journal* half-seriously insinuated in a talk before the UP Writers' Club that such was mere "propaganda" and therefore "dishonest," he walked out on Mr. Robb, pausing to say he was "sorry Mr. Robb has abused our hospitality."

"I am one of those working for the propagation of Spanish in the Philippines," Bocobo declared, "and I don't see how Mr. Robb can call our work dishonest."[53]

In fairness to Bocobo, however, it should also be mentioned that as part of the activities of his Committee on Culture, "public lectures in Tagalog were given by Lope K. Santos."[54]

Patriotism Enlivened by Pageantry

Celebrations are important elements of the socialization process and can further enhance nationalist feelings, specially if they revolve around symbols of national identification, like heroes.

Bocobo came around to this view as early as his acting presidency of the University when, on November 30, 1927, he initiated a National Heroes Day celebration at the University,[55] which he expanded when he became regular president. His purpose was, in his own words:

> ...to foster reverence for our heroes because they are the concrete examples of what our country's ideals are. Respect for them, for their memory, for their deeds, and for what they typify, constitutes a great uplifting power for the young people, and a firm unifying force for the whole country. Great nations are invariably those that have an abiding respect for their heroes. Respect for heroes unites the living and the dead and makes for the continued growth and progress of the race.[56]

Of the "expanded" celebrations, Bocobo's daughter has this description of the 1934 and 1935 festive affairs:

> ...National Heroes Day celebration consisted of a pilgrimage to the Luneta Rizal monument via Fort Santiago,... Five thousand students and faculty members went bareheaded and on foot.... In the afternoon, native games were demonstrated and a re-enactment of famous revolutionary events such as the Battles of Tirad Pass and Zapote Bridge were [*sic*] presented by the Department of Military Science and Tactics. In the evening a patriotic drama was performed at the grandstand. There were also contests in poetry, sculpture, painting,... and hymn composition of a nationalistic theme.[57]
>
> The major feature of the 1935 celebration... was the unveiling on November 11 of the "Oblation" statue by Doña Gregoria de Jesus Nakpil, widow of the great Katipunero, Andres Bonifacio. President Quezon was guest of honor and speaker.... In accepting the statue, President Bocobo said that it was of great spiritual value in the university where it was created.[58]

Still on ceremonies:

> In 1939, President Bocobo initiated a ceremony of allegorical significance by the graduating class of the UP before the "Oblation" monument. It was featured by responsive readings of excerpts from Rizal's *El Filibusterismo* and Mabini's "Decalogue," and a symbolical dedication and recitation of the patriotic pledge by the graduating class. Other numbers included the singing of "Philippine Triumphant" and "Aking Bayan".... Leading the entire graduating class in the responsive reading of Rizal's challenge to [the] youth and Mabini's moral invocations was Ahmed Garcia. Felix Makasiar, as the "Spirit of Ibarra," handed a lighted torch to one of the seniors, enjoining the new graduates to

> spread enlightenment to their countrymen.... Marciano Evangelista, as the "Spirit of the Revolution," gave a sword to a representative of the class, asking the seniors to defend their country as their fathers did in 1896 while Luz Balmaseda, as "Mother Philippines," passed the Filipino flag to another member of the class, telling the graduates to consecrate their lives to the people.... The graduating class [then] recited the following patriotic pledge:
>
> "I hereby renew my love of the Philippines, my country. This I do out of full-hearted gratitude to those who dared and died to make the Philippines lift up her head in rightful pride. Further, I hereby resolve to consecrate my life, my noblest thoughts, and my utmost endeavors to the freedom, the strength, the prosperity, and the happiness of my beloved country and people."[59]

It was typically Bocobian, a bit ostentatious but not frivolous and, in a way, Bocobo's redemption of a forecast by an obviously ardent admirer, at the time, that "his rise to the presidency of the university is most fortunate for the youth of the land in whose welfare [and sound training] he has always been interested."[60]

Unfortunately for Bocobo, it was to be the first and last such ceremony during his presidency. Shortly thereafter, Quezon appointed him Secretary of Public Instruction, breaking yet another tradition by making him the first non-occupant of a political office to become Secretary of Public Instruction since 1916.

RAMIFICATIONS OF MANAGEMENT TO ENHANCE STUDENT AND FACULTY PARTICIPATION AND WELFARE

"THE undersigned devoted special attention to student life and welfare, believing that this problem fundamentally affects the University." Thus did Acting President Bocobo begin his report to the Board of Regents in 1928.[61] This pre-figured what he planned to do for the students of the University as their regular president. Thus, next to character training as part of his 16-point program, Bocobo proposed a "deeper solicitude over the students' personal welfare."[62] A related objective, which could also be regarded as a means to promote student welfare, was vocational guidance; indeed, one may even consider Bocobo's early call for more effective teaching and the study and application of the latest pedagogical methods, also among his 16-point program, as devices intended to promote student welfare broadly viewed.

To the chagrin of many easy-going and fun-loving, or even just less serious or casual students of the University, Bocobo's prescription for student welfare also laid emphasis on the creation of the proper and congenial atmosphere, or environment, for serious study and "earnest endeavor"; it eschewed "thoughtless frivolity," claiming that such would be "shockingly out of tune with the serious temper of this era." He said further: "Moderation should be our slogan. This institution is not a ballroom or a fashion show." This was part of his address upon being sworn to office on September 1, 1934. Instead, he called for the deflection of student vigor and enthusiasm "towards pursuits literary and intellectual"—among them, "dramatics, oratory, debating, literary and musical programs, folk dances. . . ." As regards student welfare *per se*, he enjoined his listeners, most of whom were faculty and students, to look after such things as the students' "health, housing, food, budgeting, study habits and methods, manners and morals."[63]

Data on the various thrusts of the Bocobo administration in the domain of student welfare are available in the annual reports for the years 1934 to 1939. Here, only highlights are provided, for want of space.

Bocobo labelled his programs for the promotion of student welfare "areas of reform" or "new activities"—giving the impression that except during his ten-month acting presidency in 1927-1928, these activities had been given perfunctory attention or gave way to more pressing concerns of administrators and faculty alike. This was particularly true in the case of student dormitories and health services.

Student Housing Upgraded

One of the first committees created by Bocobo was the President's Committee on Dormitories and Living Conditions. Its chairman was Dr. Hilario Lara of the School of Hygiene and Public Health, with the following as members: the Dean of Men, the Dean of Women, Dr. Jose V. Santos, and Mrs. G.M. Albert. The Committee visited as many dormitories, private and public, as possible, including many boarding houses where non-Greater Manila residents stayed. The committee, using an appraisal system employed by the School of Hygiene and Public Health, rated these living quarters.[64]

Bocobo reported in 1935 that as a result of closer supervision through ocular inspection of such dormitories and boarding houses, there was a "general improvement" of living conditions in such places.[65] The safety of the dormitories was also given due attention. Thus, during the 1935-1936 academic year, fire drills were conducted with the cooperation of the Manila Fire Department. Additional fire escapes were installed or set up where necessary.[66]

The committee also visited annually the dormitories run by the Ateneo de Manila nearby, the Philippine Normal School and Philippine Women's

University. They found those dormitories to be much better than the privately or individually owned boarding houses or dormitories. This they attributed to the presence of a permanent staff and the fact that service rather than profit motivated the operations of these dormitories. This led the committee to recommend, in its reports to the President for 1936-1937 and again in 1937-1938, that the University itself should put up its own dormitories.[67]

Safeguarding Student Health

There was a vigorous campaign for "prophylactic inoculations" each year among the studentry by the University Health Service. This explained the non-occurrence of widespread illnesses during Bocobo's presidency. There was also emphasis on "ambulatory services" to students, treating them in their boarding houses or dormitories or residences. Consequently, in 1934-1935 for instance, there was a decrease in the number of infirmary admissions from 763 during the previous year to 564.[68] The desire to provide more and better services to students was behind the construction of an infirmary annex, for which the amount of ₱15,000 was set aside in 1936; in the same year, a dental clinic was installed in the infirmary.[69]

Student Counseling Initiated

Effective teaching through the latest teaching methods (Dalton Plan, Workshop Plan, All-Embracing Subject Matter Plan, etc.) was applicable to all students regardless of their abilities or circumstances. Bocobo went farther by calling for a "scientific and comprehensive plan for advising [the] weak students and of developing means for removing the causes of their failure. . . ."[70] That was the responsibility entrusted to the Committee on Study Habits and Methods under the chairmanship of Dr. Agerico B.M. Sison, with the following members: Prof. Winifred O'Connor-Pablo,[71] Prof. Casimiro del Rosario, Prof. Consuelo Barrera, Dr. Emilio Bulatao, Prof. Emma S. Yule, Dr. Miguel Manresa, Prof. Alejandro Melchor, and Prof. Gerardo Florendo (committee secretary).

The committee's work was carried out through faculty counsellors or advisers: 109 were appointed as such during the first year of the committee, the number increasing to 149 in 1935-1936, then levelling off at 100 in 1936-1937 and finally decreasing in 1937-1938.[72] The latter phenomenon may be indicative of the success of the program.

Through questionnaires addressed to both faculty and students, the committee was able to prepare a list of the top 12 causes of student failures:

bad study habits, slowness, inefficient methods, poor physical health, poor preparation for course, lack of interest in course, lack of general intelligence, peculiarities of temperament, too much courting, love affairs, self-support, and extracurricular and undergraduate activities."[73]

President Bocobo's commitment to the program, fortified by its potentiality for upgrading the overall scholastic standing of the UP studentry, was highlighted by the creation in May 1937 of a permanent office for the committee, under an executive secretary with the complement of a clerical staff. Dr. Paterno Santos of the Department of History was appointed executive secretary.[74] With this development, the program of individual advising of students and on-going studies of their problems was given a great impetus.

Bocobo's annual reports are replete with praise for the work of the Study Habits and Methods Committee, perhaps because the program was favorably received by the parents of students who had gone through the counselling and advising program. The program certainly not only helped delinquent students "improve their study habits," but also helped attain another of Bocobo's "desiderata," closer relations between the faculty and students.[75]

Vocational Guidance

Paralleling in some respects the work of the Study Habits Committee in the domain of student welfare was that of the Committee on Vocational Guidance, created by the University Council on February 20, 1937.[76] As amplified during the third year of its existence, the purposes of the Committee on Vocational Guidance were:[77] "(1) to advise the students in the Common Freshman Year on the mental qualities needed for each profession, and on the probable demand of the various professions in the future; (2) to seek the cooperation of high school faculties regarding vocational guidance; and (3) to gather data and literature on the subject of vocational guidance for the information of the faculty of the University, parents and students."

The guidance and counselling program was entrusted to a committee of fourteen (14) members composed of:[78]

Dr. I. Panlasigui, Chairman
Prof. Jose Apostol
Prof. Francisco Capistrano
Dr. Macario Corden
Prof. Narciso Cordero
Prof. Luis Gonzaga
Prof. Antonio Isidro (Secretary)
Prof. Francisco Sacay
Dr. Paterno Santos
Prof. Juan L. Tiongson
Prof. Patrocinio Valenzuela
Prof. Victorino Villa
Prof. Lope M. Yutuc
Prof. Gregorio Zamuco

Because of lack of facilities and resources, the work of the committee during the Bocobo years was limited to testing the intelligence of students to find out whether they may be readmitted to units of the University other than their original colleges, from which they had been dismissed.[79] But it was an auspicious beginning for what became one of the permanent offices of the University.

Fostering Cultural Awareness

A salient aspect of President Bocobo's program for the promotion of student welfare was the "fostering of more culture among the students." To implement what he regarded as the sixth innovation of his presidency, President Bocobo appointed the Committee on Culture. Prof. Gabriel Bernardo was made chairman of this 15-member committee, the largest among the president's several committees.[80] The work of the committee was carried out through subcommittees, such as those on book reviews, art exhibitions and musical presentations, the latter under the young and talented Ramon Tapales. The activities may be divided into:

1. A traveling or rolling library, consisting of the best 100 books ever written and sent from college to college during the schoolyear.[81] This gave way to the opening of a Browsing Room in the Main Library starting in academic year 1936-1937. The combined readership during the first two years of the Browsing Room totaled almost 11,000.[81]

2. Book reviews and round-table discussions by faculty members and eventual publication of the reviews in the *Philippine Social Science Review*. (Examples: Encarnacion Alzona's review of Lewis Mumford's *Technics and Civilization* and V.G. Sinco's review of Jose Ortega y Gasset's *La Mision de la Universidad.*)[82]

3. Art exhibitions, the first of which was a ₱250,000 art exhibit in the UP Library "composed of original pen drawings done by Callot around the time the Philippines was discovered by Magellan, three original Rembrandt pen and wood, one Carraci painting, two by El Greco, one by Andres Mantegna, and a pen sketch by Guilio Romano, the most skillful pupil of Raphael."[83] Another exhibit, this time of Filipino paintings was held, also, in 1934-35. This "happy idea" of Bocobo, to use ex-Manila Mayor Felix Roxas' words, had to be extended for one week by popular demand.[84] Succeeding annual exhibits, usually in four series (A, B, C, D) featured paintings and sketches by faculty and alumni of the School of Fine Arts or other Filipino artists, like Lorenzo Guerrero and Rafael Enriquez, Victorio Edades, Galo Ocampo, Diosdado Lorenzo and others. The 1937-1938 art exhibits drew a record of over 8,000 visitors, compared to only 3,200 the previous year. Lectures on art were also scheduled.[85]

4. Musical activities, which the President never failed to characterize as very encouraging, consisted of symphony concerts (during which compositions by Tapales and other Filipino composers were featured) and recitals, interrupted only by Tapales' going on leave in 1937-1938. The following year, with a ₱500 subsidy from University funds, the Filipino Composition Concerts were resumed, in connection with the fifth Alumni Institute and the 29th annual commencement festivities.[86]

5. Sponsorship of public lectures, e.g. Lope K. Santos' two lectures in Tagalog in 1936-1937 on "Sources and Means for Further Enrichment of Tagalog as our National Language" and another lecture on February 19, 1938 by Jose N. Sevilla on "The Wonders of the Tagalog Particles."[87]

6. Exchange of publications.[88]

Intensive Courtesy Campaign

Among the more controversial, if not also the most publicized or written about of the Bocobo initiatives, was the "fostering of courtesy among the students." This "fourth reform" was prompted by the observations of both faculty and visitors to the University that the Filipino treasured traditions of courtesy and respect had been flaunted by many university students. "Also, it was noticed that some of them had been writing indecent words on walls and blackboards, put their feet on chairs and used improper language."

To correct the unflattering and uneviable image and with a view to reestablish courtesy and proper decorum on campus, Bocobo appointed a Committee on Courtesy composed of faculty members and student leaders with Prof. Melquiades J. Gamboa as chairman.

The Committee's methods included:

1. Issuance every two weeks of "courtesy appeals" to students, written by the irrepressible and hardworking committee chairman, through the faculty members, who were requested to read them before their classes.

2. Sponsorship of an essay contest on courtesy, with the President of the University donating the prize (committee members acted as the board of judges).

3. Publication in the *Philippine Collegian* of appropriate articles on courtesy and enjoining the student organizations to support the campaign.[89]

In 1936, the committee published in pamphlet form all the 20 "courtesy appeals" then available.[90] Copies were given each student during the registration or enrolment period of the first semester. Such appeals ranged from No. 1: "Classroom Courtesy" to No. 20: "Telephone Courtesy." The pamphlet was reissued in 1937. A Spanish version was published in 1938,[91] containing an additional nine appeals, the last one being: "*Como se debe tributar la cortesia A.S.E. El Presidente de Filipinas.*" The 25th appeal, on "Tarjetas," reads in part: "3. *La tarjeta no debe ser fantastica en el tipo, forma o material. No debe tener decoraciones. Estos son indicaciones de pobre gusto.*"

President Bocobo's report to the Board of Regents on this matter at the end of the academic year 1936-1937 reads: "I am happy to report the marked improvement in the manners of our students."[92] Considering that the campaign had been "purely educational," with the methods "persuasive" rather than coercive, and that no "disciplinary action against any offender was recommended by the Committee," this was indeed an impressive record of success.[93]

Then, suddenly, before high noon of Friday, July 29, 1938, the "Albert Incident" happened. As discussed more fully later in this chapter,[94] President Quezon no less saw one of Prof. Antonio Albert's students in an engineering class seated with his feet at the back of the chair in front of him. This was patently contrary to Courtesy Appeal No. 1: "Classroom Courtesy." Professor Albert later that day admitted before a special committee of the Board of Regents which inquired into the case, that while he was familiar with Courtesy Appeal No. 1 and the other appeals as well, he had regarded them only as such, *not as rules of discipline.* On this, he was absolutely right: the courtesy appeals were not, indeed, rules of discipline, any infraction of which would have meant prompt disciplinary action by the appropriate authority.

As an aftermath, no doubt, of the Albert Incident, or Albert "Discourtesy" Case, steps were taken by the University not only to intensify the courtesy campaign but also toward converting "some points in a number of the courtesy appeals," classroom courtesy in particular, into rules of discipline, violation of which would mean a penalty.[95] The Executive Committee of the University Council at a special meeting on August 5, 1938, one week after the Albert incident, unanimously approved in principle a resolution to that effect, at the same time referring the matter for "study and report" to a high-powered committee composed of Courtesy Committee Chairman Gamboa as Chairman, with the following deans as members: Bienvenido M. Gonzalez (Agriculture), Antonio G. Sison (Medicine), Edward R. Hyde (Engineering), whose faculty member had precipitated the issue, and Vidal A. Tan (College of Arts and Sciences—Baguio).[96]

Working with haste, the committee submitted its report eleven days later, during the meeting of the Executive Committee, which after some deliberation decided to refer it to student leaders of each college or school, through the dean or director, for their comments and observations.[97] Earlier, on August 15, 1938, Professor Gamboa had read a paper at the monthly faculty conference in Manila precisely entitled "Why The Executive Committee Unanimously Resolved to Convert Some of the Courtesy Appeals into Rules of Discipline."[98] If anything, the Albert incident illustrates what the historian Louis Fisher has called the play of the contingent or unforeseen in the unfolding of human history or the role that accident plays in history.[99]

Literacy and Civic Campaigns

A university service in which students played a dominant role was the literacy campaigns. President Bocobo considered this activity his "fifth new policy," and the task of formulating the programs of implementation fell upon the shoulders of a committee headed by Prof. Aurelio Ramos, Sr. with Dr. Wenceslao Pascual, Prof. Nicolas A. Zafra, Prof. Casimiro del Rosario, and Dr. Antonio de Leon as members. The initial thrust involved teaching illiterates to read in their own dialect in line with the method devised and successfully applied by Frank Laubach (hence "Laubach Method") among the Maranaws around Lake Lanao.[100] Lectures on citizenship were added as a feature starting in the summer of 1936, hence the Committee was eventually named Committee on Literacy and Civic Education.[101]

The program consisted of student volunteers undertaking literacy and eventually civic campaigns during the summer break. Some 821 volunteers did teaching in the provinces of Negros Occidental, La Union, Marinduque, Tayabas (now Quezon), Capiz, Batangas, and the former Mt. Province in 1935.[102] The number of literacy tutors increased to 1,514, or by almost 100 percent, in 1936.[103] In addition, members of the committee themselves lectured on citizenship in Rizal, Laguna and Bulacan.

A novel feature of the 1936 campaign was the Pateros project initiated by Paterno Villanueva, a faculty member from the College of Education. This consisted of a summer school for reading and writing for illiterates, as well as vocational guidance and efficiency for literates, and citizenship classes for all. This had the support of the town officials and civic-spirited citizens of Pateros.

This adult education type program would be copied by other towns like Sta. Cruz, Laguna; Pasig, Rizal; Polo, Bulacan; and Tondo, Paco and Ermita in Manila in 1936 and 1937 when some 1,500 volunteer students registered for the program.[104] Continued in 1938, these projects turned out to be the last; the University dropped its adult education and literacy campaign thereafter with the expansion of the Office of Adult Education of the national government.[105]

But the civic work continued as before, the student volunteers popularizing among the provincial folk the workings of the government.[106] This activity did not go unnoticed, as may be seen from the following *Tribune* editorial:

> In sending out U.P. student volunteers among the people of their home communities to help make clear certain matters of government and such, Dr. Bocobo is doing something really constructive. The enterprise will not only teach the people something about the activities of the government, it will help a lot in teaching the students something about the people. As an extramural course, it has no equal.[107]

Bocobo must have been extremely pleased with this encomium.

More Innovative Aids

President Bocobo's program for student welfare also included the introduction of a prefinal examination reading period, or "integration" period, a scheme for instalment payment of tuition and other fees, and the Freshman Orientation Program.

The pre-examination reading period, more popularly known as the integration period, was Bocobo's "third reform." It was patterned after the practice at Harvard University of having a period of "reading without instruction before the final examinations." The purpose was to give the students time to prepare more fully for the final examinations and to provide them the opportunity for "synthetic thinking and deep reflection" on their subjects. Another purpose was obviously to give professors enough time to prepare their final examination questions.[108]

From 1934 to the 1936-1937 academic year, professors were given the discretion to suspend their classes one week before the final examinations for each semester, but they were to remain in their offices and be available for interviews with such students as may desire to see them.[109] This voluntary activity was made compulsory for all members of the faculty by the Executive Committee—apparently, there were the usual stragglers who refused to conform to new policies if they could help it—starting with the 1937-1938 schoolyear. However, the integration period was reduced from one week to three or four days.[110]

President Bocobo noted in his report for 1936-1937 that the students were generally in favor of the integration period.[111] It has, in a way, been with us ever since.

The instalment plan for the payment of tuition and other fees was adopted by the Board of Regents upon Bocobo's recommendation on April

25, 1935.[112] Owing, however, to strict requirements, such as on surety bonds or guarantors, only around 70 students per semester, on the average, availed themselves of the plan during its first year of adoption. The amount involved was ₱6,356.77, collected in full on schedule.[113] In 1936-1937, some 154 students each semester took advantage of the instalment payment scheme, with ₱7,814.12 involved this time. This, too, was collected in full.[114] In 1937-1938, slightly more students decided to take advantage of the very low interest plan, with ₱8,778.31 involved; as in the previous years, the amount was collected in full.[115]

In June 1936, during the first week of classes for the first semester, the Committee for the Improvement of Teaching under Dr. I. Panlasigui inaugurated the so-called Orientation Week. The objective was to provide the incoming freshmen a "systematic and comprehensive guidance" program on the university. It featured lectures on university buildings, how to study, courtesy appeals, opportunities for cultural advancement, student advising and counselling, the health service, extra-curricular activities, scholarship rules and regulations and physical education at the University[116]—these were the topics of the 1936 orientation lectures. In 1937, the lectures were increased to fourteen.[117]

Faculty Conference Introduced

The improvement of teaching was a pet program of President Bocobo, amounting to obsession. In fact, he considered it as the "first reform" under his administration,[118] a reform designed, he said, "to enlist the interest of members of the faculty in the latest teaching methods and to foster a greater desire to make teaching more effective, as well as to encourage constructive thinking on general questions affecting higher education."[119] Toward this end, he appointed a Committee on Teaching headed by the imaginative Dr. Isidoro Panlasigui of the Department of Psychology of the College of Education, with Dr. Maria Lanzar Carpio, Dr. Amando Clemente, Dr. Antonio Isidro, Dr. Daniel de la Paz, Dr. Leon Gonzalez and Prof. Ambrosio Magsaysay as members.[120] Upon the latter's departure for the United States on January 1, 1935, Prof. Ramon Mariano was appointed as a replacement,[121] and in 1936-1937 the committee membership was increased to nine with the appointment of Dr. Paterno Santos and Prof. Cristino Jamias.[122]

Through the sponsorship of the committee, monthly faculty conferences were held during the academic year, conferences which the "members of the various faculties including the instructors and assistant instructors, [were] expected to attend." Papers read during such conferences, held in both the Manila and Los Baños campuses, were collected and published in the monthly *Bulletin of the President's Committee for the Improvement of Teaching*, the first issue of which came out in July 1935.[123]

A new type of faculty conference was conceived by the committee's chairman and inaugurated in May 1936—the Baguio Faculty Conference.[124] Amidst the invigorating climate of the City of Pines, a selected number of faculty members—not necessarily the senior ones—would leave the lowlands during the summer and for one week devote themselves to a review or summary of the questions and views presented during the conferences of the past academic year, as well as the "necessity of formulating new educational policies whenever advisable for the ensuing academic year."[125] The last Baguio conference under President Bocobo was held in April and was to have lasted for two weeks instead of the usual one—indicative of how much Bocobo valued the annual gathering.[126]

It might be instructive to know how one of the discussions went during the first conference, which focused on several topics with the first being on university goals.[127] After brief remarks by the conference chairman, Dr. Leandro H. Fernandez who in a way acted as host because he was the director of the Summer Institute, Dean Bienvenido M. Gonzalez rose to explain that the university's objectives were three: the making of scholars, the production of learned professionals, and the "discovery of scientific and philosophical knowledge" which he considered as more a "consequence of the method used rather than as an objective."

Acting Dean of Veterinary Science Angel K. Gomez then took the floor and said:

> I would like to raise a question with regard to these objectives.... which of these should the university emphasize under present conditions?... the making of scholars, learned professionals or good citizens? To me... as far as the scholars are concerned we do not need much of those at the present time; we might even do away with that objective. As far as learned professionals are concerned I think we are taking care of that very well. At present the plan of the University is to cater to that tendency.... No doubt we need good citizens[,] otherwise[,] if we have communists and the life [like?] our government will certainly fail. I presume that the bringing up of good citizens is a thing for the university at the present time....[128]

"I disagree with the third item," interjected Dr. Vidal A. Tan. "Citizenship is not a function of the university. Leave training of citizenship to the lower schools, I mean, before they [i.e., the students] reach the university." Dean Gonzalez did not also think that the university should teach citizenship in particular because that would be constricting learning and eventually "becomes antagonistic." But Dean of Women Ursula Uichangco felt good citizenship did not stop with the primary or even high schools, and that the "justification for carrying on the training of citizenship in the university is that learning never ceases and therefore we can still learn."[129]

From the record of discussions in one of the workshops during the fourth Baguio annual faculty conference, we get an idea of how things were at the library and of the propensity of professors to assign references, copies of which only they possessed, if at all:

> Prof. Saniel [the librarian], after examining a list of references assigned by Professors stated that the list proved that the bulk of teaching is done at the library. He regretted that the University of the Philippines library did not even meet the requirement[s] of a college library in the United States. He told the delegates that in one course Social Science [i.e., one Social Sciences course], there are but six (6) copies of a book for 1,000 students. . . .
>
> Dr. Acosta Sison told of the experience of her daughter on being assigned references that were not available anywhere in Manila.[130]

In another workshop at the same annual conference:

> Professor Barrera informed us that the problem children ot the Philippines came from the better class homes. The delegates felt that this unfortunate situation was caused by leaving the children in the hands of servants.[131]

Presumably, the participants at the monthly conferences and the select few[132] who attended the annual conferences at Baguio became better teachers, at least, or got themselves thinking on the larger issues affecting higher education.

But emphasis on teaching methods was not quite welcome to an observer and a future faculty member who eventually became one of a handful of university professors. Because of President Bocobo's emphasis on teaching methods, he said, "many students of the college of education have been wallowing in the delusion that teaching methods are the most important things in . . . education. Consequently, many of them have become afflicted with a false superiority complex." He naturally blamed Bocobo for such an "error which is very difficult to repair." To Leopoldo Y. Yabes, the youthful commentator: "It is what to teach, not how to teach, that matters most. And in teaching, the right relations between student and teacher is much more important than teaching methods."[133]

Promotion of Deserving Personnel

Due partly to the Great Depression and partly also to President Palma's having opposed Quezon over the Hare-Hawes-Cutting Act, the appropriations for the University had declined during the three years prior to Bocobo's assumption of the UP presidency. The result was the suspension of promotions and salary increases, except in cases where vacancies occurred in higher positions due to retirement or death and the faculty members or employees occupying the lower positions were shifted upward.[134] As the late Regent Tomás S. Fonacier used to narrate, not with the intent of being sacrilegious or irreverent, even as he did so with chuckles, junior members of the faculty would go to church every day not so much to pray but to beseech the Almighty to call their seniors to their final resting places, so that they (the juniors) could get "shifted upward."[135]

Freezing of promotions was, of course, bad for morale, and Bocobo had to act quickly to cope with a deteriorating situation. He was in a good position to do so, having sided with Quezon on the Hare-Hawes-Cutting Act issue, and could therefore expect to get a sympathetic reception from the Board of Regents on the issue of salary adjustments.

He finally got ₱23,000 for the first "mass promotions" in three or four years in the University, effective March 1, 1935.[136] Thirty-seven faculty members and three employees were either promoted in rank or salary (or both). No. 18 on the list, one of six under the College of Liberal Arts, read:

> Tomas S. Fonacier, from Instructor in History at ₱1,700 (net) per annum...
> to Assistant Professor of History at ₱2,550 (net) per annum....[137]

Bocobo explained to the Board that the 40 lucky personnel constituted just one-half of the "urgent cases," hence he pleaded for an additional ₱5,000, but the Board of Regents said they would rather wait for the figures on the June registration collections before making a decision.[138] True enough, at the August regular meeting of the Board, a yearly appropriation of ₱12,000 (₱4,000 effective September 1st) for "personnel adjustments for the faculty and administrative personnel" was approved.[139] This made it possible to promote 89 faculty members and 22 employees in position and salary in 1935-1936 and another 56 faculty members and 26 employees in 1936-1937.[140]

Bocobo wrote in his report for 1934-1935 that the Board action in approving the first promotions in three or four years, was a "wise step," restoring as it did the "incentive and enthusiasm" among the university personnel "which had been seriously impaired when no prospect of promotion could be discerned."[141]

New degree programs

Bocobo believed that as a tax-supported institution, the University of the Philippines must not only serve as an effective instrumentality of the state in working out state principles and policies, through the training of leaders "who will guide the masses along the policies of the State, as declared in the Constitution."[142] It must also make its services available for the down-to-earth programs of economic and social development. As he had announced upon his election by the Board of Regents, there must be "increased stress on such courses as are required by the exigencies of the times."[143]

One of his first actions as President, with a view to making the university curricular offerings more relevant, was the appointment of a committee to look into the introduction of new courses of study or degree programs and the "amplification of existing ones." The study group included Dr. Amando Clemente, Dr. L. Gonzaga, Dr. Jose Feliciano, Dr. Cornelio C. Cruz, Dean Edward Hyde, Capt. Fidel Segundo, Dr. Hilario Roxas, Dr. Deogracias Villadolid, Dr. A.K. Gomez, Dr. Leopoldo Clemente, Dean Bienvenido M. Gonzalez, Dr. Isabelo Concepcion and Dean Conrado Benitez.

Upon the committee's recommendation, the University Council promptly approved, among others, the following during the 1934-1935 academic year:[144]

1. Introduction of the four-year course in industrial chemistry leading to the degree of Bachelor of Science in Industrial Chemistry.
2. Adoption of the four-year course in foreign service, leading to the degree of Bachelor of Science in Foreign Service; and
3. Installation of the two-year course in education, leading to the degree of Bachelor of Pedagogy.

The Council also approved in 1935-1936, courses in mining engineering and industrial engineering; a 4-year course in architecture and specialized courses in ceramics and fisheries;[145] and in 1936-1937, the four-year curriculum leading to the degree of Bachelor of Science in Geodetic Engineering.[146]

Worried about the availability of funds to implement the proposed degree programs, Bocobo approached Quezon for assistance not long after his formal assumption of office. Thus on October 25, 1934 he wired Quezon, then in Washington, DC, beseeching him to "request legislative leaders here to please appropriate ₱200,000 for industrial engineering, industrial chemistry, mining [engineering] and improvement of agricultural instruction. . . ."

"These courses," he said, "*are essential to national program for economic development.*"[147] Throughout his presidency, Bocobo, on the advice of the committee he had appointed, would encourage the faculties to keep on making their programs more relevant to the nation, through continuous curricular reform.[148]

ADMINISTRATIVE PROBLEMS AND ORGANIZATIONAL ISSUES TO CONTEND WITH

BOCOBO'S otherwise placid term—his constant nationalist advocacy and appeals for moral rectitude and proper decorum were beginning to sound tiresome after three years at the presidency—was jolted by two spectacular cases during the academic year 1938-1939.

The first grabbed the headlines, as all incidents involving President Quezon did, but created no lasting damage to the Bocobo presidency and the University. The second—likewise a headline grabber—was more serious despite its happy ending. It elicited from President Quezon, again, and the Board of Regents, also, what may be correctly construed as a mild rebuke and at the same time a blot that tarnished Bocobo's leadership.

It may even be said, in retrospect, that the textbook probe or cases convinced President Quezon and, with him, the Board of Regents of the University, that Bocobo had lost his grip over administrative affairs and that the time had come to appoint a fresh, firmer steward of the institution. This view rests on the fact that a few months after the textbook cases were considered definitely closed, Bocobo was literally kicked upstairs to become Chairman of the Board of Regents via his appointment as Secretary of Public Instruction. To be sure, Bocobo was not exiled from the University, which "remained his great love" and in whose "cherished halls, he beheld the good of his beloved country,"[149] but no longer was he directly and immediately involved, let alone responsible, for the operations of the university.

Albert "Discourtesy" Case

"QUEZON REPRIMANDS PROFESSOR" bannered the final edition of the *Philippines Herald* on July 29, 1938. That was how the world outside came to know, on the day it happened, about one of the most dramatic incidents ever to occur on the campus during Bocobo's presidency.[150]

The one-day spectacular had for *dramatis personae* the colorful, temperamental and impetuous President Quezon, Chairman of the Board of Visitors, and Assistant Professor Antonio Albert, a man of integrity and "one of the youngest and most promising members of the engineering faculty."[151] Between the two stood an embarrassed President Bocobo who had no choice but to take the side of his powerful patron and of that of the University but who also wanted to retain on the faculty one of his finest recruits[152]—Professor Albert had joined the faculty of civil engineering in October 1934, four years after his graduation at the top of his class in UP, two of which he had spent at the Berlin Polytechnic Institute.[153]

The discourtesy case was triggered by a "most disagreeable incident," to use Professor Albert's words,[154] which occurred at around 11:30 in the morning of July 29, 1938. Apprised of the incident by President Bocobo at its regular meeting in the afternoon of the same day, the Board of Regents decided to hold an extraordinary session after the agenda of the meeting had been disposed of, suspended Professor Albert pending a formal investigation of the incident by a three-man special committee of the Board, declared a one-hour recess to enable the committee to conduct its inquiry, called in Professor Albert for further interrogation before considering the report of its special committee, then before adjourning at 9:00 p.m., "approved the recommendation of the special committee to the effect that the resignation of Prof. Albert be accepted, with a reprimand, to take effect immediately."[155] It was all over in less than ten hours from the time it happened.

To Professor Albert, who became an instant celebrity, it was a "most disagreeable incident" indeed. But not for long. Thanks to the intercession of the very man who may have caused it all, President Bocobo would reinstate Professor Albert at 8:00 a.m. the following day—but the reprimand stood; the provisional reinstatement was confirmed by the same Board of Regents at the next regular meeting less than a month later.[156]

The resolution of the Albert case stands out as a record of speedy action in the annals of the University. If only for this, the case merits consideration in this chapter. But it is also worth discussing as an example of what it cost to pay only lip service to one of the commandments of a moral crusader as university president—and the price for being caught by, of all people, the President of the Philippines in the process. Lastly, the case is illustrative of how an overworked member of the faculty, who had started his day badly because of sloppy work by his freshman students, could stand up to the President of the Philippines and a Quezon at that, at the risk of sacrificing an academic career at the State University. The case is at the same time a classic illustration of Quezonian impetuousity or impulsiveness later to be mitigated by a capacity for forgiveness. When all is said and done, the case shows that men are only human.

Unpropitious Happenings

The incident was preceded by Quezon's visit to the construction site of the Armory-Gymnasium on the Isaac Peral side of the UP campus in the morning of July 29, 1938, to find out if the structure being built would drastically reduce the ground for ROTC drills and parades. With Quezon were Vice President Sergio Osmeña, Secretary of Public Instruction and Chairman of the Board of Regents; Elpidio Quirino, Secretary of the Interior;

Jose Yulo, Secretary of Justice; and presidential aide-de-camp Major Manuel Nieto.

From the construction site, Quezon decided to visit the University, stopping briefly at the shooting range. On his way to the College of Engineering, President Quezon met four ROTC cadets in uniform who, probably because they were surprised to see the presidential entourage, had forgotten to salute. Quezon promptly gave them a stern lecture on how to treat the Commander-in-Chief of the Armed Forces of the country, i.e., Quezon.[157] The President was thus in a bad mood when he went up to the second floor of the engineering building. Let Professor Albert continue the story:

> I was in my class at 11 o'clock—Materials of Construction. I had a heavy day. I had my freshmen drawing. I had to go about commenting on the work and this was quite irritating. I was not in very good humor. My students did not know what they were doing. Of course, if you start the day like that you will not be quite right for the rest of the day. I had consecutive classes—from 7 to 9, 9 to 10, and 10 to 11. Shortly after 11 o'clock, while I was starting my lecture, I saw the door open and in the portal was His Excellency, the President. Whereupon I approached the door and went to him and he met me. My class stood up and thereupon the first question that he asked me was whether the first student near the entrance was a member of the class. I answered, yes. The next thing he asked was why I permit the student to sit with one of his feet resting against the back of one of the chairs in front of him. I might have been excited at the moment but I did not have any intention of offending him. I did not reflect on what to answer, and my words came out of my mouth; my exact words were: "I never concern myself in calling down the students from this position." About which, of course, the President felt irritated. He felt it was my duty to call my students down. I believe the President did not like the answer to his question, so he asked for President Bocobo. President Bocobo was not in the room at the moment, and when President Bocobo came in, His Excellency asked him whether it was our duty to require the attention of the students to such things. President Bocobo told His Excellency, that it was our duty because it was in the Courtesy Appeals, not to put their feet on the back seats. Precisely, in one of the courtesy appeals, I remember this provision distinctly. And, of course, the President started to call me down because of something I had said that it was not my concern, and frankly I always felt that way whenever my students sat down to hear my lectures; as long as they did not disturb the class, I let them that way. Moreover, I feel that the students may sit in any way they like so long as they do not disturb the lecture. Evidently, of course, if I should have seen them with the soles of their shoes sticking over the chair, I should generally call their attention. So I did not think it was an act of discourtesy or disrespect on the part of the students, nor a manifestation of lack of discipline. I don't quite remember what transpired thereafter, but I was made to feel that as a Professor I was not cognizant of what my duties and obligations were, and in fact His Excellency called attention to the fact that I was standing not at attention while talking to him, and this perhaps also irritated him. I said before, I was very tired. I did not mean to be disrespectful to him. Having been made to feel that I did not know

> my duty as professor, I tendered my resignation. To which the President answered (addressing President Bocobo): "accept it." He left after that.[158]

And what did Professor Albert feel afterwards? He was so upset he had to dismiss his class for the remainder of the hour. He later wrote a letter of apology, at Bocobo's suggestion, admitting that he may have been rash in his repartee to the President of the Philippines.

Was he aware of the courtesy appeals, particularly on classroom courtesy?[159] Professor Albert continued:

> Of course, I am cognizant of the fact that in one of the courtesy appeals, we asked them [the students] to sit upright and straight and not to put their feet on the back of the seats in front. I have considered the appeals as just mere appeals and not rules that are binding, and I never thought it my moral obligation as a professor to call down the students and embarrass them. When I find them seated in that manner, because I myself used to sit in that position when I was a student, I did not mind them so much.[160]

How about the courtesy to the President of the Philippines?[161] Well, Professor Albert said he knew about it too. But, when asked whether he had read it to the class, his reply was: "I don't quite recollect." Most likely, he never read it to his students.

Albert's Resignation Waived

Regarding his resignation, which he had initially offered orally, he said that he did so because "I felt that I was being accused of not being cognizant of my duties as a professor." That being the case, he felt that "for the good of the University, I should sever my connection; as it can be shown very plainly that if a fellow does not know what his duties are, he has no business staying in the University." Professor Albert would later say in an interview, upon his reinstatement, that he had answered the way he did, including the tender of his resignation, "because at that moment I felt the urge to preserve my professorial dignity before my class."[162]

The happy ending for a chastened, and presumably wiser, Professor Albert came after he went to Malacañang to apologize personally to President Quezon, accompanied by his father Vicente Albert, clerk of court of the Supreme Court. President Quezon would thereupon instruct President Bocobo by phone to reinstate Albert; this was followed by a formal letter,[163] which reads like its contents had been dictated by Bocobo, if he did not personally write the letter himself.

In that letter, the full text of which was published in the Manila papers, the President took the occasion to remind students and faculty alike that proper decorum must at all times be observed; that character training was important; that if the people in the barrios with little or no classroom education could behave properly, he couldn't see why the youth in the colleges and the university should be lacking in courtesy and politeness and the like. He concluded with the exhortation: "Let us reeducate ourselves and drink from the fountain of our true Filipino traits." The phrasing is reminiscently Bocobian.

Textbook Imbroglio

On November 18, 1937, President Quezon wrote in alarm to the Secretary of Public Instruction (i.e., Vice-President Osmeña) that he had received complaints "to the effect that certain professors of the University... practically compel their students to buy" reading materials, like books or mimeographed notes, which they themselves had written for their courses. Although this practice had admittedly been "tolerated for many years even during the administration preceding President Bocobo's," still Quezon considered it as "fundamentally wrong,... especially as some of these books and notes appear to be mere compilations... and [were being sold] at prices entirely out of proportion to their worth to such an extent that mere profit... seems to be the animating purpose" of the authors or mere compilers. "I request that you ask the Board of Regents to order an investigation of this question, and to take appropriate action," Quezon ended his letter.[164]

Not satisfied by the subsequent action of the university authorities,[165] the Board of Regents decided to conduct what came to be known as the textbook probe, appointing for the purpose a Special Committee on Textbooks under the chairmanship of Regent Gil (hence for our purpose Gil Committee);[166] for obvious reasons, President Bocobo was not named to the Committee even in an *ex-officio* capacity.

After more than ten months of investigation—apparently conducted *ex parte* for the most part[167]—the Gil Committee, with two sub-committees, was ready with its report. As fate would have it, President Quezon was Acting Secretary of Public Instruction and as such was Chairman of the Board of Regents when such a report of the probe prompted by his letter would be up for consideration by the Board, Vice-President Osmeña having gone to the United States at the time.

The Board initially discussed and took formal action on some of the Gil Committee's recommendations for the first time on December 1, 1938. A brief news item about the meeting the following day gave the impression that the only important thing that happened was President Quezon's merely reiterating the "ideas he gave in the condemnatory letter addressed to the Board recently," (i.e., his November 1937 letter?);[168] but in reality a lot more was expressed by President Quezon on some of the recommendations, and a few important decisions were in fact adopted by the Board. Recommendation No. 1, on "procedure in the matter of the adoption" of textbooks and other reading materials, for example, was readily adopted after a brief discussion.[169]

Recommendation No. 2, "that an investigation be made of the conditions in the Department of Botany of the College of Liberal Arts with a view to the re-establishment of harmony and cooperation therein," aroused the President's curiosity and he "inquired as to the circumstances which [had] led the Committee to make the recommendation." He was informed this had its origins in the charges of plagiarism and technical errors in the book on "Experimental Botany" recently filed by a junior member of the Botany faculty against Dr. Jose K. Santos, the book's author; that the charges had been referred to a technical committee appointed by President Bocobo, which exonerated Dr. Santos; that President Bocobo had referred the technical committee's report to the Gil Committee which, in turn, was now recommending also Dr. Santos' exoneration, "but that he should be required to revise said book with a view to removing typographical errors."

> His Excellency then stated that he was surprised why nothing was done to correct the mistakes pointed out by [complainant]. . . notwithstanding the fact that the matter was officially reported some nine months ago; that the allegations of [complainant] were so concrete that even Dr. Santos himself could have verified them. . . .

When Bocobo remarked that he could not have acted sooner because his own technical committee took nine months to conduct its investigation, President Quezon countered by stressing the point "that he believed that when a member of the faculty came out with a formal complaint. . . it was the duty of those *in charge*[170] of the administration of the University to have attended to the complaint and that certainly Dr. Santos should have made the necessary corrections in his book."

Quezon added that inaction could very well be construed as "an attempt to 'cover up' the situation." While he expressed the hope that this was not the feeling of the university authorities, he nevertheless felt constrained to point out that it was "not right nor proper to condone [by inaction] faults committed by the faculty," and that on the contrary those in charge of the administration should have acted swiftly to protect the good image of the University; "and that this had been his feeling with regard to the textbook question." The exoneration of Dr. Santos was approved as recommended, but it must have struck President Bocobo too plainly that President Quezon was dissatisfied with Bocobo's failure to be more decisive on this matter.

Textbook Committee Chairman Dismissed

Then followed the Board's decision to relieve the chairman of the President's Textbook Committee and to reprimand him "severely . . . for dereliction of duty and gross negligence in the enforcement of the regulations" adopted by the Board of Regents on October 13, 1930. Another member of the Textbook Committee escaped a similar punishment when the Board amended the Gil Committee's recommendation to that effect, but it was understood that Bocobo would replace him.

But more was in store for President Bocobo as President Quezon moved on to the Gil Committee's recommendations for six faculty members of the College of Law, including the Dean no less.

The College of Law was President Bocobo's special preserve, it was his "baby" so to speak, having served on its faculty from its creation in 1911 to 1934 or a total of 23 years including 17 years as college dean. The current dean, Prof. Jose Espiritu, he had handpicked as his successor; like Bocobo, Dean Espiritu had been with the first batch of government *pensionados* in 1903. Any unflattering, or just even a neutral remark about the College of Law, its dean and faculty, would make Bocobo react sensitively. If Quezon sensed that such was the case, he chose to ignore it as he commented on Recommendation No. 4 of the Gil Committee that the case of Prof. Vicente G. Sinco "was a very serious matter where a faculty member was charged of violating a resolution of the Board of Regents" regarding engagement in private business and work outside the University. This was all the worse because that private business was a publishing house, and that "this company published books of the University, using therefor the facilities of the U.P. Press," of which Sinco was, by designation of the Board of Regents, general manager. In the case of Dean Espiritu, it was his having sizable investments in shares or stocks.

President Quezon then proceeded to give a lecture (monologue) on the exacting demands of the legal profession when it came to ethical and moral principles, "referring particularly to the case of Prof. Sinco and Dean Espiritu . . . [and] that certainly the University of the Philippines should have the one College of Law wherein the highest standards of professional ethics should be inculcated among the students. . . ." Obviously, this would be impossible if the professors themselves were violators of rules and regulations. Perhaps pausing briefly to ascertain the Regents' reactions, particularly President Bocobo's, President Quezon then emphatically said:

> ... that he should like the Board and the Committee to consider further this case of Prof. Sinco and Prof. Espiritu to determine whether they should be dismissed or compelled to resign.

As for the case of the four other law professors,[171] Recommendations Nos. 6 and 7, the Gil Committee urged that they be reprimanded, but no final action was taken except that the offenders be furnished each with a copy of the report pertaining to them, "so that they may, if they so desire, present a written answer to the pertinent findings and recommendations of the Committee," to which the "punitive recommendations" had been referred back.

The Committee's amended recommendations, taking into account the memoranda of the parties concerned, were considered by the Board at its meeting a fortnight later.[172] All of the professors were merely "admonished" for having been "remiss"; it would not be fair, in the Committee's revised thinking, to "reprimand" them because they had "committed these several acts in the honest belief that they were not prohibited from so doing...." However, Professor Sinco was additionally "ordered to dispose of his interest in the Community Publishers" within 90 days, and was relieved as manager of the U.P. Press "effective February 1, 1939."

Regents' Noblesse Oblige

The above recommendations were adopted by the Board, with President Bocobo absenting himself from the meeting. Perhaps aware of possible repercussions to President Bocobo's administration, the Board adopted a further resolution:

> ... That notwithstanding the approval of the recommendations of the Committee, it is the sense of the Board that the usefulness of the President of the University is in no way impaired by the action hereby taken, and that in his administration of the University he continues to enjoy the confidence of the Board.[173]

This is open to misinterpretation; in fact, considering what followed for Bocobo, it might even be considered as a dubious statement.

The decisions of the Board were published in the *Philippines Herald* on December 16, 1938 and in the *Tribune* on the following day which coincided with the culmination of week-long activities commemorating the 30th (Pearl) Anniversary of the founding of the University.[174] For the next four or five days, the textbook probe would be front-page news, with eye-catching headlines and given more prominence than the meeting of President Quezon and the Regents with the educational experts (Elliott and

Packer) on the reorganization plans for the university.[175] Dean Espiritu immediately tendered his "irrevocable" resignation from the University, while the others said they would do likewise, depending on developments. A student rally on campus, sans permit,[176] ended at Malacañang with Executive Secretary Jorge B. Vargas accepting a student council petition to the Board of Regents, via President Quezon, asking for a "reconsideration" of the Board's action. President Quezon had to meet with student council leaders headed by Sotero B. Laurel, then a law junior, the next day.

Finally, on the morning of December 20, President Quezon met with the law professors and their Dean, together with President Bocobo, after which he issued a statement[177] to the effect that "the character and integrity of the six law professors had not in any way been impugned" by the action of the Board of Regents; that as far as Quezon was concerned, what the Board did was merely to "express an opinion" on a practice it had considered wrong. With respect to Professor Sinco's actuations as U.P. Press Manager, President Quezon said he "was satisfied beyond doubt that what he [i.e., Sinco] did was in the best interest of the U.P. Press." President Quezon thus persuaded the professors, including Dean Espiritu, to withdraw their resignations and to continue serving the university with honesty and integrity and even exhorted them to write more books the sale of which would now be subject to the new regulations prescribed by the Board.

Having achieved a "neat *finis*,"[178] President Quezon did not even bother to request the Board to reconsider its earlier decision when it convened briefly in the afternoon of the day he met with the professors—to the chagrin of the latter who would have preferred such a reconsideration to reflect what actually took place. However, President Quezon wrote President Bocobo shortly before Christmas Day of 1938,[179] presumably by way of an answer to the professors' request that his "personal statement" be officially made a part of the Board's records,[180] "expressing [his] satisfaction over the attitude of Dean Espiritu and [the professors] in accepting as final his opinion. . . ." The Board, adverting to this presidential missive and his earlier statement to the press, would on March 10, 1939, consider "the matter closed since its action on December 15, 1938."[181]

"All's Well that Ends Well," thus appropriately editorialized the *Herald*.[182] True, indeed. Dean Espiritu retired as Dean of the College of Law on December 31, 1953,[183] while Professor Sinco succeeded Dean Espiritu to the deanship from which position he was later elected to serve as President of the University (1958-1962).[184]

As for President Bocobo, the textbook incident turned out to be, in retrospect, the beginning of the end of his presidency. Within 40 days after the Board of Regents had considered the probe closed for the last time on March 10, 1939, he would be deftly removed from his post by President Quezon who appointed him Secretary of Public Instruction instead.

Reorganizational Survey

Two major studies and surveys, one of which was to fundamentally affect the physical features of the University after World War II and is therefore historic, were undertaken by the Board of Regents during Bocobo's presidency. The surveys or studies seemed to have been embarked upon not on Bocobo's initiative, but rather on that of a member of the Board of Regents, or of someone even higher, e.g., President Manuel L. Quezon, in the case of the transfer of the University to another site. The other survey on the reorganization of the University, which we shall discuss first, was proposed by Regent Manuel A. Roxas.

The survey was formally authorized by a resolution of the Board of Regents of the University adopted during its meeting on January 28, 1938, and was to be undertaken by its Committee on Educational Policy with the assistance of "three competent advisers... appointed by the Board of Regents for the purpose."[185] The enterprise was meant to be a "thorough study of all courses, personnel, and equipment of all colleges and departments of the University" with the end in view of recommending means for their improvement; eventually, as we shall see in the next section, this mandate was expanded to include a study of possible sites for the Manila units of the University.

Bocobo had included a self-survey of the University as part of a 16-point program, already adverted to, which he had announced upon his election as president, but the initiative for the survey seems to have come from Regent Roxas. This is inferred from the few documents on its origins in the Roxas Papers in the National Library, *viz.* Quezon's telegram to the US Secretary of War dated August 4, 1938, quoting Osmeña's earlier identical telegrams to President Edward C. Elliott of Purdue University and Dean Paul C. Packer of Iowa University's College of Education, who had met with Roxas during the latter's trip to the United States in June 1938.[186]

Parenthetically, it might be mentioned that this was the first survey of the UP since 1925 when the Monroe Commission studied the Philippine educational system which, of course, included the State University. But it was intrinsically a UP self-study. Mention may also be made here that in 1958, almost 20 years after, another survey would be undertaken by a group which would be headed by an American, Dr. John A. Hannah (of Michigan).[187]

The Committee on Educational Policy of the Board of Regents which conducted the survey had been created during the Acting Presidency of Bocobo, who was himself the author of the proposal.[188] In 1938, its chairman was Regent Roxas, who was at that time the Secretary of Finance, and it had the following members: Regent Celedonio Salvador, Regent Jose Gil, and President Bocobo, *ex officio* non-voting member.

The committee's procedure involved submitting to the educational experts—President Elliott and Dean Packer—"An Outline of Problems" confronting the University as identified by members of the faculty and brought to the attention of the committee by President Bocobo during the third and fourth meetings of the committee, respectively, on September 3 and 30, 1938.[189] The advisers were given access to pertinent data and would interview as many members of the University constituency and even outsiders as they desired. They then prepared an advisers' memorandum on each vital problem which would be presented to and discussed with the committee between October 21 and December 23, 1938—totalling 27 in all, including the Final Advisers' Memorandum.

Samples of these memoranda are Advisers' Memorandum No. 2: Relating to the Location of the University of the Philippines, submitted to the CEP on October 21, 1938; Memorandum No. 3: Relating to the Government of the University, presented on October 22, 1938; Memorandum No. 6: Relating to Academic Freedom, November 21, 1938; Memorandum No. 10: Relating to Class Size, December 19, 1938 meeting. After each memorandum was thoroughly discussed the advisers would revise it and present it at the succeeding meeting. The committee explained in its report that this method, a cooperative endeavor between the Board and its advisers, "is one that is gaining favor in the United States."

President Bocobo, at the request of CEP Chairman Roxas, prepared a draft of the Committee's Report, forwarding the same to Chairman Roxas on January 16, 1939.[190] It was submitted to the Board of Regents on March 31, 1939, and printed and released in June of the same year.

It would be impossible to give even brief summaries of all the recommendations in the report; indeed, it is not necessary to do so, since most were never carried out immediately, nor during the remainder of the Bocobo presidency.[191] But it might be instructive to discuss at least two of these, namely, that pertaining to the College of Liberal Arts and that relating to the government of the University, together with some of the less salient recommendations, even if it means going beyond Bocobo's term.

Revamp of Main College

For the College of Liberal Arts,[192] the Committee recommended the adoption of a division plan of consolidating allied departments into four divisions, namely: Division of Biological Sciences, Division of Physical Sciences, Division of Social Sciences, and Division of Literature. A fifth—Division of Fine Arts—was also envisioned, in case the committee's recommendation to transfer the Conservatory of Music and the School of Fine Arts should be implemented.[193]

The thinking of the members of the committee was that the divisions should eventually *replace* the fifteen (15) departments then existing in the College. However, the committee realized that their recommendation would take some time to accomplish. As a first step toward their gradual consolidation, it recommended that the four divisions be created immediately, each to be "presided over by a director appointed from among the heads of the various departments composing the division." The departments were to remain in the meantime as such, but "all the faculty belonging to the Department under each division would constitute the Division and as such would decide on matters of *larger policy* affecting the Division." (Emphasis supplied.)

In proposing the gradual abolition of departments and the creation of divisions to replace or absorb them, the Committee on Educational Policy adduced two specific arguments, namely: (1) better coordination and (2) "neutralizing," if not arresting altogether, what it considered or judged as the "baneful" trend in tertiary education of "dividing human knowledge into numerous pigeon-holes." In short, the committee cited administrative and philosophical considerations behind its recommendation.

Perhaps on account of the changing of the guard, as it were—President Bocobo would resign as president in April 1939 because of his appointment as Secretary of Public Instruction and Dean Bienvenido M. Gonzalez would take over the UP presidency—and because of more urgent concerns such as settling the issue of transferring the University to a new site, the intervening Japanese invasion and occupation (1941-1945) and the pressing and costly rehabilitation and reconstruction activities thereafter, and finally, the physical transfer of the University to its present location and the need to cope with the problems attendant thereto, none of the abovementioned recommendations for the College of Liberal Arts was adopted and implemented until 1957. In June of that year, the Board of Regents, upon the recommendation of College of Liberal Arts Dean Tomás S. Fonacier, approved the reorganization along a divisional scheme of the academic departments of the College of Liberal Arts and other departments of the University offering courses in the fundamental disciplines.[194] The Board of Regents created four divisions, namely: Division of Biological Sciences, Division of Physical Sciences, Division of Humanities (which included Architecture, Fine Arts, Library Science, History and Philosophy) and Division of Social Sciences. Each division was to have a chairman appointed for a term of five years.

As explained by Dean Fonacier, who later became a regent of the University, this divisional scheme was academic and not administrative. There was therefore no impairment of the administrative integrity of the departments (to say nothing of particular colleges). However, since the divisions were expected to look into curricular offerings and to recommend interdisciplinary programs, the possible diminution of the academic autonomy of departments was foreseen.

The rationale behind the adoption of the divisional scheme was to foster, engender and ensure "cooperation and friendly rivalry" among allied departments/disciplines instead of "destructive competition" between them.[195]

University Governance Reexamined

The second set of recommendations in the survey report had something to do with the government of the University, and covered such matters as the Board of Visitors, the Board of Regents (its freedom from external pressure or control, its composition and tenure of members, its committees and its relationship with the University Council), the President of the University—whose recommended title was "Rector"—and the Office of Vice-President (or Vice Rector).

With respect to the Board of Visitors, the committee recommended a change in its composition from the Governor General, the President of the Senate and the Speaker of the House of Representatives—these having become since 1935 mere "historical terms"—to the President of the Philippines, the Speaker of the National Assembly, and the Chief Justice of the Supreme Court. As regards the composition of the Board of Regents, the committee did not accept the Advisers' recommendation to terminate *ex officio* memberships, "except in the case of the President of the University."

The committee endorsed the abolition of the election of the three Alumni Regents; instead, the President of the Philippines would appoint these regents plus one more to make it four Alumni Regents. The *Report* states that freedom of the Board from external control could still be maintained despite the continuing ex officio membership of the Secretary of Public Instruction (who is, of course, the Chairman), the Director of Education, and the Chairman of the Committee on Public Instruction in the National Assembly. The denial of ex officio membership to the President was justified thus: "It would be conducive to greater and more sustained interest on the part of the members of the Board of Regents, especially the Chairman . . . if leadership of the Board were squarely placed upon the Chairman." This proposal was contrary to what Bocobo had written in his draft of the *Report*, that the president of the University should continue to be a member of the Board of Regents.

At the March 31, 1939 meeting of the Board, a resolution was adopted endorsing the above recommendations with Bocobo abstaining from voting.[196] The same resolution was reiterated during the April 20 meeting of the Board presided over by Quezon, as Acting Secretary of Public Instruction, except in the case of the Board of Visitors which, because Quezon thought it was useless, would instead be abolished.[197] During the 470th meeting of the Board, however, it was resolved to recommend an amendment to the charter along the lines recommended by the Survey, "and, in the event of the re-creation of the Senate, that the President thereof be added to the membership of the Board of Visitors."[198]

The recommendation discontinuing the membership, *ex officio*, of the president of the University in the Board of Regents was withdrawn by the Committee on Educational Policy itself during the 470th meeting of the Board of Regents; at the same time, it disapproved the change of title of President to that of Rector of the University.

The proposed semi-annual joint conferences between the Board of Regents and the University Council were approved, likewise during the 470th meeting of the Board, but "with the understanding that the representatives of the University Council shall be limited to the Deans, Directors, and Department heads."

Finally, the appointment of a vice-president was implemented when the Board appointed Prof. Hermenegildo B. Reyes as Vice President of the University, effective October 13, 1939.[199]

Search for New Campus

On December 14, 1937, during a Board of Regents meeting Vice-President Sergio Osmeña, the Board's chairman, appointed a five-man Special Committee "to gather data on possible new sites" for the University's Manila units.[200] Regent Horace B. Pond was named chairman of the *ad hoc* committee, with the following as members: Regent Fernando E.V. Sison, Veterinary Science Dean Gregorio San Agustin, Dr. Eugenio Hernando and Mr. A.D. Williams. Pond was the logical, if not the ideal, choice for chairman: he had on October 28, 1937, submitted a "confidential memorandum" to President Quezon—upon the latter's request—on "comments [which included his own] on the proposal to transfer the University of the Philippines from its present site in Manila to a site in the provinces."[201]

The Special Committee met five times. All except the first were held in March 1938. Bocobo was invited to the third meeting on March 14 to give his comments on a proposal that all Manila units, except the Graduate School, and the Colleges of Medicine, Law, Education and Business Administration, be transferred to Los Baños.

Bocobo was against the proposal in general, specially the feature concerning Los Baños: he favored the "clinical courses" of Medicine and Veterinary Science remaining in Manila and the transfer of all others to "one place," but not necessarily Los Baños, which in his view, "didn't quite fit in with the general idea of a College of Liberal Arts—which should also be cultural." To Bocobo, Los Baños was a cultural desert. He preferred a site 15 to 20 kilometers from Manila, the nation's cultural center. On this, he was supported by Regent Sison, but was rebutted by Pond who very early seemed to have come to the view that the only alternative site for the Manila units whose transfer was envisioned, was Los Baños.[202]

Perhaps, it might be worth mentioning here that Dean Leandro H. Fernandez of the College of Liberal Arts objected to the proposed transfer of his college to Los Baños on the grounds that other colleges depended on the College of Liberal Arts for some of their courses, thus creating a problem; and also because of a predicted "radical slump"—at least 50 percent—in enrolment and he was not sure that those who opted to follow the College to Los Baños would be the best.[203] Another dean, Dr. Bienvenido M. Gonzalez of Agriculture, on the other hand, was emphatic that certain colleges could "profit by being in Los Baños," citing Los Baños' isolation as "conducive to study and students would be less likely to be distracted" and the opportunity to develop a "cooperative spirit" among the faculty. Gonzalez, however, thought that only "at least some units" be outside Manila.[204]

The Special Committee in the end produced a majority and a minority report, with the Chairman among the majority of three.

Debate on Los Baños Site

In their majority report,[205] Chairman Pond and members Williams and Hernando recommended that the Colleges of Liberal Arts, Engineering and Pharmacy be transferred to Los Baños, while the "Senior Colleges" (Medicine, Law, Education, Business Administration, Graduate School, Hygiene and Public Health; Dentistry and Fine Arts, then merely schools; and Music, then a conservatory) were to remain in Manila.

Regent Sison and Dean San Agustin, on the other hand, disagreed with the majority report. They complained that the Committee had ignored altogether the procedure it had formulated during its first meeting on January 6, 1938; that "Los Baños seems to have been thrust into the midst of the Committee, to the exclusion of other possible places;" that it was their understanding that the Committee was supposed to contemplate the transfer of all the Manila units, not just some; and that the choice of the site must be anchored on the possibilities of realizing the "ultimate aims and purposes of the University"—whose re-examination must be a precondition. They then enumerated what they felt were the disadvantages of a transfer to Los Baños, as recommended by Pond and his two associates.[206]

Osmeña submitted both the majority and minority reports to the Board of Regents during its meeting on May 26, 1938, which promptly referred them to the Committee on Educational Policy, "for study and recommendation."[207] The latter committee took official cognizance of the mandate during its July 27, 1938 meeting,[208] although as of August 26th the Board of Regents was informed by Regent Roxas, Educational Policy Committee Chairman, that it was the desire of the Committee "to secure the comment of the education advisers [President Elliott and Dean Packer], before finally considering the matter."[209]

It seems, however, that by the time the advisers formally entered the picture in early October, [210] a consensus had more or less emerged among the members of the Committee and the Board of Regents to relocate the Manila units to a site near Manila. Thus, during the Committee meeting on September 30, 1938, a place in Marikina near the "Diliman Estate" and a scenic location "between Cainta and Tay-tay, part of the hacienda of Mr. Wolfson," were mentioned;[211] Los Baños was not considered anymore. And on October 14, 1938, during the 456th meeting of the Board of Regents, Regent Roxas said that the new site "under consideration" was "adjacent to the Diliman Estate," with an area of "approximately six hundred hectares" belonging to the Philippine National Bank. Finally, during the same meeting, Board of Regents Chairman Sergio Osmeña, whose views on the proposed UP transfer Regent Roxas wanted to solicit before Osmeña left for abroad, expressed himself as in favor of the transfer of the University, "if the new site was near the city of Manila."[212]

Marikina Site Favored

By the time the two educational advisers met with the Committee on Educational Policy on October 21, 1938, the latter had already decided to recommend to the Board of Regents the transfer of the University to the proposed site in Marikina, [213] adjacent to the Diliman Estate; President Bocobo was requested to draft the Committee's report in time for the next Board of Regents meeting "to be presided over by President Quezon."[214]

Dean Packer had already a draft memorandum on the proposed transfer when he and President Elliott were invited to the Committee's meeting. It contained the advantages and disadvantages of the proposed transfer, possible sites, problems which might be involved in case of transfer, etc. He informed the Committee that the memorandum would be ready in its final form "early next week." President Bocobo suggested that the memorandum should include "whether after the initial appropriation for buildings and other facilities on the new site, the Government would be willing to appropriate additional funds to meet the enlarged and future needs of the University." This was reflected in the revised memorandum submitted and further discussed at the Committee meeting on October 28, 1938.[215]

Earlier, on October 22, 1938, the President of the UP Alumni Association had forwarded to CEP chairman Roxas the report of the Committee of the Alumni Board on the transfer of the University under the same date.[216] The report "endorsed" the proposed transfer to the Marikina site, this being in the direction of the "trend in metropolitan expansion, and would place at the disposal" of the State University rich "opportunities" of potential utility. The report also contained the prayer that "government solicitude... should extend further than providing the institution with building and other physical facilities on the site"; that there must be the assurance of "continued adequate financial support with which to insure high academic standards...."

Transfer Strongly Advocated

The Committee on Educational Policy (CEP), therefore, had the reports of the Pond Committee, briefly discussed earlier, an alumni board Committee Report, and that of CEP's educational advisers. It came out with a "Report on the Advisability of Transferring the Manila Units of the University of the Philippines to Another Site," dated October 27, 1938.[217] Predictably, the CEP's report relied heavily on the one submitted by its advisers. The "Report" is worth summarizing and/or excerpting at length.

It starts by tackling the issue of the proposed transfer of some units to Los Baños, which it had already discarded, and the question of "whether the present site of the University could be so improved and expanded as to make possible [the attainment] of the principal objective behind the proposed transfer." After extensively quoting the Advisers' Memorandum No. 2

on this aspect as regards the advantages and disadvantages, specially monetary, the "Report" read:

> Your committee is convinced that the present site... is decidedly inadequate to meet present and future needs. [It] is likewise convinced... that complete relief may not be had by expansion of the present campus through expropriation of surrounding blocks at an unusually large initial outlay.

The prescriptive portion of Recommendation 1 reads in part:

> After a thorough consideration of all the data... your Committee recommends that the University of the Philippines be transferred to a place contiguous to the City of Manila and that for this purpose that portion of the Mariquina Estate (adjacent to the Diliman Estate) which is owned by the Philippine National Bank, with an approximate area of 600 hectares, be selected.

Recommendation 1 also expressed the view that it would be "desirable" to consider the advisability of acquiring an additional area of 150 hectares for future expansion and of forestalling the establishment of business or recreational centers that might frustrate the sound program of the University.

With the additional land, the contemplated University boundaries would be the Marikina River on the East and the provincial road to Marikina (now Aurora Boulevard Extension) on the South, the Payatas and Piedad Estates on the North, and Marikina Estate West. The present Balara Filtration Site was to have been within UP's borders.

Bocobo's Reactions on Relocation

On October 28, the day after the CEP "Report" was submitted to the Board of Regents, President Bocobo issued a "Statement of View" on the UP transfer to the Board of Regents. Bocobo said he "heartily" endorsed the Committee's recommendation—it after all jibed with his own view that the new site should be within 15-25 kilometers from Manila and many of the Committee's supporting arguments echoed his own. He then went on to say that President Quezon, the initiator of the idea of the University's transfer, had a "great vision for the University" and on various occasions had expressed desire that the University of the Philippines "should be one of the leading universities of the world."

Bocobo doubted, however, whether the Quezonian enthusiasm and "breadth of view regarding the State University" would be shared by his successors. Neither was he certain, he said, whether future National Assemblies, after 1941, would be "willing to support a comprehensive and long-term program for a first-class State University." He, therefore, requested that the Board of Regents petition President Quezon and, through him, the National Assembly, "to set aside a cash grant of ₱10,000,000 to be separate from the usual annual contribution to the University, and to be exclusively devoted to the strengthening of the faculty and the carrying out of research within the next ten years." This would be over and above the ₱10,000,000 "which is requested by your Committee on Educational Policy for the construction of buildings on the new site"—which amount, should the ₱10,000,000 "cash grant" not be forthcoming, Bocobo proposed to use, instead, for research and the strengthening of the faculty and for new buildings on the old campus.

In other words, Bocobo would not recommend the transfer of the University unless he had the extra ₱10-million "cash grant." This alternative proposal, Bocobo argued, "would be more effective for the economic development" of the Philippines, as well as for its "social and moral regeneration," specially at a time when the nation is "girding itself to assume a separate existence." "When all is said and done," he concluded, "[the] University can best serve the country by having a qualified faculty."[218]

This was probably well taken by the Board of Regents because at its meetings on November 25, 1938 and December 15, 1938, it discussed and finally approved the rules to govern the "contest for the best architectural style for the proposed buildings for the University of the Philippines on its *new site* adjacent to the Diliman Estate, Mariquina, Rizal." It set 10:00 a.m. of March, 1939, as the deadline for submission of entries, which date was later extended to May 1, 1939.[219]

Meanwhile, a bill on the transfer of the university was submitted to the National Assembly. The latter's Committee on Public Instruction, with Assemblyman and *ex officio* Regent Guillermo Z. Villanueva as Chairman, had by March 10, 1939 approved such a bill (No. 938) in principle.[220] Finally on June 3, 1939, President Quezon signed Act 442 authorizing the University of the Philippines to transfer to a site "suitable for the proper development of the institution." The Board of Regents was, under the law, empowered to choose the site, "with the approval of the President" (i.e., Quezon). The law also provided ₱17,500,000, of which ₱8,5000,000 was to be made available immediately, the balance to be released from time to time within the period 1940-1949.[221] In a way Bocobo's wishes were met to a substantial degree, but he no longer was at the helm as president at the time, having been appointed Secretary of Public Instruction on April 19, 1939; he, of course, became *ex officio* Chairman of the Board of Regents.

30th Year Commemorated

The University reached a milestone during President Bocobo's administration—the 30th, or Pearl, anniversary of its founding. To mark the occasion, appropriate activities were scheduled for a whole week from December 11 to 17, 1938.[222]

Among the highlights of the Jubilee celebration were: (1) an art exhibit at the Main Library, featuring 120 paintings and drawings, 49 of them by guest artist Gaston O'Farrell, who was described as belonging to the "old school taught by the immortal Juan Luna," and those by leading local artists like Diosdado Lorenzo, Eduardo Salgado, H.R. Ocampo, Jose B. David, and others, and which was extended to December 24, 1938;[223] (2) the holding of a Higher Education Conference wherein leading educators and professors from UP and other universities discussed for five days various aspects of Philippine education in at times parallel academic sessions;[224] and (3) the presence as guest speaker during the second day of the Higher Education Conference, of the American High Commissioner to the Philippines Paul V. McNutt.

The climax of the activities was the conferment of the degree of Doctor of Laws, *honoris causa*, on the venerable ex-President Rafael Palma in the morning of December 17, followed by the address of Assemblyman and former Justice Secretary Jose Yulo.[225]

Statistical Record

The academic year 1938-1939, the 30th anniversary year of the University, turned out to be the last under President Bocobo. This is probably the most appropriate place, therefore, to indicate some "vital statistics" on the more than four years of Bocobo's stewardship of the University.

We begin with student enrolment at the collegiate level, not counting summer enrolment. The academic year 1934-1935 registered the lowest enrolment record since 1927, with only 5,225 students in the first semester; obviously, this was a continuing effect of the economic depression which had started to affect the country at the onset of the 1930s.[226] By the first semester of the 1937-1938 schoolyear, the previous high of 7,412 students enrolled in the first semester of 1930-1931 had been exceeded by almost 300; the following academic year, 1938-1939, the first semester enrolment was just 41 students shy of 8,000!

The enrolment by years and semesters during President Bocobo's term is given below:[227]

Academic Year	*1st Semester*	*2nd Semester*
1934-1935	5,225	5,004
1935-1936	5,756	5,433
1936-1937	6,860	6,161
1937-1938	7,711	7,101
1938-1939	7,959	7,377

Because student enrolment had steadily declined, on the average by 600 annually between 1931 and 1935, it was understandable why the number of graduates during the five commencement exercises under President Bocobo would decline from 656 in 1935 to 584 in 1936, to a record low of 510 in 1937, rising slightly to 588 in 1938 and finally 597 in 1939.[228]

The holdings of the University libraries, however, steadily increased from 102,744 books as of May 31, 1935, to 126,356 four years later; pamphlets from 31,857 to 37,661; and serial publications from 2,909 to 4,394.[229]

These increases, albeit not impressive, took place in spite of frozen or even lower annual contributions by the national government to the University's total income available for expenditures, except during the last academic year under President Bocobo. The figures below tell the financial assistance given to the University starting with the 1933-1934 academic year to 1939:[230]

Academic Year	*National Government's Contribution*	*Total University Income*
1933-1934	₱1,018,067	₱2,255,977
1934-1935	1,018,067	2,125,777
1935-1936	977,163	2,046,552
1936-1937	977,163	2,179,696
1937-1938	995,663	1,887,940
1938-1939	2,158,697	3,509,028

LINKS ESTABLISHED WITH ALUMNI AND THE PUBLIC FOR A WELL-ROUNDED PRESIDENCY

MORE than his predecessors, Bocobo attempted to make relations with alumni of the university more fruitful and meaningful, if not also more reciprocal. He had given an inkling of what could be done in that direction when, as Acting President in 1927-1928, he suggested to the UP Alumni Association that class reunions be held every ten years.

Bocobo also planned to send out a newsletter and a questionnaire to all alumni of the university. The newsletter was meant to inform the alumni on the "progress and needs of the university," while the questionnaire was intended to gather information from the alumni such as their "present work and accomplishments" and to solicit their thinking and suggestions on the "academic programs and methods of teaching in the University."[231] When, therefore, he was finally chosen president on August 11, 1938, he expectedly announced that part of his 16-point program would be to foster "closer contact between the university and the alumni."[232] His efforts toward that end may be discussed under three rubrics, although by no means the only ones:

1. **Contact with the Alumni**

On September 15, 1934, a fortnight after taking his oath as the fifth President of the University, a questionnaire almost along the same lines of the one he said he would send out six years earlier as acting president, was mailed to each alumnus of the University.[233] Another mailing was done in 1936, although the original intent was to mail the questionnaires annually.[234] Perhaps on account of the expenses involved, and because replies to the second mailing continued to be received by the Registrar's Office until the end of academic year 1937-1938,[235] it was not deemed necessary to send out another one in 1938. Perhaps, also, the number of alumni who responded had something to do with it: only 30 percent in 1934 and 28.86 percent in 1936.[236]

Notwithstanding the low percentage of replies, Bocobo could not have been but satisfied with their contents. From the 11 "typical suggestions" received as late as 1938,[237] at least nine were an indorsement of his pet projects or ideas, while the rest were also the ones he desired. Among the nine were No. 4: "The University should have an independent source of income and be independent of legislative aid as much as possible"; No. 6: "To emphasize things Philippine"; No. 9: "The administrative policies should enliven and strengthen the students' love and pride for their race and country, and should endeavor to solidify their spirit of patriotism"; and No. 11: "That the teaching of character and ethics be included in the curriculum and that initiative on the practice of good conduct and the creation of right attitudes be encouraged." Among the desirable suggestions were No. 5: "To release faculty by turns for study and research," and No. 10: "To open a business laboratory for business students in order to acquaint them with the routine work in business houses." One item—reduction of tuition fees—was recommended by the 1934 and 1936 respondents.

What did Bocobo do with the suggestions? One may assume that since they jibed with policies he had been pursuing or had been suggesting, he did not hesitate to use them as proofs that his administration was "on course." Not surprisingly, he sent them to the various faculties, presumably for them to discuss or take into account.[238]

2. Organization of Provincial Chapters

Bocobo's new deal for the alumni was also reflected in his own efforts and with those of Dr. Vidal A. Tan, Dean Francisco Benitez, Dr. Patrocinio Valenzuela, and Dean Leandro H. Fernandez in 1934-1935 to help the UP Alumni Association organize new chapters in the provinces, e.g., La Union, Bulacan, Cagayan, and Isabela.[239] A year later, similar chapters were organized with the faculty's assistance in Leyte, Samar, Bukidnon, Cotabato and Sorsogon.[240]

3. The Alumni Institute

The most significant, in many respects, was the holding of an Alumni Institute for the first time in 1935.[241] He had already conceptualized this before his formal inauguration in December.[242] Constituting Bocobo's "seventh reform," the Alumni Institute's objectives were:

> 1. To offer progressive alumni a chance to keep themselves posted upon new tendencies and experiments along their specialties;
> 2. To give assistance to professionals who had only two years of preparatory course in college, so that they may acquire broader culture by taking up a course in the natural and social sciences and in literature.
> 3. To provide a medium of contact between the professors and the alumni, so that they may discuss ideas that may tend to render the University of the Philippines still more useful to the country as a whole.[243]

Despite the low attendance at the First Alumni Institute (only 88), Bocobo was undismayed and organized the second in 1936. This time, 201 attended. More (237) participated in 1937 and still more (265) in 1938. In 1939, the attendance (238) was less than that of the previous year, but still the second highest among the five institutes in Bocobo's time.

The Alumni Institutes were usually held during the last week of March, except the first which was held on April 3-17 and, therefore, the longest. Except for the last two institutes under Bocobo, all the lectures were given by the faculties from the Manila units, with the College of Medicine and the College of Liberal Arts providing a large share of the lecturers; the College of Agriculture, which had tried to organize its own alumni institute in 1934 but failed for want of attendance, participated only during the last two institutes, and at that sending only four lecturers on each occasion.

Although organized principally for the alumni, many participants were non-alumni of the university, specially during the 3rd, 4th, and 5th institutes. University of Santo Tomas alumni formed the largest non-UP contingent, with 40 in each of the 3rd and 5th institutes and 29 in the 4th. There were even alumni from such foreign universities as Chicago, Utah, Chulalongkorn and Fook Tah.[244] Other than simply doing something valuable for the university's sons and daughters, therefore, the Alumni Institutes were performing a service to the nation at the same time.[245]

Manifestations of Alumni Support

What did the University get from its alumni in return for all these, other than the satisfaction that came with increasing participation?

According to Bocobo, in 1935-1936 the UP Alumni Association assisted the University through "the formation of listening groups among our alumni in connection with our radio lectures; the lending of University books and magazines to alumni chapters, and the printing of the Radio and Alumni Institute lectures."[246] For the following year, the UP Alumni Association helped encourage research through two research fellowships with a yearly ₱360-stipend for each recipient, and assisted needy but deserving students by increasing its loan fund "from ₱500 to ₱1,000."[247]

Last but not least, the UP Alumni Association financed the construction of the Alumni Hall. Inaugurated on March 27, 1938, it housed among others the UP Press and "a section of the Home Economics Department that maintains a sandwich stand which is of great help to the student body."[248]

In sum, Bocobo's programs for the alumni were an investment that produced returns, some concrete and some psychic. It also generated contacts or interactions between alumni, the faculty, and indirectly, with the third of the University's constituents: the students. And since presumably several, if not most, of the alumni had children studying in the University, such interaction also involved the parents—the fourth constituent reached.

Information Program

The creation of the UP Information Service in May 1936 was a more direct and immediate manifestation of Bocobo's wish that the institution be of service to the nation.[249] The Information Service's mission was three-fold:

1. To secure reports, memoranda, and articles from various members of the teaching staff of the University on any social, economic, educational, agricultural, financial, scientific, or professional problem and to furnish copies—if so requested—to any legislative committee or

any member of the National Assembly, to any administrative board or commission, any government official, or any newspaper, magazine, or private citizen.

2. To encourage and co-ordinate investigation by the instructional staff of current national problems and to enlist the interest of the student body therein.

3. To organize conferences and lectures on current public questions.[250]

Although only the first objective was all that the Service was able to carry out during the Bocobo years, still its accomplishments were not meager. Under its hardworking Executive Secretary, Prof. Bernabe Africa of the Department of Political Science, College of Liberal Arts,[251] it commented in 1936-1937 on 14 bills, drafted three bills and submitted 15 memoranda on various topics at the request of members of the National Assembly and the executive branch of the government. Additionally, it answered 38 questions from private individuals on a wide range of topics such as social credit system, Filipino poets, nutrition, gold production, and the health, physique and manpower of the Filipino race.[252]

For 1937-1938, the score was 16 bills commented upon, nine memoranda prepared, and seven opinions on legal questions rendered.[253] Its increased service to the National Assembly elicited a letter of gratitude from the Hon. Gregorio Perfecto, chairman of the Committee on Third Reading of that body, acknowledging the invaluable cooperation which the Service had extended to him. He labelled it as "a very commendable contribution to the public good."[254]

There would be less service to the National Assembly starting 1938-1939 because of the reorganization of the latter's legislative research office, "which is well-equipped and adequately staffed." But still it commented on seven bills, rendered six opinions, and answered 25 private queries.[255]

Writing for Publication

In addition to the activities mentioned above, the UP Information Service obtained during its first year 51 articles from various members of the teaching staff for dissemination to the public through the print media. Of these, 33 or a majority, were published in local papers and magazines,[256] thus reaching a wider audience and, therefore, of greater usefulness to a larger number of people.

The number of articles gathered from the faculties in 1938-1939 was 82, of which 71 or 86.6 percent were published.[257] This did not include articles released by the faculty without the intervention of the Information Service from 10 colleges of the University which had responded to a survey undertaken by the Service. There were, in 1938-1939, the last academic year of Bocobo's presidency, 263 such articles, of which 163, or 62 percent were published in local papers and magazines.[258]

Recognizing the importance of the UP Information Service, President Gonzalez would later reorganize and strengthen it on November 7, 1939, with Prof. Africa taking charge as chairman and no longer as executive secretary.[259]

BOCOBO'S PRESIDENCY IN RETROSPECT

JORGE C. Bocobo sought and got the UP presidency at a crucial phase in our national history. We were just emerging from the depths of the Great Depression and soon made to assume the awesome responsibilities of a semi-sovereign existence, as a prelude to full nationhood. It was a challenging moment in light of the current state of our unity and development.

Bocobo took immediate steps to ensure that the University of the Philippines, as a tax-supported institution, performed its mission in nation-building—beyond those that are intrinsic to the life of a university—effectively and, because of financial constraints, economically. Thus, he sought to make the University the steadfast promoter of national discipline and the nurturer of Filipinism; and the stern molder of socially conscious community leaders imbued with civic responsibility and at the same time leading exemplary lives. Last but not least, President Bocobo strived to make the University the dynamic engine of progress—economic, cultural and social—through timely curricular reform and effective teaching, research and outreach programs.

Bocobo, whose "sterling quality" was, according to a contemporaneous estimate of his presidency,[260] an unusual capacity for hard work, seemed in a hurry to implement the programs of his administration as he had defined them even before formally assuming the presidential mantle. He mobilized a number of working committees of the faculty and students and even the alumni. By the time of his inaugural in December 1934, less than four months after assuming office, he could inform his audience that his committees were hard at work on their assigned tasks.

To Bocobo's lasting credit, while a few of the committees could show only passable performance after four years, others did magnificently. A number of UP "traditions," practices and even institutions had their roots in the Bocobo era—thanks to the imaginativeness and ingenuity of some committee chairmen and members. If Filipinos, specially UP alumni, displayed a deeper sense of commitment to the common good, a greater appreciation of the national purpose and ideals, as well as reverence for national symbols before and during the Second World War, it was partly due to their UP training under Bocobo's administration. Unexpected developments during the last years of his presidency, like the textbook scandal and the Albert "discourtesy" incident, which may have triggered his replacement as UP president, do not in any way lessen the significance of Bocobo's legacy.

On the occasion of Bocobo's inaugural, the highest official of the land had expressed the hope that the University of the Philippines,

> ... initiated in humility, ... will continue under the splendid leadership of President Bocobo to give to the service of the community men and women who will not shirk social responsibility, who will do their duty to their country and their kind, because they are possessed of that enlightened moral leadership needed for our guidance in the momentous days ahead of us.[261]

In light of what the Bocobo administration accomplished in less than five years, Governor General Frank B. Murphy was remarkably prophetic.

VI

Gonzalez as an Adamant Visionary (1939-43, 1945-51)

The University Resurrected from the Ashes of War

by Guillermo R. Lazaro

Gonzalez as an Adamant Visionary

ON April 20, 1939, at the meeting of the Board of Regents presided over by no less than the President of the Philippines, Manuel L. Quezon, the resignation of Dr. Jorge C. Bocobo as President of the University of the Philippines was accepted and, in his place, Dr. Bienvenido M. Gonzalez was nominated and designated as Acting President of the University. Dr. Bocobo was earlier appointed by Quezon as Secretary of Public Instruction. After further deliberation, however, the Board amended the nomination and resolved that Dr. Gonzalez be appointed as the sixth President of the University of the Philippines to be effective immediately.[1] *

Dr. Gonzalez, formally inducted into office on October 19, 1939, a date which he himself chose because on that same day his father was sworn into the presidency of the "Universidad Literaria de Filipinas," the university established by the Philippine Revolutionary Government, was then the youngest and the first alumnus president of the University of the Philippines since its foundation. The formal induction was held amidst impressive ceremonies highlighted by the attendance of the highest officials of the Commonwealth headed by President Manuel L. Quezon, Speaker Jose Yulo, and Chief Justice Ramon Avanceña.

From Dean to President

The inauguration was the highest point in the career of the man who had steered and guided the administration of the College of Agriculture as Dean for more than ten years. Nonetheless, the appointment to the presidency did not come as a complete surprise for Gonzalez. A letter to Edwin Copeland, the first dean of the College of Agriculture of the University of the Philippines and whom he first met during his intermediate course at the Philippine Normal School, reveals that he had secretly longed and, consequently, prepared himself for the position for years.

> I do not know that there is anybody that could rejoice with me more in the attainment of this new position than you. It is a secret (ambition, perhaps) that you and I shared all these years. I revealed it to the Board of

*Footnote references are compiled in the NOTES section at the end of this book.

> Regents when I told them that I preferred a temporary appointment. It was my way of telling them that I was not a beggar for a job, and that if they wanted me to take it, they would have to put it on a silver platter.[2]

Early Years in Pampanga

Bienvenido Maria Gonzalez was born in Apalit, Pampanga, on March 22, 1893. He belonged to a family of boys and was the eighth of ten sons of Joaquin Gonzalez Angeles and Florencia Sioco y Rodriguez. His father died when he was barely seven years of age and so the brunt of rearing him and his brothers to manhood fell on the shoulders of his mother. Florencia Sioco was a strict disciplinarian who stressed, above all, self-discipline, but whose influence upon her sons was so great that, before she died, all of them had finished their courses and were embarking on illustrious careers.

Start of a Career in Agriculture

Gonzalez had manifested during his early school years a love for science and mathematics and, to satisfy this inclination, he enrolled at the College of Agriculture in 1910. After a year of residence, he was appointed student assistant in this College, his mentors and classmates readily recognizing and admiring his talent and dedication to duty.

Two of his superiors in particular, C.F. Baker and E. B. Copeland, were very much impressed by his unimpeachable character and by his ability and diligence. Portions of their letters attest to this.

> This is to attest my good opinion of Bienvenido M. Gonzalez, who has been one of the most reliable students we have had, a man who seems to have his own self-respect as a gentleman, and a man from whom we have known only courtesy, and attention to duty.[3]
>
> This is to say that Bienvenido Maria Gonzalez graduates this week from the University of the Philippines, with the degree of Bachelor of Agriculture. He has been three years in residence at the College of Agriculture having entered with advanced credit from the Philippine Normal School. The general character of his work here has been excellent.[4]

In April 1913, Gonzalez graduated from the College of Agriculture, obtaining the degree of Bachelor of Agriculture at the age of 19. Right after his graduation, he went to Apalit to be with his mother and for a much needed vacation. During his short stay in Apalit, his brothers, who believed that his chosen profession was not dignified enough, advised him to take up law. But he was not inclined to it. He was also not inclined to be a physician, although he had a scientific mind, because he felt that since three of his elder brothers had already finished their medical courses, he did not want to go into a field where they would be crowding each other.

Dean Copeland, meanwhile, had foreseen a bright future for Gonzalez. On December 1, 1913, less than eight months after the latter's graduation, Copeland took in Gonzalez as assistant in animal husbandry at the College of Agriculture. He was satisfied with the performance of Gonzalez. After a year of service, and upon Copeland's advice, Gonzalez applied for a University fellowship to specialize in animal husbandry in an American college. After it was held in abeyance due to a technicality, the application was approved and Gonzalez's fellowship was granted by the Board of Regents.

Graduate Studies in Wisconsin

Gonzalez enrolled at the University of Wisconsin in Madison. He matriculated in more subjects than was the normal load, so that he could finish his course quickly enough to enable him to spend what time remained of his fellowship term in visiting other colleges in the United States. His performance at the University of Wisconsin was so outstanding that on October 26, 1914, he was appointed Filipino Scholar in Agriculture, at a salary of $100, by the board of regents of that university.[5]

In record time, Gonzalez was able to obtain his master of science degree, even earning the distinction of being one of the two best students in the history of the Department of Animal Husbandry of the University of Wisconsin.[6] After graduation, Gonzalez visited other American universities, as he had planned, before coming home.

Gonzalez returned to the Philippines in May 1916. On January 1 of the following year, he married Concepcion Rafols of Cebu in the San Juan de Letran College Chapel.

Appointment to the Faculty

Very soon after his return from the United States, on June 12, 1916, Gonzalez was promoted to the position of instructor in the College of Agriculture. He attained the rank of professor on January 1, 1920 after a series of well-deserved promotions. This was exactly six years and one month since his first appointment as assistant in animal husbandry on December 1, 1913.

A close colleague of Gonzalez commented that aside from demonstrated competence, Gonzalez's phenomenal rise was partly favored by his having been elected first alumni regent of the University on September 2, 1918 at the age of 25 years.[7]

At about this time, Copeland was succeeded by C. F. Baker as Dean of the College of Agriculture. Dean Baker, foreseeing the greater role that Gonzalez would play in the University, convinced him to go back to the United States for a doctorate degree. Gonzalez, who was not very enthusiastic about the idea, agreed on the assurance that he would work for his doctorate under the guidance of Raymond Pearl, noted geneticist of Johns Hopkins University. Thus assured, he was awarded his second University fellowship.[8]

Doctorate Earned Leads to Deanship

Gonzalez decided to visit some universities in Europe before coming back to Manila after earning his doctor of science degree, thus requiring an extension of his fellowship term. On October 6, 1923, shortly after his return to the Philippines, Gonzalez was promoted Head of the Department of Animal Husbandry in the College of Agriculture.[9] Higher university officials were becoming more convinced of Gonzalez's capabilities, so much so that he was chosen commencement speaker of the University graduation exercises at the end of that academic year. On April 27, 1926, he was sent as representative of the Philippine government to the 3rd Pan Pacific Science Congress in Japan.

The Board of Regents on August 26, 1927 voted and appointed Gonzalez as Acting Dean of the College of Agriculture to replace Dean Baker who had fallen ill. On October 23, 1928, on the strength of the report of a committee of the Board of Regents and the recommendation of President Rafael Palma, Gonzalez was appointed permanent Dean of the College of Agriculture.[10]

LAYING THE GROUNDWORK FOR EFFICIENT ADMINISTRATION

BIENVENIDO M. Gonzalez began his job as President of the University of the Philippines with the confidence of one who had prepared himself for the task. Indeed, he appeared to know at once what kind of job he had to do and how to do it. During his early days as President of the University, a question of responsibility regarding the administration of that institution arose. The then Secretary of Public Instruction Jorge Bocobo had a misunderstanding with him on the administration of the University. Gonzalez wrote President Quezon for a clear-cut ruling on the line of responsibility of the Office of the President of the University and that of the Chairman of the Board of Regents.[11]

Presidential Responsibility Clarified

President Gonzalez asserted that while the President of the University was responsible to the Board of Regents as the policy-making body of the

University, he was not directly responsible to the Secretary of Public Instruction, the Chairman of the Board of Regents, in the management of his office.[12] The matter was settled when the Board of Regents supported Gonzalez's view. Secretary Bocobo's attitude about the incident is revealed in this statement:

> When I was appointed Secretary of Public Instruction in April 1939, I became Chairman ex officio of the Board of Regents. As I said in one of the faculty banquets at the time, I was a mere grandfather, and President Gonzalez was the father of the University constituency.[13]

Gonzalez's first year in office was a very eventful one for the University and for himself. The Board of Regents, in line with its resolutions instructing the Committee on Educational Policy to make a thorough study of all courses, personnel and equipment of all colleges and departments of the University, considered in its various meetings during the year the report submitted by the said committee which contained specific recommendations on the organization, administration and policies of the University.

Reexamination of Objectives

Some of the specific resolutions approved by the Board were: 1) a resolution requesting the President of the University to present a revised set of by-laws and codification of all general and special rules and regulations governing the university; 2) urging the authorities and faculty to look as often as possible into the aims and objectives of the university; 3) transferring the schools and colleges in Manila to Quezon City; and 4) creating the position of Vice-President of the University and the immediate appointment of Prof. Hermenegildo B. Reyes thereto.[14]

In connection with the recommendation to examine constantly the objectives of the University, President Gonzalez submitted the following statement as an administrative objective:

> To set high standards in the acquisition and interpretation of knowledge so that the pronouncements of faculty on any subject will be authoritative. As a concomitant, I expect the people will eventually learn to look up to their State University as a real fountainhead of knowledge.[15]

Early that same year, Gonzalez began the codification of the University rules.

Upgrading Faculty Ranks

Consonant with the policy of the Board of Regents to reorganize the University personnel, the President in a regular meeting with the University

Council raised the question whether or not it would be to the best interest of the University to further uplift its standards by the reorganization of the faculty. The voting showed that majority favored removing some members of the faculty, thus prodding Gonzalez to effect a revamp.

How he performed the painful but necessary task of dispensing with the services of some members of the faculty is recounted in a report to the Board of Regents:

> In the reorganization of the University, in accordance with the various resolutions of the Board, it was not found necessary to notify officially any faculty member or employee that his services were no longer needed. The undersigned conferred privately with the various deans, administrative officers and faculty members concerned and as a result thereof resignations were duly filed and submitted to the Board for its approval.[16]

New and amended rules were passed. Specifically amended were the rules on sabbatical leave. The former rule banning priests or ministers from speaking in the University was lifted. The Post-Graduate School of the College of Medicine was established and the Department of Mechanics in the College of Engineering officially created. To further improve and promote understanding between the students and the administration, Gonzalez set a two-hour weekly conference with the students.

Aside from the designation of Dr. Gonzalez and Prof. Reyes as President and Vice-President of the University respectively, there were other important appointments and promotions during the year. Among them were the designation of Dr. Leopoldo B. Uichanco as Dean of the College of Agriculture succeeding Dr. Gonzalez, Dr. Jose S. Reyes as Acting Dean of the College of Business Administration replacing Dr. Conrado Benitez who had resigned, Dr. Vidal A. Tan as Dean of the College of Engineering, and Prof. Fernando C. Amorsolo as Acting Director of the School of Fine Arts.[17]

Scholarships for the Deserving

An outstanding event of the year was the decision of the Board to liberalize the rules on scholarship and grant free tuition to honor graduates of high schools and colleges as long as they maintained an average of "2" or better. Highly commended by the studentry, this decision was front-page news in the *Philippine Collegian.* The *Collegian* said this move of the Board was tangible proof that the program of the administration was geared to raise further the academic standards of the University by extending to a larger number of students the privilege of scholarships. It said:

> It is expected that these scholarships will serve not only as a means of bringing to the University the best brains among the student population in

the country but also as an added incentive to those already enrolled to improve scholastic work.[18]

Distinguished Alumnus

During that same year, when Secretary Bocobo resigned as Chairman of the Board of Review of Moving Pictures, Gonzalez was appointed to succeed him. The following February, he was chosen the most distinguished alumnus of 1939 by the Board of Citizens for his appointment as the first alumnus president of the University and for his contributions to science.[19] The Board of Citizens had been formed by the U.P. Alumni Association in 1932 to take charge of the selection each year of the two most distinguished alumni of the University. The other distinguished alumnus chosen for 1939 was Fernando Amorsolo. The *Collegian* editorial had this to say regarding the selection of Gonzalez and Amorsolo:

> The Board of Citizens of the Alumni Association in its recent meeting elected President Bienvenido Gonzalez and Director (Fernando Amorsolo) most distinguished alumni of the University of the Philippines for the year 1939. No other selections could have been more fitting. The two honorees deserve the congratulations of the nation in general, and of the University constituency, in particular. Incidentally, we extend our hand to the Board of Citizens for its judgement.[20]

At the end of the academic year, the University Alumni Association presented Gonzalez a resolution unconditionally supporting his policies as president and congratulating him for his meritorious work as head of the University. The faculty endorsed this and so did the students.

Alumni and Faculty Activities

The Alumni Association actively cooperated in the different programs of the administration. To promote a closer link between the University and the alumni, the monthly journal of the Association, *The U.P. Alumnus,* started publication in January 1940. A special guest room was set apart for the first time in the Alumni Hall to accommodate alumni from the provinces who were in Manila for a visit. The Alumni Hall also housed the University of the Philippines Press and the Home Economics Sandwich Stand on the ground floor; the Institute of National Language, the U.P. Student Council, the *Philippine Collegian,* and the *Philippinensian* on the second floor; and the social hall for the use of the alumni and students on the third floor.[21]

Worthy of mention is the 1940 Faculty Conference in Baguio. Started in 1936, the Baguio Conference was initiated so that faculty members might exchange ideas on the problems of higher education. The 1940 Conference was the first in which all the colleges of the University were represented. It also had the largest attendance: a total of 94 delegates attended the conference compared with 50 delegates the preceding year.[22]

A High Regard for Decorum

Gonzalez had a delicate sense of propriety pertaining to the use of government property as shown by an incident that occurred during the early years of his presidency.

One day when the President was ready to leave for the University in the official car, his wife asked if she could come along. But Gonzalez thought it would not be proper for her to ride in the official car. He ordered his chauffeur to return to the office and the couple used their private car and driver instead. Gonzalez made it a point never to use his official car whenever a member or members of his family would have to ride with him or when his trip was for a personal purpose.

The succeeding years were also eventful. In January 1941, a mammoth rally was held in the University campus welcoming the arrival from abroad of Speaker Jose Yulo of the National Assembly. Students of different universities were gathered in large numbers to participate that afternoon. The activity lasted until late afternoon. Some male participants took advantage of the growing darkness by mashing the women participants. This resulted in great commotion and disturbance among the crowd. Some people blamed Gonzalez for this lack of discipline among the menfolk to the point that an assemblyman presented a resolution in the National Assembly to declare the Office of the President of the University vacant. Congressman Tomas Oppus of Leyte, however, made such a good defense of Gonzalez that the resolution was not even put to a vote.[23]

Leadership in Educational Policy

At the time, the Catholic Educational Association of the Philippines proposed the shortening of the grade school, high school and bachelor's courses from the then existing seven years, four years and four years respectively to six years, three years and three years or "6-3-3" as the plan was called. This became the subject of discussion in University circles. While some well-meaning people might have considered the feasibility of introducing it in the entire educational system, President Gonzalez was foremost among those who opposed the idea. Vocal in his criticism of the system, he never favored the shortening of college courses. The University Council unanimously supported his views.

> With the passage of the resolution of the University Council endorsing the views of the President in connection with the current proposals to reform the educational system in the country, the stand of the administration about

> that question is unanimous. The University Council is on record as being opposed to the shortening or reduction of the courses leading to the degree of Bachelor of Arts and to other Bachelor's degrees.
>
> President Gonzalez is not in favor of the proposal advanced by the Catholic Educational Association of the Philippines to revise the prevailing four years requirement in college work leading to bachelor's degree, it was learned. U.P., being the state university, has to set the standards of college education in the Philippines. Not only that, the institution has to keep up with world standards in education by adhering closely to American standards. This is so because the U.P. itself is a member of the Association of American State Universities, and many of our colleges are members of similar bodies. Accordingly, an inspector was recently brought to examine the College of Medicine; the bringing of inspectors for the college of Engineering and Education in the near future is also being contemplated. Then, it is asserted that U.P. degrees and credits are taken on their face value for advanced credit by American and also European universities.[24]

On December 31, 1939, Tagalog became the national language of the Philippines. This decision of the Institute of National Language was greeted by the University with optimism in the hope that through a national language, the Filipino may finally discover his own soul and identity.

Another significant event is the controversy that President Quezon created when he advocated partyless democracy. Gonzalez was against it but he did not voice out his opinions publicly. However, he allowed freedom of discussion of the issue in University circles. Quezon was criticized by certain segments of the University. Prof. Bernabe Africa of the Political Science Department openly disagreed with Quezon. A member of the Board of Regents wanting to win the good graces of Quezon proposed a bill limiting academic freedom for which he was strongly opposed by the faculty and the press.

THE UNIVERSITY IN PERIL DURING THE JAPANESE OCCUPATION

PRELUDES to the Pacific War were noticed by political observers as early as November 1939. Japan was extending her hegemony of East Asia and was expanding her Empire southward. Dr. Pedro E. Abelarde, for one, pointed out the importance of the Philippines to the Japanese in their expansionist drive and took notice of how they had penetrated and increased their participation in the business and trade activities of the country.[25]

Grim Reality of War

As the country was about to enter the Second World War, the University, especially its studentry, could not ignore the horrible predicament that was then confronting the world. When the University celebrated the Christmas season in December 1940, it did so in an atmosphere of sympathy for those people who had become the unfortunate victims of the war.

When the University was closed on December 13, 1941 because of the war, some units nevertheless continued their operations because of their immediate importance. These were the Schools of Dentistry, Forestry and Hygiene, and the Colleges of Agriculture, Medicine and Veterinary Science. In July 1942, a Junior College was opened for other students who might want to continue their studies. Later, the College of Engineering and the School of Pharmacy resumed classes.

The holding of classes in Manila was faced with difficulties because only the buildings of the Philippine General Hospital and the College of Medicine were available. There was also the shadow of repression by the Japanese military adminstration which hampered the freedom of intellectual pursuits. The academic independence which characterized learning before the war was lost and the atmosphere that loomed in the University was one of fear discouraging academic growth and excellence.

Gonzalez Replaced by Dr. Sison

Gonzalez tried to save the University from becoming an instrument of Japanese propaganda during the early part of the Japanese occupation. He discouraged the holding of convocations in order to prevent the Japanese propagandists from using the sacred halls of the University. When he sensed that the Japanese were getting wise to his moves and with the subsequent loss of academic freedom, he tendered his resignation as President of the University to the Commissioner of Education, Health and Public Welfare on September 13, 1943.[26] He did not permit himself to be used by the Japanese as a tool of their propaganda.* His resignation was officially accepted in a letter dated October 11, 1943 signed by the Chairman of the Executive Commission Jorge B. Vargas.[27]

After the resignation of Gonzalez, President Jose P. Laurel appointed Dr. Antonio G. Sison to the presidency of the University. Dr. Sison, thus,

*In a letter to Jorge B. Vargas dated July 7, 1978, then UP President O.D. Corpuz cited a letter written by Dr. Bienvenido M. Gonzalez to Dr. Leon J. Cole of the College of Agriculture, University of Wisconsin, dated August 27, 1945. As reported by Dr. Corpuz: "Dr. Gonzalez intimated that previous to the 'discovery of widespread subversive activity at the Los Banos campus,' which apparently precipitated his resignation, he 'was torn between two conflicting viewpoints.' He said that 'On one hand, I did not want to serve under the Japs, and on the other, I could not just abandon my responsibilities by the University, and more particularly expose its constituency without guidance to the influence of Japanese ideologies and pressure.' His resignation was 'voluntary,' he said, 'although it might have possibly become forced had I given (the Japanese) more time to examine my attitudes and utterances'."

Dr. Corpuz's letter was appended to the Minutes of the 903rd Meeting of the Board of Regents on June 29, 1978 as a formal acknowledgment of Dr. Antonio G. Sison's having served as President of the University of the Philippines from October 14, 1943 to February 1945.--Editor became the University's seventh president. This was the first official act of President Laurel as head of the Philippine Republic during the Japanese occupation. Dr. Sison, who was U.P. President from October 14, 1943 to February 1945, took his oath before Vice-Minister of Education, Health and Public Welfare Gabriel Mañalac. He was concurrently Dean of the U.P. College of Medicine and Director of the Philippine General Hospital.

Instruction No. 72 issued in August 1942 provided for the opening of some colleges of the University of the Philippines. The first units to be organized were the Colleges of Medicine and Agriculture.

Japanese Influence on University Affairs

The Japanese were aware of the significant role of the University in moulding the minds of the Filipinos. Certain reforms were introduced and restrictions were imposed in the University system. The Japanese saw to it that their advice was sought in instruction, teaching and research. It also became necessary to study the Japanese language and culture before one could graduate.

Eight colleges were opened: agriculture, dentistry, engineering, forestry, junior college, medicine, pharmacy and veterinary science. For the academic year 1942-1943, 791 students were enrolled in the first semester and 1,279 in the second. These figures exclude the enrolment in the non-collegiate units such as the School of Nursing and the Rural High School. If the enrolment in the non-collegiate units is added, the total number of students enrolled was 1,115 in the first semester and 1,648 in the second. Compared with the enrolment on the eve of the Japanese occupation which was 7,567 in the first semester of 1941-1942 and 6,659 in the second semester, the enrolment for 1942-1943 was very much smaller.[28]

It should be noted that only colleges in the technical and scientific units were authorized to open. Courses in the social sciences and the humanities were not allowed. The Japanese saw to it that no opposing ideology critical of the new order was permitted in the University of the Philippines.

GONZALEZ RETURNS TO A WAR-DEVASTATED CAMPUS

THE Commonwealth was reestablished in February 1945. A few months afterward, the Board of Regents was reconvened. Bienvenido M. Gonzalez was reelected President of the State University on June 28, 1945 and hence, became the eighth President of the University, acquiring the distinction of having been elected to the University presidency twice. Gonzalez accepted the reelection unhesitatingly. Others would have refused, considering that the plant and facilities of the University of the Philippines had been reduced to rubble by the war. And then there was the extremely difficult task of reconstituting the faculty. But Gonzalez's love for the University and his determination to put it back in operation proved to be greater than all the odds he faced.

Rising from the Ruins

The extent of the damage wrought on the University by the war is recorded in the President's annual report:

> When the din of battle died down, the University found its buildings severely damaged. Ruined edifices and twisted steel, halls once imposing, now shell-pocked or sprawled in rubbish, were telltale evidences of the terrible ordeal the University had gone through. The records, libraries, offices, laboratories, and the valuable scientific equipment in these, were a total loss. A conservative estimate based on original values of the material losses sustained by the University approaches the P10,000,000 mark. In view of the foregoing, when the time came for the University to reopen, the first problem that presented itself was the location.[29]

Since not even one building on the main campus was available for use, the University requested the Philippine General Hospital for the temporary use of the Institute of Radium Therapy. The University opened its first academic year after the war on August 6, 1945. The first units that reopened were the Colleges of Liberal Arts, Medicine (including the School of Dentistry), Pharmacy, Engineering, Law and Education (including the U.P. High School) in Manila; Veterinary Science in Pandacan; and Agriculture, the School of Forestry and the Rural High School in Los Baños. Other units which subsequently resumed functioning were the Cebu Junior College, the School of Fine Arts, the School of Nursing and the Conservatory of Music.[30]

Reconstruction of Academic Records

The war had prevented students from either finishing their courses or pursuing their studies. The University Council formulated emergency rules for students whose scholastic records had been destroyed, and recommended to the Board of Regents the graduation of those students who had completed all their requirements for their respective college degrees during the Japanese occupation. It also approved a pre-collegiate year course, known as the common first year, that would supplement the education of those students who had only ten years of education prior to their collegiate studies.

Two of the important actions taken by the Executive Committee of the University Council were the offering of completion courses for students who were unable to finish their work during the second semester of 1941-1942, and the examination of the affidavits of students, whose academic records were destroyed, regarding the courses which they had already taken and passed.[31]

Efforts Toward Recovery

The first academic year after the war covered only a period of eleven months from July 1, 1945 to May 31, 1946.[32] This was due to the late reconstitution of the Board of Regents on June 21, 1945. As a consequence, the statements and reports of income and expenditure for the school year covered only an eleven-month period.

Prof. Hermenegildo B. Reyes resigned from his position as Vice-President. As a result, the Board of Regents created the Office of Business Manager of the University and appointed Dr. Enrique T. Virata thereto. Dr. Bienvenido M. Gonzalez temporarily served as Acting Dean of the College of Education in the absence of Dean Francisco Benitez, who had been appointed by President Sergio Osmeña as Secretary of Public Instruction. Dean Leandro H. Fernandez of the College of Liberal Arts was designated Acting Dean of the College of Business Administration and Prof. Ramon Tapales Acting Director of the Conservatory of Music.[33]

Before the outbreak of the war, the Board of Regents had decided to transfer the University to its new site at Diliman, Quezon City, the projected transfer to take place in 1942. But with the start of the Pacific War on December 8, 1941, the construction of the buildings at Diliman was suspended. When the Japanese army occupied the premises of the new site, two three-story buildings, one for the College of Liberal Arts and the other for the Colleges of Law and Business Administration, were almost ready for use. When the Japanese army withdrew, the buildings were not left unscathed as the Japanese tried to destroy them. The construction of the buildings could not be resumed right after the war, as the United States Army occupied the Diliman site and signed a lease on the property to expire on June 30, 1948.[34]

The destruction of the University campus and the fact that some units were not able to reopen and resume operation resulted in the great decrease in enrolment for the academic year.[35] The enrolment for the year represented only 33 per cent of the enrolment before the war. The units that failed to reopen were Business Administration, Arts and Sciences, the Institute of Hygiene, and the School of Public Health Nursing.

Excellence Upheld Despite Privations

In spite of the tremendous physical handicap of the University, President Gonzalez undauntedly stood up to the challenge. The problems were great but they were not insurmountable. Little by little, unceasingly, Gonzalez the builder undertook the rehabilitation of the University. Competent faculty members who returned to work and were willing to serve the University at great financial sacrifice gave untold encouragement. Gonzalez took pride that as far as the standard of education was concerned, the quality of U.P. instruction immediately after the war did not deteriorate.

> The University may have been badly handicapped in material means, but from the spiritual and intellectual standpoints, it has fortunately survived the ravages of war. While several outstanding members of the faculty have been drafted by the government in positions of equal or greater responsibility and several more have been attracted to remunerative positions elsewhere, those recalled to duty have been specially chosen for their energy, steadfastness, resourcefulness and competence in their various specialties. As far as intellectual gifts and mastery of the subject-matter and loyalty to the institution and its ideals in the face of a most difficult situation are concerned, there has been no serious deterioration in the quality from pre-war standard.[36]

Gonzalez sent promising young instructors to the United States and, notwithstanding the inadequate financial support of the government, he made the best use of the appropriations set aside by Congress for the University.

Rebirth of Philippinensian

Student representatives of the different graduate classes embarked on preparing the yearbook of student graduates from 1942-1946. The yearbook was entitled the *U.P. Phoenix* or *The Phoenix* after the mythical bird which is believed to have a life span of 500 years. It is fabled that the bird consumes itself by the fire of its own creation, and then rises again from its ashes – new, fresh, youthful and vigorous as ever.

The Phoenix is a fitting symbol of what the University of the Philippines should be after its devastation in the war. Conscious of its obligation to lead the nation in transmitting knowledge and liberating the spirit, the U.P. must, in the words of Paul V. McNutt, the last American High Commissioner to the Philippines and speaker at the 1946 commencement exercises: "Like the Phoenix. . . rise renewed and revitalized from the ashes of destruction. From this very group must come the teachers to take the place of those who have died in the great struggle of the past half-decade. You are the shock troops of the post-war struggle for rehabilitation."[37]

The yearbook was a labor of love. It was prepared after graduation so that it became difficult for the yearbook staff to contact the graduates who were already scattered throughout the Philippines. Letters were sent as far north as Batanes and as far south as Davao and Zamboanga. Notices and announcements were printed in newspapers and broadcast over the radio. Although some letters were unanswered without any trace as to the whereabouts of the addressees, the response from the graduates was generally encouraging. When the yearbook came out, a large number of the graduates were included.

Nationhood as a New Challenge

Aside from the task of rebuilding the University after the war, equally important was the challenged posed by the proclamation of Philippine independence. With its changed political status, the country had to adopt fresh approaches and give new directions to its national policies as it became a part of the world community of free and sovereign nations.

Against this background, the University of the Philippines continued to lead in the search for truth, equality, freedom and justice; to give "light where there is darkness, hope amid ruin, and life arising from the ashes of destruction."[38]

The proclamation of Philippine Independence on July 4, 1946 affected the University in two ways. First, with the changed political status of the country, revisions in the curricula of the various schools and colleges were made. Secondly, as certain branches of the government increased their needs and activities, the University became favorite recruiting place resulting in great loss to the academic ranks of the institution.

Replenishing Personnel and Physical Plant

Aside from defections caused by inadequate salaries and the recruitment by certain branches of the government, there was a shortage of personnel because of deaths during the war, lack of replenishment, and the refusal of University fellows who had been overtaken abroad by the war to return to the Philippines and fulfill their obligations to the University.

In order to cope with the shortage of academic personnel, President Gonzalez, upon the suggestion of the President of the Philippines, resuscitated the faculty with Americans.[39] As an initial step, the University appointed Prof. H.H. Bartlett of the University of Michigan as Visiting Professor. Bartlett had been twice a visiting professor before the war. The University also tried to ameliorate the salaries and wages of its personnel by curtailing some activities for which it received no additional funds from the government.

Meanwhile, the Board of Regents had resolved to ask the permission of the President of the Philippines to allow the University to undertake planning and construction in the new site in Diliman since the Bureau of Public Works was too busy working on its other projects.[40] The Board also made representations to the President of the Philippines and Congress for the retention of the Manila campus upon the transfer of the University to its new site.

When the University entered the second academic year after the war, it was still faced with the same problems and handicaps so that it was able to admit only a small number of students. Although it tried to maintain its high academic standards, the University could not within a short period of one year regain its pre-war status. Inflation was acute and the cost of maintaining the institution mounting. With the low scale of salaries, it could not prevent the defection of its faculty members. More space nevertheless became available for use as the U.S. Army, which had been occupying the main campus in Padre Faura, vacated the place and returned it to the University. Consequently, additional units were able to reopen and to resume their operations, enabling the University to admit more students.[41]

Recalcitrant Fellows

A number of faculty members on fellowship or special detail had been overtaken in the United States by the war. A few of them failed to report to the University after the war and to fulfill their obligations to render service to the institution, in spite of repeated instructions that they return. The Board of Regents, therefore, adopted this resolution:

> WHEREAS, some of these University Fellows have secured higher degrees and others have so far advanced in their studies as to be in a position to render greater service to the University. The Board of Regents, however, views with regret their failure to comply with instructions to return to the University because other offices or entities of the government, of which the University is a part, had offered them positions with larger stipends. This practice obviously undermined the whole University Fellowship System, and if it is sanctioned and allowed to continue, a time will come when the University, insecure in its program of further training personnel for its work, can hardly discharge its proper functions not only as an educational institution but also as an instrumentality of the government for the training of competent personnel for public service.[42]

The Board called the attention of the President of the Philippines regarding these reneging fellows. It appealed for the recognition by other branches or departments of the government of the right of the University to claim the services of its faculty who were beneficiaries of the UP fellowship system.

Role of the Alumni

The Alumni Association for its part continued to contribute and cooperate in the solution of important University problems. It participated in

University activities and devised ways of collecting donations for the use of the Alma Mater. It planned to erect a memorial for those alumni who died during the last war. But it especially took pride in the fact that a large number of those who were in control of national activities were University alumni, proof of the success of the University in training leaders for the country and thereby fulfilling the objectives for which the University was established.

Revival of Student Activities

The *Philippine Collegian* was reborn in September 1946. President Gonzalez himself sent a congratulatory message and reminded the *Collegian* staff of its duty to maintain, as in the past, a proper sense of sobriety in moulding public opinion and in working for progressive and constructive reforms.[43]

A number of student organizations, associations, clubs, leagues and councils were revived, and university activities became almost regular. Perhaps the most important organization that was revived was the UP Student Council whose officers and committee members were elected right after its restoration. Other organizations that were reactivated were, to name only a few, the UP Woman's Club, the UP Dramatic Club, the UP Oratorical-Debating Club, the University Junior and Senior Student Councils, and the UP Writers' League. Military training was also resumed with the revival of the UP ROTC and the organization of the UP Vanguard by the UP Cadet Corps.

Earlier, news was circulated in one of the local dailies that the University of the Philippines was not satisfied with the administration of Gonzalez.[44] To disprove such allegations, the Board of Regents of the University passed a resolution affirming its faith in the presidency of Gonzalez and assuring him of University support for his policies. The student body was particularly riled by the news and moved to petition the Student Council to adopt a resolution expressing the students' faith in and support for Gonzalez.

Cause for Debate

The relationship of the studentry with the administration was warm and cordial as the former was sympathetic with the policies of the latter. Cases of misunderstanding were very rare. A minor controversy arose, however, when the studentry decried the prohibition by the University authorities of the use of Villamor Hall for the first post-war debate of the students. The activity was a revival of the annual student debates held before the war.

The University officials did not permit the students to use Villamor Hall because the debate was on the controversial "parity" issue, and they could not risk having the opposing groups engage in mudslinging accusations that would debase the sanctity of the hall. The students were taken aback by this attitude of the authorities. They protested the officials' lack of faith that they could have an orderly debate and handle themselves well. Contrary to what the authorities feared, the students felt that the debate would help enlighten the minds of the studentry for an intelligent consideration of the "parity" issue.[45] The students saw that the "parity" agreement would mean the dependence of Filipinos on American economic aid. Rather than enabling us to be on equal footing with the Americans, "parity" would make us their mendicant "brothers."

ANXIETIES AND REWARDS OF UNIVERSITY STEWARDSHIP

PRESIDENT Manuel A. Roxas recognized the ability of Gonzalez and named him to several other important positions. He appointed him chairman of the Board of Regents of the Institute of Science and a member of the National Economic Council, a policy-making body headed by President Roxas himself.

Gonzalez related how he managed to discharge his manifold duties in a letter to Dean Copeland:

> To the list of eight that Gonzalo must have shown you when he came to see you, one more has been added recently – a membership in the United States Educational Foundation in the Philippines. These organizations are fairly active and when they start forming committees and sub-committees, as they often do, they begin to eat up time. It is not unusual for me to have three meetings in a day, and an average of six a week is quite ordinary. There are also three directorates in private industrial organizations. And socials where they load you with food, rather, where they give you an opportunity to stuff yourself come about three times a week, conservatively. How one is able to do one's work with all these affairs is difficult to explain. I manage somehow by starting work at 7:30 A.M., and not admitting callers before 9:00. Papers requiring study are taken home and memoranda written there. Then come regular conferences with visitors, local and foreign, and consultations of personal or semi-official nature by members of the faculty, students, and outsiders. On the side I have to personally keep up my files of these different organizations. I have adequate help in so far as the University business is concerned but for the other organizations, I have to do my own filing to forestall confusion.[46]

Gonzalez was, however, not spared from apprehensions during the intervening years. After the death of President Roxas on April 15, 1948, Gonzalez felt that his position in the University was becoming more difficult and less encouraging. This he expressed in the same letter to Copeland.

One of the most annoying features of my work is the occasional appearance in the papers of news that someone wants my job and that I would be shifted, often kicked upwards, to this position or that. Had these materialized, I would have become Vice-President of the Philippines, ambassador to the Court of St. James, ambassador to Europe with residence in Paris, manager of some Government industrial enterprise, Director of the scientific work of the government, Secretary of Education, and last but not least, a private citizen. I have learned not to be bothered unduly by these news and the deliverance from a difficult and a thankless job may be considered as sufficient compensation for anything that might happen. It is rather annoying, however, to feel that one's work is neither recognized nor appreciated and one must find consolation and encouragement in the thought that one is doing an onerous job that is more than likely to be messed up by one's successor whose best qualification is likely the wish to be honored by the position, or in its use as a stepping stone for something "bigger" and juicier. After one has lost his life work in the destruction of the breeds of animals he has sought to establish that would have meant a great deal to the economy of the country, the serious setback in the educational work in which one has taken an active part, the defection of carefully selected youngsters to carry on the work after he is gone, the loss of a small competence one has built painfully slow during a lifetime devoted to public service for the winter years ahead, can you blame one if he turns out a cynic. Yet one's background of breeding and training, and an idealistic philosophy that inspiring teachers have led him into, and the cold fact that one has to do something to live and to avoid boredom as long as he exists, and may I say one's responsibility for his share of the general clamor for freedom he voiced in his aggressive youth. All these cannot be ignored and one goes on with the work pretty much regardless of his feelings. What is more incongruous however, is that I can even go to a great expense to prepare my son to follow in my footsteps – to continue the seemingly constructive but probably futile work I am attempting to do.[47]

Appreciative Student Leaders

Prior to this, however, at a luncheon tendered by President Gonzalez for student leaders to discuss university problems and improve faculty-student relations, the student leaders unanimously approved the policies of Gonzalez and gave him the assurance that they would support his administration. Letters of appreciation were written by these student leaders thanking the President for the luncheon meeting and reiterating their support for his leadership. Some of the important portions of these letters read:[48]

We fervently wish you more success in your undertakings and please rest assured that each and every one of us will endeavor to harmonize completely professor-student relationship and coordination.

In reiteration, allow us to extend our profound gratitude for an inspirational manifestation of your fatherly solicitude for the welfare of the university constituents.

Delfin J. Villanueva
President, U.P. Student Council

. . . . In you, Mr. President, we have a leader whose presence awakens in us admiration and kindles in us the urge to push on. You are not only a leader, but also a true comrade and a father to the thousands of students of the University of the Philippines.

Lourdes L. Lontok
U.P. Woman's Club

The PHILIPPINE COLLEGIAN hopes you will keep (SIC) the good work – and the good fight. And if you need any help, please be assured that the editorial staff of the University paper is always at your side, ready to help in its small way, for the good fight which is yours – is ours.

Mariano V. Ampil, Jr.
Editor-in-Chief

This, Sir, shall be our lasting manifests (SIC) of gratitude to you – not the glory of praises or honors or medals of merit bestowed upon us – but the brave and undimmed light of truth, wisdom and knowledge shining in the eyes of our youth. Then shall we point with just pride to the man who taught us, through blameless example, our great lesson – our beloved President who is first among educators, first among leaders and administrators and last but not the least, first among fathers.

Annie Ramos
College of Education

So close was the relationship of President Gonzalez with the student body that a column appeared in the October 1948 issue of *This Week Magazine* which charged the *Philippine Collegian* of being used as a tool by President Gonzalez to serve his personal ambitions and to establish a one-man rule in the University. The *Collegian* staff was so incensed at this accusation that it deemed it proper to ask the columnist to apologize to the *Collegian* for his unfounded article. The *Collegian* declared that it had not broken faith with its noble tradition of free inquiry and militant thinking. It asserted that it had not been subjected to any administrative pressure, and said that "if there are those who doubt the integrity of the *Collegian* as a member of a respectable press, we wish to declare that should anyone dare silence this paper, he can only do so over the dead vigilance of a staff that cherishes freedom above anything else."[49]

Administrative Problems

The University steadily progressed toward normalization as it entered its third academic year after the war at its site in Manila. For this school year, only one academic calendar was followed in contrast to as many as ten academic calendars when the University reopened. Conditions were still not entirely normal, however, as the academic calendar had to be adjusted to the time schedule of public schools whose students graduated in the middle of the year. Consequently, regular classes had to be adjusted until the summer period, to the discomfiture of the faculty and the students.

Still the most immediate problem was the inadequate financial support of the government after the large-scale destruction that the University suffered. Angel Martinez, the Dean of Men, summarized into five main topics the problems of the University: (1) lack of sufficient funds to pay salaries to the faculty; (2) reconstruction of the buildings destroyed in the last war; (3) establishment of an adequate library and library facilities; (4) insufficiency of dormitories near the campus of the University; and (5) absence of gymnasiums and places of recreation in the U.P. premises.[50]

The President of the Student Council observed that a major problem in the University was the deficiency of the students in their command of English. President Gonzalez attributed this shortcoming to the shortening of the academic calendars and the curriculum of secondary schools resulting in the inadequacy of student preparation for collegiate students.

To prevent the exodus of faculty members and to induce them to render their services to the University instead, the rates of faculty compensation were steadily improved so that the salaries for the academic year were higher by approximately 50 per cent compared with that before the war.[51] Gonzalez nonetheless found the compensation still inadequate because of the high cost of living. The University was further saddled financially by the admission of Philippine veterans who did not have to pay any fee because they enjoyed educational benefits from government legislation. These factors plus the rapid rehabilitation of the University and the increase in the student population led to the increase of expenditures by a little above ₱400,000 over the last academic year.[52]

Faculty Concerns

Aside from the death of President Manuel A. Roxas, the University also grieved over the loss of Dr. Leandro H. Fernandez who was for many years Dean of the College of Liberal Arts and Chairman of the Committee on Graduate Studies. As a result of the death of Dean Fernandez, Dr. Enrique T. Virata was appointed Dean of the College of Liberal Arts, Acting Dean of the College of Business Administration and permanent chairman of the University Council Committee on Graduate Studies. Other important promotions during the year were the designation of Prof. Angel Martinez as permanent Dean of Men and the appointment of Prof. Ramon Tapales as permanent Director of the Conservatory of Music after both had served in an acting capacity.[53]

Prospects for the rehabilitation of the depleted faculty ranks, begun the preceding year, brightened with the signing by the United States and Philippine governments of an agreement in line with U.S. Public Law 584, otherwise known as the Fulbright Act. The agreement provided for American professors to be brought to the Philippines to teach here. Prof. H.H. Bartlett was appointed educational consultant in the United States to facilitate the selection of the right personnel for the University of the Philippines.[54]

Dr. Tomas S. Fonacier was named Dean of the College of Iloilo which opened during the year. The groundwork for the elevation of the pre-war School of Public Health Nursing to the College of Nursing was laid by the University, with the opening set for the next academic year. The Alabang Vaccine and Serum Laboratories, which for 11 years had been under the Institute of Hygiene of the University, was transferred to the Department of Health, while the Philippine General Hospital, formerly under the Office of the President of the Philippines, was transferred to the University.[55]

The first postwar Baguio Faculty Conference was held in June 1948. The faculty discussed and stressed the importance of maintaining the leadership of the University in national education and even upgrading its standards for the improvement of college education.[56]

Fund for Reconstruction

Under the Philippine Rehabilitation Act of 1946, the U.S. Philippine War Damage Commission received an appropriation of ₱240,000,000 from the U.S. Congress. A total amount of ₱13,000,000 was set aside for the University by the War Damage Commission as the reconstruction of the University buildings was covered by the Rehabilitation Act of 1946. The reconstruction program that followed was not inconsistent with the plans to transfer to Diliman in Quezon City.[57]

The Board of Directors of the U.P. Alumni Association made representations to the alumni members of the Congress of the Philippines for financial assistance essentially needed by the University. It also sponsored a resolution addressed to President Roxas to request Congress to pass a law which would grant permanent ownership by the University of its campus, buildings, and physical properties in its site in Manila even as it transferred to its new site in Diliman, for this would enable the University to use the old campus as a source of income. The Alumni Association was also able to work for the amendment of the Charter of the University to enable the Board of Regents to confer honorary degrees upon those who merit them, including graduates of the University. Previous to this, the University was not allowed to confer honorary degrees on its own alumni. The Association also resumed the publication of *The U.P. Alumnus.*[58]

Transfer to Diliman

The operations of the University were almost normal during the academic year 1948-1949. But what made the year significant was the transplantation of the University from its 10-hectare site in Ermita to its 493-hectare campus in Diliman.[59] The transfer marked a new era in the history of the University and acquired greater significance because it coincided with the 40th anniversary of the University. The transfer, which took place from December 16, 1948 to January 11, 1949 was timed and implemented by the late President Manuel L. Quezon to provide better facilities for the state university.

But the decision to transfer the University to Diliman met with serious opposition. Adverse criticisms were especially hurled against Gonzalez, often questioning his capacity as a leader. An ex-regent of the University even asked for his immediate ouster.[60] A local columnist lambasted Gonzalez several times in his column.

Despite the adverse criticisms from the detractors of President Gonzalez, the general attitude regarding the transfer was one of enthusiasm and optimism. University officials, faculty members, employees and students stuck to their belief and confidence in Gonzalez, affirming their faith in his administration and giving their wholehearted cooperation to the transfer of the University. The studentry was especially vocal about its unwavering faith and support for the "exodus" of the University.

> You are become a very misunderstood man, Mr. President. But those who do not understand are people who have never really known you. They are people who are motivated more by the desire to malign than by the desire to tell the truth. But no matter what these detractors say or write, we know that you do not rise or fall to what they think of you. To us, Mr. President, you are the symbol of our idealism, and not even the most caustic pen can diminish your influence upon us.
>
> We believe in you, Mr. President; we believe in your leadership. We believe that you are leading the U.P. in a progressive crusade. The mere thought, Mr. President, that we, your students, believe in you, should be sufficient shield for you against the attacks of irresponsible critics.[61]

> . . .the transfer of the U.P. to Diliman is a big event, one that can easily become shrouded in disagreements. Yet, while we remain impassive to the colored propaganda of unscrupulous detractors, we owe it upon ourselves as students of this university, to strengthen our resolves by looking into our consciences for the answers to whatever doubt we may have.
>
> The transfer to Diliman is a pioneering venture. It is essentially a movement designed to open a more progressive era in our educational history. We, the students of this University, should feel the burden of our participation in this great event. We should condition our hearts and minds toward a deeper dedication to this big task of leading a movement, to give freely of our talents and be willing to forego personal conveniences so as to help bring about a climate of thought and attitude favorable to the realization of a greater University of the Philippines.[62]

The University faculty, except for a few detractors, stood behind their president. The College of Law faculty passed a resolution reiterating its faith and confidence in Gonzalez.[63]

Start of a New Era

The quadragesimal anniversary celebration on February 11-12, 1949, held in the new campus in Diliman, signalled the beginning of a new era in the history of the University. Open house was declared for the public to visit the new location. The celebration was marked in the morning of February 11 by the transfer of the Oblation from Padre Faura to its new site. The Oblation was greeted by the cheers of the students and the enthusiastic welcome of University officials. The transfer of the Oblation which had stood for 13 years in the Manila campus saw the end of the Padre Faura era. The celebration also featured a forum on higher education in which the University reaffirmed, and rededicated itself, to its role in leading and serving the nation through quality education.

The transfer of the ever-growing and progressive University of the Philippines to its present locale is now accepted as the product of the vision and determination of President Gonzalez. Indeed, it should serve as a lasting memorial to the man who dared all opposition and overcame all obstacles to make a "magnificent obsession" a reality.

Incidents shortly after the transfer of the University to its present site show some facets of the character of Gonzalez.

One day in 1949, following a heavy downpour and strong winds, Dr. Paterno Santos, then registrar of the University of the Philippines, approached President Gonzalez and suggested the construction of waiting sheds for the students. The color of the President's face changed visibly, warning Santos that he had come at an inopportune moment. Gonzalez told him that such a suggestion was unthinkable at that time. He pointed out to the roofing of the quonset hut housing the Department of Chemistry, which had collapsed as a result of the storm, and which obviously needed more immediate attention than the proposed waiting sheds. Santos withdrew his suggestion. However, after several days, he again approached the President to take up the same matter. He was not disappointed this time. Gonzalez readily approved his suggestion.[64]

Another incident was related by his son Gonzalo.

> . . . Once, a few years ago, when the University had just come to this place, I visited my father here because he had told me that he wanted me to see something. I waited in his office wondering what it could be. The whistle blare marking the end of another class hour sounded and he finally stood up from his work and led me to the window. Below us and in the distance we saw the wide expanse of campus green that, as if by magic, had suddenly come to life with young people. Without turning his gaze, he asked, "Doesn't that make you happy? " He was not looking at the foundations and forms of these halls of learning that were fast taking shape nor at the young trees that

had just been planted and were growing. He was looking at the students changing classrooms, some hurrying, some walking slowly, the women in gay colors and the clean young men talking with them. "This makes everything worthwhile," he told me. "Whenever I am tired or when things seem trying I come to this window and I look at them." I knew then why my father had spent his life with this University.[65]

Staff and Faculty Appointments

Incident to the operation of the College of Nursing which started at the beginning of the school year, Prof. Julita V. Sotejo was appointed dean of this newly established College. Other important appointments were the designation of Dr. Ignacio Salcedo as acting Dean of the Iloilo College to succeed Dr. Tomas S. Fonacier, who had been recalled from the deanship of the College to serve as vice-dean of the College of Liberal Arts, the designation of Prof. Jose E. Velmonte as acting dean of the College of Business Administration to succeed Dr. Enrique T. Virata, and the designation of Dr. Victorino G. Villa as dean of the College of Dentistry following its conversion from a school. Dr. Salcedo was later transferred to the College of Liberal Arts, and Prof. Soledad Aguirre of the College of Education was named dean of the Iloilo College to replace him.[66]

The rehabilitation of the depleted academic ranks saw some activity as the United States Educational Foundation, the body in charge of executing the program of the Fulbright Act, called for the assignment of 20 professors to the Philippines. Out of this number, nine were to be assigned to the University of the Philippines, six as regular professors, one as extension professor, and two as research professors. These were Dr. Robert Conklin in English, Dr. Milton C. Cummings in economics, Dr. Edward Jones in psychology, Dr. John T. Salter in political science, Dr. Bernard F. Mann in pathology, Prof. Gertrude Lienkaemper in textiles and clothing, Prof. Fred Eggan, research scholar in anthropology, and Prof. Karl J. Pelzer, research scholar in geography. In addition; the program provided 40 travel grants to Filipino students to study in the United States. It also scheduled four American students to study in the Philippines and six Filipino students to study in American institutions in the Philippines.[67]

Construction Program Carried Out

On October 21, 1948, the Executive Committee on Development and Construction was reconstituted to direct the construction program. The Committee was composed of B.M. Gonzalez as chairman; Dr. Enrique T. Virata, business manager; Prof. Angel Martinez, consulting engineer; Cesar H.

Concio, University architect; and Julio F. Nakpil, consulting architect, as members. Dean Vidal A. Tan of the College of Engineering was appointed to take the place of Prof. Martinez after the death of the latter on March 3, 1949. Immediately after the transfer of the University to its new site, the institution started construction at the new campus with the allotment of ₱10,000,000 given for this purpose by the United States War Damage Commission.[68] The University prosecuted the task at a rapid pace because the Commission set June 30, 1950 as the deadline for the expenditure of war damage funds.

At the end of the academic year, the Executive Committee on Development and Construction approved the construction of the following buildings:

(1) Library building, with a shelving capacity of 800,000 to 1,000,000 volumes and reading room accommodation of about 2,000 students sitting at one time. The building was planned with ample allowance for future expansion. Excluding the book stacks, it would cost about ₱2,350,000 and would have a total floor area of 14,613 square meters.

(2) College of Engineering building, partial, costing approximately ₱2,500,000 of which ₱1,340,000 will come from war damage payments and having a total floor area of 16,200 square meters when completed.

(4) Women's residence, costing about ₱650,000 and having a total floor space of 4,515 square meters, four house mothers' and assistants' rooms and a capacity of 245 beds.

(5) Men's residence, costing about ₱650,000 and having a total floor space of 5,000 square meters and a capacity of 234 beds.

(6) Conservatory of Music building and auditorium, costing about ₱1,200,000 and having a total floor space of 10,204 square meters, excluding a carillon tower having a floor area of 324 square meters. Its concert hall would have a capacity of 1,222 seats including 542 balcony seats, and the open-air auditorium a capacity of 5,964 seats.

(7) Administration building, costing about ₱670,000 and having a total floor space of 4,948 square meters.

(8) President's residence, costing about ₱75,000 and having a total floor area of 475 square meters.[69]

At this point, actual construction of the women's residence, main library, and College of Liberal Arts was in progress. Out of the total of ₱13,000,000 awarded to the University by the War Damage Commission, ₱1,000,000 was set aside for equipment, ₱2,000,000 for the repair of the damaged buildings in Los Baños, Cebu, and Iloilo and the medical units in Manila, and ₱10,000,000 for new constructions and for the repair of pre-war buildings in Diliman. Also during this period, only a total of ₱4,241,592 out of the ₱13,000,000 had so far been released by the Commission. The Commission also deducted ₱1,000,000 from the amount originally allocated, forcing the University to readjust the construction program.[70]

Alumni in Full Support

The University Alumni Council passed three important resolutions during the year. These were: (1) urging the President of the Philippines and the Congress for a substantial increase in the appropriation for the University of the Philippines, (2) urging the increase in the scale of salaries and wages of the members of the faculty and personnel of the University of the Philippines, and (3) appealing to our alumni and to non-alumni to endow professorial chairs and scholarships in the University of the Philippines.[71]

The Alumni Association conferred the gold medal of honor upon President Elpidio Quirino. The medal was a new award given to an alumnus for outstanding accomplishments. The Association resolved to donate to the University a carillon costing ₱70,000. It also presented a resolution to the Congressional Committee on Education requesting that a provision be made for greater and more adequate annual legislative aid for the University of the Philippines. The transfer of the Oblation to its new site, already mentioned above, was done under the auspices of the Alumni Association.[72]

The first commencement exercises in the new campus took place on April 26, 1949. A total of 576 students graduated with Dr. Carlos P. Romulo as the guest speaker. During the ceremony, an honorary doctorate of laws was conferred on Dr. Romulo, then Philippine delegate to the United Nations Organization; on Justice George Malcolm, first Dean of the College of Law; and on Dr. Edwin B. Copeland, first dean of the College of Agriculture.[73]

UNIVERSITY FIRMLY SETTLED IN DILIMAN AS GONZALEZ BOWS OUT

THE first academic year of the University in its new site at Quezon City was characterized by the rapid prosecution of its building construction so that at least seventy-five per cent of the projects financed by the War Damage Commission were completed after the year.[74] There was also a steady and significant improvement in the academic standards of the institution. New courses were instituted and existing ones enriched. Local and foreign educators gave greater recognition to the accomplishments of the University of the Philippines and visitors from abroad commented on its speedy growth and recovery after the war. Academicians of the University were invited to attend world meetings of academic bodies and its graduates gained ready admission to American universities for graduate studies.[75]

The return to the service of members of the faculty sent abroad for post-graduate work and the assignment of six Fulbright professors to the University considerably improved the teaching staff. Recognizing the importance of fellowships and desiring to hasten the rehabilitation of the teaching personnel, the University added an amount equal to the sum alloted by the government for fellowships. But because of the high expense of travel, the University could not send as many fellows abroad as it did before the war.

The Fulbright professors assigned to the University proved to be beneficial to the institution. They taught higher courses in their respective departments and compared experiences with the local faculty on the methods and the use of teaching materials.

A tragic accident occurred, however, resulting in the untimely death of Prof. Robert J. Conklin, Fulbright professor in English, and Prof. Marvin S. Pittman, regular faculty member of the Department of Geology and Geography. They died during the Christmas season while on a journey to the hinterlands of the Mountain Province.

Adherence to Principles

Several noteworthy incidents occurred during the last years of Gonzalez as President of the University of the Philippines which particularly depicted his independent-mindedness, the firmness of his convictions and his refusal to compromise the principles he believed in.

One incident took place when President Soekarno of Indonesia visited the Philippines. Because the University Committee on Honorary Degrees failed to endorse an honorary degree for the visiting head of state, Gonzalez incurred the displeasure of the powers that be. Higher authorities had made an announcement regarding the conferring of the degree. Even before the committee had met, Gonzalez took this as an encroachment upon the powers of the Committee and an intrusion into the affairs of the University. Some of the committee members shared this view, so the committee's endorsement of the conferment of the degree was doubtful, a unanimous vote being necessary.

It was the opinion of some that, had Gonzalez exerted a little pressure on the committee members, the degree could have been granted. Gonzalez was, however, the last person who could be expected to do that. Whether or not he approved of a proposition, and in this instance he did not feel that the honorary degree was merited, he would never try to influence others especially in the delicate matter of granting an honorary degree.[76]

The selection by the Executive Committee of the University of then Senator Claro M. Recto to be the commencement speaker of the University of the Philippines in 1951, was another issue which put Gonzalez on the spot. Some deans had suggested the name of Recto as the 1950 commencement speaker. Gonzalez told them that it was not advisable to invite Recto, who had been a persistent critic of the Quirino administration and whose name was anathema to the administration. The deans did not insist on having Recto; another man was chosen commencement speaker.

Coincident with the approach of the 1951 commencement, local newspapers reported that President Quirino had appointed Senator Recto ambassador to Spain. This was opportune. The deans, thinking that it would no longer hit a snag, proposed Recto again for speaker. Gonzalez, apprised of the renewed proposal and shown the newspaper report, smiled. The Executive Committee thought that since Recto was now apparently acceptable to Malacañang, there could be no question as to his fitness to be commencement speaker. It selected Recto unanimously.

Trouble started, however, when shortly afterwards, the newspapers reported that Recto refused his appointment as ambassador to Spain. Pressure from Malacañang was exerted on Gonzalez to change Recto as speaker. Gonzalez ignored Malacañang and upheld the Executive Committee.[77] This widened the rift existing between him and Malacañang.

Then there was the beer incident during the University of the Philippines' College of Law Alumni Homecoming in 1951. Despite the standing University rule against bringing liquor into the University campus, the celebrating alumni, relying on President Quirino's presence, he being one of the celebrants, brought beer. Gonzalez ordered the beer out. After that he left for home. President Quirino later asked for him. Two professors were sent to Pasay to request Gonzalez to return to the festivities but were politely told by Mrs. Gonzalez that the president was indisposed and could not see them.

When Two Presidents Disagree

After these incidents, Gonzalez was called to a conference by President Quirino. President Quirino offered to make Gonzalez a cabinet member or an ambassador. Gonzalez was told that, because of his training and experience, he could be of great service to the nation in either capacity. Gonzalez understood that what Quirino really meant to tell him was that his services in the University were no longer needed. He expressed his desire to retire and declined President Quirino's offer. Gonzalez could not be prevailed upon to accept any other position. He felt that his job was in the University and if his services were no longer appreciated in the task he had been trained for and to which he had devoted the best years of his life, he would rather leave public life.

Gonzalez tendered his resignation on March 20, 1951. At a special meeting, the Board of Regents accepted Gonzalez's resignation.

Prof. Enrique M. Fernando, one-time secretary to President Gonzalez, wrote:

> Finally, when it was clear there was no stopping the pernicious intrusion of partisan politics in university affairs and he was to be eased out, a group of distinguished lawyers offered their services to test the validity of such a move. He was grateful but he would not go to the courts. To do so might lead to misunderstanding. People might consider that he was interested in his position rather than in the principles. Besides, he could not find it agreeable to remain where he was not wanted.
>
> It was not so. The Quirino government wanted him out, but certainly not the faculty and the student body. That was an impressive demonstration of loyalty the students spontaneously staged for him. Some were surprised. They should not have been. True he did not take pains to ingratiate himself with them. Nor was it necessary. The warmth of his personality, his sense of humor, his sympathy and understanding, won their affection. In a real sense, he was one of them. For if youth be measured by the power to assimilate what is new, by freshness of outlook, by quickness of response, he remained young to the end.[78]

A Final Review

A number of noteworthy events occurred during the last academic year of Dr. Bienvenido Ma. Gonzalez as President of the University of the Philippines.

The Cebu College, established in 1918, was closed because of financial problems.

Important changes in personnel were the designation of Dr. Enrique T. Virata as Executive Vice-President of the University, and the election of Dr. Vidal A. Tan as President of the University of the Philippines to succeed Dr. Bienvenido Ma. Gonzalez.[79]

The following buildings financed mainly from war damage funds were completed during the year:

> *In Quezon City*: South Concrete Building (reconstruction), North Concrete Building (repair); Main Library, Liberal Arts, Engineering, Women's residence, Men's residence, and Administration.

In Manila: Pharmacy (Medicine Annex), Medicine Building and Institute of Hygiene (repair).

In Los Baños: Animal Husbandry, Chemistry, Infirmary, Makiling School, Plant Pathology, Poultry Husbandry, and Rural High School (reconstruction); Bungalows, Students' Dormitories, and Mess Hall.

In Cebu: Cebu College (repair) and Cebu Girls' Dormitory. (The work continued even after the College closed in fulfillment of contracts regarding it.)

In Iloilo: Iloilo College (repair) and Iloilo Gymnasium (70%).[80]

The War Damage Commission added ₱5,118,631 during the year for the rehabilitation and construction program of the University. As of May 31, 1951, the total war damage funds released by the Commission amounted to ₱10,996,953.55.[81]

As in the previous years, the U.P. Alumni Association made representations in both houses of Congress for more financial aid to the University. It also appointed the Committee on Endowment to "solicit from alumni, industrial concerns, and friends of the University, endowment for research work in the technical and scientific fields with a view to helping the country in its total economic mobilization."[82]

When Gonzalez left the Presidency of the University, the state institution still faced the same major problems: inadequate buildings and extremely low salaries of the faculty.

Gonzalez's Resignation Opposed

The news of the resignation of Gonzalez spread quickly. It was the headline of most of the leading newspapers in Manila on March 21, 1951. The students of the University were the most outspoken in their protest against the ouster. From the Diliman campus, they marched to Malacañang on March 29, 1951 and petitioned an audience with President Quirino. The audience was granted but their efforts to make Quirino reconsider were futile. They were, however, granted their request that President Gonzalez be permitted to preside over the year's commencement exercises and to sign the diplomas of the graduating students. The University Council, meeting on April 12, 1951, passed a resolution of confidence and appreciation. Excerpts from this resolution read:

> Whereas, by his efficient and wise administration he was able to secure the stability of the University in spite of the limited financial resources by pursuing policies unaffected by outside pressures that usually affect human institutions;

> Whereas, by his steadfast devotion to duty, by his loyalty to principles, and by his integrity of character he set out an inspiring example of leadership to the youth of the land that seek his guidance.[83]

Farewell to the President

Gonzalez terminated his official duties with the University on April 23, 1951. Loyal faculty members and employees of the University who visited him in his office shared the heaviness of heart of their President. Not a few of them shed tears. Gonzalez made one request of every group who visited him and that was to maintain their loyalty to the University and do their best for the good of the institution.

Before leaving the University campus, Gonzalez made a tour of the place in his car. As he finally departed, he waved his hand in farewell to the deans and faculty members who were waiting at the administration building.

With a heavy heart, Gonzalez severed his official relationship with the institution where he had spent 40 years of his life. Yet, his love and interest for the University did not change even after he had resigned. During visits to his daughter Eva, who became an instructor in the University after his resignation, he still expressed his concern for the University. A foreman in charge of ground beautification used to tell of the several instances when the former president had requested him to take the best care of the trees in the campus.

Affectionately Remembered

Gonzalez was again offered the presidency of the Pampanga Sugar Development Company after his departure from the University. He accepted. Having also resigned all his other positions in the government, Gonzalez was able to devote all his time to his new job in private industry.

His failing health, however, did not permit him to do his work as he wanted to. He had to stay at home most of the time. Papers requiring his study and signature were brought to his home.

One consolation he had was that his friends in the University continually visited him during his retirement. This made him happy. Student leaders of the University of the Philippines were among his frequent visitors.

It was during a visit of his brother Joaquin when Gonzalez felt that the end was imminent. In the course of their conversation, Gonzalez suddenly lost his speech. Although weakening fast, he faithfully kept his diary. Gonzalez was able to make his last entry on December 28, 1953 – two days before he died: "Feeling very weak. Left part of body paralyzed."

Footnote to History

Gonzalez died on December 30, 1953, a few minutes after noon, in the San Juan de Dios Hospital. It was a significant date, for it coincided with Rizal's death. Only a few hours before, President Ramon Magsaysay had been sworn into office.

Unfortunately, President Gonzalez did not live to see the new administration vindicate him. It is consolation, though, that it meant to do so. The orations of some of the new administration's leaders at the necrological services in the Senate Session Hall on February 5, 1954 are testimony to this.

VII

Tan's Devoted Presidency (1951-1956)

A Campus Shaken by Strife Until Redeemed by Sobriety

by Rosario Mendoza Cortes

Tan's Devoted Presidency

TWO months before he was chosen the ninth president of the University of the Philippines, Dr. Vidal A. Tan was asked to deliver the welcome address at a convocation of the Writers' Club of the Far Eastern University of which he was then the President. He said he was complying with the request, although there were at that hour some very interesting tennis matches going on at the Rizal Memorial Stadium, because he had a very wholesome respect for, if not fear, of that species of humanity known as writers. It had also been subtly suggested to him that the Writers' Club would not take *no* for an answer; but he was advised that he should not speak too long because he was not the main speaker.

Tan also revealed that he had once aspired to become a writer and that the first money he ever earned was the princely sum of three pesos for a story he submitted to a weekly magazine in 1911. In those days, three pesos was a lot of money but he never spent it and he kept the check to that day. After that successful debut, he tried a few more times but with no success, until finally, some 30 years later, he received ₱30 for an essay. By that time, however, he had given up his ambition to become a writer and decided instead to become a teacher.[1] *

The ninth president of the University of the Philippines was a man of varied interests and accomplishments, a recognized writer and a playwright. His primary interest was in the field of the physical sciences but he had obtained his bachelor's degree in the arts and throughout his life, he retained a love for letters and the humanities. He was therefore that rare combination – a scientist-humanist who viewed scientists as being men first and only secondarily as scientists. He also believed that there should be no moral ambiguity in science; that all efforts of science must be directed toward the preservation of man's dignity.[2]

Tan was no stranger to the University when he became its president in 1951. In fact, for almost all of his adult life, he was an intimate part of the University, first, as one of the very first students of the College of Liberal Arts, and later, as member of the faculty. He also served on the administrative side and on the board of regents as faculty representative.[3] He had therefore a well-rounded view of the University, an intimate familiarity with all its problems and needs, and an intense commitment to its fundamental principles.

***Footnote references are compiled in the NOTES section at the end of this book.**

SEARCH FOR A COMPETENT LEADERSHIP

ON March 29, 1951, the Board of Regents held a special meeting at the Council of State Room, Malacañang, to consider the successor of President Bienvenido M. Gonzalez, who had earlier applied for retirement. The Secretary of Education was *ex officio* Chairman of the Board of Regents but at that time, President Quirino was himself the Acting Secretary of Education, hence the meeting was held in Malacañang. Present were the following Regents: Manuel T. Cases, Lino J. Castillejo, Teodoro Evangelista, Modesto Farolan, Gumersindo Garcia, Aurelio Montinola, Camilo Osias, Benito Pangilinan, Pio Pedrosa, and Jose Yulo. Undersecretary Cecilio Putong was also present; President Gonzalez was absent.[4]

When the meeting was called to order at 9:10 in the morning, President Quirino was still away in Baguio and the Board designated as temporary Chairman, Camilo Osias, then the Chairman of the Senate Committee on Education. The Special Committee created by President Quirino to canvass the field of possible nominees for the presidency of the University submitted the following names for the position in question: Dean Francisco Benitez, President Florentino Cayco of the Arellano University, and President Vidal A. Tan of the Far Eastern University.[5]

Regent Garcia was for the postponement of the election to give the other regents a chance to study the matter further. But the Board decided to accept the report of the Special Committee without prejudice to any member of the Board making additional nominations. No other nominations, however, were made and the nomination was closed.

Among the rules adopted by the Board were that the nominee receiving the majority vote was to be declared elected by unanimous vote, and that six (6) votes would be considered a majority, but he was not to be considered elected until after he had signified his acceptance.

In the balloting, Yulo abstained from voting because he was related to Mrs. Vidal Tan and Garcia also abstained because he had favored postponement of the election. Putong was designated to canvass the votes and he reported that Dean Benitez had obtained two votes while Dr. Tan had six votes. When contacted by Regent Evangelista, Tan indicated his acceptance of the presidency of the University of the Philippines. Thereupon, Dr. Vidal A. Tan was declared elected as President of the University effective April 24, 1951.[6] Tan was inducted into office by President Elpidio Quirino at the Council of State Room, Malacañang, on Tuesday, April 24, 1951.[7]

Welcome to the New President

A highly respected academician in the field of science, Tan was the first Filipino to be conferred the doctorate in mathematics from the University of

Chicago. If academic leadership and experience in academic affairs were the criteria, Tan had both in ample measure. This perception was reflected in one of the first congratulatory messages received by Tan. It came from the Secretary of Foreign Affairs, Carlos P. Romulo:

> Your appointment is one of the happiest made by Pres. Quirino and he deserves credit for choosing the one man who by all accepted academic standards is prepared to be the head of our State University . . . an office so pivotal in our national life . . . .[8]

But Gonzalez's retirement had been attended by so much controversy that when Tan assumed the presidency, placards were still conspicuous around the campus, one of them proclaiming: "We prefer a U.P. run like hell by an independent-minded man to a U.P. run like heaven by Malacañang."[9] Describing the situation in the campus at the time he took over, Tan reminisced at the end of his own presidency:

> When Pres. Gonzalez left the University, he was considered a victim of circumstances, if not a martyr. His successor took over; and for a while he was looked upon as an interloper even if he had nothing to do with the change. He therefore started with a handicap and it took him almost a year to win over the various elements on the campus.[10]

Dr. Tan started his administration without any fanfare, quietly establishing his office on the second floor of the College of Liberal Arts (in what is now called Palma Hall), a building completed a few months earlier on February 21, 1951.[11] When the *Philippine Collegian* interviewed him, he issued the following statement:

> I am accepting my new responsibilities with humility and courage, acutely aware of my shortcomings. In all my actuations, the paramount criterion shall be the welfare of the students, the faculty and the country. Every fundamental principle cherished by institutions of higher learning will be zealously guarded.[12]

At his own request, his formal inauguration took place a year after, in conjunction with the 38th commencement exercises of the University.

When Dr. Tan took over, he made no changes in the administration of the University. In fact, he announced, "No one will be removed from office except for cause."[13] Changes in the composition of the Executive Committee of the University Council were occasioned only by the death of members or their retirement at age 65.

Faculty Dominance: The University Council

The University Council is composed of all the faculty members holding the rank of assistant professor and up. Its Executive Committee is composed of all the Deans of the various units of the University, and takes final action on disciplinary matters involving the studentry.

At the start of the Tan administration, the Executive Vice-President and Business Manager was Dr. Enrique T. Virata. He took charge of the mundane affairs of the University. The Registrar was Dr. Paterno B. Santos, also a professor in the department of history. When he retired in 1953, he was succeeded by Prof. Arturo M. Guerrero.[14]

The biggest unit of the University with a student population of over 2,500 in June, 1951, was the College of Liberal Arts and at its helm was Dr. Tomas S. Fonacier with the following department heads: Anthropology, Prof. Marcelo Tangco; Botany, Prof. Gregorio T. Velasquez; Chemistry, Prof. Amando Clemente; English, Prof. Cristino Jamias; Geology and Geography, Prof. Mateo H. Tupas; History, Prof. Nicolas Zafra; Mathematics, Dr. Raymundo A. Favila; Oriental Languages, Dr. Cecilio Lopez; Philosophy, Dr. Ricardo R. Pascual; Physics, Prof. Mariano de la Cruz; Political Science, Dr. Pedro L. Baldoria; Sociology, Prof. Petra de Joya; Spanish, Prof. Antonio Abad; and Zoology, Dr. Leopoldo S. Clemente. In 1955, some changes occurred as follows: Prof. Jose Vera Santos for Botany; Dr. Ignacio S. Salcedo for Chemistry; Dr. Alfredo T. Morales for English; and Dr. Francisco Nemenzo, Sr. for Zoology.[15]

At the College of Education was the venerable Dean Francisco T. Benitez. He died in July 1952 and was succeeded by Dr. Isidoro Panlasigui.[16] When he retired on April 2, 1956, Dr. Antonio G. Isidro replaced him.[17]

Other units on the Diliman campus had the following heads: College of Business Administration, Dean Jose F. Velmonte; College of Dentistry, Dr. Victorino G. Villa; College of Engineering, Prof. Juan L. Tiongson, who was succeeded in 1953 by Prof. Crisostomo Ortigas; School of Fine Arts, Prof. Fernando Amorsolo, who was succeeded on his retirement in 1953 by Prof. Guillermo F. Tolentino; College of Law, Dean Jose A. Espiritu, who was succeeded in 1954 by Dean Vicente G. Sinco; Conservatory of Music, Prof. Ramon Tapales; College of Nursing, Dean Julita V. Sotejo; College of Pharmacy, Dr. Patrocinio Valenzuela; College of Veterinary Medicine, Dr. Angel K. Gomez; and the Department of Physical Education, Prof. Candido Bartolome.[18]

Directly under the Office of the President were the Deans of Men and Women, Andres Abejo and Ursula Clemente, respectively; Francisco Arcellana was Press Relations Officer while Ramon Portugal was Secretary to the President. When he was sent abroad to specialize in public administration in

1953, he was replaced by Josefina Constantino. In 1955, she was replaced in turn by Felixberto Sta. Maria. An important unit of the University was the Library system headed by Prof. Gabriel Bernardo.[19]

At Los Baños campus, Prof. Leopoldo B. Uichanco was Dean of the College of Agriculture while Prof. Florencio Tamesis was Director of the School of Forestry. He was succeeded in 1954 by Prof. Felipe R. Amos.[20]

The College of Medicine and the Philippine General Hospital in Manila were under the charge of Dr. Agerico B.M. Sison, while the nearby School of Public Health was headed by Dr. Hilario Lara, later upgraded into the Institute of Hygiene. The School of Nursing had for its Principal, Prof. Rosario Sison-Diamante.[21]

The Administrative Staff

Keeping the machinery of the University running is the task of the non-faculty staff and employees. The principal officials in charge were: Domingo Cervantes, Chief of the Administrative Section and also Secretary to the Board of Regents; Elias Manalang, Property Supply Officer; Antonio Perez, Accounting Officer; Luis O. Yap, Comptroller; Cesar H. Concio, University Architect; and Fructuoso Aquino, Superintendent of Grounds and Buildings.[22]

TOWARD A UNIVERSITY OF GREATER ACADEMIC EMINENCE

AT the first University Council meeting he presided over on June 12, 1951, the new President announced his policies. He declared that every president who had preceded him had done some good work on which he must build and on which he intended "to build a structure of greater academic eminence"; that the primary goal of the University was "to exert every effort to maintain and improve its position of leadership in the field of scholarship." The University, he said, would be governed by two major plans of activities: a long-range plan to achieve the stated primary goal, and a short-range plan to keep the University sensitive to the needs and problems of the nation. These were to co-exist, one reinforcing the other but never to interfere with one another. He further declared that his earnest endeavor would always be the academic improvement of the University and his ever present wish the economic betterment of its personnel.[23]

Basic Functions of the University

In his inaugural-commencement address a year later, he defined the unique role of the state university as subdivided into four major functions:

1. To serve as a measuring stick in our educational system;

2. To serve as a training ground for the nation's future leaders;

3. To serve as the chief repository of the nation's cultural heritage and traditions; and

4. To serve as our principal contributor to the world's stock of knowledge.[24]

These then were the guiding principles of the Tan regime.

President Tan's contributions to the growth of the University are not as easily visible nor as dramatic as the concrete structures rising on the central campus. Quezon Hall, Palma Hall, Melchor Hall, Benitez Hall, Gonzalez Hall, and Malcolm Hall easily remind the professors and the non-academic personnel of the eighth president of the University.

But tucked in a shady corner of the main campus, behind the Faculty Center and the College of Arts and Sciences, is a tall edifice, screened from the street by a cluster of trees, its name half-hidden by leafy foliage, almost as self-effacing as the man it was named after – the Vidal A. Tan Hall. Dedicated to the sciences and research, it is fitting that it should be named after the ninth president of the University for that was one of his principal concerns and where much of his accomplishments lay – the impetus and stimulus given to research. Another was also in the field of academic development – the development of instruction and of the faculty. These two concerns of education, namely, the nature of instruction and the productive scholarship of faculty and students, do not easily yield tangible results nor do these lend themselves to measurement in the same manner as material products do. The effects of Tan's policies and endeavors would not be felt until long after he had left the scene, but these would be of lasting benefit to the University and ultimately to the country.

Tan's general program of university improvement and expansion was planned along five lines: instructional rehabilitation and enrichment, research, faculty development and cultural growth, extension services, and physical plant.[25] These were not separate but complementary programs, all with the end in view of maintaining and improving the University's position of leadership in the field of scholarship.

Instructional Expansion

This program was carried out through the revision of existing curricula and the institution of new curricular offerings, the replenishment and improvement of laboratory facilities, equipment and supplies, and the revitalization of teaching techniques. The program was greatly facilitated by contracts entered into by the University with certain American institutions of learning and financed by an assistance program jointly undertaken by the United States Mutual Security Agency (MSA), later named the Foreign Operations Administration (FOA), the Philippine Council for United States Aid (PHILCUSA), and other non-legislative sources.[26]

The first year, 1951-1952, was the year of preliminaries, of the preparation of FOA–PHILCUSA projects and contractual agreements: with the University of Michigan for the establishment of the Institute of Public Administration; with Cornell University for the improvement of the College of Agriculture; with Stanford University for the upgrading of the Colleges of Engineering, Business Administration, and Education, and the Library System; with the University of Connecticut for the establishment of a Labor Education Center; and with Johns Hopkins University School of Public Health for the development of the Institute of Hygiene. The last project was actually a four-party agreement with the Rockefeller Foundation and the World Health Organization (WHO) as the other two participants.[27]

The second year saw the formal launching of some programs, particularly at the Institute of Public Administration, which opened at Rizal Hall on the old university site at Padre Faura. This year also saw the initial implementation of the agreement with Cornell, with the arrival of the first four agricultural specialists at Los Baños, and of the four-party agreement for the development of the Institute of Hygiene.[28]

The third year, 1953-1954, was the year of full-blast operations when more than 40 American professors came to the Diliman and Los Baños campuses to reinforce the University faculty. They taught younger members of the faculty, guided them to evaluate and revise curricular offerings, to make intelligent use of the new laboratory equipment coming in a steady flow, and trained them in better teaching techniques. The visiting professors worked closely with their Filipino counterparts in the respective college faculties who would then carry on after the former would have left.[29]

The same year, 1953-1954, saw the holding of two international congresses in the Diliman campus: the Eighth Pacific Science Congress and the Fourth Far Eastern Prehistory Congress on November 16-28, 1953. The holding of the Eighth Pacific Science Congress was an activity of the National Research Council of the Philippines, which is the counterpart of the National Research Council or similar bodies of such countries as Argentina, Canada, France, Denmark, the United Kingdom, United States, and many other countries. Preparations for the hosting of the Congress had been initiated by former President Bienvenido M. Gonzalez as Chairman of the National Research Council of the Philippines (NRCP). When President Gonzalez retired in 1951, he was succeeded by President Tan as Chairman of the NRCP. The Philippine Government set aside the amount of ₱61,500 for the operation and maintenance of the NRCP to enable it to stage the Congress.[30]

The Eighth Pacific Science Congress brought together 353 foreign scientists and 1,090 local delegates for a common exchange of views and information – the largest assemblage ever of anthropologists, prehistorians, geologists, volcanologists, oceanographers, meteorologists, botanists, soil scientists, biologists, zoologists, agriculturists, foresters, nutritionists, and workers on public health, social science, and power resources. Twenty-nine countries were represented and 800 papers were read.[31]

In his welcome address to the delegates, President Tan expounded his view on the moral responsibility of the scientist in the evolution of mankind's destiny. He invited the scientists gathered to formulate a scientific philosophy that would recognize the true role of man in science, that would make possible the recognition of an international conscience based on universal moral values and human friendship.[32]

The successful handling of the two Congresses brought the University into the limelight, its prestige acclaimed by many nations. It was a gain the University would never lose, having earned it with justice and grace. Representative of the congratulatory messages received by the President was the following wire from Dr. Edward Bullard of the National Physical Laboratory, Middlesex, England: "The organization and running of the Conference were a real triumph. I have never been to one before where everything went so smoothly."[33]

Toward the close of the academic year, the College of Education was the site of the Pacific Regional Seminar on "Teaching about the United Nations" and "Education for International Understanding." The two seminars held on April 4-11, 1954 at Benitez Hall were under the auspices of the United Nations Educational Scientific and Cultural Organization (UNESCO), the World Federation of United Nations Associations and the United Nations Association of the Philippines.[34] Dr. Tan was chairman of the UNESCO National Commission of the Philippines from 1952 to 1954 and president of the United Nations Association of the Philippines from 1950 to 1951.[35]

One of the most important accomplishments of this period was the successful implementation of the project on library improvement and rehabilitation which was part of the UP-Stanford agreement. It resulted in the cataloguing of more than 150,000 volumes accumulated since the end of World War II of which only 7,000 had been properly catalogued as of 1952 and made available for use. The University was now provided with a union catalog, the first of its kind in the country, a catalog of all library materials owned by the University and located in 17 branch libraries. Needless to say, the implications of this improvement were tremendous, considering that the library is the heart of any university.[36]

The University received from the MSA a total of $1,671,679 and from PHILCUSA, a counterpart fund of ₱1,548,761 in equipment, supplies, construction materials, and cash to make possible the construction of buildings necessary to carry out the functions of the University, enlarge and strengthen its laboratories and faculties, engage the services of specialists from the United States, and institute new courses. As a result, the University was able not only to recover completely from the ravages of the war but even to surpass pre-war equipment, faculty resources, and programs of instruction. The contract programs were also planned so as to provide a tapering off of assistance for the University to attain its goals on its own resources.[37]

New Curricular Offerings

The Tan presidency started under the Quirino administration which had launched an "Economic mobilization program." Midway in the period, newly-elected Ramon Magsaysay took over and the focus of government shifted to "Rural development." The University was responsive and therefore kept pace with these programs of government.

To help meet the industrial needs of the country, the University Council approved in 1952 a five-year curriculum in Industrial Pharmacy, a one-year course leading to Master of Industrial Management, and a course leading to Master of Engineering. To meet the needs of the rural areas, the University Council instituted courses leading to bachelor's degrees in agricultural engineering, home technology, and agricultural education in 1953. A special honors curriculum in agriculture was also developed to prepare leaders in agricultural research and technology. The growing need for technologists led to the approval in 1955 of a five-year curriculum in metallurgical engineering, a three-year course leading to the title of Associate in Surveying, and a course leading to Master of Arts in Statistics. Modifications in various engineering curricula to upgrade the standards of technical education were also made in 1955.[38]

Courses in archival science were offered for the first time in the country in 1954 when the University acquired the services of Prof. Isidoro Montiel, Spanish librarian-archivist of the *Biblioteca-Nacional* in Madrid. In the last months of the Tan period, the Council recommended and the Board of Regents approved five new curricular offerings reflecting the increasing variety of the country's needs: a five-year course leading to Master of Home Economics; a four-year curriculum leading to Bachelor of Fine Arts in Art Education; a five-year curriculum leading to Bachelor of Science in Architecture; and a four-year curriculum leading to Bachelor of Fine Arts in commercial design.[39]

President Tan had very strong feelings on the subject of liberal education. He defined a liberally educated man as one who "must not only know the facts and the accomplishments and ideas of the masters," but one who was also familiar with the various disciplines or methods of thought applied in the fields of social sciences, the humanities, the natural sciences and mathematics and steeped in the liberalizing influence of great literature. He advocated an educational system that would be less materialistic but would instead be more "spiritual and cultural in emphasis," one fortified "by a certain philosophy of life and a certain spirituality based on deep-seated customs, virtues, and traditions."[40] He urged the infusion of the professional courses with larger doses of the humanities and the social sciences emphasizing literature and Philippine culture. As a consequence, the preparatory curricula in medicine, dentistry, pharmacy, and engineering were revised to include more of the humanities and the social sciences.[41]

In 1953, the College of Liberal Arts was prompted to begin work on a scheme of general education. Although the fuller implementation and establishment of a program of general education was carried out by a later administration, the germinal idea was inspired and the gestation phase of this program took place under Tan's administration.

Founding of New Units

Academic expansion was also evident in the establishment of new units. In June 1951, the University Extension Division was opened in Manila to enable students who could not study at the main campus in Diliman, Quezon City to avail themselves of the educational offerings of the University. With Dr. Enrique T. Virata as its first Acting Director, complete preparatory courses in business administration, education, and law, and the first two years of the general course were offered in the evening for the convenience of those who had to work in the daytime. Classes in law were also opened and a complement of graduate courses leading to the degrees of Master of Arts and Master of Education. On April 5, 1952, Dr. Antonio G. Isidro was named Associate Director and in 1953, he assumed full responsibility as Director. The same year, another extension unit was established at Clark Air Force Base in Angeles, Pampanga.[42]

The Institute of Public Administration (IPA) was created to raise the level of performance and efficiency of government employees and stimulate interest in public administration as an important field of study, and to make the Philippines the center of such an educational endeavor in Southeast Asia. The institute opened in July, 1952 with a staff of American professors from the University of Michigan whose services were acquired through a grant of $375,000 from the MSA. For its part, the Philippine Government through PHILCUSA granted ₱150,000 to cover the outlay for services and administrative personnel of the Institute.

PHILCUSA also undertook the reconstruction of Rizal Hall at Padre Faura to house the Institute. In return for this building and the lot occupied, the University ceded to PHILCUSA its Zamora athletic field of 43,071.4 square meters.[43] In July, 1955 the IPA received a grant of $68,000 from the Rockefeller Foundation for the exchange professor program of the Institute and to fund the American professors in the program up to October 31, 1958, after the expiration of the UP-Michigan contract in 1956.[44] The first of its kind in Asia, the IPA has become the regional center for training in public administration of the peoples around the Southeast Asian basin (ASEAN). In 1953-1954, there were ten of these scholars from Burma, Thailand, Malaya, Indonesia, Indochina, and Taiwan, all of whose expenses were financed by the Board of Fellowships and Exchange Professors for Southeast Asia, with the University providing free tuition and dormitory facilities.[45]

Another unit established in response to the needs of the government in particular and the country in general was the Statistical Training Center. It was organized with the assistance of the United Nations and was also conceived to be an international training center for Southeast Asia. On June 23, 1953 it opened with a faculty of five with 40 students enrolled, half of whom were government employees.[46]

The University Preparatory High School was founded to experiment on a program of instruction that would best prepare high school students for college work.[47] Noting the high rate of delinquencies among students every year leading to warnings, probations, and dismissals, an experimental school to upgrade the secondary school curriculum was opened in June, 1954 at Rizal Hall in Padre Faura. Its program of instruction was enriched with more subjects in the natural and social sciences, the arts and the humanities than in the ordinary high school. Placed under the supervision of Dr. Antonio G. Isidro of the College of Education, its first Principal was Prof. Nemesio R. Ceralde. Much later in 1972, having paved the way for secondary schools of its kind, it was integrated with the University High School in Diliman.

Another response to the needs of the country, this time in the field of labor-capital relations, was the establishment of the Asian Labor Education Center in July, 1954. Designed to effect a labor education program throughout the country, it was organized under a contract with the University of Connecticut, with the latter furnishing an advisory staff. Training was also provided a stand-by staff to insure the permanence and growth of the program in the Philippines.[48]

The Institute of Asian Studies (IAS) was formed in May, 1955 in response to a directive from President Ramon Magsaysay to establish a center that would be "a common ground in which to bring together scholars and students of Asia to develop among themselves a spirit of greater kinship, mutual helpfulness and solidarity. . ."[49] A survey team was sent abroad to confer with scholars and administrators in the field of Asian Studies. The team was composed of Dean Tomas Fonacier of the College of Liberal Arts, Prof. Marcelo Tangco, Dr. Alfredo T. Morales, and Dr. Jose V. Aguilar. They visited 25 universities and colleges in the United States and Europe, 12 research organizations and 10 government agencies.

The IAS was placed under the College of Liberal Arts with Dr. Alfredo T. Morales as Acting Director. Initially, it was an interdisciplinary body of professors from the social sciences and humanities. The intent was to intensify study and research in these fields starting with the Philippines as a nucleus and then expanding into the neighboring countries of Southeast Asia. The Institute was the recipient of financial aid and of books and journals from the Asia Foundation.[50]

The Institute of Economic Development and Research (IEDR) had its beginnings in 1956 when President Magsaysay wrote the Chairman of the Board of Regents indicating a desire to see established in the University of the Philippines a center that would "provide not only our students but also those of the neighboring countries with the advanced training essential to accelerate development."[51] On April 18, 1956 a bill proposing such an Institute of Economic Development and Research and prepared by Dr. Amando M. Dalisay was submitted to Malacañang for endorsement to Congress.[52]

Impetus to Research

Corollary to the program of instructional improvement and enrichment was the emphasis given to research. President Tan had declared that the Philippines was duty bound to contribute to the world pool of human wisdom if the country was to remain a self-respecting member of the family of nations.[53] Intensity of research was, however, limited by the heavy academic load of the faculty and the paucity of available funds. But endeavors in that direction were not neglected. A research center to encourage and coordinate research efforts was immediately created in 1951.[54]

The next year, separate research centers for the natural and social sciences were organized. The Natural Science Research Center (NRSC) was enjoined to intensify and direct research activities of the pure and applied sciences. The center was headed by Dr. Amando Clemente with Prof. Crisostomo Ortigas as Director of Research and with the following members: Dean Patrocinio Valenzuela, Dr. Gregorio Velasquez, Dr. Jose M. Feliciano, Dr. Leopoldo S. Clemente and Prof. Enrique Ostrea.[55]

The Social Science Research Center (SSRC), on the other hand, was directed to give special attention to social problems that have immediate impact on social conditions. The center had for its first chairman Dean Tomas S. Fonacier. The members were Dr. Cecilio Lopez, Dr. Severino Corpuz, Dr. Ricardo R. Pascual, Dr. Pedro L. Baldoria, Dr. Antonio G. Isidro, Dean Jose F. Velmonte, Prof. Carmen P. Talavera, Prof. Nicolas Zafra, and Prof. Gabriel A. Bernardo.[56]

In 1953, the research fund was doubled from ₱50,000 to ₱100,000. The most important project of the SSRC, entitled "A Pilot Study on Communication Problems on a Barrio Level," was completed in 1955. An annotated bibliography of the Philippine social sciences in the field of economics was also finished in 1955 and a similar work on education was started.[57]

In the College of Agriculture, important studies were continually being undertaken to raise the level of agricultural productivity of the country. Experiments were conducted on the production of a high-yielding hybrid corn variety; on rice strains; on the optimum use of fertilizer; on nitrogen and phosphorous deficiency in soils; on livestock, poultry, and other related problems.[58]

In the College of Engineering, a big stride in technological research was taken with the approval by the Board of Regents in October 1954 of the Industrial Research Center. This was a non-profit unit designed to extend technological services to other units of the government and the general public.[59]

President Tan was at that time also the Chairman of the NRCP and was instrumental in giving grants-in-aid to the faculty for studies on dietary surveys, thiamine, Vitamin C, and survey of blood levels,[60] among others.

Finally, the Board of Regents adopted in 1954 the policy of giving a reduction in the teaching load to the faculty engaged in research by giving research an equivalent number of academic units. In sum, the different measures taken together – the upgrading of the laboratories, the augmentation of funds, the creation of research centers to coordinate activities, the reduction of the academic load for those engaged in research – all these worked to give increasing stimulus and impetus to research.

Faculty Development

Parallel to the program of improving instruction and stimulating research was the continuing effort to upgrade human resources, directed primarily at the faculty. To President Tan, the faculty was the most important component of the University for, he said, the University is primarily made up of men. Libraries, laboratory equipment, and buildings follow in the order of importance.[61]

Starting in 1951, an increasing number of faculty members were sent abroad each year to do graduate or post-graduate work to observe the latest educational trends. In addition, local fellowships, consisting of a reduction of the school fees to 25 per cent of the total fees, were awarded each year in an increasing number from 1951 to 1955. The table below summarizes the fellowship grants and other privileges:[62]

TABLE I. Fellowships Granted for Faculty Development, 1950-1956

	1950-51	1951-52	1952-53	1953-54	1954-55	1955-56
Full Fellows	6	4	14	15	17	10
Partial Fellows	1	5	15	19	11	18
Special Fellows	1	5	–	–	13	10
Special Detail	1	6	16	10	10	9
F O A Fellows	–	–	–	26	55	25
Local Fellows	63	78	89	112	128	105
Sabbatical Leaves[63]	13	12	37	50	54	30
TOTAL	85	112	173	234	291	208

The number of faculty members sent abroad for advanced training constituted 16 per cent of the full-time faculty in 1953 and 1954. This constituted a drain on the University's human resources, but the contribution they made in upgrading the instructional staff upon their return was of lasting benefit to the University. With a sizable number of faculty members possessing Ph.D.s, the graduate and post-graduate programs of the University were subsequently enhanced such that the University was enabled to upgrade its faculty right here instead of spending for their studies abroad.

Many of these fellows served the University faithfully until their retirement. Some of them left to take up responsible positions in various agencies of the government and a number later rose to national eminence. A conspicuous example is Prime Minister Cesar E.A. Virata who returned in 1954 with a Master in Business Administration from Wharton School of Finance, University of Pennsylvania. He and some others were a loss to the University but a great gain to the nation at large.

Extension Services

The University rendered services either directly to the public or indirectly by coordinating its work with governmental agencies and private institutions. The College of Engineering undertook a technical counseling and laboratory service program which performed a variety of services for governmental agencies. The Institute of Hygiene had a program of malaria control in the Diliman area and coordinated with the Bureau of Health in operating the Rural Demonstration and Training Center, giving in-service training to public health personnel. The College of Veterinary Medicine participated in the rat control work of the government and established an Animal Disease Control Center, extending its animal hospital facilities to the public.[64]

The College of Business Administration conducted forums on exchange controls, tariff policy, development plans and overall trade policies. In cooperation with visiting Stanford professors, it conducted a series of countrywide seminars in management designed to assist the business community, particularly small enterprises in Malolos, Bulacan, Baguio City and Manila.[65]

Physical Plant

The University received generous aid from the Mutual Security Agency, later the Foreign Operations Administration, and the PHILCUSA in the rehabilitation and expansion of the physical plant. The assistance centered on the technical and scientific branches with special emphasis on agriculture. The College of Agriculture received $962,000 from the MSA and ₱1,171,000 from the PHILCUSA which it utilized in acquiring farm machinery, laboratory equipment, and supplies, including an electron microscope, the only one of its kind in the country at that time. The most modern equipment were also acquired for the Colleges of Engineering, Veterinary Medicine and Pharmacy. The Engineering building was completed while proper housing and equipment were acquired for its various laboratories: its soils mechanics and hydraulic laboratory, and the chemical engineering laboratory including the boiler room annex; the electrical engineering department, which was equipped with a high-voltage laboratory apart from an electric and power laboratory; and the mining engineering department which set up the Philippine Metallurgy and Metallurgraphic laboratory, a Batch Fishery laboratory, pyrometallurgical pilot plant, and the chemical laboratory for the analysis of ores.[66]

In the College of Pharmacy, the Chemical laboratory of Pavilion I Annex, which housed the laboratory of the industrial-pharmaceutical manufacturing department, was completed along with the Pharmacy-Chemistry laboratory and the balance room. At the College of Education, the Education library, the curriculum laboratory, the audiovisual room, and the first unit of the University High School building were completed.[67]

Other units were also repaired, improved or provided with permanent homes. Rizal Hall was repaired with PHILCUSA funds to the amount of ₱750,000 to house the Institute of Public Administration. It also came to be the home of the University Extension Division, the Statistical Training Center, and the University Preparatory High School. In 1953, through the efforts of Dean Agerico B.M. Sison, the Science Hall of the Philippine General Hospital was finished and inaugurated on June 4, 1953. It also housed the Medical Library, the only one of its kind in the Far East, made possible by a grant of $200,000 from the China Medical Board, a subsidiary of the Rockefeller Foundation.[68]

The College of Veterinary Medicine acquired its permanent home on the Diliman campus with the blessings of FOA-PHILCUSA funding and moved into its new quarters in October, 1954. The year 1954-1955 also saw the completion of the ₱335,000 Forestry building in Los Baños with the assistance of FOA-PHILCUSA in the amount of ₱167,000.[69]

Faculty and student welfare were not overlooked. Four permanent structures for dormitories were completed during the period, a North and

South dormitory for each of the sexes, while more than 20 units of faculty homes were built through a loan from the Rehabilitation Finance Corporation. In Los Baños, similar residences for the faculty and dormitories for girls were also constructed.[70]

In October, 1955, the University obtained a three-million-peso loan from the Government Service Insurance System (GSIS) to give the University's building program an initial push. The five-year building plan included the construction of the Infirmary building, the Conservatory of Music auditorium, the Home Economics building and other units not yet properly housed.[71]

The President and Faculty Welfare

At the first University Council meeting President Tan presided over on June 12, 1951, he announced: "The first little relief you will receive is through the abolition of the present time record." In its place was instituted the honor system. All that would be required of the faculty was a statement that "on his word of honor," he had "rendered full service to the University" and his word would be accepted.[72] The abolition of the time record did not confer any material benefits but it strengthened the faculty's feeling of self-respect and sense of gratification that the nobility of his profession was recognized. First granted only to members of the University Council, it was later on extended to all members of the faculty.

President Tan was aware that productive scholarship can flourish only where there is freedom from financial insecurity. Thus, his first official act was to address an appeal to the President of the Philippines requesting greater financial support for the University.[73] His initial effort failed but he never relented in his efforts to obtain more funds for salary increases. Much later, he was finally able to convince the Budget Commission to increase the University appropriation by ₱600,000. The budgetary request was not approved by Congress until 1953 and the release of the amount of ₱600,000 for salary increases in 1954 was attributed to the generosity of President Magsaysay.[74]

Meanwhile the financial difficulties of the University personnel, especially of those with children of school age, had been alleviated in some measure when Tan successfully pushed through the Board of Regents in December, 1951 the proposal to exempt the children of permanent full-time personnel from the payment of tuition fees at all levels of the University, from the elementary to the graduate level. The only qualification was that such students must maintain a general passing average in at least fifteen units or its equivalent in the elementary and secondary levels.[75] The same year, 1951-1952, the University started negotiations with PHILCUSA and MSA for a low-cost housing project that envisioned the construction of 200 houses with modern conveniences to be rented to low-salaried employees at nominal rates. Tan also arranged a ₱2-million loan from the Rehabilitation Finance Corporation to finance the construction of faculty houses.[76]

Within the modest resources of the University, more frequent promotions of faculty members were effected. In 1951-1952 alone, 325 faculty members and personnel were given salary increases through promotion in step or in rank.[77] Ironically, his program of upgrading faculty resources through the award of scholarships abroad, and of promoting faculty welfare through promotions in rank or in salary, became a source of dissatisfaction among some members of the faculty. Because funds were meager and scholarships limited, the awards and promotions were necessarily selective in nature and these elicited charges of favoritism among those not benefited. Complaints of discrimination and favoritism found their way into the columns of the *Manila Chronicle.*[78]

Cultural Presentations

It was not all work and study for the faculty and the students. The university community was also brought under the civilizing influence of the theatre and other cultural media such as the exhibits room and the concert hall. The President's Committee on Culture regularly sponsored quality programs for the students at popular prices.

In 1952-1953, concerts were given by Benjamin Tupas, renowned pianist, Arigo Pola, a tenor from *La Scala,* Milan, and Helen Traubel, famed soprano; an organ recital by Bruce P. Frampton, and a violin recital by Oscar Yatco. In 1953-1954, there were musical presentations by the Manila Symphony Orchestra under the baton of Dr. Herbert Zipper, an All-Beethoven Symphony concert by the U.P. Symphony Orchestra conducted by Dr. Walter Hendl, a Band concert by the Philippine Constabulary Band, a violin concert by Gilopez Kabayao,and a Symphonic Ballet: Tchaikovsky's "Fifth Symphony" under Ricardo Cassel.[79]

The Conservatory of Music presented annually a Christmas concert featuring the Conservatory of Music Symphony Orchestra and the Conservatory of Music Chorus. In 1955, its opera department presented Gian Carlo Menotti's *Amahl and the Night Visitors.*[80] Dramatic presentations were also given annually by the University Little Theatre Group under the direction of Prof. Wilfredo Ma. Guerrero. In 1954, it staged *A Streetcar Named Desire,* and in 1955, Moliere's *Tartuffe.*[81]

Extra-Curricular Activities

Student organizations are a vital part of the University for these provide outlets for the creative energies of the students and constitute the training grounds for national leadership. Providing leadership in extra-curricular activities was the University Student Council as the highest student organization. It was composed of two representatives from each of the colleges granting bachelor's degrees and one representative each from the other units. Next in prestige were the University Senior and Junior Councils which had similar compositions. Exercising general control was the University Council Committee on Student Organizations and Associations (UCCSOA), but each organization had a faculty adviser, approved by the UCCSOA, without whose presence no meeting or activity of the organization could be undertaken.[82]

The University Student Council sponsored convocations to which the most important figures of the land were invited to air their views on national issues and problems. The Woman's Club sponsored monthly socials and when these became infrequent and reduced to a once-a-semester social, the club officers became the target of good-natured ribbing from male *Collegian* columnists. The Junior Student Council annually held the Junior prom at which a Lakambini was chosen, the candidates coming from the various colleges and usually featured in the society page of the *Collegian.* Fraternities and sororities held their annual socials as did other campus organizations. The religious groups also had their own associations: the UP Students Catholic Action (UPSCA) and the UP Christian Youth Movement (UPCYM). The various student organizations provided color and spice to campus life by sponsoring dramatic presentations, oratorical contests, debating jousts and other similar activities.

But there was also a dark side to this student activity. Because of the prestige attached to leadership in the councils, elections to the University Student Council (USC) and the Senior and Junior Councils were hotly contested affairs especially among the elitist Greek letter societies.

The USC also determined who was to be the editor-in-chief of the *Philippine Collegian,* official organ of the student body, from among the top three candidates adjudged the best in the editorial examinations conducted by the University Committee on Publications. This added still another source of rivalry which gave rise to charges of intrigue and vote buying during electoral contests.

Another source of dismay to university constituents was the recurrence of reports of physical brutality in the initiation rites conducted by the fraternities and sororities. Despite efforts to solve this problem, it surfaced again and again.

Death of a Neophyte

In July, 1954, Gonzalo Mariano Albert, an Upsilon Sigma Phi neophyte who had undergone initiation rites, died while being operated upon for acute appendicitis. The incident created such an uproar that President Magsaysay created a committee to look into the student affairs of the University and make proper recommendations.[83] The committee headed by Executive Secretary Fred Ruiz Castro uncovered no evidence to show that hazing had or had not contributed to the death of young Albert and his death was attributed to "cardiac failure secondary to coronary sclerosis."[84]

However, it was established that the Upsilon Sigma Phi had conducted pre-initiation rites and held a meeting to screen the candidates without the presence of the faculty adviser, and had tolerated physical hazing, all in violation of the UCCSOA rules. The Castro committee recommended harsh penalties: expulsion for the top officers, and one-year and one-semester suspension for some members.

The Executive Committee of the University which has the final action on matters involving student discipline decided as follows: four Upsilon officers, namely Efren Pascual, Teodoro Peña, Nereo Andolong and Jose Maronilla, were to be suspended for three months effective January 11, 1955, while 26 others were suspended for varying terms of one week to one month depending on the extent of their participation in the hazing rites.[85] The effect of the three-month suspension was to delay the graduation of the affected students from the College of Law to 1956.

During the investigation of the incident by the Castro committee of Malacañang and the Executive Committee of the University, President Tan suspended the circulation of the *Collegian* for printing a news item claiming that the Executive Committee would "summon" the Castro committee. This incident later on became a part of the charges against Tan for infringing on the freedom of the student press.[86]

In a way, the Gonzalo Mariano Albert case cast a shadow on the Tan administration because it appeared to indicate ineptness on the part of the officials of the administration in controlling and supervising the activities of the fraternities. The Albert case brought once more into the open the unfortunate excesses committed by fraternities and sororities and these, together with rumors of unsavory practices in campus politics, brought demands from certain quarters for the dissolution of the fraternities and sororities. It is difficult to assess how much damage the Albert case caused the Tan administration, but in retrospect, it appears to have catalyzed certain forces within the University to challenge the Tan presidency.

THE PRESIDENCY IN CRISIS: COPING WITH DISSENSION, PAROCHIALISM AND BELLIGERENCE

THERE were certain changes in the year 1954 that appear to have exerted an influence on the events of 1955. The first was a change in the national administration with the Nacionalista victory in the presidential elections of 1953. The Magsaysay administration appointed Arturo Garcia, Vicente Lontok, and Ernesto Y. Sibal to the Board of Regents to fill the vacancies created by the departures of Jose Yulo, Aurelio Montinola, and Pio Pedrosa. Together with Gumersindo Garcia, new Regents Arturo Garcia and Ernesto Y. Sibal came to compose a minority on the Board that was not exactly friendly to Tan.

Regent Arturo Garcia, in particular, frequently visited the University campus, encouraging complaints against Tan and creating "an atmosphere most unwholesome to smooth administration." In consequence, Tan would later on reminisce, "there was considerable rocking of the boat, and many faculty members," he said, "resorted to intrigues and gossips instead of getting busy improving themselves in their fields of specialization."[87]

The other change was in the editorship of the *Collegian.* Luis Q.U. Uranza, Jr. became editor-in-chief in August, 1954.

Charges Filed against the President

Early in 1955, a month after the resolution of the Albert case, Amelita Reysio Cruz filed charges against Tan and his secretary Josefina Constantino. Reysio Cruz had volunteered to work in the office of Constantino and subsequently was given an item. In 1955, she had a disagreement with the Dean of Men, Andres Abejo, over the handling of foreign students. President Tan upheld the Dean of Men, and Reysio Cruz tendered her resignation. Upon the recommendation of Miss Constantino, Tan accepted her resignation.[88]

Thereupon, on the date her resignation became effective on February 21, 1955, Reysio Cruz filed charges against President Tan and Constantino. In her letter to the Chairman of the Board of Regents, Hon. Gregorio Hernandez, she charged

> Dr. Tan and his secretary, Prof. Josefina D. Constantino, of bigotry and mental dishonesty, of using their positions jointly and individually for their personal interest, of illegal and unconstitutional promotions of sectarian interest and for practicing openly favoritism.[89]

Reysio Cruz furnished the Manila newspapers with a copy of her charges but only the *Manila Chronicle* published her letter in the "Letters to the Editor" section.[90] The following day, however, the *Chronicle* came out with an editorial declaring that the charges could not be dismissed "as it affects the very integrity of the administration and the manner in which promotions are given and salary increases distributed."[91]

The charges were shocking, to say the least, but what lent them greater impact was the publication of the charges by the *Collegian* as an enterprise story, giving it smash play in the issue of February 28, 1955. Prof. Francisco Arcellana, the editorial adviser in the absence of Prof. Cristino Jamias, held up the printing of the student newspaper on March 1, 1955, on the ground that the issue was running a story that was "sensational, fantastic, and untruthful," and that created a greater furor.

The metropolitan newspapers picked up the suspension of the *Collegian,* and the *Manila Chronicle* assailed it as an act of censorship. The *Manila Times* also publicized the suspension of the *Collegian* and quoted Uranza, its editor, as the source of the story. Uranza was also reported to have quoted Dean Sinco of the College of Law as saying that "the story in question was merely a narration of events of general concern to the University population."[92]

Both the *Chronicle* and the *Times* reported that the university students to be led by Uranza, Elias Lopez of the University Student Council, and Cesar Pangalangan of the Senior Council would stage a rally against the suspension.[93]

President Tan met with the student leaders, lifted the suspension of the *Collegian* and defused the rally. On March 3, the February 28 issue of the *Collegian* came out with the bold headline: "CHARGES AGAINST TAN SENT TO THE REGENTS."[94]

Subsequently, the Board of Regents created a five-man committee to investigate the charges made by Reysio Cruz. It was composed of Arturo Garcia, Gumersindo Garcia, Ernesto Y. Sibal, Vicente Lontok, and Carmen Dinglasan-Consing as Chairman.[95] The Board of Directors of the UP Alumni Association (UPAA) offered to act as *amici curiae* and formed a committee composed of Hermogenes Concepcion, Jovito Salonga, and Jose Africa. Hearings were conducted by the five-man committee on March 11, 14, 21, 22, and 29; and on June 24 and July 1, 1955. The UPAA committee was allowed access to the records of the Board committee and the transcript of the testimony.

On July 1, 1955, three members of the Board committee namely, Arturo Garcia, Gumersindo Garcia and Ernesto Y. Sibal submitted a majority report, while the other two, Vicente Lontok and Carmen Dinglasan-Consing submitted a minority report. But the UPAA committee had submitted its report much earlier on June 13, 1955 and its findings and conclusions became much of the basis of the majority report. It was also published in the papers while the case was still *sub judice* before the Consing committee and could have prejudiced the case of the respondents before the public, if not before the Consing committee itself.[96]

The hearings of the Consing committee were opened to the public at the request of Tan himself. At the first hearing on March 11, 1955, the complainant withdrew the charge of bigotry and mental dishonesty, on the advice of her counsel, alleging inability to substantiate the same. The Lontok-Consing report condemned the complainant for withdrawing the charge after it had been amply ventilated in the metropolitan dailies, declaring that it indicated the highest kind of irresponsibility, more so when the complainant was now beyond the reach of the authorities of the University.[97] On the other hand, the Garcia-Garcia-Sibal and the UPAA reports made no mention at all of the withdrawal of these charges as if it were of no significance at all and had no bearing on the case.

The charges finally crystallized into the following specifications: against President Tan, the charge of favoritism in matters of appointment and promotion, and the curtailment of freedom; against Miss Constantino, the charge of intrigue, of submitting the names of colleagues to the Military Intelligence Service (MIS), of propagating secular literature and speaking ill of the interests of the minority on official time and with the use of official facilities, and of collecting funds for denominational interest; and against Dean Abejo, the charge of incompetence as Dean of Men and head of the Student Personnel Service.[98]

"Censorship" of the Philippine Collegian

To support the charge of "curtailment of freedom" against President Tan, three instances were cited when Tan allegedly suppressed the *Collegian.* The *Collegian* issues referred to carried streamers as follows: the first –– "Regents Junk Tan's Retirement"; the second, a flash story in which the Executive Committee was reported to have "summoned" the Castro committee; and the third pertained to the *Collegian* issue of February 28. Tan admitted responsibility for the first two instances but disclaimed responsibility for the third. He predicated his suspension of the *Collegian* in the first two instances on the ground that it involved the public interest. He declared:

> . . . No university paper has any business publishing information about the University which is factually wrong because it should consider it as its primary duty to be accurate about its own institution.[99]

In the first instance, the Board never acted on his retirement, therefore, it could never have "junked" it. Since the Board had not expressed its stand one way or the other, the *Collegian* headline, Tan said, would have created the impression on the Board that he had allowed a misinformation in his favor to impress upon the public that the Board was for him. This would have hurt his relations with the Board, which in turn would hurt the University. And if it hurt the University, it would hurt public interest.[100]

In the second instance which happened during the Albert case, Tan explained that the Executive Committee had never decided to summon the Castro committee. Such a wish may have been expressed by a member of the Executive Committee but it should not be taken as an action of the whole committee. The publication of such an item could have angered the Castro committee or even Malacañang itself and would have strained relations between the University and a powerful individual or a group of individuals which would in turn hurt the University and consequently public interest.[101]

In the third instance, Tan denied responsibility for the suspension of the February 28 issue, but Arcellana, the faculty adviser designated to act in the absence of Professor Jamias, owned full responsibility for the act. Lontok and Consing accepted Arcellana's statement that he acted in good faith. In effect, both upheld Tan when they declared that the power of the University president to suspend any issue of the student publication came under his administrative functions as President of the University; that it was part of his responsibility to the parents of the students and even to the Board of Regents as its executive officer.

Consing and Lontok declared, "To contend that although he has the power to decide appeals from the decisions of the Faculty Adviser, he has no power *motu proprio* to suspend the *Collegian*" notwithstanding the fact that under the rules, he alone could decide what constituted 'public interest' is to "deny him authority for his responsibility towards the constituencies of the University."[102] Consing and Lontok averred that "an irresponsible, immature and radical *Collegian* leadership poised on the student body by the fortunes of student elections" could easily "create panic in the campus unless University authorities, particularly the President of the University," were "endowed with adequate control and supervision over student publications." To maintain otherwise, it added, "would make possible student excesses of all kinds."[103]

It was a measure of the distrust that some elements of the University felt for Dr. Tan that the Garcia-Sibal-Garcia trio would not believe his word when he denied responsibility for the suspension of the February issue but would rather believe that Arcellana was covering up for the President. The UPAA committee report presumed as much. It made much of Arcellana's letter to the *Manila Chronicle* dated March 2, 1955, wherein he allegedly curiously omitted mention of the alleged desire of President Tan to 'go ahead' with the publication.[104] Both reports practically accused Arcellana of prevarication in order to shield the President.[105]

On this point, Arcellana said that when he wrote the *Manila Chronicle* on March 2nd, his intent was mainly "to defend myself and it was all I could humanly do – defend myself against the abuses that had been heaped upon me by the *Chronicle* writers."[106]

Both the Garcia-Sibal and UPAA reports also took Arcellana to task for his objection "to the manner in which the charges, subject of the news story, were played up," which constituted the basis for his suspension of the printing of the student organ.[107] Justifying his action, Arcellana explained that when a newspaper 'breaks' a story, giving it first publication and taking the initiative of making it public, it is normal sound journalistic practice to make sure that it has enough proofs to substantiate the story. He reminded them that the story of the complaint had been brought to the metropolitan papers "but not one of them would touch it," that the most that the *Chronicle* did was to print the Reysio Cruz bill of charges in the column 'Letters to the Editor' where the following note usually appears: "Opinions expressed in this column do not necessarily reflect the views of the *Chronicle* and this paper assumes no responsibility for them." Thus, Arcellana further explained, when Uranza and the *Collegian* broke the story, and not only broke it but gave it smash play, and not only gave it smash play, but treated it as an enterprise story, "they assumed responsibility, endorsed the story, committed themselves editorially, entered upon a crusade, and elected to stand or fall by the story." The *Philippines Free Press,* he declared, had also published enterprise stories and in all instances, proofs had been required, photostats, signed statements, testimonies, even photographs.[108]

With the exposition made by Arcellana on the ethics of journalism, Regent Sibal, who was by implied consent the spokesman for the majority in the investigating committee, withdrew the portion of the majority report pertaining to Mr. Arcellana.[109]

Alleged Violations of Academic Freedom

One of the more interesting aspects of this case was the issue of how far a president may go in the exercise of his prerogative as the educational leader of the university. According to Tan, by long-standing practice everywhere, the president is the educational leader of the university and that this leadership is also vested in him by the University Code (Section 17, Article III, Chapter III).[110]

The issue of presidential leadership surfaced when Reysio Cruz introduced evidence tending to show that Tan had "essayed to cripple or emasculate the department of Philosophy," simply because he did not believe in the school of thought represented by its head, Dr. Ricardo R. Pascual. The evidences presented were: (1) the dangling of scholarships to Cesar A. Majul, Ruben Santos Cuyugan, and Alfredo V. Lagmay in fields other than philosophy; (2) the appointment of Dr. Jose Eleazar, graduate of Fordham University, as lecturer in scholastic philosophy; (3) the substitution of Mathematics 0 for Philosophy I; and (4) the offering of the directorship of the Asian Labor Education Center to Dr. Pascual.[111] The counsel for the complainant argued that the four incidents were "so closely interrelated with each other, all leading to one purpose and objective," namely, the emasculation of the department of philosophy. This line was adopted by the UPAA committee and the Garcia-Sibal-Garcia report agreed.[112]

In rebuttal, Tan pointed out that Lagmay actually got his scholarship under former President Bienvenido M. Gonzalez, while Dean Tomas S. Fonacier testified that it was on his initiative that Majul and Cuyugan were given scholarships in Political Science and Sociology respectively in order to strengthen those particular departments. Dr. Pascual also testified that the extension of scholarships to his colleagues "in lines other than Philosophy was with his consent." He justified his action by stating that "by permitting his men to embrace other lines, he was expanding the usefulness of his department."[113] It was also shown that Mr. Lagmay was replaced by Jose Encarnacion, Jr., while Mr. Majul was replaced by Armando F. Bonifacio, both upon the recommendation of Dr. Pascual, and both known as belonging to the same school of thought as Pascual.[114]

The appointment of Dr. Eleazar was justified on the ground that this would not only strengthen the department but also enrich it because Eleazar was of a different persuasion. Tan averred that he did not know of any department of philosophy in any big university which would consider it wise to have all its men of the same school of thought.[115]

As for the substitution of Mathematics 0 for Philosophy I, Tan explained that he had from the beginning consistently supported the teaching of Logic (Philosophy I), as a tool in clear thinking, to all students as part of their formal training. He recalled that before the time of Dr. Pascual, Logic was handled in the classical way but under Pascual and his staff, it was presented as symbolic logic which, Tan claimed, failed to achieve the desired objective. There were several complaints from students who took the subject in symbolic form. But rather than infringe on the academic freedom of the department by forcing it to change its manner of presentation, Tan had preferred to give the students the option of taking Mathematics 0 which was applied logic as designed. This was simple justice to those students who desired to improve their power of thinking, Tan declared.

Charges Convincingly Refuted

He argued further that instead of giving these four incidents "a collective but fancied meaning," the impartial observer would consider the Mathematics 0 and Eleazar incidents as signs of unwillingness on the part of the head of the department of philosophy to cooperate with him in his educational policies. And any administrative official under him who would not support his educational plans had only one honorable thing to do. If he had not asked for the resignation of Pascual as head of the department of philosophy, it was because he believed in the wisdom of allowing divergence of opinions and ideas for the healthy growth of the university.[116]

And in the matter of the Labor Education Center, Tan explained, its directorship had been offered to Pascual as a result of a conference held with various persons, one of whom was Vice-President Virata. It was thought that Pascual's broad interests and training fitted him for the position better than anyone else. However, Tan himself realized that the department of Philosophy might be crippled and so he had not pushed his offer.[117]

Consing and Lontok accepted Tan's explanations and declared that "based on the observations and facts gathered, there had been no attempt on the part of Dr. Tan to displace faculty members of the philosophy department for ulterior purposes."[118]

An interesting revelation was made during the hearing on March 14, 1955 which the complainant attempted to use as evidence for violation of academic freedom. Mrs. Eugenia Zaballero Luna, an instructor then at the College of Education, testified on an incident that allegedly occurred sometime in February, 1954.

She related that Father Delaney, the Catholic chaplain had come to her house and asked her to discontinue any mention of religion in her classes unless he was present to dispute with her on the point she presents. Although an extraneous matter to the investigation, Garcia, Sibal, and Garcia regarded the incident as an attempt on the part of the Catholic chaplain to interfere with the academic freedom of Mrs. Luna. Since the incident occurred in February, 1954, the three Regents made the presumption that President Tan had been informed of the incident by the Dean of the College of Education and assailed Tan for his failure to take remedial measures, declaring , "He must be deemed guilty of tolerating this gross infringement of academic freedom."[119] This despite the claim of Dr. Tan that he had not been informed of the incident, that the first time he had heard of it was at the hearing on March 14, 1955.

In the face of this statement, Dr. Tan asked, "Why presume? And why presume when the dean and the head of the department could have been asked? Why such a readiness to convict? " Tan further inquired, "Since when in this enlightened country of ours are people presumed to be guilty unless proven innocent." Tan declared that even criminals are presumed to be innocent until proven guilty, and that in the Luna case, he had been judged guilty without a hearing. [120]

President Tan Exonerated

The Board of Regents met on July 12, 1955 to consider the reports of the investigating committee. President Tan withdrew from the meeting when the Board started to deliberate on the cases. Sibal brought in the Delaney-Luna incident but Consing and Farolan expressed themselves in favor of separating that incident from the question at hand. It was decided to consolidate that particular reference to religion in the testimonies with other communications pending before the Board on the matter of religion on the campus.[121]

After a lengthy discussion, the Board took action as follows: on the charge of favoritism against President Tan in matters of promotion and appointment, the Board accepted the unanimous finding of the committee that there was no evidence to sustain this charge and President Tan was therefore exonerated. On the second charge of curtailment of freedom, the following Regents voted for exoneration: Consing, Farolan, Laurel, Lontok, and Hernandez; while three abstained: A. Garcia, G. Garcia, and Sibal.[122] The last three regents did not dissent from the motion to exonerate Dr. Tan, they merely abstained. The motion for exoneration, having obtained a majority vote of six out of nine, actually a two-thirds majority vote, was declared carried.[123]

The *Collegian* heading on this action of the Board was as follows: "President Tan exonerated; is based on Minority Report; Regents adopt Minority as basis to clear President," a fact which covered the truth. This news item was also overshadowed by the main headline: "RECTO TO SPEAK ON VIET ISSUE." While the charges against Tan had been played up with screaming black headlines in huge bold type, his exoneration was downplayed by the same editor, Luis Q. U. Uranza in the July 28 issue.[124]

With regard to Miss Constantino, the Regents, including the members of the investigating committee, agreed to eliminate the charge of "propagating secular literature and speaking ill of the interests of the minority on official time and facilities," when it was pointed out by Dr. Tan that one of the papers Constantino was accused of distributing was the baccalaureate speech of Father Horacio de la Costa, printed copies of which were distributed by the Office of the President.[125]

However, Constantino was found to have committed a breach of official duty when she reported the names of two faculty members to the MIS as having communistic leanings. As secretary to the President, "her official obligation was to report the matter to the President, her immediate chief, so that appropriate action could have been taken." She was also found to have promoted sectarian interests when she admitted having collected contributions for a former UP student, who had entered the Carmelite convent in Cebu, on official stationery, utilizing the services of a university employee on official time. Such efforts, it was declared, should be divorced from official action "not only to obviate possible preference for, and discrimination against, a particular sect but also to prevent the University from becoming vulnerable to criticism."[126] In consequence, six regents voted to have her relieved from her position as secretary to the President and be issued a "warning".[127]

As for Dean Abejo, the investigating committee recommended his relief and the Board decided to approve this recommendation. His relief was not based on any evidence adduced by the complainant but on the findings and recommendations made by the Castro committee in the Gonzalo Mariano Albert case.

Dean Abejo fought back. He not only filed a motion for reconsideration with the Board of Regents, he also filed a suit with the Quezon City Court of First Instance for "prohibition and certiorari" before the sala of Judge Nicasio Yatco. Abejo contended that he had never been formally charged and that the Board had relied on the testimonies of witnesses behind his back.[128]

Eventually, the case was amicably settled. In a special meeting held on October 4, 1955, the Board of Regents sitting *en banc* decided to clear Dean Abejo of the charge of incompetence embodied in its resolution of July 12, 1955 after finding out the premises of the resolution had been based on other attendant circumstances.[129] Soon after the decision of the Board, the case pending at the Quezon City Court of First Instance was also dismissed.[130]

Having been cleared of all the charges against him, President Tan presented at the next meeting of the Board on July 28, a request that he be allowed to retire at the end of his terminal leave which he desired to commence on September 1, 1955.[131] The request, however, was not taken up until the board meeting of August 29, and then the resolution of the board was "to defer action on the request of President Tan indefinitely for a while."[132] By that time, the so-called religious controversy was raging on the university campus.

Religious Controversy as an Explosive Issue

Since the transfer of the University to the Diliman campus, the Catholic and Protestant groups had shared a community chapel, a bamboo-and-nipa relic from "liberation" days. When Tan became president, the chapel was already under the custody of the Catholic chaplain, Fr. John P. Delaney, and the UP Students Catholic Action (UPSCA) organization. The Catholics had spent over ₱12,000 and the Protestants about ₱50 for the repair of the structure, fixing the roof and the walls, and putting in two rooms in the sacristy and a bathroom. Tan did not change the arrangement to save the University the cost of a janitor's services.[133]

However, the chapel could no longer accommodate comfortably the number of worshippers each Sunday, particularly the Catholic populace. Hence Catholics and Protestants had plans to build their respective chapels. The Protestants were first to apply for permission to lease from the University a piece of ground "in a non-academic area of the campus on which to erect a chapel, a minister's residence, and a fellowship center."[134] Actual construction began in May, 1954 and the Chapel of the Risen Lord was completed on May 31, 1955.[135]

The Catholic group also applied for a lease of land for a similar purpose on February 24, 1955 and the Board of Regents approved the lease on

March 4, 1955. At this same meeting, the Board created a special committee "to define the sphere of activities of the religious groups on the campus."[136] As a result of the Delaney-Luna incident revealed in the Consing committee hearings, this special committee was reactivated at the July 12 meeting and its membership was revised to include the following: Regent Jose P. Laurel as Chairman, and Regents Consing, G. Garcia, Lontok, and Sibal as members.[137]

The reactivation of this committee appears to have been only the curtain raiser to the great drama of 1955, the religious controversy that would engulf the campus from August 1st to the end of the year. It did not, however, involve a conflict over religious beliefs and practices. Rather, it was a dispute over the role of a priest on the campus and the right of organizations defined by adherence to a particular sect to engage in student politics.

Father Delaney's Catholicism

The campus was stirred by accusations of interference with academic freedom and counter-accusations of abridging the constitutional right of organizations to exist, by rallies, and counter-rallies, and denunciations over the radio and the press. In the center of the storm was John Patrick Delaney, S.J., chaplain of the Catholic community of Diliman. He had "contributed much to the material and spiritual welfare of the community and sought to put a stop to the brutalities in fraternities and sororities, and cleanse student politics."[138] He had preached that the Catholic should "live his religion, carry it into every phase of living, anywhere and everywhere, and bring Christ and his principles into even campus political life."[139] In the process, however, he earned the displeasure of other groups in the community who saw in his activities a threat to the secular nature of the university.

During the investigations on the Gonzalo Mariano Albert case, Delaney had denounced the excesses of the fraternities and called for their dissolution. The Castro committee had then recommended that the rules of the University governing student organizations be revised to enable University authorities to exercise stricter control over them. Dean Sinco of the College of Law was appointed to head the Committee on the revision of the rules. On January 5, 1955, the University Council approved the Revised Rules as recommended by the UCCSOA and the Executive Committee. On January 10 the Revised Rules were sent to the Board of Regents and then forwarded to Malacañang because the President of the Philippines had expressed a desire that his committee be given opportunity "to go over the new rules and regulations before their approval and promulgation."[140]

The Revised Rules contained a controversial provision which pertained to the illegality of organizations that "foster racial or sectarian prejudices."[141] The UPSCA felt that the provision was aimed at the abolition of their particular organization. With chapters in every college, the UPSCA had been welded into one strong solid organization and its entry into student politics in 1954 threatened the dominance of the fraternities, particularly the Upsilon Sigma Phi and the Sigma Rho.

The adviser of the Upsilon fraternity, Prof. Jose C. Campos of the College of Law, had, however, revealed that the UPSCA was not averse to seeking an alliance with Upsilon against Sigma Rho. Such a coalition, he claimed, had been proposed by Delaney in the student elections of 1954. But instead, Campos related, the Upsilon made an alliance with Sigma Rho and the UPSCAN candidates were defeated in the elections. According to Campos, this was what caused Delaney to denounce the Upsilon Fraternity before the Castro committee in 1954.[142]

Specter of Sectarianism

The above incident together with the Delaney-Luna incident was regarded by Regents Garcia and Sibal as evidence of interference by Delaney in University affairs. It led to fears that the state university would be converted into "a sectarian institution contrary to the provisions of the Constitution, particularly the principle of separation of Church and State."[143] Thus, the Garcia-Sibal-Garcia report recommended that the Board of Regents consider the "legality of according University recognition to sectarian organizations."[144] Hence the creation of the special committee already mentioned.

On August 1, 1955, a petition signed by 177 faculty members and university employees was submitted to the Board of Regents. It requested that Sibal and Garcia be inhibited from sitting on the committee on the ground that the two could not sit on the committee without "bias and prejudice inasmuch as they already publicly and openly expressed their opinion on relevant matters."[145] The petition was taken up by the Board meeting of August 29 and was denied on the ground that the "reasons advanced in the petition were not sufficient for unseating the two committee members."[146]

Meanwhile the special committee had held its first meeting on August 3 to which Fr. Delaney was invited to air his views. The latter took the occasion to make a denunciation of the three Board members: Garcia, Sibal, and Garcia. The following day, August 4, a large delegation of faculty and students, reportedly estimated at almost a thousand, went to Malacañang to denounce the same three members of the Board for their persecution of Dean Abejo and Miss Constantino. They expressed "fear and apprehension over the threat against the security and tenure of the faculty" and further complained of the unethical behavior of a certain Regent which had a demoralizing effect on the members of the faculty. That same day, Dr. Gumersindo Garcia "lashed out at Tan in a radio interview."[147]

While the UPSCANS were holding a rally at Malacañang, the Chairman of the University Student Council, Fernando Campos, convoked the Council to an emergency meeting. Although the Council members belonging to UPSCA failed to attend the meeting, the Los Baños representatives were able to make it. Later the UPSCA representatives would claim that they had not been informed of the meeting. The Council passed a resolution expressing support of the three regents and concretized their support by holding a counter-rally demanding the ouster of Fr. Delaney. President Ramon Magsaysay assured them that he would retain the three regents as no charge had been filed against them.[148]

On August 9, a manifesto was prepared and circulated to gather signatures from the various faculties and staffs of Diliman, Manila, and Los Baños. It appealed to the University President and the Board of Regents and the President of the Philippines to uphold and maintain the principle of separation of Church and State and to safeguard academic freedom in the University.[149]

Appeal for Sobriety

Whether or not Tan knew the contents of the manifesto, he issued an appeal to the University constituency to "Bring Peace Back to Diliman." In his appeal, he said that he had kept silent because he knew from bitter experience that whatever he would say would be "maliciously twisted and misunderstood by certain elements." He enjoined everyone, students, faculty, and personnel to "refrain from adding further fuel to the fire," and to stop participating in any activity that might increase the trouble that the press had "already exaggerated beyond reasonable proportions."

Tan asked for a moratorium on "unethical practices, gossips, rallies and counter-rallies, accusations, and counter-accusations." He pledged all in his power to help solve the problem with absolute fairness and justice to all. He promised that he would encourage equally all efforts to improve the religious character of the community but he would not permit any professor to talk in favor of or against any religion nor to inculcate sectarian tenets. He decried the fears expressed as being "exaggerated if not unreal."

Finally he tried to calm down the community by asking them not to work themselves to a pitch fighting for a "cause that does not exist, for a principle that is not endangered, for a right that is not involved." He asked the community to examine its heart and conscience and "see to what extent our mistaken concern for principles has contributed to the present misunderstanding."[150]

Shortly after, Tan suspended the Delaney lectures being held every Monday noon at Benitez Hall. Permission to hold the lectures had been granted three years before on the assumption that the University came under the classification of 'public schools' as used in the Administrative Code and to which the Constitution refers in connection with optional religious instruction.[151] However, the Registrar, Arturo M. Guerrero, had expressed his doubts on the legality of the lectures and Tan suspended the lectures pending the receipt of the official opinion from the Secretary of Justice. Delaney immediately assailed Guerrero and Tan's action as part of "an organized move to stamp out religion on the campus."[152]

On August 25, eight student leaders filed a petition with the Board of Regents urging the expulsion of the Catholic chaplain from the campus. On August 26, the Board of Directors of the UPAA adopted two resolutions: one seeking the expulsion of Delaney and another urging the President of the Philippines and the Board of Regents "to act favorably on Dr. Tan's retirement pursuant to his manifest wishes."[153]

But even as the winds of conflict swirled around the campus, students and faculty packed the University theater to capacity on August 25 to hear William Faulkner, famous American novelist and Nobel Prize winner literature.[154]

Support from Malacañang

On August 29, Malacañang returned the Revised Rules to the Board of Regents recommending approval. The Board approved the Revised Rules on September 5. It contained the controversial provision prohibiting associations that "foster racial or sectarian prejudices."[155]

The constitutionality of the provision was immediately questioned by Prof. Bernardo who claimed that it would violate the freedom of worship and the right to form associations on the campus. Delaney attacked the provision as "anti-religion" and charged that Dean Sinco drafted it to drive out religion from the campus and to dissolve the UPSCA. On September 12, the Board of Regents decided to re-study the disputed provisions. The enforcement of Sections 67 and 90 of Article III of the University Code was suspended and the matter referred to the Laurel committee for re-study.[156]

The *Collegian* issue of September 15 carried an editorial acknowledging the role of Fr. Delaney in the "religious revival" of the Diliman community but expressed its deep regret that in his "zealous care for his flock," he was destroying so much of what he had built by his intemperate attacks and accusations. On the same page, the *Collegian* printed a letter from an Upsilon alumnus, Juan Hagad, defending Fr. Delaney for choosing to live among our people, "leaving home and family to dedicate his life for our youth's welfare, without personal material benefit," despite his alien birth. Hagad chided his fellow Upsilonians for seeking to expel Delaney and to disqualify UPSCA from participating in student politics. He voiced the suspicion that UPSCA posed a threat as a potent opponent but he expressed the hope that his "fraternity's victory in all campus contests" would "be clean and clear-cut."[157]

The effect of Padilla's editorial and Hagad's letter to the editor may have been to put the issues and the parties involved in the proper perspective for in the succeeding weeks, the controversy appears to have simmered down. In November, the UPSCA-Upsilon war flared up anew when four members of the USC, all UPSCANS, filed charges against Fernando Campos, the Council Chairman and an Upsilonian, with the UCCSOA. Enrico Feliciano, Amado Lagdameo, Jorge Sta. Maria and Fernando Lagua charged Campos with illegal alteration of the student council resolution of August 4, grave abuse of power, and shameful conduct unbecoming his office.

It was alleged that Campos had added the phrase "and also the appropriation of ₱530" to the resolution upholding the council stand against the "move to usurp to its sectarian aims the academic freedom of the University." In the investigation, it was revealed that the amount of ₱530 was used to defray the expenses of the council rally held at Malacañang on August 5. In turn, Campos accused the four representatives of obstructionism and retaliated by filing a counter-charge that the complainants were conducting a systematic campaign of vilification against him.[158]

Regents against Tan's Retirement

On November 25, the Board finally took action on the retirement request of President Tan. Regent Consing seconded by Regent Farolan presented a motion to reject the retirement of President Tan.[159] The reason for rejection was based on a previous resolution of the Board adopted on January 13, 1955, wherein the Board expressed the Board's sense of satisfaction that the "highest center of learning, notwithstanding shortcomings and handicaps" was moving "steadily forward and adequately meeting the challenge of the times." According to the resolution, "the expert view of many leading educators and observers credits the University administration with competence, with the fruitful character of its stewardship and with much admirable achievement," and they regarded "the quality of its leadership as of a high order." [160]

When the motion to reject the retirement bid of Dr. Tan was put to a vote, four regents, namely, Consing, Farolan, Hernandez, and Lontok voted in favor of the motion while the two Garcias voted against. Sibal and Trinidad voted to accept his retirement at the end of the schoolyear. Since there were four definite votes for and two against, the motion to reject retirement was declared carried. President Tan was then requested to come into the meeting and he was informed that his application for retirement had been rejected.[161] Tan expressed his appreciation for the confidence expressed by the Board.[162]

Guidelines from the Secretary of Justice

On November 26, the Secretary of Justice issued an opinion on the use of Benitez Hall for sectarian lecturers. Secretary Tuason avoided the constitutional issue and based his opinion on a provision of the University Code which provided that priests or ministers of the gospel may speak before student groups provided that in every case, the written permission of the president shall have been previously secured, and provided further, that "speakers do not discuss questions which might provoke dissension in the university." This section, Tuason declared, constituted the president's sole guide in matters relating to the use of university halls or rooms by ministers of the gospel and was not in conflict with the Constitution.

The Secretary of Justice also defined religious and sectarian lectures as those "which expound or inculcate doctrine and dogma peculiar to a particular sect." Such lectures, he observed, "would be apt to arouse dissension in a place like the University of the Philippines" whose population included not only "militant adherents of different sects" but also "articulate persons who have no sympathy for any religion whatsoever."[163]

On December 5, President Tan ruled out the use of university buildings for sectarian lectures. He said such lectures may very well be given in the chapels.[164] The *Collegian* commended Tan for taking a definite stand on the matter, saying his firm action would "do much to reassure the country that the officials of the University will neither fall prey to casuistic interpretation of Secretary Tuason's opinion nor yield to pressure groups."[165]

As for the charges against Campos, the UCCSOA had held hearings on November 22 and 28 and with a vote of five-to-four decided to acquit Campos. The addition of the phrase appropriating a certain amount of money was considered justifiable after considering the original intent of the resolution. The countercharges Campos had filed were also dropped on the ground of insufficiency of evidence.[166] The *Collegian* did not take kindly to the decision. The editor declared that while the decision was "overflowing with the spirit of the season," it had set "a bad precedent."[167]

If the Tan ruling restricting the sectarian lectures to the University chapel disheartened the UPSCAns, they could take comfort in the fact that the Chapel of the Holy Sacrifice was nearing completion. An architectural marvel designed by Leandro Locsin, an alumnus of the University, it cost ₱300,000 raised over a period of five years by the Diliman Catholic community. With a seating capacity of over 900, it could easily accommodate another five hundred.

Catholic Chapel Built; Chaplain Departed

On December 20, 1955, the Chapel of the Holy Sacrifice was formally blessed by Archbishop Rufino J. Santos at four o'clock in the morning.[168] But as the Spanish saying goes, "Hombre propone, Dios dispone." When the students came back from their Christmas vacation, it was to hear that their beloved controversial spiritual mentor had suffered a stroke which was to prove fatal. A four-thousand crowd joined the procession that brought back his mortal remains from the Ateneo chapel to the Diliman chapel, and among them were members of the fraternities and sororities with whom the late chaplain had disagreed on many an issue concerning the university.[169]

The controversy over the role of religious organizations in the campus did not die out with Fr. Delaney although it became muted. The fight did go on. Despite the threat to its existence as a student organization, or probably because of it, the UPSCA, running as a political party, unseated the Upsilon fraternity to take full control of the UP Student Council in the student elections of July 1956. Soon after a rigid contest between the religious group and the fraternities, Fernando Lagua and five other UPSCAns captured the University's top student organization from the presidency all the way down to the minor posts. Eddie Sinense of the allied fraternities lost his bid for the presidency. Lagua won by a margin of 29 to 21.[170]

Meanwhile, President Tan had tendered his irrevocable resignation on June 22, 1956. Whether or not UPSCA or other religious organizations would still be able to participate in campus politics would be left to a later administration to decide.

A Mission Faithfully Served to the End

EVEN while some sectors of the University were engaged in verbal conflict, President Tan had been working toward the development of the University as a regional center of learning in Southheast Asia. Late in October, 1955, he attended a conference in Rangoon, Burma where he formally proposed the formation of an association of Southeast Asian Institutions of Higher Learning, whose purpose was to be cultural in nature and was to consist mainly of the exchange of students, professors, publications, and research work, and to promote mutual understanding among the member universities.[171]

In April and May, 1956, Dr. Tan made an extended trip to the United States as the Philippine delegate to a series of cultural conferences. During this trip he did spade work toward getting help from the Eisenhower $100-million fund for the "United States Asian Development Program." Tan later revealed that no counterpart fund and strings would be attached to this aid "except the readiness of the University to admit more students from Asia and Southeast Asia."[172]

As the schoolyear opened in June, 1956, Dr. Tan had three concerns and he asked the Board to define its policy regarding these matters: (1) the University of the Philippines as a regional university; (2) the support of the Institute of Asian Studies; and (3) the role of the University in the Association of Southeast Asian Institutions of Higher Learning. Tan inquired, "Did the University wish to invite the Association to meet in Diliman during the semi-centennial celebration of the University?"[173]

Before these items on the agenda could be discussed, Regent Lontok called attention to another item on the agenda which concerned the emolument that Dr. Alfredo T. Morales would receive. In addition to his salary as a professor of English, he would get ₱4,000 annually from the Asian Foundation as Acting Director of the Institute of Asian Studies. Lontok averred that this would destroy the salary scale of the University and bring about demoralization among key faculty members. Dr. Tan took exception to the comments of Lontok and after further verbal exchange of opinions on the issue, Tan "verbally tendered his irrevocable request for retirement effective at the end of his terminal leave, adding to it his personal insistence." Thereafter, he left the meeting.[174]

President Tan Determined to Retire

The following day, June 22, the Board met at the office of the Chairman in the Department of Education building at Arroceros, Manila. Secretary Hernandez read to the Board Tan's request for retirement. Tan had written, "I realized how increasingly difficult it is for me to remain in my present position." He added, "The pleasure and peace that I used to find during the first three years of my five years of administration, I now no longer have." He said he "suddenly felt just plain tired," and concluded it was time to end his "forty-three and a half years of service to the University." Regent Laurel, however, suggested that the matter be postponed to the next regular meeting as he was not ready to act on such an important question.[175]

A week later, the Board met again but postponed anew action on the retirement bid of Dr. Tan. Laurel pleaded for more time to study the matter. Regent Farolan told reporters that the Board wanted to explore all possibilities and all problems that might arise in case the Board accepts or rejects the retirement request. Secretary Hernandez, Chairman of the Board, reportedly told the regents that the President should leave the University without any ill feeling.[176]

On July 5, 1956, the Board finally took action. Except for President Tan, all the other eleven members were present. Regent Arturo Garcia, seconded by Gumersindo Garcia, moved that the Board take action on the retirement of Dr. Tan by secret ballot. However, only three voted in favor of secret balloting and the motion was lost. Regent A. Garcia, seconded by Regent Sibal, moved that the application for retirement be approved. The motion as drafted by Regent Lontok read as follows:

> WHEREAS, Dr. Vidal A. Tan has requested retirement from the University of the Philippines as President thereof, effective at the end of his terminal leave;
>
> WHEREAS, Dr. Tan has made his request for retirement irrevocable in nature;
>
> WHEREFORE, BE IT RESOLVED, as it is hereby resolved, by the Board of Regents to accept with regrets as it hereby accepts with regret, the voluntary retirement of Dr. Vidal A. Tan as President of the University of the Philippines, effective as desired;
>
> BE IT FURTHER RESOLVED, that the Board of Regents makes of record: (1) that it has been constrained to accept Dr. Tan's retirement because of his personal insistence, and (2) that the Board collectively and individually acknowledges the efficient and faithful service and the educational leadership of Dr. Tan during his incumbency as President of the State University.

Before the proposed resolution was put to a vote, Regent Laurel, as did Regent Farolan, expressed a desire to talk to Dr. Tan. A recess was declared and when the meeting was resumed, Dr. Tan was requested to come in. Regent Laurel then tried to persuade Dr. Tan to "remain a little bit longer." He expressed the feeling of the great majority of the Board that as far as practicable, they "wanted him to leave without any bitterness in the heart."[177]

In reply, Dr. Tan voiced his appreciation of the sentiments expressed, but said it would be unwise for him to stay inasmuch as he had indicated the irrevocable nature of his request. He also assured him that there was no bitterness in his heart, that he just felt very tired; that he did not expect the Board to vote always for everything that he recommended; that it was to be expected that the Board would differ with him from time to time since it was a body of independent minds. But he said that he sometimes found the going very difficult, and he felt that if he had greater support from the Board there would have been less rocking of the boat inside the University. He said he had not experienced this during his first three years in the University.

After reassuring them that he had no bitterness in his heart, he bade the regents good day and withdrew from the meeting.

Farewell to the President

The Board then adopted by unanimous vote the resolution and also passed a vote of thanks to Senator Laurel for the role he played in bringing about a happy solution to the question of the retirement of Dr. Tan.[178] The Board also agreed to tender a testimonial banquet at which a plaque would be presented to Dr. Tan and Regent Lontok was designated to take charge of these arrangements. Finally, the Board took notice that under the University Code, the Vice-President would automatically take over the function of the presidency.[179]

Reflective of the atmosphere in the University at the time of Tan's retirement was the *Collegian* editorial of Sabino Padilla. According to the *Collegian,* the real reason for the retirement of Dr. Tan was because he was tired of the intrigue, the gossips, and the unfair attacks hurled against him, "that he chose to press his retirement rather than wait a little over a year when he could have retired according to law."

The *Collegian* added that Tan's retirement did not really solve the problems that had plagued the last two years of his administration, that the intrigues and scramble for his position would become more bitter and intense; that the "unfair publicity waged by a certain newspaper" would probably continue if the successor by misfortune happened to be related by affinity to a family not to the liking of the publisher, and that the "spectacle of a regent roaming the University the whole day and asking for complaints against the President would probably continue." Concluding, the *Collegian* said, these were the real problems that the regents must face "before looking for a successor."[180]

And expressive of the attitude of the perceptive studentry toward Dr. Tan was the column of Perfecto V. Fernandez. He paid tribute to Tan saying, "Perhaps, they are right who say he is a victim of injustice and intrigue. Perhaps they are wrong who think him too weak and too old for the great responsibilities of his position." But, he said, "the time for recrimination is past" and that "what remains is a moment of tribute to an old soldier of higher education who guided with lonely passion this Republic of Learning and Letters, who fought unceasingly for his vision of the scholar as a cultured and sensitive human being," and "who, if not always in the right, nevertheless had the courage to be guided by the light that was in him." Concluding, Fernandez declared, "not even his detractors will refuse our invitation to bid him goodbye thus: Sir, well done!"[181]

Above the Turmoil: In Retrospect

The period 1951-1956 covered by the Tan presidency marked a distinct phase in the post-war growth of the University. In pursuit of its president's vision of an academic structure of greater eminence, the University carried out five programs that complemented each other: instructional rehabilitation and enrichment, research, faculty development and welfare, cultural growth and physical plant expansion.

In consequence, various curricula were modified and new curricular offerings were added particularly in the Colleges of Agriculture, Engineering, Education, Business Administration, and much later, even in the School of Fine Arts. Corollary to the program of instructional enrichment was the greater stimulus given to research, the expansion of the physical plant, the replenishment and improvement of laboratory facilities and equipment, and the rehabilitation and improvement of the Library and its facilities.

To complement these programs, faculty human resources were upgraded. Each year an increasing number of faculty members were sent abroad to do graduate or post-graduate work or observe the latest trends in education. New academic units were also established, notably: the University Extension Division (which later became the U.P. College Manila), the Institute of Public Administration, the Statistical Training Center, the Asia Labor Education Center, and the Institute of Asian Studies. The last four units were intended to serve not only the needs of the country but also those of the neighboring countries. Together with the College of Agriculture, in Los Baños, the Institute of Public Administration attracted scholars from neighboring countries bolstering further the role of the University as a regional center of learning for Southeast Asia. In 1955-1956, there were 97 students from Vietnam, Burma, Indo-China, Thailand, Taiwan, Indonesia, and Malaysia.[182]

The growth of the University may also be measured in terms of three elements, namely, the faculty, the number of students and graduates, and the physical plant.

The number of the faculty increased from 651 in 1951 to 1,176 in 1955-1956; the number of students enrolled almost doubled from 8,744 in 1951-1952 to 16,393 in 1955-1956. The number of graduates also increased appreciably. In 1952, 916 degrees and 505 certificates were awarded for a total of 1,421 graduates. Four years later, in April 1956, 1,415 were awarded degrees while 621 more were given certificates for a total of 2,036 graduates. In April 1954, the University conferred its first Ph.D. in Science on Dr. Carmen G. Velasquez. Her doctoral dissertation entitled "Studies on resistance and dissemination of ascaris ova for the control of ascaris infection in rural districts" was a significant contribution in the field of public health.

The sudden and unprecedented increase in enrolment despite selective admission procedures bore witness to the rising prestige of the University in the country and in the region of Southeast Asia. But the value of the physical plant or fixed property of the University showed only a slight expansion from ₱17,600,000 in 1951-1952 to ₱20,500,000 in 1955-1956. As a result of the great rise in enrolment, the specter of over-population, with its inevitable ills, loomed before the University horizon for the first time.[183]

The expansion of the University gave rise to many problems, among them the problem of supervision and administration of extracurricular activities. The incessant attacks by columnists of a particular newspaper whose publisher was antagonistic to the university president and the unfriendly actions of a regent who encouraged complaints among the faculty vitiated the atmosphere and exacerbated the stresses and strains within the university. The zeal of Fr. Delaney in protecting his Catholic flock from ideological corruption and his militant attempts to transform them into a truly Christian community according to his best lights evoked fears among the liberal elements that the University might lose its secular character. This coupled with the decision of the UP Students Catholic Action to enter campus politics aroused the enmity and hostility of the Greek-letter societies and the Protestant elements, whether among the faculty, the students, the board of regents or the alumni. All these factors came into play in the year 1954 when there was a change in the national administration and came to a climax in the controversial year of 1955.

Despite the attacks hurled against him, there appears no evidence that Tan practiced favoritism, whether in the awards of promotions or scholarships given to the faculty, or in the treatment of religious groups, or that he ever allowed any religious group to influence any of his decisions. Tan weathered the malice and the slander cast against him and won full exoneration from the Board of Regents, except from the "unfriendly minority of three" who merely abstained when the moment of truth came.

In the end, Tan resigned not because of the "religious controversy" but because he felt that he was no longer getting enough cooperation from the Board on his academic policies, particularly on the Institute of Asian Studies. He knew he had served faithfully and well and that he had done his part in the building of the University as a citadel of learning.

At the beginning of his administration, he had said that he could not tell what the future held for his administration, that he realized only too well that the history of every university presidency had an unhappy ending, but if his administration should not prove to be an exception, he pledged it would not be for lack of trying.[184] Concluding, he had quoted Abraham Lincoln:

> I do the very best I know how, the very best I can; and I mean to keep doing so until the end. If the end brings me out all right, what is said against me won't amount to anything. If the end brings me out wrong, ten angels swearing I was right would make no difference.

Dr. Vidal A. Tan retired in the thought that "when the mist of passion and pettiness shall have cleared," a calm and objective appraisal would in the end bring him out in the right.[185]

VIII

Sinco's Clash with Conservatism (1958-1962)

(Preceded by Virata's Transitional Administration as Acting President, 1956-1958)

by Milagros C. Guerrero

Sinco's Clash with Conservatism

Until Vicente G. Sinco was elected President in February 1958, the University struggled to carry on without a leader. The Board of Regents, responding to political pressure both inside and outside the University, postponed action on the election of a new president for almost two years since President Tan's resignation in June 1956. The responsibility, therefore, for administering the University fell upon Enrique T. Virata who had served the University for many years in various administrative capacities. At the time of his appointment as interim President, he was Executive Vice-President of the University and Professor of Mathematics and Engineering.

VIRATA'S RETICENT ROLE AS CARETAKER OF THE UNIVERSITY

CAREFUL research into the administration of acting President Virata failed to yield adequate data on the significance of his contributions to the University.[1]* Partly, perhaps, because of the temporary nature of his administration and also because of his obviously unassertive and neutralist disposition, his presidency could easily be regarded as uneventful. Although well intentioned and a capable administrator, Virata was, after all, only an acting president. He had no set policy or program for innovations. In the interests of the University, he devoted himself to executive functions until President Sinco was appointed in early 1958.

Despite the temporary and uncertain character of his administration, the University achieved notable progress in several fields. The year 1957-1958 was marked by the construction of buildings at the total cost of ₱1,963,241. These included faculty houses, men's and women's dormitories, the Physics pavilion of the College of Liberal Arts, the Infirmary building, rowhouses in the laborers' quarters, the textile plant of the Home Economics department and the President's residence.[2]

The physical expansion of the University proceeded in various ways: The University leased out about five hectares on the northeastern edge of the Diliman campus to the Interdepartmental Commission on Atomic

*Footnote references are compiled in the NOTES section at the end of this book.

Energy. While the yearly rental amounted to a token one peso, all the buildings constructed for the purpose of nuclear research would become University property upon the termination of the 25-year lease.[3]

There were other agreements with a number of government and international agencies under terms that would enhance the physical plant and building facilities. In September 1956, the University approved the proposal of the Philippine Assistance for Community Development to construct buildings within the campus of the College of Agriculture that would become the operational base for training personnel for community development. After 15 years, such buildings would become the property of the University.[4] A similar arrangement between the College of Agriculture and Cornell University for a period of three years (1957-1960) provided much needed technical facilities and assistance to the campus in Los Baños.[5]

The University constituency was not unaware of the need to commemorate the University's golden jubilee the following year. Members of the English department formed with others a writing group that would prepare and edit a history of the University from 1908 to 1958 as well as publish histories of the different units and entities of the University. The leading members of this group were Professors Leopoldo Y. Yabes, Cristino Jamias and Rony V. Diaz. Out of this endeavor, Cristino Jamias' *A History of the University from 1908-1923,* the first volume of a projected two-volume work, was published.[6]

REGENTS IN PROTRACTED SKIRMISH OVER SELECTION OF UNIVERSITY PRESIDENT

THE academic community, however, was most concerned during the interim Virata administration with the failure of the Board of Regents to elect a president for the University. A month after Tan's resignation, the Board of Regents created a special committee, headed by the Chairman of the Board and Secretary of Education Gregorio Hernandez, to canvass for suitable nominees to the presidency. The committee came up with a list of 18 candidates, all prominent men representing government, education and industry. The nominees were Emilio Abello, Fred Ruiz Castro, Teodoro Evangelista, Tomas S. Fonacier, Gonzalo Gonzalez, Gregorio Hernandez, Jr., Antonio Isidro, Salvador P. Lopez, Camilo Osias, Gil Puyat, Jose S. Reyes, Carlos P. Romulo, Juan Salcedo, Vicente G. Sinco, Pedro Tuason, Enrique T. Virata, Jose Yulo and Ambrosio Padilla.[7] This list was eventually narrowed down to seven: Evangelista, Isidro, Puyat, Salcedo, Sinco, Virata and Yulo.

After the list was made, however, the Board hedged on resolving the matter. Since Tan's resignation in June, the Board met ten times but discussed the issue of the presidency desultorily during the meetings of September 6 and 12 only to postpone the election indefinitely, per motion presented at both meetings by Regent Jose P. Laurel and endorsed unanimously by the Board.[8]

Only one regent expressed dissatisfaction with the Board's inaction and indecision. On November 29, 1956, Regent Gumersindo Garcia, Sr. wrote Hernandez that since he was embarrassed by the "flood of criticism" against the Board, he decided that he would not attend any of its meetings until the final election of the new university president was decided upon by the nominating committee.[9] Hernandez was the chairman of this committee. The Board's immediate response was to create a special committee of three to study the implications of Garcia's letter.[10]

Delays Caused by Politics

Indeed, as a result of the delay in the election of a permanent University president, the University became the subject of much adverse publicity, both in the metropolitan press and the campus publications. Critics tended to put the blame directly on political interference in university affairs. The editorial of the *Manila Chronicle* of 7 January 1957 attributed the sole responsibility for the "comedy at UP" to President Ramon Magsaysay who closed his eyes to the "shameless irregular activity" of the few regents who were resorting to delaying tactics in order to put a man in the presidency who would promote the interests of certain groups they were committed to protect.[11] Critics in the University hinted at an attempt of some regents to install a president partisan to sectarian interests.

The problem of finding a permanent president of the university, wrote Alfredo V. Lagmay in a lengthy article "The Attack on the State University," was due to the difficulty of getting a president "acceptable to the Catholic group." Lagmay alleged that the maneuvering of the Archbishop of Manila through President Magsaysay and Secretary of Education Hernandez to get a university head sympathetic to the Catholic Church was an "open secret." Such a president would also be expected to be sympathetic to the Catholic student group on the campus.[12]

When the Board elected its chairman, Secretary of Education Gregorio Hernandez, acting president while interim president Virata was abroad, the *Philippine Collegian* denounced the Board's move as one clear proof of the body's "totally insensitive and nonchalant" attitude to the popular disgust prevailing against it on the campus.[13] The Board's appointment of "a UST man" (Hernandez was an alumnus of the University of Santo Tomas) was reportedly regarded by the faculty as "an insult to the UP alumni."[14]

Regents Dillydally on the Issue

In early 1957 the University community began to express disappointment over the failure of the Board to elect a president. On 17 January, the faculty of the College of Liberal Arts sponsored a symposium which urged the Board to fulfill its commitments to the University. Two regents who participated in the program, Gumersindo Garcia, Sr. and Arturo Garcia, alluded to the operation of political intrigues in the Board that kept the body from electing a new president.[15] With a sense of impatience and frustration, faculty groups urged the Board to select immediately a new university head.[16] The prolonged exchanges during the meetings of the Board, however, suggest that the regents would not be moved to act expeditiously. Regent Modesto Farolan warned of the danger of "undue haste" in the election of anyone who did not command the absolute majority of the Board.[17]

In its meeting of 23 May 1957, the Board seemed ready to elect a president. The new Philippine President, Carlos P. Garcia, who had succeeded Ramon Magsaysay after the latter's death on 17 March 1957, had sent the Board a telegram assuring its members "absolute freedom" to choose the President of the University. The Board adopted a few rules for secret balloting, the most important of which was the rule that there would be no further balloting until a majority of 6 votes was cast in favor of one candidate. In the three ballotings that followed, Vicente G. Sinco obtained 5 votes against 4 of Gonzalo Gonzalez. Salvador P. Lopez, Juan Salcedo and Enrique Virata obtained one vote each. As Sinco was one vote short of obtaining a majority vote, the Board decided to postpone the election once more.[18] It was not until mid-February of the following year that the Board finally elected a new president.

That politics was of paramount importance in the selection of the University head was evident in the decision of the Board in its meeting on June 1 to postpone the election until after the November 12 national elections but not later than December 30, 1957. This was in fact the thirtieth postponement of the election. This time the Board made the election of the new chairmen of the Committees on Education and Instruction in both chambers of Congress a precondition to the election of the president of the University.[19]

More Postponements

On December 3, the Board went through the motions of electing a president once more, but this meeting, like the previous ones, was just as indecisive. Regent Jose P. Laurel moved for the postponement of the election. Regent Benigno Aldana opposed the postponement in view of the temper of the public – there had been a scathing editorial against the Board that day in the *Manila Times* – as well as the problem of the University's golden jubilee in the following year. He was convinced that "a further postponement" of the election would not promote the best interests of the University. Regent Carmen Dinglasan-Consing, Chairman of the Committee on Education in the House of Representatives, felt that she must do her duty before stepping down from political office, particularly in light of all the criticisms made by the newspapers and numerous private citizens.

Regent Modesto Farolan, on the other hand, said that the University needed the support of Congress and if the regents would choose a president before the new chairmen of the committees on education in both chambers of Congress were installed into office, the University might have a difficult time securing the necessary appropriation for the University. Regent Laurel contended that since the University was dependent upon the State for monetary support, its president should be installed only after the newly elected members of Congress had taken their oath of office. Most members of the Board took the cue from Laurel, who presented a resolution postponing again the election of the University president until after the election of the new chairmen of the committees on education and instruction in Congress.[20]

The watchful and waiting University constituency mounted their opposition to the Board after this new postponement. Speculation was rife on campus that the Catholic Church was pulling strings so that the Board would elect a candidate acceptable to the sectarian groups within and without the University as well as sympathetic to the gains and future objectives of the UPSCA (University of the Philippines Student Catholic Action), the strongest campus organization. The frequent postponements of the election and the expression of some Regents of their misgivings about certain candidates known for their liberalism, independence of mind and non-sectarian stance, lent credence to this speculation.

Resentment Spreads against Regents

Aries Cruz, a columnist of the *Philippine Collegian,* said that the Board of Regents proved once more their "disloyalty" to the University with their failure to elect a president on December 3. He singled out President Virata for his "habitual abstention and the lack of backbone to cast his vote."

"If that one precious vote," noted Cruz, "had been in stronger hands, it would have created a deadlock. Then it should have looked as if the Board really tried to elect a President." Cruz further alleged that the Catholic hierarchy would like to see "a good sheep in the President's chair." Thus, while Dean Sinco, who had obtained the most number of votes ought to have been elected president, he would not make it because he was not "loved by the Catholics."[21]

Homobono Adaza, the *Collegian* editor, lashed out against the regents whom he accused of wanting "postponements in terms of decades." In his editorial, "The Regents and the Big Farce," he wrote that the postponement of the election by the regents, who behaved like "some regimented members of an athletic squad," constituted an "insult" to the University.[22] The "pachydermous insensitivity" of the board, Adaza noted in another editorial, had no parallel in the history of the University, for despite a lapse of almost two years, it could not even do the simple task of electing a University President.[23] Adaza was convinced that the only alternative left to the students and faculty was to combine and join forces and demand that the presidency issue be settled once and for all. The only way that the University constituency could salvage "the joke that is the University presidency" was to strike against the university authorities.[24]

Students Restless and Aggressive

"Strike! " was the battlecry of the students against the inaction of the Board of Regents. On December 16-17, 1957, Fernando Lagua, President of the University Student Council, and Adaza led the students in "a peaceful and spontaneous strike" against the Board for its failure to choose a president. Against Acting President Virata's injunction, the students absented themselves from their classes, carried posters denouncing the Board and demanding the immediate election of a president. The University Council's Executive Committee on December 17 was constrained to advance the start of the Christmas vacation to that day.[25]

The students considered this gesture as a sign of weakness on the part of the University authorities. On the third day of the "strike", the students went on a "victory" motorcade around Quezon City and Manila. Upon passing by Malacañang Palace, the students shouted, "We want a president! We want a president! " The students, however, did not have any permit for this demonstration.[26]

They threatened to continue the "strike" even after the Christmas vacation but a conference between the Executive Committee and the student leaders on January 2, 1958 succeeded in averting it. The strike was discontinued, so the student leaders maintained, because they had decided to drop their plans for a protracted mass absence from their classes.[27]

New President Finally Elected

A new Board of Regents was constituted in early January 1958.[28] It took this new body less than two months to resolve the dilemma over the presidency. On February 18 the Board elected Vicente G. Sinco, then Dean of the College of Law and Chairman of the Monetary Board of the Central Bank of the Philippines, new head of the University. To Congressman Manuel Enverga and Senator Decoroso Rosales, chairmen of the House and Senate Committees on Education, might be attributed the credit of resolving in minutes the two-year impasse over the presidency of the University.[29] Sinco obtained a clear majority of six votes; Dean Juan Salcedo and Enrique Virata obtained two votes each while Ambassador S.P. Lopez, one vote. Upon the motion of Director of Public Schools Benigno Aldana, ex-officio regent, the Board made Sinco's election unanimous.[30]

SINCO ASSUMES PRESIDENCY WITH EMINENT QUALIFICATIONS

AN outstanding scholar, a lawyer and economist of experience and long training, an educator of non-sectarian orientation and an "insider" who was most conversant with the University's peculiar problems, Sinco was indeed highly qualified for the presidency of the country's highest institution of learning.[31] As Dean of the College of Law, he distinguished himself for undertaking reforms intended to reduce rote learning and enhance among the law students a deeper understanding of the law and the administration of justice. At the time of his election, he was 64 years old and was, therefore, just one year short of the age of retirement. President Carlos P. Garcia, aware of this situation, expressed his desire to the Board of Regents to see Sinco continue in the Presidency of the University for as long as he was physically fit and mentally able and willing to do so. Sharing this view, the Board unanimously approved on December 10, 1958 the extension of his term indefinitely.[32]

Sinco's election ended a long season of discontent and low morale in the academic community. The faculty and the student body expressed hopes that the years under the Sinco administration would be a time for healing the antagonisms, intrigues and jealousies of the Tan administration and that the new president would "stabilize and liberate the University from sectarian controversy."[33]

Diverse Problems of the University

Sinco was not unaware of the serious and urgent problems that awaited solution. He considered the Presidency as coming to him as "a call," an "unsought" appointment which he accepted with "some degree of diffidence and even of apprehension." His fears, he explained in his first meeting with the University Council on 22 March 1958, were due to (1) "the state of confusion, almost amounting to disorder in the University, in a degree never known or experienced before the last four or five years," and (2) the inadequate financial resources of the University. So meager was the income available to the University that "nothing we could do would enable us to elevate very much the level of the University's achievement." He declared that "money in sufficient amounts is the indispensable factor – money for competent professors and for good equipment."[34]

Sinco took cognizance of the pervasive and inimical effect of sectarian influence upon the University. The Tan and interim Virata administrations had failed to define a clear-cut policy, for example, on the right of the UPSCA to participate in campus politics. The university community must certainly have expected the new president to take action on this issue. Much of the "state of confusion" on the campus was due to this but Sinco was convinced that it was wholly within the power of the community to solve.

He also made it clear that the sole concern of the members of the University was intellectual work, their exclusive interest was intellectual training and their one and only objective must be the pursuit of knowledge. The functions, duties and decisions of University professors must be "confined exclusively in intellectual affairs without any dictation or bias from political or sectarian sources." He warned the professors that anyone who would violate the provision of the University Charter prohibiting the teaching of sectarian tenets for or against any church or religious sect would be dismissed from the University.[35]

Sectarianism and insufficient funding, however, were not the only problems. An undated list of "problems of the University" – which Sinco must have prepared around the time of his assumption into office – shows how Sinco was painfully conscious of the formidable tasks that lay ahead for his administration. These concerned (1) a more logical definition and distribution of function and responsibility between the Board of Regents and the

President; (2) a change in the composition of the Board by removing those elements that cannot ordinarily be expected to have a deep personal interest in the affairs of the University and the problems of higher education; (3) reform in the administrative structure of the University to relieve the president of routine work so he could devote more attention to the implementation of higher policies; (4) a more permanent source of income, in addition to tuition fees and yearly Congressional "handouts" to raise the level of faculty salaries and finance research projects; (5) an effective method of faculty recruitment; (6) an effective way of selecting students; (7) concentration on basic subjects of study in the College of Liberal Arts to do away with course proliferation and "scatterization" of subjects, and (8) a good system of establishing and maintaining closer relations between the alumni and the University.[36]

Regents Amiable to the President

The relationship between the Board of Regents and the University President, the first in Sinco's list of problems, did not develop into a particularly worrisome concern, at least not until the very end of his administration. During the Gonzalez and Tan administrations, the Board of Regents had wielded so much power that left the President little room within which he could exercise his prerogatives. But the new Board that elected him seemed disposed to give up some of its powers and grant the president wider authority.

The Board, for example, had the sole power to investigate cases involving students and the faculty. On March 3, 1958, the Board adopted a resolution asserting that it stood for the maintenance of the authority of the University and for the compliance of the rules governing the institution. The Board also recognized that the President would and could "enforce the regulations of the University as they should have been enforced." The Board also approved a motion, which was submitted by Regent Manuel Enverga, that disciplinary matters involving students and faculty members, be left to the charge of the President.[37] In a later meeting, the Board granted the President exclusive powers, i.e., without further action by the Board, on retirements, resignations, scholarships and leaves of absences.[38]

Need To Discipline Errant Students

Thus, one of the first things that Sinco had to do as President of the University involved the exercise of disciplinary power to resolve the problems posed by the student demonstrations of December 16-17, 1957. The student leaders had presumed that they would not be called to account for their violation of the provisions on discipline and conduct of the University Code. Acting President Virata did not call their attention to this plan of the University authorities. For their part, students Johnny B. Antillon, Emmanuel T. Santos, Epifanio San Juan, Jr. and Romulo Villa petitioned the University authorities on January 20, 1958 to expel Adaza and Lagua; the first for the illegal and immoral use of the *Philippine Collegian* to malign the Board of Regents and the University administration, and the second for instigating the student strike and inciting thousands of University students to join it.

Between January and March, hearings were conducted by the following duly constituted bodies: the Committee on Student Publications, a sub-committee of the University Council Committee on Student Organizations and Activities (or UCCSOA), and three sub-committees of the Executive Committee of the University Council headed by Dean Ricardo Pascual, Dean Crisostomo Ortigas and University Registrar Jose C. Campos, Jr., respectively. Throughout the investigations, Lagua and Adaza maintained that the inquiring committees had no right and jurisdiction over their case. The various committees found the *Collegian* editor guilty of maligning the members of the Board of Regents, not just ambiguously, but in specifically mentioning the names of some Regents as well as the Acting President. They also found Adaza and Lagua guilty not only of disrupting the regular and official functions of the University but also of influencing and inciting others to follow their example, a clear violation of Section 92 of the University Code.[39]

On March 30, 1958, the Executive Committee sustained the recommendations of the investigating bodies that Lagua be suspended from the University for a nine-month period (March-December 1958) and removed from his position as president of the University Student Council, and that he be further disqualified from holding any position in student organizations in the University during the period of suspension. The Executive Committee also endorsed the recommendation that Adaza be permanently dropped from the rolls of the University, without prejudice to the issuance of the transcript of his records. The Executive Committee required the two student leaders to apologize personally and in writing to the Board of Regents.[40]

It fell to the University president to implement the recommendations of the committee. Sinco's hand was strengthened by President Garcia's statement that if the students wanted the case reopened, he (Garcia) would leave the matter entirely in the hands of the university officials.[41]

Sinco's Action Supported, Assailed

On the basis of letters from readers published in the metropolitan papers, public reaction could be roughly divided into those who felt that Sinco should not have imposed disciplinary action upon the two student leaders and those who believed that he should be given utmost leeway in the administration of university affairs. Teodoro Valencia's column, "Over a Cup of Coffee," readily accommodated critics who did not agree with the decision of the university authorities to punish the two student leaders. Prominent alumni of the University from Pampanga were said to have denounced the 'drastic penalty' while Alfonso Ponce-Enrile, a member of the Council of State, was quoted as saying that the Regents who allowed it should have 'their heads and hearts examined.' Valencia himself denounced the Regents for "behaving like children" while he chided the university authorities for penalizing the students for "behaving like adults."[42]

In Congress, Senator Emmanuel Pelaez, who spoke in behalf of the two student leaders, declared that Adaza and Lagua had suffered from a serious miscarriage of justice. Adaza's editorials, he urged, were the expression of the sentiments of the University's student population and not merely of the author. Lagua and Adaza were being "penalized" and required "to pay the price of leadership." He called upon the University authorities to review the case and urged the Senate Committee on Education to look further into what had brought about the confusing situation in the University.[43]

Assertion of Autonomy

Though he himself did not have a hand in the investigation of the student leaders, Sinco was quick to defend the decision of the University to punish the student leaders. The basic issue in the disciplinary action against Adaza and Lagua, the president said, was "the authority of the University to run its own affairs and enforce its rules and regulations within the law." They were punished for violations of University rules enacted for the proper administration of the activities of the University, as embodied in the University Code. In rendering these decisions, Sinco stressed, the University authorities were fully conscious of their grave responsibility to the nation and the academic world with respect to the mission of the University.[44]

Proceeding from the Crossroads

How might the University meet its obligations to the nation and the academic world? In 1958, when Sinco assumed office, the University was very clearly at the crossroads; it could surge forward to become the best academic institution in the land or it could choose to remain quagmired in the problems that slowed its growth in the past years. The problems that Sinco was called upon to face were grave ones. He, however, did not inherit any established administrative and academic policy. At the beginning of the University's semicentennial, the President and the University officials believed that to take any step forward, it was first necessary to subject the University (its administrative structure, faculty, curricula and resources) to an objective and critical assessment.

Thus, upon the authority of the Board of Regents, the University invited in early 1958 four American educators to make an impartial and thorough evaluation of the University's resources and progress. The United States International Cooperation Agency (ICA) and the Philippine National Economic Council (NEC) provided the financial assistance in securing the services of the following professors who constituted the survey group: Dr. John A. Hannah, President of Michigan State University, as chairman; Dr. William T. Middlebrook, Vice-President for Business Affairs of the University of Minnesota, member; Dr. Floyd W. Reeves, Professor and Consultant to the President of Michigan State University, member; and Dr. Thomas H. Hamilton, Vice-President for Academic Affairs of Michigan State University, member.[45] Dr. Hamilton was retained as consultant to the University after the survey team had tendered its report.[46]

The findings and recommendations of the Hannah Survey Team and their subsequent implementation bear a lengthy treatment in this chapter because they provide insight into the state of affairs in the University during its golden jubilee and they would indicate the direction of reorganization that the University would follow under the Sinco administration.

A Comprehensive Evaluation

The Hannah Survey Team inquired into practically all aspects of university life: the role of the University within the nation, the problems of higher education in the Philippines, the policies and procedures of the Board of Regents, and the external and internal organization and government of the University; budget making and control, the University's resources and investments, and government and foundations' assistance; course offerings, teaching loads, faculty research and field work, and faculty appointments and promotions; faculty and student housing and student guidance, organizations and extracurricular activities.

Among the findings of the survey team, the following were perhaps the most significant: (1) excessive centralization of operations which prevented prompt action on the part of the University administration; (2) a Board of Regents with far too much power that should have been given to the University President and other administrative officials; (3) the urgent need for more and better research by members of the faculty; (4) an inadequate graduate program; (5) the tendency of the University to automatically grant tenure to faculty after a probationary period of one or two years; (6) proliferation and superficiality of courses in different units of the University; (7) inadequate textbooks and reference materials for both faculty and students; (8) dispersed and uncoordinated student personnel service; (9) A University budget highly dependent upon Congress; (10) an internal operating budget that did not foster the wide sharing of authority and responsibility among university administrators; (11) salary levels of academic staff that lagged behind the cost of living changes and unreasonably uncompetitive with non-teaching opportunities; (12) the absence of any central office for recruitment, testing and in-service training of the non-academic staff; (13) the lack of adequate and efficient custodial system of personnel records; and (14) the lack of any long range planning for physical growth and expansion, particularly on the Diliman and Los Baños campuses.[47]

Faculty Underpaid but Competent

The Hannah Team discovered that about 70 percent of the University professional force was receiving salaries below the scale specified by the Wage Administration and Position classification scale.[48] The survey team, however, believed that despite their low salaries, the University faculty ranked "well above the average for comparable institutions, above average for the Philippines but somewhat less than what characterizes the University of first rank in the United States." The survey team noted that nothing is of "greater importance" to an institution of higher learning than the morale of its faculty. The group recommended that the criteria for promotion be studied by a joint faculty-administration committee and that a small advisory committee composed of elected faculty assist the administration in deciding on the promotions. Care, however, should be taken to "keep the process from becoming simply one of faculty election."[49]

President Sinco created a Committee on Reorganization which he instructed to study the Hannah Survey Report and to work out a plan for its immediate implementation. This committee was headed by Prof. Ricardo Pascual who went to the United States on an observation tour of leading American universities so that he might be guided in formulating a program for administrative innovations in the University.[50] Sinco also appointed Dr. Antonio Isidro, Vice-President for Academic Affairs, to head a committee that would work out a comprehensive plan with the International Cooperation Administration for the purpose of funding the reorganizational changes called for by the Hannah Survey Team.[51]

Reorganizing the University

In line with the proposed reorganization of the University administration and aware of the greatly expanded activities of the University since the end of World War II, President Sinco created the position of Vice-President for Academic Affairs. All research programs, all recommendations for the appointment of research personnel as well as the study of the curricula of the University became the responsibility of the new Vice-President. Thus, the office of the President was relieved of a heavy burden that would allow him more time to deal with other difficult aspects of administration.[52]

For the Los Baños campus, the President recommended the creation of the Office of the Vice-President for Agricultural Affairs. This new office, which the Board of Regents duly approved, was empowered to supervise the activities of the College of Agriculture and Forestry as well as the Forest Products Research Institute. Dean Dioscoro L. Umali of the College of Agriculture was appointed to this position.[53]

Sinco was also concerned that a substantial part of his time was being devoted to routine work and details of administration which could very well be attended to by lower level officials. The President then proposed to the Board of Regents the creation of the Office of the University Provost. This office, which was also recommended by the Hannah Survey Team, would enable the President to devote most of his time to overall policy and top-level decisions as well as attend important meetings and negotiations. The Board approved the proposal with the proviso that an executive assistant be appointed instead of a provost. Upon Sinco's recommendation, Dr. Ricardo Pascual, head of the Department of Philosophy and chairman of the University Reorganization Committee, was appointed Executive Assistant to the President.[54]

In 1960, the Board of Regents created four more important positions in general administration: (1) Director of the Physical Plant; (2) Director of Non-Academic Personnel; (3) Internal Auditor of the University; and (4) Director of Auxiliary Enterprises.[55]

An International Perspective

The President travelled widely, visiting universities in the United States and Europe where he discussed aims, objectives and methods of higher institutions of learning with leading academic administrators.[56] The purpose of such travels was to obtain guidance in the improvement of the University's course of study and to raise funds for the University. His trip to the United States in 1958 (October 4 – November 21), for example, was essentially a fund-raising one. He visited the headquarters of the Asia, Ford and Rockefeller Foundations, China Medical Board, and the American Council on Cultural and Economic Development to obtain much needed funding for the University.[57] The subsequent Romulo presidency later shared the ensuing benefits generated by aid received from these foundations especially in the support given to the faculty development programs. President Sinco also conferred with Secretary of State John Foster Dulles on the prospect of obtaining funds to enable the University to build an Asian Center.[58]

At the headquarters of the International Cooperation Agency (ICA), he presented a formal request for direct aid to the University. In conversations with Dr. Raymond T. Moyer, the agency official in charge of assistance to the Far East, the President obtained tentative commitments of aid to the University equal to ₱1 million a year for a period of five years starting in 1958. Such funds would come out of monies made available by US Public Law No. 480 (or the Agricultural Trade and Development Assistance Act of 1954). This aid, however, was contingent upon keeping the University budget intact without reducing the share of the national government. After a year of negotiations between the officials of the University and the agency's branch office in Manila and the head office in Washington, DC, the United States government allocated the sum for a five-year period to provide for salary increases to the faculty through selective promotions and to give assistance in housing projects.[59]

ACADEMIC PROGRAMS REFURBISHED AGAINST WIDESPREAD CONSERVATISM

THE achievements for which President Sinco will be most remembered are, of course, in the field of educational reorganization and curricular reform. His vision of the University growing into "the stature of the best institution of its kind" in the Philippines and abroad was described in his inaugural address, "The University of the Philippines and its Mission." He said that such a goal could only be achieved if the University were to follow a pattern of functions that covered three main activities: instruction for liberal or general education, training for the professions, and research work.[60]

The President deplored that for many years, the first function received "more lip-service and platitudinous praise than serious consideration." And yet there was

> an urgent and pressing need for this University to develop a program of general liberal education which shall constitute the basic intellectual training for every man and woman who must be enlightened and free citizens of this Republic. Such a program should include those disciplines that have relevance to a better understanding of man as a unit of civilized society and as a member of a democratic community.[61]

Requirements for Basic Education

He announced a plan of establishing in the University "a common core of basic education" that would provide the cultivation and development of the following traits and skills: (1) the ability to communicate thought effectively and to read with understanding materials of great value; (2) the ability to think critically and to make relevant judgments; (3) knowledge of the present status and past history of the culture and society of which the students are a part; and (4) an understanding of the nature of science as an intellectual process.[62]

Sinco deplored the fact that the College of Liberal Arts, which was supposed to assume "full responsibility" for the basic education of men and women had been gradually converted into "a dumping ground of all sorts of subjects," resulting in the "bewilderment and the superficiality of the average student." Sinco feared that without basic education, the University would turn out professionals who would be nothing more than "modern barbarians." Only liberal education would humanize the specialization gaining ground in the University. He stressed:

> Precisely because our need for specialization is great that we should promote and encourage liberal education with zeal and determination as a counter-balancing force for the maintenance and development of a well-ordered society.
>
> It is general education alone that can be depended upon to intervene as the integrating factor that works for harmony, order, and understanding among the different elements constituting our social system. Without this unifying factor, the danger of community and national disintegration, with all the evils it brings, is likely to be most difficult to arrest.[63]

Sinco also proposed a new orientation in the academic and cultural life of the University and called for the creation not only of incentives for faculty improvement but also for a fresh, imaginative and scholarly approach to teaching. He counselled against narrow nationalism and arrogant regionalism.

Opposition to Political Interference

The mission of the University, however, would not be achieved, Sinco warned, if the "limiting and cramping interference of politics" would continue to flourish in the University. In the past administrations, it had weakened the University's internal government and had lowered its academic standards.

> A university would be a dead institution when it can no longer advance the frontiers of human knowledge; when it ceases to be an instrument of intellectual freedom; when students and professors in their classrooms and laboratories grovel in abject obedience to authority; when it submits its judgments to outside directives.

The President, however, was confident that against such threats to the integrity of the University, the institution would prevail. For the University, he said, was not "a party of political zealots, or a guild of sectarian fanatics or a body of business adventurers but is a society of men and women devoted to the search for truth and knowledge."[64]

Search for Truth Emphasized

Indeed, the full stature of the University as an institution devoted to the search for truth and knowledge was revealed in the Golden Jubilee celebrations, which ran through the entire academic year of 1958-1959. The opening ceremonies, which coincided with Sinco's investiture and inauguration, were held at the new University Theater. Sinco's investiture was attended by representatives of leading colleges and universities in the United States, Asia and Europe; by numerous delegates from learned societies, cultural associations, and philanthropic foundations; as well as by high officials of the Philippine government.

This was followed by a series of jubilee celebrations which included an elaborate round of public lecture series and an international conference on University Education in Asia; roundtable discussions on higher education, scientific progress and national development; an alumni-faculty tour of the Visayas and Mindanao; the installation of a new bronze statue of the Oblation in front of the Administration building; and a Gala Symphony Concert.[65] Most of the participants were alumni of the University who had achieved distinction in their respective fields.

Inaugural Message

In his inaugural address, Sinco made a clear presentation of his far-reaching plans on the institution of a program of general education for the

University. Until his time, the idea of general education received "more lip-service and platitudinous praise than serious consideration." Sinco's first and most important objective as President was to develop such a program and in the first year of his administration, 1958-1959, he led the faculty in instituting university-wide curricular reforms which, according to him, were essentially a return to fundamentals.

He stressed that the mistaken belief that knowledge was equivalent to information had led to the proliferation of subjects in the University which caused the "superficiality of the education" of many students. If the curriculum of the first two years in the College of Liberal Arts were pruned, thus limiting the student's work to the basic and essential subjects in English, Spanish, physical and biological sciences, social sciences and the humanities, then the University would be able to provide the "indispensable foundation" of every professional education of any man, be he a teacher, physician, lawyer or any other professional.[66]

Curricular Reform

On May 22, 1958, Sinco created a committee to study and formulate a curriculum on general education with the following objectives in mind: the development of the ability to write and speak English effectively and to read with understanding materials with some complexity; the development of the ability to think critically; the understanding of the present status and past history of the culture and society of which the student is a part; and the understanding of the nature of science as an intellectual process.[67]

On June 21, 1958, the University Council approved the curriculum of the first two years of basic general education in the Colleges of Liberal Ats, Education and Business Administration. The curriculum prescribed 63 units, which includes 9 units of English, 12 units of Spanish, 6 units of Mathematics, 3 units of Logic, 9 units each of courses in the Humanities and the Social Sciences and 6 units each of courses in the Biological and Physical Sciences. Another three-unit course, Philippine Institutions I (also called the Rizal course) was considered an indispensable part of the curriculum.[68] Aside from providing a broad liberal education, the new curriculum included subjects intended to familiarize the students with the concept and development of Philippine and Asian nationalism.[69] It also emphasized the development of skills in the English language.

The general education curriculum covered the period of two years and was prescribed for all students of the University. Students entering the University were required to complete the general education program before they could be admitted to the professional colleges. Before these curricular changes were instituted, the University offered only what was called "preparatory courses" for various professional curricula, which differed from one profession to another to the extent that the only learning experience common to all students in the University were English, Spanish, Physical Education, Military Science (or Euthenics) and Philippine Institutions.[70] General education was thus given its rightful place in the academe, equal in importance with the two other major concerns of the University, professional studies and research.

New Courses Introduced

Various departments in the College of Liberal Arts introduced new courses especially geared to the tenets of the general education plan. The History Department offered two subjects intended to develop in the entering freshman students "a better appreciation of the cultural tradition and history of the Philippines and Asian Countries." The department offered a 5-unit course in Philippine History and Institutions and a 3-unit subject on Eastern Thought and Institutions, both of which were required in the new curriculum. Compared to the older courses, History 5, which had "a very narrow scope and limited interest," the new Philippine History and Institutions I gave the students a better perspective of their country's history; in fact, it introduced them to almost all fields or areas in Philippine History. The new course called for a Filipino point of view in teaching the subject for the intention in including it in the general education plan was to lead the student to think of himself not as a colonial but as a Filipino.[71]

In Social Science 1 (Eastern Thought and Institutions), the cultural and social traditions of China, Japan and India were interpreted on the basis of selected philosophical, literary and social documents. The course was not intended to be just a historical survey, for the documents used would be analyzed "not for the facts about the culture and the society which produced them but more for the enlightenment they might shed on the nature of the interrelationship of ideas and institutions within the social and cultural context of a particular time and place."[72]

The Department of Political Science, for its part, offered Social Science II (Western Thought), a five-unit course on social philosophers and their works similar to Harvard University's two-semester course on "Ideas of Man and the World in Western Thought." Like its counterpart at Harvard University, Social Science II stressed the works of Plato, Aristotle, Tomas Aquinas, John Stuart Mill and other great Western thinkers. The course, according to one of its proponents, Dr. Onofre D. Corpuz, was intended to develop the student's ability to "consider and criticize social philosophies, independently of one's subjective attitude and values."[73]

Pilot Classes and Textbook Writing

The departments offering new courses in the General Education Program offered pilot classes handled by selected faculty members. Dr. Cesar

Adib Majul, Messrs. Emmanuel Orara and Silvino V. Epistola, and Mrs. Ellen Capiz offered the first classes in Social Science II. In the English Department, a core group composed of Professors Alfredo Morales, Concepcion Dadufalza, Dionisia Rola, Wilhelmina Ramas, Teodoro Locsin and Dolores Feria presented lectures to help prepare their colleagues for the innovative courses the department was planning as its contribution to the General Education Program. Syllabi or outlines for various general education courses were also prepared.[74]

To complement the teaching of these courses, the administration encouraged the writing of textbooks and other instructional materials. Those who engaged in research and writing for this purpose were allowed a reduced teaching load of at least six units, a definite inducement to creative work and research inaugurated by the Sinco presidency. Dr. Raymundo Favila and Prof. Felina Mapa prepared *Mathematics for General Education,* the textbook for Mathematics I, while Prof. Francisco Nemenzo, Sr. and Dr. Agustin Rodolfo and Dr. Joventino Soriano prepared the syllabus for Natural Science II (Principles of Biological Science). Prof. Teodoro A. Agoncillo and Prof. Oscar M. Alfonso wrote the textbook for the general education course in Philippine History entitled *A Short History of the Filipino People.* This book was used for the first time during the academic year 1961-1962.[75]

A New University College

The implementation of the program of basic education, however, called not only for new courses and textbooks but for a core faculty that would constitute the University College, that would be vested with the responsibility of pursuing Sinco's goals. The University, already operating under severe budgetary constraints, was ill-equipped to recruit a huge number of professors. It was not also possible for the University to carve a new college from the old College of Liberal Arts. Moreover, if a new unit would have to come from the College of Liberal Arts at all, the urgency with which the General Education Program must be implemented gave the administration and the liberal arts faculty little time to make a permanent selection of faculty slated for the University College apart from a faculty slated for the College of Arts and Sciences, the new unit that would take the place of the College of Liberal Arts.

The obvious solution to the problem was the reorganization of the College of Liberal Arts into three academic units: the University College, the College of Arts and Sciences, and the Graduate School of Arts and Science. All three units, however, would constitute one single body of faculty.[76]

The University College, which began its operations in the first semester of 1959-1960, was vested with the task of teaching general education courses in the humanities, the social sciences and the natural sciences for the first two years.[77] By improving the foundations for a liberal education, the college would serve the purpose of continuing the general education that the high schools had started to provide. President Sinco, however, recognized that due to the "inadequate instruction" provided by the country's high schools, the instruction provided by the University College would have the effect of not only giving "some completeness" but also some "correction" to secondary general education.[78]

College of Arts and Sciences Founded

The name of the College of Liberal Arts was changed to College of Arts and Sciences. It was responsible for the third and subsequent years of undergraduate studies in the humanities, social sciences, natural and physical sciences, mathematics, and languages.[79] These were the disciplines that the college offered as fields of specialization. Thus, the Junior and Senior years of a student were built around a single subject, or a major, for concentrated advance work, in addition to other related subjects called free electives. The University required the student working for the degree of Bachelor of Arts or Bachelor of Science to finish a total of 70 units, including major and elective subjects, for graduation.[80]

The separate functions of the University College and the College of Arts and Sciences required separate administrations. President Sinco appointed Dr. Augusto Tenmatay (Professor of Chemistry) and Oscar M. Alfonso (Assistant Professor of History) as the first Dean and Secretary, respectively, of the University College. Dr. Tomas S. Fonacier continued as Dean of the College of Arts and Sciences. To prevent any duplication of subjects by the two closely linked colleges and to integrate the various disciplines in the old College of Liberal Arts, three major divisions were created to take the place of the academic departments. These were the Division of Humanities, Division of Social Sciences, and Division of Natural Sciences. The traditional academic disciplines operated under their corresponding divisions without any departmental head.[81]

Shuffling Faculty Assignments

The deans of the two colleges were directed to jointly decide the assignments of the faculty members who would teach in either one of the colleges.[82] Such an arrangement, however, was obviously unsatisfactory for the University College had yet to be provided a faculty of its own. Five months after the establishment of the new unit, its organizational relationship with the College of Arts and Sciences, existing divisions and departments had yet to be defined.

Dean Tenmatay, in a letter to President Sinco, pointed out that budgetary considerations posed an "undesirable complication" that could destroy the existing organic unity of the faculty. For one thing, most of the faculty of the University College were junior instructors. Moreover, there were even then few professors to meet the needs of both colleges. While the Divisions of Humanities, Social Sciences and Natural Sciences had provided a working organization for the University College, the divisions had nevertheless direct supervision only over the faculty members assigned to the College of Arts and Sciences. Tenmatay suggested that the jurisdiction of the Division chairman be extended to all faculty members in the two colleges.[83]

Professional Colleges Give Way

The adoption of the General Education program brought about some conflict between the College of Arts and Sciences and the professional colleges. The professional schools held that the addition of new courses in the first two years would lead to a corresponding drastic reduction of many of their curricular offerings. The professional colleges believed that general education should be introduced without sacrificing the professional competence they wanted to develop in their students. The University Advisory Committee met with representatives of the College of Arts and Sciences and the professional colleges many times during the schoolyear 1959-1960 to thresh out the problems created by the introduction of the General Education Program. As a result, four professional colleges prolonged the curricular requirements for their degree courses by one year in order that their respective programs might dovetail with the general education plan.

The College of Veterinary Medicine extended the five-year course leading to the Degree of Doctor of Veterinary Medicine to six years of which two years must be taken in the University College. The College of Law required the four-year Bachelor of Arts course, as precribed by the Supreme Court, as a requirement for admission into the College of Law. Both the College of Nursing and the College of Business Administration increased the requirement from four to five years for the degrees they were offering.[84]

Term System Introduced

Another change introduced by the Sinco administration was the concentrated study plan, which took effect in June 1959. This was patterned after those in operation in tertiary institutions in the United States such as Harvard College, Mount Holyoke College and Sarah Lawrence and Bennington Colleges.[85] According to Sinco, the semestral system had many disadvantages not the least of which was its failure to provide the student enough time to concentrate and accumulate the subject matter of his courses.[86] The concentrated guided study plan, which came to be known as the term system, would in Sinco's view provide the students wider opportunities for learning.

The guided study plan which the University adopted had the following characteristics: (1) the number of subjects to be enrolled in simultaneously was limited to no more than two; (2) the class session was used for study and discussion of the assigned subject or lesson, and (3) daily class sessions were held five times a week, each class lasting at least one and one half hours for each subject.[87] President Sinco suggested that the maximum load should not exceed eighteen units; such a load would allow sufficient time for reading, reflection and understanding of the reading assignments.[88] The academic year was divided into six terms of six weeks each: three terms each semester or a total of six terms in an academic year. The student took the final examination on his two subjects before proceeding to his next two courses.

Widespread Opposition Noted

There was, to be sure, considerable opposition to the term system. The Conservatory of Music, for example, found it impractical and cumbersome for many courses that required long periods to accomplish and quickly reverted to the semestral system.[89] The College of Medicine did not even attempt to experiment with the new system and continued to adhere to the semestral arrangement for it was the consensus of the college faculty that the end-to-end system would be "deleterious" to the clinical instruction of the students and would make it difficult, if not impossible, for medical students to undertake chronic animal experiments that required many long weeks to complete.[90]

Many members of the faculty, particularly those of the College of Arts and Sciences which adopted the guided study plan in its entirety felt that while the term system might be useful for casework study in the College of Law, where it had been in operation for several years before the University adopted it for the other units, it could not provide successful training in courses such as science and mathematics where understanding in depth is essential and could be arrived at only after a time of gradual gestation. H. Fairfield Smith, an agricultural statistician of the Food and Agricultural Organization and visiting lecturer in statistics, warned that the continuation of the guided study plan would serve only to encourage the fundamental weakness of Philippine education – learning by rote. He warned that it would be rash to enforce on all "a university revolution" opposed by the large majority of the faculty.[91]

The College of Arts and Sciences, the unit most affected by this innovation, nominated and elected early in 1959 a special committee to study the problem of teaching loads under the new system. The eight-member committee, which was headed by Prof. Mateo H. Tupas (Geology), prepared a draft resolution which opposed the two-subject plan and advocated a return to the old academic calendar. This draft resolution, which was prepared for the faculty by Asst. Prof. Emerenciana Y. Arcellana (Political Science), contended that the end-to-end system, as the term system was popularly known, compared unfavorably with the semestral system for the former increased the faculty members' teaching burden, thus precluding intensive research and creative work as well as other activities toward general self-improvement and the advancement of knowledge. At the same time, the draft resolution also claimed that the new study plan gave the University a budgetary saving which corresponded to a virtual reduction in pay for the faculty members.[92]

Conflict and Confrontation

Dean Fonacier provided President Sinco a draft resolution before the College faculty could discuss it in a meeting scheduled on 30 April 1960. In a letter to Dean Fonacier dated 19 April, mimeographed copies of which were distributed to the faculty on the date of the meeting, President Sinco admitted to feelings of "disgust and disappointment" over the faculty's "unreasonable," "unfair," and "prejudicial" judgment on the term system. He refused to admit that the term system exploited the faculty. He reminded the faculty that they had contractual obligations with the University and the students. The term system had in fact saved the faculty time otherwise needed for their research. He pointed out that his administration was the first to reduce the teaching load from fifteen hours to only nine hours a week. The University had no intention of overworking its teachers without giving them due compensation. "High salaries alone do not necessarily produce superior professors, . . . for teaching, as every good teacher knows, is as much a passion as it is a craft – and even Hollywood cannot teach passion." Since the University was not a commercial institution to begin with, "those faculty who see no reward for its labor in anything but cash" should not be in the University but in business.[93]

Responding to President Sinco, Prof. Arcellana deplored that the "merest voicing" of faculty thinking on "a subject vital to their interest" had aroused the "unkindest insinuations" and pleaded for a more "enlightened attitude" towards a faculty who were, after all, "responsible people, conscious of their duties" to themselves, to the University and to the world.[94] The College faculty, however, did not take any action against the term system.

The University administration thus continued to support the term system. A year after it was introduced at the University College, the Registrar reported that the new system had helped reduce the number of failing students, the increased proportion of passing students being those in the General Education curriculum. The highest rates of passing were in Political Science I (from 48% to 70.07%); Sociology (from 48.8% to 79.54%) and Psychology I (from 51.3% to 73.49%).[95]

Grading System Modified

The Board of Regents also radically changed the rules on graduation with honors. Students who obtained grades lower than "3" could graduate with honors provided that the total average of the grades taken met the prescribed standards for graduation with honors.[96]

Another innovation the Sinco administration introduced was the grade of "4" or low pass. The Board of Regents on 6 January 1961 approved the grade of "4" as the equivalent of a low pass, instead of being the equivalent of a conditional failure. This took effect during the fifth term of the second semester, 1960-1961.[97] However, the colleges offering technical courses opposed the institution of the new grade on the ground that their course offerings were more difficult than those offered by the non-technical colleges of the University. A poor standing in the technical colleges, it was pointed out, could be offset by obtaining good or high grades outside them.[98] This innovation was criticized as a bold attempt at lowering the standards of the University. The *Philippine Collegian* editorialized that the institution of the grade of "4" was "an invitation to sterility and stagnation."[99]

After a year from the introduction of the low pass grade, the Executive Committee reported that the new grade was creating confusion among the students. Apparently as an effort to eliminate the confusion, a sub-committee of the Executive Committee proposed that the University adopt the letter grading system used by American universities and colleges. The faculty of the College of Arts and Sciences, often the sounding board of new measures endorsed by the administration, vigorously opposed this recommendation and voted to keep the old numerical system of "1," "2," "3," "4" and "5." Some members of the faculty declared that the old system had been functioning smoothly and that the proposal was "impractical and unwarranted."[100]

Academic Reforms Unwelcome

Criticisms of the experimentation with the general education program in particular, and of Sinco's administration, in general, were brought out into the open with the publication of Josefina Constantino's "The Slow Death of an Institution," and the ensuing debate between her and Armando Bonifacio, an assistant professor of Philosophy, in the *Sunday Times Magazine* in September and October 1960.[101] Constantino charged that because of the reckless changes initiated by President Sinco in the academic programs of the University, the institution was facing "threats of corruption and decay."[102] The relaxed admission rules that allowed ill-prepared freshmen into the University ("everybody" was supposedly admitted during the school year 1960-1961) and the introduction of the term system and the general education program merely wasted faculty resources and lowered student morale. The administration's insistence on continuing such policies only proved that the Sinco presidency had lost its appreciation of the University's mission.

Constantino denounced the Sinco presidency for excluding the faculty from important University deliberations and reducing it into "a voiceless entity." The University Council, on the other hand, had become "a mere rubber stamp," content to receive administrative orders from the President. The faculty, she alleged, was never consulted on the adoption of the term system. Sinco's condemnation of the resolution of the faculty of the College of Arts and Sciences and Mrs. Arcellana's defense of it, vividly demonstrated the "truly autocratic nature" of the Sinco administration and the "unhappy condition" of the faculty.[103]

Moreover, Sinco allegedly played favorites with the faculty and ignored time-honored traditions in his dealings with the academics. Textbooks written by professors who enjoyed the official patronage were reportedly rushed into print and adopted for use by the University. The "publish or perish" rule, "no matter how" led to a race in "mediocre textbook writing" by professors "eager to make a mark." This contributed to a further "debasement" of scholarship in the University.

Innovations Explained and Defended

Prof. Armando F. Bonifacio took exception to Constantino's charges. Far from abandoning its time-honored ideals, the University according to Bonifacio's appraisal was in fact "undergoing a process of reconstruction and resetting its perspectives." In instituting new features and programs, both in the administrative and academic aspects, the University had had to contend with traditional notions and encounter difficulties posed by "habits of mind and somatic dispositions acquired through the years."[104] Bonifacio wrote that the semestral system, one of those old features the new administration wanted to abolish, only resulted in "the deterioration of the quality of the student's work," an argument that Constantino countered by pointing out that she and Bonifacio and a host of outstanding graduates of the University, who were products of the semestral system, proved that the system was not all that bad.[105]

When asked for his reaction to Constantino's charges, Sinco questioned the motives of the author in criticizing the changes taking place in the University. He said that Constantino resigned from the University in disgust over her failure to reinstate Homobono Adaza who was expelled for writing derogatory articles about the University.[106] On the other hand, various officials of the University administration denied that the University had deteriorated under Sinco. In fact, asserted Prof. Rex D. Drilon, Secretary of the University, "for the first time after fifty years," the University underwent "an unmistakable invigorization on the academic front."[107] Constantino's charges, noted Drilon, were nothing more than "half-truths" which were "more misleading than outright lies."

Alumni Prompted to Investigate

Dean Hermenegildo R. Reyes, president of the University of the Philippines Alumni Association, did not agree. Spurred by Constantino's denunciations, Reyes created a seven-man fact-finding and survey committee to investigate the alleged deterioration of the academic standards of the University. Ricardo Paras, just retired as Chief Justice of the Supreme Court, headed the committee composed of Justice Marcelino Montemayor, Congressman Rogaciano Mercado, Regents Gumersindo Garcia and Florencio Tamesis, Mrs. Geronima Pecson and Salvador San Juan.[108] The Committee appointed prominent alumni who in turn constituted themselves into sub-committees which inquired into the consequences of the implementation of the concentrated study plan upon the various sectors of the University, particularly the four colleges most affected by the innovation: the University College, the College of Law, the College of Education and the College of Arts and Sciences.[109]

The results of the inquiry were mixed; the various opinions obtained from different sectors of the University indicated that since the previous semestral system had functioned effectively, a thorough study and small-scale experimentation should have been done before the end-to-end system was introduced. The college deans were divided in their reaction to the term system. Dean Oscar Baguio of the College of Engineering declined to comment on the merits of the system even though he was in favor of it. Dean Vicente Abad Santos of the College of Law, where the system had been in effect since 1953, declined to provide any opinion.[110] Both Dean Tenmatay and Dean Fonacier of the University College and the College of Arts and Sciences respectively favored the continuation of the system. Tenmatay, however, said that it was "too premature" to give an appraisal of the results of the system.[111]

Term System Evaluated

The Committee discovered that the term system was not accepted "gracefully" nor with "any degree of unanimity" by either the student body or by the members of the faculty.[112] Indeed, the following objections of the faculty and students of the College of Education echoed the sentiments of the constituency of the other units affected by the term system. The college administrators thought it was easier to preserve the continuity and sequence in scheduling classes during the year but they recognized that the new system made it more difficult for the professors to teach their majors because both professors and students were provided very little respite from one term to the next. The professors contended that while their preparation might have been reduced, as the proponents of the system claimed, their work load, in fact, more than doubled. Bright students would not find the term system particularly burdensome but weak students would have little time and opportunity to make up in case of a few absences.

The system was particularly disadvantageous for graduate study as there was too little time for research and the writing of term papers; consequently, the graduate students would be forced to engage in "scissor and paste work." The psychology professors in the College of Education contended that the system contradicted learning theories and principles of growth and development. The learning process, like human growth, could not be hurried even if the nutrition and other elements necessary for such growth were doubled.

Professors at the University College and College of Arts and Sciences agreed with this view and expressed their doubts about the "pedagogical soundness" of the system because the concentration process involved could produce in the student "a feeling of surfeit, listlessness, lack of interest or even hostility to the subjects taught, frames of mind not conducive to the very objective the term system sought to achieve."[113]

In defense of the term system, President Sinco pointed out that to gain mastery of any subject, there could be no substitute for concentrated attention and strenuous efforts. "Those who talk of the so-called leisurely development really encourage the pernicious *mañana* habit. They are misleading our youth."[114]

The San Juan Committee did not think its findings were conclusive. Owing to the controversial aspects of the end-to-end system, the Committee recommended that all the faculty members concerned be polled secretly on the desirability of the system. The Committee did not seem to have followed up this recommendation and the colleges concerned did not conduct any survey. In any case, the term system continued until the end of the Sinco presidency.[115] One of the first administrative measures implemented by his successor, Carlos P. Romulo, was to return the four colleges to the semestral system.

New Building Reflect Progress

The new direction in scholarship, teaching and research of the Sinco administration was accompanied by considerable material or physical improvements in University facilities. New colleges were established, new buildings were constructed and existing facilities on the Diliman and Los Baños campuses were improved.

In 1961, ten new construction projects were completed, nine of which were built entirely with University funds. These included the University Theater, the Convervatory of Music Building (Abelardo Hall), the Baguio College Building and the Radiological Health Laboratory of the Institute of Hygiene. The last was funded by a grant from the National Economic Council and the United States International Cooperation Agency.[116] On the Los Baños campus, the national government relinquished the administration of the Makiling National Park and Reserve– all the forests, plantations and nurseries– to the University.[117]

Expansion of Academic Units

Several disciplines, which used to function as mere departments within the colleges, were transformed into full-fledged autonomous units to meet the growing demand for further specialization. In August 1961, the Board of Regents elevated to college status the Department of Home Economics, which had been under the Graduate College of Education for 35 years. The curriculum of the former department, which was designed to train girls to become high school home economics teachers, had so expanded to warrant the creation of an entirely new college capable of offering specialization in the home arts.[118] Housed in a new building constructed with Rockefeller Foundation and University funds, the only college of Home Economics in the country and in Southeast Asia could boast of the most complete and modern laboratory equipment and facilities.[119]

The Department of Library Science, which was also administered by the College of Education, was elevated into an institute for the purpose of meeting the need for trained librarians not only in the Philippines but also in other countries of Southeast Asia.[120] A grant from the Rockefeller Foundation helped in setting up the Institute. Through representations made by the Foundation and the University President, the American Library Association agreed to send to the Institute within four years after its founding in 1961 four American professors to help in the organization and implementation of the Institute's graduate program.

The reopening of the Baguio branch in April 1961 brought the services of the University to the mountain areas of Northern Luzon.[121] A branch had operated in Baguio before World War II but it was only in May 1960, after alumni in the upland city and nearby communities worked tirelessly for the revival of the college, that the Board of Regents appropriated and made available sufficient funds for the college. A small building was constructed in a site assigned to the University at Baguio City's Government Center. The College reopened in April 1961 with modest administrative offices, a small library and a laboratory.[122]

The College of Agriculture in Los Baños played a key role in the establishment of the multimillion-peso International Rice Research Institute (IRRI), which opened in February 1962. Its primary purpose was to conduct a continuing research on rice under the sponsorship of the Ford and Rockefeller Foundations. Scientists at the Institute were expected to work closely with professors and researchers of the University.[123]

Serving the Alumni and the Public

Indeed under Sinco, the University was not an isolated institution that rarely communicated with the world outside its two main campuses. It had long been his goal "to bring the University to the people." On April 10, 1958 the Board of Regents approved a resolution creating the Office of Information and Alumni Relations. This would function as a clearing house of facts about the University and would coordinate with agencies, institutions, groups and individuals whose goodwill and cooperation were essential to the welfare and progress of the University.[124] Extramural services, on the other hand, increased the influence of the University upon other areas of the country.

In February 1960, Sinco established the Department of Extramural Studies for the purpose of carrying out university-level instruction in areas far from the campuses of the University. Teachers, businessmen, professionals, farmers and others who wanted to improve themselves educationally but found it impossible to enrol in the University's four campuses could enrol in the extramural studies center near them. Instruction would be done partly through correspondence and radio and partly through personal attendance in actual classes offered during the summer months.[125]

External study centers were established in Davao City, Ilagan (Isabela) and Bayambang (Pangasinan) with course offerings for the improvement of the teaching of English and science, specially in the elementary schools.[126] Sinco also signed a memorandum agreement with the Provincial Governor of Laguna for the purpose of stimulating greater interest in scientific agriculture and aiding the agricultural development of the province. A Laguna Farm Development Trust Fund of ₱10,880 was initially set up for this purpose.[127]

A MOVE TO COUNTERACT *UPSCA* DOMINANCE OF STUDENT ORGANIZATIONS

IN the midst of all these far-ranging academic and administrative innovations, President Sinco had to take into account the unsettled problem of sectarianism in the University and the growing influence of only one student group, the University of the Philippines Student Catholic

Action (UPSCA), in student politics. Its domination of student politics in the years before Sinco's presidency underwent a proliferation never before seen in the history of the University. The Tan administration encouraged this expansion while the interim Virata administration appeared indifferent to it. Sinco's attempts to reduce the UPSCA into a less powerful organization brought him into an open conflict with the student group and its partisans.

Father Delaney's Influence

Indeed, the UPSCA had become the only student organization within the University capable of "instant mobilization on an overall basis." During the schoolyear 1956-1957, the UPSCANS, whom the late Father John P. Delaney, S.J., had shaped into a strong political machine, captured a clear majority of the University Student Council, the junior and senior student councils as well as the Board of Management of the *Philippine Collegian.*[128] For the first time, the fraternities and sororities lost their control of student politics which they had wielded for decades.[129] Scholars in the University, aware that the gains of the UPSCA during the Tan administration constituted a real threat to scholarship and academic freedom, were dejected by persistent efforts of the Catholic group to gain control of affairs on the campus. After President Tan resigned, fears that a sympathetic and sectarian President might be appointed mounted, particularly because the administrative policies of such a president might eventually converge with UPSCA's sectarian policies and goals.[130]

Regents Too Wary and Ineffective

The Regents during the interim Virata presidency did not help ease this apprehension for they continued to be divided on basically the same issues that beleaguered the Tan administration. The Board of Regents had created a committee, headed by Senator Jose P. Laurel, to define the sphere of activities of the religious groups on campus but for lack of a consensus among the Regents, the Board conveniently shelved the committee's recommendations.

The Laurel Committee had recommended that the Board revise existing rules and regulations governing student organizations, that religious organizations limit their activities within their respective chapels and grounds, and that no religious organizations should be allowed to engage in student politics and elections. The Committee had also recommended that "no priest may speak before students or organizations of the University without a written permission from the University President."[131] If these proposed amendments to the University Code were adopted by the Board, the UPSCA would have been seriously emasculated for the Code, so revised, would have practically banned all those activities that had made it the strongest and most militant student organization in the University.[132]

Sinco's Strategic Move

The failure of the Board of Regents during the late Tan and interim Virata administrations to act on the Laurel recommendations must have prompted President Sinco to implement his own radical policy regarding student organizations. President Sinco, at the time he assumed office, faced these alternatives: to deprive the UPSCANS of all privileges to take part in student activities on the campus and thus deny them the advantages they had gained in campus politics, or to treat them on the same level as all other student organizations.

On June 24, 1958, he issued Administrative Circular No. 1 which limited the representation of any student organization to one representative only in each of the student councils.[133] Sinco's purpose was to increase the participation of students in extracurricular activities and to prevent the concentration of privileges in any one group of students as well as drastically reduce friction and dissatisfaction among students in extracurricular affairs.[134] Thus, no student organization, including the UPSCA, could have complete control of student politics in the University.

UPSCANs Take Issue to Court

The circular had the effect of nullifying UPSCA's hold on campus politics and on the student organizations. Indeed, the circular was tantamount to "a death warrant" for the Catholic organization. UPSCA's leaders described the circular as "illegal, discriminatory, unreasonable, undemocratic and arbitrary."[135] Convinced that the circular was directed only at their organization, the UPSCANS sought judicial redress against it.[136] Judge Bienvenido A. Tan of the Manila Court of First Instance ruled that the circular was illegal and unconstitutional. Tan also gave the UPSCANS the opportunity to question, in a higher court, the validity of Circular No. 1.[137]

In response, government lawyers filed in behalf of the University a petition which sought to block the UPSCA move on the ground that the latter failed to include the Board of Regents as defendants.[138] The final approval of the circular lay with the Board of Regents; it followed that President Sinco was not the proper authority to sue in court.

The UPSCA appealed to the Supreme Court but this body dismissed the petition on the sole technical ground that the petitioners had not exhausted administrative remedies within the University. Indeed, the organization had not even appealed to the Board of Regents.[139] The Supreme Court decision, however, came only in November 1960. Thus during the schoolyears 1958-1959, 1959-60 and 1960-1961, student government and student politics came to a virtual standstill, pending court decision on the UPSCA case.

Ruling Made Part of UP Code

In January 1961, a committee created by President Sinco to propose changes in the University Code adopted Circular No. 1 as an important new provision in the Code. It became Article 448 which provided that "not more than one member of any student club, society or fraternity or any other form of association of a permanent nature" could be appointed or elected to any particular term to any office or employment in the Student Union.[140] The Board of Regents also approved Article 437 which provided for a student union which would take charge of the cultural and social programs and activities of the student body "under such rules and regulations as may be issued by the Dean of Student Affairs."[141] In effect, the Student Union took the place of the University Student Council. The way was clear for preparations to constitute that Union.

The UPSCA charged that Article 448 was neither presented to nor approved by the University Council and that the Board of Regents did not hold a hearing on Article 448 before adopting it. It also charged that the Sinco administration used Article 448 against the UPSCANS with a particularly "heavy hand and an evil eye," oblivious of the fact that the Catholic student body enjoyed the "active support and sympathies of the overwhelming majority" of the student population.[142] UPSCA sought an indefinite postponement of the election of the Student Union officers by obtaining a writ of preliminary injunction from the Rizal Court of First Instance. In seeking the annulment of Article 448, the UPSCA challenged its legality, contending that the disputed article should have been enacted by the University Council.[143]

Supreme Court favors UP

The University Legal Office sought the dissolution of the writ, countering that the Catholic actionists could not have acted in innocence and in good faith for they had been aware all along of the controversial codal provision.[144] The Supreme Court decided in favor of the University authorities. It allowed the Dean of Student Affairs to organize the Student Union. The Dean, however, allowed only one member of the UPSCA to run for a position in the Union; 28 other members were disqualified.[145]

Greek-Letter Societies Subdued

Although the UPSCA was at the center of the controversy, it was not the sole target of reforms instituted. President Sinco also sought to reduce the problems brought about by the activities of the fraternities and sororities. In April 1959, President Sinco asked the Registrar to send to the parents and guardians of the students a questionnaire to determine whether or not they were in favor of their children joining the fraternities or sororities. The Registrar reported that less than 10% preferred fraternity or sorority membership for their children.[146] This seems to have been the basis for an UCCSOA ruling that required all applicants for admission into the fraternities and sororities to first obtain the written permission from their parents or guardians before they can be admitted into these societies.

Romulo S. Gatilao, an officer of the Sigma Rho fraternity, criticized the ruling as unreasonable and unfair for it not only reduced the university students to "mere children" but also presumed the "hurtful" influences brought by membership in the Greek-letter societies.[147] The ruling, however, seemed to have been discontinued or suspended – perhaps it was found impracticable – for nothing in the University records showed that it was ever implemented.

In any case, it was easy to understand why President Sinco sought to discourage the students from joining the fraternities and sororities. The minutes of the Executive Committee of the University Council indicated that not a single semester during his term passed when the Executive Committee over which he presided did not have to investigate a case involving violent fraternity hazing or some disturbance caused by members of fraternities.

Sinco was cordial, kind and sympathetic, friendly but frank to the students. Just as he sought to establish greater rapport with the University faculty by frequent conferences and meetings at the Executive House, his official residence, so did he seek student participation in free and full discussions of leading issues of the day.[148]

Stern Way of a Disciplinarian

He did not, however, pass up any opportunity to instill discipline among erring students. In this regard he appeared to the students and to some members of the academic community as a very stern disciplinarian. This is illustrated by the so-called "flag hauling incident" involving Niceto S. Poblador and two other students. Under the influence of liquor, on December 17, 1958, Poblador unceremonoiusly hauled down the Singaporean flag, which flew over the library during the Asian Conference on Cultural Cooperation (15-19 December) and slashed it. This caused the Embassy of Singapore to lodge a protest with the Department of Foreign Affairs. Subsequent investigation confirmed Poblador's guilt.[149] Poblador was suspended from all classes and from any association with the University for three months. He was also required to make a public apology in a University convocation.

On January 12, 1959, when the President reported on his tour of various universities abroad in a University convocation, he called Poblador to the stage. The latter confessed his guilt and apologized for his misdeed to the academic community. The *Philippine Collegian* severely criticized President Sinco in its editorial of January 14, 1959. However, this was heavily censored; patches of black prevented the reader from gaining any further insight into the sentiments of the editor.[150] But on May 14, 1959, another editorial expressed resentment that Sinco's presidency had become "too paternalistic and, to some extent, patronizing." The administration, the editorial said, had not exerted any attempt to understand the students and their feelings nor did it show any conscious effort to make the students understand that policy innovations were designed for their welfare. Thus, the students interpreted every policy change as "an authoritative imposition."[151]

RAMPAGE OF WITCH HUNTERS ON A BELEAGUERED CAMPUS

THE problems brought about by student discipline, sectarianism and administrative innovations in curricula and teaching methods constituted a real challenge to the resources of the University President and the academic community. But these were not as serious and menacing as the so-called witch hunt in the University during the fourth year of Sinco's presidency. His attempts at bringing about a renaissance on the campus were interrupted in early 1961 when Congressman Leonardo Perez (Nacionalista, Nueva Vizcaya), Chairman of the House Committee on Anti-Filipino Activities (CAFA) called for a "loyalty investigation" of the faculty of the University because there were "strong grounds" to believe that a significant number of the University faculty could be considered sympathizers of the Communist Party of the Philippines. He was persuaded that it was urgently necessary to verify reports of "communist incursions" into the state university.[152]

Perez offered as evidence "seditious materials" published in the University such as the anonymously written "Peasant War in the Philippines," an 84-page "communist-oriented" historical essay which appeared in the Golden Jubilee issue of the *Philippine Social Sciences and Humanities Review;*[153] and the anonymously written articles entitled "Tower of Babel and Tower of Ivory" and "Human Dignity – The Myth and the Heresy" which appeared in the 1959 *Philippinensian.*[154] He also declared that two professors from the College of Arts and Sciences, Dr. Ricardo Pascual of the Department of Philosophy and Dr. Agustin Rodolfo of the Department of Zoology were Communist sympathizers if not actually members of the Communist Party.[155]

Flushing Out Alleged Communists

Perez held public hearings to ferret out the "communist sympathizers" hiding in the UP campus. On March 9, 1961, the first day of the hearing, he presented as witnesses Miss Josefina D. Constantino, associate professor in the Department of English, who had just resigned from the University and had joined the Development Bank of the Philippines, and Miss Amelita Reysio Cruz, a former student of Dr. Pascual and a reporter for the *Manila Daily Bulletin.*

Constantino said that she resigned from the university because she could no longer stand its "repressive atmosphere." She complained that "intellectual ferment" had increased considerably under the Sinco administration.[156] She accused Pascual of creating in his classes an atmosphere "receptive to communist indoctrination" through his "logical positivistic approach" to philosophy, a denunciation which, according to the *Philippine Collegian,* she had been making since 1954. She failed, however, to provide categorical proof that Pascual was indeed a communist. She had heard reports that Dr. Pascual had been attending *buklod* (or Communist Cell) meetings.

Dr. Pascual later contended that by *buklod* meetings, the witness probably meant the meetings of the Philosophical Association of the Philippines, which met regularly at its headquarters in Tondo. He attended these meetings because he was the organization's adviser and frequent lecturer.[157]

The CAFA also pinpointed Dr. Agustin Rodolfo as a card-bearing member of the Communist Party. Rodolfo did not deny this accusation and admitted having been a member of the "inner sanctum" of the *Hukbong Mapagpalaya ng Bayan* (HMB or People's Liberation Army) under the direct and personal command of its supremo, Luis Taruc. However, he had "violent disagreements" with the HMB supremo on crucial matters such as dictatorship and the use of force to bring about economic reforms. He also severed his ties with the Huks when he went to the United States under a plan which repatriated to the United States Filipinos married to American wives. Indeed, a Huk document seized by the Army on August 20, 1950 during a raid on a Politburo meeting mentioned Rodolfo's trip to the United States as one of "rank opportunism" resulting in his suspension from the Communist Party.[158] The CAFA, in the end, failed to come up with any convincing evidence of Rodolfo's continuing links with the Communist Party.

Faux Pas for the CAFA

Indeed, the CAFA investigation floundered shortly after it had been launched. Firstly, the members of the committee could not themselves agree unanimously on a clear-cut definition of "communism" and "Communist sympathizers." Secondly, the committee found that Constantino's claims on the Communist infiltration of the University were nothing but hearsay. Miss Reysio-Cruz, the committee's other "star witness", when summoned to the witness stand, denied ever having made any allegations of Pascual's *buklod* meetings outside the campus, where communist doctrines were reportedly discussed.[159] Thirdly, the committee could not get any respectable witness to lend credence to Constantino's denunciations. Finally, the committee members disagreed among themselves whether the evidence, flimsy and silly as they were, justified the charge of communist infiltration against the professors and the University.[160]

Failing to provide any concrete evidence about the presence of Communists among the university constituency, the committee indefinitely suspended the hearings after Congress adjourned in May 1961.

Turmoil in Congress

The "loyalty check" on the University drew a mixed reaction from the members of Congress. Congressman Emilio Cortez (Pampanga) denounced the investigation as "a smear campaign" that had cast "a shadow" on the prestige of the University.[161] Congressman Marcelino Veloso declared that "no amount of effort and money should be spared to save our State University from becoming the citadel of an alien ideology – an ideology sharply at variance and in conflict" with the tenets of democracy.[162] Congressmen Delfin Albano and Leonardo Perez maintained that the investigation was initiated "precisely to protect the good name and integrity of the university" and alleged that Communism had already infiltrated the thinking of some professors and students, thus contributing to threats against the security of the state.[163]

Congressman Felicisimo Ocampo, for his part, declared that if the CAFA were probing into teaching at the University without proceeding from a *prima facie* case of any professor's communist affiliation or subversive behavior, the CAFA was encroaching upon the University's academic freedom. To condemn agnostics and atheists in the University "smacks of a pure and simple affront to the freedom of religion guaranteed by our Constitution."[164] Congressman Jacobo Gonzalez believed otherwise and announced that he was preparing a bill that would penalize any person who did not believe in God. If his proposed measure were adopted into law, then any professor in the University who declares to his class that he did not believe in God automatically violates the law and is punishable by the State.[165]

Senators Ambrosio Padilla, Estanislao Fernandez and Francisco "Soc" Rodrigo, however, believed that the investigation was called for, considering that the State University was being supported with government funds. The State, therefore, had the right "to screen its officials, teachers and employees as to their fitness to maintain the integrity of the schools as a part of ordered society." Thus, an agnostic professor like Pascual had no business teaching in the University for he could be a very "unwholesome influence" upon the students.[166]

Sinco's Appeal for Sobriety

Such were the threats upon the very existence of the university as a free institution that President Sinco called upon the university community to defend and uphold its academic freedom.

> Every professor has the obligation to observe at all times those principles directly contributing to the respect for truth, the promotion of justice, the devotion to freedom, and the enhancement of the spirit of love for one's fellowman. A university that is worthy of its mission should stand and insist on these principles. It should not hesitate to back up its faculty and its students who fight for them. On the other hand, it should not have anything to do with the pusillanimity of any of its constituents.
>
> The constitutional provision on the academic freedom of the University of the Philippines, as a State University, is as legally impregnable as the independence of the judiciary or of any other independent unit of the government. Every person and every official of the government are bound by an oath to observe and respect our Constitution. It follows, therefore, that all of them are bound to observe the academic freedom of the University of the Philippines. To refuse that observance or to ignore it is to commit an act of disloyalty to the nation.[167]

Skirmishes on Issues and Implications

The different sectors of the University community reacted to the CAFA investigation in varying ways. Some members of the Board of Regents expressed concern that any further move by Congress and other official agencies with regard to the CAFA investigation might inimically affect the interests of the University. Regent Decoroso Rosales, in particular, proposed that the Board establish a committee to find out if Communism, agnosticism and atheism existed in the University.

The Board accepted the proposal and created a committee of three, consisting of Executive Vice-President Virata, Vice-President for External Affairs Antoñio Isidro and Dean Vicente Abad Santos of the College of Law for the purpose of making a study that would determine whether there were in fact communists among the University faculty.[168] This study seems to have been abandoned when the CAFA suspended its investigation of the University.

Regent Rosales also believed that since Professor Pascual was a professed agnostic, he should not be allowed to teach. Regent Jose Romero (also Secretary of Education) proposed that, if the Board were amenable, it could expel Pascual. Pascual might then present a test case in court to decide the issue of a professor's right to teach in the University if he did not believe in God.

President Sinco reminded the Board that both the University Charter and the Constitution provide that a religious test "shall not be required for the exercise of political or civil rights or for the appointment of professors nor shall religious opinions of professors be a matter of inquiry." At this sobering remark, Rosales admitted that Romero's view was too drastic and instead suggested that the philosophy professor be removed from the classroom and be given some other kind of work, even if this would mean a promotion. The Regents later arrived at a consensus that gave the President the power to decide what was best with regard to Pascual.[169]

Reactions of a Befuddled Faculty

On the other hand, while many members of the faculty objected to the CAFA investigation on the ground that it constituted "an encroachment" upon academic freedom,[170] there was hardly any unanimity of opinion regarding the position that the faculty might take against it.

This is illustrated by the deliberations of the Faculty Association of the University on March 14, 1961. When Dr. Pascual Capiz (of the Institute of Asian Studies) presented a motion that the Policy and Coordinating Council of the Association should urge the CAFA "to desist from continuing its current probe in a manner that amounted to checks on the faculty's right of conviction and expression," the council refused to take a stand. Instead some of its members argued that the CAFA, as a duly constituted body of the Congress, had indeed the right to inquire into the problem of Communist infiltration of the University. Faculty indecision during the meeting precipitated the resignation of Dr. Onofre D. Corpuz, political science professor and newly elected president of the Association, from his post and from the organization.[171]

Members of a smaller faculty group, the Society for the Advancement of Academic Freedom, urged the CAFA to end the investigation and challenged the congressional body to bring the cases of the suspected professors to a proper legal indictment. If this were not done, the society declared in a resolution similar to the above defeated Capiz motion, the investigation could only be interpreted as undue harassment of the faculty. This eventually would do "more harm in discrediting the integrity of the University than the good in being able to identify one or two more persons who had been unfortunate in their past associations."[172]

Students Impatient and Furious

The students, for their part, expressed more vehemence in their protest of the CAFA investigation. On March 14, 1961, as ten professors of the University appeared in Congress in response to the committee's summons, over a thousand placard waving students arrived at the Congress building to express their indignation over the investigation. A policeman's demand for a rally permit provoked what may be called a riot. The demonstrators rocked and almost rolled over a police car. They attempted but failed to force their way into the hearing room. The angry students broke the window glass inside the room. Upon seeing the committee chairman, Congressman Perez, they cried "Down with Perez." The latter, visibly agitated, turned on them and issued the challenge "Choose your weapons."[173]

The student demonstration, according to Teodoro M. Locsin, editor of the *Philippines Free Press,* was nothing new; "it was part of the UP tradition." He recalled that in 1933, during President Rafael Palma's administration, the students of the University protested a bill reorganizing the government personnel – except those of the legislators. At that time the students also broke some windows. Lawmakers who went to the university campus to defend the measure were booed and heckled. Palma sent for the ailing Quezon who prevented the demonstration from deteriorating into a riot. But in 1961, observed Locsin, there was no Quezon to charm the students.[174]

However, the Democratic Youth Forum, a student minority led by UPSCA leaders and supporters Angel Sto. Tomas, Conrado Pascual and Generoso Gil, Jr., refused to express sympathy for the student mass demonstration. It echoed the denunciations of the congressional committee and insinuated in a leaflet circulated in the University that sufficient evidence pointed to "traces of Marxist elements" on the campus.[175] It further charged that the University administration had encouraged and financed the student demonstration. Despite such thinly veiled innuendoes, there is no evidence that the Forum had had any impact upon both the faculty and student constituency of the University.

Soliongco Sizes Up the Conflict

Support for the University came from leading columnists in the metropolitan press – leading intellectuals in their own right. I.P. Soliongco, writer of the popular column "Seriously Speaking" in the *Manila Chronicle,* minced no words and denounced the CAFA investigation as a "witchhunt" that made the professors of the University unfortunate victims of "legislative sadism." This "fishing expedition," however, would simply drive the real Communists "to dissemble their methods and play the part of democratic chameleons."[176]

Soliongco, moreover, saw the CAFA investigation as the extension of the continuing conflict between two schools of thought in the University. One school regarded the world "as an ever changing and ever expanding universe where rules, principles and ideas must be subjected to rigorous and constant tests and analysis" while the other school, which was "dominant" during the "dark, sectarian time" of the Vidal Tan administration and was now "behind" the investigation, would view the world as "a completed universe with fixed ideas and harsh, immutable jurisprudence."[177]

Of the professors of the first school who were proving that the University of the Philippines was a real *universitas,* one could count Teodoro A. Agoncillo, professor of History, who daily was "destroying the myth that Philippine history was merely a recounting of the glories of Spain in a heathen land and was expounding the idea that the history of the country was the history of the Filipinos." In his classes in political science, Prof. Onofre D. Corpuz was telling his students that discipline could be learned "not in terms of meaningless definition of the state but in terms of how elections are won and lost" and was insisting that Philippine-American relations be examined not in terms of McKinley's Benevolent Assimilation Proclamation and the glorious Manifest Destiny but in terms of the Bell Trade Act, the Bases Agreement and other onerous documents. Philosophy professors like Ricardo Pascual and Cesar Adib Majul, on the other hand, were developing in their students the capacity to doubt and were enjoining them "to accept the hypothesis of philosophy not because of the authority behind them but because of their inherent plausibility."[178]

Other Columnists in Sympathy

Another popular columnist, Carmen Guerrero-Nakpil, reminded the public that no university "worth its salt" could ever be free from "the attacks and suspicions of the established order." The faculty of the University, by refusing to conform, had become the natural target of conservatism and the status quo. The CAFA, Nakpil petulantly remarked, should perhaps have been congratulated for in conducting the investigation of the university professors, it was proving in the process that the University was a real *universitas.*[179]

Jose Ma. Sison, a columnist for the *Philippine Collegian,* called the members of the congressional committee "enemies of intellectual freedom." He noted that the published materials under investigation had "a high and strong nationalist character and temper" and predicted that "as nationalism keeps on becoming stronger – the bogey of Communism – the most convenient bogey of them all" would be raised "frantically and desperately." However, investigations based on such a flimsy reason would inevitably fail.[180]

Indeed, as Sinco recalled a year after the investigation, the CAFA investigation was "a dismal failure," which proved nothing that could be rightly called subversive. "The only thing it accomplished was to smear the University and some of its professors."[181]

Sidelight on Albert's Gyrations

However, Quezon City councilor Carlos Albert, who was formerly director of the National Intelligence Coordinating Agency (NICA), believed that the charges of "Redism" against the same suspect faculty and students should not be put to rest. In April 1961, while the CAFA investigation was still going on, Albert called for action on the part of the Board of Regents against the publication in official university journals of works that called for "the destruction of our free society and [incited] readers to rise against the present order." These constituted "a clear and present danger to the nation" particularly in light of communist expansionism in Southeast Asia and Huk activities in the Philippines.[182] He denounced the university administration for its laxity, negligence and collusion with Communist sympathizers for these resulted in the publication of seditious materials.

Albert called attention to the publication in the *Philippine Social Sciences and Humanities Review* of the anonymously written "The Peasant War in the Philippines," which he alleged contained an "out-and-out praise for the Huks and the Communist Party of the Philippines, an outlawed subversive organization." The Quezon City councilor noted that the article was full of hatred for the United States. He observed the same inflammatory and subversive orientation in three anonymously written articles, published in the *Philippine Collegian:* "Requiem for Lumumba," "Human Dignity – The Myth and the Heresy," and "The Tower of Babel and the Tower of Ivory."[183] All three articles were said not only to be "fraught with communistic jargon and scurrilous libels" against the government and the duly constituted authorities but also tended to instigate, suggest and incite rebellious conspiracies and riots.[184]

On April 17, 1962, at Albert's instance, Quezon City Assistant Fiscal Miguel F. Halili, acting like "a timorous old maid afraid to peep under the bed," filed a case of sedition against Dean Tomas S. Fonacier and Prof. Leopoldo Y. Yabes, respectively editor and managing editor of the *Philippine Social Sciences and Humanities Review.*[185] In the hearings that followed, not a single witness presented by both the defense and the prosecution admitted having been incited to sedition by the so-called subversive writings. Far more interesting to note was Albert's admission that the "seditious" articles were "incomprehensible" to him and that he was not incited to rebel against the government when he read "The Peasant War in the Philippines" in 1959.[186] On March 30, 1964, the Court of First Instance of Rizal dismissed the case against Fonacier and Yabes for want of evidence.[187]

TAINT OF POLITICS HASTENS PRESIDENT SINCO'S RETIREMENT

THE excitement and furor over the CAFA probe had hardly died down when in 1962, politics once more intruded into the affairs of the University, leading to the "early" retirement of the President. In January of that year, soon after the assumption into office of President Diosdado Macapagal, he announced that he had "offered" the Presidency of the University to General Carlos P. Romulo. The latter was reported to have "accepted" the appointment. Macapagal's embarrassing announcement flew in the face of University tradition – which was backed by the provision of the University Charter that the Board of Regents was the sole body to formulate policies governing the University and to fix the tenure of the University President.[188]

It may also be recalled that the Board had passed a resolution fixing the university president's term of office to six years. Thus while the Sinco appointment would expire on April 30, 1963, his tenure would actually end two years after this date. On September 1, 1962, Justice Secretary Alejo Mabanag ruled that the Board of Regents could not legally extend President Sinco's term beyond April 30, 1962, when he would reach the age of sixty-five and would then be covered by the Compulsory Retirement Law.[189] Thus, Macapagal's move was construed by many as the first step in what appeared to be a determined effort to force Sinco's retirement.

Disquiet and Discontent

The Board of Regents was silent, with the exception of Regent Gumersindo Garcia who, expressing some misgivings about the announcement, said that the Board must have the autonomy to choose the head of the University. The faculty, at best, was non-committal. Hermenegildo Reyes, president of the Alumni Association, welcomed the 'appointment' because Romulo's standing would attract the American foundations to extend 'more liberal' financial aid to the University.[190]

The officers of the Student Union, representatives of various schools and colleges, and fraternity and sorority leaders protested Macapagal's offer to Romulo and accused the former of placing the Presidency of the University on the "auction bloc" at his "personal disposal." Through a resolution and manifesto adopted on January 6, 1962, the student leaders denounced this attempt "to turn the University into a mere object of political intrigues."[191]

Under the leadership of Enrique Voltaire Garcia, Chairman of the University Student Union, the students staged a demonstration in front of the Administration Building to affirm their trust in the Board of Regents.[192]

But the students were not united. As in 1957, the students were divided between UPSCA supporters and sympathizers and non-UPSCANS. The UPSCANS who had opposed the Student Union rally, staged their own counter-demonstration. The UPSCA president, Gemino H. Abad, implied in a statement that because the Student Union was organized mainly for cultural and social activities of the students, it had been divested of the power to organize a rally.[193]

Outside the University, this latest political intrusion into the academe did not fail to affect various sectors of the country's intelligentsia. The Civil Liberties Union branded the Macapagal "offer" to Romulo "a violation of presidential power" for which "no justification could be found."[194] Congressman Leonardo Perez, Chairman of the Committee on Anti-Filipino Activities, broke his silence since the aborted "loyalty check" of the University in March 1961 and alleged that 'a leftist clique' was responsible for the Student Union-supported demonstration against the appointment of Romulo. This 'leftist clique' consisted of members of a supposed 'student politburo' and the National Progress Movement.[195] Macapagal for his part did not comment on the furor created by his offer of the University Presidency to Romulo; the latter, in his post in New York, was non-committal.

Ceremonious Rigmarole

Then, during the months of March and April, politicking on the part of some members of the Board of Regents and the Alumni Association resulted in a much criticized and embarrassing mix-up in the selection of the commencement speaker for the University's graduation exercises in April 1962.[196] The Executive Committee of the University Council (which was composed of Deans and Directors of various units of the University), in performance of its powers provided by the University Code, had chosen former Speaker Jose Yulo as commencement speaker. The Committee also decided to grant Yulo the honorary degree of Doctor of Laws. According to tradition and a standing resolution adopted by the committee, the recipient of an honorary degree would automatically deliver the commencement address. The Board of Regents approved, by a clear majority, the decision of the Executive Committee.

However, some five hundred members of the University of the Philippines Alumni Association, which was composed of 30,000 members, under the leadership of Regent Hermenegildo R. Reyes (a Macapagal appointee and supporter),[197] offered Macapagal the "Most Distinguished Alumnus Award" through a committee headed by Senator Gaudencio Antonino. Such an award would acknowledge the fact that the President had finished an Associate in Arts course in the University.[198] The Malacañang protocol office, however, informed the Antonino committee that if the President of the Philippines would be present at the commencement exercises, he should be the only one honored, and no one else.[199] If Yulo were retained in the same commencement exercises as speaker, his presence would pose a problem in protocol as it would constrain Macapagal to take a back seat to a private citizen who would play the "starring role."

Who Else but President Macapagal?

Regent Reyes, who attended the meeting of the Board of Regents for the first time on March 29, 1962, proposed that President Macapagal be the commencement speaker. President Sinco asserted that the Executive Committee of the University Council had exercised the power of selecting the commencement speaker for the past 30 years and there had never been an instance where the Board of Regents revoked the decision of the Executive Committee. Sinco added that Yulo had been duly invited and had already accepted the invitation. To put another speaker in his place would be difficult as well as embarrassing. The President, therefore, suggested that Macapagal be invited at some other time.[200]

Regent Reyes disregarded the argument on the University's 30-year-old tradition by pointing out that since the Committee was "only a creation" of the Board, its decisions were "still subject" to review, modification, amendment, approval or disapproval of the Board.[201]

To avoid "embarrassing" President Macapagal, the Board of Regents, headed by Secretary of Education Alejandro Roces, adopted the handy solution of withdrawing the invitation to Yulo and postponing the conferment of honors upon him to the commencement exercises in November. Rebuffed, the Executive Committee adopted a resolution formally expressing the embarrassment it suffered from the Board of Regent's reversal of its decision. The Committee also asked that it be relieved of its function of choosing the speaker for the university's commencement exercises.[202]

Inauspicious Ending

This latest controversy during the Sinco administration was "an academic mayhem" – which an alumnus of the University described as "a result of a deliberate cold blooded killing of morality and principle in the State University" – that was interpreted as the gesture on the part of Macapagal's supporters that finally forced Sinco's retirement.[203] On April 10, 1962, a few days before the University's 55th graduation exercises, President Sinco announced to the Board of Regents his retirement from the University.[204] A month later, on May 9, the Board of Regents elected former Ambassador Carlos P. Romulo President of the University after a short deliberation, without benefit of any nominating or screening committee which the Board of Regents traditionally created before the selection of a University President. It seems clear that the election was held in obedience to Macapagal's signals and orders. At no time in the past history of the University had such a manner of election for a president taken place.[205]

ASSERTION OF INTELLECTUAL FREEDOM AS A LASTING LEGACY

HOW meaningful was the Sinco administration for the University? Two appraisals suggest how students came to appreciate and value the competence, scholarship and creativity of the Sinco presidency. The editorial of the *Philippine Collegian* on April 14, 1962, on the occasion of the last University alumni homecoming reunion over which Sinco presided, recognized the multifarious contributions of his controversial administration:[126]

> Dr. Sinco is one of the most liberal of the U.P. Presidents. He stood for intellectual freedom, for the autonomy of the mind. During his term the University has witnessed one of the happy creative years of its existence as an institution of learning not merely among the faculty but among the students. This in itself is a challenge. Since the tenure of the Office of the University President is not permanent, this particular achievement of Dr. Sinco in liberalism and protecting the freedom of intelligence from the infringements of lies, orthodoxy and mediocrity is a challenge to anyone in the future who will occupy the office.

Probably the best assessment of his four-year administration is expressed in a plaque the Student Council presented to him for "his firm commitment to the preservation of the free and secular nature of the University, for his support and enhancement of the liberal intellectual tradition, for his encouragement of scholarship and research and for his efforts in making the University assume a more definite position in the national life as the premier institution of learning in the Philippines."[207]

Penchant for Educational Reform

The University faced, at its semi-centennial, many difficult challenges. General dissatisfaction with past shortsighted policies required the adoption of radical steps to elevate the standard of instruction in the University. As the Sinco years were a period of experimentation, it was inevitable that many elements in the University should express at that time their apprehension as to the feasibility and reasonableness of the innovative policies Sinco introduced and implemented. The term system, for example, was a highly controversial innovation that turned many members of the faculty against Sinco. Whatever their defects and however intensely criticized, the Sinco innovations and educational reforms constituted a milestone in the growth of the University, marking a sharp turning point in the development of values, attitudes and standards particularly adapted to the Philippine setting and responsive to the needs and demands of a rapidly growing and modernizing society.

Of the many contributions of the Sinco presidency to the University, perhaps the most important was the establishment of a concrete, definite and substantial general education program. His interest in such a program encouraged considerably continued efforts and increasing interest in the following areas: (1) reassessment of methods of instruction, (2) the preparation of textbooks and other teaching materials, and (3) interdisciplinary approaches to teaching and further refinement of new patterns and techniques of instruction.

Survival with Honor

The CAFA probe during his administration, however, was a portent of things to come. As the University continued to influence life and society beyond its boundaries, it was bound to meet challenges to its academic freedom. Various sectors of Philippine society were concerned that the University was encouraging allegedly perilous tendencies toward dangerous philosophies and experimental academic procedures. It is heartening to note, however, that at the end of the Sinco presidency, the fact-finding and survey committee headed by former Chief Justice Ricardo Paras gave the University a clean bill of health: indeed, under Sinco's able stewardship, the university was headed in "the right direction, ideologically and academically;"[208] its faculty outstanding in ability and unselfishly dedicated to the cause of education and the academic community unsurpassed in its dedication to liberty and the dignity of the human spirit.

IX

Romulo's Design for the Filipino University (1962-1968)

The Vision That Brought on Student Activism and Faculty Dissent

by Silvino V. Epistola

Romulo's Design for the Filipino University

DILIMAN first heard of Carlos P. Romulo as prospective President of the University of the Philippines when it was rumored early in 1962 that Diosdado Macapagal, then President of the Philippines, had offered the Presidency of the University to the then Ambassador of the Philippines to the United States who had at once accepted the proferred office.

Most of the people who heard about this were skeptical. How could Macapagal offer the post to anyone when it was not even vacant? The incumbent UP President then had a term that was not due to expire until April which was several months away. Moreover, the Board of Regents had passed a resolution in 1961 fixing the term of office of the President of the University. This resolution would in effect extend the term of the incumbent beyond April 1962.[1*] Besides, did not Macapagal know that under the provisions of the University Code, the Board of Regents had the sole prerogative of electing the President of the University of the Philippines?

Others more vigilant reacted in anger. In their eyes, Macapagal's action was a brazen assault on the freedom and integrity of the University of the Philippines. Even the President of the Philippines might not legally do what Macapagal had done.

Protests at the Outset

Newly installed Editor-in-Chief Luis V. Teodoro, Jr., of the *Philippine Collegian*, official organ of the student body of the University of the Philippines, used the front page of his term's maiden issue to inform the studentry and the rest of the Diliman community that Macapagal had offered and Romulo had at once accepted the Presidency of the University.[2] And faithfully reported in subsequent issues of the *Collegian* were the remarks on and the disapproval of the community of these rather unusual happenings.

---

*Footnote references are compiled in the NOTES section at the end of this book.

The January 5 issue of the *Collegian* carried on its front page the Manifesto of the students, which opened with this paragraph:

> The undersigned students, officers of the Student Union and representatives of the various schools and colleges, clubs, publications, organizations, fraternities and sororities, confident that they express the sentiment and determination of the student body, vigorously assert their confidence in the Board of Regents and strongly protest against the act of President Diosdado Macapagal, in virtually placing the presidency of the University of the Philippines on the auction block at his personal disposal.[3]

The signatories were Enrique Voltaire Garcia II, chairman of the Student Union; Benjamin N. Muego, editor-in-chief of the 1962 *Philippinensian;* Luis V. Teodoro, Jr., editor-in-chief of the *Philippine Collegian;* Rafael S. Tinio, acting president of the Students' Cultural Association of the University of the Philippines; Petronilo Bn. Daroy, chairman of the Graduate School Association; Crisanto T. Saruca, Lord Chancellor of the Alpha Phi Beta; and many other prominent student leaders.

This Manifesto together with the Resolution of the Student Union Board of Management were formally handed to Prof. Rex R. Drilon, secretary of the Board of Regents, during the students' demonstration in front of the administration building on the afternoon of January 12.[4]

However, the sentiment in Diliman was by no means unanimous. The University of the Philippines Student Catholic Action (UPSCA) attempted to stage a counter-demonstration that same afternoon in front of the administration building under the leadership of its president, Gemino H. Abad. To justify their action, the UPSCA students asserted that the demonstration led by the Student Union was neither timely nor necessary and that it was really inspired by ulterior motives. They explained that Romulo was anti-communist and therefore anathema to the leftists who hoped to keep their positions in the University's administration system as well as their positions of responsibility in student affairs with the help of the incumbent president. The counter-demonstration fizzled out, and the demonstration led by the Student Union went on without further distraction.

President Macapagal Assailed

On January 18 the Student Union met for two hours to pass a resolution calling on President Macapagal to withdraw the offer of the University presidency to Romulo "in order that the independence and prestige of the State University may be restored."[5] As the *Collegian* had noted, 38 students voted for the resolution and three voted against. Of the three, Lincoln

Drilon of the University College and Reynaldo Maceda of the Kanlaon Residence Hall explained that they had voted against the resolution because it was too mild.

The Civil Liberties Union also had something to say about the matter. This civic organization issued a press statement on January 26, branding Macapagal's "offer" of the University presidency to Romulo as an instance of "abuse and violation of the presidential power and discretion in its avowed desire to implement what it pleases to call the people's mandate."[6]

However, President Macapagal attended the traditional general homecoming of the University alumni as the main speaker for the occasion. He departed from the text of his prepared speech to apologize personally and publicly to President Vicente G. Sinco. Macapagal explained that he had been carried away by his enthusiasm when he offered the presidency of the University to Romulo. As the *Collegian* reported it, "Macapagal continuously repeated his deep admiration for President Sinco." Then the paper quoted Macapagal as saying, "I do not know what he thinks of me, but I admire Dr. Sinco's administrative ability and academic record that never had I thought of having him replaced. When he lays down the burdens of office, he can look back with pride to his great accomplishments and to a job well done."[7]

Unexpected Turn of Events

After the commencement exercises, the tempest simmered down, and everything in Diliman seemed normal again. In all that seeming quiet and serenity, few realized that nothing would be the same again in Diliman. President Vicente G. Sinco left for the United States on April 24, 1962 to receive a special award from the Southwestern Legal Foundation and its Comparative Law Center in Texas.[8] Before his departure, he had announced his desire to retire from the Presidency of the University at the end of the academic year which was May 31, 1962.[9]

The Regents of the University were called to a special meeting on Wednesday, May 9, 1962, in their Board Room on the second floor of the administration building in Diliman. Except for President Vicente G. Sinco, all eleven Regents were present.[10] Executive Vice-President Enrique T. Virata attended the special meeting in his capacity as Acting President of the University.

At the beginning of the session, the Board formally confirmed the previous action of Secretary of Education Alejandro R. Roces, chairman of the Board of Regents, "in approving the application for retirement of President Vicente G. Sinco, effective at the close of business hours on May 31, 1962."

Then Regent Encarnacion Alzona was designated to draft the resolution expressing the Board's appreciation and gratitude to Dr. Vicente G. Sinco for valuable service rendered as University president.

The next item on the agenda was the election of Dr. Sinco's successor. The question was raised as to whether the Board should itself nominate the candidates for the office at that meeting or should it create a nominating committee for this purpose. The question was put to a vote. Nine of the Regents were for the Board itself nominating the candidates while two Regents voted for the creation of a nominating committee.

Acting President Virata thereupon presented President Sinco's cabled request that the nominations be postponed until his return. Because two of the Regents were going abroad shortly while another Regent's term was due to expire on May 17, and with classes scheduled to begin in the first week of June, the Board denied the request and proceeded with the elections. Six persons, including Ambassador Carlos P. Romulo, were nominated.

Romulo's Election to the Presidency

The *Collegian* reported that Regent Maria Kalaw Katigbak nominated Ambassador Romulo and cited his "democratic dynamism" as the nominee's outstanding qualification. She also said that he could rid the University of leftists and communists.[11]

With the other nominations acknowledged, the Board resolved to adopt, on motion of Regent H.R. Reyes, the same rules followed in the election of Dr. Vidal A. Tan as President of the University.[12] The rules were:

1. The election shall be by secret ballot.
2. Election to the position shall be by a majority vote. Six (6) votes shall be considered a majority.
3. Only the first balloting shall be made if a majority vote is cast in favor of one candidate. If there is no majority, the nominee receiving the least number of votes shall be eliminated, and there shall be further balloting.
4. The nominee who gets the majority shall be considered unanimously voted for. However, he shall not be considered elected until after he has signified his acceptance. No announcement of the election shall be made until after the nominee had been declared duly elected.

Secretary of the Board Rex Drilon read the names of the nominees, after which the Regents cast their votes by secret ballot. The Acting President did not participate in the balloting. Nine of the Regents cast their ballots for Ambassador Carlos P. Romulo. (The *Collegian* later identified the Regents who voted for another candidate as Gumersindo Garcia and Encarnacion Alzona.) Ambassador Romulo was therefore "considered unanimously voted for."[13]

The following Wednesday, May 16, the Board of Regents met in another special session at the conference room of the Institute of Public Administration at the Rizal Hall on the Padre Faura campus of the University.[14]

New President Accepts Post

The Chairman of the Board opened the special meeting by reading the telegram he had received from Ambassador Carlos P. Romulo:

> PLEASE CONVEY TO MEMBERS BOARD REGENTS MY ACCEPTANCE OF RESPONSIBILITY THEY HAVE ENTRUSTED TO ME WITH MY ELECTION AS PRESIDENT OUR UNIVERSITY OF THE PHILIPPINES AND MY DEEP APPRECIATION OF UNANIMITY BEHIND MY SELECTION STOP TO YOU PERSONALLY MY THANKS FOR YOUR CONGRATULATORY MESSAGE.
>
> CARLOS P. ROMULO

The telegram fully satisfied the provisions of Paragraph 4 of the rules adopted by the Board, and Carlos P. Romulo was declared duly elected to the presidency of the University.

While he was in Washington, President Sinco received a totally unexpected telephone call from Ambassador Romulo who was in New York. President Sinco talked to a reporter in London about this phone call.[15] His story was carried in a news report that came out later in a Manila daily and then picked up by the *Collegian*.[15]

President Sinco told the reporter that Ambassador Romulo had promised that should he be elected President of the University, he would do three things. He would strictly follow the policies laid down by President Sinco which he would leave unchanged. He would closely observe the separation of church and state because the University was a secular institution. He would guard against a "witch hunt," as McCarthyism had no place in a university. President Sinco said he was happy about the assurances made by his successor.

Phasing Out the Old

However, the Board of Regents had one more piece of business to attend to. At its special meeting the previous Wednesday, the Board had accepted from Regent H.R. Reyes the Report of the UP Alumni Fact-Finding and Survey Committee which had been chaired by the venerable former

Supreme Court Chief Justice Ricardo Paras.[16] The Board had decided then to transmit to the University Council the report which had to do with the selective admission of students and the short-term system which President Sinco had instituted three years earlier to make full use of the facilities of the University. The Board asked the University Council to return its recommendations within one week.

The University Council was duly called to a special meeting on the morning of Wednesday, May 16, at the second-floor theater of the Arts and Sciences building in Diliman. Present at this special meeting were 168 members of the University Council. By *viva voce* a clear majority of them voted to end the three-year-old short-term system under which classes met every day during the term. However, those who had not voted with the majority requested that they be counted, and they were 38 in number.

Now on the very afternoon of that same Wednesday, Acting President Virata reported verbally to the Board that the University Council had decided to end the short-term system. On motion of Regent H.R. Reyes duly seconded by Regent Maria Kalaw Katigbak, the Board passed a resolution on the short-term system (as amended by Regents Gonzalo Gonzalez and Ernesto Y. Sibal) stating:

> That effective as soon as possible but not later than October 1962, the University should return or go back to the semestral system of instruction, with the reservation, however, that each college or unit be allowed to adopt the term system, or any other system in whole or in part, upon recommendation of the faculty to the dean of the college concerned, and upon recommendation of the dean to the President of the University, who shall submit the said recommendation to the Board of Regents for approval.[17]

Commenting editorially on these two events which followed each other within hours of the same day, the *Philippine Collegian* said:

> It is to be hoped that the action of both the University Council and the Board of Regents on an issue as vital as this one is not indicative of the way deliberations are to be carried out in the future; as the policy-making and governing bodies of the University, the gravity of their functions is such that they can determine, to a very large extent, the future of the University itself.[18]

THE CHALLENGE OF CONTRIBUTING SOMETHING OF VALUE

IN 1962, the University of the Philippines had already passed its Golden Jubilee. It had campuses in Diliman, at Padre Faura and Herran in Manila, and in Los Baños, Iloilo, Baguio and Cebu. It had had a succession of presidents, and it had educated and graduated generation upon generation of students. Professors had grown old and retired. Young instructors had taken over classrooms and laboratories where they had once been students. Now the University even had traditions and the legends that went with all these. As a matter of fact, it had even become fashionable for people to think of the University of the Philippines as something more than the institution of higher learning described in its Charter. Those who had spent part of their lives in its grounds and buildings, had even begun to speak of the University as a separate "Republic."

If the Republic did not exist, pure thought would have given it being. But then it would have been a long time in the making. Each generation of scholars and academicians had in its own time contributed something to the making of that Republic of the spirit. The first Presidents of the University had, so to speak, laid out the avenues which one traveled to reach any of the many parts of the Republic. Their successors widened the avenues. Some even paved roadways and planted acacia trees that could not but make traveling around the Republic a pleasure to be savored.

Some presidents put up buildings on this or that avenue to serve some academic purpose or another. Many of these still stand, magnificent monuments to a president's far-reaching vision. A few have not survived reexamination, torn down to make way for new construction in the name of some latter-day academic ideal. Several have been renovated and enlarged to serve an expanded, because more clearly perceived, purpose.

As one old graduate had once observed while he looked over the haunts of his youth: "Why, the place has not changed at all!" The old avenues still run in the same old directions. A few of the dirt roads in the old days have been paved, but don't let that fool anyone. They are really the same old roads. Just get on the avenue you remember best, and you will surely get to the places that had been the haunts of your youth. Well, perhaps some of the places you had known are no longer there, and some that are, no longer look the way you remember them. For instance, what you remember as a cogonal patch of nothing-at-all may now be the site of a spanking new building full of busy classrooms and bubbling laboratories. But for all that, the place still looks and feels like the old place you had once known so well. Really, as old grads like to say, nothing ever changes in the UP Republic.

Dimensions of Growth

What, then, can a new President, even if his name is Carlos P. Romulo, hope to add to this Republic?

If he tried to lay out a new avenue, would he not run at once into some old tradition? Would he not run afoul of some academic ideal made awesome by long practice? If he tried to put up a new building, would people rush to put it to good use? Would the older professors see in its construction the significance of a long-cherished ideal? Would the younger members of the faculty see it as progress itself? Would they accept the building as something modern and yet of lasting value that it would most likely endure and in enduring give the Republic a measure of strength?

Actually, there is nothing anyone can add to the Republic that is not already part of it. A president can, of course, lay out a new avenue or put up an imposing edifice for no better reason than that the money for it was available along with the rhetoric that would give it a justification of sorts. However, if the avenue or the building did not serve a real academic purpose in the pursuit of an academic ideal, neither avenue nor edifice would last beyond one presidential term. Ultimately, only the Republic knows in the collective wisdom of its faculty what is and what is not of itself.

Necessarily, therefore, the history of the University of the Philippines cannot but be the history of what its presidents and its academicians had done together in the pursuit of a commonly held ideal. No event or development in the University of the Philippines can be adequately explained except in these terms.

Concept of the University

Carlos P. Romulo began his presidency with a speech. Emerging from the oath-taking ceremony, he delivered his first presidential statement:

> Ours is a university of the people, and therefore, it has no particular political affiliation. It is a secular university, and therefore, it has no religious sectarian adherence. Its mission is to constantly search for knowledge. Scholarship is its primordial concern, research its indispensable arm and unfailing source of strength. It believes in and values above all things else human freedom without which there can be no creative ingenuity that can make of knowledge a blessing for society.[19]

His audience readily recognized the traditional ideals of the traditional university. The more perceptive among his listeners noted at once that he had said something none of his predecessors had ever said. He had neatly linked the old ideals to the altogether new concern for human freedom and through this he connected the traditional university to modern society. However, the idea that made of knowledge a blessing for society might have been old in heaven but in 1962 it was new in Diliman.

President Romulo closed his first speech as President of the University of the Philippines with the solemn promise: "From this day onward, Mr. President and Members of the Board of Regents, to keep faith with (the

University) and to install in our youth its ideals, I pledge the best that there is in me, and I promise to devote all my waking hours."[20] With this solemn oath, President Romulo put the seal on the old-new ideals by which he would guide the University in the coming years of his tenure as head of this public institution.

New President at the Helm

The day was Friday, June 1, 1962, and the place was Malacañang Palace.[21] The President of the Philippines, Diosdado Macapagal, had himself administered the oath of office to Carlos P. Romulo, Brigadier General of the Philippine Army, Ambassador of the Philippines, erstwhile journalist, newspaper editor, publisher, and one time associate professor of English and acting chairman of the Department of English in the old College of Liberal Arts of the University of the Philippines on Padre Faura.

The new President of the University had taken his oath of office, stood before his well-wishers, delivered his first presidential speech, and acknowledged the applause of the throng gathered around him. Thus began the history of yet another UP presidency.

There had been no time for specifics that June morning in Malacañang. True, President Romulo had enumerated the ideals by which he would guide the affairs of the University during his term. This, he would deal with in a series of meetings with the various constituencies of the University of the Philippines.

President Romulo began with the Executive Committee of the University Council, a body made up of the chief administrative officers of the University. He met them on his first working day as President of the University on Monday, June 4, 1962.[22] After some remarks on punctuality and seating arrangement which would be "in accordance with seniority," he directed his attention to the faculty.

Faculty First and Foremost

In broad strokes he outlined to the administrators what he would like to do for the faculty, because "the first and primary consideration in the university is the faculty."[23] He noted that unless the faculty felt secure and contented, "there cannot be a good university." Then he invited the members of the Executive Committee to study his plans for the faculty, making it quite clear to the University's executive officers that he would welcome suggestions for the effective implementation of those plans. He emphasized, however, that these were not promises but objectives. He placed before them four items:

1. To make the University a citadel of truth, a true community of scholars enjoying academic tenure and freedom, non-political and non-sectarian in nature;

2. To set new goals, values and directions consistent with the purpose and function of the University in this day and age;

3. To inspire the faculty to reach new heights of academic vision and achievement; to make the faculty feel that they belong to the University and to each other, and to the larger community of scholars;

4. To elevate the faculty to their proper place in the University and the community by improving their working conditions, their status, and their relations *vis-a-vis* the President of the University and other administrators.

Later that month of June, it was the turn of the faculties of the College of Arts and Sciences and of the University College to listen to the new President of the University.[24] Instead of talking to them about plans for the faculty, President Romulo discussed the changing concept of the university. For the traditional function of the university to provide basic and advanced instruction had by now changed in response to the demands of developing conditions in a world in ferment.

Basic Functions of the University

The President proceeded to outline the seven university functions:

1. The unifying function: to meet the divergent, sometimes clashing interests of modern society, making clashing interests understand their places in the social system and their participation in basic values and larger national goals;

2. The integrating function (related to the unifying function but characteristic of a transitional society, the Philippines): to create a synthesis out of the various "subcultures" which exist in the country;

3. The diversifying function (diversification of skills as needed in modern society): to equip the citizen with a diversity of skills to prepare him for involvement in the larger society;

4. The symbolic function: to serve as the symbol of the nation's abiding greatness in recognition of the many functions that the university performs for society;

5. The obligatory function: to lead in the advancement of knowledge not only in teaching but also in research as a matter of obligation;

6. The service function: to encourage members of the university staff to participate in national, governmental programs and committees, or private enterprises, whether as consultants or as members of policy boards and planning bodies; and

7. The regional function: to serve the needs of countries in East and South East Asia as a regional university.

Nationalist Orientation for Students

The turn of the students came on Tuesday, July 10, 1962, at a University Convocation.[25] At this gathering of students, Romulo spoke of what is now recalled as "the bedrock" of his policies as President of the University. He began by expressing his desire "to make the University the center of Philippine nationalism." He considered this as basic to his policies as President. The expression of desire and the declaration of policy occurring at the very beginning of his address startled no one. To be sure, some of the earlier Presidents of the University had uttered similar sentiments regarding nationalism in the University. He had, however, said something none of his predecessors in office had ever said, when he declared that he would "make the University the center of nationalism."

At least one listener took in this happy phrase as nothing more than a rhetorical device. Certainly, a man noted for his oratory would have a supply of such devices ready to be hauled out as occasion demanded to startle an indifferent audience into paying attention. At this point, the President recounted Henry David Thoreau's reply to Ralph Waldo Emerson's comment: "Did you know that Harvard is now teaching all branches of learning?" "Yes," answered Thoreau. "All of the branches but none of the roots."

This was Romulo's signal to his youthful listeners that he was about to talk of fundamentals. No, the President had not chosen this story to argue that nationalism had a place in a modern university. He was already sure that it had. What he really wanted was to use the story to illustrate in a most graphic manner that in a modern university, teaching the branches of knowledge for the sake of teaching them was simply not enough. For that would be nothing more than vanity. Knowledge must be linked to a "for what." To explain this view, he said:

> If aside from seeking knowledge you know that you are here because of something noble, something profound and inspiring, something that will accrue in unlimited benefits to our country and people—if, indeed, aside from mere book-learning you know that you are here to devote the best years of your youth to the sharing of the ideals which, through our heroes and martyrs as exemplified in their deeds and thought, we Filipinos have learned to live by, then you know—and must be proud to know—that you are here for the noblest of reasons. You are not merely swinging from the branches of learning but have gone to its very roots.

He had said it at last. The roots could not but be the ideals exemplified in the deeds and thought of the heroes, ideals by which latter-day Filipinos had learned to order their lives. Then he went on to the specifics of his argument, asserting that the roots could not but lie deep in the Filipino people's sense of belonging to a national community. He said:

> This, to me, is the most practical meaning which you, as students of this University, can offer in the name of nationalism. This is scholarship that has a direction and goal, and this is nationalism born not out of expediency and motivated by chauvinism but out of the profoundest love of country which, in your circumstances as students preparing here and now for your future roles in our society, you are in the best position to express.

In short, President Romulo was telling the students and the rest of the University as well as the world beyond Diliman that the University under his administration would teach all the branches of learning but would also delve deep into the roots where lie the ideals Filipinos had learned to live by, and thereby provide the wherefore of learning. He had, in effect, linked knowledge to life as well as the personal life of the student to the life of the nation.

Projecting Filipinism on Campus

In line with the nationalistic orientation that he was fostering, Romulo started to fill the University with images that would give tangible form to the ideas which his rhetoric had evoked as the substance of the basic policy for his administration. On the walls of the Board of Regents Room appeared the portraits of the heroes and martyrs whose deeds and thought exemplified the ideals which President Romulo would make the roots for the branches of learning being taught in the University of the Philippines.

The first symbol President Romulo installed on campus was the flag. At precisely ten minutes of four o'clock on Friday, August 3, 1962, the first flag ever to fly over the administration building was hauled up from the ground to the top of the mast which had been attached to the roof of that splendid edifice.[26] The widow of the former President of the University who had made the move from Padre Faura to Diliman, Mrs. Concepcion Rafols Gonzalez, raised the flag assisted by President and Mrs. Carlos P. Romulo and two cadet color guards. The UP ROTC Band conducted by Capt. Eliseo Clamor played the national anthem, and for the first time ever a cadet contingent had appeared in public in their resplendent new *rayadillo* and *salakot* uniform to do the military honors.

To underscore the significance of the flag-raising ceremony, Romulo told his audience that the flag "wraps up, as it were, all the ideals that we have to know under the name of Filipinism; and so, as it waves over this campus, it waves as a symbol of our determination here at the University to translate Filipinism into as many concrete activities of the heart and mind that spirit can inspire." To make the intended symbolism really clear, he added:

> It is no mere coincidence, therefore, that above such a symbol as the Oblation rises the flag, our country's flag. For this underscores the fact that nationalism may well be meaningless without the spirit of offering and sacrifice that is embodied in the Oblation.[27]

The raising of the flag atop the administration building which its architect meant to stand as the gateway to the University of the Philippines was followed on August 19, 1962, by Quezon Day.[28] On the morning of that day, which was also the anniversary of Quezon's birth, Zenaida Quezon Avanceña and Manuel A. Quezon, Jr. unveiled the plaque which formally gave the administration building a name, Quezon Hall. A faculty-student symposium on Quezon was held at the Arts and Sciences theater. Jose David Lapuz read his paper, "Quezon and the Foundation of Filipino Policy"; Alejandro M. Fernandez, "Some Political and Social Ideas of Quezon"; Irene R. Cortes, "President Quezon and Our University"; Alejandro J. Casambre read Napoleon J. Casambre's "Quezon as Resident Commissioner," the author having left for the United States on a grant to pursue advanced graduate studies in history. In the afternoon, the Honorable Emmanuel Pelaez, Vice President of the Philippines, addressed the University Convocation at the University Theater. He dwelt on the special role Quezon had envisioned for the University of the Philippines as "a spawning ground of Philippine nationalism."[29]

Interaction Between Ritual and Reality

Other "days" followed, other heroes were honored. Attached to buildings, streets and geographical districts, their names became part of the Diliman landscape. Also, as President Romulo hoped, of the University's intellectual landscape. It was clear from the outset that he intended all these to stand as symbols for the ideals of nationalism upon which he wanted to base the academic endeavors of the University. As far as he was concerned, knowledge for its own sake was useless. Only knowledge that led to action for the uplift of the Filipino people was worth the bother. To understand what Romulo was trying to do, however, it would be necessary to see the symbols and then look at what lay beyond them.

In its August 21, 1962 issue, the *Collegian* commented editorially on President Romulo's program to project nationalism. The editorial expressed its misgiving that nationalism might become equated with the gestures "that accompany its spirit."

> The overemphasis on rituals like flag-raising and laying wreaths, and on external symbols like the *rayadillo* and *salakot* uniforms of the UP ROTC Color Company, would in the end tend to make nationalism in the minds of the students nothing more than a performance of commonplace ceremonials and would make of gestures a chauvinism which neither the place nor the time calls for.

Certainly, this was not something Romulo would disagree with. Perhaps, he was elated by the following paragraph in the same editorial, for it points where further action might be taken:

> These gestures are meaningless and their observance inane if the spirit behind them is not revitalized. Filipino nationalism as we know it today is still inchoate. Probably a great cause of its slow growth may be traced to a lack of perspective—the need of a broad viewpoint that encompasses not only appreciation of an indigenous past, but also a recognition of the value of the exogenous influence on the present.[30]

Language as a Crucial Factor

Having taken his position on the side of nationalism, Romulo could not have failed to touch on the language issue in the Philippines. The first plenary meeting of the Philippine Academy of Science and Humanities at the Philippine General Hospital Science Hall on August 30, 1962 provided him with a forum for his thoughts on the subject.[31] Following the eminent Jorge Bocobo, Romulo expressed his total agreement with the contention that the great Filipino literature would be written in one or another language spoken by Filipinos in the Philippines. Posing the rhetorical question, "Why is this so?" he gives the not totally unexpected answer, "Because great literature is a full-grown flower of the national soul. That soul has its habitation in the life of the common people." For all that, there was still a Filipino problem of language, and it was right there in the University.

> A decline of English similar to that of Spanish is likely to happen within the next fifty years. The quality of college-level English leaves much to be desired—a problem that is drawing nearly all the resources and efforts of the University on account of the patent inadequacies of those who come from the public high schools.

Romulo warned that the situation would continue "if no forthright language planning is adopted to provide for the multilingual character of the learning environment as for the gains we have made in the use of English as *lingua franca.*" He said nothing about how the problem might be dealt with, but he did underscore its gravity as a means of ushering in a cultural renaissance and attaining national integrity.

Guidelines to Practical Planning

What President Romulo had in mind for the University of the Philippines received its first full treatment in an address entitled "Unity in Diversity: Planning for the University," which he delivered at the 217th meeting of the University Council on September 14, 1962, at the Arts and Sciences building.[32]

Romulo spelled out the basic policy which he would pursue in office even as he announced the establishment of seventeen (17) *ad hoc* committees which would eventually involve more than 50 of the highest ranking members of the faculty. He would ask these *ad hoc* committees to look into the affairs of the University and to recommend structural as well as procedural changes in policy. The President began his address by quoting that part of his June 1 statement in which he had said, speaking of the University of the Philippines:

> Its mission is to constantly search for knowledge. Scholarship is its primordial concern, research its indispensable arm and unfailing source of strength.

Having established that as the principle of inquiry, Romulo proceeded to examine "the existing goals, programs, organization of the University." What he had found, he said, was the University's utter diversity. This brought him to the realization that his position as President of the University of the Philippines would be a difficult one.

> I was given to understand that "every problem is exposed to a complex of interests and angles, some of them intersupporting, some quasi-conflicting, some mutually contradictory, each of them significant to somebody, all of them meriting a degree of consideration." I was further warned that to approach "any campus decision from a unilateral point of view is to court failure" and that "indeed, if any single rule of university administration can be evolved, it is this: only by continual balancing of many perspectives can a campus administrator achieve success."

Even if the University were to keep its unstructured diversity as its desirable trait, the President would still have to "provide leadership, unified direction and support to all the diverse plans, objectives and methods of the several academic units and individual scholars." This, then, was the challenge a university administrator must confront.

In accepting that challenge, Romulo set the direction that his presidency of the University would take. Actually, this solved nothing for him, but it did clarify matters sufficiently for him to recognize the basic problem of his administration which he phrased in the form of a question: *How do we achieve necessary unity in a desirable diversity?*

Answers to a Basic Problem

That problem was not all that unique to the University of the Philippines. However, the three answers that President Romulo offered certainly were.

First, he would "orient the University with its new goals and directions imposed by the changing place and function of the state university in the total scheme of higher education in the Philippines." The validity of his answer would certainly depend on the correctness of his perception of "the total scheme of higher education in the Philippines." But he would not rely on his own perception. He would place the matter before the faculty of the University for the fullest discussion possible. This, he said, he was most anxious to do, for in the few months that he had been in office, he had discovered the faculty to be "a veritable powerhouse of academic wisdom, insight and experience." He was certain that anything placed before the faculty for appraisal would be thoroughly discussed and, thereby, gain rather than lose clarity.

Second, he would involve "the most searching minds among our faculty" in the study of the state the Univerity was in, and he would ask them to recommend changes in policy. He would, therefore, appoint faculty committees. He would provide each of these its general and specific objectives, and he would also see to it that every one would enjoy the widest latitude of freedom possible. All these committees would be free to report every observation that they might consider worthwhile and to recommend any change that they might deem advisable under the circumstances.

Third, he would do an "exhaustive University self-study." He noted that studies of the University in the past had been undertaken by outsiders, such as the team that put together the Hannah Report and the Paras committee of the UP Alumni Association. He pointed out that these committee studies were useful but only to the extent that they provided perspective or generated support for the University from the larger community. As far as Romulo was concerned, only a carefully chosen group of scholars, students, university employees and administrators would be capable of producing the exhaustive self-study which would give the University of the Philippines what it needed to achieve "the necessary unity in a desirable diversity." He promised that he would constitute such a group, justifying what he planned to do with this statement: "By knowing where we are in every significant respect, we should be able to project our educational plans with better vision and understanding."

But would not he be creating thereby a pressure group that would in time hold the President of the University in bondage? He saw the possibility. Against such a dire eventuality, he interposed his belief that "the university administrator cannot possibly sacrifice to any professor or group of professors his own mature and enlightened assessment of academic and organizational problems."

He promised there would neither be "authoritative instructions" nor "mandates" raised by pressure groups, for "these are utterly unknown to a sound perspective of academic administration." In other words, he would listen to professors, ignore mandates drummed up by pressure groups, and keep his counsel.

The Ad Hoc Committees

At the same meeting of the University Council on September 14, 1962, President Romulo announced the creation of seventeen *ad hoc* committees, ranging in subject matter from long-range planning through landscaping to national heroes. In general, these committees would look into and report on the existing state of affairs in a particular aspect of university life and make appropriate and feasible recommendations to change the existing situation for the improvement and strengthening of the University. To these committees, the President appointed "the most searching minds of our faculty."

The Ad Hoc Committee on Long-Range Plans[33] was instructed by the President to plan and develop a scheme "to guide the various units of the University in preparing development plans for a five-year period." The committee was also asked to develop a guide for the central administration of the University in "integrating the unit plans and planning those aspects of long-range planning for the University which transcends the scope of any unit or units."

Romulo established several committees to deal with the faculty and its multifarious problems. In his instructions to the Ad Hoc Committee on Faculty Status and Welfare,[34] Romulo noted that the evaluation of faculty performance as a basis for advancement or separation from the University had always been a problem, and no satisfactory solution had so far been found for it. He also referred to the "iniquities in the present status of faculty members," the existence of which had long been an open secret in the

University. The most flagrant example of this, he said, was the unusually long time that a faculty member spent in the same rank. He instructed the committee to put an end to all these "iniquities" by formulating standards and procedures for the recruitment, selection, probation, permanent appointment and promotion of faculty members.

With regard to the welfare of the faculty, the President asked the committee to make a comparative study of the salary scale of the University vis-a-vis those of other public and private colleges and universities and comparable government agencies. He wanted the committee to look into ways and means of increasing fringe benefits for the faculty and other academic personnel and of improving their physical working conditions. In addition, he told the committee to look into inducements which the University might give in recognition of superior scholarly performance, such as professorial chairs for meritorious work.

Faculty Development and Research

As for faculty development, Romulo created the Ad Hoc Committee on Faculty Development,[35] with Dean Cesar A. Majul as chairman. He instructed the committee to study and report on current policies, procedures and programs for faculty development not only on the level of the school or college but also on that of the entire university. In particular, he enjoined the committee to take up the UP fellowship program and the arrangements by which faculty members might go abroad for further study under other auspices.

He asked the committee to recommend policies, procedures and plans that would promote the faculty development programs of the University. In particular, he asked the committee to look into the means by which such a program might be promoted. He suggested that the committee examine how faculty members might be employed properly upon their return to the University with advanced training and specialized capabilities. He also asked that the committee consider such other means of faculty development as sabbatical leaves, faculty seminars and colloquia, the exchange of professors with other universities here or abroad, the provision of library and laboratory resources, the participation of the faculty in scholarly conferences and their membership in national and foreign learned organizations.

The promotion of research among the members of the faculty was given to the Ad Hoc Committee on Research.[36] The President asked the committee to examine the organization, policies and procedures for individual as well as organized research work in the University and to recommend policies for the promotion of research and for the funding of research projects.

Survey of Management Problems

The central administration of the University and its relationship to the various units of the University as a problem area was given to two bodies, the Ad Hoc Committee on Central Administration[37] and the Ad Hoc Committee on the Executive Committee and College Autonomy.[38] The President named Dean Cesar E.A. Virata as chairman of the first committee and Dean Vicente Abad Santos as chairman of the second.

The President asked the Virata committee to study the University's central administration and to recommend such changes as would enhance the capacity of the Vice Presidents and other administrative officers to assist the President and serve the needs of the faculty. In particular, he asked the committee to delineate and redistribute the authority and the responsibilities of deans and directors vis-a-vis the President and his administrative assistants so as to enable the various academic units to function with optimum efficiency, initiative and resourcefulness.

As for the Ad Hoc Committee on the Executive Committee and College Autonomy, it was asked by the President to report on undesirable limitations on the authority of deans and directors vis-a-vis the President of the University and the officers of the central administration and to recommend policies and rules which would enable deans and directors to provide decisive leadership which would be responsive, responsible and dynamic. Moreover, the President asked the committee to suggest changes in the central administration which would relieve the University president of unnecessary demands on his time and energy. He also asked the committee to develop plans for enlarging faculty participation in administration once autonomy was granted, as proposed, to colleges and schools and their respective deans and directors.

To deal with the problem of financing the operations of the University, President Romulo created the Ad Hoc Committee on Finance[39] which was instructed to look into the sources and the forms of financial support for the University, formulate plans for funding the University's five-year plan, develop potential sources of financial assistance, and recommend plans and techniques for raising funds to underwrite such projects as the University might undertake in the next five years.

The matter of student affairs in the University was handed to the Ad Hoc Committee on Student Scholarship and Extra-Curricular Activities.[40] Its task would be to examine the different offices and programs which were intended to enhance student scholarship, serve the students' social and physical needs as well as foster extra-curricular activities among them. The committee was expected to formulate, on the basis of its findings, a coherent plan for the offices and programs concerned with students.

Romulo created other committees and appointed faculty members to these bodies, though he did not give them detailed instructions. These included such committees as were necessary to deal with archival materials which had been dumped in the Main Library building, with the beautification and landscaping of the campus, and with other peripheral matters. The principal burden of these presidential actions was clear. The President wanted to effect changes in the University and give it a new direction, but the President also wanted to enlist the academicians in this difficult endeavor.

TO BUILD THE BEST UNIVERSITY FOR FILIPINOS

THE reports of the committees created by President Romulo were mimeographed and published as *University Perspectives; Reports of the President's Ad Hoc Committees* (University of the Philippines, Quezon City, 1962-1963). It was made available to the faculty members involved in this intensive analysis and evaluative survey.

The reports dealt with long-range plans, financing and central administration, the Executive Committee in its relation to college and school autonomy, faculty status and welfare, faculty development, faculty turnover, the promotion of research, the graduate program, student affairs, the proposed medical center, university housing, and the University's relations with the public.

In a sense, the volume contained the collective wisdom of the faculty in the form of advice to the President of the University. It is also a volume of incalculable importance, for it reveals the thinking of the faculty on what the University of the Philippines should be.

Long-Range Planning

The Ad Hoc Committee on Long-Range Planning presented a five-year development plan on the operating budget of the University which included the substantive functions of teaching, research and extension services as well as provisions for the auxiliary services division of the University, staff development and general administration.[41] On the recommendation of the committee, the President approved an estimate of the magnitude and pattern of expenditures for the five years (1963-1968) covered by the development program. The President set the upper limit at ₱41 million and the lower limit at ₱31 million, which was deemed adequate for the University to run its educational programs at a respectable level commensurate with its responsibilities as an institution of higher learning.

During the five-year period mentioned, emphasis would be shifted from teaching to research. This meant that percentage-wise, funds for teaching courses leading to academic degrees or certificates would decrease over those five years, although in absolute terms it would increase by 300 per cent. Across the board increases in faculty salaries would rise by 70 per cent, and selective salary increases and promotions would rise by 30 per cent. Funds would be allocated for the creation of new positions for junior and senior faculty as well as for the establishment of scholarships and grants to cover cost of living and other contingency items for both undergraduate and graduate students.

The recommended pattern of expenditures would allow for a 50 per cent increase in enrolment while maintaining the 1961 faculty-student ratio of 36 students per faculty member. However, most of the additional enrolment would be on the graduate level, and the program would provide for 400 to 600 graduate scholarships. Emphasis, then, would be on graduate education. Clearly, this fitted the President's decision to give the highest priority to research.

The committee singled out staff development as the most important feature of the five-year development plan. The success of the program, which envisioned self-sustained growth, would depend on the success of the staff-development plan. Accordingly, the committee alloted to staff development an amount that closely approximated what it had alloted to teaching in relative as well as absolute terms.

The staff-development program would eventually alter the composition of the faculty of the University: 31.15 per cent would have the doctorate, 38.59 per cent would have the master's degree, leaving 29.22 per cent with the bachelor's degree. This, the committee believed, would compare favorably with the composition of the faculties of many universities in the American mid-west.

The committee stated that through an extension and consultation program, the University would be able to serve the larger community as well as help unify, integrate and diversify Philippine society. Among the activities cited were home and farm development, refresher courses for public elementary and secondary school teachers, technical assistance and consultation for agencies of government, technical assistance and consultation for various social groups, and so on.

To support the principal substantive functions of teaching, research as well as community service, the committee allocated ₱6.150 million to ₱7.690 million for medical services, library facilities, security and physical plant maintenance. The largest amount would go to the purchase of 175,000 to 225,000 volumes of books at a cost of ₱3.5 million to ₱4.5 million. The current appropriations for medical services, security and physical plant maintenance would be increased by 100 per cent representing an outlay of ₱1.05 million.

The committee in effect envisioned a university with a high-powered faculty, two-thirds of whom would have advanced training in their various fields of specialization. It would do some teaching, but mostly on the graduate level. Its principal activity would be research, basic as well as applied. However, it would also serve the community, the public sector as well as the private sectors.

Evidently, the faculty and the President of the University had dreamed the same dream.

Financial Capability

The plans which would turn the vision into reality would naturally cost something. The University might never have enough money to implement those plans, if nothing were done to find new sources of funds.

The Ad Hoc Committee on Finance[42] made nine proposals to improve the financial posture of the University: (1) to invest idle funds of the University which then stood at ₱2.9 million, (2) to develop portions of the campus not needed at present for academic purposes into an industrial or commercial center, (3) to build more dormitories and expand food service, (4) to develop the UP land grants systematically along more modern lines, (5) to increase tuition fees which could be collected periodically, (6) to campaign for contributions among the alumni, (7) to amend the Tax Code to make gifts and donations to the University tax deductible, (8) to work for the amendment of the Assessment Law so that one-eighth of one per cent of gross receipts imposed on real estate would go to the University as part of the national contribution to the promotion of higher learning, and (9) to analyze the expenditures of the University to determine which ones could be reduced without impairing efficiency.

It was clear from its recommendations that the Committee expected enough funds to be generated for self-sustained development of the University.

Central Administration

In the main, the Committee on Central Administration recommended the revision of the organizational setup of the University as well as the staffing of the Office of the President of the University and the decentralization of personnel administration while maintaining centralized control.[43] To justify what it had recommended, the committee asserted the principle that the University should not be administered as though it were a business corporation or an agency of government. The committee cited John J. Carson who wrote in his book, *Governance of Colleges and Universities* (N.Y., McGraw-Hill, 1960, p. 120):

> "Good" administration is not necessarily reflected by a "smooth-running machine" nor by a no-nonsense, tightly coordinated system of activities. "Good" administration is better reflected by the capacity to keep the eye focussed on basic ends and to adapt activities to the attainment of these ends.

The committee also cited Burton R. Clark of the Center for Higher Education at the University of California, who wrote in his essay, "Faculty Authority," which appeared in the Winter 1961 issue of the *AAUP Bulletin* (pp. 300-301):

> In colleges and universities, the work of the specialist is more nearly an entity in itself. Especially in research and scholarship, the specialized effort follows its own logic, it is not done to order, and it is itself what the organization wants to put out. What the individual professor does on his own, or in the company of a few other workers, is what the organization sets out to do. Rationality in college organization is the creation of conditions that support the free, specialized inquiry and teaching of the professor.
>
> The implications for authority are clear; the authority structure does not need to be clearly knit or as hierarchical, as in most other settings. The loose, meandering, overlapping structure of authority we see in colleges may be there because it is in the service of rationality rather than madness.

The ideas of these two men formed the basis of the committee's recommendation to create the position of Academic Vice President. The academic holding this post would have administrative supervision over all units whose services were related to instruction, and he would also serve as Dean of Faculties, but he would have no administrative supervision over any dean or director. The committee also recommended the creation of two positions in the Office of the President. One was the Assistant to the President for Business Affairs who would have the function of advising the President on all business matters of the University. The other was the Assistant for Administrative Services who would have the function of supervising all units performing administrative, custodial, housekeeping as well as auxiliary services.

The committee also recommended that Deans and Directors be placed directly under the President's supervision. The committee further recommended the creation of an executive committee in each of the colleges and schools comprising the University with their respective deans or directors as chairman and representative members of the faculty as members.

The committee endorsed the recommendation of the Ad Hoc Committee on Long-Range Plans for the adoption of performance budgeting even at the college level. Likewise endorsed was the establishment of another committee to make an intensive analysis of the budgetary procedures currently being followed in the University and to "set up a budgetary system that should, as a general principle, reflect respect for college autonomy, wide faculty participation, and little intervention from central administration other than that from the President."

These various recommendations would give the central administration control over the various units of the University while at the same time fostering a decentralized administration. This meant that the schools and colleges would have autonomy, and the faculty would have a say on matters of administration.

College Autonomy

One problem still remained to be resolved. How should deans and directors relate to the Central Administration?[44]

Invited to deal with the problem, the Ad Hoc Committee on the Executive Committee agreed with the President of the University that "a definite line must be drawn to separate, on the one hand, matters which can be left solely to academic administrators and, on the other, matters which require presidential intervention."

The committee worked on two assumptions in the determination of such a line. One was that academic administrators were capable officers who should be responsible for the operation of their school or college, but who should be given commensurate authority. The second assumption was that academic administrators were, or ought to be, the servants of the scholars. For the University is a community of scholars engaged not only in the dissemination of knowledge but also in extending the frontiers of knowledge.

The committee recommended that deans and directors be given some freedom to deal with financial, personnel and academic problems pertaining to their units. Accordingly, deans and directors should participate in the making not only of their own school or college budget but also in that of the entire university.

Faculty Status and Welfare

The Ad Hoc Committee on Faculty Status and Welfare prefaced its report[45] and recommendations with their own exposition of principle:

> It has been observed that the many imperfections of the university today are due largely to the failure to appreciate the full meaning of the idea of a university. In essence, the university is a community of scholars. Its mission is not only to conserve and disseminate knowledge through teaching, but also to advance the frontiers of knowledge through research and creative work. The faculty, composed of teacher-scholars, constitute the heart of a university: they must therefore assume a role of prime importance in university affairs.

On the basis of such an understanding of what really constituted a university, the committee recommended the adoption of general principles and standards of faculty recruitment and selection for the entire University. The committee noted that there should be a standard procedure for recruiting and selecting people to be appointed to the faculty. To this end, a personnel committee should be created in each college or school to conduct a regular survey of the needs of the college for instructors, to publish a bulletin of information for prospective candidates for faculty positions, administer competitive examinations, and evaluate the overall records of those being proposed for appointment to the college faculty.

The committee recommended the amendment of the *Revised Code of the University of the Philippines* and the inclusion of new rules which would govern appointments to the faculty.

It also urged the formulation of a uniform, accurate and fair system for rating the performance or efficiency of faculty members. The procedure should be so devised as to maximize uniformity and accuracy, and encourage full faculty participation in the whole process.

Regarding faculty salaries, the committee made two policy recommendations: (1) the salary policy should be understood, it should be consistent, and it should be progressive; and (2) in the allocation of the University's resources, top priority should be given to salary increases, which should be substantial in order to give instructors and assistant professors sufficient compensation to enable them to maintain a decent standard of living. Compensation should be commensurate with the educational and social standing of the faculty in the community.

To stimulate scholarship, the committee recommended the reduction of the regular teaching load of the faculty to no more than twelve (12) hours a week, the limitation of lecture classes to no more than forty (40) students and of English classes and the like to no more than twenty (20) students, the systematic canvassing of faculty potential through seminars, the assignment of topics for research and publication, the holding of public lectures, the relief of the faculty from such duties as classcard distribution and checking during registration as well as from semi-academic and clerical tasks, and the giving of adequate honoraria and lighter teaching load to faculty members doing research for which grants should be awarded.

Evidently, the committee wanted a faculty for the University that will not only teach but also do research. As far as the committee was concerned, as shown by its recommendations, the faculty must be given adequate means to do these tasks well, and they must be richly rewarded for work well done. The faculty must also be paid well for their work and allowed all the fringe benefits which would enable them to live in more comfortable straits. But then that is because the committee had gone along with the President of the University to whom the faculty was the all and be all of a university.

Faculty Development

The Ad Hoc Committee on Faculty Development began with a study of the composition of the faculty of the University.[46] It found that the ratio of low ranking faculty members to those holding the higher ranks was too much out of kilter. There were too many instructors and assistant professors and too few associate professors and full professors.

The committee took this to mean that young people were continually being taken into the faculty and that only a few of these new instructors stayed long enough to be promoted to assistant professors. These low-ranking people, then, had to carry out the major objectives of their respective schools and colleges. The committee also learned that too many associate professors and full professors were leaving the University. Many had retired, but many more had resigned. Yet not enough assistant professors were promoted to the now vacant associate professorships. And since only a few associate professors were being promoted, many full professorships remained vacant.

When the committee looked into the total number of resignations from the faculty as a whole, it learned that most of those who had resigned their positions in the faculty were instructors and assistant professors. Further inquiry led the committee to the inevitable conclusion. Deepening despair of ever reaching the higher professorial ranks had led these young members of the faculty to resign from the University. It was then that the committee came to the sad realization that the University of the Philippines had had to make do with an ever-new and untrained faculty to fulfill its mission as an institution of higher learning.

By polling the faculty, the committee learned that in no unit of the University was research not desired. If research had not been done, it was because the unit lacked the necessary facilities for research or did not offer incentives for the faculty to do research. But these conditions, the committee learned, did not deter some members of the faculty from continuing research, which many considered a normal supplement to teaching.

The committee noted that in 1962, a dramatic shift had occurred toward research. The shift was even more dramatic in the more recently established units of the University as well as in those that were more exposed to outside pressure to contribute to programs for national development. The committee felt, therefore, that the basic mission of the University had to be reassessed.

Although no member of the faculty had ever served as an exchange professor in any university or college in the Philippines and elsewhere from 1958 to 1963, the committee noted that some faculty members in certain units of the University had expressed the belief that faculty exchange with foreign universities could bring new ideas and new influences into the University, expose the faculty to new methods of teaching as well as to recent developments in the various fields of study, and forge close relations between the University of the Philippines and other universities. The committee suggested that the University look into the possibility of instituting a program of faculty exchange with those nations with whom the Philippines had concluded cultural exchange agreements, particularly the Asian universities.

In order to increase the number of Ph.D. holders on the faculty, the committee recommended the immediate institution of a program to send more faculty members to universities abroad under a UP fellowship or under some other sponsorship. The committee did not see anything wrong with allowing members of the faculty to accept scholarship grants or even assistantships in foreign universities.

The committee would make teaching efficiency and research output as the principal criteria for promotion. Research work should be given due recognition in material as well as symbolic forms. In other words, the committee was saying that a suitable cash award should be given, and appropriate academic honors should be bestowed on faculty members for achievement of high distinction. To stimulate research, the committee recommended that faculty members known for their research work should as much as possible be relieved of teaching duties in whole or in part and provided with ample funds to buy books and learned publications in their respective areas of research interest. Of course, once they had formulated their research projects, they should be given generous grants to enable them to undertake relevant research work.

In the interest of continuous faculty development, the committee recommended that methods be devised to encourage a broad segment of the faculty to participate in seminars which would deal with substantive matters. Topics might be determined beforehand, and members of the faculty might be asked well in advance to choose from among these the topics they would develop into suitable seminar papers.

It was quite clear from their recommendations that the committee saw faculty development as an institutional responsibility. The University should do more than send junior faculty members abroad on fellowships to work for doctoral degrees. More importantly, it must see to the continuing development of the faculty. The committee put emphasis on research. It must, therefore, make research grants available to all who wish to undertake research, and it must maintain adequately stocked research libraries and well-equipped laboratories. It must reward achievement with generous cash awards and high academic honors. This should encourage faculty members to sharpen analytical skills and broaden intellectual capabilities through constant work-outs in research and in seminars.

It was clearly the hope of the committee that the faculty would in time develop into a really first-rate academic body for a really fine university for the Filipino people.

AN AUSPICIOUS START TO MATCH THE DEFT APPROACH TO THE GOALS OF MANAGEMENT

ELEVEN months after the oath-taking at Malacañang Palace, Carlos P. Romulo, one-time associate professor in charge of American literature courses and acting head of the Department of English in President Palma's time at the UP campus on Padre Faura, was formally inaugurated President of the University. The ceremonies were held on Sunday afternoon, April 7, 1963, at the commencement grounds behind Quezon Hall.[47]

The Inaugural Spectacle

The color and pomp of the inauguration would be hard to forget. The academic purple, maroon, red, green, blue, black, and gray of the world's universities mingled in spectacular fashion as academicians marched in solemn procession beneath the acacias on their way to the stage fronting the commencement grounds. Delegates from the world's oldest as well as youngest universities followed the graduating class of 1963 and the faculty of the University of the Philippines. Many more lined the wide avenues of the campus and wondered at all the resplendent colors being flaunted before their eyes, each one a symbol of some scholarly persuasion or bend of intellect. As some guests observed then, it was just too much pomp to grace a single occasion.

This was the spectacle to cap the festivities that began on Monday, April 1,[48] with the open house of colleges, schools and institutes and university departments, art exhibits and competitions at Vinzons Hall. On Tuesday, April 2, there was a symposium at the theatre of Palma Hall on "The Challenge of Leadership to the University." On Wednesday, there was a tea-musicale for friends of the University at the Tea Room in the Teodora Alonzo Hall. On Thursday, the Board of Regents of the University of the Philippines tendered a dinner in honor of President Romulo at the Tea Room. On Thursday also, a Gala Concert was presented in honor of President Romulo featuring the UP Symphony Orchestra, the UP Mixed Chorus, the Speech Choir of the Department of Speech and Drama, and the Children's Chorus of the UP High School and the UP Elementary School. On Saturday, which was UP Alumni Day, there was a luncheon in honor of the UP Alumni Council at the Executive House and a reunion dinner of the faculty and the alumni of the University at the Vinzons Hall Court. During the dinner, Dean Roy D. Ribble, Dean Emeritus, Farleigh Dickinson University, presented the Presidential Collier to President Romulo. On Sunday, the inauguration exercises were followed by a buffet dinner at Teodora Alonzo Hall.

Outstanding Artists in Concert

The Gala Concert on Friday evening at the University Theater in honor of President Romulo was memorable not for its pageantry and color but rather for the stunning display of creativity by the artists of the University.[49] The concert opened with Bernardino Custodio conducting the UP Symphony Orchestra for Nicanor Abelardo's *Cinderella Overture*. Then Lucio San Pedro mounted the podium to conduct his *Concerto in D minor, Op. 51 No. 1* with violinist Sergio Esmilla, Jr. as soloist. For this performance, a special cadenza was composed for Esmilla.

And then Eliseo M. Pajaro conducted his *Prelude and Testament* with Aurelio Estanislao, baritone, as soloist. This was easily the most stirring of the masterpieces performed that evening. Pajaro had set to music President Romulo's first Presidential Statement of June 1, 1962.[50] The orchestra entered with the principal theme, a four-tone motif. The chorus then took up the motif as it sang, "The University is a citadel of truth. Let no one make of it anything else." The motif was repeated with variations by male voices, then by female voices and later by the speech choir.

Aurelio Estanislao's participation heightened the impact of Pajaro's musical tribute. The baritone solo enthralled the audience and set the stage for the concluding part of the composition. Developed as a choral fugue, the

Grand Finale opened with the various voices singing the main burden of the closing line of President Romulo's statement: "May the Almighty give me His divine guidance." The different sections of the orchestra entered in fugal fashion and kept pace with the UP Mixed Concert Chorus. Beginning quietly as prayers do, the Grand Finale gradually worked up to a powerful climax and closed with quiet dignity and profound serenity.

Thunderous applause followed the last dying note. The audience leaped to its feet, clapping wildly. The UP was applauding what it had always believed in about itself. But Romulo had put it so well, and Pajaro had given it the stirring music that was its due.

The President's Vision

When the moment arrived, President Romulo approached the bank of microphones and began to address an audience which had come to hear an orator's orator. He began with the past, talking of his predecessors and the part each had played in the making of the University of the Philippines.[51] Coming to his own times, he announced:

> I have come to dream new dreams; I am to attempt what has not been tried; I am to carry out all the good but stillborn plans of our admired and late lamented leaders. But, above all, I must keep faith with an ideal shared by all: with an eye single to the one task for which you, in being here today, shall remember this era.[52]

Could it be that in speaking of new dreams, of attempting what had not been tried before, of carrying out "all the good but stillborn plans of our admired and late lamented leaders," he was in reality talking of the one ideal, "a great university in this country, the best university for the Filipino"? But then this had always been the way UP thought of itself.

In 1963, the idea of a university for the Filipino was not all that new. Dr. Murray Bartlett as the first President in 1911 had already dreamed that dream, and he had actually tried to make the UP that University. After him President Ignacio Villamor worked hard to give the University a permanent faculty of Filipino scholars. President Guy Potter Benton in turn drew up a plan for growth and expansion, and he did succeed in implementing a faculty development program which had "considerably enriched the University's intellectual fare." President Rafael Palma had his "Our Country" university program, which his successor, President Jorge Bocobo, enriched with pageantry, symbolic presentations, and scholarly research in what many now call "Philippine Studies." President Bienvenido M. Gonzalez set the stage for all subsequent growth and development of the University by moving it to Diliman, where it could begin to perform duties no one had ever dreamed before as proper functions for a university. President Vicente G. Sinco strengthened the academic functions of the University, giving full support to the liberal and general education program.

Then President Romulo asked, "Where then are we heading?"[53]

Insofar as the UP community was concerned, there could only be one answer. It could not possibly be anything but to go on doing "what it is that we are trying to build in the University." And this, as President Romulo was at pains to make clear, was the whole effort to produce the educated men and women needed by the country at any particular time and age.

Higher Education Redefined

Of course, President Romulo was thinking of a liberal and a general education that could not possibly be dependent alone on "a rigid system of formal course work, prescribed curricula, and enforced attendance." The kind of higher education that he was concerned with took place whenever one confronted ideas, actions, and things. If the core of such an education were a habit of mind and a mode of thought, then it could also be found outside the classroom and the laboratory, "in research activity, even in travel to distant places." Many, however, had lived out their lives without understanding the wealth around them. They might have had "more useful and fuller lives for themselves and for their society."[54]

It was for such people that it had been necessary to establish the modern and all too complex system of higher education. No other system had so far been devised for widening one's capaciy to enjoy and use as well as for giving one the discipline that lent existence a meaning and an order. To give Filipinos this kind of higher education was what the University of the Philippines was all about.

Many in his audience that afternoon were not entirely prepared for the kind of higher education Romulo had in mind. In those days, one normally thought of the deficiencies of the educational system in the Philippines in terms of the inability of Filipinos to speak correct English or to comprehend the elegance of an algebraic equation. President Romulo had other things in mind:

> It is my wish to give it amplitude, insofar as it provides a common background for professional or vocational programs, insofar as it makes up for gaps in the student's early training and insofar as it corrects deficiencies in orientation in the Philippine educational system, notably the neglect of the understanding and the appreciation of our culture, thought, achievements, as those of our Asian

> neighbors. This is also the period for the instilling of attitudes and skills, by means of so-called "tool" courses, which will stand the man in good stead in professional pursuits and make for competence and usefulness in any endeavor.[55]

If modern higher education were a complex system, then, Romulo argued, its base could not be other than the University program in liberal and general education. This would consist of two components: (1) the "understanding and the appreciation of our culture, thought, and achievements, as those of our neighbors," and (2) the "instilling of attitudes and skills, by means of so-called 'tool' courses."[56]

However, since higher education was an unfolding process at every level of academic life, the active exercise of freedom became all important. At this point, Romulo proposed that instead of just protecting academic freedom, he would actively espouse its positive and constructive expression. As though to underscore his resolve, President Romulo said, "It is better for the University to be slightly on the side of excess than on the side of suppression, especially where educated, mature persons are concerned, if the spirit of free inquiry is to prevail and not to be discouraged or stultified."[57]

Freedom as Fountainhead

There were still other aspects of freedom for the individual as well as for the corporation, and President Romulo expressed his resolve to investigate them. And as he looked deep into the matter, it became all too clear that he had to react to demands no UP president had ever entertained.

> I have noted the desire of the faculty for more participation in decisions affecting their work, their welfare, and their living conditions. Along a similar vein, colleges have asked for more unit autonomy, and students greater say in their affairs and in their relations with the administration and the faculty, in which they had always been at a disadvantage.[58]

Having founded his system of higher education on freedom, Romulo turned to "a sense of one's capacity and worth as an individual in a society of free and fully-functioning individuals." He identified this as one of the cherished aims of higher education, but he explained it in a manner that was most unusual for the UP of his time. He said:

> To my mind, what is this but self-identification which, carried to its most exalted purpose, becomes nationalism? With this clear before us, it is evident that nationalism becomes consistent with the idea of a university. Indeed, it becomes a necessary component, for no one has ever achieved universality without the integrity that comes from a realization of one's unique position in the cosmos.[59]

What his audience had so far heard was President Romulo's explanation of what constituted higher education. Some in the audience marvelled at the seriousness with which he had tackled the problem, even as they wondered how he would go about formulating that which would concretize what he had been dreaming about. Eventually he put at ease those who were wondering about the matter as well as those who were skeptical about the feasibility of his goals for the University of the Philippines, when he brought up what he had simply called the "Five-Year Development Program for the University." He discussed twelve of the most important features of the Program.

Development Program Described

President Romulo began with the promise that he would seek to establish the bases for sustained growth at all levels of the University for the next five years. "Every unit," he said, "will be encouraged to develop in accordance with its own urgings and the principle of unit autonomy."[60] For the sake of balanced development, internal resources would be allocated and outside aid would be actively solicited for those units of the University which appeared to fall behind for reasons of past neglect. And he called attention to the plight of the basic disciplines.

Regarding the teaching programs of the University, undergraduate enrolment would be maintained at the current level by simply putting admission on a more selective basis. However, more scholarships would be made available to allow a greater number of "high-performance but economically disadvantaged students" to be admitted. Stress would be placed on high quality undergraduate education through the institution of better conceived undergraduate curricular programs to be handled by "better developed" staff members using improved teaching methods and instructional devices.

While reducing its role in undergraduate education, the University would encourage the growth of graduate programs by expanding facilities, increasing scholarships for graduate students, establishing graduate assistantships, and appointing additional staff. The desire here, as pointed out by Romulo, was "to increase the proportion of graduate activity to the undergraduate, to the level characteristic of reputable universities abroad." But this did not mean that undergraduate education would be sacrificed. Rather, it would thereby be enriched. As the President saw it, the emphasis on graduate education would enable the university not only to achieve "the status of a true university" but more importantly to respond to the urgent need of a developing society by producing "the workers with the highly specialized training and the research orientation" required in national development.[61]

Hand in hand with the projected expansion of graduate education, research would be intensified in all units of the University.[62] Funds for research would be increased, research institutes or centers would be established as required, and research professorships and instructorships would be provided, faculty members doing research would be relieved of some of their teaching duties. Moreover, the status of the researcher would be given due recognition, and an adequate incentive plan would be set up. And the President promised to have the library developed to the level that it would be able to support the University's expanding programs in graduate education and research.

Upgrading Faculty Ranks

Of course, it would be necessary "to accelerate the development of the academic staff qualitatively, in the main,"[63] but also in point of numbers. The President pointed out that by 1968 forty to fifty new doctorate degree holders would be needed in order that 16 per cent of the whole faculty would be made up of people wih this kind of advanced training. This would force the University to send a great number of University Fellows to universities abroad, but as soon as the University's graduate programs attained higher levels of development, it would no longer be necessary to send so many members of the academic staff overseas.

Staff development would have to proceed hand in hand with the replenishment of the thinning ranks of associate and full professors. The systematic and judicious promotion of faculty members in every unit mainly on the basis of merit would have to be done to achieve a rational distribution of ranks as rapidly as possible, so that the anomalous state in which half of the staff were Instructors could be corrected. The policy regarding the transfer of faculty members from temporary to permanent status would be subjected to continuing examination so that the granting of tenure would not be so difficult and complicated a process. Romulo said the promotions and tenure policies of the University would continue to be scrutinized in order to more "effectively reward good work and retain promising young instructors."[64]

The President likewise noted that communities had already developed in Diliman and Los Baños, presenting the University with some problems as well as with the rare opportunity to create "in these places islands of productive scholarship and congenial fellowship among scholars and their helpers."[65]

As President of the University, Romulo declared that in his relations with the students, "there should not be a sort of tug-of-war." His premise was that the "student and his groups have been given the chance to join the academic community as full members, being the mature and responsible persons they have become." This, he noted, was a view many people felt was risky, considering the existence of contrary evidence. Nevertheless, he had proceeded on his own assumptions, abolishing censorship of the *Philippine Collegian*, and restoring both the University Council Committee on Student Organizations and Activities and the Student Council.[66] Other steps had been taken. All were meant to further ingrain the habit of leadership among UP students and not to deflect the student from his basic aim of learning but to further enrich his path to it.

His confidence seemed even then to be well-founded. He knew his faculty quite well, and his experience with them served as the basis of his understanding of the men he was to lead as their President.

> Under ordinary circumstances the academic personality is an autonomous being, needing no prod to move him along ways which are his by preference and vocation. It is important, then, to remove all obstacles to free expression of his inner compulsion toward academic excellence. This free spirit now manifests itself in the eagerness to re-examine curricula, courses of study, and the willingness to participate in symposia, departmental and interdepartmental seminars and public lectures.[67]

In other words, the creativity of the UP faculty had come out into the open, finding expression in many forms of intellectual endeavors under the leadership of the President of the University.

Problems of Implementation

The history of the implementation of the *Five-Year Development Program for the University* became the history of the University of the Philippines to the end of the Romulo Presidency. It was a time of great undertakings and breathtaking changes in the University, and when President Romulo went down the front steps of Quezon Hall for the last time, he left everywhere in Diliman the indelible mark of his Presidency. And the people who were with him then speak of that era with a glow in their eyes. They remember how exciting it was to scale the heights of academic excellence, to be lifted by the creative intelligence of a whole community that had nothing to bank on except their scholarly good sense. But it was never easy. The program was always in danger of floundering. It was touch and go all the time, and failure was not just a dire possibility. It was a distinct probability.

By the time it was two years old, the grandiose plan had run into the most serious difficulty of all. The country had fallen into hard times, and some of the budgetary requests of the University went unheeded. In his report to the faculty on October 16, 1964, Romulo acknowledged that the "second phase of salary adjustments for the faculty and the non-academic employees, while patently difficult to carry out due to the absence of additional funding from national sources, remains a commitment of this administration."[68] The almost ₱2-million needed for the purpose would have to be obtained from internal sources. Naturally, some projects would be handicapped. By making full use of the resources available as well as of external assistance, Romulo hoped that these projects would not be too adversely affected.

The ₱1-million scholarship program for the academic year 1964-1965 failed to get any funding from the government. However, the University received funds for such specific projects as the Natural Science Research Center, the Law Center, the Institute of Geodesy and Photogrammetry and others.[69] The University resolved to keep the scholarship program for implementation as soon as money for it would become available. Financial support did not come for the much-postponed establishment of the Institute of Mass Communication, and Romulo thought of putting up a Department of Journalism and Communication in the College of Arts and Sciences, if only to exert some influence in this vital profession.

More Funds for Research

The University, however, was not so strapped for funds that it could not proceed with the research component of the *Five-Year Development Program for the University*. The Natural Science Research Center did receive a ₱2 million allocation in the General Appropriations Act of 1964.[70] The University also obtained ₱1.5 million in grants for research. Research professorships and fellowships had already been established on an affiliate basis with the various research institutes or centers of the University. The plan to develop the University Library to the level that it could effectively support research did not have to be shelved. In his trip to the United States in September 1964, Romulo obtained a Ford Foundation grant of ₱1,442,550 for the library. In sum, the University increased its allocations for research in the natural sciences, social sciences and humanities by 500 per cent over those of the past year.

Faculty development continued at a faster rate than before. As of October 16, 1964, there were 113 members of the faculty working for their doctorates. Of these, 108 were in universities abroad. Some of these faculty members were granted either a full fellowship or a partial fellowship by the

University. The others studied abroad on scholarship grants from the Rockefeller, Ford, Guggenheim and other foundations and from the NEC-AID, Fulbright-Hays and Colombo Plan programs. Many faculty members were also working for advanced degrees on local fellowships which might be University-funded or Foundation-supported.

Better Deal for the Faculty

No longer would it be necessary for the younger members of the faculty to anticipate a discouragingly bleak future in the University. As President Romulo said in his October 16, 1964 report:

> We have succeeded, I believe, in stabilizing procedures with which promising young scholars, as well as established scientists and artists, are identified, attracted, tested and retained. The fact is, the promise of unlimited intellectual rewards, within the framework of an expanding material recompense and facilities, makes employment attractive in the University, and prevents abnormal attrition by outside interests.[71]

Romulo categorically stated that there would be promotions. The University was now in a position to "advance toward the rational distribution of ranks as originally proposed to unit heads, emphasizing, as always criteria of productivity and excellence, service and promise." To the instructors, the future never looked brighter or rosier.

From the vantage point of the Presidency, the University seemed to hum with hectic activity. The various faculties were hard at work, updating their curricular offerings. Numerous courses and degree programs were instituted, revised or abolished with the approval of the University Council. In this stream of continuing change, Romulo noted that his challenge toward a new orientation to Asia had received a critical response. A course on Asian Civilizations was already part of the general education program. A program of studies toward the Bachelor of Arts degree in Pilipino had been instituted.[72] The program of studies toward the Master of Arts degree in Asian Studies had been enriched, and it was now attracting more students than in previous years. In support of the new curricular offerings, research on Asian, particularly Philippine, matters had increased significantly.

Construction and Expansion

The landscape had by 1964 begun to change.[73] Covered walks now led to the University Library. The University Gymnasium was nearing completion on the knoll behind Malcolm Hall. The construction crews were still busy with the east wing of Melchor Hall to build the facilities for the Institute of Geodesy and Photogrammetry and the Instrumentation Center. The building for the Child Development Laboratory was going up. The architects had already finished the plans for the International Center and the Faculty Center, and they would soon start on the projected Natural Science Research Center and the Physical Plant and Maintenance building.

In October 1964, the Instituto de Español was already a going concern. The Ford Foundation had just allocated $208,500 for the establishment of a Population Institute. Government financial support for the Institute of Mass Communication was still being awaited. Recognizing that the University had evolved into a semi-residential, cosmopolitan university town beset by peculiar problems its novel status had entailed, the President organized the Committee on Housing and Community Welfare. His aim was to create by this means a dynamic, productive community of scholars.

To unify the scattered efforts of the University at maintaining relations with each of the 34,000 alumni, the President established an alumni office.[74] The UP Alumni Endowment Fund was incorporated with an operating capital of ₱250,000. The Fund would serve as an independent private foundation which would subsidize chairs for exceptional scholars, award scholarships for children of alumni and deserving but economically handicapped students, as well as provide compensation for retired faculty members who continue serving as teachers, researchers, and administrators.

Focus on the Collegian

A series of events which led to the grant of greater freedom to the *Philippine Collegian* under the Romulo administration could be traced back to the time when the Fact-Finding and Survey Committee established by the University of the Philippines Alumni Association completed its investigation of the University of the Philippines. In its issue for June 28, 1962, the day the officers of the alumni association were to submit the Committee's report, the *Philippine Collegian* emblazoned on its front page the headline, "Alumni report says sectarianism one cause of conflicts and confusion in the campus."[75] The student paper had somehow gained access to the report.

Under the headline was Florante G. Reyes' news story which opened with this sentence: "Overly enthusiastic sectarianism in the State University has been one of the main sources of conflicts and confusion in the campus for the past few years." Then he went on to relate what the committee headed by Ricardo Paras, former Chief Justice of the Supreme Court, had found about the various aspects of the University, which included its administrative setup, its curricula, the term system, the non-selective admission of students, the examination board, the communist infiltration of the University, and the alleged "godlessness" within the campus.

The news story was avidly read by all in the University. The investigation conducted by the Paras Committee had been going on for two years, and the University community eagerly awaited the results of the inquiry. The *Collegian* related what these were in the news story, but the student paper also had ideas of its own regarding the matter.[76] Its editorial concluded:

> The existence of a closed and monolithic organization whose very nature is diametrically opposed to everything a free and secular university stands for, only serves to prevent adequate student unity in times of university crises when its principles and ideals are questioned by a powerful majority which would make of mediocrity a national creed.

The next day, June 29, 1962, the adviser of the *Collegian* suspended Editor-in-Chief Luis V. Teodoro, Jr. and Managing Editor Ferdinand S. Tinio for one month on the ground that they printed the entire issue of the paper for June 28 without the prior approval of the adviser. In their places, the adviser designated Rene J. Navarro, Editor-in-Chief, and Florante G. Reyes, Managing Editor.[77] The Dean of Student Affairs upheld the suspension of Teodoro and Tinio on the finding that they had indeed violated Article 450 of the University Code when they ordered the printing of the June 28 issue of the *Collegian*.[78]

To Free the Collegian

At the induction of the officers and members of the Student Union on August 10, 1962, President Romulo indicated in his brief remarks for the occasion the possibility of abolishing the position of adviser of the *Collegian*.[79] He said he would recommend to the University Council and to the Board of Regents the suspension of Article 450 of Chapter 75 of the University Code, which gave the *Collegian* adviser administrative and editorial powers over the student paper. At its meeting on September 14, the University Council approved the limitation of the administrative and editorial powers of the *Collegian* faculty adviser to post-publication review under circumstances to be determined by the President of the University.[80]

On the surface, it looked as though Romulo had intervened in the chain of events started by the June 28 issue of the *Collegian* on the side of liberal idealism. Actually, he had done nothing less than to strike down one more of the many obstructions to student freedom which had remained in the University Code since the days of the American governance of the University of the Philippines. However, what Romulo had done did have a more fundamental meaning than that.

It was not readily apparent at the time that by suspending Article 450, he had in effect raised the students to a new position of responsibility in the University. The students were at last free as full members of the University constituency to exercise their creative intelligence and to act accordingly. To be sure, they would still have to account for their actions, but no longer would they have to look back to see if the faculty would approve and permit them to go ahead and act as intelligence dictated. From then on, the students never looked back.

To be sure, President Romulo had his difficult moments with students after that, but he never gave even the slightest indication to anyone that he ever regretted what he had done in granting the *Philippine Collegian* a greater measure of press freedom. In fact it was a move in keeping with his own eminent career as a journalist in charge of the *Tribune* and then the *Philippines Herald* way back in the 1930s.

Fund-Raising for Survival

By February 1964, lack of funds became a major cause for anxiety. It had become apparent that the University might not get the increased allocation from the national government for the 1964-1965 phase of the Five-Year Development Program.[81] To head off the impending debacle, President Romulo sent vigorous personal appeals to the financial managers of the national administration. Toward the end of April, it became all too clear that the vigorous personal appeals had failed. Romulo then started making plans for a fund-raising trip to the United States. He presented the plans to the Board of Regents at its May meeting. With Dr. O.D. Corpuz and Miss Iluminada Panlilio of his staff, Romulo left for the United States on June 2, 1964.

The week before his departure, Romulo completed arrangements for a formal meeting with the officers of the Bacolod Rotary Club, and the meeting took place just as May was ending.[82] The men from Bacolod were briefed on the University's background, its status and programs, its plans for future growth, its wide-ranging services to the nation, and its new expanded services which could further be extended, with additional support, to the youth and to the economic development of the nation. On this occasion, the leaders of the sugar industry pledged a million pesos to the UP Endowment Fund over the next five years, and the President received a check for ₱200,000 representing the first annual contribution.

The donation was crucial. Romulo mentioned it in his conference with American foundation and government officials. Together with the unprecedented ₱4.4-million increase in the appropriations for the University in the 1963-1964 national budget, the donation was accepted as clear evidence of the high rating enjoyed by the University in the eyes of leaders of industry and government in the Philippines. Undoubtedly, this made it easier for Romulo to convince American benefactors to contribute funds to support the University's development program.

An Array of Foundations

In San Francisco on June 4, Romulo presented the Five-Year Development Program of the Institute of Asian Studies (1963-1968) to President Haydn Williams and the principal officers of the Asia Foundation.[83] He discussed the original philosophy and purposes of the Institute, its lack of marked growth since its establishment, the development and new orientation which had been brought about since the beginning of his Presidency. Then he turned to the history of the Asia Foundation in the Philippines, noting how its resources could be re-directed, with richer results and more lasting impact, through closer and increased support of the Institute of Asian Studies. From Dr. Williams, Romulo received the categorical promise that the Asia Foundation would provide the resources to support the expanded operations and development of the Institute of Asian Studies.

Romulo arrived in New York City on June 5, and by lunch time he was in the Time-Life building offices of the Rockefeller Foundation. In the absence of Dr. J. George Harrar, President of the Rockefeller Foundation, Dr. Kenneth J. Thompson, Executive Vice President, hosted the luncheon. Romulo reported to the executives of the Foundation present on the progress of Rockefeller-assisted projects, new projects launched or planned, and the generally stable state of the University. Asked to remark on developments in Southeast Asia, which were causing the Foundation a great deal of concern, Romulo discussed the matter at some length. Among other things, he dwelt on the significant role of the University of the Philippines "as a center of higher education in the region, an institution which annually registers hundreds of Asian students in its various faculties." He had an interested audience which reacted favorably to his remarks. After all, the Foundation had appropriated in May 1964 about ₱2.8 million for the University's social sciences and humanities projects. At this luncheon-meeting, he presented the University's development program for the natural sciences in Diliman. He also handed to the Foundation a brochure on the new Faculty Center for the social sciences and humanities staff, saying that he would formally request aid for equipment and a library for the Faculty Center as soon as it was feasible to do so.

In later meetings with Dr. Thompson, Romulo discussed details of the implementation of Rockefeller-assisted projects. Visiting professors would be arriving shortly together with a consultant to look into the development of the University Library and an advisor for the improvement of the University's cultural program. A grant of ₱40,000 for the acquisition of books, and another of some ₱50,000 for the purchase of equipment needed for cultural presentations and art projects, were due to be released to the University.

From June 8 to 12, Romulo was in Toronto and Ottawa, Canada.[84] He visited the University of Toronto and McGill University. He also addressed the convention of the Rotary International on "the inadequacy of the traditional education of the Westerner about Asia," and he asked the Rotarians to understand "the historical and contemporary issues in the development of new Asian nations." While he was in Canada, he sought out Filipino students in the area, and he was surprised to find no fewer than 400 of them. In his conversations with UP scholars, he elicited suggestions on how the needs of UP fellows and scholars abroad might be better served, and he directed that appropriate action be taken on the matter.

More Benefactors Pursued

On June 15 he was in Washington, DC, calling on an old friend, Rutherford Poats, Assistant Director in charge of Far East Operations, Agency for International Development (AID). He mentioned the fear that a cut in AID appropriations would result in the phasing out of the NEC-AID program for the construction of UP faculty housing. Under the program, which had started before Romulo's presidency, 50 faculty houses would be put up every year for five years. Now 150 units still remained to be constructed. Without AID assistance, the cost of building these would be a serious drain on the resources of the University. The President was assured that AID would continue to fund this housing project for the faculty. The President was also informed that his request for equipment to be used in the UP Basilan Land Grant had been acted upon favorably.

On June 17, Romulo gave a luncheon at his hotel for Mr. Poats, Minister James Ingersoll of the AID mission in Manila, and seven other AID and State Department officials.[85] On this occasion, the "agreements" arrived at on June 15 were "confirmed." Then President Romulo strongly suggested the continued detail of John Rork as AID advisor to the University of the Philippines, and he was assured that Rork would not be recalled from his post.

On June 19, Romulo went to a luncheon meeting hosted by J. Burke Knapp, Vice President of the International Bank for Reconstruction and Development. He learned then that minor revisions were required on some of the details of the College of Agriculture development program. Consequently, the $6 million loan could not be finalized. However, he was told that the delay had only been caused by a procedural technicality.

On June 24, Romulo was back in New York City, having lunch with executives of the Rockefeller and Ford Foundations.[86] Like the Rockefeller Foundation, the Ford Foundation had evinced a readiness to help in the development of certain social science and natural science departments. In line with Ford Foundation procedure, Dr. Harry Case was sent to Manila as resident representative to confer with Dr. Enrique T. Virata and Dr. O.D. Corpuz. Dr. Case told Romulo that the Ford Foundation was already considering five of the six UP proposals for eventual implementation. The five were (1) the acquisition of a computer for the Institute of Economic Development and Research, (2) the establishment of a demographic institute, (3) assistance to the University Library, (4) assistance to the science teaching improvement program, and (5) assistance to the behavioral sciences improvement program.

During the luncheon which had been arranged by Dr. K. W. Thompson at the Century Club in New York, Romulo talked specifically of the broad scope of the programs for the Asian Center, the Medical Center, and the Institute of Asian Studies.[87] He also talked of his recent trip to the universities of Southeast Asia to an interested and receptive audience which included Ford Foundation Vice President Forrest P. Hill, Dr. George Gant and Dr. David Fanner of the Ford Foundation; and Mr. Boyd Compton, Dr. Art Mosher, Dr. A. H. Moseman, and Dr. William Spencer of the Rockefeller Foundation. In his report to the University Council, Romulo commented on the experience, "As usual, I received encouraging words of support for the University, and even words of praise for what has been done along the lines of growth and new purposes in the last two years."

On July 2, Romulo concluded his campaign for funds to support the University development plan. In closing his report to the University Council, he once again referred to his relation to the faculty: "To go out on a fund-raising trip is always wearisome to the body, and often worrying to the mind, but the assurance that I had the Faculty's confidence had made it infinitely a lighter task."[88]

Matching Hindsight with Foresight

President Romulo again stood before the University Council at its 230th meeting on August 18, 1966, to review the past and look to the future of the University of the Philippines.[89]

The penetrating studies conducted by the faculty contained in the report of the *ad hoc* committees, which had led to the rediscovery of the University, had riveted the consciousness in the academic community to the social, economic and cultural ferment in the nation. The liberal impulses of the University could not remain aloof to what was going on in the rest of the country. As Romulo had put it: "We knew that the situation called for bigness in conception and imagination and ambition but we were willing to risk the dangers of our dream and we assumed its concomitant responsibility."

From its inception, the 1963 to 1968 development program of the University had never been regarded as sacrosanct. It was subjected to critical review and evaluation with the intention of creating the opportunity "to do some re-thinking or revising or modifying not only of the goal we set but also of the scheduled sequence of phases indicated in the plan."[90]

Romulo reminded the University Council that the Program aimed at nothing less than to make the University of the Philippines "the best University for the Filipino." Toward the fulfillment of this objective, the Program concentrated effort on seven major areas. These were: (1) the shift from undergraduate to graduate instruction; (2) the sustained expansion of research; (3) the widening of community service rendered by the University for the benefit of the nation; (4) the upgrading of faculty salaries and the elevation of faculty competence; (5) the continuing increase of the financial resources of the University; (6) the development of the University's physical plant; and (7) the streamlining of the administration not only for the reduction of costs, but also for the elimination of red tape, the simplification of administrative procedures, the effective control in the expenditure of resources, and the greater autonomy of the colleges in development planning and in securing external assistance for development.[91]

Goals Accomplished

The biggest strides were taken toward the upgrading of faculty competence and the raising of faculty salaries. In 1962, a total of 70 faculty members were abroad working for advanced degrees. This grew to 305 in 1966, and the cumulative total from 1962 to 1966 was 655. As of July 1966, more than 70 had returned with the Ph.D. degree and 82 with the Master's degree. The cost of this undertaking was defrayed mostly by grants given by the Rockefeller, Ford and Asia Foundations and by the Agency for International Development of the United States government.

In 1962, the starting pay of an instructor was ₱3,480 a year and that of a full professor was ₱8,100.[92] Under the Five-Year Development Program, it was planned to increase this by 50 per cent by 1968. However, in 1966, the pay of faculty members had been increased by 32.8 per cent over the 1962 level. This meant that the starting annual pay of an Instructor had gone up to ₱4,623 and the maximum annual salary of a full professor had become ₱13,800. At this point, Romulo broke the good news to the University Council. The faculty would get the projected increase in pay of 50 per cent over the 1962 salary scale not in 1968 but as of January 1, 1967. If the Board of Regents approved the new salary scale, Instructors would receive an annual salary of ₱5,220 to ₱6,660; Assistant Professors, ₱7,440 to ₱9,120; Associate Professors, ₱9,840 to ₱11,400; and Professors, ₱12,120 to ₱14,880.

The University's physical plant had been expanded.[93] In the first four years of the Five-Year Development Program, an annex to the College of Dentistry, a building for the College of Fisheries, the Abelardo Hall for the College of Music, the University Gymnasium, the facilities for the Institute of Geodesy and Photogrammetry in the east wing of the College of Engineering building, and the new auditorium for the UP College in Baguio had been constructed.

Out of the proceeds of the loan granted by the International Bank for Reconstruction and Development, 18 new buildings would be constructed and equipped at a cost of ₱29,753,000. Two new dormitories for men and the International Center had been built on the campus in Diliman. At Vinzons Hall, student offices were renovated and additional rooms were built. A new restaurant, the Drive-in Canteen, was constructed near the swimming pool, the cafeteria in each of the residence halls had been renovated, and canteens for students in the various colleges had been opened. Roofed walks had also been constructed leading to the University Library. The 250 houses under the five-year faculty housing program had been built and the area had been landscaped.

In the name of extension service under the Five-Year Development Program, the University employed its faculty and used its resources in continuing professional education in national and community projects and in specialized key governmental activities.[94] In addition, the University operated programs, such as the Institute for Small-Scale Industries, the Asian Labor Education Center, the UP-Wisconsin Program in Development Economics, the Institute for Services to Education for the development of graduate programs in the College of Engineering, the Inter-University

Program in Business Administration, the Law Center, the Science Education Center, the Population Institute and the Philippine Executive Academy.

The University had renewed the contract of the UP-Cornell Graduate Education Program, and it had supported the operation of the Extension Service of the College of Forestry, the Dairy Training and Research Institute, as well as the training programs for organizers of cooperatives, rural bankers and organizers for non-cooperative enterprises. As of August 1966, 35 members of the University faculty were dôing full or part-time work in key positions in agencies of the government, and 11 were in foreign agencies.

Looking toward the Future

When President Romulo turned to the decade of the '70s and on the year 2000, he said: "We believe, for instance, that the University as it is now would not be able to fully and adequately fulfill the needs of 1970 or the year 2000 A.D."[95]

Since scholarship and creative thought and research would be impossible in a squalid milieu, and since the life of ideas would be incapable of being sustained by leaking faucets or eternally dry plumbing, by poor ventilation and an electrical system that went off and on and caused brownouts in the University campus, by a sewerage system so old it could not be anything but a disgrace, then community development and physical plant would become a matter for immediate concern. The University, therefore, projected a plan for campus and physical plant development. This included the modernization of the sewerage system, the construction of buildings to house new or still to be established units and to accommodate much-needed classrooms, the building of new dormitories adequate for the University to maintain a residential campus for 4,000 to 5,000 students, and the installation of a modern telephone and electrical system.

Research being central to the teaching function of the University, the University would continue to strive toward the ideal situation where the teacher would not merely be a passive disseminator but an active discoverer of new knowledge.[96] Faculty members would therefore be supported as they work for advanced degrees abroad. They would likewise be given grants to do research, to write as well as observe anywhere in the Philippines and in any part of the world where their scholarly interests might lie. The aim here was nothing less than the strengthening of the curricular offerings of the University. But President Romulo had something more grand in his vision:

> By 1970, the University must be prepared to offer a full-scale program of graduate and post-graduate studies, and the program itself conducted by Filipino teachers and experts. This calls for nothing less than the nationalization, as it were, of knowledge. Expertise and competence need not be exclusively based, for us, in American universities, but should be made available here, promoted by Filipino scholarship, Filipino discipline, Filipino passion for truth.[97]

ROMULO'S FAREWELL TO ARMS

IN 1968 Carlos P. Romulo came to the end of his term as President of the University of the Philippines. He thought that was also a good time to end his career in the public service.

At the 770th meeting of the Board of Regents of the University, President Romulo who was presiding in his concurrent capacity as Secretary of Education, informed the Board that his term as President of the University would end on May 31 and that he had decided to retire from public service effective June 1, 1968, to close his career in government which had begun in 1918 in the Bureau of Commerce and Industry.[98]

Relentless Social Change

On that May morning, he presented to the Board a prepared statement entitled "After Fifty Years."[99] He was looking back over the past five decades, and he was accepting the inevitability of change.

> It has been a lifework subsumed by great events, not the least of which is our own people's ceaseless struggle for freedom and search for well-being in a continually changing world. It is not weariness that informs our leave-taking after such an experience, but it is, rather, utter humility before the inexorable, in the face of intransigent change.[100]

However, he was not one to bewail the changes which had occurred in the University. Toward the end of his statement, he said:

> The University of the Philippines is one area where, in the view of some, the focus may have altered in recent years. I refer to some criticism levelled at our studentry and our professoriate, of the activism of the one and the dissent of the other. I make special reference to this as I take my leave because I consider it important. For were this not the case, we should have real cause for worry. The University's vigor, and indeed its very life, is in its ability and potential for dialogue on such themes and issues that are vital to the nation. By its very

> nature, knowledge is crucial and is the fiscalizer that questions and doubts, that searches and discovers, only to question and doubt once more. This is as it has been, and I bow out, as it were, within full sight and hearing of the throb and hum of an academic machine in high gear, a power plant generating that force, that electricity, which brings light to every dark corner of our lives.[101]

Student Activism, Faculty Dissent

As an outgoing President of the University, he had no doubt that after his departure the University would go on as vigorously as before. To prove his point, he called attention to the activism of the students and the dissent of the faculty. These in themselves were important, he said, for without them, the University of the Philippines would be nothing.

Romulo was not to have his pleasure and pride "to watch that great tasks continue to be accomplished in the workshops of the word and thought where his modest skills had been put to the test in their time."[102] He retired from the meeting to enable the Regents to deliberate on his decision to retire from the government effective June 1, 1968. Regent Eva Estrada Kalaw took over as temporary presiding officer. Copies of the Board's Resolution of June 14, 1961, fixing the tenure of the President and the members of the faculty of the University were distributed together with the signed appeals of the faculty and the resolution of the Executive Committee of the University Council petitioning the Board of Regents to extend a second appointment to Romulo as President of the University.

Regents' Avowal of Confidence

Regent Eva Estrada Kalaw drew the attention of the Board to the fact that Romulo's 70th birthday would fall on January 14, 1969. She said that the Board had been called upon to decide whether it would accept Romulo's application for retirement or extend his term to the age of 70, which would be in accordance with the Board's resolution of June 14, 1961. The provisions of Republic Act No. 3963 which amended the Charter of the University, empowered the Board of Regents to extend the tenure of faculty members to the age of 70 years. The Board, with the approval of the President of the Philippines, could also extend the term of the President of the University to the age of seventy.

In accordance with the Board's Resolution of June 14, 1961, and Republic Act No. 3963, as well as the signed appeals of the faculty and the Executive Committee of the University Council, the Board of Regents, on motion of Regent Rafael M. Salas, *unanimously resolved* to extend the

Presidency of Romulo to his 70th birthday on January 14, 1969. The Secretary of the University then fetched President Romulo from his office, and Regent Kalaw informed him, upon his return to the meeting, of the Board's decision to keep him in office until his next birthday.[103]

While Romulo gratefully acknowledged the decision of the Board of Regents, he reiterated his wish to retire, but he would defer to the expressed desire of the Board. Pleading that he had made commitments that he could not but respect, such as his attendance at a conference of former presidents of the United Nations General Assembly which would be held in Yugoslavia in June 1968, he asked that he be allowed to go on leave for three months. The Board assured him that it would discuss the matter if he formally presented his request for leave of absence. When interviewed by the *Philippine Collegian*, Romulo insisted that his decision to retire from the government was irrevocable but that he could not just ignore the unanimous resolution of the Executive Committee of the University Council.

President Emeritus

Nevertheless, Romulo did not serve the extended portion of his tenure. On December 20, 1968, he informed the Board of Regents at its 777th Meeting that his retirement as approved by the Government Service Insurance System took effect on November 30, that his terminal leave began on December 1, and that he had designated an officer-in-charge of the Office of the President of the University.[104]

After he had left the meeting, the Board approved on motion of Regent Pio Pedrosa a resolution conferring on President Romulo "the lifetime honor and title of President Emeritus." The citation ran as follows:

> In recognition of invaluable services rendered the University of the Philippines during his tenure, setting a remarkable pace of progress for more than six years unequalled in the history of this institution of higher learning, and through vigorous leadership impressing upon the scholarly mind the exacting demands of excellence to spur both the faculty and the studentry to unparalleled endeavor in the quest for knowledge.[105]

Regent Pedrosa explained that the title of President Emeritus conferred neither academic nor administrative power on the recipient and entailed no duties and responsibilities. It was an honorary title. Its sole intention was "to clothe the retiring President with a measure of academic dignity—dignity but not authority—so that he can render such voluntary service as he can give the University during his remaining years with the knowledge that he still belongs to the University community."[106]

The Board of Regents elected Romulo's successor at a special meeting called for that purpose on December 23, 1968.[107] In the afternoon of January 23, 1969, while he watched, his successor took the oath of office as President of the University of the Philippines in appropriate rites presided over by the President of the Philippines at Malacañang Palace.[108] President Emeritus Romulo then moved on to other posts in the service of the government.

The Passing of the Old Order

Carlos P. Romulo's Presidency had already ended long before January 23, 1969, when his successor was sworn into office, even before December 23, 1968, when the Board of Regents elected his successor, and indeed even before November 30, 1968, his last day as President of the University of the Philippines. As a matter of fact, it would be impossible to fix a precise date. It might be easier to say that the Romulo Presidency began coming to a close as the year 1968 wore on. And President Romulo saw the end coming with the passing of the old order in the University of the Philippines.

On Monday, July 1, 1968, at the traditional exercises to open the new academic year, President Romulo had proclaimed 1968-1969 "The Year of Enlightened Activism."[109] He recalled that student demonstrations, picketing, pamphleteering had been student-organized activities in the University since 1918, and he stressed his judgment that these had already become part of the University's tradition.

He told his audience which had filled the University Theater that what the UP was then facing was the second phase of the student movement which he called "enlightened activism." This, he explained, was nothing less than the freedom to decide on issues and evaluate decisions in terms of interests that did not necessarily subvert the general welfare, even when these decisions and evaluations negated tradition or introduced ideas radically new to the culture.

Enlightened Activism Takes Over

At the end of that July, UP students took to the streets to oppose the Second Philippine Civil Action Group bill then being discussed by the Congress of the Philippines. Under the sponsorship of such UP student groups as the Student Council, the *Philippine Collegian*, the Katipunang Makabansa, Kalayaan, Pagkakaisa, and Partisans, the rally drew 14 busloads of students to the Congress building.[110] The students in UP Los Baños rose up in protest when the suspension of classes which would have permitted them to join the rally in Congress was suddenly rescinded.[111]

Another grouping of UP student organizations—the Samahan ng Demokratikong Kabataan (SDK), the Student Cultural Association of UP (SCAUP), and the Kabataang Makabayan (KM)—prepared to join a massive demonstration on August 16 at Malacañang and the American Embassy to protest the so-called Special Relations between the Philippines and the United States.[112] The demonstration was carried out as planned on August 16. The Manila Police and the Metropolitan Command (Metrocom) dispersed the students massed in front of the embassy grounds. At least five UP students and one worker suffered bruises in what might well be the first violent student demonstration in Manila.[113]

Closer to home, the *Collegian* asked in an editorial, "Has DOW Chemicals brought the Vietnam war to the campus?"[114] The reason for the editorial was the contract entered into by DOW with the College of Forestry for the use of an area in the Makiling National Park in Los Baños for testing chemical defoliants. To be tested was Tordon-Brushkiller, which was described as a pellet-type substance more deadly than the powder type defoliant. The Tordon-Brushkiller was absorbed into the soil and thence into the roots of trees and such plants as garden beans, soybeans, potatoes and manioc. The head of the Los Baños unit of the University replied to the *Collegian* editorial by saying that their researches had political implications. "But as scientists," he stressed, "our interests are for knowledge."[115] The protest put the scientists in Los Baños in a most unfavorable light. The President ended the whole noisy affair by rescinding the agreement with DOW Chemicals.

The Dream Romulo Left Behind

Another big blow came in the form of a letter from Senator Lorenzo M. Tañada, the head of the organization known as the Movement for the Advancement of Nationalism (MAN), protesting the undue Americanization of the University of the Philippines.[116] The specifications of such a charge included discrimination against Filipino members of the faculty who got less pay and poorer housing than the Americans teaching in the University, the curtailment of nationalist expression, the propagation of anti-nationalist causes, the tying up of UP funds in the implementation of American "aid" projects and programs.

Romulo answered the letter which Tañada had released to the press, but the hurt had been inflicted, for what MAN had attacked and held up to public ridicule was an important component of the Five-Year Development Plan—the help the University had solicited and obtained from American governmental agencies and private foundations to support faculty fellowships in the United States, staff housing in Los Baños and Diliman, local scholarships for junior faculty members, physical plant expansion, and the like.

President Romulo had insisted on making the UP "the best University for the Filipino people," giving it a nationalist and an Asian orientation. At the same time, however, he had sought to upgrade the competence of the faculty by sending them to schools in the United States and by welcoming American professors to the University of the Philippines. To the men of MAN this was nothing more than blatant Americanization. Romulo argued that this was to the interest of the University, and he insisted that the nationalist impulse had given this its impetus.

By this time, President Romulo knew that the time to go had arrived, and he went, leaving behind a UP that was uniquely Filipino in its orientation yet manifestly American in its academism. In all the years of his Presidency he did endeavor to give, and he was confident he had indeed given, the University the resources and intellectual power to decide for itself, to build its own splendid academism. That was his dream.

X

Lopez's Beleaguered Tenure (1969-1975)

Barricades on Campus at the Peak of Student Discontent

by Oscar L. Evangelista

Lopez's Beleaguered Tenure

"The true mark of a guerrillero is instinct, pure instinct. All you need to be a good guerrillero is a good pair of legs. Keep running, that's all. General Romulo here was a good guerrillero who knew how to run away from danger. *S.P. also had a good pair of legs, but he was running in the opposite direction.* (Underscoring ours.) Safe in the foreign service, why, he came in with all the enthusiasm, zeal and dedication of a loyal alumnus to serve the University. As a veteran of Bataan and Corregidor, he must have known that there was an ambuscade somewhere waiting for him. Notwithstanding which he went in."[1]*

AN ambuscade it was as Salvador P. Lopez "exchanged the problems of the world for the problems of the campus"[2] when he took over the presidency of the University on January 23, 1969 amidst a Philippine society going through a period of ferment and radical change. As the eleventh President of the University, he was to survive the ambuscade and steer the University through its most tumultuous years, keeping it intact despite the challenges of student activism and the declaration of martial law.

The first three years of his presidency was a period of trial, testing and survival, with the University's energies spent living with, and reacting to, student-faculty activism; the remainder of his term was essentially a period of growth and development despite the restrictions of martial law.

Successor to Romulo

Salvador P. Lopez was elected President of the University on December 23, 1968. He was selected from an original list of 21 names earlier nominated by an *ad hoc* committee of the Board of Regents to consider the selection of a university president. Carlos P. Romulo had earlier declared his intention to retire in January 1969, making the selection of his successor an urgent matter. Of the seven finalists, Lopez garnered the majority vote, with two other nominees getting one vote each.

S.P. Lopez came to the position an outsider, having spent 23 years of his life in the diplomatic service. His UP connection dated back to 1927, when he enrolled as a freshman in the College of Liberal Arts, majoring in

*Footnote references are compiled in the NOTES section at the end of this book.

English, with political science as his minor subject. Even as a freshman, he began publishing short stories and articles in the *Philippines Free Press* and the *Tribune.* He eventually became a member and later president of the Writers' Club, editor-in-chief of the *Literary Apprentice,* dramatic critic and later city editor of the *Philippine Collegian,* and president of the Philosophy Club. He earned his Ph.B. degree in 1931, and then his M.A. in Philosophy in 1933 with "The Social Philosophy of Trinidad H. Pardo de Tavera"[3] as his thesis. His last connection with the university was as Instructor in English in 1941.

From Journalism to Diplomacy

As an outsider looking in, he therefore had a fresh view of the problems of the University unfettered by political ties with any one group on campus. His reputation as a liberal was well established. His book, *Literature and Society,* won the Commonwealth Literary Award in 1941, and was, according to S.P. Lopez, in itself "an intellectual autobiography showing the main strands" of his "emotional and mental attitudes" and philosophy of life.[4] As a newspaperman, who worked as a reporter, daily columnist and later as associate editor and editorial writer (1933-1941) of the *Philippines Herald,* he demonstrated his liberalism and critical-mindedness, for instance expressing concern in his column over the growing stature and political power of President Manuel Quezon.

His liberal spirit was further nurtured in the various positions he held in the diplomatic service, from technical adviser to the Philippine Mission to the United Nations in 1946, to Chief of Mission in France, United States, and the United Nations, and then Secretary of Foreign Affairs. He held wide-ranging positions in the diplomatic service, from representing the Philippines in various committees and agencies of the United Nations to attending international conferences in which the participation of the Philippines was crucial. He drafted UNESCO's resolution on human rights.

S.P. Lopez, the humanist and consummate diplomat, accepted the presidency of the University as a call of duty and vowed to make UP "an institution more hospitable to the positive idealism of our youth, and more relevant to the true priorities of our national life, an instrument more responsive to the irrepressible clamor of our people for the rapid transformation of our society so that all may enjoy the blessings of a better life in larger freedom."[5]

Defining the University Goals

As he started his presidential term, Lopez was fully sympathetic to the growing role of the youth in aspiring for change and the people's desire for the transformation of society. He had then committed the University to the guiding principles of *relevance* and *social transformation.* Like all his predecessors in the presidency, Lopez recognized the importance of academic excellence to the role of the University "in the search for truth and tireless pursuit of knowledge."[6]

These goals he would reaffirm, seven months after he assumed office, during his inauguration as President of the University. His determination heightened by the developments that had taken place during those seven months, he stressed further the role of the University as a social critic and as an active agent for change. He likewise viewed the University as a major instrument for national development.

Lopez was the first President to live in the Executive House, to make himself more readily available to his constituency. Lopez had barely begun familiarizing himself with the University when the University Student Council, and the Council of Leaders representing 49 campus organizations, presented him with demands, which represented sore points with, and problems left behind by, the Romulo administration. The demands and the first confrontation of Lopez with student power were symptomatic of the trend that the University would be experiencing for the next three years. President Lopez had come face to face with student activism.

Confrontation with Student Activists

Overt student unrest had surfaced in the mid-60s. It started as an ideological movement influenced largely by the nationalism of Recto. The issues centered on the American domination of Philippine economy, US military bases in the Philippines, parity rights, etc.

Students of the University of the Philippines were at the forefront of early student demonstrations. The Student Cultural Association of the University of the Philippines (SCAUP), the Kabataang Makabayan (KM), formed in 1964 by a UP student and later Instructor, Jose Ma. Sison, and the UP Student Council led demonstrations against the Vietnam War and the Philippine participation in that war, oil monopolies, implementation of the retail trade nationalization law, and American imperialism. When US President Lyndon B. Johnson attended the Manila Summit to try to influence Asian countries to support American presence in Vietnam, the first massive demonstration took place at the Luneta. By then, the tide of student activism had become world-wide, set by the patterns of American and European universities where demonstrations, teach-ins. and cupation" of university buildings had become commonplace.

During the last years of the Romulo administration, the target of the activists was the alleged "Americanization" of the University coupled with other local issues easily grasped by the studentry.

The wide-ranging issues raised in the 77 demands represented a cross-section of student, faculty and non-academic personnel concerns. For the students, interest centered on control over student funds and publications, recognition of all university and college organizations, release of government funds for the construction and improvement of some academic buildings, the move to make faculty advisorship of campus organizations and publications optional. The faculty was concerned with security of tenure. The non-academic personnel advocated security of tenure, improved housing conditions, and increased salaries. Issues of general concern were the revision of the University Code and the University charter to do away with their colonial orientation, termination of contracts with the allegedly CIA-backed Asia Foundation, a medical program for the community, and allowing access to official documents upon request of interested parties.

Dissatisfaction with Previous Administration

The demands brought to the surface the students' impatience with the University Council Committee on Student Organizations and Activities (UCCSOA), the handling of student activities by Dean of Student Affairs Crisolito Pascual, the powerful role played by Iluminada Panlilio in the Romulo administration, the "incompetence" of some faculty members, the police and military presence on campus, and the more ideological issue of the colonial nature of the University. Heretofore, these issues were held sacrosanct and considered beyond the jurisdiction of students.

The movement to present the "state of the University" to the new President was started by the Committee on Public and National Affairs of the University Student Council and quickly snowballed into a university affair as student organizations of all persuasions saw their chance to present their demands. The participation of some faculty members and the non-academic sector gained more ground for the movement, for the first time uniting the three sectors of the University in a common undertaking.

Lopez's diplomatic background was immediately put to a test when he began an eight-hour period of negotiating with the students who presented him with 77 demands on the evening of January 30th. At one point in the discussion, the group led by the *Kabataang Makabayan* virtually gave the President an ultimatum on the immediate resolution of the demands, and threatened to lead a University strike. The group walked out of the discussions, but not before the President reminded them that while it was their right to call a strike, the University would not tolerate any act of violence leading to destruction of property or injury to persons.[7] As consensus emerged on some of the issues, he prevailed upon the remaining students to pare down the list to the most urgent issues, a move which the students promptly complied with as they came back the next day with the demands reduced to 18.

Assertions of Student Power

On January 31, the KM/SCAUP-led activist groups started the general strike by stopping vehicles at University Avenue and asking students to join in the protest. The initial move did not succeed and led to the arrest of five students by Quezon City policemen for obstructing traffic.

The student leaders decided on a boycott of classes that afternoon. But the general strike did not gain headway until Tuesday, February 4. The day before, Lopez issued Executive Order No. 1 giving greater autonomy to all student organizations in the handling of funds collected by the University, lifting on a case-to-case basis existing restraints on student organizations, and making optional the appointment of faculty advisers for student organizations and publications.

The fact that President Lopez's first Executive Order dealt with student autonomy showed a sensitive understanding and recognition of the students' desire to run their own affairs, subject to certain constraints. This order also contained implicit recognition that freedom must be met with responsibility: the supplemental order to Executive Order No. 1 issued on February 5 assumed that student organizations would adopt appropriate measures and set up the necessary machinery for self-government and discipline.

President Marcos Takes a Hand

On the afternoon of February 4, President Marcos himself came to the University and dialogued with the student leaders. He was able to resolve student demands involving the release of funds by the national government by ordering the immediate release of ₱3 million for the Philippine General Hospital; ₱1.5 million for the Natural Science Research Council building; ₱300,000 for the Institute of Mass Communication building; and ₱1 million for the retirees. President Marcos also committed himself to the release of ₱9 million for the operation of the University.

The visit of President Marcos was unique because it was the first presidential visit since the late President Quezon came to the University to discuss vital matters of state with the students and faculty. As reported by Lopez to the Board of Regents, "the dialogue was conducted with candor and firmness on the part of the protest groups, but equally with abiding respect for the office and person of President Marcos."[8]

Between the actions taken by President Marcos and Lopez, the 18 demands of the students were substantially met. Student autonomy was granted; Miss Iluminada Panlilio had gone on leave; Dean Crisolito Pascual resigned effective the end of the semester; all documents, papers and books of accounts of the University were opened to all parties with legitimate interest; some funds were released; deans and directors were ordered to recommend eligible faculty members for permanent appointment; an agreement was forged with Mayor Norberto Amoranto that the Quezon City police would not enter the campus without any written request from the University. Other issues were placed under study, notably the contracts with the Asia Foundation, with a view to terminating some of the projects being funded by this agency.

More Campuses Involved in Protests

The resolution of the outstanding issues did not end the strike. While the students gave their approval to the measures taken on their demands, the protest continued in sympathy with UP Los Baños students who came up with their own demands, and with other colleges having their own grievances. Students in the UP branch in Iloilo also joined the fray. The downtown universities, Far Eastern University, Lyceum of the Philippines, San Beda and La Salle staged their own strikes on such issues as lowering of tuition fees, demand for readmission of students arbitrarily dismissed, press freedom and student rights.

Between February 5 and 12, Lopez helped in negotiating the settlement of the UP College of Agriculture strike; met with the UP Prep Student Council which demanded a permanent school site; and averted a walkout by draftsmen and utility men in the Physical Plant Office who were demanding the ouster of Director Romeo Tomacruz. By February 12, the last striking group returned to resume classes.

The 77 demands and the first University strike set the tone for the next three years. For the students, it was an initial victory which would be followed by more demonstrations, teach-ins, boycotts. Issues of local and national concerns were freely ventilated in the pages of the *Philippine Collegian* and in other student publications. Faculty members were no less active in the progressive movement. The *Samahan ng Guro sa Pamantasan ng Pilipinas* (SAGUPA), among others, joined student groups in protest movements and the clamor for reforms.

As even the once-guarded privilege of the University to recognize the existence of student groups was replaced on May 29, 1969 by merely asking any student group wishing to make use of University facilities to register their organization with the Office of Student Affairs, student organizations proliferated as a necessary concomitant of student autonomy. Only where national student organizations with members from UP wanted the use of campus facilities was the approval of the University President needed.

Proliferation of Militant Groups

The campuses of the University became the home of different organizations of all kinds of persuasion and ideology, whose influence was nation-wide in scope. The most active was the national democratic front led by the SCAUP – KM – SDK (Samahan ng Demokratikong Kabataan), referred to as the "Maoist" group since its ideological model was Mao-Tse-Tung's leadership in transforming Chinese society. The Maoist's rival group, the BRPF (Bertrand Russell Peace Foundation) and the MPKP (Malayang Pagkakaisa ng Kabataang Pilipino) purported to be under "Russian" influence, drew their support from the old Communist Party of the Philippines. The moderates, coming from some fraternity groups like the Upsilon Sigma Phi and other campus organizations, were linked nation-wide with either the National Union of Students of the Philippines (NUSP) or the National Students' League (N.S.L.) By November 1969, an umbrella organization of student groups from different universities and colleges had been formed under the auspices of the Steering Committee of the Election Protest Movement of UP, to be later known as the Movement for a Democratic Philippines (M.D.P.).

The call of the times was active involvement, and the cry was "serve the people." Linking up with labor unions, workers and peoples' groups in mass action was common fare, where clenched fists went with shouts of "*Makibaka, huwag matakot*" (Dare to struggle, don't be afraid). UP students were out in the streets either denouncing American imperialism or supporting striking workers' groups. It was not uncommon to see groups of students in the lobbies and hallways discussing issues of the day among themselves.

Student Pressure to Oust a Dean

This was the milieu within which the Lopez administration and the University operated as the schoolyear 1969-1970 was ushered in. Militancy and radicalization was further boosted by the election of Fernando Barican as Chairman of the Student Council, and the selection of Victor Manarang as editor-in-chief of the *Philippine Collegian.*[9]

Barely sworn into office, the Barican Council supported the strike in the College of Education seeking the ouster of Dean Felixberto Sta. Maria for inaction on student demands. Faced by a University-wide boycott which threatened to spread outside of Diliman, President Lopez on July 23, 1969 transferred Dean Sta. Maria to the Office of the President as Special Assistant with the rank of Dean, involving no reduction in salary. This decision was sustained by the Board of Regents.

Dean Sta. Maria protested the transfer, raised the question of "rule of law" and accused President Lopez of "rule of mob."[10] In his defense, Lopez cited the existence of an emergency situation which compelled him to act so as to protect and preserve the University.

Even as the faculty became divided on the issue, Sta. Maria elevated his case to the Supreme Court which subsequently ruled in his favor.[11] He was reinstated but decided instead to retire from the University.

Collegian Intensifies Nationalist Drive

Meanwhile, the *Philippine Collegian* under Victor Manarang committed itself to the nationalist progressive line, and inaugurated issues published in Pilipino or Pilipino-English combined.[12] It exposed the plight of the *sacadas* of sugarlandia; supported the striking personnel of Pantranco, San Miguel Corporation and New Frontier theater, sponsored the presidential election boycott and condemned the electoral frauds.

Before 1969 ended, a rally against the visit of then US Vice-President Spiro Agnew on December 29 sparked another bloody confrontation between the police forces and the students, setting the stage for the second major crisis to be faced by the Lopez administration.

FROM THE FIRST-QUARTER STORM TO THE BARBED WIRE OF AROUSED STUDENT ACTIVISM

THE events of the first quarter of the year 1970 have been romanticized by militant groups as the "first quarter storm." Amidst police brutality, the rise of fascism and militarism, American imperialism and militant nationalism, the militant students ushered in the "second propaganda movement of the nationalist struggle" through the *Philippine Collegian.* The *Collegian's* first issue for the year had an 8-page supplement which carried militant articles such as those of Jose Ma. Sison on "Student Power," Eleanor Gomez-Palma on "A Teacher's Open Letter to a Revolutionary Youth," Bertrand Russell's "Towards a New International," and Ernesto "Che" Guevara's "The Human Factor in a Socialist Society."[13]

The impending storm was building up as UP students returned to the campus in January 1970 after the Christmas break. The arrest and detention for eight hours of three student leaders, Renato Ciria Cruz, Gary Olivar and Jorge Sibal during the anti-Agnew rally and the brutality of the truncheon-wielding Manila police rookies brought nearer home the growing state power and what the militant students called the "militarization" of society.

Testing the President's Mettle

Teach-ins were held and a convocation on the "rise of fascism" followed at the Arts and Sciences theater where Sibal and Olivar, among others, spoke. As the University Student Council, the SDK, the Arts and Sciences

Council, and about 50 faculty members led by Dean Cesar A. Majul, through their declaration of concern, reacted to the "repressive tolerance towards organized dissent,"[14] student leaders suddenly became critical of President Lopez, first, for allegedly refusing to sign a faculty declaration denouncing police brutality; secondly, for "praising" the ground rules to maintain peace during student demonstrations which resulted from a meeting attended by the President and some UP student leaders with Mayor Antonio Villegas of Manila (the students felt that the ground rules favored the police rather than the students); thirdly, for issuing two memoranda on "Guidelines on Student Demonstrations" stating that participation in mass actions be on a voluntary basis, that classes would not be suspended unless ordered by his office, and that coercive measures should not be countenanced; and a circular suggesting that the Dean of Student Affairs be officially informed in writing of any "demonstrations, rally or picket organized by UP students at least one day before it takes place, so that appropriate measures can be taken."[15]

Until this time Lopez had enjoyed a relatively high rating among student leaders.[16] Suddenly, he was the object of a picket in front of the Oblation, the beginning of a "strained" relationship between the administration and the militant students.

On the day of the picket (January 7), the students staged a boycott of their classes beginning at 1 p.m. in Diliman and some Manila units, and thereafter proceeded to the different colleges in Diliman inviting students to join a mass rally that afternoon in front of Malacañang to denounce police brutality. A number of UP students responded, joined by students from other universities, in staging the rally without any outbreak of violence.

Involvement in National Issues

Meanwhile, preparations were being made for the holding of a mass rally and demonstration in time for the opening of the new Congress on January 26, 1970. Sponsor of the rally was the National Union of Students of the Philippines headed by Edgar Jopson of the Ateneo de Manila. While the radicals were talking of revolution as evidenced by the "second propaganda movement," the N.U.S.P. and its affiliate organizations pinned their hopes on the holding of a non-partisan constitutional convention for the re-structuring of Philippine society. The target was the election (1971) of delegates to the constitutional convention, without the participation of political parties. That this was an idealistic dream was apparent from the very beginning because of the structure of party politics in the Philippines and the existence of family dynasties. Nevertheless, the January 26 rally was purposely timed to remind the legislators of an avenue for change still hoped for by the moderate groups. Although the leadership of the UP Student Council and the M.D.P. did not share this dream, the University was well represented in the rally, as were the other radical groups which were more interested in exposing the true state of the nation.

What started out as a peaceful demonstration of some 40,000 students (according to the *Philippines Herald)* turned into a bloody riot as a flying mock "coffin," a cardboard crocodile, rocks, sticks and other objects were thrown at President Marcos and party as they were leaving the halls of Congress. What followed was a violent confrontation between students and police that found students scampering in different directions but fighting back as they were relentlessly pursued by helmeted and truncheon-bearing policemen. Those apprehended were brought to the Manila City jail.

As expected the University Student Council called for a boycott of classes from January 27 to the end of the week. With vivid reporting from the mass media specially through television cameras, on the incident that occurred the night before, it was not difficult for the militant students to gain the spontaneous sympathy of the University constituency. Lopez told a group of some 500 students milling around the administration building that he would suspend classes the next day and call a meeting of the faculty to assess the situation. In a speech delivered that same evening at Centro Escolar University, President Lopez declared:

> . . . the night of January 26 must be regarded as a night of grave portent for the future of our nation. It has brought us face to face with the fundamental question: Is it still possible to transform our society by peaceful means so that the many who are poor, oppressed, sick and ignorant may be released from misery, by the actual operation of law and government, rather than by waiting in vain for the empty promise of "social justice" in our Constitution?[17]

Meanwhile, the students at that point had already set a bigger indignation rally for January 30 and were anxious to get faculty support for it.

Faculty Move to Support Students

The decision to call a faculty meeting came from many faculty members who went to see Lopez on the morning of January 27. The well-attended meeting, presided over by Lopez, gave birth to the Faculty Assembly as a forum for the discussion of relevant issues of University and national import. In that meeting, the following decisions were reached:

1. The faculty was to take a stand through the adoption of a resolution denouncing police brutalities committed against the students on January 26, 1970;

2. A faculty delegation was to be formed to present the resolution to President Marcos and Congress;

3. Faculty members were to be free to join other rallies and demonstrations;

4. Faculty members were to contribute at least one per cent of one month's salary for a Legal Defense Fund for use in defending any members of the University constituency arrested during a demonstration;

5. Faculty members were to conduct "teach-ins" on relevant issues and propose specific terms to attain social justice for the people.[18]

The Assembly named seven faculty members with Dean Cesar A. Majul as Chairman to draft a resolution for consideration by the whole assembly that same afternoon.[19]

Faculty Assembly's Declaration

Guided by certain points enunciated in the discussions, the Committee submitted the following declaration of concern which the Assembly approved by acclamation:

> We, the Faculty of the University of the Philippines, strongly denounce the use of brutal force by state authorities against the student demonstrators on January 26, 1970. We support unqualifiedly the students' exercise of democratic rights in their struggle for revolutionary change.
>
> It is with the gravest concern that the Faculty views the January 26 event as part of an emerging pattern of repression of democratic rights of the people. This pattern is evident in the formation of para-military units, such as the Home Defense Forces, the politicalization of the Armed Forces such as the National Defense College, the existence of private armies, foreign interference in internal security, and the use of specially trained police for purposes of suppression.
>
> We strongly urge that congressional and other investigations be so conducted and concluded as to reaffirm democratic principles. Under no condition must there be a repetition of the congressional investigation following the October 24, 1966 demonstration which turned into a veritable mockery of students' and citizens' rights.
>
> The Faculty holds the present administration accountable and responsible for the pattern of repression and the violation of rights. It expects full redress for all injuries suffered by the students.
>
> We call on the faculties of other universities, church leaders, peasants, workers, writers, and other sectors of our society to join us and the students in this struggle for liberty, justice, and national democracy.

The Assembly likewise decided to hold a peaceful demonstration the following day, January 29 in front of Malacañang and Congress.

The Faculty March was another historic first for the University. Meeting at the Agrifina Circle, faculty members from Diliman, Manila, Los Baños and Tarlac, with many non-academic personnel and students and a delegation from the Philippine Normal College, marched peacefully to Malacañang, with Lopez leading the group.[20]

Confrontation with President Marcos

What followed was a supposed "confrontation" between President Marcos supported by the highest officials of the Government, and the UP delegation composed of Lopez, 16 faculty members and 4 students. In the ensuing discussion, President Marcos demanded an explanation for the statements contained in the Declaration of the faculty, to which the UP side argued that the nature of the resolution was a declaration of concern rather than an accusation, that the faculty members were morally obliged to support their students on an issue deeply affecting their welfare, and that "the President of the Republic himself would be ashamed of them if they failed to speak up and assumed instead a posture of being intimidated."[21]

In the same report President Lopez said that the "meeting was a full, frank and cordial exchange of ideas and opinions" between an aggressive President and a firm but respectful UP group, both sides engaging themselves in a "wide-ranging discussion and hard-hitting dialogue of give-and-take."[22]

Reactions to the Faculty March and the "confrontation" with President Marcos varied. The Manila Press generally reported the incident as involving an angry President who chided, scolded, and lectured the intimidated UP group.[23]

S.G. Del Rosario, purported expert on communism, testified before the Joint Congressional Committee investigating student unrest that Lopez and the UP faculty could be charged for "inciting to sedition" based on his analysis of the UP Faculty's Declaration of Concern. He charged that the declaration had "identity with the 'programme' of the Maoist Communist Party of the Philippines."[24]

Appraisal of the Faculty March

The UP students were divided in their reaction to the March. The radical group charged the faculty with elitism as it wanted the faculty to join them in the January 30 rally. They showed their displeasure by going to Quezon Hall while the March was taking place, where they "turned the flag upside down, removed the plaque under the picture of Gen. Romulo, and covered the Oblation with a sack."[25]

Another group appreciated the move of the faculty and joined the March. Some members of the UP Student Council joined unofficially despite a disavowal by the Council of the March.

The January 30 rally in front of Congress started at 4 p.m. and ended peacefully after 5 p.m. Then a group started marching toward Malacañang and what followed was the storming of the gates of Malacañang, the spread of violence to Mendiola, Lepanto, the "University belt," and beyond. In the long drawn-out "battle" which raged the whole night, four students were killed, including Ricardo Alcantara, a UP freshman; 117 injured according to the *Herald,* and 293 arrested, including Fernando Barican; 131 were charged with sedition, according to the *Manila Times.*[26]

Student Militancy Gains Momentum

The militant UP students were in the thick of the fight as the radicals launched the "peoples' congress" (February 15 and 26), and the "peoples' marches" (March 3 and 17). The scenario was essentially the same, complete with a demonstration in front of the US Embassy and the inevitable military confrontation.

The people's marches inaugurated the strategy of hiking around Manila's populous streets denouncing fascism, feudalism and imperialism through banners, streamers, leaflets and bullhorns. Subsequently, it became a pattern to congregate in different areas of the City, march around the major streets and converge in a common place, usually Plaza Miranda.[27]

In March, Lopez submitted statements to the joint congressional committee to inquire into the causes of student unrest. A UP panel also submitted a position paper on points touched upon in the Faculty Declaration of Concern of January 28, 1970. Through the position paper, the UP panel was able to give concrete evidence in support of the Faculty Declaration regarding the pattern of repression. Documented were repression of the people's rights, American policy of counter-revolution, foreign interference in internal security, politicalization of the Armed Forces, formation of para-military units, special training of police forces for the purpose of suppression, and existence of private armies.

The academic year ended with the graduation of militant student leaders all of whom finished their courses with honors. Fernando Barican, Victor Manarang, Orlando Vea, Vicente Paqueo, Ericson Baculinao and Rafael Baylosis led other graduates in protest moves. Even invitations to join the prestigious Phi Kappa Phi Honor Society were turned down by some graduates as a protest against "bourgeois education" and "American cultural aggression." To secure the safety of the guest speaker, United Nations Secretary General U Thant, the University decided not to make him appear in the commencement rites.

Student Activists at the Helm

The election of Ericson Baculinao as Chairman of the Student Council and the selection of Ernesto Valencia as Editor-in-Chief of the *Collegian* for the academic year 1970-1971 heightened the hold of militant students on campus politics and portended bigger headaches and challenges for the Lopez administration. Local issues were given as much weight as national concerns as the *Collegian* and the Council protested what the student leaders contended were administration attempts to stifle the *Philippine Collegian.*

The administration supported a move made by leaders of Upsilon Sigma Phi Fraternity to call for a voluntary subscription to the student newspaper allegedly due to its biased political position[28] to which not all students adhered. The Council and the *Collegian* then supported the strike at the Philippine General Hospital in September which led to the creation of the Regents' Commission, which in turn became the body responsible for instituting reforms at the P.G.H. The students then confronted Lopez on October 5 with 57 new demands. What was termed by the Council as a "walk-out, occupation (of Quezon Hall), mass action"[29] was a move to "welcome" Lopez, who had just arrived from abroad, and to present him with their "state of the University" declaration.

The demands were apparently designed to "liberate the University" to "ultimately help in the emancipation of society."[30] Symbols like inverting the Philippine flag at the top of Quezon Hall and placing an Uncle Sam hat on the Oblation accompanied the alleged "occupation" as the dialogue was going on in the President's Office. The "57 demands" were grouped into five mass headings: democratization, Filipinization, academic affairs, student welfare, non-academic affairs and faculty welfare.

Demand for Reforms Intensified

The more substantive issues raised, reflective of the time, were those of Democratization and Filipinization. With regard to Democratization, the demand for equal faculty-student and non-academic personnel representation in the Board of Regents recognized and reiterated the need for a broader representation of the different constituencies in the highest governing body of the University. The proposal for the revision of the entrance examination by using Pilipino as medium of instruction was in line with the nationalist orientation. The demand for the election of the chairmen of departments by students and faculty also reflected a desire to have a wider role for students and faculty members in the selection of chairmen of departments and deans of academic units beyond mere nomination.

In relation to Filipinization, the proposal for the inclusion of 9 units of Pilipino in the General Education Program and the encouragement of the use of Pilipino as medium of instruction by initiating experimental classes using Pilipino in all subjects, were obviously meant to develop a nationalistic educational program.

The year ended with the traditional lantern parade assuming an activist line: "Parada sa Pakikibaka." Instead of the gaiety and laughter of past lantern parades, the tone of this parade was sombre. That one of the categories in giving awards was "militant interpretation of the theme" made this parade different. Aside from lanterns, there were more torches, adding a touch of "revolutionary" fervor to the activity.

From Blockades to Barricades

1971 came with the government's announcement of a gasoline price hike. This prompted workers, jeepney drivers and students to demonstrate. UP was again in the frontline as on January 11 some 200 to 300 students formed a "human barricade" at the intersection of University Avenue and Emilio Jacinto to stop cars and other vehicles from entering the campus in a show of unity with the striking jeepney drivers. They asked passengers of public utility vehicles and drivers of private automobiles "to walk to their destinations on campus showing their willingness to share the sacrifice imposed by the strike."[31]

Since University Avenue was a national road, Lopez requested the protestors to lift their barriers but they refused. Due to numerous complaints received from those who were inconvenienced by the blockade, the Quezon City Police and Metrocom soldiers came at around 11:30 a.m. and forcibly drove the students from their outpost. Lopez himself went to the checkpoint, interceded in behalf of the students, and succeeded in asking the police to withdraw but only after he had guaranteed full responsibility for peace and order.

The blockade continued for the rest of the day and the next, but the UP Security Guards were able to open the rear gate on the morning of January 12 making possible the flow of cars in and out of the campus.

On what would have been the third day of the blockade, the administration's decision to man the main entrances as early as 7 a.m. prevented the students from continuing with their blockade.

The jeepney strike lasted for two more days, but Diliman was spared from the blockade and more importantly, violence. UP Los Baños had a more violent confrontation with the police and a lengthier blockade (January 12-17) resulting in injuries to some students and the arrest of 49 persons.[32]

Skirmishes with the Police

The first jeepney strike left two legacies: it gave students a potent tool, the barricade, as a means of protest; and it was apparently the first instance in which the police forces had withdrawn voluntarily and peacefully from the campus.

The experience of the two-day blockade served as a "trial run" for the second round, when the students decided to put up a more massive human blockade on February 1, 1971, as the jeepney strike was resumed by the Pasang-Masda and Mapagsat, striking unions of jeepney drivers. National student organizations of moderate and progressive persuasions had earlier forged an agreement with the drivers' organizations that they would actively support the second strike. It was in this light that the student leaders started rallying students of the College of Arts and Sciences at around 9 a.m. of February 1 to join them in forming a human barricade at the entrance of the University to keep public vehicles from entering the campus, while a small contingent group manned the back gate at Katipunan road.

Shortly after 11:30 a.m., the UP Security Force arrived at the front barricade, allegedly on orders of President Lopez who, acting on complaints of faculty members wanted to see to it that private vehicles, specially those belonging to residents of the community, be allowed to enter. A scuffle with the students resulted when the security force refused the students' move to reinforce the left lane barricade with logs brought by a pick-up truck. Word about the scuffle spread to the College of Arts and Sciences and Vinzons Hall, prompting the arrival of more student reinforcements at the front barricade.

Tangling with an Irate Professor

While the student leaders were confronting the security guards, Prof. Inocente Campos of the Mathematics Department appeared on the scene. Professor Campos had previously established a reputation among the students for ignoring boycotts and continuing with his classes despite threats from boycotting groups. On three previous occasions (the January 26, 1970 demonstration; the P.G.H. rally on September 7, 1970; the December 4, 1970 rally condemning the death of a Philippine Science High School student Francis Sontillano), he tangled with students who wanted to get inside his classes to invite his students to join the respective rallies. He had also gained a reputation for carrying a gun since on one occasion, he fired three warning shots to drive the boycotting students out of his classroom. Despite his eccentricities (he was remembered for orating in faculty meetings), there was no question that he was a dedicated teacher. To him teaching was not only a public duty but a sacred duty as well.[33]

Professor Campos was on his way to the campus to conduct his classes after he called the University Secretary's office and received word that no order for the suspension of classes had been given.

As he entered the first checkpoint on University Avenue, he slowed down but was not blocked by the human barricades. Someone recognized him and soon pillboxes were thrown in the direction of his car. He continued driving but since a tire had been damaged, the car stopped. As students started advancing toward him, he went out of the car, put on a vest, got his shotgun from the back seat and tried to fire to scare the students, but the gun was jammed and did not go off. He then got his automatic .22 caliber rifle and started firing it, then drew his revolver and fired some more.[34] During a short lull, a Security Force jeep coming from the direction of the barricaded area sped toward Professor Campos, arrested him and brought him to the Quezon City police station.

As a result of the Campos incident, a student, Pastor Mesina Jr. was seriously wounded. He was taken to the UP Infirmary and later transferred to the Veterans' Memorial Hospital. He died four days later.[35] But more importantly, the incident was crucial in determining and influencing later developments in the University. For one thing, the students were to vent their ire over the incident on Lopez, with about 50 irate students storming Quezon Hall, shouting invectives at and berating the President. For another, it invited the entry of the Quezon City Police and Metrocom into the campus. From that point on, the issue was no longer the gasoline price increase but the military intrusion into the campus.

Police Intrusion Authorized

The burning of Professor Campos' car by the students, his subsequent arrest, and the complaints received at the Quezon City Police Department about the disorderly situation at the University made it imperative for the Quezon City Police to intervene, backed up by a decision made by the Peace and Order Council under the chairmanship of Secretary Vicente Abad Santos of the Department of Justice, for the Quezon City Police to enter the University. The meeting of the Peace and Order Council was called in the afternoon of February 1 to assess the situation in the University. Lopez, who was invited to the meeting, stressed that he would resist the entry of the police on campus, pointing to an earlier agreement forged between him and Mayor Amoranto during the first jeepney strike in January. The Council made it clear to Lopez that the laws took precedence over a mere agreement.

At 4:30 p.m. the Quezon City Police backed up by Metrocom troopers forcibly broke up the human barricade and pursued students fleeing toward the campus, apprehending 18 of them.

The confrontation between the students, the University administration, and police had begun and was to be repeated several times in the succeeding two days as the militant students defied the police intrusions, raised more barricades—this time physical rather than human, and took firmer control of the campus.

Students Battle Policemen and Soldiers

On February 2, the Quezon City Police and Metrocom again entered the campus to clear the national road of barricades and obstructions. Efforts made by the faculty delegation and later by Lopez himself to convince the police to withdraw and give the University authorities time to solve the problem proved to no avail as the Chief of Police of Quezon City gave an ultimatum, made a countdown, gave Lopez five minutes to go back to the students' line, broke through and went as far as the area in front of Quezon Hall.

Hundreds of retreating students went to the College of Arts and Sciences, which for the duration of the barricades, became the center of activities. Chairs, tables, benches, bulletin boards, etc., were used for barricading the area around Palma Hall.

The tense atmosphere extended to Kamia and Sampaguita Residence Halls due to their proximity to the College of Arts and Sciences. Late that afternoon, the two residence halls were assaulted by the police who apparently were in "hot pursuit" of male students who sought refuge there. The police lobbed tear gas cannisters into both residence halls, ordered the "refugees" to come out, with some policemen entering the buildings complete with gas masks and white helmets. About 50 students were arrested.

The "warlike" invasion of the University and the sensationalized media reporting of the incidents increased the sympathy of many sectors of the community for the barricaders.

Campus Completely Barricaded

On February 3 the campus assumed the appearance of an embattled area, with around 15 barricades spread all over the campus; those previously removed by the police were set up again. A community meeting called by Lopez in front of Palma Hall reached a decision to continue with the barricades as a manifestation of opposition to "militarization" and the "proposed closure" of the University. The meeting was, however, interrupted by the entry of the police. Commotion followed as more chairs were piled on top of the existing barricades. A delegation met the police forces and succeeded in negotiating their withdrawal on condition that faculty members would help direct vehicles at the entrance of the University.

Late that afternoon, Lopez prevailed upon President Marcos to withdraw the police forces from the campus on condition that the former would be held responsible for the situation. More time was then given to the UP administration to settle the question.

The developments from February 4 to 9 were inconsequential compared with the erupted events. Tension erupted now and then. Even after the official withdrawal of troops, fear of military attack continued. Helicopter teams kept a close watch from the air, prompting the students to improvise their "long-range missiles" (kuwitis) to scare the helicopters away. Sporadic gunfires could be heard from the rear of the campus.

High Spirits behind the Barricades

Within the barricaded areas, teach-ins and mass meetings were regularly held, while molotov cocktails and pillboxes were hand-made and stockpiled by the students. Student marshals took care of security because of constant fear of military assault. Thus the use of the password to cross a barricade, the setting up of self-igniting molotov cocktails to deter trespassers, and the close scrutiny of incoming vehicles on campus.

A food committee was set up under the president of UP Woman's Club and the Kamia Residence Hall Student Body Organization. From the evening of February 3 to the lifting of the barricades on the 9th, free food was served to the barricaders, funded by contributions from residents of the UP Community and by outsiders who responded to student appeals through Radio Patrol. A commandeered taxicab was used later for buying supplies and distributing food to the barricaders.

Despite the tension, there was an air of romanticism, adventurism, and "revolutionary fervor" as the barricaders "liberated" Palma Hall; renamed some buildings on campus after progressive leaders of the Left; set up the "Diliman commune"; took over DZUP; "liberated" the UP Press and published "Bandilang Pula"; splashed the Oblation with red paint; and displayed red flags on "liberated" buildings.

Barricaders in the Limelight

Reactions of the UP Community varied. Some faculty members openly supported and even influenced the decisions made by the barricaders. Others were sympathetic although they were inconvenienced by the barricades. Residents of Krus na Ligas and Area 11 were actively involved in the student cause.

On the other side of the spectrum were irate residents who condemned the barricades and criticized Lopez for not having coped more decisively with the situation. As the barricade reached its fifth day, many residents evacuated the campus with their families and dormitories were emptied of students, more so as news spread on the commandeering of taxicabs by barricaders, the presence of strangers and cases of theft.

The barricaders drew nationwide attention even as the barricades ended on the ninth day without any major destruction to property. Just as the barricaders were in the limelight, Lopez was as much a central figure. He had staked his presidency on upholding the integrity of the University by opting against a hard line solution to the problems. That there was a breakdown of administration in the first few days of the barricades was obvious. But in exercising restraint, in refusing to merely enforce the law, he was able to diffuse a volatile situation which could have led not only to destruction of property and loss of lives, but even to the extinction of the University itself.

Tension Gradually Diffused

The barricades served as the climax to the series of dramatic challenges which characterized student activism in the University of the Philippines. After the barricades, there were no more forms of dissent that could surprise the UP administration and the nation except perhaps a revolution which was in fact avoided. During the barricades, the radicalization of the studentry had been heightened, and the image of the University in revolutionary ferment could no longer be challenged. After the barricades, protest classes, boycotts, demonstrations became almost a daily spectacle that would beset the University until the declaration of martial law.[36]

Martial Law Declared

The declaration of martial law on September 23, 1972 (retroactive to September 21) shocked the entire country. The suspension of the writ of *habeas corpus,* the discovery of the M.V. Karagatan, the "bombing" of several places in Metro-Manila and the arrests of known militants were handwritings on the wall that presaged the declaration of martial law.

The University had a full schedule of teach-ins, convocations and pickets within three days before the declaration of martial law. Opposition leaders like Senator Jose Diokno and Benigno Aquino, Constitutional Convention Delegates Bonifacio Gillego, Heherson Alvarez and Voltaire Garcia, Broadcaster Roger Arrienda, and other outspoken critics appeared at a number of mass gatherings protesting fascism as well as the imprisonment of political prisoners.

The editorial of the September 21 issue of the *Philippine Collegian* ominously warned that martial law was merely a matter of time based on developments of the last few days. It pointed to the pattern being drawn by the Marcos administration to condition the minds of the people toward military control, although predicting that the masses would strongly resist such a move. The charged atmosphere of uncertainty was further heightened by a torch parade around the campus on the night of September 22 with students chanting revolutionary slogans. The imposition of martial law was not farfetched but nobody seriously believed it would actually happen.

Initial Shock and Confusion

On the morning of the next day, the campus woke to the shock of the announcement that martial law had been declared. Word spread around later on that the transmitter and equipment of DZUP had been wrecked and immobilized by the military and that the nearby *Iglesia ni Kristo* compound had resisted the entry of soldiers bent on taking over the radio station there.

At that point, all that the University administration could do was to cautiously keep track of developments until Malacañang announced, among other things, that all schools, colleges and universities were declared closed and classes suspended until further notice.

Surprisingly, the predicted violence did not occur. "Quiescent" conditions prevailed and the University braced itself for the reopening of all units by October 19 under stringent conditions imposed by Proclamation 1081 and other Presidential Orders, Decrees and Instructions. President Marcos ordered the reopening of the University on condition that Lopez assumed the responsibility for the maintenance of order and discipline on campus. The big question uppermost in the minds of the faculty was whether academic freedom and the right to teach one's discipline unhampered by restrictions had been seriously undermined by martial law.

Concern within the Academe

The question was to be clarified by Lopez when he sought President Marcos' view on the matter. The latter made a distinction between "teaching" and "advocating," giving at the same time assurance of normal guarantees of academic freedom, provided that the classroom was not used "as forum for advocating subversion, revolution and the overthrow of government by violent means."[37]

With the Government having banned activist organizations, the University administration saw it fit to give members of the faculty, staff and students a chance to clear themselves should their names be included in the military's lists of radicals to be furnished the University. At the same time the University took security measures to prevent physical violence, disorder and other unlawful acts. Entry to the various campuses was strictly regulated so that only students, faculty members, administrative staff and other persons properly identified to do business would be allowed to come in. Bags and attache cases were inspected for any weapon or incendiary material. Everyone had to wear his ID for easier identification. Curfew hours in academic buildings were maintained from 10 p.m. to 6 a.m.

The big blow was directed at student organizations and activities with the suspension of the student government, Woman's Club, and all other student groups. However, the University, through the Office of Student Affairs, took the lead in the restoration of student organizations a few months after the imposition of martial law, bringing back to the campus a certain air of normalcy even as the University and College Councils remained suspended.[38] Despite an earlier order suspending all student publications, the *Philippine Collegian* resumed publication in January 1973 after it subscribed to the rules of the Mass Media Council.[39]

On September 13, 1973, Lopez recognized the creation of the Consultative Committee on Student Affairs (CONCOMSA) whose members were elected from among the officers and designated representatives of recognized student organizations. The CONCOMSA was given authority by the President to make use of the Student Council funds for student welfare projects, subject to the approval of the President and the Board of Regents, and likewise to pertinent government accounting and auditing rules.[40]

Expectedly, the student leaders accepted with misgivings the CONCOMSA and used it to further their cause toward reviving an "autonomous, democratic and representative" Student Council.

Diminishing Protests

Mass actions or group meetings were not allowed, but on the whole, this rule was not thoroughly enforced. Generally, student organizations did not exceed the bounds of the law, but neither did the spirit of dissent die down. Underground manifestoes continued to be circulated while janitors had a hard time erasing revolutionary slogans written on the walls of comfort rooms and lecture rooms. During the editorship of Emmanuel F. Esguerra (1974), the *Philippine Collegian* began renewing its nationalist commitment through issues published in Pilipino and by featuring basically critical materials.

FLEXIBILITY WITHIN THE UNIVERSITY THAT GAVE SHAPE TO THE SYSTEM FOR SURVIVAL

THE tumultuous years from 1969 to mid-1972 shaped the directions that the University took, and conditioned the responses of Lopez and his administration in laying down goals and programs more in keeping with the critical times. After the imposition of martial law, some programs started earlier managed to carry on and even gained ground after 1972. Under a controlled situation, the University was able to devote more time to expanding existing programs and planning new ones. Consequently, the University went through a renewed period of growth from late 1972 to 1975 notwithstanding the restraints of martial law on academic life.

The militant members of the faculty and students were either arrested and detained by the military, or went underground. By the end of the year 1972 and early 1973, some 15 faculty members who had allegedly gone underground were dropped from the rolls of the University for unexplained long absences.[41] Those who were identified to be under detention were given a chance to clear themselves and rejoin the university upon their release. To the credit of President Lopez and the members of the Board, those who were detained and subsequently released made use of their leave credits and were allowed to get some backpay.

Roots of Democratization

The lessons gained from student-faculty activism guided Lopez in setting forth "polestars" in administering the University:

1. "Democratization of the University in terms of sharing responsibilities of decision making with the elements that constitute it" would be instituted; and the University would be made "accessible to all who, regardless of social and economic status, have the ability to benefit from its programs";
2. University programs would be made "more relevant to the needs of the national society without, however, neglecting the needs of individual fulfillment and perfection";
3. University autonomy in running its own affairs while receiving adequate financial support from the State and people would be granted.[42]

That "democratization" took precedence in Lopez's program was not surprising. His background as a liberal and the mood of the University on his assumption of office made it imperative for him to share the governance of the University with its constituents, and to open channels of communication with the students, faculty, administrative personnel, and the nation at large.

Coping with Student Activism

Lopez's policy of student autonomy recognized the role of the students as the most dynamic sector of the University and therefore the most dynamic agent for change. Student activism made this fact possible. Confronted with student power, the University had to recognize legitimate student interests, accepting its "duty to enhance them within limits of available resources."[43] Thus a policy of tolerance evolved, even as unconventional methods resorted to by the students strained to the utmost the patience of the University administration.

To do away with further outbursts of violence, Lopez made it clear that the true character of student activism must be recognized, "that it is part of a world-wide movement which we may deplore but cannot escape, which we may seek to regulate but cannot ignore, which we may try to tame or even master but dare not thwart or repress by force or intimidation."[44]

But the policy of toleration did not mean "coddling" the students. Where the University could give in within reasonable bounds, it did; but where it was not possible to do so, the University firmly took a stand. Lopez, for example, went out of his way to protect the students, even visiting the city jails to look after those arrested by the police for participating in riotous demonstrations. But when a university councilor of the UP Student Council was summarily suspended by Dean Amado Castro of the School of Economics for allegedly creating unnecessary noise in the lobby of the School, Lopez supported the move of Dean Castro despite the pressure exerted by the Student Council and the *Collegian*. While the "noise" was a result of student reaction against the suspension of the writ of *habeas corpus*, validity of the University rules was upheld by the President.[45]

The University likewise recognized "the validity of the students' desire to relate their studies to the dynamics of life and experience."[46] It emphasized the role of the University as primarily a citadel of learning but it also accepted that learning was not confined to books and the classroom: the University was a place to study life itself.[47] Necessarily, student activism was viewed as a "supplement to, and not a substitute for the process of learning."[48]

Extent of Student Autonomy

Student autonomy provided the students with mechanisms to participate in the decision-making process, premised on the principle that the final decisions were to be made by the faculties, the administration and the Board of Regents. Starting on the college level, students were represented in departmental and college committees, with the privilege of attending faculty meetings involving curricular matters but without voting rights. Generally, the extent of student participation in the local units varied from one college to another. As expected, the widest latitude of student participation was in the College of Arts and Sciences, where students voted during the democratic consultation for the selection of a successor to Dean Cesar A. Majul.

On the University level, student representatives sat with voting rights on committees involved with student rights and welfare, e.g. the Committee on Scholarships, Grants-in-Aid Committee; Food Committee; University Student Loan Board; University Library Board; etc.

The biggest concession to the students was representation in the highest governing body of the University, the Board of Regents. Fernando Barican started as a non-voting observer in September 1969 and ended up becoming the first duly-appointed student member of the Board on February 25, 1970.[49]

Communication Lines Kept Open

To maintain channels of communication, the President reactivated the Student-Faculty Relations Committee in every degree-granting unit and created through Executive Order No. 14 the position of Student Relations Officer to chair the Committee. The main task of these two offices was to deal expeditiously with student problems on the unit level. Another body, the Board of Student Petitions, was created by Executive Order No. 13 to act on complaints from student organizations and associations.

When martial law was declared, the operations of all student organizations were temporarily suspended but Jaime Galvez Tan, who was elected Chairman of the University Student Council for the schoolyear 1972-1973, and who was sworn in as student regent on November 27, 1972, kept the position until his term expired in July 1973. For a while, therefore, the students had a channel for their activities in the office of the Student Regent. After Tan's term, the position of Student-Regent was left unoccupied.

With the creation of the CONCOMSA, student representation resumed in University Committees affecting the students. Despite martial law, students also won for the first time the right to be represented in the editorial examining committee to choose the editor-in-chief of the *Collegian.* Nominations for the first student examiners as well the faculty examiners were received by the Office of Student Affairs from student leaders in a meeting called for the purpose. On the recommendation of Dean of Student Affairs Armando J. Malay, the President appointed Roberto Crisol and Ma. Carmen Jimenez as the first student members of the *Collegian* Examining Committee.

Role of the Faculty

Faculty participation in the governance of the University centered on two time-honored traditions which were formerly the exclusive preserve of University administrators: the selection of deans and chairmen of academic departments, and the promotion of faculty members.

The institution of "democratic consultation" was based on the principle that the University was made up of three major and co-equal constituencies: the faculty and academic non-teaching staff, the students, and the administrative staff. Each sector had a theoretically proportionate share in the selection of deans and department chairmen through the process of consultation, but because the academic sector was more directly involved in the choice of academic heads, in practice, more weight was given to the nominees of the faculty. While the final selection of deans and department chairmen was left to the President and the Board of Regents, generally the nominees eventually got the posts.

Viability of Democratization

The concept of democratic consultation was brought out in earlier policy statements of President Lopez but its institution was a result of the opposition of some faculty members in the Department of History led by Prof. Teodoro Agoncillo against the appointment of Dr. Oscar M. Alfonso as Chairman of the Department. The petition for democratic consultation was publicized in the *Collegian*[50] even as the matter reached the Board of Regents at its August 28, 1969 meeting. At that meeting, the petition of the opposing group signed by seven members of the faculty and a counter-petition supporting Dr. Alfonso signed by eight faculty members, had been merely noted by the Board after Lopez informed the Board that conditions in the Department had stabilized under Dr. Alfonso's chairmanship.

The opposing group, however, pressed for voting rights and again aired through the *Collegian* its decision to hold "protest classes" until its demand was met by the Administration. The "protest classes" involved holding regular classes but instead of discussing their subjects, more relevant issues of national and local concerns were taken up, apparently using the classroom "to air their personal grievances and advocate private views."[51]

It is significant to note that in February 1970, a group of faculty members and students under the banner of the "Movement for Democratization of the University," proposed, among other things, the direct election of deans/directors and department chairmen by the faculty members of each unit, and by the department staff respectively with the participation of student representatives with full voting rights in both cases. It also proposed the participation of student majors with full voting rights "in all matters governing the appointment, promotion and dismissal of faculty members, as well as in all questions governing curricular changes." The significance of these proposals becomes more meaningful if placed within the context of the demands of those against the chairmanship of Dr. Alfonso.

Respect for Democratic Process

On February 19, 1970, Lopez met with the staff of the Department of History and thereafter, he and Dean Majul agreed to seek a consensus on the appointment of the next department chairman. Dr. Alfonso chose to cut short his term and resigned on February 23 to give way to the holding of a democratic consultation, committing himself in writing to his agreeing to a proposal made at the February 19th meeting that he was not going to be available for the position in the next academic year. He had earlier informed Dean Majul and the President on several occasions, that he was for democratic consultation even before he was unilaterally recommended by the former for the chairmanship.[52]

In March 1970, the department staff was thus consulted, leading to the appointment of Dr. Honesto A. Villanueva by the Board of Regents on April 4, 1970. His appointment as chairman was the first made with consultation of the faculty. In that meeting, the Board stressed that selection by consensus did not mean that it was giving up its power to make the final selection, upon recommendation of the President, as mandated by the University Charter.[53]

Despite the participation of the faculty in the nomination process, a first in the history of the University, several groups opted for no less than the direct election of not only the department chairmen, deans, and directors, but also the University President. The nomination process itself was severely criticized by the *Collegian* and by faculty and student groups when it was taken to determine the successor of Dean Majul in 1971, not only because they were for "electing" the Dean, but also because of the creation of four sectors: senior faculty, junior faculty, non-teaching personnel, and students; where it was pointed out that the faculty was over-represented, and where, moreover, the weight of the senior faculty, who were less in number, was the same as that of the more numerous junior faculty.[54]

In January 1972, the University Student Council unanimously endorsed a resolution requesting Congress to give students the right to "democratic election" in line with the move to completely democratize the University.

Faculty Participation Enlarged

Another erstwhile preserve of department chairmen, deans, and the university administration was faculty promotion. Lopez took the bold step of sharing this power with faculty members through a promotion procedure centering on the establishment of academic personnel committees on three levels – department, college, university. The department academic committee was headed by the department chairman, with two to four faculty representatives (depending on the size of the department) elected at large by the faculty; the college academic personnel committee had the Dean as chairman with the chairmen of various department personnel committees in the college as members; the university academic personnel board was composed of the Vice-President for Academic Affairs as chairman and four senior faculty members. This procedure introduced the concept of collegial decision-making, allowing wider faculty participation.

The need to widen faculty participation in the discussion of local and national issues was partly answered by the establishment of the Faculty Assembly. Its creation was in response to the bloody confrontation between the students and the military in the wake of the January 26, 1970 demonstration in front of Congress. Unlike the University Council whose membership was limited to faculty members on the professorial level, the Faculty

Assembly included the Instructors. The first Faculty Assembly called on January 28, 1970 decided on the Faculty March.

A second Faculty Assembly which met on March 19 was a follow-up of developments since the Faculty March. It took stock of faculty moves from the Faculty March to the congressional hearings to investigate the causes of student unrest. The second meeting resolved that the root causes of popular unrest should be attacked for the nation to avoid violence and bloodshed.[55]

The assembly, which might have continued to be a good avenue for a fruitful dialogue between the faculty and administration, was not convened again after its second meeting. During the crisis posed by the barricades, the President met not only with the faculty but with the entire community several times.

Role of Administrative Personnel

The participation of the administrative personnel in the decision-making process was minor in comparison to the direct and decisive roles played by the students and the faculty. Nonetheless, they did have a share in the form of negotiations undertaken by the Organization of Non-Academic Personnel (ONAPUP) and the UP Supervisors' Association (UPSA) with the administration on matters involving salary increases and working conditions. The temper of the times was concern for the masses, putting the non-academic personnel, specially the janitors, laborers, and gardeners in the limelight.

The militant students and faculty members supported the administrative personnel's cause in the first university strike and in succeeding negotiations with the administration, going to the extent of holding boycotts of classes for salary raises and for giving permanency to daily wage employees. Not to be outdone, the administration as a policy accepted the principle that the University was composed of three sectors: the students, the faculty and the administrative employees. The administrative personnel participated in the democratic consultation process and were appointed to university committees like the Committee on Housing.

Likewise for the first time the administrative personnel and the students were represented by speakers from their sectors at the Faculty Conference held in 1970. In 1973 the Administrative Personnel Committee was formed to handle staff promotions.

Benefits from Democratization

The administration instituted other measures to democratize the University. The minutes of the Board of Regents were initially made available to Deans and Directors and heads of units; then through the founding and publication of the *U.P. Gazette* in 1970, important decisions of the Board as well as those of the President, were made known to a larger sector of the University. The founding of another publication, the *U.P. Newsletter*, in 1972 was intended to inform the community of developments in the University. An aftermath of the first University strike was the issuance in 1969 of an Executive Order opening official records of the University to interested parties as long as they made an official request in writing to examine these records.

Salary increases and adjustments for faculty and staff took into consideration their needs to live decently in the wake of the eroding value of the peso, and the need to provide incentives through merit increases. At least four times during the administration of Lopez, upward salary adjustments were given to the faculty and staff of the University "even at the risk of incurring budgetary deficits."[56]

One notable aspect of the salary scale instituted by the administration was the step to lessen the salary gap between the faculty and the administrative staff and to apportion the scale more equitably.

Grants-in-Aid Program Introduced

The selective admission process of the University through the UP College Admissions Test was maintained despite pressures to democratize admission and convert the UP into a University of the People similar to the Chinese experience in which academic studies and work in the field and factories were combined. But a concession to the clamor for equal opportunity between the rich and the poor for quality education was the institution of the University Grants-in-Aid Program, giving the intellectually deserving but financially deprived students an opportunity to study in the University.

The program started modestly with only full and partial tuition fee privileges being extended to those whose parents' income was not more than ₱4,000. There was an arbitrary cut-off point between free and reduced "single fee" depending on the availability of funds. But behind this modest enterprise was the recognition that the majority of the students came from financially well-off families and that efforts should be made to divert part of the University funds to the poor. The first step was to increase the tuition fee by 15 per cent, the increase going to the G-I-A fund. Then entrance, university and college scholarships were made honorific instead of granting tuition discount privileges. The amount saved also went to the G-I-A coffers.[57]

In 1972, a book allowance of ₱200 and ₱100 per year were given to full and partial grantees; then in July 1973, monthly stipends for 10 months were added to the financial benefits as follows: ₱60 and ₱40 per month for full and partial grantees respectively.

Requirements for Grants and Scholarships

The rules governing the G-I-A program were revised in 1974 to do away with the arbitrary cut-off point, and the "partial" and the "full" categories, and a new formula was instituted to determine the financial need of a family. Depending on the need, the corresponding grants were classified into 26 categories, the recipient getting a tuition discount from 10 to 100 per cent; a stipend of up to ₱60 monthly; and a book allowance of ₱25 to ₱100 a semester. The academic rules were also liberalized to give due consideration to the principle that financially poor students have built-in disadvantages and therefore must work harder for their grades. Room was allowed for a varying number of units passed depending on the year classification of the recipient.[58]

The number of recipients during the academic years 1971-1972 and 1972-1973 were 1,529 and 1,653 respectively from Diliman, Manila and Los Baños. The number of grantees increased to 2,870 and 2,668 during the years 1973-1974 and 1974-1975 respectively, when the financial benefits were increased.

Republic Act 5549 passed by Congress on June 21, 1969 appropriated ₱1 million yearly for scholarships at the University of the Philippines. The Republic Act itself stipulated that 60 per cent of the grantees should be in such specific fields as natural and physical sciences, engineering, agriculture, fisheries, forestry, economics and public administration, with the purpose of developing manpower in these areas but left to the University the drafting of specific rules to govern the scholarships. As a product of the time, the University saw fit to limit the granting of these scholarships to financially needy but intellectually deserving students. The academic rules governing these scholarships were more stringent than the requirement for G-I-A, with financial benefits enough to sustain the needs of the grantee until he graduated provided that he made the semestral average grade requirement of "2.5". This scholarship program was to be known as the UP-Government Scholarships.

Due to the stiff scholarship rules, there was a high attrition rate among the recipients of the program. Of the first batch of 176 scholars, only 23 graduated four years after the program was inaugurated. By the academic year 1974-1975, the program was supporting 291 scholars.

Genesis of the University "System"

The birth of the University of the Philippines System on November 21, 1972, was a high point in the administration of President Lopez. Just as he had democratized the University in "unprecedented" ways, the creation of the UP System was as much an extension of democratization, with Diliman willing to surrender its centralized functions to the autonomous units to be created.

The idea of a UP System was already in the mind of Lopez when he came to the University in 1969. The reference point was a University plan for the nation, with the external units and UP Los Baños as focal points for the expansion of the State University System. Necessarily, this would mean a revamp of the educational system, the University of the Philippines in Diliman serving as the nucleus of the new system.

Meanwhile, the Presidential Commission to Survey Philippine Education (PCSPE) had proposed that UP be designated as the National University of the Philippines, with only three other regional state universities, one each in Luzon, Visayas and Mindanao to be created out of the existing geographic groupings of state universities and colleges, but excluding the teacher training and technical colleges. The PCSPE recommendation would not have impaired the autonomy of the University.

Thrust towards Reorganization

Given the PCSPE recommendation and the impending reorganization by the Commission on Reorganization of the executive offices, which included the University of the Philippines as an autonomous unit under the Office of the President, but governed by its own charter, the idea of the UP System was not given the necessary push except as a model for the future development of the external units.

The resignation of Dr. Disocoro L. Umali as Vice-President at Los Baños effective August 1, 1971, in a way triggered the move to resuscitate the idea of the UP System. As a result of the President's consultation with the Board of Regents on whether to leave the position of Vice-President at Los Baños vacant or to appoint an officer-in-charge, at the same time expressing the hope that UP at Los Baños would eventually become an autonomous university headed by a chancellor, the Board authorized the President to study the possibility of abolishing the position of Vice-President at Los Baños. A committee was appointed by the Board headed by Regent Abel Silva as Chairman and the Deans of the Colleges of Agriculture and Forestry as members to make a study of the operations of Los Baños, including the phasing out of the office of Vice-President.

As the Silva committee was re-examining the structure of UP at Los Baños, Lopez directed the deans and directors of the Los Baños units to plan for the establishment of an autonomous unit in that region. This move was followed by the creation in February 1972 of a committee for the establishment of a College of Arts and Sciences in UP at Los Baños (UPLB), a necessary ingredient in the establishment of an autonomous unit.

Autonomy for UP Los Baños?

Meanwhile, it became apparent to the Silva Committee that there was a strong feeling among UPLB administration and alumni in favor of the creation of an autonomous agricultural university in Los Baños. It was not however clear what was the role of the Silva committee in approaching Executive Secretary Alejandro Melchor and Secretary of Agriculture Arturo Tanco and asking their support in convincing President Marcos to approve a decree providing a charter for a separate and independent University in Los Baños. Nor was it clear whether the proposed charter was drafted by the Silva committee.[59]

When Lopez heard of this move from Secretary of Education Juan Manuel, he forthwith sent President Marcos a letter on October 18, 1972 objecting to the proposal for an independent agricultural university on the following grounds:

1. Most, if not all of the outstanding Agricultural Colleges abroad are not independent institutions but members of a large university complex . . . improved and strengthened by association with other disciplines. An independent agricultural institution deprived of this contact with other disciplines would turn into a second or third-rate university.
2. The international reputation and prestige which the UP College of Agriculture now enjoys derives mainly from the over-all prestige and international reputation of the University as a whole. Conversely, the international prestige and standing of the UP is based partly on the excellence of its College of Agriculture. Both the UP and the College of Agriculture would suffer from a decision to separate them.
3. . . . The inevitable lowering of its academic standards and of its international reputation would diminish its effectiveness as an instrument of national development.
4. The notion that establishing Los Baños as an agricultural university would advance economic development also overlooks the fact that agricultural growth can best be promoted not by itself alone but as part of a larger agro-industrial or socio-economic development program.

Lopez ended by saying that the proposal to establish an autonomous UP at Los Baños under a Chancellor but under the authority of the UP Board of Regents, was in keeping with the recommendation of the PCSPE to make the UP the National University of the Philippines, maintaining that it was inconceivable for the national university of an agricultural country not to have a college of agriculture nor a college of forestry.[60]

Issue of Autonomy Debated

On October 25, Regent Silva wrote Secretary Manuel on behalf of his committee reacting to President Lopez's letter of October 18. Answering point for point the arguments of Lopez, Regent Silva said that (1) UPLB would not become a second or third-rate university since it could draw from the world market place of humanities and philosophies, aside from what UP Diliman and other liberal Philippine universities could offer; (2) UPLB students were trained and produced by Los Baños units, with little or no direct influence from Diliman; there was therefore no reason why UPLB and UP Diliman would lose prestige due to the separation; (3) the separation of UPLB from Diliman would make it possible for the former to concentrate on its functions on a closer and more mundane level; (4) inter-disciplinary programs could continue even with an autonomous UPLB; (5) the move made by his Committee was in accord with the spirit of the PCSPE report on the strengthening of the educational system to support national development, and in consultation with the Chairman of the PCSPE, Dr. Onofre D. Corpuz.

Regent Silva expressed further the concern of his committee for the strengthening of agricultural education as an instrument of national development, a step that could be achieved if UPLB were "released from the inherent fiscal, administrative and academic trap of a liberal university so that it could be given the full freedom to grow and chart its course in accordance with the pressing needs of a developing agricultural country."[61]

On the same day, Lopez wrote another letter to President Marcos reiterating his objections to the establishment of an independent agricultural university, and instead proposing the creation of a UP System with modifications in the composition of the Board of Regents and an autonomous UPLB as a member of the System.

Reconciliation through a UP System

The Board of Regents, at its October 26 meeting, with Lopez presiding due to the absence of Secretary Manuel, discussed the issue of an autonomous UPLB as part of the UP System. Regents Sicat, Pedrosa and Fonacier supported President Lopez's proposal and considered Regent Silva's objections as his stand on the matter. Secretary Tanco, in the meantime, had a change of heart and decided to submit to President Marcos an amended proposal along the lines proposed by Lopez.

With the Board's approval and the support of Secretaries Tanco and Manuel, the question was submitted to President Marcos for approval.

A last-minute effort on the part of Regent Silva to water down the Lopez proposal proved to no avail. The UPLB administrators on the other hand, were unanimous in essentially supporting the Lopez proposal but with guarantees to ensure the academic, administrative and fiscal autonomy of their unit. These points were eventually discussed with Lopez and three of the five points were incorporated in Presidential Decree No. 58 granting autonomy to UP at Los Baños and establishing the University of the Philippines System on November 21, 1972.

What was achieved in a month's time could not have been possible under normal circumstances. Martial law made it easier to realize the emergence of the UP System.

UP System Firmly Established

The birth of the UP System marked the development of the University into a multi-campus university, allowing for the growth of not only one but multiple centers of learning dedicated to excellence. It was then the hope of Lopez that the establishment of the UP System would rationalize the situation of state colleges and universities, and the system of higher education in general, through the integration and coordination of state colleges and universities throughout the country. This hope did not materialize but it gave incentive for the regional units to improve themselves and strive to create an impact on their respective areas.

The autonomous UP at Los Baños which emerged was composed of the following units: the College of Agriculture, College of Forestry, Agricultural Credit and Cooperatives Institute, Dairy Training and Research Institute, the Graduate School, and the Agrarian Reform Institute, which was transferred from Diliman. On December 31, 1972, the College of Humanities and Sciences was established by the Board, and on May 1, 1973, Dr. Abelardo G. Samonte became the first Chancellor of UP at Los Baños.

As plans were being drawn for the expansion of the System and the creation of more autonomous units, Presidential Decree No. 342 established the Philippine Center for Advanced Studies (PCAS) on November 22, 1973 as another autonomous unit of the UP System. The PCAS, which grew out of the original Asian Center based in Diliman, was composed of the Institute of Islamic Studies, Institute of Philippine Studies, Institute of Asian Studies, Institute of Strategic Studies, Division of Basic Research, and Division of Academic Instruction. Like UPLB it was under a Chancellor but unlike UPLB, PCAS had its own Board of Trustees which was responsible for formulating and reviewing objectives and policies, and for nominating the officers and staff of the unit.

PCAS Infiltrates the System

The Board of Regents at its 839th meeting of November 29, 1973, merely noted the creation of the PCAS after some discussion. All it could do was to suggest that the University President seek clarification of Presidential Decree 342 on points like the relationship of the PCAS with the UP System, and the role of the Board of Regents and the President of the UP System.

The creation of the PCAS established an empire within an empire. Particularly vexing to the UP community was the fact that it was imposed from above without consultation or agreement. Funds of the Asian Center were transferred to the PCAS budget. In addition, the UP had to appropriate ₱1.5 million from its budget annually to finance recurring operational expenditures of the PCAS beginning June 1974.[62]

The minutes of the 844th meeting of the Board of Regents on April 8, 1974 recorded the discussion of Letter of Instructions 179 to the UP Board of Regents and the PCAS Board of Trustees, amplifying the jurisdiction of PCAS and its relationship with the UP System, and reflected the implied annoyance of the members of the Board as they commented on the provisions of the Letter of Instructions.

Lopez referred to the PCAS as a unit affiliated with the University. Implicity, Lopez also had PCAS in mind when he mentioned attempts "to erode the unity and integrity of the UP System."[63]

RAMIFICATIONS OF RELEVANCE WHILE STRENGTHENING THE FRAMEWORK OF UNIVERSITY RESPONSE

WHEN President Lopez committed the University to live up to the aspirations of the vast majority of the Filipino people, he was keeping in mind the dynamic changes taking place in Filipino society. Toward the attainment of this goal, the University had to strike a balance between the traditional role of the University as a "conservator of the truth," and the demands of the Filipino people as expressed by the militant students and faculty members.

The University through Lopez recognized that developments in the campus were mere reflections of the national scene and that the University could not be isolated from the country at large. Seen from this perspective, the University, if it was to be relevant, had to be in the forefront as a social critic and an agent for change. The direction called for was to make the University's academic programs, research and extension services relevant to the demands of society during both the years of activism and those of martial law. Commitment to this direction was, in effect, a commitment to keeping the University's nature as a Filipino University, with nationalism "as the basis for a coherent philosophy of action."[64]

Reevaluating the Curriculum

The Lopez administration took cognizance of the antiquated and colonial nature of the University curriculum when it appointed on February 18, 1969 a faculty-student committee to set basic considerations for the review of the curriculum.[65] In its report, the Committee established the following guidelines in helping the academic units to review their curricula: (1) in the examination of all curricular offerings, the role of extra-curricular activities in the learning process should be looked into; (2) the curriculum should help develop the student into an educated man, one imbued with critical thinking, social awareness, and social consciousness; (3) an examination of the role of each college, through its curriculum as an instrument for national development should be undertaken; (4) an examination of the needs of Philippine society in relation to what the curriculum was trying to meet should be considered; (5) the role of each college curriculum in contributing to the University's role as an agent for change should be evaluated; and (6) the need for a proper balance to enable the University to fulfill its obligation "to the student as a person seeking self-fulfillment; to the community of scholars and professionals striving for excellence; and to the society in search of solutions to its many problems" should guide the evaluation.[66]

The years 1969-1972 witnessed sufficient gains in curricular changes, fulfilling some of the guidelines enumerated above, specifically those with regard to the growth of Pilipino, institution of social change, and introduction of courses linked to national development.

Importance of Pilipino Recognized

On March 25, 1971, the Board of Regents suggested that a study be made on the validity of the courses in the General Education curriculum. Consequently, the College of Arts and Sciences spearheaded the re-examination of the GE curriculum leaving practically intact most course requirements, with minor revisions, but coming out with a major proposal recognizing the important role of Pilipino (renamed Filipino by the Batasang Pambansa in 1974) in the University. The college plan would have required at least 3 units of Pilipino, but as approved by the University Council on September 11, 1971, a student could opt to take 12 units of English and/or Pilipino, thereby giving the option for the students to take any combination of English and Pilipino, or to take only one of the two language requirements.

The blooming of Pilipino in the University was inevitable given the flowering of nationalism during the period. This was evident in the use of Pilipino as medium of instruction in some Chemistry, History, Mathematics, Philosophy, Physics and Psychology courses, even in English 3 and 5. The Physics Department reported that for the schoolyear 1970-1971, 56.8 per cent of all class sections were taught in Pilipino.[67] The Colleges of Medicine and Engineering also experimented on the use of Pilipino as medium of instruction.

Prodded by the interest in Pilipino, other symbolic gains for Pilipinization made headway. The Commencement Exercises in 1970 held several "firsts" along this line. The oath of loyalty to the alumni association and to the University were recited in Pilipino, while the University Hymn, "U.P.

Beloved," was given a Pilipino translation, put together by a committee which selected the best lines and words from seven translations received for the purpose, and first sung in this commencement as "U.P. Naming Mahal."

Other signs of Pilipinization evident in 1970 were the lead taken by the *Philippine Collegian* in publishing issues in Pilipino; the publication of *Literary Apprentice,* organ of the UP Writers' Club, in English and Pilipino; and the offering of cultural presentations in Pilipino by campus organizations.

Likewise the University Student Council and the UP Woman's Club pilipinized their names into Sanggunian ng mga Mag-aaral and Samahan ng mga Kababaihan sa Universidad ng Pilipinas (SKUP) respectively.

The important position of Pilipino did not detract from the bilingual policy enunciated by Lopez in 1969, which became the official policy of the Government through the National Board of Education in 1973 on the recommendation of Lopez.

New Course on Social Orientation

A survey made by the UP Woman's Club led to the recommendation to abolish the age-old Euthenics courses and substitute Social Change I and II. Social Change I was to discuss relevant issues like drug addiction, cooperatives, leadership, sex education, disaster relief, etc. while Social Change II was to serve as practicum where female students would do field work in line with the need to expose students to the bigger community outside of the University. The Administration responded to this proposal promptly by calling a special meeting of the University Council on June 15, 1970 to discuss only one subject: the institution of Social Change I and II.

In the discussions that followed, Vice-President Abelardo Samonte, Chairman of the Curriculum Committee, stressed "rapid changes and developments, which oftentimes cannot be postponed since decisions in order to be effective must be sensitive to the timing."[68]

The Council likewise responded favorably by instituting the new courses with a different title: Social Orientation, the course to be handled on an interdisciplinary basis, with the College of Home Economics administering the program.

The institution of the new courses was significant in a number of ways. For one, it symbolized the cry for relevance, while the swift response of the administration and the faculty to institute the courses underlined their own commitment. Ordinarily curricular changes of this sort went through the mill and took time to institutionalize. For another, its institution was student initiated, based on consultation with the women students of the University.

Growth of Curricular Programs

During the years under review (1969-1972), thirty new curricular programs were instituted, distributed as follows: 1969-1970 –four; 1970-1971 – eighteen; and 1971-1972 – eight. In terms of relevance to national development, i.e. training of needed manpower in new fields, the following curricula substantially met this need: Bachelor of Science in Hotel and Restaurant Administration, Master of Statistics, Master of Community Development (1969-1970); Bachelor of Science in Agricultural Business, Bachelor of Landscape Architecture, Bachelor of Science in Business Economics, Master of Agricultural Business Management (1970-71); Bachelor of Science in Community Nutrition, Bachelor of Science in Business Economics, Bachelor of Science in Applied Mathematics (1971-1972).

Three of the above programs (B.S. in Hotel and Restaurant Administration, B.S. in Agri-Business and B.S. in Business Economics) were administered not by one but by two colleges pooling their resources. A post-doctoral course was opened by the newly established Anesthesiology Center Western Pacific.[69]

The College of Arts and Sciences reported that during the academic year 1970-1971, the major's curricula were upgraded by "revising antiquated courses and institution of new ones geared towards modern trends, specially in the fields of science and technology."[70]

The changes during these years reflected no drastic move along the lines demanded by the militant sectors of the University. Seen from these militants' point of view, some of the changes merely served the interest of the "ruling elite" and were still "irrelevant." Unit curricular offerings remained parochial in outlook largely because of departmental autonomy. This fact was accepted by the University administration when Lopez alluded to a study made of curricular changes between 1961 and 1972, showing the lack of a unified direction for curricular proposals. He blamed the autonomous departmental approach which resulted in "piecemeal, fragmentary changes and a proliferation of courses and programs, some of which have persisted beyond the limits of utility."[71]

The course content basically did not change but the perspectives and interpretations may have varied according to the ideological persuasions of the faculty members handling the courses.

Peripheral Benefits under Martial Law

Signs of growth in curricular matters were evident from the schoolyear 1972-1973 until the end of the Lopez administration in 1975. Several factors were responsible for this development. The "quiescent" atmosphere after the declaration of martial law made it easier for the University to draw long-range plans and carry them out. There was more time for development projects and for energies to be directed toward academic changes. For example as early as December 1972, development proposals for the academic years 1974-1976 were completed.

Getting the funds for programs was also made easier by the martial law administration as it did away with the erstwhile prerogative of the defunct Congress to scrutinize and approve the budget. Budget-making was simplified and releases facilitated for programs geared for national development. Aligning some of the University programs with the new thrusts of the national government, like land reform, population research and expansion of cooperatives, assured their funding.

Curricular review that was started during the period of activism continued during the martial law regime with a new emphasis: meeting the socio-economic challenges of the latter period and the strengthening of graduate offerings specially on the doctorate level. The goal was a proper balance between undergraduate and graduate courses, keeping in mind the traditional role of the University and the new demands of national development goals.

Courses Made More Compact

Significantly, curricular changes in the undergraduate level centered not on new degree offerings (there were only two new bachelor's degrees instituted: Bachelor of Science in Interior Design and Bachelor of Arts in Islamic Studies) but on integrating and redesigning some existing courses, abolishing others and reducing unit requirements, making the curricula shorter but more meaningful. For four-year courses, the administration pegged the goal to the completion of a minimum of 120 units to satisfy graduation requirements. Records of the University Council for 1974 show the academic units' compliance with the call for curricular review by the abolition of more courses in comparison to the smaller number of courses instituted. Thirteen curricular offerings in six colleges cut down on the number of units required for graduation.[72]

There were marked gains in graduate course offerings, reflecting the pioneering role of the University in exploring new fields of learning.

In 1972, the University's concern for the quality of its graduate offerings prompted the administration to create a committee to study the graduate programs and institute measures that would emphasize "academic excellence, relevance, and effective utilization of University resources."[73]

Scope of Graduate Program

In 1972, there were 146 masteral and 23 doctoral programs. Nine new master's programs, mostly in the biological and natural sciences, were instituted in veterinary parasitology, veterinary pathology, educational psychology, biochemistry, marine biology, marine geology, oceanography, veterinary public health, and fisheries.

On the doctoral level, the College of Arts and Sciences launched programs in geology, environmental science, Philippine studies and psychology. The College of Education added language teaching and social studies education to its existing doctoral programs. Doctorates in business administration and in food science completed the list of new doctoral programs instituted during the Lopez administration.

The Ph.D. in Philippine Studies represented the University's interest in Philippine culture on the highest academic level. Other units of the University contributed offerings on things Filipino as in the case of the College of Music and some departments in the College of Arts and Sciences.

Auxiliary Academic Activities

Non-curricular programs likewise appeared zealous in the propagation of Philippine culture. The work of the Science Education Center in publishing primary and secondary textbooks using Philippine materials; the University Library in actively soliciting the donation of the private collections of famous Filipino writers like Magdalena Jalandoni, Hermogenes Ilagan, Vicente Alcoseba, Julian Cruz Balmaseda and Aurelio Tolentino; the University Press and its publication of scholarly works in history, economics and literature, among others; the UP Writers' Club, revived in 1974, and its role in holding creative writing workshops like the Palihang Aurelio Tolentino; the UP Repertory Company in staging plays only in Pilipino; all these did more to highlight interest in Philippine culture.[74]

Primacy of Teaching Sustained

Stress on academic excellence and the primacy of teaching, first enunciated by Lopez early in his administration, was not sacrificed even as the University went through troubled times. The community learned to adjust and live through frequent interruptions of class days brought about by boycotts, natural calamities and forced closure of the University. The prevailing policy was to keep the University open, as it was after the barricades, and for professors to conduct classes even with few students in attendance. At one time though, as a result of the suspension of the *writ of habeas corpus* in 1971, 52 per cent of Arts and Sciences faculty members in a meeting called for the purpose, favored a faculty boycott of classes.

The University experimented with the use of tutorial classes, take-home examinations, self-study (laboratories and the library were kept open), optional lectures and other similar techniques in an effort to maintain minimum requirements while keeping up academic standards. A spirit of tolerance prevailed among faculty members as shown by giving enough time for students to catch up and take make-up examinations and allowing them to drop their subjects without a grade of "5" beyond the prescribed period up to the end of the semester.[75] But notwithstanding all these, the faculty judiciously graded their students according to their best judgment.

Innovations Attuned to the Times

Another experiment approved by the proper University bodies was optional attendance in lecture classes at the College of Engineering effective the schoolyear 1970-1971 for a one-year trial period, but thereafter made permanent after the experiment proved to be a success. Its approval was recommended by a University Council Committee created to study the matter. In recommending its approval, the Committee took note of the consensus reached by the students of the College of Engineering favoring the move, the unanimous endorsement of the college faculty, and the fact that the students of the College were already in their third and fourth years and therefore more mature in outlook.

The University's share in the students' clamor for the integration of academic programs with the masses was somewhat met with the setting up of the Comprehensive Community Health Program in 1970. This multidisciplinary program trained community health service workers in environmental sanitation, first-aid, communicable disease control, nutrition and health education. As a novel project, it likewise served as training ground in rural health practice for students from the Colleges of Medicine, Nursing, Pharmacy, Dentistry, Agriculture, Home Economics, Veterinary Medicine and Education, and from other institutes and units such as Public Health, Social Work and Community Development, Nursing, Allied Medical Professions and the Philippine General Hospital. The direct exposure of medical and paramedical students to rural health conditions helped in changing their traditional urban orientation.

To highlight the primacy of teaching, the Administration urged senior faculty members to handle introductory courses and thus be accessible to the younger students who may be influenced beneficially thereby rather than limit their interaction to advanced students and their activity to research functions. This was also meant to highlight the role of the University as still primarily a teaching University instead of one giving priority to research or extension services.

Centers and Institutes with Development Goals

While curricular programs were generally tied up with national goals and policies, the impact of these programs was neither easily discernible nor quantifiable. The task of public service was, therefore, more prominently discharged by specialized University Centers and Institutes whose link-up with government units in the solution of national problems was on a more regular basis.

Between 1969 and 1972, three units geared to national development needs were created: the Council on Regional Development Studies, Agrarian Reform Institute, and Center for International Studies. The Council on Regional Development Studies was in charge of coordinating the organization of regional development centers[76] by units belonging to the public affairs complex. The Agrarian Reform Institute was intended to serve the land reform program through research and training of personnel. The Center for International Studies was to undertake research on issues of international concern and was intended to be a training arm in the upgrading of diplomatic personnel.[77]

The existing service-oriented units belonging to the public affairs cluster continued providing their counsel and expertise to various government agencies. These included the Local Government Center, which helped local and provincial executives with their administrative needs, and the Philippine Executive Academy,[78] which trained executives from government and industry, while the Institute of Environmental Planning,[79] the Labor Education Center, the Institute for Small-Scale Industries and the Law Center did their share in sponsoring developmental projects for the government.

Academic units like the College of Agriculture, the College of Fisheries, the Institute of Mass Communication, the Population Institute and the School of Economics contributed the expertise of their faculty members either as resource persons or consultants in allied government agencies.

Bifocal Role within the New Society

From the point of view of the administration, the University continued to remain relevant as it both pursued purely academic goals, in line with its being a citadel of knowledge, and aligned itself to national development goals, being an agent of change.

The dichotomy between the academic degree-granting units and the specialized centers made it thus convenient for the University to discharge its avowed functions as spelled out by Lopez when he took over the Presidency of the University. This was made more obvious during the martial law years when the national government turned to the University for the implementation of the new programs of the New Society in the fields of agrarian reform, cooperatives, agricultural development, government reorganization and educational reform, among others. University professors like Gerardo P. Sicat, Onofre D. Corpuz, Jaime C. Laya and Manuel S. Alba were "drafted" to assume high positions in the national government.

At the same time, the University continued to be an outspoken critic of the national administration on more sensitive issues like freedom, human rights, the new constitution and the absence of electoral processes. Lopez set the pace, as he spoke on the new constitution, the role of social scientists and writers under martial law, the need for more freedom in the campus and especially his appraisal of the martial law regime itself in the Dillingham lectures he delivered in Hawaii and other academic centers in the United States. Some faculty members and students tested the limits of the martial law administration as they continued to speak out their minds on martial law issues in public forums, in the pages of the *Philippine Collegian,* in unsigned manifestoes and various graffiti.

Regional Units in Perspective

The establishment of the University of the Philippines System in 1972 placed in focus the role of the regional units vis-a-vis the System. As envisioned by Lopez, the regional units would eventually serve as the core of other autonomous units of the system. They were, therefore, urged to develop specializations suited to their respective regions and to gradually develop themselves as worthy intellectual centers in the area.

In rationalizing the operation of the provincial units, the University closed UP Tarlac after the provincial government repeatedly failed to give its financial share in running the unit, and opened UP Tacloban to serve the needs of the eastern Visayas region. The opening of the latter branch in 1973 was moreover premised on the wholehearted support of the Provincial Government.

A lump sum of one million pesos for each regional unit beginning fiscal year 1974 was provided for in the University budget to help boost the growth of each unit. In addition, financial incentives were offered to faculty members from Diliman, Manila and Los Baños who were willing to serve in the regional units for at least two years.

The expansion program of the University in terms of the regional units, which included proposed new branches in Davao and Bicol, was in line with the institution of the National College Entrance Test which was envisioned to lead to the closure of diploma mills due to the expected reduction of the number of students going to college. The UP would be prepared to fill the needs of regions affected by the closure of these substandard schools. The idea was to make the University Campus co-extensive with the Republic of the Philippines.

Faculty Welfare Assured

Based on the premise that a competent faculty is the backbone of the University in the training of students, Lopez in 1979 set four goals to promote faculty welfare: promotion of a climate "conducive to free inquiry, meaningful intellectual interchange, and academic excellence"; continuation of the faculty development program; promotion of faculty research; and formulation of "sound policies on faculty selection, promotion, compensation and tenure."[80]

In no instance was the freedom to teach and to learn hampered during the Lopez administration. This freedom was a policy made sacrosanct by the liberalism of Lopez.[81] Not even the turbulent years of activism when the political consciousness and ideological bent of some faculty members ran counter to the President's views, nor during the early years of martial law when the very foundation of academic freedom was oftentimes challenged by military rule, did Lopez and his administration ever transgress against this fundamental policy. Circumstances brought about by activism and martial rule may have occasionally impaired the implementation of this policy, as in the case of disruption of classes due to boycotts and student strikes, or in the imposition of self-censorship under martial law, but as a principle, the freedom to teach was upheld by the Lopez administration.

Opportunities for Advancement

Faculty development proceeded further despite the cutback of support from American benefactors, notably the Ford and Rockefeller Foundations, whose influence on the "Americanization" of the University was the object of criticism by the radicals. In 1969, there were 211 faculty members on study programs abroad, broken down as follows: 152 for Ph.D.; 35 for MA./M.S.; and 24 for special studies. Most of these personnel were sent under the Romulo administration. As of June 30, 1974, the number of fellows abroad decreased to 124 (excluding fellows from the Los Baños units which became autonomous in 1972) distributed as follows: 71 for Ph.D.; 20 for M.A/M.S.; 33 for diploma training.[82]

In the absence of dollar funding for studies abroad, faculty training centered on local fellowships. From 258 local fellowships registered for the schoolyear 1969-1970 at the cost of ₱47,114.60 the figure remained more or less constant for the succeeding years: 267 for 1970-71; 276 for 1971-1972; 301 for 1972-1973; and 239 for 1973-1974 (excluding those for Los Baños units).[83]

Faculty members were, at the same time, encouraged to attend conferences, seminars, and short-term training programs abroad even when travel was restricted by Malacañang during the early years of martial rule.

Lopez made representations with Malacañang to allow faculty members and University cultural groups to travel on official missions abroad.

Support for Faculty Research

Faculty research work continued to be given high priority by the University administration. Scholarly pursuits of faculty members as a necessary complement of their teaching functions went on unabated, despite the troubled times. Funding sources came from the University, American and European foundations, private corporations, and government agencies like the National Science Development Board.

In 1971, the University Research Council was created by the Board of Regents to coordinate and effectively integrate the activities of research units and research councils, like the Natural Science and the Social Science Research Councils, and relate them to the goals and priorities of the University. It is difficult to judge whether this Council succeeded in its tasks, but this fact notwithstanding, various research programs were reported, most of them as "parochial" in outlook as the academic units' curricular programs.[84] Units like the Industrial Research Center of the College of Engineering, Institute of Fisheries Development and Research, Community Development Research Center, and the research arms of the UP at Los Baños, generally came out with projects directed at national development goals.

Faculty Compensation Upgraded

The faculty's share in the selection of new teachers and in the promotion process has been discussed earlier. On the matter of compensation, salary increases and merit promotions were given to faculty members and other personnel of the University at least four times during the Lopez years. The University had to increase the number of steps per rank to allow for salary increases for those who could not be given rank promotions, and in the case of topmost Professors, the additional four steps were meant to reward deserving faculty members who otherwise had reached the maximum step. The first three Professors who reached the highest rank of Professor 8 in January 1973 were Cesar A. Majul, Jose Vera Santos and Carlos P. Ramos.

To augment faculty salaries and at the same time share the expertise of UP faculty members with other Universities, the Board of Regents, on the recommendation of Lopez, amended the University Code to allow the faculty to teach in other universities, provided that a faculty exchange agreement was duly entered into between the University and the other educational institution. This was meant to correct the earlier practice of "moonlighting" in other universities.

In 1972, the faculty teaching load was reduced from 15 to 12 units, followed by a policy statement from the Board of Regents that it discouraged overload teaching and frowned upon "moonlighting." The Board, however, accepted the fact that with a 12-unit load, the faculty could earn extra money through an overload of three to six units. According to Lopez, this move reflected the practical consideration that faculty members needed extra compensation due to the high cost of living.

Faculty members continued to receive honoraria from private projects on the condition that the total sum of the honoraria should not exceed their basic annual salary. This was to emphasize the primary obligation of the faculty members to the University.

Numerous Professorial Chairs

Professorial chairs grew in number from six before 1969 to 79 by September 30, 1974. Most of the chairs were obtained between 1972 and 1974 from private entities, alumni donors and proceeds from the University's investment portfolio. According to the President's Report, the College of Arts and Sciences and the Graduate School of Los Baños had the largest number of chairs (16 each), but based on the size of the college faculties, the College of Business Administration, with 13 chairs, had the prize plum, enabling it to give chairs even to Assistant Professors. Most of the chairs provided for an honorarium of ₱6,000 per annum.

More than the honorarium was the prestige attached to the chairs since the recipients were mostly the top professors of the University. Some of the recipients were Raymundo A. Favila, Leopoldo Y. Yabes, Melecio S. Magno, Carmen Velasquez (Arts and Sciences); Jose Solis (Veterinary Medicine); Jose Encarnacion, Jr. (Economics); Gelia T. Castillo (Rural Sociology); Lourdes Vera Lapuz (Psychiatry); Dolores F. Hernandez (Education); Irene R. Cortes (Law); Jaime C. Laya (Business Administration); and Pedro Escuro (Plant Breeding).

Another incentive for qualified and deserving faculty members in the creative arts (literature, fine arts, music) was the creation of titles of Writer-in-Residence, Artist-in-Residence or Musician-in-Residence by the Board of Regents on August 29, 1974. The benefits included a reduced teaching load of from three to six units per semester; honorarium of ₱3,000 per annum; and temporary enjoyment of cumulative vacation and sick leave.

These numerous benefits including salary increases, provisions for overload teaching, more relaxed rules on consultancies, and professorial chairs, made the University competitive with other private universities in terms of attending to the welfare of its teaching staff.

Permanent Appointments to the Faculty

A more rational and definite policy on tenure was adopted by the administration on June 28, 1973 based on a study made by the Executive Committee of the University Council. The old practice of giving permanency to Instructors without Master's degrees was replaced by the rule that Instructors should be given temporary appointments for five years, within which time the persons concerned would be given the chance to earn a Master's degree and be recommended for Assistant Professorship. Tenure would be at the level of Assistant Professor. For those initially appointed to the ranks of Assistant Professor, Associate Professor and Professor, their temporary appointments should be for three years, two years and one year respectively, after which time they could be considered for permanency.

The new policy on tenure not only encouraged Instructors to work for their M.A.'s within the specified time, but it also made promotion to Assistant Professorship more attainable in a shorter period of time. There were many examples in the past of Instructors who were made permanent after a few years of service with the faculty, but who remained in that rank for several years. It also did away with Instructors who, because they attained permanent status easily, took their time in earning graduate degrees.

Student Activities Geared to Relevance

For the militant students, relevance of student activities was measured in terms of doing away with frivolous and expensive social activities. Instead their energy was directed toward heightening love and interest for the masses through integration with the peasants and the urban poor. Distinctions between "burgis" (Bourgeoisie) and "masa" (masses) permeated student activities as well.

Seen in this light, the lantern parade and its beauty contest aspect (selection of the Lantern Queen) were deemed irrelevant. After the 1970 "Parada sa Pakikibaka," the lantern parade had to go, only to be revived in 1978 during the Corpuz administration.

The Cadena de Amor Festival was not held in 1969, purportedly due to lack of funds. Its sponsor, the UP Woman's Club, renamed Samahan ng Kababaihan sa Unibersidad ng Pilipinas (SKUP), had changed its directions and perspectives. Thus, the Cadena de Amor Festival and the Pink and White Ball had to go in the name of relevance.

Another tradition that "died" shortly after 1971 was the University annual, the *Philippinensian.* The last issue came out in 1971 edited by Bienvenido Noriega. The troubled times and the lack of interest to manage the publication of the University annual was partly responsible for its death. Printing costs had gone up making it very expensive to publish a University-wide annual. A series of problems plaguing its publication ended in the failure of *Philippinensian '69* to come out purportedly due to the nervous breakdown of its editor-in-chief, and the delay in the publication of *Philippinensian*'70 and '71.

But the flowering of Pilipino and its wide usage in rallies, demonstrations and symposia, as well as in student publications as earlier discussed, was a high point of the period. The staging of plays, skits and other dramatic presentations not only in Pilipino but with a "revolutionary" orientation, usually formed part of rallies and demonstrations. Even under martial law, the UP Repertory Company, formed in 1973, and other cultural groups produced plays with a "message."

External Relations Reexamined

President Lopez had to cope with the issue of "Americanization" of the University as articulated by the Movement for the Advancement of Nationalism (M.A.N.) in 1969 to the effect that American "educational aid" and grants from foundations had a great influence on the University's curriculum, research and teaching, thereby impeding the growth of nationalist expressions. Lopez deemed it necessary to terminate the University's contract with the Asia Foundation and to form the University Committee on Contracts which took charge of scrutinizing all contracts with foreign agencies and foundations before these were approved by the President's office and the Board of Regents.

However Lopez rejected the students' demand that the University cut itself off from American institutions and do away with American visiting professors. He was for diminishing the American presence in the campus but he believed that to completely de-Americanize the University was to run against modernization. He then emphasized the importance of not closing windows already open and opening windows still closed to the University, stressing that nationalism should not be xenophobic and a barrier to internationalism.

The Ford and Rockefeller Foundations understood the extent of anti-Americanism on campus, and thus agreed to continue with their existing programs only but to refrain from starting new ones. For example, the Ford Foundation-assisted Wisconsin-UP training program in Development Economics which started in 1965, involving the participation of faculty members from the University of Wisconsin, was terminated in 1973. But faculty members of the School of Economics completely took over the training program, including its funding requirements. Likewise, the Rockefeller Foundation-funded UP-Cornell University Graduate Education Program ended in 1970.

The University continued to receive foreign assistance from, among others, various United Nations agencies, U.S. Agency for International Development, several European countries, and the South East Asia Regional Center for Graduate Study and Research in Agriculture (SEARCA).

Exploring International Links

As early as 1970, the University, through President Lopez, was already laying down the foundation for educational exchange agreements with the USSR and other socialist states of Eastern Europe, with special emphasis on science, when the Board of Regents authorized him to explore the possibility of entering into specific arrangements with said countries. He made more definite commitments in 1974 for academic exchange with the University of Moscow and the Institute of Oriental Studies.

Relations with the Association of South East Asian Institutions of Higher Learning (ASAIHL) and ASEAN countries continued as Lopez participated actively in their conferences on topics dealing with faculty sharing, admissions requirements for graduate programs in South East Asian Universities, resources and information, and promotion of joint programs in teaching and research.[85]

University units like the Anesthesiology Center; the Science Education Center; the Colleges of Agriculture, Education, and Economics; the Institute of Mass Communication and others, sponsored training programs, seminars, workshops, and conferences participated in by Asian and Western scholars.

To rationalize the existing UP foreign scholarship program, the rules were centralized and specific funding provided (₱72,000 per annum), to give substance to reciprocal programs entered into by the Philippine Government with foreign governments. Four scholarships in the undergraduate and graduate levels were provided in each of the following areas: (1) Southeast Asia; (2) West, East and South Asia; (3) Africa; (4) Latin-America; (5) Europe and North America. In addition, four scholarships for non-selfgoverning territories were created in 1974 at the request of the United Nations.

Sharing of Academic Resources

On the local level, sharing the UP's expertise with private and other state universities was done not only through faculty exchange programs, provided for by the University in 1970, but also with the establishment of consortium arrangements with the Pamantasan ng Lungsod ng Maynila, the Mindanao State University, the Philippine Military Academy, Brent School, the Centro Escolar University, the Central Philippine University and the West Visayas State College. The consortium agreements called for the sharing of facilities, resources, and personnel on a reciprocal basis.

Rapport with the Alumni

Ties with the alumni could not have been any better under the Lopez presidency. Realizing that the alumni are an important segment of the University community, at the alumni homecoming for 1969 and 1970 Lopez took pains to inform them of important changes taking place on campus in response to the times. An alumni "teach-in" conference for this purpose, on the topic "U.P. Today," was organized in 1970 by the Alumni Relations Office and the UP Alumni Association.

In September 1969, Eduardo Escobar, President of the UP Alumni Association, became ex-officio member of the Board of Regents, representing the alumni sector. In that capacity, the "Alumni Regent" participated in the policy-making process of the University.

The construction of the offices of the alumni groups and the recreation hall, the initial components of the UP Alumni Center Complex, was completed with the full support of the Lopez administration. In 1974, the University signed an agreement with the UP Alumni Association for the former to build a hostel within the Alumni Center Complex for the use of alumni participating in the University's continuing education programs. The funds to build the hostel came from a GSIS loan for the construction of dormitories and housing units in the University.

Oblation Plaza and Other Donations

To commemorate the 25th anniversary of the University's transfer to Diliman, the Alumni Association undertook the beautification of the area fronting the administration and built the Oblation Plaza out of donations from the alumni.

Generous support from the alumni came in the form of donations for the construction of the Llamas Science Pavilion in the College of Arts and Sciences and of the German Yia Engineering Research Shop; in raising funds from private sources through the UP Endowment Foundation, Inc., which has funded professorial chairs and given loans for student welfare projects; and in donating professorial chairs funded by the UP Alumni Association and the College Alumni Chapters.

PERSPECTIVE ON SIX YEARS OF TURBULENCE ASSUAGED BY DEMOCRATIZATION

THAT the University underwent a significant transformation during the Lopez years can not be questioned. The nation was in turmoil and the University had no other option but to respond to changes brought about by student-faculty activism.

The nature of the response could, however, have taken a different direction had it been contrary to that taken by the Lopez administration. A hardline President could have misread the signs of the times in a manner that would have evoked violent confrontations between the radical students and faculty members. Moreover, he could have marshalled the resources of the University and the State to muzzle the student activists, or to "throw the book" at the activists and impose stern disciplinary measures. The events would certainly have taken a different turn with another man at the helm of the University.

Rational Approach to Relevance

The goals that Lopez had set for himself and the University at the start of his administration were substantially implemented through his efforts at democratizing the University and keeping the University relevant through the re-orientation of programs involving teaching, research and extension service. Lopez set the pace in leading the University constituency to these goals as reflected in his speeches and in his programs.

A closer look at his programs would, however, show certain flaws which were interpreted by some quarters as signs of weakness.

The democratization program was faulted by the radicals for introducing a limited type of participatory democracy. If they could have their way, the radicals would have wanted more power for students and faculty members in curricular and administrative matters, such as the institution of "free" courses through which students and faculty members could initiate new subjects and courses without being encumbered by bureaucratic procedures; or they would have made all administrative positions in the University subject to elections.

The conservatives, on the other hand, would have wanted to preserve the status quo which gave the prerogative of selection and appointment to department chairmen, deans and directors of UP units up to the University President. Some conservatives had, in fact, resented the President's supposed coddling of student activists, and the President's acquiescence to the demands of students for a say in curricular matters.

Admissions Policy and Elitism

The move to democratize the student mix in the University was limited by the UP College Admissions Tests (UPCAT) which was culture bound and catered to students coming from better schools. Although some reforms were instituted such as combining the three-year high school average with the UPCAT score in the selection of freshman students, the UPCAT remained the stumbling block in getting students from the lower social classes and the rural areas. Moreover, in the initial phase of the Grants-in-Aid program, the financial benefits were not enough to completely support financially handicapped students. Thus the University remained basically elitist despite the goal of Lopez to open the University to the Filipino masses.

Options intended to give a larger voice to the lower sectors of the faculty, like the Faculty Assembly, were called only during the crisis posed by police brutality and the barricades.

Uplift of the Masses

In keeping the University relevant to the times, the Lopez vision was to link the University and its programs to the transformation of Filipino society to the end that the happiness and well-being of the masses could be guaranteed. The idea then was to promote curriculum changes to meet the needs of society, research geared toward improving the life of the people, and extension services that would benefit the majority of the people.

Seen in terms of these lofty goals, the University failed to respond to the challenges of Lopez. Curriculum changes were slow in coming, research generally remained individualized, and extension services had no central direction, with the exception of some centers or institutes which were public-affairs oriented.

But seen from the standpoint of academic and scholarly activities, there were evidences of growth: the propagation of Pilipino and Philippine culture, the new and innovative undergraduate curricula, the doctoral programs, the big number of research projects completed covering topics of great diversity, and the involvement of faculty members in national programs, among others.

Despite the above limitations and apparent weaknesses, Lopez introduced significant innovations. Democratization in terms of governance of the University opened the floodgates to the sharing of functions with the three sectors of the University constituency, and to more benefits for these sectors.

Filipinism Enhanced by Relevance

By democratizing the University, Lopez initiated the move to keep the University relevant as it was buffeted by all kinds of pressures and winds of change. Thus, he pushed further the role of the University as a Filipino University, keeping in mind its function as a social critic and agent for change.

As he kept the University relevant, he managed to save the University from possible destruction physically and intellectually. The various crises brought about by student-faculty activism, capped by the barricades, could have led to untold violence and to loss of lives and property if they had not been properly handled.

That relevant posture was maintained under martial law. For one, the attempt to "dismember" the University by a move to establish an independent agricultural university was checked by the Lopez administration through the establishment of the University of the Philippines System. The birth of the UP System was one of the more tangible accomplishments of the Lopez administration. Its establishment provided the foundation for the expansion programs undertaken by the succeeding administrations.

A Perceptible Conservatism

From another angle, the above developments showed the basic conservatism of the University where its basic concerns of curriculum and research were involved, even as the university projected the image of radicalism and militance.

The assertive students and faculty members fulfilled the main role of the University during this period as a social critic. Lopez himself was not wanting in this role. He provided the balance between the radical stance of the activists and "conservative" quarters, represented primarily by government agencies like the police and the military. But there were irritants. The University President was caught in the middle: he was sympathetic to the activists but at the same time he had also pledged the University to national development. The "blueprints" for national development radically differed between the two contesting groups. It was this "balancing act" that was interpreted by some quarters as a sign of weakness, a sign of "fence-sitting."

Another irritant was the clash between Lopez's brand of nationalism and the radicals' militant nationalism. To Lopez, nationalism should not be the xenophobic type that would discourage the growth of universalism. On the other hand, the radicals saw nationalism as a vehicle to completely remove foreign, i.e. American, influences and establish a non-elitist society.

Upholding Institutional Integrity

Lopez read the signs of the times and reacted accordingly. He thus preserved the integrity of the University specially from outside interference, and by so doing kept the University intact, allowing its constituents to seek the truth in a relatively free atmosphere.

Lopez had the ability to work with the different sectors of the University, and even in an atmosphere of antagonism and confrontation, he patiently kept the communication lines open. A love-hate relationship existed between him and the militant students, but these students were to realize that he kept the University going against all odds, and that he was a friend who helped them gain the rights they won during the height of activism.

The faculty generally appreciated his policies and his efforts in promoting faculty welfare.

Lopez enjoyed a good working relationship with the Board of Regents. He had the support of, and his decisions were upheld by, the Board of Regents in his handling of student activism, in the different crises faced by the University, and in his academic programs. Lopez admitted to enjoying "an exceptionally fine working relationship" with the Board of Regents. In his description of the situation: "No University President has worked more closely and cooperatively with the Board, and the Board with the President."[86]

The relationship of Lopez with the national government and with President Marcos was generally cordial. The University with him at the helm continued to get the necessary funding from the national government despite Lopez's and the University's role as critics of the government. The University budget increased considerably every year until the end of Lopez's term.

Duty Fulfilled with Deep Satisfaction

By the eve of the end of his term, Lopez had become the object of testimonials from all segments of the University. As early as September 1974, he was given a testimonial luncheon by various constituents of the University in Diliman; honored at a concert where Dr. Eliseo M. Pajaro played a new work entitled "The Lopez Years 1969-1974"; and feted as a special guest at a testimonial dinner tendered by UP at Los Baños. On the last occasion, Lopez good-naturedly said: ". . . one wonders whether this is a warm welcome or a warm send-off."[87]

Unlike a previous president who stepped down from the presidency under unhappy circumstances, Lopez ended his term enjoying a wide latitude of support from, and credibility with, all sectors of the University. These groups clamored for his reelection to let him "continue making the UP relevant."

He was readying development plans and would have wanted to serve the University for a second term, but a decision for a change had been mandated.

On January 16, 1975, he issued a statement at the special meeting of the Board of Regents that he did not seek the renewal or extension of his term, and summed up his administration thus:

> "I have served the University in a troubled time, without stint. It is today in reasonably fine shape—safe, sound and solvent. This is therefore a good time to lay down the burden of its administration, and I do so with a deep sense of relief and satisfaction."

XI

Corpuz and Soriano's Bifocal Administrations (1975-1981)

Toward a Realignment of the Academe to National Realities under a Crisis Government

by Jose N. Endriga

Corpuz and Soriano's Bifocal Administrations

HARMONY between the national and the university leadership, considered significant even in normal times, took on an added dimension during the period of an authoritarian regime which in essence strives for greater concordance among the various institutions in society. Where disharmony arose in the past, some university presidents, such as Palma and Gonzalez, resigned from their positions for their own principled reasons, and thus earned the deep respect of the University constituency, and even of their own adversaries.

The expiration of the term of an incumbent university president could also provide a convenient and gracious way out from an irreconcilable conflict. Such was the case with Salvador P. Lopez. His words and deeds, manifesting his consistently liberal outlook, endeared him to a significant portion of the university constituency, but made his position more and more untenable, given the political context of the country.

Nevertheless President Marcos was to acknowledge in early 1975 that President Lopez's handling of the University's troublous affairs during the early 1970s was responsible for the preservation of the University's intellectual, moral and physical integrity. "It is a monument to his flexibility, resiliency and wisdom that the University still stands," the President declared in a gracious public acknowledgment.[1] *

However, the University that President Lopez helped in surmounting the gravest crisis was not to be his to run after the expiration of his six-year term on January 23, 1975. In late 1974, Lopez in a sense had sealed his fate by delivering his much publicized Dillingham lecture in Honolulu.

Inauspicious for a Liberal

Before a foreign audience he tried valiantly to present a balanced picture of the martial law regime in the Philippines, but he ended on a more unequivocal stance. He, in fact, called for the dismantling of martial law, a process which he however thought

*Footnote references are compiled in the NOTES section at the end of this book.

> . . . must be deliberate and measured so as to ensure a smooth transition from the present "command society" to a democratic policy. The indefinite prolongation of martial law or its complete and precipitate withdrawal by a stroke of the pen could result in anarchy and civil strife. These alternatives seem, thus far, to be unacceptable to most Filipinos who, despite the admitted shortcomings of the martial law regime, continue to give it their support.
>
> Their patience, however, is not endless; they will not wait forever.[2]

Thereafter, various elements of the University constituency expressed their desire to have President Lopez continue in office. The UP Faculty Organization, the *Philippine Collegian,* the Consultative Committee on Student Affairs, the Organization of Non-Academic Personnel, the Supervisors' Association and the Alumni Association, among others, all passed resolutions endorsing the President's continuance in office.[3] They specifically singled out "his enlightened policies towards students, faculty and other personnel,"[4] "his vigorous and imaginative infrastructure program,"[5] his pursuance of policies which were in accord "with the principles of the times–Filipinization, democratization, and the affirmation of the University's integrity."[6]

Quite apart from their recognition of Lopez's demonstrated merits in his administration of the University, the resolutions were perhaps also signs of the apprehension of the University constituency who believed that the UP should continue to be led by someone more in sympathy with the cherished liberal traditions of their university. Their words, to be sure, were to no avail.

A BRILLIANT POLITICAL SCIENTIST AND ADMINISTRATOR FOR UNIVERSITY PRESIDENT

AT its 855th (Special) meeting the Board of Regents on January 16 1975 unanimously elected Dr. Onofre D. Corpuz as President of the University for a six-year term commencing on January 24, 1975. The new President was not a newcomer to the University and was, in the words of former President Lopez, simply taking on a "resumption of his love affair with the University."[7] He had previously spent two decades in the UP as student, teacher and administrator. On the basis of his academic background and related experience, he appeared to be eminently suitable for the presidency.

Corpuz had a brilliant academic record, graduating *magna cum laude* from the UP in 1950, going on for graduate studies in the United States, first at the University of Illinois, then at Harvard where he shone as a graduate student.[8] He capped his stint there with a Master's degree in Public

Administration in 1955 and a year later with a Ph.D. in Political Economy. His doctoral dissertation, published locally as *The Bureacracy in the Philippines,* is not only an excellent piece of scholarship but is indubitably the best work ever done in that area in the Philippines.

From the UP to the Cabinet

Returning to the country in 1956, he resumed his faculty position, rose quickly in the academic ladder while establishing a reputation as a brilliant, kindly, soft-spoken teacher, whose pen produced provocative pieces that found publication in learned journals and in popular magazines. Following a probably dysfunctional University tradition, whereby a bright young faculty member would not be left to his academic pursuits, he became variously secretary of the Graduate School, chairman of the Political Science department, secretary of the University, Acting Business Executive, and special assistant to UP President Romulo. The latter, when he moved over to the Department of Education as Secretary, took with him Dr. Corpuz as Undersecretary of the Department. When Romulo became Secretary of Foreign Affairs, Dr. Corpuz succeeded to the Education portfolio in 1968. He thereby became the chairman of the UP Board of Regents, and together with President Lopez, saw the University through the troubled times of the early 1970s.[9]

He subsequently retired from government service. As a private citizen, he became president of the Fund for Assistance to Private Education, while increasing his participation in the private sector by becoming chairman or member of numerous boards. In 1973 he became the President-Founder of the Development Academy of the Philippines, an institution that became very active in working for the New Society, developing programs and projects and training civil servants in the new dispensation.

Thus, at 48, when he became one of the youngest presidents of the University, Dr. Corpuz might not have achieved the national stature or the international prestige of some of his predecessors, but he brought to his position incomparable academic credentials as well as a perspective shaped not only by academia but considerably altered by exposure to the world of politics and action. He was going to manifest as university president the non-puristic outlook of such a man, a fact which might explain partly some of the problems he was to encounter with the vocal university constituency. Then, in addition to his formal credentials, he also had an ideological affinity with the regime, being its most brilliant and articulate spokesman.

Spokesman for the New Society

President Corpuz had earlier written a brief treatise on "Liberty and Government in the New Society," a scholarly as well as a polemical justification of the martial law regime. Drawing upon his rich knowledge of political philosophy and history, he demonstrated in that tract the necessity for the Filipinos' ridding themselves of Western-derived concepts of liberty and functions of government.

In place of political liberty, which in his analysis was shown to be a narrow concept, he offered the idea of human liberty which he defined as an instrument for human liberation. In achieving the latter the government was shown to be a primary vehicle, whose enlarged powers and sphere of activity would lead to that liberation. The essay succeeded brilliantly, and the piece remains, on theoretical grounds alone, as the finest defense of the martial law regime. It also contributed to apprehensions within the University that such a philosophy might mean an alignment of its activities with the priorities, or even the dictates, of the regime.

Oath-Taking in Malacañang

Some of that apprehension might have been allayed by the remarks of President Marcos during the induction of Dr. Corpuz on January 24, 1975 at the reception hall in Malacañang.[10] Speaking before a fairly large crowd composed of such dignitaries as the First Lady, Foreign Minister Romulo, former President Lopez, the deans and directors of various units and some faculty members of the University, President Marcos expressed nothing but the finest liberal sentiments in relation to the role of the University in society. He did deliver a cryptic statement to the effect that "as the tradition of civility recommends, there is no liberty, of course, without authority; these must go hand in hand if man's life in society must be fulfilled" – a statement which he did not elaborate upon–but the gracious occasion yielded its share of ringing passages, the most eloquent and reassuring of which is the following:

> . . .If the University is only going to reflect current realities, where will the critical thought–the transforming criticism of society come from? There has to be a zone of sanity, of clear uncluttered thought, so that the turmoils can be seen at a distance and hopefully provide an approach to accommodating them or putting them at the service of society. This the University is ideally suited to do.[11]

The President ended his remarks by giving the assurance that "whatever the plans for the future, the University will receive the support of the government."

Message of Self-Liberation

It was not until four months later, on April 13, 1975, that President Corpuz was formally invested, during the sixty-seventh commencement exercises of the University. His investiture address, entitled "The Self-Liberation of the Filipino," reiterated his familiar theme on the new and expanded meaning of liberty and government in the New Society. He said that "if we recognize the fact of our conditioning by foreign ideas, and resolve to liberate ourselves from bondage to obsolete concepts, we can begin to make contributions to the exciting adventure of building our nation."

Continuing, he spoke more specifically of the role of the University in this context:

> The University will assume a major role in this task of self-liberation. We will review the Filipino experience, and derive wisdom from it. In doing so, perhaps we will be enabled to realize, among others, that the true minorities in our national community are not the ethnic or religious groups but that in fact the true minorities are the majority of millions of Filipinos who receive only a small share of the values and products of our national growth and development.[12]

He also called for an examination of "the conventional and romantic stereotype of the University as a battleground of ideas." He observed that many of those who wanted the University to be a battleground "have never seen the blood and violence, nor smelled the smoke of gunpowder on a real battlefield." He considered it "rather odd" for the Filipino people "to support a battleground with their taxes."[13]

Instead, he saw the value of the University in this way:

> The intellectual life of the University is in the seeking, and questing, for ideas, so that we may have a surer sense and understanding of truth. This has nothing to do with warring opinions. Nor should the University offer itself as a cockpit for fighting ideas, especially if those ideas are merely orthodoxies for, or orthodoxies against, an issue of partisan nature. If the University should engage in the politics of ideas, it should lend itself to the expression of ideas other than the conventional and established orthodoxies, so that it be neither advocate nor adversary, but a catalyst and an enriching agent.[14]

The views expressed in the investiture address were in fact tested even before they were actually delivered and expectedly became productive of controversies, thereafter to erupt sporadically and to bedevil the administration from its beginning to the end.

Clashes with the Studentry

This was specially true in the administration's relationship with the students which was described at one time by President Corpuz himself as an "adversary relationship."[15] The details and lineaments of such a relationship can be told, and the quality of the discourse indicated, by drawing from records of the first year of administration with its series of lively controversies.

As if to quickly put to a test the divergent perspectives of the new President and the active segment of the University constituency, President Corpuz issued within two weeks of his oathtaking his memorandum circular No. 3. This circular, which sought to govern discussion in the University of issues pertaining to the February 27 referendum, provided among others that "no outside discussants shall be invited to any such discussions." The circular provided the reasons for the prohibition: ". . . we attach no special value to intellectual brilliance or sophistication from outsiders, although the members of the University are not deficient in this respect. What is to be stimulated and promoted is the expression of honest ideas and feelings of University campus residents, who may not have the glamour of famous or powerful personages, but whose thoughts are fully as legitimate."[16]

The reactions to the memorandum were swift. The staff of the *Philippine Collegian* complained that the guidelines automatically cancelled the series of symposia which nine campus organizations had scheduled for three different days in February, to which in fact, famous outside personalities had been invited. These included former Senators Gerardo Roxas, Jovito Salonga, and Jose W. Diokno; and Supreme Court Justices Roberto Concepcion, Fred Ruiz Castro and Calixto Zaldivar.[17]

Sharp Words Leading to Concession

The Student Steering Committee for Information on the Referendum Issues, composed of 50 campus organizations, argued in a position paper that "the guidelines assume that if speakers are invited, the University can no longer think independently." It went on to emphasize that the University position and thinking "can be 'independent' only to a certain degree, but not to the extent of isolation from the rest of Philippine society." Since the referendum involved a national question and not only a University issue, "it is only proper to invite speakers, besides those from the University, who are knowledgeable on the questions involved, so as to help crystallize views and opinions." Borrowing the language of the memorandum itself, the steering committee pointed out that "this step will certainly stand in the way of stimulating and promoting the 'expression of honest ideas and feelings of the University campus residents.'"[18]

That argument elicited from the President a reply of uncommon fervor:

> If the rest of the U.P. constituency think like you do, I am almost tempted to conclude that this University is beyond salvation. Your views and your choice of speakers reflect the most unmitigated elitism which I personally commit myself to destroy.[19]

In a well-attended dialogue held at the Abelardo Hall auditorium on February 18, President Corpuz agreed to rescind the controversial item in his memorandum. He replied to the position paper of the steering committee by declaring eloquently that "the guidelines. . . were promulgated not from disguised partisanship, but from a raging dissatisfaction on my part at the insensitivity of the University to many of the real issues in our national life."

"The University," he continued, "should take a stand, not merely by adopting one orthodoxy or the other, but must whenever it can, seek to generate unorthodox views." It must, therefore, welcome not only "knowledgeable speakers" but must "learn from the wisdom of the common citizen."

Learning from the Humblest

Accordingly, his rescinding of the inhibition on outside speakers was based on the condition, stated with much feeling, that "you invite a fisherman whose house is not lighted by electricity and who goes into the cold wind and waters of dawn to feed his family and eke out a livelihood. Let us open the University to them and to common Filipinos like them, and learn from them about dignity and issues of welfare."[20]

In the series of symposia that followed the resolution of the controversy, three groups of speakers in fact had their say: University professors, famous personalities from outside the campus and common people. Among the first group were Dean Raul P. de Guzman and Prof. Felipe V. Oamar of the College of Public Administration, who argued respectively for the retention of elective (as against appointive) officials and for a metropolitan authority which was subsequently realized in the Metro Manila Commission headed by the First Lady. Prof. Jose F. Espinosa of the College of Law, addressing the main question of the referendum, concluded that it was a futile exercise because it was merely a consultation and had no binding effect on the President who could merely ignore a negative vote.[21]

Former Senators Salonga and Roxas spoke before a jampacked audience at the University theater. The former argued that it was a "supreme injustice" for the people to be compelled in a "managed, manipulated referendum" to say that they approved of the way the President was exercising his powers and of his continuing to do so. He claimed that the questions themselves suggested the desired answers. He argued further that there was no such thing as a consultative referendum, meaning that, if the results were adverse, they would not be binding, and if they were favorable they would be interpreted as a mandate.

As if to lend credence to the accusation by the opposition of prosecution by those in power, Salonga while speaking was interrupted three times by electrical brownouts. Roxas had to speak without a microphone as he gave his "separate but concurrent opinion" to Salonga's views. Calling the referendum a "farce," a "streetshow," and a "moro-moro," he said he could not in conscience participate in the exercise and expressed his willingness to risk imprisonment for holding such a view.

Four ordinary Filipinos, the ones whose views President Corpuz wanted the University constituency to hear, had their say at another symposium. Marcial Lucero, a lawyer and a former mayor of Meycauayan, Bulacan (and therefore not an ordinary Filipino) argued in favor of the manager-commission type of government as well as in support of martial law. Nick Sevilla of Constitution Hill, who introduced himself as "an ignorant squatter," noted that discipline prevailed under a martial law regime and hence advised students that before thinking of the wrongs that President Marcos had done, they should think first of the good he had also done. Fely Latorena, a Kanto-Katipunan driver, declared that the country had "an overdose of referendums." He asked: "Since President Marcos has all the power in the country, why does he have to call for a referendum? " and then pointed out that this could only confuse the people. Josephine Domio, a social worker from Tondo, asked the question, "Are we free?" She proceeded to reiterate the four demands of the Catholic bishops of the Philippines.[22]

Advent of More Disagreement

This particular controversy was by its nature short-lived, and although subsequent national referenda were to exercise the University again, the resolution of the issue in favor of free discussion remained in the books. Against this background, however, other conflicts also developed, principally those on rules governing the *Philippine Collegian* and the convening of the Student Conference. Both issues, interestingly enough, were triggered by separate actions taken on the same day, May 29: the New Rules Governing *Philippine Collegian* being approved by the Board of Regents and Memorandum Circular No. 19 being issued by the President to call for a Student Conference. Of these, the second was the more important since it concerned what to the students was the most fundamental matter of the restoration of the Student Council which in fact resulted in a prolonged combat between the administration and the students that lasted until late 1979.

EXECUTIVE VICE-PRESIDENT TO EASE BURDEN FROM THE UNIVERSITY HEAD

ACADEMIC year 1975-1976 opened with these controversies and the appointment of a high administration official to a newly recreated post to help handle the conflict. The Office of Executive Vice-President (EVP) had been restored on April 10, 1975 by the Board of Regents with much broader powers:

1. Subject to review and instructions of the President of the University, the EVP shall have executive supervision of the University of the Philippines System to ensure the implementation of the policies of the Board of Regents;
2. In the management of the affairs of the UP System the EVP shall act in the name of the President, subject to the latter's instructions and the policies of the Board of Regents;
3. The EVP shall exercise such other powers and discharge such other responsibilities as may be delegated to him by the President of the University and the Board of Regents.

In addition, Executive Order No. 1 dated April 22, 1975 provided that "for the expeditious and sound administration of the affairs of the UP System, and in order to reduce the volume of matters submitted to the President for consideration, approval or review, it is hereby directed that all matters which are now or may hereafter be subject to consideration, approval or review by the President of the University, except matters transmitted by the Chancellors of universities in the System, shall first be submitted to the Office of the Executive Vice President for evaluation and determination. Such determination shall be considered final until and unless modified, reversed or set aside by the President of the University."[23]

Soriano to No. 2 Post

The choice for the position was 39-year-old Emanuel V. Soriano, professor of Business Administration, past director of the UP College in Cebu, a doctor of business administration from Harvard University, and consultant both to the Ayala Corporation and to the Development Academy of the Philippines (DAP). It should incidentally be noted here that President Corpuz during his term continued to serve as DAP president in a concurrent capacity.

The grant of very broad powers meant, in practice, that the EVP would be running the affairs of the University, an arrangement that enabled the President himself "to devote a more substantial portion of (his) time to policy-making and long-range planning."[24] It also meant that Dr. Soriano bore a major brunt of the conflicts that continued between the students and the administration.

Rationale for Student Conference

Such was the situation when President Corpuz called for the student conference to be held in Diliman to enable student representatives "to discuss and to formulate recommendations on basic issues affecting student welfare."[25] According to Executive Vice-President Soriano, this was the mechanism decided upon by President Corpuz in response to "petitions, opinions, and other resolutions from many sectors in the past" asking for the revival of the Student Council and for participation in University affairs.[26]

The Memorandum provided that such a Student Conference would be under the supervision of the Dean of Student Affairs or his representative, and composed of representatives of the University units in Diliman as well as in Baguio, who were entitled to one representative each, except for the College of Arts and Sciences which was entitled to two. It provided for a grade requirement of 2.5 or better for representatives but disqualified those who had obtained a grade of "5" or "incomplete," dropped any course during the previous semester, or were subjected to "any disciplinary action for misconduct of any kind."

The mechanics of the organization would have the Executive Vice-President call a preliminary session of all the elected representatives in order to elect from among themselves a chairman, a vice-chairman and a secretary, which officers would confer with the EVP and the Dean of Student Affairs on the details of the organization and operation of the Student Conference. It was supposed to appropriate amounts for its operation from student fees, subject to the approval of the Dean of Student Affairs and the EVP.

Dissent from Student Side

Such provisions could not but raise objections from the student side. The CONCOMSA took the stand that there was no student participation whatever in the drafting of the guidelines; no guarantee that any of the proposals coming from the Conference would be accepted or implemented; that the terms of the representatives were uncertain; and that the funding for the Conference would be drawn from the Student Welfare Fund.

One student leader, Oliver Juma-os, labelled the Conference as "a mere palliative to the demands for student autonomy and representation."[27] The *Collegian* editor, Abraham Sarmiento, Jr., raised the question of representation, the autonomy of the Conference from the University administration, and the vagueness of the functions of the Conference.

The *Collegian* itself questioned why the College of Arts and Sciences, which constituted 45 percent of the student body to be represented in the Conference, would have only 2 out of 29 representatives. It also considered the qualification requirements too stringent. It pointed out that the circular did not stipulate that the conference could carry out student welfare projects, its function being merely recommendatory. It said that the circular granted unlimited power to the EVP "for the accomplishment of the purpose" of the Conference, and said further that the representatives were supposed to hold office "for as long as it takes them to discuss Soriano's agenda."

Modifications Proposed and Carried

More specific proposals were subsequently made, and these included the following: modification of the grade requirements and greater student participation in the election process.[28] A Consolidated Stand was drawn up led by the CONCOMSA and several student organizations which reiterated the points raised earlier by CONCOMSA and added: "The Student Conference, with all its limitations, can only be of value to the students if it works for the immediate restoration of the Student Council – a body the entire studentry has long been fighting for. The general call for the restoration of an autonomous, democratically mandated and representative student Council therefore remains."[29]

After all this lively exchange between the students and the University administration, which by now had become a characteristic of their relationship, an amending memorandum circular was issued on August 26, 1975 which lowered the grade requirement to 2.75, increased the representation of the CAS to eight, provided that the tenure of the Conference be determined by the representatives themselves, and that the recommendations of the Conference be presented to the students for approval.[30]

The changes elicited qualified praises from the *Philippine Collegian* in an editorial in the August 29, 1975 issue: "The guidelines are still far from ideal, but the Administration has been both reasonable and flexible in acceding to valid proposals submitted by various student groups . . . the Administration may be willing to give us a foot but the students will have to fight for that inch by inch."

Excitement Generated by Elections

Elections were thus scheduled for September 12, which were moved to September 18, a postponement that triggered another round of objections from many student groups. Apparently, the Executive Vice-President had acceded to requests for postponement by other student groups who cited as reasons the lack of time for campaigning, the possible declaration of September 11, President Marcos' birthday, as a holiday (it was not so declared), the presentation of cadet sponsors, and other University activities.[31]

Despite such a disagreement, however, the campaign fever hit a high pitch, with the College of Arts and Sciences being the most active and even the residence halls joining in various activities. As one student leader put it: "The Student Conference marks the first time that elections will be held in a major institution after martial law. Even our parents do not have this right to vote."[32]

The elections were won by the Students Rights and Welfare (STRAW) group, which garnered 32 out of the 38 seats.[33] The Conference expectedly reiterated the four main demands of the campaign, and embodied these in their first six resolutions, which advocated: (1) reactivation of the Student Council; (2) restoration of the local councils; (3) restoration of the Woman's Club; (4) adoption of general guidelines for the operation of all local councils; (5) restoration of student representation in the Board of Regents; and (6) student representation in the Program Development Staff on an institutionalized basis.[34]

Edgy Relationship Recalled

Earlier the student conference had sent President Corpuz three letters (Jan. 5, Feb. 2 and 5) the first of which contained the resolution on the reactivation of the Student Council. This elicited a strong, chiding letter from the President, in which he argued against the student demands. On the suspension of the Student Council itself, the President asked: "Why was it suspended? You yourselves know this. As for me, I was not yet in the University then, and can only guess at the reasons considered by the supreme authorities of the land." His reference of course was to the suspension of all student councils in the country by martial law. But he allowed that "the University President can decide on the matter." Then, explicitly defining the prerogative of authority, he said: This does not mean that when you *demand,* I shall acquiesce. To decide means to have options, for or against and *the authority to decide favorably includes the authority to decide negatively."*[35] He raised a number of questions, "your answer to which will influence my final decision."

The first one concerned the Conference's demand that the University is and ought to be "autonomous," and Corpuz explained why this was not possible:

> . . . . the University is supported by the people's taxes which proceed from their labor. The President of the Republic approves the budget of the University, which is an allocation of a portion of the people's taxes to the University. At the moment of Presidential approval, however, that money allocated in the budget does not exist. It is still to be raised; that farmers, laborers, clerks, managers and other *adults* engaged in production of wealth must first produce that wealth through their labor, and other services. Then the government collects taxes, allocates these proceeds to government programs, and then releases the corresponding share of the University. Question: How can the University assert autonomy under the circumstances, when it is supported by the labor and wealth of the people allocated to it by the government? It can do so only by earning the *confidence* of the leaders of our government that the University's operations are contributive to national goals. Only stupid leaders of government will yield to petulant University demands.

The letter also demolished the demand that the student council must participate "in all major policy-making bodies of the University." *"I will attribute this to the immaturity of the membership and/or leadership of the*

Student Conference," he suggested strongly, and continued, "what you are saying arises from ignorance, because the charter of the University provides that policies . . . are formulated by specific bodies which are to be constituted by qualified persons by virtue of faculty status or by proper appointment by authority of the government."

Plethora of Arguments

He gave the example of the University Council which "includes only persons who were once students, who dedicate themselves to teaching, research and other functions of the academic life, who have served the University adequately and competently and have thereby *earned* the rank of at least assistant professor in the University." Then paternalistically, he added: "You should work some more, then as an adult serve in some profession or occupation, so that you can qualify for these policy-making bodies in our University."

Then he offered the information that student participation in the past in the Board of Regents was "lamentable," as a result of which a retired University employee with an otherwise excellent record of service, could not get his retirement benefits.

He further chided the Student Conference by pointing out that other groups in the University, such as the faculty and administrators, had made concrete suggestion to the University's planning for its welfare and improvement. "I had hoped that the . . . Student Conference would also make similar contributions. But all you could recommend was a student council. You were thinking of political structures, not community purposes."

Finally, the President gave the assurance that he had "not eliminated the matter of a student council in the University." But first, he went on, "it is my duty to try and see to it that the diverse and heterogeneous values and interests of the thousands of students of the University are provided with mechanisms for representation in student politics."

Such values and interests he described in specific terms:

> Many students have come to me complaining of letters and other materials which they send to the student newspaper but which are never printed because they are opposite to your views. Many student leaders have come to me proposing student activities which the Student Conference has ignored. Many student groups have suggested to my office projects independent of politics but relevant to students' day-to-day concerns. These values, sentiments and interests are as valid as yours because they belong to a significant, in my opinion, number of other human beings.
>
> I am also advising you that I am aware that many students, like many adults, do not interest themselves in politics. They are quiet, they do not proclaim they are crusaders and champions. But they are the masses of the University

> community. They have a profound wisdom: they resolve to attain professional competence as a result of their University studies, so they can improve their individual capabilities and make contributions in their adult lives. They are the "not-activists." I do not claim to speak for them. But neither do you. Nevertheless, because I was elected by the Board of Regents to manage the affairs of the University as chief executive officer, I have to interpret their interests as best as I can, in the same way that I try to read and serve the interests of the faculty, administrators and more humble workers of our community.[36]

Rejoinder from Students

The last word was heard from the Conference itself. It strongly took exception to the President's assertion that students are not qualified for the major policy-making bodies of the University. "This is not only an affront to University constituents who are scholars of the Filipino people, but a feudal conception of student representation,"[37] the letter said.

Concluding, the Conference argued trenchantly that "we have no intention of preventing you from fulfilling your tasks as chief executive officer of the UP from trying to interpret the interest of the masses of students. We share common objectives. But we want to tell you that it is not totally a profound wisdom to fully commit oneself to the sole pursuit of a University degree and defer social contribution to adult life. . . to be sure, you would not want the University to break off its tradition of building students who shall commit themselves to taking up the social demands."[38]

By the time the schoolyear ended no plebiscite had been held on the decisions of the Student Conference. In an April 7, 1976 letter to Diwa Guinigundo, EVP Soriano said there would be no plebiscite because the Conference became *functus oficio* as of March 7. The matter, in fact, would drag on and intermittently erupt, until its final resolution with the restoration of the Student Council in late 1979 when Soriano himself was President of the University. We shall have occasion to discuss this later.

Antipathy Much in Evidence

Conflict characterized the relationship between the administration and the students and pervaded the student politics and press of the time. Whether the issue was new rules for the *Philippine Collegian* or dormitory rules providing for a single-fee system, or limited tenure for residents, or a memorandum providing for prior approval by the Office of Student Affairs of written materials for dissemination on campus, or the cancellation of the freshman convocation in June 1976, and many other controversies, the lines were always drawn between the administration and the students.

In his first annual report to the Board of Regents, President Corpuz offered his own thoughts on the phenomenon. Although he described the administration's relationship with the "generality of students" to be "reasonably good," he continued and said that

> . . . there is an obvious problem with the more politicized individuals or groups. The latter tend to regard the University administration, as well as others not belonging to their camp, in adversary terms. I understand that such an attitude is natural, in consequence of historical situations and experiences. In some cases, I must surmise that it is due to temperament or personality, or in something attendant to the student leader role. My own roles as the father of five children in the University and as University President rule out a desire or intention to engage young people in adversary relationships. I listen to them and try to divine their interest, just as I do those of the University's other constituencies, and then act according to reason, or prudence or boldness as circumstances suggest.

THE UNIVERSITY AS AN IMMENSE DOMAIN FOR ANY ADMINISTRATOR

FOR indeed, the constituency of the President was not only multi-sectoral but also large. In 1975 the University as a whole had a student population of over 28,000[39] and a faculty complement of 2,173.[40] It had two autonomous units, the UP at Los Baños and the Philippine Center for Advanced Studies, in addition to several campuses outside of Diliman: Manila, Baguio, Clark Air Base, Cebu, Iloilo and Tacloban. Altogether the University had 36 colleges, schools and institutes. It offered 14 under-graduate programs leading to baccaulaureate degrees, 144 leading to masteral degrees and 29 leading to doctoral degrees. Using corporate language President Corpuz placed the University among the top 26 or so corporations in the country which had assets of P300 million or more.[41]

As of December 1977, the University had expanded to include 46 colleges, schools and institutes and offered academic programs in 156 fields of concentration leading to bachelor's degrees, 295 areas leading to master's degrees and 83 fields leading to doctoral degrees.[42] Two years later it had more than 33,000 students,[43] about 3,700 faculty members, 8,500 administrative personnel and 2,004 academic non-teaching personnel.[44] By this time also two new autonomous units had been established: the UP in the Visayas and the Health Sciences Center, both formally created in 1979. The University administration also presided over the dissolution of the Philippine Center for Advanced Studies in 1979.

All in all, under the Corpuz-Soriano administration, the University underwent an expansion and organizational growth unprecedented in its history. The bare data alone imply a world very different from the smaller and simpler UP of as late as a decade ago. From another point of view, the statistics imply the dimensions of the demands that would be made on the administration of the University that had become both very large and complex. The expansion and the resulting size and complexity of the University exhibited in general a responsiveness to national concerns and environmental imperatives that came to be viewed as both a bane and a blessing.

Development Aligned to National Goals

But whatever the later verdict on it, the development was certainly along explicit goals as defined by President Corpuz himself. In his first annual report, he identified these as consisting of the following:

> To relate University operations more closely to national development goals, whilst preserving intact the nature of the University as an academic institution;
>
> To effect a closer correspondence between state University goals and University operations; and
>
> To improve the internal government systems of the University.[45]

Operationally, the goals would be pursued in the University's policies, programs and projects, more specifically in such areas as the organization of new academic and non-academic units, curricular programs, admission policies, research priorities, policies toward extension services and consultancy, and management practices. The plethora of developments in all these areas could not, however, be discussed in detail in an account such as this one. We can simply single out a few significant developments to highlight important characteristics of the administration.

For example, as far as the first goal was concerned, one of the earliest steps that President Corpuz took was to develop a project for the establishment of a new university in the UP system. It was to be an answer to the top priority given to food and nutrition in the national development plan. Envisioned to be devoted to aquatic and marine sciences, the new university was to evolve from the UP College in Iloilo (UPCI) and the College of Fisheries in Diliman. Development planning for the new university was to last for four years and culminated in the establishment of a full-blown university in 1979.[46]

An Integrated Health Sciences Program

In October 1977, the Board of Regents established the Health Sciences Center (HSC) to be comprised of established units such as the Colleges of Medicine, Nursing, Dentistry, Pharmacy, the Institute of Public Health and the Philippine General Hospital; newer ones such as the Institute of Ophthalmology, the School of Allied Medical Professions, the National Teacher Training Center for the Health Professions, the Anaesthesiology Center Western Pacific, the Comprehensive Community Health Program, and the Institute of Health Sciences. Aside from putting all the University units concerned with the health sciences under one organizational umbrella, an arrangement that would yield obvious benefits to the units concerned, there was an innovative curricular approach started by the HSC which was implemented through the newly established (1976) Institute of Health Sciences (IHS).[47]

The establishment of the IHS was an earnest of "a modern university seeking to make itself directly relevant to the needs of the national community."[48] It was also a response to the serious problems of health manpower development, more specifically, the phenomenon of the brain drain of medical personnel migrating to other countries, the inequitable distribution of medical personnel within the country itself and the extraordinary long training period for medical doctors.

The IHS started a ladder type curriculum with various points of entry and exit. The first stage is a barangay health worker program, after which the students return to their barangay to apply their knowledge and skills. Favorable endorsement by the barangay qualifies the students for the next program, called the community health workers program, which entitles them to a UP-awarded certificate. The third level is the community health nursing program, while the next one, the Bachelor of Science in Rural Medicine program (BSRM), is a baccalaureate degree, which qualifies the students for the Doctor of Medicine Program. The most distinctive feature of the curriculum is its "self-conscious emphasis on community-based training," which in practical terms means very little dependence on a hospital setting for training purposes.[49] The program hopes that the strategy being tested at the IHS would be "replicable in other parts of the country as well as in countries similarly situated as the Philippines."

Tourism in the Limelight

Another academic unit created in response to national government concerns was the Asian Institute of Tourism (AIT). Established through an agreement between the University and the Department of Tourism and the Philippine Tourism Authority, the AIT's main purpose is to "train manpower badly needed by the fast growing tourism industry not only in the country but in other Asian countries as well."[50] To pursue this aim, the Institute developed degree programs in tourism development and management, hotel and restaurant management, and in food service. To establish the AIT, President Marcos released an appropriation of ₱16 million.

On campus the new institute at once became the object of critical comments, for example, from the *Philippine Collegian* which viewed its establishment as "manifest state intervention in the affairs of the University." In answer to such a criticism, EVP Soriano wrote the student paper: ". . . With its expertise and resources, the University is in a position to support the growth of the tourism industry by assisting in its professionalization. Thus, the University should involve itself in an area whose development would benefit not only the University and the academic community but also the general public." Then on the matter of government intervention, he said: "The proposed AIT is not a project imposed on us by the national government. It is simply another opportunity identified by the University to make a contribution to public welfare."[51]

The AIT ultimately became the whipping boy on campus, representing what was perceived as state intervention in the affairs of the University. Its academic program was regarded somewhat superciliously by other units as merely vocational in nature. Its physical structures also presented a glaring contrast to most of the old, poorly maintained buildings and facilities on campus, and this fact aroused mixed sentiments of envy and disdain from many of the University constituency, even as they ventured to enjoy its carpeted and air-conditioned comforts.

Proliferation of New Units

Certainly less controversial than the AIT, but just as reflective of the responsiveness to national concerns, was the establishment of other academic units such as the Institute of Sports, Physical Education and Recreation (SPEAR) which expanded from a University department to an institute, and was envisioned to be a national training center for sports and physical education; the Institute of Agricultural Engineering and Technology (INSAET) in Los Baños, which specialized in formulating and implementing programs in development-oriented engineering sciences and related fields; and the Institute of Agricultural Development Administration (IADA), also in Los Baños, which integrated contributions from agriculture, forestry, agrarian reform, human ecology and other fields that bear on agricultural development.[52]

Research centers and training institutes were also established: the Transport Training Center (TTC), which offers programs in traffic planning, traffic engineering and traffic management and enjoys generous support from the Japanese International Cooperation Agency; the Post-Harvest Training Center (PHTC) in Los Baños, which offers a course on fruit and vegetable handling to participants from ASEAN member countries, and has the assistance of the government of Australia; the National Institute of Biotechnology and Microbiology, which undertakes research and other activities required to establish industries based on biotechnology and microbiology, and which received a ₱30 million grant from President Marcos; the National Engineering Center (NEC), which links the research and extension service capabilities of various engineering programs and pioneers in technology development; and the Public Affairs Research and Development Center, a joint project of the UP College of Public Administration and the Commission on Audit, which serves as a research arm of the State Accounting and Auditing Center.[53]

Apart from new curricular offerings, various non-degree programs were also established, and these included the Extramural Studies Program and the Third World Studies Program, both of the College of Arts and Sciences in Diliman; the Linking with Community for Development Program with the apt acronym LINK COD of the Institute of Social Work and Community Development; the Integrated K-10 Program of the UP Integrated School; and the Comprehensive Preparatory Music Program of the College of Music.[54]

Democratic Basis for Admissions Policy

Perhaps the most distinctive program evolved during the Corpuz-Soriano administration, which was faithfully reflective of President Corpuz's own social equity concerns, was the democratization of admissions program. He had, for instance, made the earlier observation regarding Filipinos "who receive only a small share of the values and products of our national development."

One specific reference of such an observation was a fact, hitherto recognized and even systematically studied by some of the University's academicians,[55] that certain socio- economic factors adversely affected the chances of the poor to enter the University. Early in 1976, in response to a concern identified in various workshops, surveys and concept papers prepared by faculty members, the Program Development Staff came up with a paper entitled, "Admissions and Enrollment: Towards a More Equitable Distribution of U.P. Educational Benefits." This paper showed that the student population of the University, far from being representative of the country's population, tended to come largely from the higher socio-economic classes. It also suggested means for redressing the inequitable distribution of educational benefits under the established system.

President Marcos took cognizance of the problem in his address delivered at the 65th commencement exercises of the University on March 28, 1976. After noting the specific fact that some ₱4,000 of tax money is added by the University and the government to the ₱600 to ₱700 tuition fees per year paid by a UP student, he issued a call to "the officers of our administration, from the President to the Board of Regents, and with the cooperation of the faculty, to institute early reforms that will democratize its admissions system."

"These reforms must ensure," he said, "that there be an increasing participation by our poorest young men and women in the life (of the mind) that the University promotes so well." He even admonished the University that until it presents "a suitable program consistent with this policy, there shall be no untoward increases in freshman admissions, except in those fields where our professional manpower requirements for national development indicate otherwise, and except in the regional units of the University."[56]

Faculty Support for Democratization

The University's response was quick and significant. The Faculty Conference of 1976 held in Los Baños from July 6 to 8 had for its theme "Democratization of Admissions Policies." In his keynote address in that conference, President Corpuz declared: "If the University wants to increase equity, it must go beyond the problem of admissions. Thus, it must allow more children of low-income families into the University, and to graduate them with the end in view of inevitably marking them for leadership in future years. If the University produces graduates which exclude the low-income groups, it produces a group of graduates who cannot feel the life, problems and aspirations of most of our people."

The Faculty Conference ended with a resolution of great significance by acknowledging two important givens in the environment, namely: that "the University of the Philippines is an instrument of national development," and that "the national condition is one of inequity." Accordingly, it passed the following resolution: "That the University adopt and implement immediately a democratic admission policy to make its studentry more representative of the nation's population."[57]

An excellent study later undertaken by the Program Development Staff entitled "Democratization of Admissions" fleshed out the compelling reasons for the program. The study, which used the distribution of the 1976 UPCAT applicants, revealed the following:[58]

1. Of the 18,205 students who applied for admission, 24.33% came from families with annual incomes of at least ₱20,000. The study concluded that "the higher the student's annual family income, the greater are his chances of being admitted into the University."

2. Students from private schools registered greater chances of qualifying for admission (28.05%) than students from public general schools (15.53%), public vocational schools (8.15%) and public barrio schools (1.64%).

3. Students from Metro Manila registered the greatest chances of qualifying (33.44%); those from rural areas had the least chances of qualifying (11.20%).

4. The sons and daughters of professionals had the greatest chances of qualifying (34.81%), while those of farmers and fishermen registered 7.91%, production-process workers, 12.72% and manual laborers, 13.51%.

5. 62.52% of the students who qualified had fathers who had at least a bachelor's degree; 0.43% had fathers who had no schooling at all. In general, "a student's chances of qualifying for admission improve with his father's educational attainment."

6. The same pattern with respect to the mother's occupation and educational attainment was shown by the study.

Program Carefully Implemented

With official policy now formed by executive mandate, by faculty resolution, and by studies which showed the dimensions of the problem, the democratization of admissions policy was implemented on an experimental basis at the College of Arts and Sciences in Diliman during the academic year 1977-1978. Ninety-four freshmen constituted the first group of XDS (for Experimental Democratization Sample), who were selected on the basis of the following criteria: (1) an annual family income lower than ₱8,000; (2) an UPCAT score slightly below the Diliman cut-off; and (3) as much as possible, at least one representative from each province.

Each XDS was extended a financial assistance package of approximately ₱4,850 a year which included transportation expenses, tuition and other fees, book allowance, board and lodging and personal stipend. For them a new UPCAT admissions criterion was used: the University Predicted Grade (UPG) instead of the Weighted Combined Rating (WCR). The former was adjudged to be less prone to the biases of the latter.

Learning and psycho-social assistance programs were also designed which, in general, would assist the students in overcoming not only the problems of adjustment peculiar to freshmen, but also those which had been aggravated by their disadvantaged socio-economic backgrounds. These included housing on campus, special guidance and counselling services, extra-curricular activities, and assignment to classes in English and Mathematics handled by the teachers of reputed excellence.

Success of Democratic Approach

The record of the first three groups was adjudged creditable, with the first one doing as well as the regular freshmen, with a general weighted average of 2.39 and four achieving scholar status. The second group of 166 students performed as well as the first group, and the third group, now only 78 strong performed even better than the first two, with one student achieving University scholar status and eleven becoming College scholars. They were also praised as a group by the residence hall staff as "well-balanced and respectful, concerned with their fellow residents and persevering in their studies."[59]

In other campuses of the University, XDS were also admitted. In Los Baños, for example, the program was implemented through the Agricultural and Rural Development Scholarship, established by President Marcos in 1977. In the UP College Iloilo, 48 XDS were admitted in academic year

1979-80, whose mean grade average at the end of their first semester was higher than their University Predicted Grade.

Financial Aid for Students

Corollary to the democratic admission policy was the launching in 1977 of the most extensive student financial assistance program undertaken in the University. This policy was based on the important findings, among others, of various studies conducted earlier.

One such study, already referred to above, found that UP students were each being subsidized an average of ₱1,650 per semester, or ₱3,300 per year. The study raised the question: Why should the University grant a rich student an educational subsidy of ₱1,650 per semester when the student can very well afford to finance his education anyway, if not in a school such as the Ateneo (which charges about ₱1,270 per semester) then in the University but paying a more reasonable fee than merely ₱270 per semester? [60]

To remedy the situation, the new policy aimed at a more democratic distribution by reducing the subsidy for students from rich families and redistributing the amount to poorer students who cannot afford the cost of a UP education.[61] The Board of Regents accordingly revised the tuition fee structure. Thus the "raising" of the amount was explained as a move toward "rationalization" since degree programs which are costly to administer but which appeal to the high-income groups were made to charge higher fees than those which are less costly to maintain and are oriented toward countryside development.

Specifically, under the new structure, students with an annual family income below ₱30,000 were entitled to benefits ranging from a 5 percent tuition fee discount to the maximum benefit of free tuition and other fees, plus a ₱100 semestral book allowance and a ₱150 monthly stipend. Numerous lower and middle-income students throughout the University benefited from this new structure: in academic year 1978-1979 a total of 5,372 students were granted tuition fee discounts in varying amounts.

Increase in Tuition Fees

The tuition fee hike, implemented in 1977, sparked another conflict between the administration and the students. The *Collegian* once more headlined the issue, e.g. "Law Students Denounce Tuition Hike,"[62] and "Protest Mounts vs. Tuition Hike."[63] Law students denounced the increase as "totally arbitrary and unconscionable" in reference to the 250 percent jump in their tuition. They also charged that the decision to increase was arrived at without "procedural due process" since students were not given the opportunity to be heard.

To the latter charge, President Corpuz said that the students had been represented in the discussion of the democratization policy during the faculty conference and that they did not voice any protest either against the policy or its financial component.[64] Dr. Romeo L. Manlapaz, a staunch advocate of the democratization policy, emphasized that not all tuition fees registered an increase since tuition in ALEC decreased from ₱50 to ₱44 per unit; for the master in management program in the regional units, the decrease was from ₱50 to ₱37 per unit; and for B.S. Nutrition, the reduction was from ₱166 to ₱150 per semester.[65] He reiterated the real objective behind the new tuition fee increase: a redistribution of UP subsidies and a rationalization of the tuition fees of the University for the various degree programs.

EFFECTIVE MANAGEMENT TO COPE WITH FACULTY AND CAMPUS NEEDS

OTHER areas of University life, by their very nature, did not provide the kind of excitement generated by student opposition and involvement. However, significant developments also occurred in those activities that more specifically concerned the faculty, and thus would leave even more enduring marks on University life.

Research, for one, was enhanced by a number of auspicious developments, particularly with respect to funding, the administration of research projects and programs, and the dissemination of research findings. Within a year of the Corpuz-Soriano administration, for example, the budget appropriation for research increased from ₱3 million to ₱4.5 million.[66] Although this level of funding from the University budget could not be maintained, a large portion of the resources devoted to research came from outside help. Generous assistance was provided by the National Science Development Board, the government's main research funding arm, which continued to support the UP-NSDB Integrated Research Program. For the fiscal year 1975-76 alone this program supported 51 research projects (excluding the ones in Los Baños) with a total appropriation of ₱2.7 million.[67]

Funding for Research

Various other sources of funding were government agencies and foreign organizations, both public and private. The former included such agencies as the National Food and Agricultural Council (NFAC), the National Research Council of the Philippines (NRCP), the Ministry of Natural Resources (MNR), the Philippine Council for Agricultural and Resources Research

(PCARR), the National Economic and Development Authority (NEDA), the Educational Projects Implementing Task Force (EDPITAF), and the Population Commission (POPCOM).

Foreign organizations which extended support were the United States Agency for International Development (USAID), Japan International Cooperation Administration (JICA), International Development Research Council of Canada (IDRC), Food and Agricultural Education (FAO), United Nations Development Program (UNDP), the Ford and Rockefeller Foundations, the China Medical Board of New York, and the government of Germany, Sweden, and Australia, among others.[68]

The above listing indicated two trends: an extensive "reaching out" to various sources of funding, and an attempt to gear research to national concerns. The first alternative had been common in the history of the University. The linking up process with outside agencies did not have to be initiated by the University but more typically, outside agencies took the initiative in seeking assistance from the University and its pool of experts.

Alignment toward Development Goals

The trend toward mutually beneficial relationships with outside organizations was enhanced by an explicit bias toward research that would meet national development needs.[69] Thus, a new type of research became part of the University vocabulary: "mission-oriented" research, which by definition meant that it was addressed to the solution of some of the society's pressing problems. More specifically, the NSDB-assisted program sought "to enhance productivity for national development."[70] Hence the bulk of research activities was in areas directly in the mainstream of national programs such as food production, public health, agrarian reform, cooperatives, labor law, nutrition, family planning and manpower development.[71]

The administration of a wide-ranging and active research program in the University was enhanced by efforts to improve coordination and monitoring through the Office of Research Coordination. By 1979 steps had already been taken for a research management information system in order to systematize and facilitate the gathering, storage and retrieval of research findings. An annual *Research Monitor* was published, which listed on-going and new researches.

Innovative Research Activities

Research dissemination also merited much attention. Aside from the traditional research outlets, an innovation was the publication of *Research Illustrated,* which presented research results in comics form and was circulated nationally, especially in Philippine schools. It has a Filipino edition entitled *Saliksik* containing translated materials.

Still another innovation was the UP Faculty Research Conference, subtitled "The Rural Agenda," which brought faculty researchers face to face with the end-users in rural areas. This was held twice, the first in Tarlac, Pangasinan and La Union in 1977 and the second in Bicol in 1978. Envisioned along the lines of mission-oriented research, it was directed toward exploring "ways in which research findings can be made more directly supportive of programs for the uplift of the people and to direct our future research efforts more consciously toward their problems."[72]

The value of such an exercise is not easy to prove, but a young social scientist has made these observations:

> . . . There is, after all, a touch of irony . . . of surrealism in the sight of an intellectual elite emerging from the heights of their carpeted and lavishly-furnished hotel, and descending upon a mass of eager individuals, all hungry for knowledge.
>
> . . . The actual encounters between this academic elite and the representatives from the various rural communities were not without redeeming qualities. As a matter of fact, we found them actually intriguing and enormously enjoyable.
>
> . . . The points raised by the local participants were simple, pragmatic, to the point and very sensible, which, truth to tell, is more than what you can say for many papers in this Conference..
>
> . . . I feel that the Conference can reasonably be declared a tremendous success . . . The impact has mainly been on our *consciousness.*[73]

Deeper Involvement in Government Programs

On still another front, the faculty rendered extension and community services in line with the University policy of relating its activities "more closely to national programs and priorities."[74] These were in the form of the conduct of training programs, preparation of research and project development studies, and participation in local and international workshops, seminars and consultancies. The latter especially was encouraged by liberal policies regarding outside involvement. Early in his administration, President Corpuz urged the various faculties

> . . . to organize themselves to extend consultancy services (for pay) in support of government programs. The rationale for this is that the government development budget includes billions of pesos. This money will be spent, whether wisely or not. It will be spent better, in my view, if our faculty's expert and professional services are contributed towards better programming, project conceptualization, feasibility studies, etc., in and of government agencies concerned.[75]

All the preceding conjure the image of a university faculty extremely busy with research and extension services and hence forced to relegate teaching into the background. Indeed, high-ranking university officials noted the development with some dismay. Los Baños Chancellor Abelardo G. Samonte's observations placed teaching in the context of the other functions of the University. He said:

> I have always adhered to the view that teaching, research and extension or public service are co-equal functions of a University; in fact, they are interrelated and mutually reinforcing. In the past two decades, incentives were extended to encourage more professors to get out of their classrooms and engage in research or extension. Today, however, I am afraid that the pendulum has swung to the other extreme. The present incentive and reward system is loaded in favor of research and, to a lesser extent, extension; teaching has become a poor equal. Indeed, there are disturbing reports that teaching has been neglected or otherwise prejudiced because of the over-commitment of some professors in research and consultancy. The results: lectures are no longer as thoroughly prepared and up-to-date; students find it hard to consult their instructors outside the classroom; the close teacher-student relationship that lies at the base of a real institution of higher learning is in danger of being lost. Moreover, there seems to be very little or no time left for scholarly reflection and interactions among a supposedly academic community.[76]

Vice President for Academic Affairs Oscar M. Alfonso explained the phenomenon in his inimitable style:

> The "enemy" has many faces: erosive, corrosive, subversive inflation: luring lucre; rewarding research; siren-call consultancies; hyperactive way station or jumping board that the U.P. often becomes for another professional career elsewhere . . . unresponsive, irresponsible round pegs in square holes . . . capable only of discommendable behavior; lenity in recruitment by undiscriminating superordinates.[77]

Repercussions on Teaching

President Corpuz himself took cognizance of the problem and acted on it by issuing a number of memoranda while he was in office. The first of these, issued on March 2, 1977, on "Delinquent Submission of Reports of Final Grades," enjoined college authorities "to apply strictly the University rules on the submission of final grades," which he said were not being observed at all.

Another one, this time longer (and with an elaborate title: "What Chaucer Says of the Teacher: 'Gladly would he learn and Gladly Teach! ' May the Joy of Teaching Flourish in our University! ") enjoined three things: (1) for the University faculty to examine himself in private and "determine for himself where he has been amiss and where he might improve himself," (2) for deans and directors to submit to the President's office a semestral "truthful assessment of both successes and failures in the college with respect to teaching," and (3) for students to report to his office both outstanding successes and resounding failures with respect to their teachers.[78]

Still another memo, entitled simply "More on Teaching," recounted his personal experiences as a teacher and his own reflections on the task: "Our problems of teaching do not start from outside the teacher; did not start from 'the system'. They start and grow from what the teacher brings to the task, and from his or her response to the system." "The economic pressures of the situation might be unbearable to some," he continued, "but in most cases this load can be lightened by the teacher's thinking again of what teaching truly means to him or her and for the University."

Then he tackled the matter of balance among the three functions:

> What to do about research, extension service, and those nice, juicy and necessary consultancies? We can do most of them and still teach well–except that most consultancies should not be done on time belonging to the students. I would like to see more group or department research or extension services, to facilitate programming of time and effort. For research specifically, I ask the Deans to look at the research proposals of their faculties and to discourage and reduce meaningless duplication.[79]

Need for Effective Management

Such a solution to a persistent and complex phenomenon might appear too simplistic, nor would it give an inkling of the President's emphasis on management concerns. For indeed management was not only considered a mechanism to cope with the University's size and complexity; it also became a matter of pride to the administration. Based on the President's views on management as "an approach to giving life to the University's real tasks"[80] and fleshed out by Executive Vice-President Soriano's own expertise, management concerns occupied much of the University's time, efforts and resources.

Specifically, this involved the introduction of more efficient management approaches and techniques to the University's complex activities and operations. This called for more effective mechanisms to coordinate planning and implementation. Planning, especially, had heretofore been unsystematic, even *ad hoc,* and there had previously been no effective structure to implement planning in the University.[81] An immediate response to this inadequacy was the organization in April 1975 of the Program Development Staff (PDS) in the office of the President, the first such body to be created in the University, whose mandate was to "undertake a planning and project development effort to facilitate the early implementation of major pending University projects as well as to formulate short and long-term directions in the University."[82]

Accordingly, the PDS, in support of its planning function, organized in the first few months of its existence two workshops to identify "areas of concern." The first of these was participated in by selected leaders and friends from within and outside the University and yielded a list of 22 areas of concern that included principally, the reward system, the funding of the University, the governance of the University, academic programs, physical facilities, and student welfare. The second workshop, attended by deans and directors, produced a slightly different list of concerns: national development and identity, curricular reforms, staff development, funding for the University, etc.[83]

Systematic Review of Problems

The identified areas of concern were subsequently submitted in a survey of the constituencies of the University. Faculty members, designated as Program Development Associates, formulated concept papers based on them, and these included such specific areas as admissions and enrolment, reward and welfare system, academic programs, faculty and staff development, physical facilities, arts and sciences, student welfare and housing.[84]

A planning process was thereby started which extended even further the consultative procedures that former President Lopez had put into practice. President Corpuz had expressed interest in institutionalizing such processes in order to give the constituencies "a keener sense of involvement in the University."[85] We can note here the paradox that such an approach did not seem to have worked with the students, who, in their numerous conflicts with the administration, invariably accused the latter of making decisions without consulting them.

That fact notwithstanding, new approaches and techniques were resorted to in order to systematize the University's complex operations. For example, the planning and budgeting process of the University was coordinated through a sophisticated scheme described by Executive Vice-President Soriano as participative, continuing, recurring, resource-seeking and goal-setting.[86] In practice, this consisted of workshops by various units among their respective faculties and staffs to formulate their plans and ascertain their budgets, a process that turned out to be a new experience for most units in the University.[87]

Perspective on the University's Future

The various unit development plans and budget proposals, consolidated by central administration, then became the basis of the University's perspective plan called "The UP System and the Future." A workshop on this plan among all heads of units generated feedback and helped set priorities on a university-wide level. An Executive Review (ER) was then held to permit discussion of the details of each unit's plan and budget among the officers of central administration and the heads of each unit. The unit budgets agreed upon at the Executive Review became the basis of the University's consolidated budget submitted to the Budget Commission.

The University also undertook to improve its management control system. It engaged the services of the Development Academy of the Philippines to develop and implement an integrated management information system (MIS), which could promptly generate information for effective planning and control. The project covered four major interlinking subsystems: (1) the physical resources subsystem to keep track of the University's numerous buildings, physical facilities, and inventories for effective planning and allocation of existing physical resources and projected needs; (2) the personnel subsystem to generate relevant personnel data such as salaries and wages, skills inventory and appraisal, training, recruitment and other information essential to sound management of the University's manpower resources; (3) the student subsystem to enhance student records management and provide information on admissions, registration, course scheduling, curricular development, and (4) the financial information subsystem to generate timely and accurate data for financial planning, control and operations.[88]

An Extensive Infrastructure Program

In consonance with its systematization of management functions in the University, the administration launched in 1975 a big Infrastructure Development Program (IDP), which established priorities in the construction and rehabilitation of buildings and utilities and coordinated all infrastructure development plans and activities. The program involved a capital budget of more than ₱150 million and envisioned the construction of some 40 structures and the repair and improvement of existing buildings and facilities in various campuses of the University, including UP Los Baños and the regional units.[89] Availing of the technical expertise of the College of Architecture, the College of Engineering and the Physical Plant Office, the program was expected to "realize substantial savings on total project cost."

A news item in late 1975[90] identified a problem that did not augur well for the program: "Some uncertainty has crept into the program due to the freezing by the national government of infrastructure projects." Conceived as a three-year program and hampered by the usual budgetary problems, it nevertheless achieved enough to credit the Corpuz-Soriano administration with the distinction of being a major builder contributing to the transformation of the Diliman landscape.

By the end of 1979, the following buildings had been constructed: the College of Business Administration and Center for Management Studies (costing more than ₱10 million), the Philippine Center for Economic Development (PCED) Hostel, the Asian Institute of Tourism, the Transport Training Center (costing more than ₱3 million), the National Hydraulics Center, the Zoology building of the College of Arts and Sciences, the Marine Sciences Center, the Coral Laboratory and Museum, the Seaweed Laboratory Pilot Processing Plant, the building of the Brackish Aquaculture Center in Leganes, Iloilo, and the UP Integrated School Annex.[91] Earlier than these, other major structures had already been built: the buildings of the Institute for Small-Scale Industries, the Philippine Center for Advanced Studies, the Educational Development Center and the School of Economics.[92]

The University also expanded its dormitory and housing facilities with the construction of the H-shaped Kalayaan coeducational dormitory for about 450 freshmen and several rows of low-cost housing units for the low-salaried employees of the University. These two projects were made possible through a ₱20-million GSIS loan obtained with the help of the First Lady, Madame Imelda Romualdez Marcos.[93]

Renovating Worn-Out Facilities

In addition to construction projects, the IDP also renovated numerous worn-out or antiquated facilities. The most notable of these was the improvement of the campus water-distribution and fire-protection system, which replaced the inadequate and outmoded facilities. The water distribution system was in fact laid out in 1945 to service an American military camp and had since then served an ever-increasing university population which by 1976, the year before the project started, had reached almost 9,000 campus residents, excluding dormitory tenants and the shifting day population of the University.[94] Plans for the complete overhaul and rehabilitation of the water system were prepared as early as 1964, but nothing came out of them because of lack of funds. The University therefore had to cope with a paradox of sorts: enduring lack of water while living next-door to the Balara filtration plant from where emanates the water supply for Metropolitan Manila.

In July 1977 President Corpuz ordered a survey of the University's water distribution system which confirmed the dearth of water. He forthwith requested funds from President Marcos for the installation of new water mains. The request was approved immediately.[95]

Lessors Accommodated on Campus

More changes in the campus landscape ensued with permission granted non-UP organizations to erect buildings inside the campus. The practice, to be sure, had some precedents, one of the earliest being the permission granted in 1960 to the Philippine Atomic Energy Commission to lease 7.25 hectares for a token one peso a year. Other such arrangements included the leases granted to the Catholic church and the National Council of Churches for their respective chapel sites.

During the period under review, lessors allowed to construct buildings were the Philippine National Bank, the Commission on Audit, the National Textbook Secretariat, the Metro Manila Commission, and Innotech. The period of the leases ranges from seven years with the Metro Manila Commission, to 25 years with PNB, and an indefinite period with Innotech. Some of the leases provide for joint use of space with the University (in the cases of PNB, MMC, and COA), and eventual transfer of ownership of the buildings to the University at the end of the lease periods. The areas covered also vary from 1,161 square meters in the case of PNB to 31,032 square meters in the case of Innotech.[96]

Surreptitious Entry of BLISS

However, exceeding all the preceding in regard to area and terms of lease is the occupation of a large portion of the University's campus by the Ministry of Human Settlements, which transformed the area into a site for a BLISS housing project. Acquired by MHS under circumstances that even some high-ranking university administrators decried, the occupation of the area was nevertheless eventually condoned with a usufruct agreement between the University and the Ministry. The agreement provides that the usufruct shall be in effect "continuously and uninterruptedly for 50 years," subject to renewal for a period not exceeding 50 years, "depending upon the needs of the owner," which is the University.[97]

As a consolation to the University constituency who were unanimously against the "land grab," the usufruct agreement also provided that 30 percent of the total units built by the usufructuary would be reserved for university personnel, an agreement that alleviated somewhat the acute housing shortage on campus. The University issued a memorandum on the availability of housing units at the Bliss housing project with the stipulation that "the number of units alloted to UP personnel shall depend on their eligibility and willingness to apply for housing lease."[98] However, the financial requirements for occupancy were rather high and beyond the means of low-salaried employees, such that the University did not gain utmost benefit from the usufruct agreement.

Krus-na-Ligas Problem

Another act of the administration, involving the "giving up" of a portion of the University Campus, was rather more welcome. This had to do with the transfer of some nine hectares occupied by barrio Krus na Ligas, which was completely within the University campus, to its bonafide residents on the basis of communal ownership. The transfer was to be effected through the Presidential Assistance for Housing and Resettlement Administration (PAHRA).[99]

The arrangement sought to resolve a 26-year-old problem between the University and the residents of Krus na Ligas. Historically, the residents of the barrio had been occupying several hectares of the campus long before the government conveyed the property to the University. Repeated petitions from the residents to the University had been to no avail, and the University authorities never gave up its right to the land.

In explaining this act to transfer the land, President Corpuz said that he had always made it a point to act in support of declared national objectives and programs which he believed to be in the interests of the general public. Continuing, he said.:

> My decision was based primarily on the recognition that the population of both the barrio and of the University community will continue to grow, and that the early solution of the land problem would avert any possible collision in the future. I also hold the opinion that it was never the intention of the University to dispossess people of their rightful ownership to the land and that the transfer of this land to them would be in keeping with the spirit of the government's national housing program for the masses.[100]

TRANSFER OF LEADERSHIP FORMALIZED A STRUCTURE ALREADY IN PLACE

PRESIDENT Corpuz must have been referring to achievements such as the preceding when, in his farewell letter to the University Council read for him by Executive Vice-President Soriano on July 28, 1979, he said: "For my part, I got my kicks trying to serve real people who happened to be either administrative workers or scholars or just citizens." He contrasted this outlook with that of others for whom he said he was full of admiration: "Those who deliver themselves fully to the great causes that seem to excite certain personalities, who at the slightest provocation wage ferocious crusades."[101]

The valedictory, suffused with emotions brought on by a personal tragedy, ended with a revelation of a private philosophy and a candor unusual for a public official. He said: "Anyway, I and my family have resolved to travel light in this world. We are not inclined to accumulations and ponderous luggage. I came to the University with little; I leave with little to carry along to the next job. Maybe it is for this that I leave very little behind."

His next job was as Minister of Education and Culture, which he had previously occupied, and which placed him in a position to have continuing influence on the University as chairman of the Board of Regents. Executive Vice-President Soriano was named acting President: then, within a month he was appointed the thirteenth President of the University, effective 31 August 1979 until 22 January 1981, the original terminal date of the Corpuz administration.[102]

EVP Appointed President

Having managed the University as Executive Vice-President since April 1975, and therefore in many ways performing Presidential functions, but now vested with full responsibility, Dr. Soriano's appointment represented continuity rather than change. This meant, for example, no drastic alterations in policy.

On the occasion of his oathtaking in Malacañang, he reiterated the theme now familiar to the University. He said:

> We in the University of the Philippines, in turn, want to support national priorities, and we want to do so with intelligence and responsibility. We believe that the leaders of our country sincerely want to know the realities in which our people live to find out what our people are thinking and feeling, and so enter into their joys and pains.

Continuing, he said:

> Inspired by this belief, we shall act freely and speak freely and try to embody in our lives the deepest meaning of freedom, which goes beyond self-assertion into the depths of self-emptying and total giving. We shall pool together our resources of heart and mind and spirit, as we try to build together, through the youth that we educate, a better world.[103]

Continuity Rather than Change

That statement might have offered a glimpse into the new President's personal philosophy, but his public concerns were really of a more mundane nature. Thus, in his first press conference, he revealed his policy of continuing with the Democratization of Admissions Experiment, the strengthening of the regional units, and encouragement and support of the extension programs of various colleges directed toward countryside development.[104]

Specifically, he followed through on the initiatives undertaken earlier in the administration and saw some of them to completion. One of these projects was the UP in the Visayas which, by the time President Corpuz resigned, had been established as an autonomous member of the University. Thereafter it was declared by the National Board of Education as the regional university in Region VI and the national center for fisheries and marine sciences. The site of the new university had also been chosen, and to hasten the acquisition of land from private owners, the Ministry of Budget reallocated ₱15 million to the University out of the budget of EDPITAF.

By December 1979 the Board of Regents appointed President Soriano as officer-in-charge of the UP in the Visayas. By this time also the World Bank had approved the sixth educational loan of the Philippine government, effective January 1980. The UPV was scheduled to receive for the development of its College of Fisheries the amount of $17.63 million or ₱132.24 million from the loan proceeds.[105]

With the onset of 1980 the campus development plan and the architectural plans for the College of Fisheries buildings had been completed for approval by the Board of Regents. By this time some 200 hectares, out of the projected total of 1,200, had been covered by letters of intent of the landowners to sell. Thus, by February, the campus was ready for groundbreaking. The ceremonies were presided over by President Soriano and the Board of Regents, and featured charming and unique rites including invoking the spirit-residents of the *bubog* trees to look upon the UPV with understanding.[106] By June 1980 the Board of Regents appointed Dr. Dionisia A. Rola, former Dean of the UP College Iloilo, as Acting Chancellor of the new university, the first to occupy this chancellorship and the first woman to have achieved such a distinction.[107]

Student Council Reestablished

Another development, one of great significance to the studentry, was the continuation of the odyssey toward an acceptable student government. As noted earlier, the clamor for a student council was a consistent theme of student demands on the administration. Practically all the mechanisms established for student presentation and participation in University affairs failed to satisfy such demands. The last of these structures was established in May 1977. This was the UP Metro Manila Student Welfare Board (UPMMSWB), which under Memo No. 22 creating it, was supposed to undertake activities of common interest to the students, It was organized after three-fourths of all UP academic units in Metro Manila had organized their own college councils.

After the organization of the UPMMSWB, developments continued apace. The student press by now echoed optimism. "Hopes raised for a University Student Council this semester" was the *Collegian* headline for its issue of November 29, 1979. Then on December 14 President Soriano announced the restoration of the University Student Council (officially known as the "Sanggunian ng mga Mag-aaral sa Pamantasan ng Pilipinas") which had been inactive for the last seven years. The announcement was the highlight of the President's first official address before the university community. He linked the council restoration with the "normalization" program of the government and cited the significance of the USC's role in "the widening participation of the students in University affairs." It was a proud moment for the new President.

This time it was the students who seemed to have been finally appeased. The faculty, research and administrative personnel were also waging their own struggle, principally for salary increases. July to September were restive months, as formerly sectoral groups joined forces and formed an alliance to press their demands for a salary hike.[108]

Agitations for Salary Increase

The last such increase had been undertaken in late 1976 when the Board of Regents approved both a salary hike and a common salary scale for academic, academic non-teaching and administrative personnel. Done as a response to inflation (the last upgrading was in 1974), a new round of inflation and price increases had nevertheless overtaken the increases earlier implemented.

By June, 1979 a 5 percent increase was approved, which the various groups considered very inadequate, and not even at par with the approved 1978 salary rates.[109] The original demand of the faculty for a 60 percent increase was dismissed by President Corpuz because of "budgetary constraints and possible antagonistic response from the non-academic personnel."[110] By the time President Soriano took over, the Alliance had been formed and the united demand was now for a mere 15 percent increase. Although that seemed extremely reasonable, the matter was complicated by Letter of Implementation No. 94 which allowed a 15 percent increase, provided that the recomputed salaries of personnel in one state university would not exceed by 40 percent the salaries for equivalent positions in other state universities, on the basis of national classification plans.

This meant that UP personnel who, as it was, were receiving better salaries than personnel of other state universities, could receive only a 9 percent increase, not 15 as they demanded. Efforts were therefore devoted to have the so-called 40 percent ceiling lifted. Protest became the order of the day as university personnel, joined by the students, staged a boycott on September 13 and marched 4,000 strong to Quezon Hall carrying placards that demanded increase in salaries, the restoration of the student council, and sectoral representation in the Board of Regents.[111]

By September 27 the Board of Regents approved a three-step salary adjustment. The decision was the result of the revision of Letter of Implementation No. 94 from Malacañang which lifted the 40 percent ceiling and allowed a 15 percent across-the-board salary increase.

Tight Financial Control

Such a conflict was of course only a symptom of the larger financial problem that the University has historically had to cope with. This familiar situation seemed to have been further exacerbated by certain regulations of the national government that put a tighter rein on the University's financial management. One of these was the infamous Presidential Decree 711, issued in May 1975, which channeled all income of the University– and of all government agencies for that matter– to the national treasury before allocation to individual agencies. Prior to this decree, the Board of Regents had full power to appropriate the University's income.[112]

Another source of difficulty was that the University could not create any new item without the prior approval of the Budget Ministry. This was a marked contrast with the earlier practice whereby the University could create new items for personnel without such a prior approval. Both regulations and many others were in line with the government's general policy of regulation and tightening that characterized financial management at the time.

Accordingly, the budgetary picture during the Corpuz administration was not as bright as the constituency expected it to be. Just looking at national government allocations for the University, there was a dramatic increase from ₱59,772,074 in 1974 to ₱95,564,325 in 1975. By 1977 the figure had reached ₱233,578,482. Then the following year it decreased to ₱206,766,742; after which it rose slightly higher than the 1977 amount to ₱242,499,865 in 1979.[113]

Such financial fluctuations were contrary to popular belief that a university supportive of national priorities, and led by an administration acceptable to the regime, would actually enjoy, and perhaps deserve, special treatment in a budgetary sense. But then that would probably be contrary to the equity concerns of both the University leadership as well as of the national government.

Furor against Education Bill

In any event, another controversy brought on by a national government action stirred the University by July 1980. This was the Education Bill which, with hardly any prior consultation with the concerned sectors as claimed by its critics, literally burst upon the scene and would exercise the University once more in a protracted struggle that was to last into the following year.

The aim of the bill seemed harmless enough: to place the entire educational system, including the chartered universities and colleges – hence, including the UP – under the Ministry of Education and Culture (MEC). The aim of integration, however, was to be pursued through specific provision in the bill that all curricular proposals would have to go to the MEC for study by the Board of Higher Education and would require approval by the Minister. Fears were aroused on the prospect of loss of curricular autonomy by the universities and colleges, and apprehension over tremendous powers conferred on the MEC.[114] Another provision had to do with giving to the MEC exclusive authority over all academic personnel, and this raised objections that the MEC might lay down policies governing the choice of teachers, the system of rewards, perhaps even the style of teaching.

The various objections to, and criticisms of, the bill were consolidated in a resolution of the University Council, passed on August 12, with a vote of 263-1.[115] In very strong language, the Council resolution raised eight fundamental objections:

> The bill is authoritarian and absolutistic in substance and spirit;
>
> It cripples institutions of higher learning by eroding their fiscal autonomy;
>
> It deprives teachers, scholars and students of their individual academic freedom under the Constitution;
>
> It sets up a machinery for the involuntary servitude of students;
>
> It constricts the inherent and Constitutional rights of parents and the larger community by subjecting these rights to policies, rules and regulations issued by the MEC;
>
> Several provisions constitute undue delegation of legislative authority;
>
> The procedure in securing the enactment of the bill has been undemocratic for the lack of consultation with the educational community;
>
> The total effect of the bill would be an Orwellian nightmare of thought and behavior control that would victimize not only the education system but also the Filipino people themselves.[116]

Soriano Placed on the Spot

President Soriano presented the resolution to the Batasan committee on education before which he also presented his own suggested amendments to the bill. Among others, he proposed that the bill contain a policy that would "uphold the rights of colleges and universities to institutional autonomy and to provide material and usual support to enhance this autonomy," and that "the right of institutions of higher learning to institutional autonomy and to the exercise of academic freedom," shall include "the right to determine on academic grounds who shall teach."[117]

Several sectors of the University were dissatisfied with the position taken by President Soriano at the Batasan. The Association of Faculty, Research and Extension Employees of the University of the Philippines (A

FREE U.P.) said that Soriano's endorsement of the bill was inconsistent with the stand of his constituency and maintained that he should not have offered at the Batasan his personal views since he was there as University head. Some University Council members even wanted the President to explain his statement of support. The students themselves were very active in the agitation against the bill and for the next few months, the student press devoted much space to the discussion of the issue aside from covering symposia, boycotts, noise barrages, and marches on the Batasan which were promptly stopped by the military.[118]

UP Community Apprehensive

These were indeed trying times for the University administration as it tried to cope with yet another round of controversies. This time it was a united community that it had to face. The faculty, hitherto quiescent, gathered their inchoate voices into one clear message, repudiating the kind of cozy relationship being maintained by the university administration with the national power-that-be. There was indeed a touch of irony and sadness in the fact that the administration, which had its baptism of fire in 1975 with the referendum issue, would come full circle in 1980 and end with another issue involving the national government.

A BASIC DIFFICULTY IN ATTEMPTING TO RECONCILE ACADEMIC INTERESTS WITH POLITICAL IMPERATIVES

SUCH drama, of course, was merely the exaggeration of constant tendencies. The administration had an explicit and unabashed policy of supporting national priorities, and tailored many of its programs along such lines. Such support was mitigated by a consciousness of the integrity of the University and of its traditional role as critic of society. In practice, the record might actually match the balancing act that was tried. What stood out, however, because they became a matter of emphasis, were organizational expansion, curricular and non-curricular innovations, and program thrusts that were explicitly in response to expressed national priorities, the determination of which the University had actually little to do about.

Even that by itself need not be a negative thing. If the University believed in the "myth of the neutral university" – as President Corpuz did not – the historical record shows that the UP has never stood apart from national concerns nor even spurned governmental resources. Such had perhaps been mutually beneficial. What seemed to occur at this point in time was an important difference in degree, since it was perceived that the University had never been such a willing handmaiden to the national leadership.

A Matter of Propriety and Timing

On the face of it, following predetermined directions, while reserving the right to alter some of them, need not connote sinister results. The achievements of the Corpuz-Soriano administrations, specially those that promise to endure in the shape of new institutions and academic programs, really still have to prove their worth, and it might be premature to make a judgment on them at this point in time. Addressed as they were to perceived problems in the society, they might in time prove themselves to be really responsive to the needs of the Filipino people. At least on the level of some of the objectives that were being pursued, even the protagonists need not argue, for example, on the matter of democratizing admissions policies in the University.

As goals were being pursued, however, the means employed were another matter. The administration's style, if not much of its substance, was technocratic. Management per se could be the most necessary tool for dealing with the complexity and size of the University. However, there is often a level of obsession with means that transforms them into ends, and this was looked upon with disfavor by many. The University constituency might have shown naivete toward computers and newfangled ways of dealing with management problems. It might actually have been more naive to open up the University to outside forces and expect it to maintain its integrity and independence.

It was perhaps a problem of both excess and timing. The response to outside priorities might have been too eager, and there are enough symbols, positive or negative, physical or otherwise, of the hospitality of the University to outside forces at this period in her history. Timing seemed to be the more crucial dimension. It is easy enough to see that many of the program and policy emphases of the administration could have met with the approval of the University constituency if they were not hopelessly identified with an increasingly unpopular national regime. Even President Corpuz's paternal, and occasionally condescending, stance toward the students might have produced some of their desired effects.

Realism against the Harsh Reality

The actual harm inflicted by over-responsiveness on the University's integrity and independence is an arguable issue. The matter of appearance is important here: the University must not appear to be in a position where it is left with little choice except to accept predetermined goals and their concomitant resources. To an important part of the University constituency, it was more than appearance; it was a matter of fundamental principle.

However, the ability to carry out a principle presupposes a strength that happened to be lacking. The University was too vulnerable to outside forces.

On the one hand, there was the explicit commitment on the level of policy. On a more practical level, it needed outside resources for its survival. In other words, the administration might have been responsible for some of that vulnerability. There is, however, a more enduring source of that weakness: the fact that the University has never in its long history been able to assure itself of resources of any adequacy that would make it stronger against outside blandishments. Paradoxically, such vulnerability works hand in glove with the value of relevance of University programs to society's problems and needs to which the institution is committed. Ultimately, integrity and independence might only become shibboleth to beleaguered University intellectuals.

Not Really Irreconcilable

The Corpuz-Soriano administrations honestly and unequivocally accepted the realities inherent in a state university and worked within their limits. In many significant ways, it was iconoclastic in its perception and its solutions to the University's problems. But its iconoclasm, of which its brilliant rhetoric promised much but achieved less, did not sit well with a constituency steeped in largely unexamined traditions.

For in the end, every administration has to build upon the bedrock of University traditions – that strange amalgam of the noble and the ignoble, of the profound and the shallow, and of the simply stubborn – on which it may leave enduring or temporary marks, perhaps a stone that strengthens the structure, or embellishments that beautify it, or scars that make complete the edifice that we call the University of the Philippines.

XII

Angara's Toughminded Leadership (1981-19)

The Diamond Jubilee Highlighted by Reform of the University System

by Leslie E. Bauzon

Angara's Toughminded Leadership

THE advent of 1981 saw the country just starting its ninth year in an era popularly known as the "New Society." The era was historically significant as having been suffused by the restrictions of Martial Law under an autocracy which President Ferdinand E. Marcos deemed a prerequisite to pursuing the development of the country. Some of the things Marcos was able to do: establish land reform, settle the Mindanao rebellion within the Muslim community, restructure and raise tax levels, and even steer the country through the oil crisis by severe efforts toward energy conservation—these would have been tremendously difficult to achieve without the sweeping authority made possible by Martial Law.[1*]

Despite these notable achievements, evident among the citizenry was a general dissatisfaction with, if not resentment against, a situation where the chief of state had near-absolute power, using a system called rule-by-decree. In 1980, however, Marcos announced that he was dismantling such concentration of authority and that he was restoring the representative system. He hinted that the "New Society" was coming to an end, to be marked by the commencement of another era, which he later identified as the "New Republic."

All over the country, this intimation of forthcoming changes drew varied reactions. Some were trusting enough to welcome this development; others who were more cynical commented that it was a mere change in name of the same thing. Nevertheless, everyone looked forward to a new life in 1981, a life promising more political freedom.

Focus on the University

Amidst these preparations for the "lifting" of Martial Law, the University of the Philippines also girded itself for a change that would affect it directly in the form of a new president. President Emanuel V. Soriano's term had just ended. In January of 1981, speculations lay heavy in the air as to who might replace him as president of the University:

*Footnote references are compiled in the NOTES section at the end of this book.

lobbyists campaigned for their choice and sought support from the University community and from the members of the Board of Regents.

But even as his identity remained still unknown, everyone agreed that the new president must have all the qualifications and capability to steer the University through a time of delicate transition to "normalization" of the political climate, as it was then popularly called. Certainly, he would be faced with problems that would call for more innovative approaches toward their solution. Erosion and possible loss of fiscal autonomy, academic freedom, and administrative independence were the general classifications of the problems facing the new president, whoever he might be.

As the *Philippine Collegian* editorialized:

> The University has found itself restricted by its lack of funds, for one thing, and its lack of freedom to allocate such insufficient funds as the needs arise. As it is the central government has the final say on funding and expenditures. The educational priorities of the government are thus reflected in the priorities given to choice units of the University, questionable as their contribution to the people's interest might be.
>
> Academic freedom and administrative autonomy are aching under the burden of various schemes like the proposed Education Act of 1980 and the Public Order Code. There is also the militarization of the campus, which lends an atmosphere of suspicion and caution to our classrooms and halls.[2]

January was to have been the month when the new man would be appointed.

Choosing the Next President

However in the flurry of the "lifting" of Martial Law, the presidential elections, the setting up of the Batasang Pambansa (National Assembly), and the proclamation of the "New Republic," an era where Philippine politics and economy were supposed to have come of age, the decision on who should be elected to the presidency of the University of the Philippines was postponed.

For one thing, some members of the Board of Regents were far too busy attending to their regular functions as high government officials rather than as Regents; and for another, it would have been awkward to turn over the reins of the University when the academic year was just ending and University affairs were geared toward preparations for the annual graduation.

Meanwhile prominent names emerged as likely candidates to the presidency. These included then Secretary of Justice Vicente Abad Santos,

Acting Budget Minister Manuel S. Alba, Dean of the College of Law Froilan M. Bacungan, Minister of Education Onofre D. Corpuz, Deputy Minister of Education Hermenegildo C. Dumlao, former Vice President for Administration of the University Alejandro M. Fernandez, Chancellor of the Health Sciences Center Florentino Herrera, Jr., Chancellor of the University of the Philippines in Los Baños Emil Q. Javier, Director Rafael M. Salas of the United Nations Fund for Population Activities, UP President Emanuel V. Soriano, Economic Planning Minister Gerardo P. Sicat, Assemblyman Arturo M. Tolentino, Assemblyman Ronaldo B. Zamora, and Department of Philosophy Chairman Armando F. Bonifacio.[3]

An Unfamiliar Name Emerges

Up until the actual elections, the name Edgardo J. Angara never came up in the list of aspirants or even of reluctant candidates prodded by supporters. The decision to choose Angara for the presidency of the University was therefore unexpected. He was nominated and unanimously elected by the members present at the 940th meeting of the Board of Regents on April 30, 1981. Very few in the University community had ever heard of his name before although a week earlier, he had been honored by the University of the Philippines Alumni Association with a professional award in law in recognition of the "impetus he had given to the Integrated Bar of the Philippines and for his exceptional leadership in the Philippine Bar in the name of law, justice and equality."[4]

Initially, the general reaction to his election, at least among his constituents: the faculty, staff, and students, was "Who is he?" Certainly, to a community such as the University of the Philippines, the most logical leader would be a scholar from among themselves with outstanding achievements in research work, and at the same time having the correct qualifications and executive ability to lead the country's prime academic institution. Angara was not then generally known in academic circles, although at the time of his election to the presidency of the University, he already had a solid reputation in his chosen field, law.

Angara in the Limelight

Angara was born on September 24, 1934 in Baler, Aurora Province. Though not very well known within the University itself in 1981, the year of his election to the presidencv, he was in fact an alumnus. He acquired his Associate in Arts and Bachelor of Laws in 1954 and 1958 respectively from the University of the Philippines. He earned his Master of Laws degree at the University of Michigan in Ann Arbor, Michigan, in 1964. While there, he was a De Witt scholar. He merited a scholarship grant in 1963 from the Columbia University Law School. Angara is life member of the international honor societies of Phi Kappa Phi and Pi Gamma Mu, and also of the Order of the Purple Feather and the University of the Philippines Law Honor Society, all of which reflect his outstanding scholastic performance. In 1958, he was admitted to the Philippine Bar.[5]

He started his career as an apprentice at the law firm of Carlos, Laurea and Associates, soon rising from the ranks. In 1962, he joined the Ponce Enrile, Siguion Reyna, Montecillo and Ongsiako Law Offices as an assistant attorney, eventually becoming a partner in 1968. He left the firm to establish the Angara, Abello, Concepcion, Regala and Cruz Law Offices in 1972 with himself as managing partner.

Seeing the need of Filipino entrepreneurs to have the same quick access to law as their foreign counterparts, he succeeded in making his law firm lead in this particular area of legal service. His efforts gained further recognition when he was elected first president of the ASEAN (Association of Southeast Asian Nations) Law Association General Assembly in 1980, followed by an award from his Alma Mater as the most outstanding law alumnus in 1981.[6]

Aside from having the signal achievement of establishing what would eventually become the largest law firm in the country, Angara distinguished himself as a delegate of his home province to the 1970 Constitutional Convention. In that constituent assembly, he was directly responsible for the inclusion of the provision in the fundamental law of the land that protected the public domain from undue exploitation and encroachment by speculators and by developers, thus ensuring that the succeeding generations would benefit from the national patrimony. Angara's successful incorporation of this principle in the Constitution of the Philippines reflected his deep social consciousness and civic responsibility, and his ability to transcend his personal interest in order to uphold the public weal.

Moreover, Angara was not unknown to the general Filipino public because long before his election to the UP presidency, he was already writing a regular column for *Bulletin Today*. He made use of this column to address himself squarely to various political, social, educational, cultural, and economic issues confronting the Filipino nation. As a columnist, he is influential in molding public opinion.

More on the New President

His identity and qualifications having thus been made public, the next question that needed to be resolved was, Why him?" Because of their unanimous vote, members of the Board of Regents obviously thought of him to be the man most capable of tackling the University's problems, specially those caused by meager funding. President Ferdinand E. Marcos, when informed of Angara's election, reacted by saying that the Board of Regents finally realized it was about time to have "an administrator rather than an educator"[7] for President of the University of the Philippines.

Angara averred he was just as surprised as anyone else on his election. But this was just the beginning of an administration marked by controversies, as is natural when unexpected change occurs. Being the dark horse for the position, Angara was the subject of speculations on how he really was chosen. His close friendship with Defense Minister Juan Ponce Enrile was suspected as being the deciding factor in his winning the University's presidency, and his actual election to this office was thought to be upon "orders from Malacañang."

In his first press conference, Angara replied to a question on his friendship with highly placed government officials: "If my friendship with people can help advance the interests of the University, I will ask for their help. I am what I am... the one who nominated me was Assemblyman (Ronaldo) Zamora, seconded by Solicitor General and Regent Estelito P. Mendoza. I don't know whether their personalities made my appointment political."[8]

Problems of Rapport and Adjustment

However, what was really foremost in the minds of those who were wary about the new president was whether he would make the University subservient to the national administration, a "puppet" as it were. "I think it is also important that we work hand in hand with the national government because the budget comes from it," he said. Angara quickly added, though, that "this close cooperation does not mean that we must abandon the interests of the University and the traditions that we all stand for."[9]

If the University of the Philippines academic community did not receive Angara with enthusiasm despite his impeccable credentials, this may be due to his lack of involvement in the University after his graduation. He had not been identified as a member of the University community. He was an outsider, and therefore still had to prove himself to his new constituency.

Making the situation more uncomfortable was the fact that his election came in the wake of the controversy created by Parliamentary Bill 524 (also known as the Education Act of 1980)[10] pending at the Batasang Pambansa (National Assembly) and threatening to further erode the academic freedom of the University of the Philippines. The offending issue here was the stripping of the University's autonomy since this bill would empower the Ministry of Education and Culture "to administer, supervise, and regulate the entire educational system."[11]

Students and faculty members alike made known their opposition to this bill. That Angara might compromise the University's interests by yielding to this bill, thereby making it less a bastion of freedom as the University had always been regarded, was a disturbing prospect. While many University officers and organizations made their formal statements of welcome, the general attitude was "wait-and-see." The academic community's reaction was tepid as Angara was inducted into office on June 5, 1981 by President Marcos in Malacañang.

Defining Basic Goals

The new President of the University of the Philippines set his visions for the institution to be more than ever "the source of national pride and an acknowledged institution of higher learning in the international academic community"[12] and the "source of alternative ideas and a crucible for their refinement and adaptation to our own Philippine context."[13]

Operationally, though, this vision was a continuation of the directions set by the outgoing administration of Emanuel V. Soriano. As Martial Law was "lifted" on January 17, 1981, foremost in the task of any administration, as Soriano said, was to situate the University of the Philippines in a new environment. Other targets were curricular improvement, more mission-oriented programs, more active participation in community affairs, strengthening of regional units, creation of a university-wide body with representation from all autonomous members of the University of the Philippines System, economic self-reliance, and stronger linkages with other institutions of higher learning.[14]

These were perhaps too much to do all at once; however, Angara committed his administration to quality education even as the University's source of funding must be made less dependent on the government, and to widening the doors of the University to a greater number of Filipinos.[15] But achieving these goals means doing away first with a number of obstacles. Angara acknowledged that the institution's "principal problem is the lack of a stable and adequate resource base which may be the key to many, if not most, of the other difficulties that beset the University."[16]

Grave Financial Handicaps

Although the University's subsidy from the national government for 1981 was more than ₱500 million, this was still inadequate if the University was expected besides to provide for its students whose number rose by 4.75 percent from 1980 to a total of 34,321 students in 1981,[17] likewise to upgrade faculty and staff salaries and benefits, improve physical facilities of the different campuses of the University system, and continue to pursue and maintain the different research programs of the University.

Financial difficulties stemmed from a restrictive situation. The national government was hard put in coping with competing demands on its budget, made doubly difficult by inflation; and whereas the Board of Regents had previously been allowed to allocate funds where it saw fit from a lump-sum grant, the Budget Ministry now required approval for practically every expenditure made. The financial worries could have been partially alleviated with funds coming from self-generated income and from various donations as well as from occasional grants from foreign countries, but Angara observed that these remained largely untapped.[18]

Other pressing problems of the University of the Philippines were identified by the new President. He noted the tremendous expansion of the University's population brought about by the usual increase from year to year and further enhanced by a policy toward democratization of the University's admission of freshmen, although the physical facilities of the institution remained the same. The passing of time and perennial use had worn out many of these facilities. Moreover, the development of the University of the Philippines as a multi-campus university had not been matched by an effective organizational structure. There were duplication of functions, lack of effective control, faulty monitoring mechanisms, and sadly, some cases of corruption.[19]

Corollary to the financial difficulties of any organization is the flight of talented personnel to greener pastures here and abroad.[20] At the point when the University could not give increases in salaries to alleviate the effects of inflation, some members of the faculty and staff left the University to join the private sector or other government agencies, or even to accept job offers abroad.

This problem could become critical for an organization, like the University, that relies heavily on the talents of its people. Angara realized this when he said, "My administration is pledged to the continued effectiveness of UP as the national center of learning. It is equally pledged to the physical well-being of the administrative staff on which that effectiveness so greatly depends."[21]

Engendered by a National Crisis

The problems inherited by Angara were not so much failures of previous administrations as they were spawned by hardships characteristic of the times. The country had experienced great upheavals in the decade of the '70s creating first, a climate of great political unrest, then a lull during the years under Martial Law, and finally transition to what was termed by the national leadership as "normalization." Furthermore, the global economic crises did not leave the University of the Philippines unaffected. The ensuing difficulties had to be met with resiliency, creativity and conviction to dispel the sense of chaos and confusion that come with them.

Many people thought that Angara was disadvantaged in having been an outsider to the University of the Philippines for a long time. On the contrary, his being an outsider actually afforded him fresher perspective and a more objective outlook on the institution's problems than someone who might have been more involved with its internal dynamics. It was perhaps this lack of attachment to individuals in the University that gave him courage to tackle its problems the way he did.

An Earnest Approach Exemplified

Moreover, his being a lawyer who had managed the operations of a big corporate enterprise gave him as it were the knowledge and the skill to handle a complex university system. He did not come in to the University presidency unprepared; he took a month off immediately after his election to divest himself of interests and preoccupations incompatible with his new office before taking his oath as President of the University of the Philippines, and he had to take a crash familiarity course on every aspect of running the University. Then he immersed himself into the institutional concerns of the University right away, with an in-depth and total understanding plus an extra advantage of non-partisanship, that perhaps enabled him to stand firm on later decisions, no matter how unacceptable those decisions may have been to the people affected. Immediately after his induction, he tackled the University's problems with an energy and a manner that in itself caused quite a controversy.

At his induction, Angara promised his constituency economic self-reliance. Even as measures would be taken to optimize the use of the government subsidy to the University, the University would take steps to lessen its dependence on it. He said he would establish an alternative resource base to support the growth and development of the University "according to its time-honored nature and purpose of teaching, research and extension service." But this effort must be "constrained by our abiding concern for the independence and integrity of the University not only as an academic institution but as a community of scholars."[22]

Getting the Money First

The first half of Angara's administration was characterized by a deep concern for the problem of funding. Angara seemed deeply preoccupied with the University's finances to a fault. This was something *new* to the academic community, which was accustomed to the UP's total involvement in the pursuits of academic excellence and participation in national political developments. Evidently Angara realized that he had to work hard to generate the funds essential for the improvement of the University. The problems called for a more pragmatic approach and basic to it all is funding which had to be settled first before progress in other phases of academic life could be assured.

SCOPE OF THE CHALLENGE AND THE QUALITY OF RESPONSE AS A MEASURE OF COMPETENCE

IMMEDIATELY after his swearing into office, Angara immersed himself with remarkable energy into projects that conformed with the directions he had set for himself and the University. Although at his election he was received with some misgivings by some quarters, by now, he had won the support of the vast majority of his constituency at the rate with which he initiated projects and made decisions.

One of the men who proved invaluable to him was Oscar M. Alfonso, Executive Vice-President. Alfonso, a highly respected academician and an experienced administrator, provided the transition and continuity between administrations and he served the University, as second-in-command, with as much energy and dedication as Angara. When Angara became deeply involved later in the campaign to rally support for the Diamond Jubilee Faculty Development Fund, Alfonso kept University affairs running smoothly within the scope of his responsibility.

In the latter part of July 1981, Angara issued a circular to freeze the hiring of new non-faculty personnel at all levels in the whole University of the Philippines System.[23] This circular came at a time when all over the country, retrenchment measures were being undertaken by the national government to comply with Letter of Instructions 1098 which called for the adoption of "policies and procedures for the effective imposition of budgetary reserves and economy measures in government operations for

CY 1981."[24] Angara's circular conformed with the national policy of discouraging the hiring of new personnel, but more importantly, it was a step toward more efficient use of University resources and a way to generate savings to enhance conditions of employment. This move might have depleted manpower for the University's programs and projects, especially in light of personnel leaving for better employment opportunities elsewhere. On the other hand, it generated optimal use of manpower resources available within the University, apart from generating savings from the unfilled items to be used for salary upgrading and promotions of deserving personnel. During this same period, allocation of funds was made for extensive improvements of physical facilities and water mains, as well as repair of roads within the campus.[25] But these were all common projects done for upkeep and maintenance. More important and requiring foresight and imagination was the planning of changes in the curricula and the organizational structure.

At the 943rd meeting of the Board of Regents on July 31, 1981, Angara obtained approval for the overall review and subsequent restructuring of the curricula and the organization of the University of the Philippines System. Shortly thereafter, he issued Memorandum Order No. 58 creating three task forces, later to be called committees. The first was to study the University's curricula, research and extension programs; the second, the organization of its manpower toward a more effective administrative service delivery mechanism; and the third, the infrastructure development and land-use program.[26]

Reviewing Academic Programs

The first committee was called the Committee to Review the Academic Programs, or CRAP. Appointed committee chairman was Jose Encarnacion, Jr., Dean of the School of Economics. The committee was directed to "assist the Office of the President in the re-examination and re-evaluation of all academic programs of the University of the Philippines System to make each program consistent with University thrusts."[27] The acronym of the committee, CRAP, with its dubious connotation in no way reflected the Committee's outputs because despite the controversy it generated, the committee was instrumental in the dramatic changes made in the University.

The second committee was the Management Review Committee (MRC), which was given the task of reviewing the organization of the University vis-a-vis the demands made on it as a rapidly expanding system, and thereafter making recommendations for its improvement. Angara tapped Raul P. de Guzman, Dean of the College of Public Administration, to head the Committee.[28] De Guzman would be named by Angara later on to the position of Vice-President for Planning and Finance.

Developing the Campus

To give attention to the physical improvement of the University were two committees. The Steering Committee on Campus Planning (SCCP) with Aurelio T. Juguilon, Dean of the College of Architecture, as chairman took charge of formulating campus development policies and strategies. The other, the Technical Committee on Infrastructure and Systems (TCIS), was to "review and update the infrastructure plans and recommendations prepared by the 1966 Campus Planning Office and subsequent modifications thereof." Ernesto G. Tabujara, Professor of Civil Engineering, was named chairman of this committee.[29] Tabujara would eventually be called upon to serve in 1984 as Acting Chancellor and from 1985 as full-term Chancellor of the autonomous unit of the University of the Philippines in Diliman.

When the committees commenced their respective work assignments, the University was filled with an air of expectancy of things to come, some of which were likely to be opposed or resisted.

Resistance to Proposed Changes

In a place such as the University of the Philippines where the right to hold, express and advocate an opinion is respected, controversies readily arise. Hence, the furor that was created when the findings and recommendations of the Committee to Review the Academic Programs (CRAP) headed by Jose Encarnacion, Jr.[30] was submitted to President Angara and then made public. The CRAP Report drew a wide variety of reactions, from serious in-depth critical analysis to the most ridiculous pun, the favorite among which was its unfortunate acronym.

The CRAP had a mission: to study the curricula of the different programs of the University of the Philippines and to find ways of improving them so that the University, as an institution of higher learning, and its graduates, would be not only relevant to the needs of the country and the global region we are in, but would themselves become leaders.[31] But because the report coincided with national loans then being negotiated with the World Bank and other financial institutions, one of the immediate reactions was that CRAP was a tool designed to align the University of the Philippines to whatever demands were being imposed on the grant of these loans. Speculations immediately spread, raising fears that the University would gradually support skill-oriented academic programs or strengthen the career-oriented courses, which are admittedly what the country needs, at the expense of other courses such as those in the social sciences that may be phased out.[32]

These turned out to be alarmists' speculations because CRAP never had such intention, plausible though these speculations might be. In fact CRAP merely intended that programs with similar objectives and courses be realigned.[33] There was not much point in duplication specially if it did not complement and strengthen, but rather demanded a thinner spreading out of resources.

CRAP Recommendations Approved

Therefore, on July 29, 1982, the Board of Regents approved the following recommendations:[34] the merger of masteral programs at the Institute of Industrial Relations into a single Master of Industrial Relations; the modification of A.B. Economics to B.A. Economics, and the abolition of B.S. Economics; the abolition of a Master's degree in Engineering (Computer Science); the revision of the Certificate Program to Diploma in Fine Arts; the creation of B.A. Communication with several specializations rather than the three separate programs of Broadcast Communication, Journalism, and Communication Research; the conversion of the masteral program at the Institute of Mass Communication into one with several specializations instead of having three separate programs, and the repeal of the Diploma in Population Communication; and the abolition of the Diploma in Statistics.

Most recommendations in this category came to pass without much comment. An exception was the decision by the Board of Regents on June 16, 1983 that the doctoral programs in Philippine Studies at the College of Arts and Sciences (later, College of Social Sciences and Philosophy)[35] and at the Asian Center be merged and then housed at the Asian Center. This was resisted by the faculty and students of the program based at the old College of Arts and Sciences, with the students formally submitting a petition containing the point that the successor College of Social Sciences and Philosophy is better equipped to handle the program, and insisting that the Asian Center should stick to Asian Studies. Administrative Order No. 154 created a committee composed of an equal number of representatives from both contending parties to study the matter further. Executive Vice-President Oscar M. Alfonso was named chairman of this ad hoc committee. Arguments and counterarguments ensued.[36] In its report to President Angara, the Committee recommended that (1) the old College of Arts and Sciences Philippine Studies Program be allowed to continue alongside the Asian Center Philippine Studies Program, (2) steps be taken within one year for the improvement of each Philippine Studies Program as outlined in the Committee's Report, and (3) steps be taken within two years for the adoption of a single Philippine Studies Program jointly administered by the Asian Center, the College of Social Sciences and Philosophy, and the College of Arts and Letters.

Another CRAP recommendation would link administratively a number of centers and degree-granting institutions with similar fields of study. This was rationalized as not only lessening the cost of administration but facilitating the technology transfer from the research center or the laboratory to the students.[37]

The following centers were therefore attached to other units, effective January 1, 1983: the Dairy Training and Research Institute to the College of Agriculture, University of the Philippines in Los Baños; the Institute of Ophthalmology to the College of Medicine; the Natural Science Research Center to the College of Arts and Sciences, or to the then proposed College of Science; the Philippine Executive Academy to the College of Public Administration; the Science Education Center to the College of Education; the University of the Philippines Creative Writing Center to the College of Arts and Sciences, or to the then proposed College of Arts and Letters; the University of the Philippines Film Center to the Institute of Mass Communication; and finally, the University of the Philippines Marine Sciences Center to the College of Arts and Sciences, or to the then proposed College of Science.[38]

This development was generally welcomed. The only source of anxiety was the prospect of confusion in organizing an administrative structure which thereafter would be common to both principal and attached units.

Survival of UP Branches at Issue

The CRAP also recommended that the Board of Regents either pump support in the form of finances and autonomy to the various units to make them more viable or phase them out.[39] Immediately endangered of being phased out were the campuses in Baguio City, Clark Air Base, San Fernando, and Tacloban City. Coincidentally this recommendation was strengthened by a similar proposal made by the Management Review Committee headed by Dean Raul P. de Guzman.

Petitions immediately poured in from students, faculty, staff and parents from the affected units. Delegations from the UP College in

Baguio, protesting the phase-out of its high school, and from the UP College Clark Air Base, trooped in to Diliman to plead their respective cases in late January 1982.[40]

While the proposal seemed logical from the viewpoint of managing a vast University system with scarce resources, it nevertheless appeared a harsh move upon those certain to be dislocated. Therefore, the Board of Regents, at Angara's suggestion, decided not to dissolve these units immediately but to place them instead under the supervision of the nearest autonomous unit. Closely related to this was the issue of "flying professors" who shuttle from one campus to another to conduct classes. The cost of their transport alone defied the need to economize. With the realignment of courses, this expense could be reduced.

In a conversation with President Angara on 24 April 1985, the President expressed his determination to carry out the policy duly approved by the University Council and by the Executive Committee for the phase-out of the UP College Clark Air Base. It was his view that the University has no business inside a foreign military installation, especially when the UP presence is regarded by the American base authorities as merely incidental to the defensive and offensive mission of Clark Air Base. Angara would simply not compromise the institutional integrity and dignity of the UP on this point. He prefers developing the UP Extension in San Fernando, thereby benefiting the province of Pampanga and the entire Central Luzon region, and increasing the positive impact of the University on Filipino society. He reiterated and amplified those views in his speech at the commencement exercises at the U.P. College Clark Air Base on 19 April 1985.

Reorganization at All Levels

Pertinent to Angara's vision of the University of the Philippines as the leader in education in the ASEAN region, the CRAP recommended the strengthening of the graduate program.

The recommendation on admissions was, in the meantime, received ambivalently. Everyone welcomed the abolition of the "discretionary" system which enabled higher officials of the University to allow admission of a number of students who did not make it in the entrance examinations. Removal of such privilege enhanced the quality of instruction, as the tests not only determined the capability of students but also assured that those who qualified did so on the basis of sheer merit.

The more controversial issue had to do with the University of the Philippines Integrated School (UPIS). Based upon the CRAP recommendations as approved by the Board of Regents on July 29, 1982, the status of the UPIS was resolved as a laboratory school for the College of Education, thereby limiting its enrolment but maintaining that its admission of students be democratic in nature. The UPIS would adopt a system of random admission of qualified students. There would be no lateral entry, and admission was to be made only at the kindergarten level. Before this, the children of the faculty and staff of the University of the Philippines had priority privileges. The new policy would give aspirants for admission equal opportunity regardless of parentage and family background. The University faculty and staff came to view this decision as the withdrawal of another incentive for them to stay in the University. Because of strong public pressure though, the University postponed enforcing the *tambiolo* or lottery system of admission to UPIS from school year 1984-1985 to school year 1985-1986.

Soon after the announcement to the public of the recommendations, President Angara began a series of consultations with sectors which would be most affected by the impending changes. It was at these consultations that the members of the academe became aware of the energy with which their leader pursued the changes he saw fit for a better University of the Philippines, and likewise noted his capacity to make decisions speedily and stand firm by them regardless of who would be affected.

The CRAP recommendations were not approved by the Board of Regents all at the same time. At each meeting of the Board, a few would be approved and thereafter assigned to be carried out. Some were accepted and implemented without question; others aroused stubborn opposition. On these occasions, Angara would compromise or characteristically postpone action to a more propitious time when his decision would be better understood by all. He was self-confident in making decisions and in the determination to make them stand.

Breaking up the College of Arts and Sciences

As if a bomb had been dropped and exploded at Palma Hall, the CRAP created a fissure at the College of Arts and Sciences, the largest unit of the University and often considered the heart of the institution. The CRAP never intended such a devastating effect in its mission to realign programs and courses. However, CRAP activated a dormant view among some of the officers and faculty members of the overgrown College of Arts and Sciences. Some faculty members of the Division of Natural Sciences and Mathematics proposed the separation of the Arts from the Sciences because of the unwieldiness of managing such a big college.

The idea caught on and spread quickly, obviously seen as a solution to the persistent problems that hamper the management of a huge college.

The idea of separation, although mentioned casually before among other prospects, was first officially articulated at the assembly of the Division of Natural Sciences and Mathematics on February 12, 1982 with the proposal for a College of Science presented by Ester A. Garcia, then associate dean of said Division, and Roger R. Posadas, then chairman of the Department of Physics.

They argued that the proposed separation would give due recognition to the identity of science as a profession and to its prime importance as an instrument of national development. They maintained that a separation would allow for a more effective academic leadership, administration, and coordination of the undergraduate, graduate, and research programs in the natural and mathematical sciences.

Garcia and Posadas furthermore stated that the creation of a college of science would provide greater administrative and fiscal autonomy to the science departments, collectively and individually. They emphasized that the proposed new arrangement would provide a stronger leverage for securing greater financial support for the basic sciences.[41]

Remigio E. Agpalo, a professor of political science and one of the principals opposed to the idea of separation, argued against the dismemberment of the College in terms of preserving the unity of knowledge in the arts and sciences, and in keeping alive the spirit of liberal education.

The original proposal of Garcia and Posadas for the division of the College of Arts and Sciences became the subject of much discussion and argumentation among the faculty and staff of the said College. The College of Arts and Sciences faculty conference on March 26, 1982 was the venue for the further articulation of opinions and ventilation of issues.

Three New Colleges from One

Although the members were obviously in favor of the move for the separation of the three divisions of the College, the proposal was nonetheless subjected to a referendum—whether or not to effect the split—which was the highlight of said conference. With surprising speed, the College of Arts and Sciences faculty decided in favor of a three-way split. The results of the referendum were submitted to President Angara by Dean Ofelia R. Angangco of the College of Arts and Sciences, and the Board of Regents approved on April 26, 1982 the creation of the College of Science and Mathematics, the College of Humanities, and finally, the College of Social

Sciences.[42] It was only on December 19, 1983, however, that their respective deans were appointed, with the names of the colleges modified. Roger R. Posadas became the dean of the College of Science; Pablo K. Botor, of the College of Arts and Letters; and Leslie E. Bauzon, of the College of Social Sciences and Philosophy.[43]

This was not to be the end of the issue. Soon, another controversy emerged on the problem of managing the General Education (GE) program after the split of the old College of Arts and Sciences into three colleges. The questions or issues went beyond that though; they now focused on the matter of the relevance of the courses, and on how much students needed them, for further education.

Discussions were again held to clarify the matter and people once again ventilated differing beliefs. The General Education issue has not so far been resolved while this is being written but continuous discussions traditionally respected within the University of the Philippines will surely lead to a solution that may well be acceptable to all concerned.

An Organizational Revamp

As mentioned earlier, one serious problem facing the University at the time that Angara took office was an outmoded organization. Through the years, the main structure of the organization of the University of the Philippines remained the same. Additional services demanded of it borne by rapid growth of the institution were met quite inadequately with the creation of offices haphazardly inserted within the organizational framework. This resulted in confusion and numerous duplications of functions. The situation was not only uneconomical; it made the task of management difficult. The second committee was created by the same order establishing CRAP precisely to attend to this problem.

The Management Review Committee (MRC) headed by Raul P. de Guzman, then Dean of the College of Public Administration and later Vice-President for Planning and Finance, was charged with the study of the structure of the University of the Philippines and likewise to design much-needed reforms.[44] Although its subsequent recommendations did not create furor and controversy as did the CRAP's, the MRC nevertheless caused as much changes in the area of organization as CRAP effected in the field of curricular programs. The Board of Regents on its part and in dealing with job displacements, saw to it (as in the case for example of the Physical Plant Office) that in the matter of reorganization, "officials and other personnel affected shall be accorded the right and protection due them, under existing laws as well as pertinent rules and regulations of the University."[45]

Restricted Hiring of Personnel

Clearly, the University needed to trim down the number of its personnel to enable it to augment limited funds set aside for its program of upgrading salaries and for supporting its policy of merit promotions. But here we see again Angara's brand of managing based on painless (or with the least pain possible) reforms. A situation which may have called for drastic reduction of personnel was handled tactfully. The policy of freezing the hiring of new personnel early in his term of office took advantage of the University's natural decrease of personnel, with many going for jobs in other government agencies, in the private sector and in other countries.

In 1981, the University of the Philippines in Diliman had a total of 3,030 faculty and staff members and this went down to 2,518 by 1982.[46] The duties left by resignees had to be absorbed by other incumbents, assuring optimal use of personnel, while at the same time making available more funds from unfilled vacancies for the benefit of those who stayed behind in the University. Outside the UP but within the general work force of the government, many people were on the other hand left dislocated and disillusioned over the loss of jobs due to retrenchment moves.

A question may be raised on the quality of people the University was left with and whether the reduced number was really capable of taking up the additional burdens and functions left by those who had sought employment elsewhere. The trade-off was inevitable but then, one could very well presume that only the best talents survive in a University which demands a high standard of performance. Besides, the resiliency of the Filipino was again demonstrated in this development, not to mention the dedication and the loyalty of the employees remaining in the institution.

MRC Proposals Carried Out

With the personnel trimmed down, the MRC's task of streamlining the University of the Philippines System into a more logical and responsive order was facilitated. Its recommendations, after careful study and close consultations with the people directly affected, were endorsed by Angara to the Board of Regents, which in turn approved the important measures.

Perhaps the most significant change was the realignment of units not so much geographically as with more allied fields. Executive Order No. 4 signed by Angara on March 23, 1983 decentralized the academic, administrative and service functions of the four autonomous units of the University of the Philippines in Diliman, University of the Philippines in Los Baños, University of the Philippines in Manila, and University of the Philippines in the Visayas.[47]

The University of the Philippines in Diliman was made responsible for units threatened to be phased out earlier: the UP College in Baguio, the UP College in Clark Air Base, and the UP Extension in San Fernando, Pampanga. The University of the Philippines in Los Baños retained all its units and was moreover asked to absorb the College of Veterinary Medicine which was to be transferred from the Diliman campus. Meanwhile, the University of the Philippines in Manila encompassed all units that formerly belonged to the Health Sciences Center, plus the College of Arts and Sciences (formerly the UP College in Manila) in Padre Faura, site of the prewar campus of the University.

New Chancellors Take Over

The University of the Philippines in the Visayas was to maintain all its existing units while at the same time taking in the College of Fisheries. The UP College in Tacloban and the UP College in Cebu were placed under the supervision of the University of the Philippines in the Visayas, but the Board of Regents deferred implementation of this matter, perhaps because of the practical difficulty of travelling between these branches via Manila.

With the move to decentralize, each autonomous unit would be headed by a Chancellor assisted by three Vice-Chancellors (four in Diliman). Thus, for the first time, under Executive Order No. 5,[48] the University of the Philippines in Diliman had an Acting Chancellor in Ernesto G. Tabujara, whose one-year term of office started on January 1, 1984.[49] Conrado Ll. Lorenzo, Jr., Chancellor of the University of the Philippines in Manila, was appointed earlier, on November 24, 1983.[50] At this point, it must be mentioned that the University of the Philippines in Los Baños and the University of the Philippines in the Visayas already had their own Chancellors: Emil Q. Javier for the former and Dionisia A. Rola for the latter. Tabujara subsequently became full-term Chancellor of UP Diliman while Javier stepped down from the chancellorship of UP in Los Baños on February 14, 1985. The successor of Javier is yet to be recommended by President Angara to the Board of Regents for appointment, although a search committee has submitted its report to the President.

A Well-Defined Hierarchy

On top of the whole University of the Philippines System is the President, Edgardo J. Angara and the Executive Vice-President, Oscar M. Alfonso, and three Vice-Presidents responsible for Academic Affairs, Planning and Finance, and Public Affairs. The Vice-President for Academic Affairs is Dr. Irene R. Cortes while the Vice-President for Planning and Finance, as already mentioned is Dr. Raul P. de Guzman. The position of Vice-President for Public Affairs is still unfilled as of this writing. Prof. Martin V. Gregorio is the Secretary of the University. A few offices were abolished, including the President's Staff on Regional Matters, the functions of which were given to central administration, and the Office of General Services, the records of which were transferred to the Human Resource Development Office, itself a newly established entity.

The new organizational structure of the University of the Philippines in Diliman is depicted in the chart[51] shown on the next page.

Democratic Representation

Another important recommendation of the MRC would give opportunity to every constituent of the University to participate in decision-making. The MRC advocated a University Assembly for the entire University of the Philippines System and a University Council for each autonomous unit.[52] The University Assembly would be composed of elected representatives of disciplinary clusters within the University Councils, Student Councils, administrative and academic personnel organizations, and of the chief executive officers of the University of the Philippines System as well as of the different campuses, with the President of the University as chairman and the Vice-President for Academic Affairs as vice-chairman.

The University Assembly's role would be to give advice and extend assistance to the Central Administration in "reviewing and formulating system-wide plans and policies on the development of academic and administrative programs in the different autonomous units, as well as plans and policies on community affairs and national issues."[53]

The University Council of each autonomous unit would be composed of all faculty members with professorial rank with the Chancellor as the Chairman, and would involve itself in like manner as the University Assembly, limiting its affairs only to those pertaining to the autonomous unit it belongs to.

At the Joint Conference Workshop of the existing University Councils on November 13, 1982, this development was hailed by the faculty as "allowing it a share in the decision-making in the University and not merely power over academic matters and student discipline as currently vested upon them by the University Code."[54]

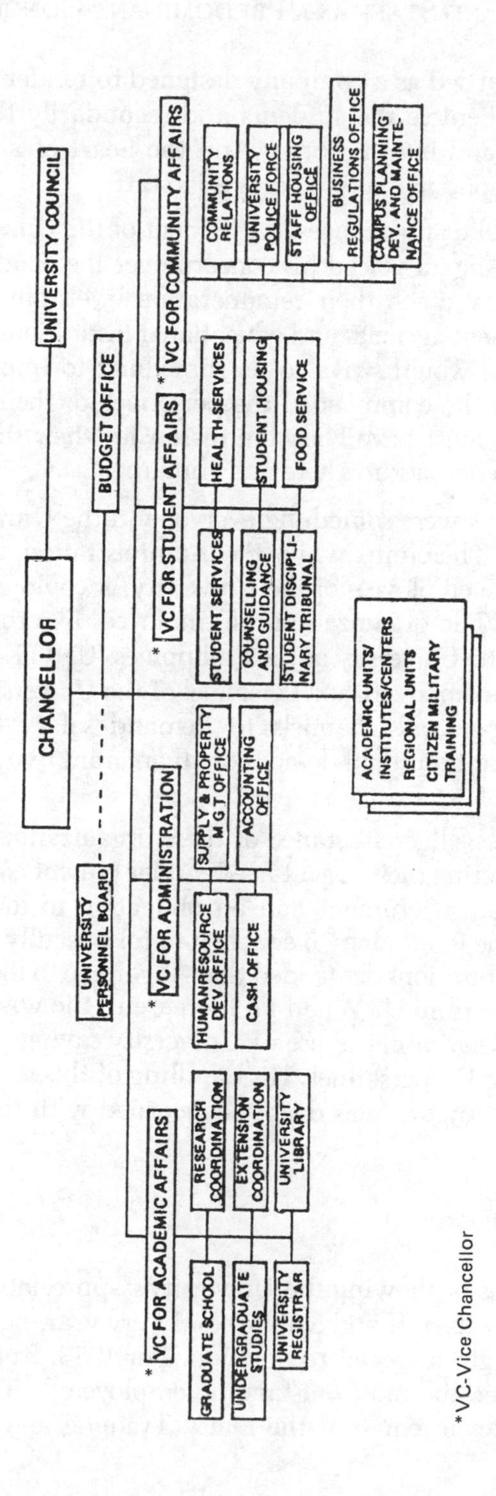

Organizational Chart

University of the Philippines in Diliman

WELFARE OF FACULTY AND STAFF AS A PREDOMINANT CONCERN

A UNIVERSITY if regarded as a company designed to render services would have as its clientele the students and secondarily the community, both local and international. And the heart of a service-rendering institution as any good manager knows is its staff.

On one of his earlier public appearances as President of the University of the Philippines, Edgardo J. Angara voiced his concern over the conditions of the University employees, how much their remuneration levels have lagged behind that of other government agencies and educational institutions, among others, and promised that he would strive to do something to improve the situation.[55] At the same time, he commended the personnel for their dedication to the University which must have been the reason for their staying on despite the enticements of greener pastures here and abroad.

Tight financial conditions were something everyone in the University of the Philippines understood. Therefore, while the Administration was concerned about the plight of the employees of the University, it could only raise salaries at minimal levels. While organizations of employees like the United Teachers and Employees of the University of the Philippines (UNITE-UP) and the Survival Action Group for Impoverished Personnel of the University of the Philippines (SAGIP-UP) sought all channels to demand salary hikes up numerous steps, the Administration could do no more than grant two steps at a time.[56]

It was not so much the belligerent stance of these organizations in submitting their demands considering their urgent needs under present conditions, as it was the contention that government had an obligation to increase its subsidy to the University of the Philippines to enable it to raise faculty and staff salaries. The employees' organizations demanded that Angara go to the government and not sacrifice the personnel. When no increase in the government subsidy was forthcoming, Angara made use of University savings to give a six-step salary increase to the UP personnel. His handling of this matter convinced his constituents that Angara was deeply concerned with their well-being.

Awards to Outstanding Employees

There were other means of showing the University's appreciation of the dedicated service rendered by its staff and employees. Every year, outstanding employees were chosen and given special recognition. For 1983, from among the rank and file were chosen the most outstanding employees.[57] They were Rogelio L. Borje, a carpenter foreman at the Dairy Training and Research

Institute of the UP in Los Baños, who had been in service for 16 years; Francisco E. Dumlao, administrative assistant of the Graduate School; Mariano Misalucha, office representative at the College of Public Administration; Ildefonso Ramos, a precision instrument technician at the College of Engineering; Pedro T. Reano, foreman at the Institute of Plant Breeding of the UP in Los Baños, who had been with the University for 28 years; Enrique A. Valera, laboratory-technician at the Department of Chemistry of the College of Arts and Sciences in Diliman; Corazon C. Villarivera, senior clerk at the Division of Humanities of the College of Arts and Sciences; Azucena M. Cabrales, records officer at the Office of the University Secretary; Liberata Zamora, administrative officer at the Science Education Center of the College of Education; and Mariano P. Zara, agricultural technician at the Department of Horticulture of the College of Agriculture at the UP in Los Baños.

In the matter of personnel, with the conditions as they were in the area of salaries, the Angara Administration was fortunate that loyalty and dedication were overriding sentiments among the faculty and staff members of the University. Had it not been for these, the University of the Philippines would have seen a bigger depletion in the number of employees, a backfiring of the strategy for staff and organizational realignment.

Meanwhile, in another effort to inspire his constituents to excel in their endeavors, Angara created in late 1984 awards for distinction in the following categories: all around outstanding faculty performance, research, administration, extension service. A UP System-wide search is now underway for the awardees in each category. The awardees will receive substantial cash prizes and proper citations on June 18, 1985, when the University will observe its 77th anniversary. A special service award named after the late Patrolman Pagasa Laurino will be given to a deserving member of the University Police Force. The most outstanding student organization will likewise be given due recognition on that day.

Improved Working Environment

When Angara took up his new responsibilities as President, he deplored the fact that physical facilities were outmoded and rundown, some to the point that they were of not much use. In one instance, Angara said that the lawyer in him was fearful about the state of the buildings because they might just give way and he would have a big liability case on his hands. This might have been an exaggeration but the point he was making was evident.

One of the first tasks he took on was the rehabilitation of the restrooms at Palma Hall, the installation of water mains, the complete repair of campus roads, and the overall restoration of buildings needing electrical, plumbing, painting, and carpentry work.[58]

The Committee to Review Infrastructure and Logistical Support headed by Ernesto G. Tabujara subsequently took charge of the physical facelifting of the Diliman campus. Thus began a massive infrastructure development in the University of the Philippines. To outsiders or old alumni coming back to the University premises, the immediate impression would be that there were a number of additions to the campus buildings.

More Structures Completed

By the end of 1981, the University of the Philippines Physical Plant Office reported that 25 percent of the four-story Law Library Building had been completed, that the National Engineering Center was in the last phase of construction, and so also the University of the Philippines Film Center. All these buildings were started under the previous administration. The first phase of the Jorge B. Vargas Museum and Fine Arts Building had been finished, as also the Storage Plant intended to house records that had accumulated over the years in Quezon Hall, making the latter a fire hazard.

Major repairs had also been done at Quezon Hall, the Science Education Center, Vinzons Hall, the UP Integrated School, and the College of Home Economics administrative staff office.[59] The University of the Philippines Sikatuna BLISS was inaugurated to help alleviate the housing problem inside the Diliman campus among the faculty and staff members.[60]

Many of these projects continued to 1982. By the end of that year, the annex of the Institute of Mass Communication was completed. Likewise finished were the new University Gymnasium, and the UP Department of Citizen Military Training/Vanguard building. On March 21, 1983, the Philippine Social Science Center, built within the campus, was formally turned over to the Center officials by the Japanese government.[61]

Diamond Jubilee Fund-Raising

The urgent need for funds drew attention to many improvement projects that were initiated, not only in the physical facilities, but also in research, instruction and extension. Starting in mid-year 1982 and throughout the year 1983, the University celebrated the 75th anniversary of its founding. This observance extended into the first half of 1984. What better way to celebrate the Diamond Jubilee of the University than by mobilizing all those who had been and were involved in the institution to support its projects. Thus, President Marcos created the Presidential Commission on the 1983 Diamond Jubilee of the University of the Philippines under the chairmanship of Prime Minister Cesar E.A. Virata. It planned, organized, and supported activities in observance of the UP Diamond Jubilee, and it worked as a major vehicle in raising the Diamond Jubilee Faculty Development Fund.

On June 18, 1982, the Diamond Jubilee Year was formally launched. Its theme, "UP's Role in the Shaping of the Filipino Nation," was further dramatized by a call to raise ₱75,000,000 for the faculty development fund of the University. The objective was to enable the University to strengthen its capability and enhance its stature to contribute more to the nation by way of its graduates and its programs in research and through its involvement in the nation's development. The fund would create more professorial chairs and faculty grants; in general, it would boost morale and make the task of instruction more rewarding other than spiritually to the teaching staff. As of June 30, 1985, the University has created 141 professorial chairs sustained by the Diamond Jubilee Faculty Development Fund.

The response was phenomenal. By the time of its launching, already ten percent of the target amount had been given or pledged.[62] Extensive media coverage of celebration activities drew more support from people who, although no longer with the University, were connected with it at one time or another. Private businessmen, government officials, civic leaders and many successful alumni representing various professions responded enthusiastically. Donations poured in, ranging in sum from fifty centavos from grade-school children to millions of pesos from individuals and organizations.

There were different fund-raising activities like sales of memorabilia, clocks, tableware, pins, cards, stickers, special Diamond Jubilee car plates, gift certificates, tickets to benefit shows and dinners, and even special varieties of crops and fish from UP in Los Baños and UP in the Visayas, respectively.

UP President Sets the Pace

President Angara with a great help from his lady, Gloria, and from officers of the University Administration, set the pace for all these activities. Willingly and perseveringly, he traveled to all the major cities in the country to raise funds from alumni and friends of the University. He flew to different countries to seek donations and support for the institution he heads.

His trip to the United States proved to be the most fruitful. The alumni there not only responded positively as proven by the impressive amount of $237,565 raised but also inspired Angara in his meetings with United States-based alumni to establish and incorporate the Friends of UP in America Foundation. This organization coordinated alumni activities mainly for the benefit of the Alma Mater. More importantly, it became a venue for a solid group of Filipinos in a foreign land to manifest their gratitude and appreciation of the role of the University in providing opportunities to their countrymen to attain a better life.

By the end of 1982, the University of the Philippines Diamond Jubilee Faculty Development Fund had already reached ₱32,040,218.[63] The suspense set in when just five days away from June 18, 1983, a year after the Diamond Jubilee Year was declared, the amount of ₱66,439,314 raised so far was still short of the target. But donations poured in faster such that on June 18, the amount committed had even surpassed the target by registering a total of ₱80,075,000 thanks to the most generous contributors to the fund campaign: President Ferdinand E. Marcos and the First Lady, Mrs. Imelda Romualdez Marcos, the Chinese Community, the Alumni Council Meeting, the Alcuaz Art Exhibit, and Central Bank Governor Jaime C. Laya, whose combined donations made up the difference of nearly ₱14,000,000.[64]

Jubilee Evokes Renewal of Ties

Perhaps the strongest attraction to support the Diamond Jubilee observance was the nostalgia that people, specially the alumni, feel for the University. No alumni would be so callous as to resist sharing their good fortune with the institution to which they owe so much in happy years spent on campus while taking on a capability to make something of themselves in the world, an ambition usually realized. And this feeling common to a great number would generate a sense of unity, goodwill and beneficence. It was therefore touching to see graduates of long ago, almost physically decrepit, sing for the cause, showing how alive the University spirit was still in them. Another group would be parents looking forward to sending their sons and daughters to the University and therefore willing to contribute as a form of investment on education the benefits of which will in due time redound to them.

With the proceeds, the University will be able to set up numerous professorial chairs and faculty grants, assure the stability of teaching as a respected profession, and raise even higher the standard of academic excellence traditionally identified with the University of the Philippines.

Malacanañg Asked to Take a Hand

As Angara saw the problem, the financial headaches of the University stemmed not only from the lack of funds but also from the lack of freedom on the part of the Board of Regents and the officers of the Administration of the

University to manage its finances. Another reason was the lack of attention given to available means of acquiring funds other than from government allocation.

In response to the first cause cited, Angara quietly worked for executive intervention to ease the pressure on the allocation of funds. This came on August 1, 1981 when Marcos signed Executive Order No. 714. However, it was not until April 1983 that a Memorandum of Agreement was finally drawn between the Ministry of the Budget, the Commission on Audit, and the University of the Philippines, putting into effect the Executive Order from Malacañang. The Memorandum of Agreement outlined the implementing guidelines for the restoration of fiscal autonomy to the University of the Philippines.[65]

Income-Generating Consultancies

Other government agencies and the private sector have always tapped the technical know-how within the University, knowing how rich the University is in terms of human talent and resources. This practice of tapping the expertise of the personnel of the University has traditionally been done on an individual basis since the University has no organized delivery of such a service. Thus, a resource of the University is being utilized without the University benefiting from such borrowing of its pool of experts and specialists.

In July 1983, therefore, the Diamond Jubilee Consultancy Project was launched.[66] This project was initiated by the Resource Generation Staff of the Office of the Vice President for Planning and Finance, and former University President Emanuel V. Soriano was appointed Chairman. The Jubilee Consultancy Project's principal objective was to provide additional income for the University of the Philippines faculty and staff members by marketing their expertise to those who need their assistance. Melito S. Salazar, Jr., Director of the Institute for Small-Scale Industries, was designated Project Director. Lawyer Florian Orendain was to take charge of the marketing aspects of the undertaking, while Celine S. Rondain, Ramon L. Nasol, and Rogelio O. Juliano were to act as coordinators for the University of the Philippines in Diliman, the University of the Philippines in Los Baños, and the University of the Philippines in the Visayas, respectively.

This Project would not only assure the University of the Philippines of a fair share but by systematic coordination, also enable faculty members to be given a chance to exercise their talents in productive programs outside the University, thus sharpening their skills further while deriving added income for themselves. The project moreover would assure clients that they will be getting the best in the field in an arrangement formally sanctioned by the University.

Aid from Foreign Agencies

Another under-utilized source of income was foreign donations. This might have been a sensitive area to explore as donations are always suspect of having strings attached, had it not been for Angara's frank and candid view of donations: "Aid is something we welcome although the University understands that such aid is basically an instrument of the donor government's policy."[67] Therefore, he stands guard on the University's prerogative to examine the terms of donations specially because it is in educational institutions where "young minds are and the future of society is determined." He cited the need for measures to be taken so that "only what is right and best be permitted to influence these minds."[68]

Increase in Tuition Fees

Another source of revenue is of course the tuition fee. Because of the government subsidy, students of the University of the Philippines pay minimal tuition fees. The government shoulders about 85 to 90 percent of the educational cost while UP students pay the rest corresponding to 10 or 15 percent.[69]

On August 23, 1983, consultations began on the feasibility of raising the tuition fee. The proposed increase ranged from 50 to 200 percent, later computed at an average of 169 percent. Naturally, discussions and arguments ensued.

Those in favor of the tuition fee increase say that this move is necessary to procure much-needed additional funds that will enable the University of the Philippines to maintain its position of leadership as the prime educational institution in the country, and also to enable the creation of more scholarships and more assistance programs for poor but deserving students. Those against an increase say that indeed, the University of the Philippines needs more funds but, as similarly contended by the faculty, students must not be made to make the sacrifice but that the government should, on the other hand, be obliged to invest more in education. In the summer of 1984, the protests escalated when word spread that the tuition fee hike would be imposed during the first semester of school year 1984-1985, and the students threatened a no-pay enrolment boycott—a barricade as the students termed it. Angara was characteristically firm about the hike. President Ferdinand E. Marcos intervened and directed Education Minister Jaime C. Laya to restudy the UP proposals. At its 967th meeting on April 24, 1984, the Board of Regents deferred action on the proposed tuition fee hike pending Laya's findings and recommendations.[70]

On May 8, 1985, Laya met with the students at Palma Hall wherein he asked them to reconsider their position saying that they would ultimately suffer the consequences of a lower standard of education should UP fail to get the funds it direly needed.

New Rates Suspended

The students likewise stood firm about their plans for the no-pay enrolment boycott should the UP Administration increase the fees as decided upon. The Board of Regents at its 968th meeting on May 31 decided to direct a modified proposal since the increase may be too drastic;[71] it approved a ₱450 increase spread over the next four semesters.

However, according to the students, the increase, even if spread out, actually amounts to a 170 percent hike over current tuition fees.[72] University officials maintained, though, that the increase is fair, reasonable, and necessary to ensure the high quality of education offered by the institution to the youth of the land.

On June 5, 1984, the students represented by Victor C. Avecilla and Louis C. Biraogo of the College of Law decided to file a suit in court just before the registration period contesting the imposition of the higher tuition fees. The Quezon City Regional Trial Court responded by issuing a restraining order directing the UP Administration to suspend the collection of the new rates pending a hearing of the case scheduled for June 15.[73]

The petitioners alleged that the "decision approving the fee increases by the Board of Regents constitutes deprivation of property entitled to protection by the Constitution" and that "no genuine consultations and hearings were made with the students and parents."[74]

Angara considered the restraining order unfortunate since the plan "to expand scholarship grants as well as to increase the salaries of our personnel has been temporarily set back."[75] The students, however, were jubilant as they proceeded with their enrolment for the first semester of school year 1984-1985.

The victory of the students over the tuition fee issue was however short-lived because after the June 15 hearing, Judge Luis L. Victor of the

Quezon City Regional Trial Court penned an order denying the petition of the students for the court to issue a preliminary injunction to prevent the UP from enforcing the newly approved rates.[76] The court decided that whereas every Filipino has the right to elementary and secondary education, "college or university education. . . is a privilege granted to those. . . able to acquire the wisdom and skill" and that the "petitioners proceed on an erroneous premise that education is property."[77]

Likewise, the court upheld the Board of Regents' approval, despite the alleged lack of "genuine consultations," on the grounds that "it is the exclusive governing body of the institution," and "it is not mandated to conduct hearings and consultations before deciding on fee increases."[78]

In any case, while the court denied the injunctive relief to the petitioners the issue of judicial review over the decision of the Board of Regents to increase the tuition fee rates was left unresolved. The position of the University on this matter, of course, is that UP is an autonomous institution and thus enjoys academic freedom in all matters affecting its internal operation.

The students quieted down on the tuition fee issue, perhaps because the matter was *sub judice*, pending in court, following the denial of their petition for injunctive relief, and following the announcement that the court still had to resolve the issue of judicial review over the decision of the Board of Regents to increase the tuition fee. Despite the lifting of the restraining order though, the University decided not to collect the new tuition fee rates for the first semester, although the new laboratory fees have been, and are being enforced. And while the court has ruled against the students in connection with their petition for a preliminary injunction, and while the matter of the tuition fee rates is still under the jurisdiction of the court, it was expected that the students would continue protest action especially if it would turn out that the decision would be adverse to them. Just the same, the University Administration was determined to pursue what it honestly believed to be the best path toward improving UP facilities and maintaining its tradition of academic excellence.

Institutional Autonomy Upheld

The suit filed by law students Victor C. Avecilla and Louis C. Biraogo contesting the University's decision to hike its tuition fees led to a definitive court ruling which upheld the institutional autonomy and integrity of the University of the Philippines. After a number of hearings, Judge Luis L. Victor of the Quezon City Regional Trial Court issued an order on September 26, 1984 dismissing the petition filed by the aforementioned students on June 5, 1984. In his 14-page decision, Judge Victor denied the claim of the plaintiffs that the UP students were not heard and consulted by the Administration of the University. On the contrary, they were given all the chances to express their views on the issue, despite the fact that the Board of Regents was not bound to hear and consult them prior to its making a decision on the increase of the student fees. Judge Victor then proceeded to point out the contradictory position of the students: they talk about keeping the UP independent from government intervention and yet by demanding increased government subsidy for the UP, they are actually opening the door for government meddling in the affairs of the institution. According to Judge Victor, it was in fact the Board of Regents which asserted the autonomy of the University, thereby safeguarding its academic freedom, by approving the tuition fee increase in order to raise much-needed monies to be used in improving the institution's academic standards.

On the crucial issue of the judicial review of the approval by the Board of Regents of the new tuition rates, the court found that the plaintiffs could give no valid and convincing evidence that the Board of Regents exceeded the bounds of its legal mandate as the highest policy and governing body of the University.[79]

Thus the way was paved for the UP to implement its new tuition rates. The court in fact recognized the reasonablenes of the increase considering the imperative need of upholding the academic excellence of the University. To keep its competitive edge in offering quality education to the youth of the land, the UP could not afford to rely on its past glories. It must always be in the forefront of higher education in this country. To be in this position, the University has the right to ask the students and their parents to pay their share in meeting the costs involved. After all, the students come from the upper crust of Filipino society. The affluent circumstances of the UP students is reflected in the severe parking problem the University faces. Many of these students spend only for a day's lunch what they pay for their tuition fee in the University. Therefore, it is only just and fair that they be made to shoulder the rising price of a UP education so that the proceeds derived from the new tuition rates can be used by the University Administration to raise faculty and staff salaries to a level that will enable the personnel to keep their dignity and self-respect, as well as to upgrade UP's physical, laboratory, and classroom facilities.

Diliman Campus Barricaded

Throughout the first semester of schoolyear 1984-1985, the University experienced a tense atmosphere brought about by student unrest. This troubled state of the studentry stemmed from the decision of the UP Administration to increase the tuition fee effective at the beginning of the said schoolyear. Rallies were a common occurrence on the steps or in the lobby of Palma Hall as well as on the steps of Quezon Hall. In these rallies, students denounced the tuition fee increase. While the student leaders welcomed the suit filed by Avecilla and Biraogo in the Quezon City Regional Trial Court against the University of the Philippines, it was clear that they did not recognize the court inasmuch as it belonged to a regime the legitimacy of which they questioned. (Ironically, they demanded more subsidy from the very government they wished to dismantle!) Therefore, the students threatened to mobilize the whole Diliman community for mass action to pressure the UP Administration into rescinding its decision on the tuition fee issue. The students recalled the days of the Diliman Commune in early 1971 and warned that they would barricade the University campus and cause utter paralysis in the operations of the institution.

Convinced that its action on the tuition fee issue was proper and reasonable, the UP Administration stood firm and refused to be cowed by the threats of the University Student Council to barricade the campus in order to achieve the stoppage of University activities. On September 19, 1984, when the students did barricade the University Avenue and the other roads leading to UP Diliman, the University community was caught literally by surprise. The student activists also padlocked some of the academic buildings inside the campus, most notably Palma Hall.

There was an element though of bad faith on the part of the students in the padlocking of Palma Hall and the other academic buildings on the Diliman campus. The previous day, September 18, 1984, the students announced that they would only barricade Quezon Hall, the building which houses the Central Administration of the University. Nobody therefore expected them to bar access to academic buildings. However, on the following day, the student activists not only barricaded University Avenue in front of Quezon Hall as well as other entry points, but also put up obstructions to bar entry into Palma Hall. As a result, many students, faculty members, and non-academic personnel were inconvenienced. Some turned back and went home, although the majority proceeded to their respective work places and classrooms, with normal University functions largely unaffected. The unit which bore the brunt of the barricading of the UP on September 19 was the College of Social Sciences and Philosophy because it occupies Palma Hall, which is always the target of mass actions of this type. Palma Hall is where the biggest concentration of students is found inside the campus.

The barricading of Palma Hall partially disrupted classes in the building in the morning. However, because only the main entry points from the Faculty Center and from the Palma Hall Annex were blocked by the student activists, majority of the students could actually enter the building via the road going through the basement and by simply climbing over the railings. The authorities therefore saw no need to confront the student activists and force them to remove the obstructions placed by them across the entrances. In any case, by one o'clock that day, the student activists abandoned their posts in order to participate in a march to the Liwasang Bonifacio (Bonifacio Plaza) in Manila where a rally to denounce what the students call the "U.S.-Marcos Dictatorship" subsequently took place. A good number of classes thus took place in Palma Hall and office workers reported for duty despite the barricading of the University that day.

Meanwhile, the faculty of the College of Social Sciences and Philosophy had an emergency meeting in the afternoon of September 19 to discuss the situation and to give suggestions on how to deal with future barricades. The faculty took the stand that while the students should be dealt with firmly, the lines of communication with them must be kept open at all times in order to ensure the preservation of the rule of reason in the University and to prevent the violation of the integrity and autonomy of the institution. Everybody agreed that while the student activists had the right to air their grievances, the rights of others should be respected.

The barricading of the University on September 19 proved to be a dry run for the events which took place in the campus on September 27-28, 1984. During this two-day period, the student activists mounted a serious and determined effort to paralyze the University by blocking the main entry points to the University, specially those coming from the University Avenue, the Don Mariano Marcos Avenue, and the Balara portion of the Katipunan Road. However, the entry via the Stud Farm coming from the UP Village remained open, and so was the entry via the Carlos P. Garcia Avenue from the Katipunan Road.

Tension in the Campus

Prior to this two-day period, the atmosphere in the campus was volatile. The students claimed success in connection with their September 19 barricading of the University, and they anticipated an even more successful paralyzation of the campus with their announced barricading of the University on September 27-28. President Angara celebrated his birthday on September 24, but that same day, the Executive Committee of the UP in

Diliman met in order to find ways and means to deal with the extraordinary situation which the University was about to experience. The Executive Committee convened again on September 26 for the same purpose of dealing with the "crisis." A day earlier, on September 25, the President's Advisory Council gathered to assess the situation likewise.

In all these meetings, the decision of the University to raise the tuition fee was unanimously upheld and supported by the deans, directors, and chancellors of the UP System. It was the consensus that the institutional autonomy of the University must be protected at all costs and that there would be no compromise with the student activists on this issue. The University firmly stated that it respected the right of students to self-expression but that the democratic rights of others must also be observed. To ensure normal operations, the University Administration called on all faculty members and employees to perform their usual duties, and the authorities moved to avert violence from flaring up in any part of the UP Diliman campus by ordering the UP police force to maintain a good distance from the barricades.

The tension in the campus rose when Quezon Hall, the building which houses the Central Administration, was hit by a fire of undetermined origin in the early morning hours of September 26, the day before the planned two-day barricading of the University by the student activists. While only the left wing was affected, the damage to the building was estimated at ₱12 million. Completely burned down were the Office of the President, the Board of Regents' Room, the Office of General Services, the Office of the Executive Vice President, and the Information Office. The Budget Office and the Office of the Secretary of the University on the ground floor sustained only minor destruction caused mostly by water coming from the firemen's hoses. Rumors spread across the campus on the probable causes of the conflagration. Many felt, rightly or wrongly, that the fire was somehow related to the unusual situation facing the University.

Palma Hall as Focal Point of Barricades

Aware that the Palma Hall building would be the primary target of the student activists during the barricading of the University on September 27-28, the administration of the College of Social Sciences and Philosophy created and mobilized a Crisis Management Committee to deal with the situation and to ensure that the premises would remain open for those wishing to teach and to attend classes. For two successive nights, on September 26 and 27, the Dean and the College Secretary, accompanied by some members of the administrative staff and by a number of custodial workers, kept vigil in the building so that it would not be padlocked by the student activists as a means of preventing students, faculty members, and office personnel from entering Palma Hall. The vigil was successful in securing the building and everybody was assured the next day of free entry to and free exit from Palma Hall. During the daytime hours of September 27 and 28, the student activists, numbering only around 50 to 60, attempted to form human barricades and to put up physical obstructions across the main entry points. However, the college administration together with some faculty members succeeded in persuading the student activists to allow those wishing to teach and those wishing to attend classes to carry on. A substantial number of classes were therefore held during this period, and no violent incidents occurred.

If there was violence, it took place some 10 kilometers away from the Diliman campus in the afternoon of September 27, when the student activists left their posts to participate in a rally involving larger national issues. This was when the police and the military violently dispersed the assembled rallyists in the area of the Welcome Rotonda where the boundary of Quezon City and Manila is located, as they were preparing to march forward to Liwasang Bonifacio. In this incident, an innocent bystander by the name of Osias Alcala was hit and killed by a stray bullet, while several persons were injured, including Fidel R. Nemenzo, son of Francisco Nemenzo, Jr., former dean of the defunct College of Arts and Sciences.

During the barricading of the UP campus on September 27-28, the student activists failed to mobilize the rank and file population of the community to join them in paralyzing the operations of the University. It was a pathetic sight they presented in Palma Hall in particular when despite their room-to-room campaign to ask their fellow students to join them, only a handful did so, while the majority demonstrated their preference to attend classes and were indifferent to the pleas of the student leaders, who shouted themselves hoarse as they tried to enlist the studentry to their side.

While the University constituents were inconvenienced by the barricading of the campus, the authorities kept their cool and equanimity and they dealt with the student activists firmly but gently, thus averting what everybody feared, and this was the deterioration of the situation to violence which would then justify the intervention of the police and the military. To the credit of both sides, a genuine effort to avoid hostile confrontation was exerted.

The barricading of the campus on September 27-28, 1984 coincided with the release of the decision of Judge Luis L. Victor upholding the right and the autonomy of the UP to increase its tuition fee. Because of the resolute stand of President Angara on the tuition fee issue, one can say that the students did not accomplish anything with their barricades except to inconvenience everybody in the community and to show their irrational and adventuristic action.

Disruption of Second Semester Registration

With the issuance of the court order, the stage was now set for the University to implement the collection of the new tuition fee. As the second semester of schoolyear 1984-1985 approached, the student activists heightened the tone of their language to the effect that they were not bound to abide by the decision of the Regional Trial Court of Quezon City because the same was part and parcel of the very governmental system they wished to see dismantled. From their point of view, the court decision was promulgated by a judicial body belonging to a regime which lacked legitimacy. Therefore, the decision was also devoid of legitimacy and was not valid.

Proceeding from this viewpoint, the student activists moved to disrupt the registration process for the second semester when it got underway in early November 1984. They asked the students to boycott the payment of fees and to skip the assessment portion of the enrolment procedure. Again, the majority of the student population recognized that the increase authorized by the Board of Regents was fair and reasonable. Many of them shunned the boycott movement of the student activists and they proceeded to complete their registration, knowing fully well that an incomplete registration would mean the loss of their status as bonafide students of the University, and this in turn would only delay their graduation. Surprisingly, the UP Diliman campus even registered a bigger number of students in the second semester than in the previous semester despite the implementation of the new rates.

Barricades Set Up Anew

Failing to disrupt the enrolment process, the student activists once again decided to bring matters to a head by announcing that they would barricade the University on November 15-16, 1984. This was basically a repeat of the barricading of the campus on September 27-28 during the first semester. The usual entry points were blocked and massive traffic jams ensued. Students, faculty members, and administrative personnel walked from where public vehicles disgorged them when these were unable to gain access to the campus, or when their drivers were unwilling to fall in line and follow the traffic which moved at a snail's pace. However, not all entrances to the campus were really barricaded as the Stud Farm entry and the Carlos P. Garcia Avenue entry from the Katipunan Road were open, albeit these routes were circuitous specially for a motorist coming from such places as Caloocan City.

As in previous barricades, Palma Hall became the focal point of the mobilization effort exerted by the student activists to rally the studentry behind them. Once again, the Dean and the College Secretary together with some administrative personnel and janitors guarded the building for two consecutive nights on November 14 and 15 to make sure that Palma Hall would be open for classes and for work in the ensuing days. Thus classes could go on and work went unhampered in the offices. The student activists seemed discouraged when they could not mobilize enough support.

Firm Stand Overcomes Resistance

Throughout the entire two-day period, the University Administration stood firm on the tuition fee issue and did not accede to the demand of the student activists for a rollback of the tuition fee to the old level. In the evening of November 16, President Angara held a five-hour talk with student leaders. His resoluteness prevailed, although he agreed to create a committee which would be empowered to review the entire financial structure of the University to find out where funds could be secured to meet the financial needs of the institution.

In retrospect, the barricading of the University by the student activists on September 19, on September 27-28, and on November 15-16, 1984, was uncalled for. The students found themselves defending the interests of the rich and affluent sectors of the Philippine society, from which the majority of the student population of the University come, when they should have been concerned with the larger issues confronting the nation.

Given the economic and social background of the students of the University, and given the imperative need of the University to raise funds to maintain its position at the apex of the Philippine educational system, the tuition fee increase approved by the Board of Regents was fair and reasonable. History will eventually prove that President Angara was right in upholding the decision of the Board of Regents. The next five to ten years will prove very crucial in the very survival of the University as an educational institution. From all indications, it will be the funds which the University expects to generate from the new tuition fee that will spell the difference between the advancement or collapse of the institution.[80]

Safeguarding Academic Freedom

The University of the Philippines has been criticized for its zealous concern over the valuable right loosely defined as "academic freedom." When he first assumed the Presidency of the University, Angara was received with reservations as one not too familiar with intellectual tradition on campus and hence more likely to compromise the University's commitment to academic freedom. But as the head of the Institution, he had to fight for his own brand of academic freedom, in his own way and in his own time.

He became aware of the stifling effect of the ruling that almost all spending of the subsidy granted by the government to the University of the Philippines had to be approved by the Ministry of the Budget, giving little elbow room for financial autonomy. Quietly, Angara was able to secure an Executive Order restoring to the University of the Philippines its fiscal authority in the disposition of funds.

The Education Act of 1980 threatened academic freedom, and since this was legislation passed by the Batasang Pambansa, it seemed that no remedy was in sight. Through the Committee to Review Academic Programs, Angara showed that the University had enough internal flexibility to reorganize and strengthen its capabilities and in this way assert its independence.

Angara moved for the appointment of a Student Regent in his recommendation to the Board of Regents at the meeting of June 27, 1983.[81] The proposal was rejected but eventually the appointment to the Board of Regents of a student representative, who can freely participate in the discussions but without voting capacity, was agreed upon.

Military Presence Dismantled

Academic freedom in the University was being tested in the continued presence of military personnel within the campus, a source of constant irritation to many academics and students. Angara therefore took the initiative of remedying the situation through a letter dated November 3, 1981 to Defense Minister Juan Ponce Enrile, asking that the military be removed from the campus. The letter reads in part:

> The scholar who thrives best in an ambience of freedom and... the soldier acting in a disciplined cast, would be hard put to understand each other's outlook and methods. We would therefore be on the side of prudence to put some distance between the scholar and the soldier, particularly as there is no known emergency that should require them to suffer each other, and because there is in fact some conscious effort away from the lingering vestiges of an emergency pronounced past by all official accounts.[82]

Soon thereafter, Enrile ordered the phase-out of the military training of non-UP students and non-students from the Diliman campus effective the second semester of academic year 1981-1982, another victory attained in safeguarding academic freedom.

Background of the Squatter Problem

UP Diliman occupies approximately 500 hectares of prime land in an area of Quezon City that is rapidly growing. Much of the land titled to the University is however idle. Of course the University has drawn up plans for the use of the land in accordance with the expansion program of the institution, but still, the greater portion of the UP real estate property remains undeveloped. Given this situation, and given the massive rural to urban migration by people in search of greener pastures in metropolitan Manila every year, it is not surprising that the University campus would become an attractive place in which folks escaping from impoverishment in the barrios could set up their shanties or makeshift dwellings.

Over the years though, these supposedly temporary structures have become permanent, with their occupants showing no signs of ever uprooting themselves. Many of the owners of these shanties probably entertain the thought that by simply staying on, their *de facto* occupation of the portions of the UP Diliman campus where their dwellings are situated would be condoned by the University and government authorities and that they would be allowed to eventually acquire titles of ownership based on the simple reality of their being there. The fact that prior to the Angara Administration, no concerted action had been taken by the University to deal with the unauthorized occupation of portions of the UP real estate property by squatters, probably contributed to the mushrooming of illegal housing structures. This tolerant attitude toward the proliferation of squatters in the University premises may be traced to the activism which reigned supreme in the University during the period of the sixties and the seventies, complemented by the coddling attitude of city politicians like the late Mayor Norberto S. Amoranto.

In the early part of the 1960s, the University could have ordered the removal of the eleven squatter houses which appeared out of nowhere in the vicinity of the Arboretum. These shanties were apparently the very first illegal structures to be erected inside the campus. However, instead of moving toward the expulsion of the intruders, the University authorities then did not take effective action to have the unauthorized man-made constructions demolished and their occupants evicted from the scene. As a result of this lack of action, the squatter problem was not nipped in the bud, so to speak, and so today, there are more than 250 shanties existing in the said area. Compounding the situation is a claim made by a man named Roberto Pael over a substantial portion of the Arboretum. Some unpleasant incidents have arisen as a result of this claim by Pael. The case has been under litigation, with the University banking on the validity of its title of ownership which has been deemed irrevocable by the highest court of the land.[83]

Elsewhere in the campus, squatter shanties appeared by leaps and bounds during the 1970s. Severely affected by the massive encroachment of illegal occupants was that area of the campus along Tandang Sora Avenue. In the mid-1970s, the residential structures in the place have grown to such an extent that they formed communities in themselves. The illegal squatter shanties were erected side by side with the houses of UP Diliman personnel who had been transferred to that place in 1972 from elsewhere in the campus. As time went by during the seventies, the communities in question came to be known as Pooks Ricarte, Dagohoy, and Palaris. These *pooks* now contain approximately two-thirds of the estimated 1988 squatter families found inside the entire campus of UP Diliman.[84] Other portions of the University real estate property affected by the entry of illegal occupants include Pook Amorsolo, Pook Amado V. Hernandez, and the areas along the Carlos P. Garcia Avenue and the Don Mariano Marcos Avenue. Many of these squatters are indeed miserably poor but some of them have been discovered to be well-off enough to build their illegal structures with the use of expensive construction materials.

Angara Disentangles Squatter Issue

Stewardship is a concept that means not just the wise and proper allocation of scarce financial resources but also the correct use of property, including real estate property, to maximize the benefits that will accrue to the owner. Good stewardship is essentially good administration and supervision. It is a position of trust wherein the steward is expected to handle the affairs entrusted to him in such a way as to bring advantages to those for whom stewardship is undertaken.

The position of university president involves stewardship over the extensive real estate property of the University in the Diliman district of Quezon City. On the surface, the squatter problem looks unrelated to the academic mission of the University. However, a deeper look will show that the solution of the said problem will ultimately affect the capability of the institution to perform its educational task. If the squatters are not relocated, they will deprive the institution of valuable land area into which the University can expand, particularly in connection with the construction of new buildings and facilities needed for instructional purposes. This seemingly mundane headache and its cure are thus vital to the future growth and advancement of the institution. The solution of the problem will contribute toward the viability of the University as a Filipino institution of higher learning.

Angara early in his term recognized the gravity of the squatter problem facing UP. The first thing he did toward tackling the vexing situation was to order in late 1982 a census for the purpose of identifying the squatters in the UP campus.[85] The electric and water bills of the University were enormous. The President realized that the squatters were consuming a large part of the supply of these basic necessities for which the University was paying huge amounts of money. The University was literally giving the squatters free commodities in the form of water and electricity and in return, UP received nothing because the squatters were non-UP personnel. Instead, the squatters contributed to the rise in the crime statistics of the campus. Many of the occurrences involving thievery, holdups, stabbings, and even homicide have been traced to persons living in the squatter colonies, with UP personnel and students being the aggrieved parties.

The census which Angara ordered was completed on February 2, 1983. This census revealed that as of 1983, there were 1,988 squatter families residing inside the campus, with two-thirds of these, or 1,325 families, found in Pooks Ricarte, Dagohoy and Palaris, along Tandang Sora Avenue in Balara.[86] It has been two years since the census was undertaken. One can therefore assume that the number of squatter families has increased considering how stealthily the squatters erect their illegal structures.

Rationale for Squatter Relocation

The rationale for the removal from the UP campus of the squatters is simple and compelling: "the protection and preservation of the integrity of the UP Diliman campus, to ensure its availability and suitability for the University's academic mission not only for the present generation but for future generations also."[87]

Accordingly, President Angara issued Memorandum No. 7 on April 18, 1983, which created the University Task Force on the Relocation of Squatters and the Relocation of UP Employees in Unauthorized Areas. Angara appointed Executive Vice President Oscar M. Alfonso to be the chairman of this task force. This body has the necessary but unenviable duty of undertaking the relocation of the squatters from the UP campus to designated places away from the University. The President mandated the task force to proceed with its job to dismantle and relocate the illegal makeshift structures owned by the squatters "with due consideration for human rights and humanitarian methods" and "in a humane and humanitarian manner."[88]

Alfonso's task force carried out its mandate by conducting dialogues with the affected inhabitants of Pooks Ricarte, Dagohoy and Palaris in 1983 and 1984, and by informing the squatters about their impending relocation to another site in Quezon City. This relocation site was later identified as Bagong Silang in Caloocan. The squatters received due notice about the University's intention to relocate them effective within the first quarter of 1984. However, the parliamentary elections of May 14, 1984 interfered with the plan to relocate the squatters during the early part of 1984. The relocation program suffered some more postponements and delays when the demolition and transfer operations scheduled for October 22, 1984, November 5, 1984, and January 24, 1985, did not push through for one reason or another.

The primary reason for the setbacks in the timetable of the University was of course the resistance of the squatters themselves, who barricaded the entrances to the three *pooks* affected and threatened to resort to bloodshed in order to frustrate the efforts of the University to relocate them. For example, during the scheduled dismantling of the shanties on January 24, 1985, the hotheads among the squatters caused rocks to rain upon the demolition crew even before it could begin touching a single house. Because the University did not wish to see anybody injured, it called off the relocation program that day. This deliberate avoidance of trouble prompted Alfonso's task force to also withdraw the demolition crew from the *pooks* on February 1, 1985, even when only four makeshift structures were demolished because the agitated squatters caused again some rocks to rain upon the workers carrying out the order for the removal of the said shanties.[89]

Relocation Pushes Through

The University showed its determination to relocate the squatters when in early February 1985 it proceeded with the dismantling operations. Actually, on February 3, 1985, the squatters had an opportunity to cause another delay in the relocation effort had they agreed to provide the University with a written commitment that they would respect the Supreme Court's ruling should their case be elevated to that judicial body for speedy disposition. That day, a man with a legal training who served as a go-between for both the squatters and the University asked President Angara to suspend the demolition of the squatter shanties so that the affected inhabitants of the three *pooks* could submit a petition to the Supreme Court and for the same court to decide on the matter on the basis of its merits. However, the squatters acted in bad faith when they indicated unwillingness to respect and observe whatever the court ruling was, nothwithstanding the understanding reached by the President and the go-between.[90] Consequently, the University was left with no choice but to proceed with the demolition and relocation effort.

Thus, on February 4 and 5, 1985, the dismantling and relocation operations proceeded as scheduled. The operations were marred by violence though in the morning of February 4 when some rock-throwing occurred again; the rock-throwing was accompanied by the throwing of a pillbox which landed on the head of a Quezon City policeman, who nearly lost his life. Some gunshots were fired too. In addition, there were truncheons which flew in every direction. After the melee, both sides counted the injured among them.[91]

Nevertheless, the dismantling operations proceeded when the violence subsided. By the end of that day, many of the squatter shanties had been dismantled, with the squatters themselves helping remove their own houses. The following day, dismantling operations continued until they were completed by nightfall, with no more violent incidents taking place. As of February 8, more than thirty shanties involving forty-three squatter families in Pook Ricarte had been dismantled.[92] Apparently, what finally persuaded the squatters of Pook Ricarte in particular to dismantle their houses voluntarily was when a few within their ranks went to Bagong Silang to have a look at the relocation site and they found that the place was to their liking.[93]

Those who were injured during the melee on February 4 received free medical assistance from the UP Health Service or were reimbursed for their medical expenses. The squatter families who were relocated to Bagong Silang were by direction of President Angara, given an outright cash assistance of ₱250 per family, 4 kilos of nails needed in the reassembling of their shanties in the relocation site, and some food supplies for their consumption during the relocation period. Moreover, the University shouldered the cost of the transport of the squatters and their worldly belongings to Bagong Silang.[94]

It may be pertinent to mention at this point that the relocation of the squatter families from the UP campus to Bagong Silang took place in accordance with the usual legislation governing squatter relocation and in congruency with the established procedures observed by the local government of Quezon City and by the National Housing Authority. The Quezon City government provided a relocation task force, backed up by

Metrocom troopers and local police, while the National Housing Authority awarded the lots in Bagong Silang on the basis of the conditions set by that agency. The involvement of the UP was in the form of the assistance it extended to the affected squatter families as described in the preceding paragraph.[95]

Reassessment of Squatter Problem

For the first time in the history of the University of the Philippines, the Central Administration faced the squatter problem frontally and it succeeded in showing to the illegal occupants of University property that it has the will and the determination to protect and uphold the territorial integrity of the campus. Angara acted true to his stewardship of the University by deciding that now was the time to put an end to the encroachment into the campus of elements who had nothing to do with the academic mission of the University whatsoever and who in fact only lived off the UP without giving anything in return.

These elements not only occupied land belonging to the University at no cost to themselves. Some of them even established thriving business operations on the rent-free premises they illegally occupied. Moreover, the squatters consumed water and electricity without paying a single centavo for them. They could do this through the *colorum* water and electrical tappings they made on University installations.

In effect, it was the University that paid for their basic utilities all these years. No wonder then that the water and electrical bills of the University reached astronomical levels. When one considers that water and electrical expenditures which benefited only the squatters could have been used by the University for material incentives to its bonafide personnel and for the improvement of its instructional facilities, then he can begin to imagine the magnitude of the loss incurred by the University, and this loss in the final analysis affected the capability of the institution to provide benefits to its legitimate constituents. Furthermore, the squatters created eyesores in the campus through their shanties, and they have been responsible for many breaches in law and order in the campus.

Therefore, it was imperative that the squatters be relocated. The squatters have been invading the UP campus on a massive scale over the past several years and if the University fails to assert its territorial right, there will come a time when the land area titled to the University will be much diminished to the UP's disadvantage. Apparently, the squatters are encouraged by the idea that if they stay long enough in a piece of property that is not theirs, that piece of property will eventually be given to them by virtue of their long and continuous occupation.

Angara is determined to rid the campus of squatter elements who have nothing to do with the University at all. In ridding the campus of squatters, Angara has ensured that the territorial integrity of the UP would be preserved and upheld. The University will then be able to use the land now and in the future for institutional expansion and growth, specially in connection with the construction of housing units for its employees, dormitories for its students, and buildings for its academic programs. The University will also be able to use the land for generating income that will supplement the subsidy it gets from the government. Moreover, the savings it will incur due to the removal of illegal water and electrical consumption by the squatters will redound to the benefit of the genuine UP personnel in the form of material incentives and better working conditions. Finally, the relocation of the squatters to places outside the campus will make the campus more conducive to living and learning from the aesthetic and security aspects.

The University cannot allow itself to be involved in the question of housing impoverished rural migrants out to make it in the city. UP is an educational institution. It is not a housing agency. Its mission is to educate the Filipino youth. As the premier institution of higher learning in the country, it cannot give the Filipino youth less than quality education. Therefore, the responsibility for providing adequate housing for the people lies with the government, not with the University. The land titled to the University is for the purpose of making the institution more effective as time goes by in fulfilling its educational mission. In tackling the squatter problem head-on, Angara has only the best interests of the University in mind. This is definitely to the credit of the President.

INTIMATIONS OF A LASTING CONTRIBUTION TO THE FUTURE OF THE UNIVERSITY

THE Angara Administration is a little more than halfway through its regular term of office, and if the preceding half is to be considered an augury of things to come, then the coming years may well be marked with significant reforms that will infuse vigor to the institutional life of the University. Reforms mean change, and sweeping changes are bound to upset the comfortable routine to which many have become accustomed, no matter how welcome the changes may be in light of the need for them.

Angara's administration thus far has given the impression of a total concern for the University's finances and a single-minded dedication to the raising of funds needed for the programs and operations of the University. However, this can be misinterpreted. Actually the funds are only the means to support programs and projects for developing even more the University's capabilities to fulfill its time-honored mission of instruction, research and extension. They are the means toward further institutional autonomy in every aspect of the University life.

Indeed the reforms were extensive, involving diverse curricular, organizational and physical changes, and to which the same single-mindedness of the man was applied. Angara at times appeared "dictatorial" in administering the affairs of the University, for despite consultations and other methods to involve the faculty, students, employees, and other constituents of the University, these would seem token and the impression left behind was that his mind had already been made up earlier and that he would stand firm on his decisions. Angara probably observed that his constituents always engage in unproductive bickerings among themselves and he perhaps felt that if he would wait for them to agree with one another, nothing would move and the University could not accomplish anything. Under the circumstances, he was compelled to act decisively and courageously, regardless of where the chips fell. Only a strong man could afford to behave in this manner.

An Exemplary Administrator

Angara sometimes had to contend with his constituencies, and quite often their opinions and wishes were contrary.

Despite the feuds, controversies and irritants that ensued, the Angara Administration managed successfully to implement the reforms envisioned. Indeed, the impression that the University of the Philippines was given an administrator for a President because that was the urgent need, was not proved wrong. The Angara Administration may have made decisions that many could not agree with, but it may be branded with courage and firmness of purpose in pursuing the best interests and upholding the highest ideals of the University, while at the same time preserving that most valuable right of the men and women who make up the community: academic freedom.

> In the Philippines, this University for the past half-century has been the fecundest source of the liberal spirit. The liberal mind, seeking the thread of logic wherever it may lead, and no matter what it may find and what gods it may topple, inherently courts danger to itself; it is a magnet for controversy. And so the University of the Philippines has had its share of controversies.
>
> This is a sign of vigor and health. If the day should come that this University can no longer excite disagreement and controversy, and the noise of debate gives

> **way to sepulchral silence, then we shall know that the children of darkness have vanquished the children of light. Then shall the figure of the Oblation be hauled down and in its place, we shall install a eunuch, yes, a eunuch, a castrated male.[81]**

Living Symbol of the Oblation

To this point, Angara demonstrated a kind of leadership which recognizes the tight-rope performance required by a militant academic community. The crucial task was to preserve and pursue academic freedom while at the same time running the affairs of the foremost Filipino University in the midst of the reforms that had to be instituted against widespread resistance to change.

Angara made firm decisions and fearlessly acted to pursue his objectives. He introduced a kind of leadership that kept faith with the symbol of the Oblation. While history reserves the right to render final judgment which can be made only after the completion of the full term of the Angara presidency, one can already say that the University did not err in installing a man with extraordinary foresight to ensure that the institution is transformed into an even greater University for the Filipino people, and endowed with the means to fulfill its noble educational mission.

Notes, Bibliographies & Appendices

Notes on Chapter I — "Bartlett as First President"

1. "The Insular Schools in the City of Manila," The Philippine Normal School, in the *Eighth Annual Report of the Director of Education*, July 1, 1907 to June 30, 1908, p. 110.

2. *Ibid.*

   See also: "Insular Schools" in the *Tenth Annual Report of the Director of Education of the Philippine Islands*, July 1, 1909—June 30, 1910.

   "Origin and History of the Junior College": Extracts from the *Report of the Dean George W. Beattie on the Junior College of Liberal Arts*, 1910, in *UP Bulletin No. 1*, pp. 24-26.

   P. O. Olayta, "History of the Philippine Normal School" in *The Torch*, Third Senior Annual, Manila, 1913, p. 13.

3. "Recommendation for the Establishment of University," *Fifth Annual Report to the Philippine Commission*, 1904, Part 3, p. 897.

4. *UP Bulletin No. 1*, p. 34.

5. *The Journal of the Philippine Commission*, Manila, Bureau of Printing, 1908, pp. 23, 24, 239-243, 314-318, 355, 356, 505.

   "Acts of the Philippine Legislature" in *War Department Annual Reports*, 1908, Vol. IX, pp. 80-81.

   A true copy of Act 1870 appears in the *UP Bulletin No. 1* under the heading "Law Founding the University of the Philippines," pp. 18-22; also in Chapter X (State University Education) in the *Joint Legislative Committee Report*, 235 *et seq.*, as amended up to Act No. 3197 enacted December 2, 1924.

6. The paper, *Assemblea Filipina* carried in its issues provocative articles on the proposed university. Two from Assemblyman Juan Alvear, a member of the Committee on Public Instruction of the Philippine Assembly, were "La Universidad Filipina," March 21, 1908, p. 3, and "La Universidad Filipina," May 26, 1908. Antonio Regidor, a *balikbayan* of those years from London, took time out to contribute his bit toward pushing the passage of the University Act. His article in the *Assemblea Filipina* of February 15, 1908 was fittingly entitled "Universidad Filipina." Still another piece on the University was V. Sanconi's "Quienes mataram la Universidad Filipina?", May 25, 1908, p. 1.

7. *The Manila Times*, May 26, 1908, p. 1.

8. The first law to amend the Charter Act of the UP, this is described as "An Act amending section four, paragraph (b) of section six, and section ten of Act Eighteen hundred and seventy," "Acts of the Philippine Legislature," in *War Department Annual Report*, 1913, pp. 33-34.

9. Secretary Donovan, "The Executive Journal of the Philippine Commission—Minutes of the Proceedings," Wednesday, October 7, 1908, pp. 309-314.

10. George A. Malcolm recalled how "in the early days" he spoke against the site chosen, "a plot inadequate in size [and] located in the heart of Manila." In his commencement address delivered in 1919, he repeated his "protest... in a more formal way" but that had to wait until after nineteen years "... before President Quezon endorsed the transfer, from the cramped Manila campus to the vast rolling plain northwest of the city. The war gave an assist to the plan by laying low the university buildings in Manila. The year 1949 found a resurgent University of the Philippines established in its new home in Diliman, Q.C."—*American Colonial Careerist*, Boston. The Christopher Publishing House, p. 209.

11. *UP Bulletin No. 1*, p. 97.

12. "Report of Newton W. Gilbert, 1908-1909" cited in C. Jamias, *The University of the Philippines: The First Half Century*, Quezon City, University of the Philippines, 1962, p. 17.

13. "Loyalty Day Address," October 10, 1958 in *Ibid.*, pp. 21-22.

14. Joseph Ralston Hayden, *The Philippines (A Study in National Development)*, New York, The Macmillan Company, 1952, pp. 537-538.

15. Lawrence E. Griffin, "The University of the Philippines" in *Cablenews—American Yearly Review*, November 1911, Sociological Section, p. 106.

16. Dean Lope M. Yutuc was interviewed by Prof. Cristino Jamias when the latter was doing research for his book, *The University of the Philippines*, p. 29.

17. There were it seems all sorts of jokes in connection with this unlikely problem in a country where there were so many real, if not urgent needs, having to do with the scientific care of work and other animals. One joke is on the *doctor ng kabayo* or horse doctor, a pejorative reference to the Vet-Med graduate.

18. *UP Bulletin No. 1*, p. 26.

19. Griffin, p. 79.

20. *Ibid.*, p. 107.

21. *Ibid.*, p. 35.

22. *Ibid.*, p. 106.

23. *UP Catalogue 1911-1912*, p. 187.

24. *The Woolsack*, College of Law, UP, 1913.

25. Jorge B. Vargas in the *College Folio*, October 1910, cited in Jamias, p. 47.

    See also: Harry Lawrence Case and Robert A. Bunnel, "The UP as an Agent of National Development," Manila, 1969, pp. 17-21.

26. President Bartlett was one of the first two professors who taught courses in Sociology, according to Sociology Professor Belen T. Medina, "unit historian" of the Department of Sociology.

    Other bio-data details of Bartlett appear in: "Biography of Murray Bartlett" in the *Carillon*, V. 10, June 10, 1958, p. 5; Lewis E. Gleeck, Jr., *The Manila Americans, 1901-1964*, pp. 108, 127; L.R. Doty, *History of the Genesee Country*, S.J. Clark Publishing Company, Chicago, 1925, pp. 223-224; Consuelo V. Fonacier, *The Role and Mission of the University*, Q.C., 1971, p. 2; *Who Was Who in America*, A.M. Marquis Company, 1950, vol. 2, 47; *The National Cyclopaedia of American Biography*, Vol. 38, pp. 317-318.

27. *Manila Times*, 12 March 1911.

    "Fifty Years with the *Times*" in the *Manila Times*, 12 March 1961.

28. This is included in Fonacier, also in Bartlett's Annual Report 1911-1912.

29. *Cablenews-American*, December 21, 1911 also devoted its editorial on the Bartlett speech that it described as "excellent." Entitled "Efficiency the Watchword," it went on to comment extensively on "efficiency as the watchword of the university."

    Under the news heading "En la Universidad de Filipinas," *Libertas*, December 21, 1911, takes the reader back to the Bartlett inauguration rites of the previous day with its more detailed account of the occasion than that of the *Manila Times*.

    El Comercio, December 20, 1911, entitled its news report "Toma de posesion" but actually took most of the space for Vice-Governor Gilbert's pronouncements and for the Bartlett speech rendered into Spanish for the still wide readership in that language of those times.

30. *Report of the Philippine Commission up to June 30, 1913*, p. 27.

31. *Bartlett's Annual Report, 1912*, p. 16.

32. *Report of the Philippine Commission, 1912*, p. 26.

33. *Report of the Philippine Commission, up to June 30, 1913*, p. 27.

34. *Bartlett's Annual Report, 1912*, pp. 26-27.

35. *Report of the Philippine Commission, July 1913—December 1914*, p. 312.

36. A discussion of the issue on the AB degree, touching particularly on the reasons behind the decision of the Board of Regents to defer action on the proposals, was submitted as part of *Bartlett's Annual Report, 1912*.

37. It is not without good reason that the Vet-Med building in the UP Diliman campus was named in memory of the first UP President, Murray Bartlett. He, more than anybody else in those early years of the University, worked hard toward making the Vet-Med course a going concern.

38. *Bartlett's Annual Report, 1912*, pp. 16-17.

39. This was a Master of Arts degree that was different from the degree of the same designation conferred in the early years of the UP upon graduates of the old AB degree who continued their studies for three more years.

40. *UP Catalogue 1913-14*, p. 48.

41. *UP Catalogue 1911-12*, p. 42 indicates the following specifics on the History requirements:

HISTORY (4 units)

a) General History, 2 units; the essential features of Greek and Roman history; the outlines of ancient Oriental history; early Medieval history to the death of Charlemagne; the rise and fall of the Holy Empire; feudalism; the difference between Medieval and Modern history; the elements of modern history to the end of the seventeenth century.

b) United States History and Government, 1 unit; from the European discovery of the new world, with special attention to the development of the British Empire in America during the seventeenth and eighteenth centuries. After the Revolution, the history and civil government of the United States only need be studied. Text-book recommended, Thomas' *United States History*.

c) Colonial History and Government, 1 unit; a brief concise summary of the history of colonization in ancient and modern times; the colonial possessions of great modern colonizing nations; the various forms of colonial government.

Textbook: Reinsch, *Colonial Government*.

42. A good number of American professors were recruited from the University of Michigan, like Dr. Paul C. Freer, second Dean of the College of Medicine and Surgery; George A. Malcolm, first Dean of the College of Law; George A. Wrentmore, first Dean of the College of Engineering. Also from Michigan was D. C. Worcester, proponent of the establishment of the College of Veterinary Medicine, and Justice E. Finley Johnson, once a member of the Board of Regents. Hayden, 536, who cited the aforementioned names added that there were "other strong personalities [from the University of Michigan] who guided the University during its early years."

43. Jamias, p. 82.

Leopoldo Y. Yabes, "Towards a Greater University of the Philippines," Quezon City, University of the Philippines, 1970 (originally published in *The Carillon*, January-February 1970, Vol. XIII, No. 1), pp. 11-12.

David P. Barrows, who did not serve in the faculty of the UP but became a member of the Board of Regents, on returning to the United States received the appointment of full professor at the University of California in Berkeley. He interpreted his appointment as a "recognition of what [he] had done." *David Prescott Barrows, 1873-1954*, pp. 108-111.

44. There were of course notable exceptions to the general rule: H. Otley Beyer, Dean and Harriot Fansler, Austin and Craig and George A. Malcom.

45. See Annex A, p. 601.

46. "Table 112" in the *Monroe Survey*, p. 616. This is cited in William Cameron Forbes, *The Philippine Islands*, p. 477.

47. *Bartlett's Annual Report, 1912*, p. 40.

48. *Ibid.*, p. 29.

49. Bartlett's strong views on the need for the university to pay attention to the moral and character development of the students was re-echoed by Quezon in 1937. Hayden, in reaction to the Filipino leader, expressed a different view representing the opposite school of thought.

Discussions on current concerns in US education have once more brought to the fore the question: "Should schools also aim for the moral development of man?" Theodore M. Hersburg ("Learning How to Do and How to Be" in *Dialogue*, No. 55, I, 1982, pp. 35-39) discussed his views that remind one of Bartlett's own predisposition in favor of teaching not only skills subjects but also subjects inculcating values in the students.

50. *Report of the Philippine Commission, up to June 30, 1913*, p. 28.

51. In *Bartlett's Annual Report, 1912*, p. 31.

52. *Report of the Philippine Commission*, July 1913. . ., p. 312.

53. *Report of the Philippine Commission*, July 1913. . ., p. 311.

54. Encarnacion Alzona, *A History of Education in the Philippines*, Manila, 1922, p. 289.

55. *Report of the Philippine Commission*, 1909, 1912.

56. Alzona, p. 291.

The annual reports of the Philippine Commission and the UP President carry accountings of the UP appropriation, a breakdown of the other sources of income and expenses.

The *College Folio* of August 24, 1911, editorialized on the UP problem of funds. It directed its call for assistance to the university to wealthy Filipinos. Fittingly, the editorial carried the title "An Opportunity for Philanthropic Filipinos."

57. *Report of the Philippine Commission*, up to June 30, 1913, p. 13.

58. *Bartlett's Annual Report, 1912*, pp. 13-14.

59. *Report of the Philippine Commission*, 1912.

60. Yabes, p. 15.

61. Jamias, pp. 77-78.

62. *Bartlett's Annual Report, 1912*, pp. 17-19.

63. *Catalogue, 1911-1912*, p. 33.

64. *Ibid.*, p. 34.

65. See footnote No. 41.

66. *Bartlett's Annual Report, 1912*, p. 18.

67. *Ibid.*

68. *Bartlett's Annual Report, 1912*, p. 19.

69. *Ibid*, p. 3.

Taken at their face value, both the "resolutions" adopted by the University Council on February 27, 1915, expressing the sentiments of that body relative to the resignation of Bartlett (Jamias, pp. 79-81) and the "brilliant reception" tendered for Bartlett by the Board, the faculty and the students on March 27, 1915 (*Manila Times*, March 28, 1915) proved that Bartlett was well-loved. Therefore it seems unlikely that Bartlett's resignation was due to difficulties emanating from those quarters.

But neither would his resignation have been triggered by some debilitating illness. W. Cameron Forbes, *The Philippine Islands*, Boston, Houghton Mifflin Company, 1928, Vol. I, p. 475 simply said that sickness forced Bartlett to quit his position. However, the bio-data of the first President of the UP gives the picture of someone who remained energetic and active long after he left the University. He was in active duty during the first World War and was President of Hobart and Wm. Smith Colleges, Geneva, New York, 1919-36. He died in 1939 or only after almost a quarter of a century since he left the UP.

One is tempted to conclude at this point that Bartlett's resignation was practically forced upon him by the Forbes government whose order of priorities (public works first) diametrically differed from those of his own. Bartlett recognized this from the very beginning as shown by the second sentence of the concluding paragraph of his inaugural message. Bartlett said, ". . . We realize that there are public improvements of great importance that may have the first claim upon the resources of the government. . . ."

70. In 1912, twenty-seven Board meetings were held in all of which Bartlett was present. Nine of these were the regular monthly meetings while the rest were convened upon the request of Bartlett. *Bartlett's Annual Report, 1912*, p. 1.

Bibliography — Chapter I

PRIMARY SOURCES

A. Reports

Beattie, George W., "Origin and History of the Junior College" (Extracts from the Report of Dean George W. Beattie on the Junior College of Liberal Arts, 1910, in *The University of the Philippines Catalogue*, 1910-1911 or *UP Bulletin No. 1.)*

A Survey of the Educational System of the Philippine Islands by the Board of Educational Survey (Monroe Survey), Manila, Bureau of Printing, 1925.

"Recommendations for the Establishment of a University," in the *Fifth Annual Report of the Department of Public Instruction*, Part 3, 1904; Full Annual Report, Manila, Bureau of Printing, 1905; Reprint: 1934.

"The Insular School in the City of Manila" in the *Eighth Annual Report of the Director of Education*, July 1, 1907 to June 1908, Manila, Bureau of Printing, 1908.

"Insular Schools" in the *Tenth Annual Report of the Director of Education of the Philippine Islands*, July 1908-June 30, 1910, Manila, Bureau of Printing, 1910.

Griffin, Dean Lawrence E., "The University of the Philippines in *Cablenews-American Yearly Review*," (Sociological Section), November 1911.

"The Executive Journal of the Philippine Commission, Minutes of the Proceedings by Secretary Donovan," October 1908 (MS).

Report of the Philippine Commission, 1909, Washington, Government Printing Office, 1910.

Report of the Philippine Commission, 1910, Washington, Government Printing Office, 1911.

"The Relationship of the Bureau of Science and the University of the Philippines," in the *Report of the Philippine Commission*, 1911, Washington, Government Printing Office, 1912.

Report of the Philippine Commission, up to June 30, 1913, Washington, Government Printing Office, 1914.

Annual Report of the President of the University of the Philippines, Manila, Bureau of Printing, 1912.

"Acts of the Philippine Legislature" in *War Department Annual Report*, Washington, Government Printing Office, Vol. IX, 1908, and 1913.

B. Speeches

Bartlett, Murray, "The University for the Filipino" in *Addresses of Rafael Palma, N.W. Gilbert and Murray Bartlett, President of the U.P.* Delivered at the inaugural ceremonies held at the campus of the University, December 20, 1911, Manila, Bureau of Printing, 1911.

Bishop C.H. Brent on the resignation of the Very Rev. Murray Bartlett as Dean of the Cathedral of St. Mary and St. John, Manila, and Bartlett's acceptance of appointment to the UP Presidency, in the *Manila Times*, 12 March 1911.

Forbes, William Cameron, "Inaugural Address," 24 November 1909.

Zamora, Jose, "Loyalty Day Address," 10 October 1958. Excerpts in Jamias, Cristino, *The University of the Philippines: The First Half Century*, 1972.

C. Periodicals

Assemblea Filipina

Alvear, Juan, "La Universidad Filipina," March 21, 1910.

___________, "La Universidad Filipina," March 26, 1910.

Regidor, Antonio, "Universidad Filipina," February 17, 1908.

Sanconi, V. "?Quienes Mataram la Universidad Filipina?," Mayo 25, 1908.

Cablenews-American

"Efficiency, the Watchword" (editorial), December 21, 1911.

El Comercio

"Toma de posesion" (editorial), December 21, 1911.

Geneva Daily Times of May 27, 1935.

Libertas

"En la Universidad de Filipinas," (editorial), December 21, 1911.

Manila Times issues of February 7, 1908, May 17, 1908, May 26, 1908, April 12, 1910, October 12, 1910, December 12, 1910 (editorial), December 13, 1910 (editorial), March 12, 1911, December 21, 1911 (editorial), and March 28, 1915.

New York Times of November 14, 1939.

D. University Student Publications

College Folio of October 10, excerpts of December 1910 and August 24, 1911 issues in C. Jamias, ***The University of the Philippines, the First Half Century,*** **Quezon City, University of the Philippines, 1972.**

Catalogues

The University of the Philippines Catalogue 1910-1911
Announcements 1911-1912
Bulletin No. 1
Manila: Bureau of Printing, 1911

The University of the Philippines Catalogue 1911-1912
Announcements 1912-1913
Bulletin No. 2
Manila: Bureau of Printing, 1912

The University of the Philippines Catalogue 1912-1913
Announcements 1913-1914
Bulletin No. 3
Manila: Bureau of Printing, 1912

The Woolsack, College of Law, University of the Philippines, 1913.

E. The UP Charter

Act No. 1870—"An Act For the purpose of founding a university for the Philippine Islands, giving it corporate existence, providing for a Board of Regents, defining the board's responsibilities and duties, providing higher and professional instruction and for other purposes."

Act No. 2024—"An Act Amending section four paragraph (h) of section six and ten of Act Eighteen hundred seventy."

SECONDARY SOURCES

Alzona, Encarnacion, *A History of Education in the Philippines, 1930.* Manila, University of the Philippines Press, 1932.

Barrows, Eve, "Memories of David P. Barrows, 1873-1954," Berkeley, July 13, 1954.

Carillon, Volume 10, June 10, 1958.

Case, Harry Lawrence and Robert A. Bunnel, *The University of the Philippines as an Agent of National Development*, Manila, 1969.

Fonacier, Consuelo V. "The Role and Mission of the University," Quezon City, 1971.

Gleeck, Lewis E. Jr., *The Manila Americans, 1901-1964,* Manila, Carmelo and Bauerman, 1977.

Golt, Rev. Camillus, *William Cameron Forbes and the Philippines, 1904-1946* (Ph.D. Thesis), Manila, 1974.

Forbes, William Cameron, *The Philippine Islands*, Boston, Houghton Miffin Company, Vol. I, 1928.

Hayden, Joseph Ralston, *The Philippines (A Study of National Development)*, New York, The MacMillan Company, 1952.

Hersburg, Theodore M. "Learning How to Do and How to Be" in *Dialogue*, No. 55, I, 1982.

Inglés, Raul R., "Fifty Years with the *Times*" in *Manila Times* of April 19, 1960, March 6, 1961, March 12, 1961, March 29, 1961, August 24, 1961, September 23, 1961, December 20, 1961, December 21, 1961, December 23, 1961.

Jamias, Cristino, *The University of the Philippines: The First Half Century*, Quezon City, University of the Philippines, 1962.

Malcolm, George A., *American Colonial Careerist (Half a Century of Official Life and Personal Experience in the Philippines and Puerto Rico)*, Boston, The Christopher Publishing House, 1957.

"Murray Bartlett, D.D." in L.R. Doty, *History of the Genesee Country*, Volume 4, Chicago, S.J. Clark Publishing Co., 1925.

Olayta, P.O., "History of the Philippine Normal School," in *The Torch*, Third Senior Annual, Manila, 1913.

Who Was Who in America, Chicago, A.M. Marquis Company, Vol. 2, 1950.

Yabes, Leopoldo Y., "Toward a Greater University of the Philippines," Quezon City, University of the Philippines, 1970.

———————, *The University of the Philippines in Perspective*, Quezon City, University of the Philippines, 1971.

CHAPTER I—ANNEX A

PIONEER FILIPINO FACULTY MEMBERS OF THE UNIVERSITY
1910 to 1915

Professors

Jose Albert, Pediatrics (1910-15)
Ariston Bautista y Lin, Clinical Medicine and Therapeutics (1910-15)
Fernando Calderon, Obstetrics (1910-15)
Sixto de los Angeles, Medical Jurisprudence and Ethics (1914-15)

Associate Professors

Luis Guerrero, Tropical Medicine (1910-15)
Baldomero Roxas, Obstetrics (1912-15)
Salvador Vivencio del Rosario, Hygiene (1914-15)

Assistant Professors

Mariano Vivencio del Rosario, Chemistry (1910-15); Baldomero Roxas, Obstetrics (1910-11); Salvador V. del Rosario, Hygiene (1912-13); Jorge Bocobo, Civil Law (1914-15); Potenciano Guazon, Surgery (1914-15); Felix Hocson, Pharmacy (1914-15); Antonio Guillermo Sison, Medicine (1914-15); Honoria Acosta Sison, Obstetrics (1914-15); and Aristeo Ubaldo, Ophthalmology, Otology, Rhinology and Laryngology (1914-15).

Instructors

Mariano Manas Cruz, Agronomy (1910-11); Jose Eduque, Surgery (1910-15); Potenciano Guazon, Surgery (1910-13); Jose Petronio Katigbak, Graphics (1910-11); Jose I. del Rosario, Chemistry (1910-13); Salvador V. del Rosario, Hygiene (1910-11); Antonio G. Sison, Clinical Medicine (1910-13);

Jose M. Asuncion, History of Art and Perspective (1912-15); Conrado Benitez, Economics (1912-15); Jorge Bocobo, Law (1912-13); Teodoro Buenaventura, Elementary Drawing (1912-15); Victor Buencamino, Veterinary Surgery (1912-13); Rafael Enriquez, Color and Composition (1912-15); Perpetuo Dionisio Gutierrez, Clinical Medicine (1912-15); Joaquin M. Ferrer, Landscape and Drawing from Life (1912-15); Jose Hilario, Pathology and Bacteriology (1912-15); Felix Hocson, Pharmacology (1912-13); Ambrosio Magsaysay, Graphics (1912-15); Daniel de la Paz, Pharmacology (1912-15); Carmelo Malabanan Reyes, Surgery (1912-15); Vicente Rivera, Drawing (1912-15); Fabian de la Rosa, Decorative Art (1912-15); Honoria Acosta Sison, Obstetrics (1912-13); Aristeo Ubaldo, Eye, Ear, Nose and Throat (1912-13); Antonio Daniel Vasquez, Surgery (1912-15); Miguel Zaragosa, Anatomy in Fine Arts (1912-15).

Appointments for 1914-15: Francisco Benitez, Education; Isabelo Concepcion, Physiology; Inocencio Elayda, Agronomy; Jose Armayor Espiritu, Spanish and Mercantile Law; Leandro H. Fernandez, History; Vicente Francisco, Sculpture; Arturo Garcia, Anatomy; Angel K. Gomez, Veterinary Anatomy; Juan Gonzales, Anatomy; Pilar Hidalgo, Mathematics; Serafin P. Hilado, Public Speaking and Practice; Arsenio Luz, Spanish; and Mariano Tolentino, Obstetrics.

NOTES ON CHAPTER II — "VILLAMOR'S FILIPINO PERSPECTIVE"

1. Minutes of the 15th Meeting of the University Council, November 21, 1914. (Bound copies of the Minutes of the Meetings of the University Council are found in the Office of the Registrar, University of the Philippines. Volume I includes the Minutes of the Council Meetings from June 18, 1911 to March 30, 1921.)
2. "History of the Appointment of the President of the University of the Philippines." (Newspaper clippings), p. 7. Ignacio Villamor Papers, Box No. 9. (The Ignacio Villamor Papers are deposited in the University of the Philippines Library. The papers relating to the Villamor presidency of the U.P. are found in three boxes – Nos. 9, 10 and 11.)
3. *Ibid.*, p. 9.
4. *Ibid.*, p. 63.
5. He became a Regent in July, 1911 until his elevation to the U.P. presidency. See *Guide to the Ignacio Villamor Papers, 1884-1966, at the University of the Philippines Library.* Diliman, Quezon City, University Archives, 1975 (Pamphlet), p. 2.
6. "History of the Appointment of the President of the University of the Philippines," *loc. cit.*, p. 25.
7. Sergio Osmeña to Manuel L. Quezon (Cablegram), Manila, January 30, 1915. Manuel L. Quezon Papers, Box No. 171 – Philippine University. (The Manuel L. Quezon Papers are deposited in the Philippine National Library. Hereafter cited as Quezon Papers.)
8. Manuel L. Quezon to Sergio Osmeña (Cablegram), Washington, D.C., January 30, 1915. Quezon Papers.
9. *Ibid.*
10. Sergio Osmeña to Manuel L. Quezon (Cablegram), Manila, February 2, 1915. Quezon Papers.
11. "History of the Appointment of the President of the University of the Philippines," *loc. cit.*, pp. 76-80.
12. *Ibid.*, p. 120.
13. *Ibid.*, p. 119.
14. *Ibid.*, p. 156.
15. *Ibid.*, p. 120.
16. *Ibid.*, p. 176.
17. Minutes of the 18th Meeting of the University Council, July 31, 1915.
18. Actually the U.P. at this time consisted of only seven separate schools and colleges. The School of Pharmacy and the School of Education were constituent parts of the College of Medicine and Surgery and the College of Liberal Arts respectively.
19. Minutes of the 18th Meeting of the University Council, July 31, 1915.
20. *Ibid.*
21. "History of the Appointment of the President of the University," *loc. cit.*, pp. 208-210.
22. *The Philippinensian 1916*, p. 18.
23. *Ibid.*
24. Cristino Jamias, *The University of the Philippines; The First Half Century.* Quezon City: University of the Philippines, 1962. Appendix C, p. 248.
25. *Ibid.*, p. 251.
26. *Ibid.*, p. 256.
27. *The Philippinensian 1917*, p. 235.

28. Jamias, *op. cit.*, p. 90.

29. Minutes of the 18th Meeting of the University Council, July 31, 1915.

30. Minutes of the 19th Meeting of the University Council, October 17, 1915.

31. Paul Monroe (et al.), *A Survey of the Educational System of the Philippine Islands*, Manila, Bureau of Printing, 1915, p. 634.

32. *The Philippinensian* 1917, p. 148.

33. Jamias, *op. cit.*, p. 91.

34. *The Philippinensian 1917*, p. 233.

35. *Seventh Annual Report of the President of the University of the Philippines, July 1, 1917 to January 30, 1918.* Manila, Bureau of Printing, 1918, pp. 9-10.

36. Monroe, *op. cit.*, p. 623.

37. *The Philippinensian, 1916*, p. 211.

38. *The 1920 Philippinensian*, p. 81.

39. Dean Bocobo's Memorandum to President Villamor to Establish Legal Clinic, August 27, 1918. Quezon Papers.

40. "University Clippings," pp. 221-222, Villamor Papers.

41. Jamias, *op. cit.*, p. 94.

42. Minutes of the 18th Meeting of the University Council, July 31, 1915.

43. Minutes of the 19th Meeting of the University Council, October 17, 1915.

44. Minutes of the 22nd Meeting of the University Council, January 27, 1917.

45. Minutes of the 27th Meeting of the University Council, September 6, 1917.

46. Minutes of the 22nd Meeting of the University Council, January 27, 1917.

47. *Ibid.*

48. Minutes of the 18th Meeting of the University Council, July 31, 1915.

49. Minutes of the 26th Meeting of the University Council, June 26, 1917. See also "University Clippings", pp. 2-3, Villamor Papers.

50. Minutes of the 29th Meeting of the University Council, March 9, 1918.

51. *Ibid.*

52. Minutes of the 20th Meeting of the University Council, April 1, 1916.

53. Minutes of the 22nd Meeting of the University Council, January 27, 1917.

54. Minutes of the 23rd Meeting of the University Council, March 10, 1917.

55. *Ibid.* 56. *Ibid.*

57. Minutes of the 24th Meeting of the University Council, March 17, 1917.

58. *Ibid.* 59. *Ibid.* 60. *Ibid.*

61. Minutes of the 36th Meeting of the University Council, March 30, 1920.

62. Minutes of the 35th Meeting of the University Council, March 31, 1919.

63. *Ibid.*

64. *The Philippinensian 1916,* p. 12.

65. Act No. 2759, passed by the Philippine Legislature on February 23, 1918, amended the Organic Act of the University. It brought about several changes in the membership of the Board of Regents, one of which was the addition of a faculty regent and an alumni regent representing the university faculties and the alumni respectively in the Board. See *Seventh Annual Report of the President of the University of the Philippines, op. cit.*, p. 9.

66. *The 1920 Philippinensian,* p. 12.

67. *The Philippinensian 1916,* pp. 12-16.

68. *The 1920 Philippinensian,* pp. 19-21.

69. *Seventh Annual Report of the President of the University of the Philippines, op. cit.*, p. 18.

70. Jamias, *op. cit.*, p. 86.

71. *Sixth Annual Report of the President of the University of the Philippines, July 1, 1916 to June 30, 1917.* Manila, Bureau of Printing, 1917, p. 18.

72. The following faculty members presented papers to that Congress: Austin Craig, "Primitive Agriculture"; Inocencio Elayda, "Ancient and Modern Agriculture"; Luis Rivera, "Rural Idiosyncracy"; Mariano de Joya, "The Influence of Religions and Morality Among Rural Communities"; Sixto de los Angeles, "Economic Value of Sanitation in Rural Communities"; and Francisco Benitez, "Condition of Instruction in Our Rural Communities."

73. *Sixth Annual Report of the President of the University of the Philippines, op. cit.*, p. 22.

74. Monroe, *op. cit.*, p. 656.

75. Jamias, *op. cit.*, p. 104.

76. One such faculty fellow was Dr. Antonio G. Sison who was sent to the United States for a year to take advanced studies in medicine. In addition to his regular salary, he was granted by the University travelling expenses. See *Seventh Annual Report of the President of the University of the Philippines, op. cit.*, p. 11.

77. Letter of Charles F. Baker to the Board of Regents, January 7, 1919. Quezon Papers.

78. Letter of Charles Banks to President Villamor, July 16, 1919. Quezon Papers.

79. Minutes of the 34th Meeting of the Executive Committee of the University Council, December 22, 1916. (Bound copies of the Minutes of the Meetings of the Executive Committee of the University Council are found in the Office of the Registrar, University of the Philippines. Volume I includes the Minutes of the Executive Committee Meetings from July 9, 1911 to June 25, 1921.) p. 73.

80. *Ibid.*

81. *Sixth Annual Report of the President of the University of the Philippines, op. cit.*, p. 27.

82. *Ibid.*, pp. 27-28.

83. *Ibid.*, pp. 26-27.

84. Jamias, *op. cit.*, p. 109.

85. *Sixth Annual Report of the President of the University of the Philippines, op. cit.*, p. 26.

86. *Ibid.*, p. 49.

87. *Ibid.*

88. *Ibid.*

89. *Ibid.*, pp. 63-64.

90. *The Philippinensian 1917,* p. 168.

91. *The Philippinensian 1916,* p. 108.

92. *Ibid.*, p. 109. 93. *Ibid.*, p. 138. 94. *Ibid.*

95. *Seventh Annual Report of the President of the University of the Philippines, op. cit.*, p. 10.

96. *The Philippinensian 1917*, p. 347.

97. *The 1920 Philippinensian*, p. 297.

98. *The Philippinensian 1917*, p. 349.

99. *The Philippinensian 1916*, p. 205.

100. *Ibid.*, p. 203. 101. *Ibid.*, p. 204.

102. "University Clippings," p. 81, Villamor Papers.

103. *Ibid.*

104. *The Philippinensian 1916*, p. 321.

105. *Ibid.*

106 Minutes of the 26th Meeting of the University Council, June 26, 1917.

107. Minutes of the 31st Meeting of the University Council, September 7, 1918.

108. "University Clippings," p. 107. Villamor Papers.

109. Domingo T. Recio, "The Incident at the University Campus," (Newspaper Clipping). Quezon Papers.

110. The petition was dated March 12, 1918, addressed to the Chairman of the Board of Regents. Quezon Papers.

111. "Mysterious Attack on President Villamor" (Newspaper Clipping), pp. 1-2. Villamor Papers.

112. *Ibid.*, p. 33.

113. *Ibid.*, p. 77. 114. *Ibid.*, p. 15. 115. *Ibid.*, p. 55.

116. Jamias, *op. cit.*, p. 121.

117. "Mysterious Attack on President Villamor," *loc. cit.*, pp. 80-81.

118. *Ibid.*, pp. 82-83. 120. *Ibid.*, pp. 1-12. 122. *Ibid.*, p. 4.

119. *Ibid.*, p. 35. 121. *Ibid.*, p. 40. 123. *Ibid.*, p. 82.

124. President Villamor's Memorandum, Re: "Elimination of the Study of German from the Curriculum of, and the Cancellation of Employment of German citizens in the University of the Philippines," August 20, 1918. Quezon Papers.

125. On March 2, 1918, Professor Scheerer's daughter and daughter-in-law sent a letter to Speaker Osmeña petitioning that their father be allowed to continue his residence in the Philippines because he "has made this country his permanent home for the last thirty-six years, and he has repeatedly given proof of his loyalty to the government of the United States in the Philippines." *Ibid.*

126. *Ibid.* 127. *Ibid.*

128. "Circular Letter to Members of the Faculty, Employees, and Students." September 13, 1918. Quezon Papers. President Villamor also issued a similar communication dated September 16, 1918, to the employees of the Philippine Census Office in his capacity as Director.

129. B. M. Gonzalez and F. M. Fronda, "Why the College of Agriculture Enlisted Wholesale in the National Guard: A Word of Explanation." Quezon Papers.

130. Minutes of the 28th Meeting of the University Council, January 7, 1918.

131. *Seventh Annual Report of the President of the University of the Philippines, op. cit.*, p. 11.

132. Bienvenido M. Gonzalez, "Report on the Advisability of Transferring the College of Veterinary Science to Los Baños," February 28, 1918. Quezon Papers.

133. Anacleto Benavides, "The History of the Class of 1922," *The 1920 Philippinensian,* p. 161.

134. Memorandum of Dean Baker to President Villamor, September 9, 1918. Quezon Papers.

135. Memorandum of Dean Baker to the Board of Regents. Quezon Papers.

136. Napoleon J. Casambre, "The Administration of Francis Burton Harrison in the Philippines, 1913-1921." Unpublished Dissertation, Stanford University, 1968. Chapter V, pp. 16-17.

137. Minutes of the 63rd Meeting of the Executive Committee of the University Council, February 20, 1920. Vol. I, pp. 124-125.

BIBLIOGRAPHY — CHAPTER II

Minutes of the Meetings of the University Council (Fifteenth: November 21, 1914; Eighteenth: July 31, 1915; Nineteenth: October 17, 1915; Twentieth: April 1, 1916; Twenty-Second: January 27, 1917; Twenty-Third: March 10, 1917; Twenty-Fourth: March 17, 1917; Twenty-Sixth: June 26, 1917; Twenty-Seventh: September 16, 1917; Twenty-Eighth: January 7, 1918; Twenty-Ninth: March 9, 1918; Thirty-First: September 17, 1918; Thirty-Fifth: March 31, 1919 and Thirty-Sixth: March 30, 1920), University of the Philippines.

Minutes of the Meetings of the Executive Committee of the University Council (Thirty-Fourth: December 22, 1916 and Sixty-Third: February 20, 1920), University of the Philippines.

Annual Report of the President of the University of the Philippines (Sixth: 1916-1917, and Seventh: 1917-1918), Manila: Bureau of Printing, 1917; 1918.

Guide to the Ignacio Villamor Papers, 1884-1966, of the University of the Philippines Library, Diliman, Quezon City, University Archives, 1975.

Ignacio Villamor Papers, Boxes Nos. 9, 10 and 11, University Archives, University of the Philippines.

"History of the Appointment of the President of the University of the Philippines" (Newspaper Clippings) in Villamor Papers, Box No. 9, University Archives, University of the Philippines.

Manuel L. Quezon Papers, Box No. 171, Philippine National Library.

Casambre, Napoleon J. "The Administration of Francis Burton Harrison in the Philippines" unpublished dissertation, Stanford University, 1961.

Jamias, Cristino. *The University of the Philippines: The First Half Century*, Quezon City, University of the Philippines, 1962.

Monroe, Paul, et al. *A Survey of the Educational System of the Philippine Islands*, Manila: Bureau of Printing, 1915.

The Philippinensian, 1916, 1917, and 1920.

Notes on Chapter III — "Benton's Fleeting Performance"

1. John A. Larkin, "Philippine History Reconsidered: A Socio-Economic Perspective," *American Historical Review* 87 (June 1982), pp. 595-628.
2. See David R. Sturtevant, *Popular Uprisings in the Philippines, 1840-1940* (Ithaca: Cornell University Press, 1976).
3. Benito Legarda, Jr. and Roberto Y. Garcia, "Economic Collaboration: The Trading Relationship" in Frank H. Golay (ed.), *Philippine-American Relations* (Manila: Solidaridad Publishing House, 1966), pp. 125-148.
4. George E. Taylor, *The Philippines and the United States* (New York: Frederick A. Praeger, 1964), p. 58.
5. Bonifacio S. Salamanca, *The Filipino Reaction to American Rule 1901-1913* (Manila: New Day Publishers, 1984), p. 49.
6. A good study on Quezon's ambitions and use of political power is Joseph F. Hutchinson, Jr., "Quezon's Role in Philippine Independence," in Norman G. Owen (Ed.), *Compadre Colonialism* (Ann Arbor: University of Michigan Center for South and Southeast Asian Studies, 1971), pp. 157-194.
7. Salamanca, *Filipino Reaction*, pp. 144-153. See also Theodore Friend, *Between Two Empires: The Ordeal of the Philippines, 1929-1946* (New Haven: Yale University Press, 1965), pp. 42-44.
8. *Fifteenth Annual Report of the President of the University of the Philippines to the Board of Regents, June 1, 1925-May 31, 1926*, p. 28.
9. Cristino Jamias, *The University of the Philippines: The First Half Century* (Quezon City: University of the Philippines, 1962), p. 42.
10. *Fifteenth Annual Report, ibid.*
11. Jamias, *The University*, p. 11.
12. Letter of Guy Potter Benton to President R.M. Hughes, August 3, 1920. Hughes was the president of Miami University with whom Benton carried on a regular correspondence. This letter, together with many others, are found in the boxes in the Miami University Archives classified as Hughes Papers.
13. This brief account on the background of Benton is a collation of data contained in the following sources: "President of University of the Philippines," *The Scroll of Phi Delta Theta* 45, 4 (April 1921), 445-446; Arthur R. Priest, "Guy Potter Benton," *The Scroll of Phi Delta Theta* 52, 1 (October 1927), 10-12; Ruth Gaddis Jeffries, "Dr. Guy Potter Benton: A Vignette," *The Lamp of Delta* Zeta (1976), 20; and "Dr. Guy Potter Benton," Hughes Papers.
14. Jamias, *The University*, p. 114.
15. *Ibid.*, p. 115.
16. Jamias, *The University*, p. 122.
17. *Ibid.*, p. 123.
18. The report is entitled, *A Survey of the Educational System of the Philippine Islands* (Manila: Bureau of Printing, 1925).
19. *The World Book Encyclopedia*, 22 vols. (Chicago: World Book-Childcraft International, Inc., 1980), Vol. V, p. 143.
20. Jamias, *The University*, p. 124, quoting the *Philippines Herald* of October 15, 1920.
21. Leopoldo Y. Yabes, *First and Foremost: A History of the College of Law. University of the Philippines* (Quezon City: The Law Center, College of Law, University of the Philippines, 1982), pp. 34-64.
22. Jamias, *The University*, p. 124, quoting the *Philippines Herald* of October 15, 1920.
23. Jamias, *The University*, p. 125.
24. *Ibid.*
25. *Ibid.*
26. Letter of Benton to R.M. Hughes, Manila, December 9, 1920. Hughes Papers.
27. *Ibid*, p. 2.
28. Letter of Benton to Hughes, Manila, January 4, 1921. Hughes Papers.
29. *Ibid.*
30. *Ibid.*

31. Letter of Benton to Hughes, Manila, February 24, 1921. Hughes Papers.
32. *Ibid.*
33. *Ibid.*, p. 2.
34. Letter of Benton to Hughes, Manila, March 1, 1921. Hughes Papers.
35. *Ibid.*
36. *Ibid.*
37. Letter of Benton to Hughes, Manila, March 11, 1921, p. 1. Hughes Papers.
38. *Ibid.*
39. *Ibid.*
40. Cited in Jamias, *The University*, p. 125.
41. *Ibid.*, p. 126.
42. The United States War Department accepted his resignation, effective April 1, 1921, with the condition that he continue to serve nominally until June 30, 1921. (Letter of Benton to Hughes, Manila, March 28, 1921, p. 1. Hughes Papers.)
43. Letter of Benton to Hughes, Manila, March 11, 1921, p. 1. Hughes Papers. Underscoring supplied.
44. Letter of Benton to Hughes, Manila, March 28, 1921. Quezon Papers, Box 172.
45. *Ibid.*
46. *Ibid.*
47. Letter of Benton to Alejandro Albert, Manila, March 8, 1921. Quezon Papers, Box 172.
48. Letter of Victoriano Yamzon to Manuel L. Quezon, Manila, March 5, 1921. Quezon Papers, Box 172.
49. *Ibid.*
50. Letter of Manuel L. Quezon to Victoriano Yamzon, Manila, April 1, 1921. Quezon Papers, Box 172.
51. *The Philippines Herald*, March 5, 1921.
52. Letter of Benton to Hughes, Manila, May 6, 1921. Hughes Papers.
53. The writer is deeply grateful to Dr. Donald N. Nelson of Miami University and to Benton's grandson, Mr. Conrad H. Minnich, for these documents.
54. Letter of Benton to R.M. Hughes, Manila, May 6, 1921. Hughes Papers.
55. Letter of Benton to Judge Elam Fisher, Manila, December 8, 1922. Minnich Papers.
56. "Greeting from President Benton," *Philippine Collegian* (December 12, 1922), p. 2.
57. "Not Aristocracy, Neither Abject Penury is Object of University Says Dr. G. Benton," *The Varsity*, Vol. 3 (April 4, 1921), p. 1.
58. *Ibid.*
59. *Ibid.*
60. *Ibid.*
61. *Ibid.*
62. *Ibid.*
63. *Ibid.*
64. *Ibid., pp. 1; 4.*
65. "Objectives of the Tax-Supported University in the Philippine Islands," Inaugural address of Benton, December 16, 1921, reprinted in Jamias, *The University*, p. 259.
66. *Ibid.*, p. 262.
67. *Ibid.*
68. Inaugural address of Benton in Jamias, *The University*, p. 262.
69. *Ibid.*, p. 263.
70. Inaugural address of Benton in Jamias, *The University*, p. 265.
71. *Ibid.*, p. 266.
72. *Ibid.*
73. Inaugural address of Benton in Jamias, *The University*, p. 267.
74. Letter of Alejandro M. Albert to Benton, Manila, March 7, 1921. Hughes Papers.
75. Inaugural address of Benton in Jamias, *The University*, p. 268.
76. *Ibid.*
77. *Ibid.*, p. 270.
78. *Ibid.*, pp. 270-271.

79. Inaugural address of Benton in Jamias, *The University*, p. 271.
80. Letter of Benton to Quezon, Manila, November 26, 1921, Box No. 172, Quezon Papers; Letter of Benton to Quezon, Manila, December 1, 1921, Box No. 172, Quezon Papers; Benton to Quezon, Manila, December 3, 1921, Box No. 172, Quezon Papers.
81. Letter of Benton to Quezon, Manila, November 26, 1921, Box No. 172, Quezon Papers; Letter of Benton to Quezon, Manila, December 1, 1921, Box No. 172, Quezon Papers; Benton to Quezon, Manila, December 3, 1921, Box No. 172, Quezon Papers.
82. "Outline of Institutional Policies and Accomplishments During the Present Administration from the Fourth of April 1921," University of the Philippines, Manila. Box No. 172, Quezon Papers.
83. *Ibid.*
84. Letter of Benton to Quezon, Manila, February 8, 1922, Box No. 172, Quezon Papers.
85. *Ibid.*
86. "Outline of Institutional Policies." pp. 3-4.
87. Quoted in Jamias, *The University*, pp. 166-167. Underscoring supplied.
88. Jamias, *The University*, p. 167.
89. Letter of Benton to Quezon, Manila, February 8, 1922. Box No. 172, Quezon Papers.
90. *Ibid.*
91. *Ibid.*
92. Letter of Leonard Wood to the President of the Senate, Manila, February 8, 1922. Box No. 172, Quezon Papers.
93. Letter of Manuel L. Quezon to Guy Potter Benton, Manila, February 11, 1922. Box No. 172, Quezon Papers.
94. Letter of Benton to Quezon, Manila, February 8, 1922, Box No. 172, Quezon Papers. See also Jamias, *The University*, p. 177.
95. Letter of Benton to Quezon, February 8, 1922.
96. *Ibid.*
97. *Ibid.*
98. Jamias, *The University*, p. 178.
99. *Ibid.*, p. 179.
100. Jamias, *The University*, p. 179; "Outline of Institutional Policies," p. 2. Box No. 172, Quezon Papers.
101. Had this sum beem approved, it would have been appropriated in installments as follows: three million for 1923; four million for 1924; four and half million for 1925; five million for 1926; five and half million for 1927; six million for 1928; six and half million for 1929; seven million for 1930; and seven and half million for 1931.
102. Quoted in Jamias, *The University*, p. 179.
103. Printed in the *Manila Times*, March 22, 1922.
104. "Outline of Institutional Policies," p. 11.
105. *Ibid.*
106. "Governor General Makes Recommendations for U.P. Support," *Philippine Collegian* (Tuesday, December 12, 1922), p. 11.
107. Jamias, *The University*, p. 219.
108. See for example, the following works: Bonifacio S. Salamanca, *Filipino Reaction to American Rule;* Norman G. Owen, *Compadre Colonialism* and Theodore Friend, *Between Two Empires.*
109. Onofre D. Corpuz, *The Philippines* (Englewood Cliffs, New Jersey: Prentice Hall, Inc., 1965), pp. 65-70; 93-95.
110. Frank Jenista, Jr., "Conflict in the Philippine Legislature: The Commission and the Assembly from 1907 to 1913" in Owen's *Compadre Colonialism*, p. 85.
111. "Outline of Institutional Policies and Accomplishments During the Present Administration from the Fourth of April 1921," pp. 3-4. Manila, University of the Philippines. Box No. 172, Quezon Papers.
112. Jamias, *The University*, pp. 176-177.
113. "Outline of Institutional Policies," p. 4.
114. *Ibid.*

115. *Ibid.*, p. 7.
116. "Outline of Institutional Policies," p. 9.
117. *Ibid.*
118. Jamias, *The University*, p. 185.
119. "Outline of Institutional Policies," p. 8. Jamias implies that the Board approved even the integration of the student paper into the planned University monthly. (Jamias, *The University*, p. 185.) Actually, as stated above, the student paper was not included among the publications subjected to centralized control.
120. Jamias, *The University*, p. 186.
121. *Ibid.*, pp. 186-187.
122. "Outline of Institutional Policies," p. 9.
123. *Ibid.*
124. Jamias, *The University*, p. 187.
125. "Outline of Institutional Policies," p. 9.
126. *Ibid.*, p. 10.
127. *Ibid.*
128. "Inaugural address of Guy Potter Benton," reprinted in Jamias, *The University*, pp. 263-264.
129. "Outline of Institutional Policies," p. 10.
130. "Inaugural address of Guy Potter Benton," in Jamias, *The University*. p. 264. Original underscoring.
131. "Outline of Institutional Policies," p. 8.
132. *Ibid.*
133. Jamias, *The University*, p. 186.
134. "Outline of Institutional Policies," p. 8.
135. *Ibid.*
136. *Ibid.*
137. "Inaugural address of Guy Potter Benton," in Jamias, *The University*, pp. 261-262.
138. "Outline of Institutional Policies," p. 2.
139. *Ibid.*
140. *Ibid.*
141. *Ibid.*, p. 3.
142. *Ibid.*
143. *Ibid.*
144. *Ibid.*, pp. 4-5.
145. *Ibid.*, pp. 5-6.
146. *Ibid.*, pp. 6-7.
147. *Ibid.*, p. 12.
148. Jamias, *The University*, p. 220.
149. "Outline of Institutional Policies," p. 12.
150. Jamias, *The University*, p. 191.
151. *Ibid.*
152. Letter of Benton to Hughes, Manila, October 25, 1922, p. 12. Hughes Papers.
153. *Ibid.*
154. *Ibid.*
155. *Ibid.*, p. 3.
156. *Ibid.*
157. *Ibid.*,
158. Letter of Austin Craig to the Committee of the House of Representatives of the Sixth Philippine Legislature, Manila, pp. 4-5. Box No. 172, Quezon Papers.
159. "Curiosities of the Craig Case," p. 9. Box No. 172, Quezon Papers.
160. *Ibid.*
161. *Ibid.*
162. Letter of Austin Craig to the Board of Regents, Manila, September 7, 1922. Box No. 172, Quezon Papers.
163. Final Answer of Austin Craig to Charge 2, pp. 1-11. Box No. 172, Quezon Papers.
164. Final Answer of Austin Craig to Charge 3, pp. 11-12, Box No. 172, Quezon Papers.
165. Final Answer to Charge 4, p. 11, Box No. 172, Quezon Papers.
166. Quoted in Jamias, *The University*, p. 195.
167. See Letter of Austin Craig to the Sixth Philippine Legislature, pp. 1-7, Box No. 172, Quezon Papers.
168. Letter of of Benton to Hughes, Manila October 25, 1922, p. 4. Hughes Papers.
169. *Ibid.*, p. 5.
170. Jamias, *The University*, p. 202.

171. Letter of Benton to Hughes, Manila, October 25, 1922, p. 6, Hughes Papers.
172. *Ibid.*, p. 5.
173. *Ibid.*, p. 2.
174. Letter of Benton to Leonard Wood, Manila, 4 November 1922. Box No. 172, Quezon Papers.
175. *Ibid.*
176. *Ibid.*
177. *Ibid.*
178. Letter of Randall A. Rowley to the Board of Visitors, Manila, November 6, 1922. Box No. 172, Quezon Papers.
179. Letter of Austin Craig to the Board of Visitors, Manila, November 7, 1922. Box No. 172, Quezon Papers.
180. Letter of Jorge C. Bocobo to the Board of Visitors, Manila, November 6, 1922. Box No. 172, Quezon Papers.
181. This refers to Jose K. Santos, a faculty member of the University sent to the United States to pursue his Ph.D. in botany at the University of Chicago. More will be said about this case later.
182. Letter of Vicente Hilario to Leonard Wood, Manila, November 9, 1922. Box No. 172, Quezon Papers.
183. Jamias, *The University*, p. 214. In the one page devoted to this matter, Jamias fails to identify the faculty member involved.
184. Letter of Guy Potter Benton to Henry Pratt Judson, *Philippines Herald*, November 10, 1922. No. 172, Quezon Papers.
185. Letter of Henry Pratt Judson to Guy Potter Benton, Chicago, September 22, 1922. Box No. 172, Quezon Papers.
186. Jamias, *The University*, p. 214.
187. Letter of Gaudencio Garcia to the Board of Visitors, Manila, November 11, 1922. Box No. 172, Quezon Papers.
188. Letter of Conrado Benitez to the Board of Visitors, Manila, November 14, 1922. Box No. 172, Quezon Papers.
189. Letter of Henry A. Townsend to the Board of Visitors, Manila, November 11, 1922. Box No. 172. Quezon Papers.
190. *Ibid.*
191. "Note to the Press" by Leonard Wood, Manuel L. Quezon and Manuel A. Roxas. No date. Hughes Papers.
192. See, for instance, the letters of Guy Potter Benton to Manuel L. Quezon, Manila, September 8, 1922 and January 7, 1923. Box No. 172, Quezon Papers.
193. *Annual Report of the Governor General*, 1922.
194. *Fifteenth Annual Report of the President of the University of the Philippines to the Board of Regents, June 1, 1925-May 31, 1926*, p. 28.
195. *Thirteenth Annual Report of the President of the University of the Philippines to the Board of Regents, June 1, 1923- May 31, 1924*, p. 30.
196. *Ibid.*, p. 34.
197. *Ibid.*
198. Jamias, *The University*, p. 216.
199. Letter of Guy Potter Benton to Manuel L. Quezon, Manila, January 7, 1923. Box No. 172, Quezon Papers.
200. Letter of Pio Duran, Secretary to the President, to R. M. Hughes, Manila, May 10, 1923. Hughes Papers.
201. Letter of Benton to Hughes, Manila, July 10, 1923. Hughes Papers.
202. "Guy Potter Benton." Hughes Papers.
203. Jamias, *The University*, p. 222.
204. *Ibid.*, p. 223.

Bibliography — Chapter III

A. Books

Corpuz, Onofre D. *The Philippines*, Englewood Cliffs, New Jersey: Prentice Hall, Inc., 1965.

Friend, Theodore, *Between Two Empires: The Ordeal of the Philippines, 1929-1946*. New Haven, Conn.: Yale University Press, 1965.

Jamias, Cristino. *The University of the Philippines: The First Half Century*. Quezon City: University of the Philippines, 1962.

Monroe, Paul. *A Survey of the Educational System of the Philippine Islands*. Manila: Bureau of Printing, 1925.

Owen, Norman G. *Compadre Colonialism*. Ann Arbor, Michigan: University of Michigan Center for South and Southeast Asian Studies, 1971.

Salamanca, Bonifacio S. *The Filipino Reaction to American Rule 1901-1913*. Manila: New Day Publishers, 1984.

Taylor, George E. *The Philippines and the United States*. New York: Frederick A. Praeger, 1964.

Yabes, Leopoldo Y. *The UP College of Law*. Quezon City. 1983.

B. Journals/Newspapers

"Greetings from President Benton," *Philippine Collegian*, December 12, 1922.

"Governor General Makes Recommendations for U.P. Support," *Philippine Collegian*, December 12, 1922.

The Philippines Herald, March 5, 1921.

The Manila Times, March 22, 1922.

"The President of the University of the Philippines," *The Scroll of Phi Delta Theta* 45, 4 (April 1921), pp. 445-446.

"Not Aristocracy, Neither Abject Penury is Object of University Says Dr. G. Benton," *The Varsity*, 3 (April 4, 1921).

Benton, Guy Potter. "Objectives of the Tax-Supported University in the Philippine Islands," in Jamias, Cristino. *The University of the Philippines: The First Half Century*. Quezon City: University of the Philippines, 1962.

Jeffries, Ruth Gaddis. "Dr. Guy Potter Benton: A Vignette," *The Lamp of Delta Zeta* (1976), p. 20.

Larkin, John A. "Philippine History Reconsidered: A Socio-Economic Perspective," *American Historical Review* 87 (June 1982), pp. 595-628.

Legarda Jr., Benito and Roberto Y. Garcia. "Economic Collaboration: The Trading Relationship," in Golay, Frank H. (ed.) *Philippine-American Relations*. Manila: Solidaridad Publishing House, 1966. pp. 125-148.

Priest, Arthur R. "Guy Potter Benton," *The Scroll of Phi Delta Theta* 52, 1 (October 1927), pp. 10-12.

Sturtevant, David R. *Popular Uprisings in the Philippines, 1840-1940*. Ithaca, New York: Cornell University Press, 1976.

C. Annual Reports

Annual Report of the Governor General. Manila, 1922.

Annual Report of the President of the University of the Philippines to the Board of Regents: 1923-1924 (13th), and 1925-1926 (15th).

D. Encyclopedia

The World Book Encyclopedia. Chicago: World Book—Childcraft International, Inc., 1980. Volume 5.

E. Documents

"Dr. Guy Potter Benton," Hughes Papers, Miami University Archives, Oxford, Ohio, U.S.A.

Letter of Alejandro Albert to Guy Potter Benton, Manila, 7 March 1921. Hughes Papers.

Letters of Guy Potter Benton to President R.M. Hughes, Manila, dated 3 August 1920, 9 December 1920, 4 January 1921, 24 February 1921, 1 March 1921, 11 March 1921, 28 March 1921, 6 May 1921, 25 October 1922, and 10 July 1923. Hughes Papers, Miami University Archives, Oxford, Ohio, U.S.A.

Letter of Pio Duran, Secretary to the President, to R.M. Hughes, Manila, 10 May 1923. Hughes Papers.

Wood, Leonard, Quezon, Manuel L. and Roxas, Manuel A. *Note to the Press.* No date. Hughes Papers.

Letter of Guy Potter Benton to Judge Elam Fisher, Manila, 8 December 1922. Minnich Papers. Conrad H. Minnich is the grandson of Benton. He lives in Ohio.

"Curiosities of the Craig Case," Quezon Papers, Box 172.

Final Answer of Austin Craig. Quezon Papers, Box 172.

Letter of Conrado Benitez to the Board of Visitors, Manila, 14 November, Quezon Papers, Box 172.

Letter of Guy Potter Benton to Alejandro Albert, Manila, 8 March 1921. Quezon Papers, Box 172.

Letter of Guy Potter Benton to Henry Pratt Judson, in *Philippines Herald*, 10 November 1922. Quezon Papers, Box 172.

Letters of Guy Potter Benton to Manuel L. Quezon, Manila, dated 26 November 1921, 1 December 1921, 3 December 1921, 8 February 1922, 8 September 1922, and January 1923. Quezon Papers, Box 172.

Letter of Guy Potter Benton to Leonard Wood, Manila, 4 November 1922. Quezon Papers, Box 172.

Letter of Jorge Bocobo to the Board of Visitors, Manila, 8 November 1922. Quezon Papers, Box. 172.

Letter of Austin Craig to the Board of Regents, Manila, 7 September 1922. Quezon Papers, Box 172.

Letter of Austin Craig to the Board of Visitors, Manila, 7 November 1922. Quezon Papers, Box 172.

Letter of Austin Craig to the Committee of the House of Representatives of the Sixth Philippine Legislature, Manila. Quezon Papers, Box 172.

Letter of Gaudencio Garcia to the Board of Visitors, Manila, 11 November 1922. Quezon Papers, Box 172.

Letter of Vicente Hilario to Leonard Wood, Manila, 9 November 1922. Quezon Papers, Box 172.

Letter of Henry Pratt Judson to Guy Potter Benton, Chicago, 22 September 1922. Quezon Papers, Box 172.

Letter of Manuel L. Quezon to Guy Potter Benton, Manila, 11 February 1922. Quezon Papers, Box 172.

Letter of Manuel L. Quezon to Victoriano Yamzon, Manila, 1 April 1921, Quezon Papers, Box 172.

Letter of Randall A. Rowley to the Board of Visitors, Manila, 6 November 1922, Quezon Papers, Box 172.

Letter of Henry A. Townsend to the Board of Visitors, Manila. 11 November 1922. Quezon Papers Box 172.

Letter of Leonard Wood to the President of the Senate, Manila, 8 February 1922. Quezon Papers, Box 172.

Letter of Victoriano Yamzon to Manuel L. Quezon, Manila, 5 March 1921, Quezon Papers, Box 172.

Outline of Institutional Policies and Accomplishments During the Present Administration from the Fourth of April 1921. Manila: University of the Philippines. Quezon Papers, Box 172.

NOTES ON CHAPTER IV — "PALMA'S MOMENTOUS DECADE"

1. Rafael Palma, *My Autobiography,* trans. by Alicia Palma-Bautista, Manila: Capitol Publishing House, Inc., 1953, pp. 124-125. [Hereafter *Palma Autobiography.*]

2. For Palma's earlier political career, see Rafael Palma, "Personal file" ("P" file), *Bureau of Insular Affairs Records* [hereafter *BIA Records*], Record Group 350, National Archives, Washington, D.C.

   Palma started his career in the Bureau of Audits (1896-1898). From there he became director of Antonio Luna's *La Independencia* (1898-1899), co-founder with Sergio Osmeña and Jaime C. de Veyra of *El Nuevo Dia* (Cebu, April-December 1900), and editor of *El Renacimiento* (September 1901-March 1902). He entered politics as representative from Cavite to the Philippine Assembly (1907). From 1908 to 1916 he was one of the Filipino members of the Philippine Commission; he served as senator from the fourth senatorial district while also occupying the position of Secretary of the Interior from 1916 to 1922. Before he retired from the Senate, he served as its President Pro-Tempore. As a political figure, Palma had formed, with Osmeña and Quezon, the "OPQ" triumvirate, recognized leaders of Filipino participation in the American colonial government from 1907 to 1922. He was also a member of the Spanish Royal Academy, the Academy of Arts and Sciences of Cadiz, and the Philippine Academy of Social Sciences.

   See also *BIA Records* 397-70 and 397-71; 3722-30; 3725-82; 3038-79; 7163-211; 10265-88 and 10265-90; and 12249-139.

3. "Inaugural Address of Rafael Palma," in *Rafael Palma, A Commemorative Brochure on His Birth Centenary,* Quezon City: University of the Philippines Press, 1974, p. 65.

4. See *BIA Records* 3828-1591; 3725-68; 3725-70; 3725-82; also Palma "P" file; Francis Burton Harrison, "P" file, *BIA Records.* See also *Palma Autobiography,* pp. 57-125.

5. Inaugural festivities at Los Baños, July 25, 1925, see in *Inauguration of Rafael Palma as Fourth President of the University of the Philippines, Manila, the Eighteenth Day of July, Nineteen Hundred and Twenty-five,* Manila: Bureau of Printing, 1925.

   See also *BIA Records* 1215-77 for account of ceremonies, addresses attending Palma inaugural. See also editorials, *Philippines Herald,* March 11 and July 11, 1925, commending the selection of Palma as UP President.

   The Board of Regents appointed Palma president on March 9, effective March 15, 1925. The BOR Committee on the selection of a permanent president was composed of Jose Escaler, Fernando Calderon, and Santiago Fonacier. See letter dated February 28, 1925, recommending permanent appointment of Palma, in *14th Annual Report of the UP President to the Board of Regents,* 1924-1925, pp. 10-11.

6. *Ibid.*

7. *Philippines Free Press,* October 6, 1923; *Philippines Herald,* October 30, 1923; *Manila Daily Bulletin,* March 10, 1925. See also Palma "P" file and *BIA Records* 1215-77.

8. Palma Inaugural Address, pp. 58, 59, 60.

9. *Ibid.*, pp. 57, 62.

10. The Commission was created by the Philippine Legislature for the purpose of identifying the defects and weaknesses of the Philippine educational system and determining ways of correct-

ing them. The Commission's report devoted a chapter to the University of the Philippines (Chapter IX). The UP Survey was conducted by Dr. Stephen P. Duggan, Director of the Institute of International Relations and Professor of International Relations, Columbia University. The Commission was headed by Dr. Paul R. Monroe, also of Columbia University.

See *14th Annual Report, UP President,* 1924-1925, pp. 7-8; also *New York Times,* November 13, 1924, p. 20; December 20, 1924, p. 27; April 30, 1925, p. 35; and August 7, 1925, p. 24.

11. See Letter, Palma to Secretary of Public Instruction, Eugene Gilmore, September 19,1925, in *15th Annual Report, UP President,* 1925-1926, pp. 15-22.

12. *A Survey of the Educational System of the Philippine Islands,* Manila: Bureau of Printing, 1925, Chapter IX, pp. 609-672 [hereafter *Monroe Commission Report*]. See also *BIA Records* 3725-129 and 3725-130-E. See also Letter, Eugene A. Gilmore to Legislature, September 18, 1925, in *Report of the Governor General of the Philippine Islands,* 1925, pp. 251-252.

13. *Monroe Commission Report,* pp. 621, 669.

14. *17th Annual Report, UP President,* 1927-1928, pp. 79-81.

15. *Monroe Commission Report,* p. 613.

16. *Ibid.*, pp. 613-614.

17. Since 1919 the Legislature had enacted statutes establishing a rigid salary scale for the instructional staff of the University, requiring the approval of the presiding officers of the two houses of the Legislature and the Governor General for the selection of a president and the employment of every teacher whose salary exceeded a certain amount. In 1923 it provided that none of the moneys expended by the University for that year should be used to increase any salaries either of the instructional or administrative staff. These acts were in direct contravention of the powers placed by the Charter of the University in the Board of Regents. The act of 1923 had a most demoralizing effect upon the staff because it froze promotion and salary increases. The discontent and threats of withdrawal became so pronounced that the act was repealed in February 1924. See *ibid.*, pp. 612-613.

Contract appointments of faculty members hired from the United States also needed the approval of the Senate President and the House Speaker, with the concurrence of the Governor General. See some of these papers in *Manuel L. Quezon Papers,* National Library, Manila, Box 172.

18. *14th Annual Report, UP President,* 1924-1925, pp. 8-9; *Monroe Commission Report,* pp. 611-612.

19. See *Philippines Herald,* editorial, July 19, 1925, p. 8; August 15, 1928, p. 8; February 9, 1933, p. 3; *Manila Daily Bulletin,* June 9, 1927; *La Vanguardia,* February 2, 1933; *18th Annual Report, UP President,* 1928-1929, pp. 10-11; Letter, Palma to Governor General, August 9, 1929; *19th Annual Report, UP President,* 1929-1930, p. 14; and Gilmore to Secretary of War, Cable No. 77, August 30, 1928, *BIA Records* 1215-88.

In April 1927, C.F. Baker, Dean of the College of Agriculture, wrote Quezon complaining about the demoralization among the faculty which had resulted from the political campaign carried on by the faculty candidates for membership in the Board of Regents. The candidates involved were Dean Maximo M. Kalaw and Dr. Arturo Garcia. Quezon presumably had a "heart-to-heart" talk with the Filipinos on the matter. See Baker to Quezon, April 12, 1927; Quezon to Baker, May 10, 1927, in *Quezon Papers,* Box 172.

The Monroe Commission had also suggested dropping the faculty representative since the views of the faculty on educational policy and administration could best be expressed through the President of the University. See *Monroe Commission Report,* p. 613.

20. *Ibid.*, pp. 645-650.

21. *16th Annual Report, UP President,* 1926-1927, p. 19.

22. *17th Annual Report, UP President,* 1927-1928, p. 22.

23. *Monroe Commission Report,* p. 651.

For instance, the College of Medicine in 1925 had 470 students receiving instruction in a building which was erected to accommodate 250. In the College of Engineering, there were only four classrooms and they were separated from each other by walls so thin that lectures and recitations could clearly be heard in the adjoining rooms. The offices for the professors were simply spaces partitioned off in the laboratories and were so hot, noisy, and dusty that the professors preferred to take their work home. The Conservatory of Music and the School of Fine Arts were far removed from the campus and were housed on rented buildings. See *ibid.*, pp. 635, 638, 641-643.

24. *Ibid.*, pp. 643-644.

25. In academic year 1923-1924, there were 5,993 students enrolled in the University and 422 teaching staff. See *ibid.*, p. 616.

From 1924 to 1928, enrollment grew at an average of 500 students a year. (See Annex A for Table on the Growth of the University.)

26. Among the buildings constructed that year were the Freer Chemical Laboratory (East Wing to Rizal Hall), Engineering Shop and Forge Building, a Sulphide Building, an Animal House (College of Medicine), and an Implement House, the Soil Technology Building and some faculty houses in Los Baños. See *13th Annual Report, UP President,* 1923-1924, p. 12; *Palma Autobiography,* p. 126.

27. *14th Annual Report, UP President,* 1924-1925, pp. 52-54; *Palma Autobiography,* pp. 126-127.

28. For Palma's building program, see the following annual reports: *15th Annual Report,* 1925-1926, pp. 16, 49; *16th Annual Report,* 1926-1927, pp. 40-41; *19th Annual Report,* 1929-1930, p. 18; *20th Annual Report,* 1930-1931, pp. 42-44. See also *Palma Autobiography,* pp. 127-129; *Report of the Governor General,* 1926, pp. 10-11; 1927, pp. 7-8; Rafael Palma, "Our New University Library," *Philippine Social Sciences Review (PSSR),* XI:3 (August 1939), pp. 334-338; and *Philippines Herald,* March 23, 1929, April 11, 1929.

29. *Palma Autobiography,* pp. 127-128; *Philippines Herald,* July 2, 20, 1932; *Tribune,* June 30, 1932; *La Opinion,* June 30, 1932.

30. *Palma Autobiography,* pp. 129-130; Rafael Palma, "The University and the People," *PSSR* (August 1939), pp. 324-325.

31. Palma Inaugural Address, pp. 65-66.

32. *16th Annual Report, UP President,* 1926-1927, pp. 8-9; *Philippines Herald,* June 24, 1933, pp. 13, 14.

The Rockefeller Foundation contributed ₱150,000 for the construction of an east wing to the College of Medicine for the School of Hygiene and Public Health. See *19th Annual Report, UP President,* 1929-1930, pp. 18-20; also *New York Times,* May 14, 1930, p. 2.

33. *18th Annual Report, UP President,* 1928-1929, p. 18.

Previous to the creation of the School, there was a Department of Economics and Business Administration in the College of Liberal Arts. The Chairman of the Department was Nicanor Reyes.

34. *17th Annual Report, UP President,* 1927-1928, pp. 10-11.

35. *19th Annual Report, UP President,* 1929-1930, pp. 57-58.

The establishment of a Rural High School was recommended by the Monroe Commission. See *Monroe Commission Report,* p. 628.

36. *BIA Records,* 27243-2; 27243-3; 27243-6; 1215-64 and 1215-64-A. The Vigan Branch was transferred to Baguio in 1938.

37. See Board of Regents Resolution, adopted June 26, 1931, amended September 26, 1931, in *Quežon Papers,* Box 72; see also pertinent documents on the "crisis" in the School of Dentistry involving Dr. J. Sandoval, Director of the School, and Dr. Eladio R. Aldecoa, Head, Department of Prosthetic Dentistry, in *ibid.* See also *New York Times,* June 27, 1931, p. 4; *Tribune,* June 30, 1932; *Philippines Herald,* editorial, July 2, 1932, p. 4.

38. *15th Annual Report, UP President,* 1925-1926, p. 20; *Monroe Commission Report,* pp. 630-631.

39. *Philippines Herald,* July 2, 1932, p. 4; July 20, 1932, p. 6; *Tribune,* June 30, 1932.

40. Palma Inaugural Address, p. 66; see also address delivered July 18, 1925 to UP faculty and alumni, in *Inauguration Commemorative Brochure,* p. 52.

41. *Palma Autobiography,* pp. 137-138; *17th Annual Report, UP President,* 1927-1928; *Philippine Collegian,* February 24, 1933, pp. 1, 10.

42. Palma Inaugural Address, p. 71.

43. *Monroe Commission Report,* pp. 669-670.

44. It was in June 1927 when acting President Jorge Bocobo presented to the Board of Regents the draft of a land grant bill. The Board endorsed the draft in July and Senator Camilo Osias presented the bill before the Legislature, which, however, did not act on it because of lack of time. The bill was presented in subsequent sessions. In 1930 it was introduced by Representatives Soliven, Domingo, Ibañez, Padilla, and Santiago. See *17th Annual Report, UP President,* 1927-1928, p. 71; *19th Annual Report, UP President,* 1929-1930, pp. 11-12; Cable No. 77, August 30, 1928, *BIA Records* 1215-88; *BIA Records* 1215-91-A; and letters, Palma to Quezon, January 8, 1929 and August 23, 1929, in *Quezon Papers,* Box 172.

45. *Palma Autobiography,* pp. 133-134; *13th Annual Report, UP President,* 1923-1924, pp. 10-12; Palma, "The University and the People," *loc. cit.,* p. 327.

A minimum of two years of service was required before promotion from one academic rank to another (from Instructor to Assistant Professor to Associate Professor to Full Professor) or five years from Instructor to Full Professor.

In academic year 1925-1926, the University Council adopted a policy on academic tenure which laid down the precise terms of appointment in the University. See *14th Annual Report, UP President,* 1925-1926, pp. 14-15. See Annex B for copy of this policy.

46. *Palma Autobiography,* p. 134.

47. The UP Budget was increasingly reduced from 1931 as follows: 1931 – ₱1,801,140; 1932 – ₱1,393,146 (27% reduction from 1931); 1933 – ₱1,018,067 (27% reduction from 1932, or 43% from that of 1931). See Minutes of the Board of Regents Meeting, August 18, 1933, *Quezon Papers,* Box 172.

48. *Philippines Herald,* June 21, 1933, pp. 1. 2.

To allay growing faculty unrest, Dean Conrado Benitez proposed giving promotions in rank, if not in salary, to deserving faculty members, at least for the time being. This recommendation was submitted by Palma to the Board of Regents, which approved it. See *Tribune,* November 5, 1933, pp. 1, 19; November 7, 1933, pp. 1, 3; *Philippine Collegian,* November 10, 1933, pp. 1, 8.

49. *Graphic,* editorial, June 2, 1932; *La Tribuna* (Iloilo), June 24, 1932; *La Opinion,* June 2, 1932; Minutes of the Board of Regents Meeting, July 13, 1932, Exhibit B; Minutes of the Board of Regents Meeting, July 15, 1932, Exhibit A. See also *Palma Autobiography,* p. 138; *La Vanguardia,* January 13, 1933; and *Philippines Herald,* January 14, 1933, p. 12.

One of the economy measures resorted to was the restriction on the use of electric fans in the University. Double compensation of some faculty members and administrative officers was also curtailed. See *Tribune,* June 30, 1932.

On December 9, 1932, some 2,000 students of Manila universities, mainly from the University of the Philippines, marched to the Legislative building and staged a protest against the "outrageous" rider provision increasing the representatives' allowance. The demonstrators refused to heed police orders to disband until Senate President Quezon and other legislators addressed them and Representative Anonas announced that he had been delegated by the House to say that an arrangement would be made with President Palma to discuss any charges that the students may wish to make at the regular university convocation. Obviously the students did not see the justification for the increase in allowance of the legislators while University funding was being cut. On December 13, UP students decided not to adopt a resolution censuring the Legislature after Quezon and other legislators explained the reason for the increase in allowance. See *Philippine Magazine,* January 1933, pp. 343-344.

50. Among the schools affected by the tuition increase were the School of Forestry, College of Veterinary Medicine, College of Agriculture, Conservatory of Music, School of Fine Arts, College of Education, and the College of Medicine.

See *Philippines Herald,* June 1, 1933, pp. 1, 2; June 3. pp. 1, 12; June 5, editorial, pp. 4, 1, 14; June 8, editorial, p. 4; *La Vanguardia,* editorial, June 3, 1933; *Mabuhay,* editorial, June 4, 1933; *Manila Daily Bulletin,* June 5, 1933; *Tribune,* July 9, 1933. See also letter, Restituto Aquino (Education) to Quezon, June 23,1933, in *Quezon Papers,* Box 172.

51. *La Opinion,* June 2, 1933; *Philippine Collegian,* July 7, 1933, pp. 1, 2; *Manila Daily Bulletin,* June 9, 1933.

In this controversy, Senator Elpidio Quirino, also Regent of the University, stood as the champion of the students. He attributed the idea of the tuition increase to Palma alone. Annoyed by this statement, Palma explained that the increase was the recommendation of the Board of Regents, of which Quirino himself was a member, and he did approve the increase during the Board meeting called for the purpose of discussing the tuition hike. See *Philippines Herald,* June 7, 1933, pp.1, 14; June 8, pp. 1, 14.

52. *Ibid.,* June 20, 1933, pp. 1, 11; July 12, pp. 1, 14.

To balance its budget for 1933, the University, among other measures, retired fifteen of its personnel – five clerks and ten faculty members.

53. Palma, "The University and the People," *loc. cit.,* pp. 330-331. *14th Annual Report, UP President,* 1924-1925, pp. 44-46.

54. When Miss Salud San Jose was chosen Miss UP (by a committee of students and faculty appointed by Palma) to join the 1929 Philippine Carnival, the Liberal Arts faculty and the Law student body opposed UP's participation in the event. Palma defended the affair by graciously

admonishing the critics that "it is alright to admire beauty," while reminding them that the University could support the Carnival without endangering "our educational mission." *Philippines Herald*, November 20, 1928, pp. 1, 8.

55. *Ang Bagong Katipunan* (or National Association for Independence) was the brainchild of Manuel Roxas. Its main concerns as stated were to unite all elements and to provide funds for the campaign for independence in the United States. See Ang Bagong Katipunan, *BIA Records* 4587-B; *Philippines Herald*, November 3, 4, 10, 15, 17, 18, 19, 21, 22, 25, 27; December 1, 2, 3, 4, 8, 19, 20, 23, 1930.

56. Palma, "The University and the People," *loc. cit.*, pp. 330-331. See also flyer sent to Quezon, dated November 9, 1928, in *Quezon Papers*, Box 172.

57. *Palma Autobiography*, p. 135; Palma, "The University and the People," *loc. cit.*, p. 331.

58. *Palma Autobiography*, pp. 135-136; Palma, "The University and the People," *loc. cit.*, p. 33.

59. *Monroe Commission Report*, pp. 665-668; *Report of the Governor General*, 1927, pp. 7-8; *17th Annual Report, UP President*, 1927-1928, pp. 54-56; *Palma Autobiography*, p. 136; Palma, "The University and the People," *loc. cit.*, p. 331; *Philippines Herald*, July 15, 1933, p. 3.

The Monroe Commission noted that of the 846 students in the College of Liberal Arts in 1924-1925, only 285 or 33 per cent lived at home, 280 in dormitories, 195 in boarding houses.

60. See *supra*, p. 163.

61. Rafael Palma, "The Promotion of the Intellectual Life of the Country," *PSSR* (January 1932), p. 56.

62. *16th Annual Report, UP President*, 1926-1927, pp. 11-13; *Palma Autobiography*, p. 136; Palma, "The University and the People," *loc. cit.*, pp. 331-332.

63. *Monroe Commission Report*, pp. 665, 667; *Palma Autobiography*, pp. 136-137; Palma, "The University and the People," *loc. cit.*, p. 332.

64. *Monroe Commission Report*, p. 667; *Palma Autobiography*, p. 136; Palma, "The University and the People," *loc. cit*, p. 332. See also *18th Annual Report, UP President*, 1928-1929, pp. 42-44.

In 1913, the UP Debating Team coached by Prof. Alejo Labrador, lost to the visiting University of Oregon Team. Palma nevertheless commended them for their performance. See *Philippine Collegian*, October 23, 1931, p. 12.

65. Rafael Palma, "Our Country," UP Convocation, July 27, 1926, *PSSR* (August 1939). p. 284.

66. Rafael Palma, "The Revolt of Youth," YMCA Student Conference, Baguio, December 28, 1928, *PSSR* (August 1939), pp. 258-267.

67. Rafael Palma, "New Mentality," Commencement Exercises, Junior College, Cebu, March 16, 1929, *PSSR* (August 1939), p. 272.

68. *Philippine Collegian*, September 1, 1933, p. 8.

69. Palma, "New Mentality," *loc. cit.*, p. 274.

70. Quoted in Jose V. Tacal, Jr., "The Life and Times of Rafael Palma," *Historical Bulletin* (Philippine Historical Association), VI: 4, pp. 384-393.

71. Many contemporaries remember Palma demanding the immediate resignation of two faculty members who had scandalized the University by running around with their women students.

See Teodoro A. Agoncillo, "Rafael Palma: A Profile in Integrity and Courage," in *Birth Centenary Commemorative Brochure,* p. 18. See also *Philippines Herald,* February 17, 1933, p. 1.

72. Palma Inaugural Address, p. 66.

73. *Ibid.,* pp. 67-68.

74. Palma, "The Promotion of the Intellectual Life of the Country." *loc. cit.,* pp. 55-57.

75. Rafael Palma, "Our Age," Commencement Exercises, Far Eastern College, March 17, 1929, *PSSR* (August 1939), pp. 280, 281.

76. In 1916 the Philippine Legislature passed an act limiting the salaries for the various grades of the teaching personnel of the University. Full Professors received a salary of ₱5,000-₱6,000 per annum; Associate Professors – ₱4,000-₱4,500; Assistant Professors – ₱3,000-₱3,600; Instructors – ₱2,000-₱2,200; Assistant Instructors – ₱960-₱1,200; Graduate Assistants – ₱360. See *Monroe Commission Report,* pp. 656-657; *15th Annual Report, UP President* 1925-1926, p. 9.

On October 10, 1932, the UP Instructors Association, presided by Aurelio C. Ramos, protested the proposed discontinuance of the privilege heretofore granted to instructors to engage in outside teaching. This proposal was made in view of the reorganization and standardization plan being pursued by the government as an economy measure. See copy of resolution sent to Quezon in *Quezon Papers,* Box 172.

77. *Palma Autobiography,* p. 131; *16th Annual Report, UP President,* 1926-1927, pp. 10-11.

The Monroe Commission also recommended the establishment of a pension system and a general policy with reference to sabbatical leave. See *Monroe Commission Report,* p. 658. Palma recommended the adoption of a uniform vacation and leave of absence policy in his last report to the Board of Regents before resigning. See *Philippines Herald,* October 14, 1933, p. 14.

78. *13th Annual Report, UP President,* 1923-1924, p. 48.

79. *Palma Autobiography,* p. 132.

80. *15th Annual Report, UP President,* 1925-1926, pp. 10-11; *Palma Autobiography,* p. 132.

One of the research projects undertaken by scientists in the University was to demonstrate the use of coconut oil as motor fuel for diesel engines. See *New York Times,* October 11, 1931, III, p. 8.

81. Rafael Palma, "Research Work by the University," Radio Address, July 3, 1929, *PSSR* (August 1939), p. 336.

82. Palma, "The Promotion of the Intellectual Life of the Country," *loc. cit.,* p. 56.

83. Palma Inaugural Address, p. 70; see also *Philippines Herald,* editorial, April 8, 1928, p. 8.

84. In 1923, for instance, Palma tried to get the appointment of Major Vicente Lim to replace Capt. Chester A. Davis as Commandant and Professor of Military Science and Tactics, but the request was denied by Governor General Wood's office because the position should go to an "experienced officer." See Palma to Governor Wood, December 4, 1923; C.W. Franks (Secretary to the Governor General) to Palma, December 5, 1923; Quezon to Palma, March 7, 1924, in *Quezon Papers,* Box 172.

85. *Monroe Commission Report,* pp. 653-655; see also *Report of the Governor General,* 1923, pp. 10-11; 1924, p. 6; 1925, p. 7; 1926, pp. 10, 11.

Three-fourths of the teaching staff, from graduate assistants to instructors and professors, were UP graduates.

The faculty of the College of Medicine was composed entirely of Filipinos by academic year 1923-1924. There were 25 full-time and 27 part-time faculty members in the college. See *13th Annual Report, UP President,* 1923-1924, pp. 50-51.

From 1926, the School of Pharmacy (except in academic year 1927-1928), the School of Dentistry (except for AY 1927-1928), the College of Veterinary Science, and the School of Fine Arts had been Filipinized. In the College of Liberal Arts, the Departments of History, Political Science, Library Science, and Spanish had an all-Filipino staff in 1926. There were also as many Filipino heads of departments as there were foreigners. The Department of Military Science and Tactics had a Filipino head in 1932-1933–Fidel V. Segundo – and an all Filipino staff. The Department of Physical Education was all Filipino in 1930. See *UP Philippinensian,* 1926; *UP General Catalogue,* 1927-1928; 1929-1930; 1932-1933.

86. *19th Annual Report, UP President,* 1929-1930, pp. 6-7; *20th Annual Report, UP President,* 1930-1931, pp. 7-9.

87. Palma Inaugural Address, p. 61.

88. In 1925, the Board of Regents adopted a policy of keeping contract American teachers for at least three years. See *15th Annual Report, UP President,* 1925-1926, pp. 8-9.

89. For details of the Artamanoff case, see *Philippines Herald,* July 30, August 3, 4, 8, 9, 10, 11, 1929; *Tribune,* August 11, 1929; Minutes of the Board of Regents Meeting, August 8, 1929, p. 270.

I am indebted to Prof. Teodoro A. Agoncillo for generously allowing me the use of his notes on the Artamanoff case.

90. *Philippines Herald,* August 11, 1929, pp. 1, 10; *Tribune,* August 11, 1929, p. 12.

91. Nicholas Roosevelt, a cousin of President Theodore Roosevelt and editorial writer of the *New York Times,* was appointed by President Hoover as Vice-Governor to replace Eugene Gilmore. The Filipinos protested the appointment because, among other things, Roosevelt had consistently and publicly opposed Philippine Independence and had advocated a "treat 'em rough" policy in relation to the Filipinos. The Filipinos also had not forgotten Roosevelt's book – *The Philippines: A Treasure and A Problem* – published in 1926, where he had written contemptuously of the Filipino leadership and had cast scurrilous aspersions on the Filipinos as a race. In view of the Filipino opposition, including direct representation from Quezon himself, Roosevelt was prevailed upon to resign his appointment. See *Philippines Herald,* July 26, 31, 1930; Nicholas Roosevelt, "P" file, *BIA Records.*

92. See *Tribune,* October 1, 1930, p. 12; October 15, 1930, p. 1; Minutes of the Board of Regents Meeting, October 13, 1930, pp. 126, 141, 148.

I am again indebted to Prof. Agoncillo for allowing me to use his notes on the Moore case.

93. See *Philippines Herald,* December 16, 19, 23, 1932; also press release, *Sunday Tribune,* December 25, 1932; Speech before Commission on Independence, December 27, 1932, in *Quezon Papers,* Box 81.

94. See *El Debate,* December 28, 1932; also *Tribune,* December 28, 1932, p. 3; *Philippines Herald,* January 14; January 18, 1933, p. 4; *Graphic,* January 5, 1933; *Philippines Free Press,* January 23, 1933, p. 4.

95. *Philippines Herald,* January 18, p. 4; January 19, 1933, p. 1. For Quezon's letter to Palma, January 22, 1933, see *Philippines Herald,* January 24, 1933, p. 3. See also *Palma Autobiography,* pp. 138-139.

96. *Tribune,* January 21, 1933, p. 3.

Dean Jorge Bocobo refuted Palma's charges and asserted that the Legislature never sanctioned the Hare-Hawes-Cutting bill. See *ibid.*, January 22, 1933, p. 8.

97. *Ibid.*, January 31, 1933, pp. 1,2. See also *Philippines Herald,* February 11, March 11, 1933, for Quezon's other remarks on the bill.

98. *Ibid.*, January 24, p. 1; January 25, p. 3; January 27, pp. 1,2; February 17, 1933, p. 2. See also Guillermo B. Guevara, *Across Four Generations,* Manila: United Publishing Company, 1973, pp. 189-190.

99. The two deans, in fact, had been articulating their views on the independence bill even before their formal press debate opened. The press debate was arranged by Carlos P. Romulo. There would have been a public debate also, but that was cancelled. See *Philippines Herald,* December 20, 22, 24, 29, 1932; January 14, 21, 24, 25, 1933; *Philippines Free Press,* January 28, 1933, p. 34. The debates were published in the *Herald* on the following dates: January 21, pp. 1, 2; January 23, pp. 1,3; January 30, pp. 2,3; February 4, pp. 1, 5, 13; February 6, pp. 1, 12, 14; February 13, pp. 6, 7, 9; and February 15, 1933, pp. 1, 4, 14, 15, 16.

Dean Kalaw, in a letter to Quezon, assured the latter that there was nothing personal in his having taken a stand different from Quezon's. See letter, January 4, 1933 in *Quezon Papers,* Box 51.

100. *Philippines Free Press,* July 29, 1933.

101. *Philippine Magazine* editorial, March 1933, p. 447.

The *Tribune* editorial of February 10, 1933 commented on how the public may have been better informed on the bill through the articles published by the two deans.

102. *Philippines Herald,* February 1, p. 4; February 10, 1933, p. 4. For editorial more sympathetic to Palma, see "Let Not the UP Suffer," in *Tribune,* February 10, 1933, p. 4.

103. *Ibid.*, February 5, 1933, p. 9.

104. See Letter, Quezon to Palma, February 8, 1933, in *Philippines Herald,* February 8, 1933, p. 5; letter, Vidal Tan to Quezon, February 9, 1933, *Quezon Papers,* Box 172; see also *Philippine Collegian,* February 17, 1933, pp. 1, 2.

The Faculty Regent at this time was Vidal A. Tan, who apparently had not impressed some sectors of the UP faculty. An unsigned letter to Quezon from "An Instructor; UP" considered abolishing the Faculty Regent a great blessing to all, except for Vidal Tan who "is losing no opportunity against you (Quezon) and your leadership, and is always praising Mr. Osmeña to the skies." The letter also accused Tan of using his position for personal aggrandizement. See letter in *Quezon Papers,* Box 172.

A strong protest against the bill abolishing the Faculty Regent was filed with the Governor General by members of the faculty. See *Philippines Herald,* February 4, 1933.

105. *Sunday Tribune,* February 5, 1933, pp. 1, 9; *Taliba,* February 6, 1933; *Manila Daily Bulletin,* February 7, 1933; *Philippines Herald,* February 6, p. 1; February 8, 9, 1933, p. 3.

106. *Ibid.*, February 6, 1933; *Tribune,* February 5, 1933, p. 1.

107. *Philippines Herald,* February 4, 1933.

The vote of confidence, Regent Vidal Tan explained to Quezon, had nothing to do with the stand of the UP President on the Hare-Hawes-Cutting law. The University Council believed that the University would be hurt by Palma's resignation. See *ibid.*, February 13, 1933.

108. See letter, Quezon to Palma, February 8, 1933, in *ibid.*, February 8, 1933, pp. 1, 5.

109. Letter, Palma to Quezon, February 9, 1933, *ibid.*, February 9, 1933, pp. 1, 4.

110. Letter, Quezon to Palma, February 10, 1933, *Quezon Papers,* Box 87. See also in *Philippines Herald,* February 11, 1933, p. 3.

111. *Ibid.*, February 11, 1933, pp. 1, 14.

112. *Ibid.*, February 13, 1933, p. 3.

113. Letter, personal and confidential, Quezon to Palma, February 16, 1933, *Quezon Papers,* Box 87.

114. *Philippines Herald,* February 18, 1933, pp. 1, 14; *Tribune,* February 19, 1933, p. 5; *La Vanguardia,* February 20, 1933.

115. *Philippines Herald,* June 3, pp. 1, 12; June 5, pp. 1, 3, 4; June 6, 1933, p. 1.

Among the members of the League were Representatives Pedro Sabido and Emiliano Tria Tirona, Resident Commissioner Camilo Osias, Speaker Manuel Roxas, and Senators Sergio Osmeña and Ruperto Montinola.

116. *Ibid.*, July 1, 1933, pp. 1, 12; *Tribune,* July 2, 1933, p. 5; *Philippine Magazine,* August 1933, p. 84.

117. *Philippines Herald,* July 27, 1933, p. 4.

118. Among those who addressed the UP students were Osmeña. Roxas, Quintin Paredes, and Romulo. See *ibid.*, June 14, p. 1; June 19; July 12, p. 3; July 19, 1933, pp. 1, 12.

Quezon was scheduled to speak at a UP Convocation on July 11, but Paredes spoke instead. Quezon declined another invitation to speak at a UP Convocation "until such time as in my opinion, my presence in the University will not be understood as, or have the effect of, adding fuel to the fire already kindled and fanned by deliberate or unconscious acts of certain officials of the University." See *Philippine Collegian,* July 7, 1933, pp. 1, 7; also letter, Quezon to Melquiades Gamboa, Chairman, Convocations Committee, July 25, 1933, *Quezon Papers,* Box 172.

Quezon spoke at the Metropolitan Theater at a rally sponsored by the Anti-H-H-C Student Federation, having agreed to speak only if the rally would not be held at the UP Campus. See *Philippines Herald,* August 25, 1933, pp. 1, 2.

119. See *Philippine Collegian,* July 28, 1933, pp. 1, 2; *El Debate,* July 28, 1933; *Philippines Herald,* September 5, 1933, pp. 1, 13. There are also pertinent documents in *Quezon Papers,* Box 172. They include the July 22 Resolution of the Anti-H-H-C Student Federation Protesting Against the Use of the Philippine Collegian as a Tool of Pro-Hare-Hawes-Cutting Propaganda in the University of the Philippines; Letter, Palma to Miss Josefina Soriano, Secretary, Anti-H-H-C Student Federation, July 27, 1933; and Memorandum to Students and Faculty Members, UP, July 29, 1933, Regarding Participation of Students, in the Name of the University, in Controversial Activities that May Unfavorably Affect the Welfare of the Institution.

The Executive Committee of the University Council ruled that "students of UP are and should be free to express their views and sympathies on any public question, subject, however, to certain self-evident and well-established limitations." Students may not appear in political demonstrations as representing the institution.

The above ruling was adopted after the directors of the UP Alumni Association addressed a letter to President Palma suggesting that a meeting be called to discuss whether or not the interests of the University demanded that students be prevented from participating in controversial activities in the name of the University. This must have been a reaction to the

UP students' participation in the parade hailing Roxas as a hero after he was ousted from his position as Speaker in the reorganized Legislature.

Asked why he allowed his students to participate in this parade, Bocobo replied: "Because I wanted to show that I am more liberal than President Palma."

See *Philippines Herald,* July 15, pp. 1, 3; July 22, pp. 1, 12; July 28, pp. 1, 12; and July 29, 1933, pp. 1, 15; also *Philippines Free Press,* July 29, 1933.

120. See Quezon's speeches. July 20, 21, 22, 1933, in *Monday Mail,* July 24, 1933; also in *Diario de Sesiones de la Legislatura Filipina,* 9th Philippine Legislature, 3rd session, Vol. VIII, No. 2, pp. 12-14; No. 3, pp. 51-54; No. 4, pp. 56-59. Also *Philippines Free Press,* July 29, 1933, pp. 5, 37-39.

121. *Philippines Herald,* July 21, 1933, pp. 1, 13.

122. *Ibid.,* July 22, 1933, pp. 1, 12.

123. *Tribune,* July 22, 1933, p. 4.

124. Jose Clarin was elected President Pro-Tempore of the Senate; Elpidio Quirino became Senate Majority Floor Leader; and Jose Zulueta became House Majority Floor Leader.

125. Palma was particularly criticized for the "magnificent building" of the Conservatory of Music (it was also referred to as an "imposing mausoleum"), when there was need really for an Armory which at the time was housed in a "veritable barn." See *Philippines Herald,* June 8, 1933, p. 4.

See article "Fruitful History of UP Conservatory of Music Reason Enough for Continuance," by Raymundo C. Banas, Music Teacher, in answer to those who would wish it closed, in *ibid.,* September 23, 1933, p. 7.

There appeared a rather facetious article in the *Philippines Herald,* when the Conservatory started to offer a ballet dancing course. See *ibid.,* September 14, 1933, pp. 1, 3.

It was estimated that the UP had spent ₱4,225,742 for buildings and improvements from 1918 to 1932. See *ibid.,* August 19, 1933, p. 12.

126. See *Palma Autobiography,* p. 140; *Philippines Herald,* editorial, July 14, p. 4; editorial, July, 27, p. 4; August 8, pp. 1, 12; August 9, pp. 1, 13; editorial, August 17, p. 4; September 5, pp. 1, 13; September 7, pp. 1, 16; September 8, p. 8; September 30, 1933, p. 14.

Representative Guillermo A. Villanueva, Negros Oriental, had written to Dean Bocobo that he would bat for Palma's resignation in his speech in the Legislature. Bocobo presumably wrote Villanueva not to push through with his demand for Palma's resignation. See *Taliba,* August 15, 1933.

Vicente Bautista, President of the Municipal Board, also called for the resignation of Palma, faulting him for "weakness of character and lack of firm impartiality." See *Philippines Herald,* September 7, 1933, p. 13.

127. *Ibid.,* July 14, 1933, editorial, p. 4; see also an earlier editorial, June 8, 1933, p. 4.

128. *Ibid.,* August 8, 1933, pp. 1, 12.

129. *Ibid.,* August 9, 1933, pp. 1, 13.

130. *Ibid.,* August 11, pp. 1, 14; August 12, 1933, p. 2.

131. *Ibid.*, August 10, p.12; August 11, pp. 1, 14; August 15, p. 11; August 19, 1933, p. 2. See Resolution of the UP Alumni Association, August 15, 1933, in *Quezon Papers*, Box 172.

132. *Philippines Herald*, August 12, p. 4; September 7, pp. 1, 16; editorial, September 30, p. 6; October 18, 1933, p. 16.

133. *Ibid.*, August 16, 1933, pp. 1, 13; see letter, Quezon to Vargas, August 16, 1933, in *Quezon Papers*, Box 172.

134. Palma was present at this meeting – he came a little bit late and left soon after the meeting ended. See *Philippines Herald*, August 24, 1933, pp. 1, 14.

Quezon was provided, upon his request, with a detailed and lengthy memorandum on the matter of the salaries and financial support of the University. The memorandum was prepared by Regent Arturo Garcia and was transmitted to Quezon on August 25, 1933. See in *Quezon Papers*, Box 172.

135. See *Philippines Herald*, August 19, pp. 1, 12; August 24, 1933, pp. 1, 14.

136. *Ibid.*, August 31, 1933, pp. 1, 14; see also September 1, pp. 1, 2; September 4, pp. 1, 16; September 5, pp. 1, 13; September 6, pp. 1, 15; September 12, p. 12; September 28, 1933, p. 15.

137. *Palma Autobiography*, p. 140; *Philippines Herald*, September 23, 1933, p. 13.

Like the College of Education students, those from the College of Agriculture also protested not only the imposition of tuition fees but also the limiting of enrolment in the college to 300 students. The order for collection of fees apparently came after the start of the semester and so the students were protesting that they had not been informed ahead of time that they were supposed to pay such fees. The Board of Regents decided to condone payment of fees for the first semester but fined Dean Bienvenido Gonzalez for failure to implement the directive from Manila. See *ibid.*, August 1, pp. 1, 13; August 2, pp. 1, 14; August 2, p. 12; August 5, pp. 1, 12; August 11, p. 2; September 13, pp. 3, 15; October 19, 1933, pp. 1, 12; also *Tribune*, August 23, p. 4; October 27, 1933, p. 8; *La Vanguardia*, August 3, 1933. See Letter, Gonzalez to Palma, September 5, 1932, opposing the levying of tuition fees in the College of Agriculture, in *Quezon Papers*, Box 172.

138. See *supra*, pp. 184-185.

139. *Philippines Herald*, September 14, 1933, p. 3.

140. *Ibid.*

141. *Ibid.*, p. 6.

142. *Ibid.*, September 29, pp. 1, 14; September 30, pp. 1, 14; October 14, pp. 1, 5; November 8, 1933, p. 1; *Mabuhay*, October 15, 1933.

143. *Sunday Tribune*, October 29, 1933, p. 1; *Philippine Collegian*, November 3, p. 1, November 10, 1933, p. 2.

144. *Ibid.*, November 3, 1933, p. 1.

145. *Philippines Herald*, November 4, 1933, pp. 1, 15.

146. *Manila Daily Bulletin*, November 9, 1933; *Taliba*, November 9, 1933; *Philippines Herald*, November 10, 1933, pp. 1, 2. The other nominee was Dean Francisco Benitez.

Acting Insular Auditor Jaime Hernandez disapproved the proposed honorarium of ₱16,000 for Palma, explaining that if the Board of Regents wanted to give Palma some kind of remuneration for his services, it could pass a resolution giving him a year's leave of absence with pay. That was what the BOR did. See *Philippines Herald,* November 16, pp. 1, 3; November 21, p. 5; December 14, 1933, p. 3.

147. *Tribune,* November 9, 1933, p. 4; see also editorial, *La Vanguardia,* November 18, 1933.

Palma, Dean Francisco Benitez, Vicente Sinco (legal counsellor), and Juan Quintos (Comptroller) wanted Secretary Abeto to reconsider his opinion on the Palma gratuity. UP professors in general also wanted the matter clarified as to whether they were entitled to gratuity under the law. They cited as precedents the case of Professors Teodoro and Reyes who retired with the approval of the Cabinet. See *Philippines Herald,* November 10, 1933, p. 3; *Tribune,* November 16, 1933.

Bocobo, on the other hand, backed Abeto's ruling on the Palma case. See *Philippines Herald.* November 11, 1933, p. 2.

148. See *La Opinion,* November 9, December 20, 1933; *La Vanguardia,* November 9, 1933.

149. *Mabuhay,* December 19, 1933.

Mabuhay was part of the *Debate-Mabuhay-Herald-Monday Mail* chain (D-M-H-M), which, on August 15, 1933, came under the management of Carlos P. Romulo, who became its vice-president and publisher.

150. *Philippines Herald,* October 18, p. 16; November 11, 1933, p. 8.

151. *Tribune,* December 23, 1933, p. 4.

152. *Philippines Herald,* December 16, 1933; pp. 1, 14.

153. *Ibid.,* December 20, 1933, pp. 2, 4; *El Debate,* December 20, 1933.

154. The entire student body presented Palma with a resolution of appreciation for "his work and his democratic attitude towards the students." See *Philippine Collegian,* November 17, 1933.

155. *Mabuhay,* December 30, 1933.

The view from Washington was that Rafael Palma was forced out of the presidency of the University because of his opposition to the reorganization policies of Manuel L. Quezon. See Memorandum for the Secretary of War from General Creed Cox, Chief, Bureau of Insular Affairs, August 22, 1934, in *BIA Records* 21553-38.

Palma donated to the UP Library 1,000 volumes on political science, sociology, and Filipiniana, including papers and letters upon his departure from the University. See *Philippines Herald,* November 11, 1933, p. 1.

Palma returned to the University on December 17, 1938 when he was conferred the Doctor of Laws, *honoris causa.* A few months later, on May 24, 1939, he died.

156. *Mabuhay,* January 3, 1934; *Tribune,* January 10, 1934, pp. 1, 2.

157. *Philippines Herald,* February 24, pp. 1, 5; June 8, p. 4; September 8, 1933, p. 8.

158. *Ibid.,* October 10, pp. 1, 15; October 12, p. 7; October 28, p. 14; December 20, 1933, p. 4.

159. The "Young Philippines" was a civic organization for young people, supposed to be non-partisan, organized by Manuel Roxas, and counted among its supporters Rafael Palma, Maximo Kalaw, Jose P. Laurel, and student leaders Arturo Tolentino and Wenceslao Vinzons. See *Tribune,* January 7, p. 28; January 9, 1934, p. 16.

160. Report of Dr. Fernando Calderon as Acting President, January 1, 1934-August 31, 1934, pp. 24-26.

161. Palma Inaugural Address, p. 71.

162. *Ibid.*, p. 72.

163. Palma, "The University and the People," *loc. cit.*, p. 321. See also Palma Memorandum to the Board of Regents, July 14, 1932, in Minutes of the Board of Regents Meeting, July 15, 1932, pp. 194-195.

Palma zealously guarded the University from outside interference to the extent that he opposed an act of the Legislature, passed during his absence and while Bocobo was acting President, which would require the President to issue rules and regulations for the use of uniforms in UP. This measure was passed ostensibly to curb the extravagance in dressing of some students, and applied to public schools as well. See *17th Annual Report, UP President*, 1927-1928, p. 10.

164. Rafael Palma, "Academic Freedom," *PSSR* V; 4 (October 1933), pp. 231-237. The University Council laid down its policies on academic freedom in 1925. See Annex C.

Rafael Palma and Conrado Benitez, both members of the Constitutional Convention, felt the need for inserting a provision in the Constitution of 1935 to safeguard academic freedom in state universities. The provision is found in Article XIV, General Provisions, Section 4; "Universities established by the State shall enjoy academic freedom." See in E. Arsenio Manuel, *Dictionary of Philippine Biography*, II, Quezon City: Filipiniana Publications, 1970, p. 136.

165. Prof. Agoncillo told me that Palma's speeches were rendered from Spanish to English by Prof. Maria Agoncillo of the English Department.

166. Palma Inaugural Address, p. 71.

167. *Ibid.*, p. 68.

168. Palma, "The University and the People," *loc. cit.*, p. 321.

169. Palma Inaugural Address, p. 70.

170. *Ibid.*, p. 65; also Palma, "Our Country," *loc. cit.*, pp. 284-291.

When Dean Jorge Bocobo became acting President, from April 22, 1927 to February 8, 1928, during Palma's visit to American and European universities, Bocobo pursued the Filipinism theme of Palma. Realizing the need for students to study and learn traditional songs and dances, Bocobo sent Miss Francisca Reyes, Assistant Physical Education Director, to the provinces to study these traditional art forms. These dances were then taught to students who performed during the National Heroes Day Celebration in 1927. As part of the celebration for that national holiday, a literary contest was held annually and prizes were awarded to the best journalistic writings dealing with anyone of the national heroes.

As the beginning of the Christmas tradition in UP, a Christmas program was held on December 19, 1927 as part of student activities for the season. The campus was decorated with flags and lanterns, and a 30-foot pine tree stood in front of the grandstand.

See *17th Annual Report, UP President*, 1927-1928, pp. 7-8.

171. Palma Inaugural Address, pp. 58, 65, 70.

172. Virginia Palma Bonifacio, "A Design for the Filipino Family," paper read at the celebration of the centenary of the birth of Dr. Rafael Palma, October 24, 1974, at the National Library Auditorium, held under the auspices of the National Historical Commission.

To a grandson who had at one time asked that he and his grandfather use the university car, Palma admonished that a public office was a sacred trust. "Don't use the University car. It belongs to the Filipino people." See Benedicto Palma Bonifacio, "I Remember Lolo Apeng," paper read at the celebration of the centenary of the birth of Dr. Rafael Palma, October 24, 1974, at the National Library Auditorium.

I am indebted to Renato Perdon of the National Historical Institute for providing me with copies of the papers read during the Palma centenary symposium in 1974.

173. Palma Inaugural Address, p. 72.

BIBLIOGRAPHIC NOTE

On the occasion of Palma's first centenary in 1974, a bio-bibliography compiled by the University of the Philippines Library listed 266 items, covering all printed and manuscript materials on Rafael Palma's life (1874-1939).

For the ten years of Palma's Presidency of the University, the *Palma Papers* in the University Archives are useful to a certain extent but the collection must be supplemented by other materials. Palma's *Annual Reports* are complete, except for the reports for 1931-1932 and 1932-1933. The Annual Reports highlight the important events of each academic year and provide statistical data as well on enrollment, graduates, faculty recruitment, fellowips, etc. The Minutes of the Meetings of the Board of Regents are also quite useful, and they supplement the Annual Reports, giving an account of how matters were decided upon during Board meetings.

There is also a clipping file in the collection, consisting of selected newspaper clippings of the Palma years. Newspaper files are quite indispensable in following developments in the University, as well as gauging public opinion of the University and its activities. The *Manila Times* (up to 1930), the *Manila Daily Bulletin*, the *Philippines Herald*, and the *Tribune*, along with a number of Spanish dailies, like *La Vanguardia*, *El Debate*, and *La Opinion* are useful sources as they usually contain articles on goings-on in the University. The Tagalog newspapers – *Taliba* and *Mabuhay* – are also useful. Of course, the *Philippine Collegian* is quite indispensable. Unfortunately, there are no indices to these newspapers and consulting them means going through every issue to locate that useful article on UP, not always found on the front page.

For manuscript sources, the *Quezon Papers* in the National Library has a number of relevant documents. Boxes 171 and 172 are University of the Philippines files. There are also some useful documents in Box 114, the Bureau of Education file. Some of Quezon's correspondence with Rafael Palma and Maximo Kalaw may be found in the Correspondence File, arranged alphabetically. There are also some useful letters in General Correspondence, arranged chronologically.

The *Bureau of Insular Affairs Records (BIA Records)*, National Archives, Washington, D.C., also contain some pertinent materials, but they are disappointingly slim for the University. There are four file numbers pertaining to the University: 1215 – general record; 22339 – employees; 25898 – College of Law; 27242 – College of Liberal Arts. Most of the records I saw, however, pertained to recruitment of contract faculty from the United States. The Personal Files ("P") of Rafael Palma, Maximo M. Kalaw, the Vice-Governors, and other people connected with the University yielded very little material related to the University. There are, however, many copies of the UP General Catalogue for several years.

The Monroe Educational Survey Commission (1925) devoted a chapter in its report to the University *(A Survey of the Educational System of the Philippine Islands,* Manila: Bureau of Printing, 1925). It is an objective assessment of the first seven years of the University's growth and development. *BIA Records* 3725 deal with the Monroe Commission Survey.

The *Annual Reports of the Governor General* usually contain a short section on the University of the Philippines, and include such matters as the extent of Filipinization in the University. buildings and improvements, and enrollment figures.

Of about 20 books written by Palma, majority of which were published posthumously, the following are useful for the Palma presidency: *Alma Mater* (Manila: Bureau of Printing, 1930); *Reminiscences* (Manila: Virginia Palma-Bonifacio, 1964); and *My Autobiography* (Manila: Capitol Publishing House, 1953). *Alma Mater* is a compilation of 76 addresses and lectures Palma delivered between 1924 and 1930 while he was President of the University. In *Reminiscenses,* Palma's eldest daughter translated into English several pieces from *Alma Mater. My Autobiography* was translated into English by another daughter, Alicia Palma-Bautista. It has one chapter on Palma's stint at the University, but the chapter did not include many details of his administration.

Several of Palma's speeches were published in a commemorative issue by the *Philippine Social Sciences Review* (PSSR), faculty organ of the University, several months after Palma's death. Among them were "The New Mentality," "The Revolt of Youth," "Understanding Our Age," "Our Country," "The Woman and the Right to Vote," "The University and the People," and "Our New University Library." The same journal also published his "The Promotion of the Intellectual Life of the Country," (January 1932) and "Academic Freedom," (October 1933). These speeches and articles embody the best thoughts of Palma. Some of these ideas were written up into an M.A. Thesis by Priscilla G. Valencia, "Educational Ideas of Rafael Palma," and submitted to the University in 1957.

There are two commemorative brochures on Palma – the first on the occasion of his inauguration as fourth President of the University. It contains speeches and addresses delivered on that occasion. The second is on his birth centenary in 1974 when the University sponsored a symposium on Palma, participated in by Armando J. Malay ("Would Rafael Palma Make a Successful UP President Today?"), Teodoro A. Agoncillo ("Rafael Palma: A Profile in Integrity and Courage"), Leopoldo Y. Yabes ("Rafael Palma as Liberal Thinker and Man of Letters"), and Salvador P. Lopez ("Palma and University Autonomy").

In 1974, a symposium was also held by the National Historical Commission (now National Historical Institute) in honor of Palma's birth centenary. Among those who delivered papers on Palma were Teodoro A. Agoncillo ("Rafael Palma: A Profile in Integrity and Courage"), Encarnacion Alzona ("Rafael Palma, Escritor"), Eva Estrada-Kalaw ("Rafael Palma – Educator by Example"), Gregorio F. Zaide ("Rafael Palma as Scholar and Historian"), Virginia Palma-Bonifacio ("A Design for the Filipino Family"), and Benedicto Palma Bonifacio ("I Remember Lolo Apeng").

There are also two papers which have been delivered by Prof. Agoncillo on two occasions: "The Old UP Revisited" was delivered in September 1979 to celebrate History Week and the 69th anniversary of the Department of History, UP; and "Rafael Palma and the Contemporary Educational System," was read in October 1981 to commemorate the birth anniversary of Palma at a program held under the auspices of the National Historical Institute.

Finally, there are a few contemporary accounts which I expected would go into some detail on the Quezon-Palma controversy. Unfortunately they mention very little of it. These include Carlos Quirino, *Quezon, Paladin of Philippine Freedom* (Manila: Filipiniana Book Guild, 1971); Teodoro M. Kalaw, *Aide-de-Camp to Freedom* (Manila: Teodoro M. Kalaw Society, Inc., 1965); Vicente Albano Pacis *(President Sergio Osmeña, A Fully Documented Biography,* II (Quezon City: Phoenix Press, Inc., 1971); and Guillermo Guevara, *Across Four Generations* (Manila: United Publishing Company, 1973). Quezon does not even mention it in *The Good Fight* (New York: D. Appleton-Century Company, 1946).

CHAPTER IV—ANNEX A

GROWTH OF THE UNIVERSITY

Years	Enrolment	Graduates*
1911-1912	1400	48
1912-1913	1398	50
1913-1914	1502	149
1914-1915	2075	222
1915-1916	2401	306
1916-1917	2975	387
1917-1918	3289	380
1918-1919	3312	532
1919-1920	3409	572
1920-1921	3838	517
1921-1922	4698	617
1922-1923	4839	679
1923-1924	5993	717
1924-1925	5540	710
1925-1926	5980	819
1926-1927	6464	867
1927-1928	7533	957
1928-1929	7498	1091
1029-1930	7828	1181
1930-1931	7924	1225
1931-1932	7597	962**

* Including High School
** High School Not Included

Sources: *Monroe Commission Report,* p. 616.
Annual Reports, UP President, 1923-1931
BIA Records 1215-96
UP Golden Jubilee Alumni Directory, Part A. 1908-1958

CHAPTER IV—ANNEX B

POLICIES ON ACADEMIC TENURE

1. The precise terms and expectations of every appointment should be stated in writing and be in the possession of both college and teacher.

2. Termination of a short-term appointment should always be possible at the expiration of the term by the mere act of giving timely notice of the desire to terminate. The decision to terminate should always be taken, however, in conference with the departmental council. It is desirable that the question of appointments for the ensuing year be taken up as early as possible. Notice of the decision to terminate should be given in ample time to allow the teacher an opportunity to secure a new position. The extreme limit for such notice should not be less than three months before the expiration of the academic year. The teacher who proposes to withdraw should also give notice in ample time to enable the institution to make a new appointment.

3. It is desirable that termination of a permanent or long-term appointment for cause should regularly require action by both a faculty committee and the governing board of the college. Exceptions to this rule may be necessary in cases of gross immorality or treason, when the facts are admitted. In such cases where other offenses are charged, and in all cases where the facts are in dispute, the accused teacher should always have the opportunity to face his accusers, and to be heard in his own defense by all bodies that pass judgment upon the case. In the trial of charge of professional incompetence, the testimony of scholars in the same field, either from his own or from other institutions, should always be taken. Dismissal for other reasons than immorality or treason should not ordinarily take effect in less than a year from the time that the decision is reached.

4. Termination of permanent or long-term appointments because of financial exigencies should be sought only as a last resort, after every effort has been made to meet the need in other ways and to find for the teacher other employment in the institution. Situations which make drastic retrenchment of this sort necessary should preclude expansions of the staff at other points at the same time, except in extraordinary circumstances.

Source: *15th Annual Report, UP President,* 1925-1926, pp. 14-15.

CHAPTER IV—ANNEX C

POLICIES ON ACADEMIC FREEDOM

1. A university or college may not place any restraint upon the teacher's freedom in investigation, unless restriction upon the amount of time devoted to it becomes necessary in order to prevent undue interference with teaching duties.

2. A university or college may not impose any limitation upon the teacher's freedom in the exposition of his own subject in the classroom or in addresses and publications outside the college, except insofar as the general necessity of adequating all instruction to the needs of immature students, or in the case of institutions of a denominational or partisan character, specific stipulations in advance, fully understood and accepted by both parties, limit the scope and character of instruction.

3. No teacher may claim as his right the privilege of discussing in his classroom controversial topics outside of his own field of study. The teacher is morally bound not to take advantage of his position by introducing into the classroom provocative discussions of irrelevant subjects not within the field of his study.

4. A university or college should recognize that the teacher in speaking or writing outside of the institution upon subjects beyond the scope of his own field of study is entitled to precisely the same freedom and is subject to the same responsibility as attaches to all other citizens. If the extramural utterances of the teacher should be such as to raise grave doubts concerning his fitness for his position, the question should in all cases be submitted to an appropriate committee of the faculty of which he is a member. It should be clearly understood that an institution assumes no responsibility for views expressed by members of its staff; and teachers should, when necessary, take pains to make it clear that they are expressing only their personal opinions.

Source: *15th Annual Report, UP President,* 1925-1926, p. 14.

NOTES ON CHAPTER V — "BOCOBO FOSTERS A VIBRANT NATIONALISM"

1. Celia Bocobo-Olivar, "Jorge C. Bocobo—His Life and Ideas as Educator and Jurist" (unpublished dissertation, College of Education, University of the Philippines), I, 324. A much too short, condensed version of this two-volume work has been published under the title *Aristocracy of the Mind*, abridged and edited by Norma Occena Yabut (Quezon City: New Day Publishers, 1981). But for deficiency in documentation, Dr. Olivar's *opus*, in its unpublished form, is a fine source of details on Bocobo's life and career.

2. Leopoldo Y. Yabes, "First and Foremost: A History of the College of Law, University of the Philippines" (Quezon City: [U.P.] Law Center, College of Law, 1982), pp. 65 and 107. Professor Yabes, a retired University Professor, undertook this study upon the "invitation of Dean Froilan M. Bacungan" which was to have been published on the occasion of the Diamond Jubilee of the University in 1983. Between Palma's retirement and Bocobo's assumption of the presidency, Dean Fernando Calderon of Medicine served as Acting President. University of the Philippines. Office of the President, *Report of Dr. Fernando Calderon as Acting President, University of the Philippines, Covering the Period from January 1, 1934, to August 31, 1934* (Manila: University of the Philippines Press, n.d.).

3. *Cf.* Olivar, "Jorge C. Bocobo," I, 325. Although he was not with the university at the time of his election as president in 1951, Dr. Vidal A. Tan is not generally considered an "outsider" because he had been away from the university only since 1949, to accept the presidency of a private university. See the chapter on the Tan presidency in this volume.

4. *Ibid.*, I, 324, quoting [Palma], *Seventeenth Annual Report of the President of the University of the Philippines to the Board of Regents for the Academic Year 1927-1928* (Manila: Bureau of Printing, 1930).

5. Olivar, "Jorge C. Bocobo," I, 11.

6. *Ibid.*, I, 27-36. The *pensionado* program has been discussed in several works. Its genesis is treated briefly in Romeo V. Cruz, *America's Colonial Desk and the Philippines, 1898-1934* (Quezon City: University of the Philippines, 1974), pp. 86-88. I have also touched upon it in Chap. 5 of *The Filipino Reaction to American Rule, 1901-1913* ([Hamden, Conn:] The Shoe String Press, 1968; reprinted by New Day Publishers, Quezon City, 1984).

7. Yabes, "First and Foremost," p. 123.

8. Olivar, "Jorge C. Bocobo," I, 293-318, discusses Bocobo's 23 years as professor and law dean.

9. Yabes, "First and Foremost," p. 65. In his unpublished work, Prof. Yabes is rather derogatory to the Bocobo presidency, calling it "an interregnum of undistinguished presidency" and "less than efficient administration of the University" (p. 108). Taking into account appraisals of the Bocobo presidency, quoted copiously in the Olivar study, one is tempted to disagree partly with Prof. Yabes.

10. Yabes, "First and Foremost," 122-123.

11. *Philippines Herald*, August 15, 1934, as quoted in Olivar, "Jorge C. Bocobo," I, 325-327.

12. The procedure was hammered out during the August 8, 1934 meeting of the Board of Regents. See "Actions Taken by the Board of Regents in Connection with the Consideration of the Appointment of the President of the University of the Philippines during the Board's Meetings on June 22, July 11, and August 8, 1934," in Minutes of the 405th meeting of the Board of Regents, August 11, 1934, Exhibit "A". Bocobo was elected at this [i.e., 405th] meeting. Almost all the Minutes of the Board of Regents meetings during Pres. Bocobo's term are available in the Office of the University Secretary, thanks to former Dean Angel K. Gomez of Veterinary Medicine.

13. This does not mean, however, that Bocobo received the votes of all the members of the Board of Regents in the balloting(s) during the 405th (special) meeting.

The minutes of the meeting tell us, for instance, that "The whole proceedings of the Board at this special meeting, touching on the election of the permanent president of the University. . . . are, by resolution of the Regents, put in two sealed envelopes, one to be deposited in the archives of the University Library and the other in the archives of the National Library." It is probably nearer the truth when we say that he (Bocobo) had received only a majority (at least 6) of the votes after several ballotings, but was declared chosen "unanimously" by virtue of a rule in the procedure that "whoever receives a majority vote shall be declared *unanimously* elected." (Italics supplied). By contrast, Bocobo's successor was elected the very day Bocobo's resignation was accepted by the Board (April 20, 1939); there was no need to keep the proceedings in sealed envelopes because there was nothing to hide about the number of votes he (Gonzalez) had received: he was the only candidate. Incidentally, Quezon no less presided at the meeting which elected Bocobo's successor with such dispatch. Minutes of the 463rd meeting of the Board of Regents, April 20, 1939.

14. Yabes, "First and Foremost," p. 108.
    There was something "unusual" among the Board's actions in the election of Bocobo, and that was the Board of Regents' formally submitting a list of candidates, in alphabetical order, to the Board of Visitors, who were requested to "indicate their objections, if any, to any or all of the persons listed above. . . ." The Board did this because "it realized the interest of the Board [of Visitors] in this matter." This was via a communication to Governor General Frank Murphy, Chairman of the Board of Visitors, dated July 11, 1934, which would be returned to the Board, August 4, 1934, with the information that the Board of Visitors had met, and had "no objection to any of the persons within named." The letter and indorsement are given in "Actions Taken by the Board. . . ." (see note 12 above.) The Board of Visitors then consisted of the Governor General, the President of the Senate and the Speaker of the House of Representatives. Quezon was, of course, the Senate President. Showing lack of *delicadeza* Bocobo himself wrote Quezon twelve days before his election that the Board of Regents "can not act on the matter unless it is informed of the stand of the Board of Visitors." Bocobo to Quezon, July 31, 1934, Manuel L. Quezon Papers, National Library, Manila Subject File 1934-1941. The box is unnumbered.

15. *Philippines Herald*, August 13, 1934.

16. *Philippine Collegian*, August 17, 1934.

17. *Idem.*, August 31, 1934.

18. *Tribune*, August 14, 1934.

19. Josefina D. Constantino, "U.P. Through the Years: Praise, Disenchantment and Hope," *The 1969 U.P. Alumni Yearbook*, p. 14. As Sister Teresa, Miss Constantino is now the head of the Carmelite Order in the Philippines.

20. *Cf.* Leopoldo Y. Yabes, "The University of the Philippines in Perspective" in Consuelo V. Fonacier (Comp.) *The Role and Mission of the University: Inaugural Addresses of the Presidents of the University of the Philippines* (Quezon City: University of the Philippines, 1971), xiv.

21. As quoted in Olivar, "Jorge C. Bocobo," I, 48-49, from the Bocobo *Memoirs*, Jorge C. Bocobo Papers, University Archives, University of the Philippines, Diliman, Quezon City.

22. *Ibid.*, I, 65-66. Bocobo's daughter considers this incident as a "highlight of the first years of Bocobo's career."

23. See Bernardita Reyes Churchill, *The Philippine Independence Missions to the United States, 1919-1934* (Manila: National Historical Institute, 1983). Appendix A of Churchill's book lists the composition of the various missions, including the names of the technical advisers.

24. An undated letter to this effect is among the Bocobo Papers. This probably was during the 1923-1924 Roxas Special Mission, following the curtailment of government funds for such missions by Governor General Leonard Wood, on advice of the Auditor General.

25. The authority on this is Theodore Friend, *Between Two Empires: The Ordeal of the Philippines, 1929-1946* (New Haven, Conn.: Yale University Press, 1965). But see also Grayson L. Kirk, *Philippine Independence: Motives, Problems, and Prospects* (New York: Farrar and Rhinehart, 1936).

26. I have developed this theme in several papers, the latest being "The Contributions of Filipino Historians to the Development of Philippine Nationalism." (Elpidio Quirino Memorial Lecture, Sponsored by the Graduate School, University of Northern Philippines, Vigan, Ilocos Sur, March 8, 1985.)

27. See Teodoro A. Agoncillo and Oscar M. Alfonso, *A Short History of the Filipino People* (Quezon City: University of the Philippines, 1960), Chap. XIX. As indicated in the preface by the senior author, Dr. Alfonso wrote this chapter of the textbook.

28. Whether it was out of honest conviction that nothing was wrong with Wood and that Quezon and company were only out to embarrass Wood, or because of certain favors received from Wood or former Governor General W. Cameron Forbes (a close friend of Wood's), cannot be determined with definitiveness. Aguinaldo owed his Junior's appointment as West Point cadet to General Wood, while Forbes was instrumental in the admission of Aguinaldo's daughter (Justice Ameurfina M. Herrera's mother) to Radcliffe, as well as having provided or loaned cash whenever Emilio, Jr. needed money. And this, to Miss Aguinaldo's continuing discomfiture, came rather frequently. See miscellaneous correspondence in the W. Cameron Forbes Papers at the Houghton Library of Harvard University, Cambridge, Mass.

29. *A Nation in the Making: The Philippines and the United States, 1899-1921* (Cambridge, Mass.: Harvard University Press, 1973).

30. I have not been able to establish the precise date of the founding of Ang Bagong Katipunan. Teodoro M. Kalaw (*Aide-de-Camp to Freedom*, trans. Maria Kalaw Katigbak [Manila: Friends of Kalaw Society, 1965], page 232 and note 4), says it was "started" in 1930; Dr. Encarnacion Alzona ("History and National Solidarity" in *The PHA Balita* for June 1980, page 1), claims that it was "organized" in 1931; and Melchor P. Aquino ("Dwight F. Davis," *Bulletin of the American Historical Collection*, II, April 1974, page 9), asserts that it was "launched by Speaker Manuel A. Roxas" during the administration of Governor General Davis (1929-1932). The few documents on Ang Bagong Katipunan in the Manuel A. Roxas Papers at the National Library do not indicate *when* the ABK was founded, either. I have reproduced the Ang Bagong Katipunan's "Decalogue" or Code, in my Elpidio Quirino Memorial Lecture.

31. The Quezon Code of Citizenship may be read in Cresencio Peralta, "The Spirituo-Moral Revolution of Our Time," *Historical Bulletin* 18: 1-4 (January-December, 1974), 103-104.

32. Olivar, "Jorge C. Bocobo," I, 215.

33. *Philippines Herald*, August 13, 1934; Olivar, "Jorge C. Bocobo," I, 336-337. The 16-point program is reproduced as Annex A of this chapter.

34. "Presidential Inaugural Address," December 17, 1934, in Fonacier (comp.), *The Role and Mission of the University*, pp. 97-108.

35. "Address at the Opening Exercises of the University of the Philippines, June 8, 1936." I am indebted to Professor Yabes for copies of this and other addresses in their typescript form.

36. "Address at the U.P. Opening Exercises, June 7, 1937."

37. "Address... June 8, 1936."

38. "First and Foremost," p. 303, and his introduction to *The Role and Mission of the University*, xiv.

39. *Ibid.* See also Olivar, "Jorge C. Bocobo," I, 234-242.

40. "Transcript of the Meeting on Professor Leopoldo Y. Yabes' First and Foremost: History of the U.P. College of Law,' June 25, 1983," p. 52. *Cf.* Prof. Armando J. Malay's column in *Malaya*, June 12, 1984.

41. Minutes of the Third Meeting of the [Pond] Committee Appointed to Gather Data on a Possible New Site for the University of the Philippines, March 19, 1938, in Roxas Papers, Series IV, Box 47.

42. Olivar, "Jorge C. Bocobo," I, 372-373.

43. As reproduced in the Minutes of the 452nd meeting of the Board of Regents, July 29, 1938.

44. See pages 231 to 235.

45. See Annex A of this chapter, p. 647.

46. "Filipino Code of Ethics" (Address at the Opening Exercises for the second semester, University of the Philippines, October 24, 1938).

47. Olivar, "Jorge C. Bocobo," I, 386.

48. *Ibid.*

49. *Ibid.*, p. 390.

50. University of the Philippines, Board of Regents Committee on Educational Policy, *Report on A Survey of the University of the Philippines by the Committee on Educational Policy, Board of Regents, University of the Philippines* (Manila: University of the Philippines, 1939), p. 40 (hereafter *Survey Report).* For Bocobo's having prepared the draft of the *Survey Report*, see his letter to Regent Roxas, January 16, 1939, transmitting the 116-page manuscript, Roxas Papers, Box 47.

51. *Ibid.*

52. *Report, June 1, 1935—May 31, 1936*, p. 17..For the visiting scholars, see *Report* for 1934-1935

53. As quoted by columnist Salvador P. Lopez in the *Philippines Herald*, October 7, 1935. Commented the future diplomat and UP President on the President's behavior: "I could not believe... that the president of a great university, whose principal contribution to higher education in this country are his rules on courtesy, could so embarrass a guest speaker at an open forum in his university."

54. See section on promotion of culture in this chapter.

55. Olivar, "Jorge C. Bocobo," I, 309.

56. *Ibid.*

57. *Souvenir Program National Heroes Day*, Manila, University of the Philippines, 1935, as quoted in *ibid.*, I, 319-320.

58. *Ibid.* The Oblation was designed by Guillermo Tolentino of the UP College of Fine Arts.

59. *Ibid.*

60. Leopoldo Y. Yabes, "Pres. Bocobo—An Appreciation." *Philippine Collegian*, August 31, 1934 , p. 4.

61. "Report of the Acting President to the Board of Regents, January 10, 1928," in *Seventeenth Annual Report..., 1927-1928*, Appendix A.

62. See Annex A of this chapter. This is point 5.

63. As quoted or reported in the *Philippine Collegian*, September 7, 1934.

64. *Report to the Board of Regents for the Academic Year 1934-1935*, p. 12.

65. *Ibid.*

66. *Report, 1935-1936*, pp. 14-15.

67. See the Bocobo annual reports through 1938.

    The Committee reiterated the recommendation in its report to President Bienvenido M. Gonzalez in *Twenty-Eighth Annual Report of the President of the University of the Philippines to the Board of Regents for the Academic Year June 1, 1938—May 31, 1939* (Manila: University of the Philippines, 1940), p. 15. Since Gonzalez took over only on April 21, 1939, almost all activities covered in the report still pertained to Bocobo's last year as president.

68. *Report, 1934-1935*, p. 2.

69. *Report, 1935-1936*, p. 2.

70. See his address on September 1, 1934, already referred to, and quoted in *Report, 1934-1935*, pp. 4-5.

71. The present writer took the course in public speaking (then English 38) under Prof. O'Connor-Pablo, a very charming, but rather portly lady then (Summer, 1949). Among his classmates was Jaime M. Alfonso, now a Brigadier General of the AFP, whose class speech—actually an oration—was on Doña Aurora Quezon who had just been killed (April 28, 1949) at an HMB ambuscade in Bongabon, Nueva Ecija.

72. See the *Reports* for 1934-1935 (pp. 4-5), 1935-1936 (p. 5), 1936-37 (pp. 4-5), and 1937-38 (p. 5).

73. *Report, 1935-1936*, p. 5.

74. *Report, 1936-1937*, p. 4.

Dr. Santos later became Registrar of the University, retiring as such in 1953. During the presidency of Dr. Gonzalez, he was dubbed the "Little President"—maybe because he was very close to the latter. A short, gentle-looking, amiable and kindly man, Dr. Santos had a surprisingly different image as a professor—he was a "terror" and hardly gave a grade higher than a "2.0". The present writer took two courses under him in modern European political and diplomatic history.

75. In his brief message to the students upon his election as president, Bocobo said that with his greetings "goes an avowal of my deep-seated conviction that faculty-student cooperation is the safest mooring on which every university can and should be anchored," and that it was his "bounded duty to foster" such a spirit. *Philippine Collegian*, August 17, 1934.

76. Minutes of the 135th meeting of the University Council, February 20, 1937.

77. *Twenty-Eighth Annual Report, 1938-1939*, p. 13.

78. *Report, 1936-1937*, p. 4.

79. *Report, 1937-1938*, p. 15, and *Twenty-Eighth Annual Report, 1938-1939*, p. 13.

80. *Report, 1934-1935*, p. 8.

81. *Report, 1936-1937*, p. 6, and *Report, 1937-1938*, p. 6.

82. *Report, 1935-1936*, pp. 7-8.

83. Olivar, "Jorge C. Bocobo," I, 355-356.

84. Felix Roxas, *The World of Felix Roxas: Anecdotes and Reminiscences of a Manila Newspaper Columnist, 1926-1936*, trans. Angel Estrada and Vicente del Carmen (Manila: The Filipiniana Book Guild, 1970), p. 349. As mayor of the city of Manila, Roxas had tried to help the School of Fine Arts of the University then on R. Hidalgo St.

85. *Report, 1937-1938*, p. 8.

86. *Report, 1937-1938*, pp. 6-7; *Twenty-Eighth Annual Report, 1938-1939*, pp. 6-8.

87. *Report, 1936-1937*, p. 7, and *Report, 1937-1938*, p. 7.

88. This was mainly with Japanese organizations or societies.

89. The above information was taken from *Report, 1934-1935*, pp. 6-7.

90. U.P. President's Committee on Courtesy, *Courtesy Appeals by the President's Committee on Courtesy, University of the Philippines*, Bulletin No. 2 (Manila: University of the Philippines Press, 1936). This was re-issued in 1937.

91. U.P. President's Committee on Courtesy, *Encarecimientos sobre la cortesia* (Manila: Universidad de Filipinas, 1938).

92. *Report, 1936-1937*, p. 5.

93. *Report, 1934-1935*, p. 7.

94. See the "Albert Discourtesy Case" this chapter.

95. Minutes of the 382nd Meeting of the Executive Committee of the University Council, University of the Philippines, August 5, 1938. Bound volume in Office of the Registrar, U.P. Diliman, Vol. V (June 4, 1937—March 27, 1940). The "Tentative Rules of Discipline," numbering eight, are in Appendix "C" of the Minutes.

96. *Ibid.*

97. Minutes of the 383rd Meeting of the Executive Committee, August 16, 1938, *loc. cit.*

98. *Twenty-Eighth Annual Report, 1938-1939*, p. 5. Based on this report [by Gonzalez] which covers the period June 1, 1938—May 31, 1939, the "Tentative Rules of Discipline" did not go into effect during the remaining months of Bocobo's presidency or even the first forty days of the Gonzalez presidency.

99. Louis Fisher, *A History of Europe*, 2 Vols. (London: Collins, 1935), I, vii.

100. *Report, 1934-1935*, pp. 7-9.

101. *Report, 1935-1936*, pp. 6-7.

102. *Report, 1934-1935*, pp. 7-9.

103. *Report, 1935-1936*, pp. 6-7.

104. *Report, 1936-1937*, pp. 5-6.

105. *Report, 1937-1938*, p. 5.

106. *Twenty-Eighth Annual Report, 1938-1939*, pp. 5-8.

107. *The Tribune*, February 9, 1939, as quoted in Olivar, "Jorge C. Bocobo," I, 379.

108. *Report, 1934-1935*, p. 6. *Cf. Philippine Collegian*, September 28, 1934.

109. In 1936-1937, the Executive Committee of the University Council adopted a resolution requiring each faculty member to "devote at least one consultation hour every day in his office. . . ." *Report, 1936-1937*, p. 28. Today, members of the faculty are supposed to allocate at least two hours a day (Monday to Friday) or ten hours per week for consultation with students.

110. *Report, 1937-1938*, p. 4.

111. *Report, 1936-1937*, p. 28.

112. *Report, 1934-1935*, p. 16. The year mentioned in the report—"1934"—is incorrect, obviously a printing error.

113. *Report, 1935-1936*, p. 18.

114. *Report, 1936-1937*, p. 22.

115. *Report, 1937-1938*, p. 24.

116. *Report, 1936-1937*, p. 15.

117. *Report, 1937-1938*, pp. 15-16.

118. *Report, 1934-1935*, p. 3.

119. This amplified version of the objectives of the "first" reform is given in *Report, 1937-1938*, p. 2.

120. *Report, 1934-1935*, p. 3.

121. See the Committee's report in *Bulletin of the President's Committee for the Improvement of Teaching in the University of the Philippines*, Vol. I, No. I, July 1935. This came out monthly, normally, but at times a joint issue was published.

122. I have not been able to find out the exact date or dates Dr. Paterno Santos and Prof. Cristino Jamias were appointed to the Committee. The *Bulletin*. . . *for the Improvement of Teaching*, however, lists them as members of the Committee for the first time in its August-September 1936 issue.

123. Three of the papers published in this maiden issue were "Teaching Methods," by Prof. Aurora F. Cole of the English Department, College of Agriculture; "A Brief Report on the 'Workshop Method' in Modern European History," by Dr. Paterno Santos of the Department of History, College of Liberal Arts; and "A Class Experiment," by Dr. I. Panlasigui of the College of Edu-

cation and Chairman of the Committee on Teaching. An interesting and unique piece, "A Course in Oral English" by Dean E.R. Hyde of the College of Engineering, appeared in the July 1936 (pp. 1-7) issue of the *Bulletin*.

124. *Report, 1935-1936*, pp. 2-3. The proceedings and pre-conference materials are available in a volume compiled by Dr. I. Panlasigui, and entitled: "Record of the First Faculty Conference, Baguio, May 11-16, 1936." Typescript.

125. *Ibid.*

126. See I. Panlasigui, "The Fourth Annual Baguio Conference, April 12-20, 1939," in *Bulletin... for the Improvement of Teaching*, Vol. V, No. 1 (August 1939), pp. 17-28.

127. These were taken from "Record of the First Faculty Conference, Baguio," pp. 1-4, *passim*.

128. *Ibid.* pp. 3-4. When asked what he meant by "scholars," Dr. Gomez said that he had in mind "philosophers, scholastics, theologists" *[sic.]*.

129. *Ibid.*, pp. 11-13.

130. Panlasigui, "The Fourth Annual Baguio Conference," pp. 86-89.

131. *Ibid.*, p. 88.

132. As previously mentioned, the monthly faculty conferences sponsored by the Committee on Teaching were open to all faculty members. The Annual Summer Conference in Baguio, on the other hand, was attended only by those recommended by their respective Deans or Directors. Thus, in 1936, only 47 attended; in 1937, the attendance was 42; in 1938, it was 65. See the *Reports* for 1935-1936, 1936-1937, and 1937-1938. For the April 1939 Conference, the last under Bocobo, 115 were recommended by their respective Deans and Directors, but only 68 acually registered as delegates. See Panlasigui, "The Fourth Annual Baguio Conference," p. 77.

133. "From the Gallery," *Philippine Collegian*, January 28, 1935.

134. *Report 1934-1935*, pp. 10-11.

135. Another "Fonacierism": "The late Father John Delaney, S.J., and I have one thing in common—belief in and love for the spirit," i.e., liquor. The present writer, who had studied under the late Regent Fonacier in the early fifties and worked closely with him as an elected member of the UP Alumni Association Board of Directors from 1969 to 1975, deeply regrets not having taken an "oral history" of the University from the grand old man before he was felled by a stroke in 1978 and eventually passed away in 1982.

136. See Minutes of the 412th meeting of the Board of Regents, February 21, 1935, *Report, 1934-1935*, pp. 10-11.

137. *Ibid.*

138. *Ibid.*

139. Minutes of 418th meeting of the Board of Regents, August 14, 1935.

140. *Report, 1935-1936*, p. 10 and *Report, 1936-1937*, p. 11, respectively.

141. *Report, 1934-1935*, p. 11.

142. *Report, 1936-1937*, p. 43.

143. See Annex A of this chapter.

144. *Report, 1934-1935*, pp. 19-20.

145. *Report, 1935-1936*, p. 21.

146. *Report, 1936-1937*, pp. 26-27.

147. As quoted in Minutes of 419th meeting of the Board of Regents, September 18, 1935. Italics added. Quezon replied *(loc. cit.)* that any increase in the appropriations for the university would have to await the inauguration of the Commonwealth, "when our general program and policy of public instruction may be fully considered. . . ."

148. See the Minutes of the Executive Committee meetings during his presidency.

149. Olivar, *Aristocracy of the Mind*, pp. 38-39.

150. I have found no official, public records of the University on the incident other than the Minutes of the 452nd meeting of the Board of Regents on July 29, 1938.

151. *Tribune*, July 30, 1938.

152. Having extracted from Prof. Albert a letter of apology "for having answered [President Quezon] so rashly," Bocobo would immediately issue a statement to the press that "Prof. Albert has not tendered his resignation." This turned out to be premature. Bocobo's statement appeared in the *Philippines Herald*, July 29, 1938.

153. These few details on Prof. Albert are in *ibid.* See also the *U.P. Alumni Directory* (Quezon City: University of the Philippines Press, 1970).

154. Albert to the Board of Regents, through the President, University of the Philippines, July 29, 1938, in Minutes of the 452nd meeting of the Board of Regents, July 29, 1938. This is Albert's formal letter of resignation after Bocobo had already issued a statement to the press through reporters waiting outside his office where the Board of Regents deliberated on the Albert case in the early evening of July 29, 1938.

155. *Ibid.* For some of the details, rather sensationalized, see the *Philippines Herald*, July 29, 1938. The *Tribune* (July 30, 1938) is my source for the sequence of events in the afternoon and evening of the incident, like the Board of Regents going into an "extra-ordinary session" (special meeting?) after its regular meeting. The minutes of the meeting do not so indicate that there was a special meeting *per se.* It was, of course, an extraordinary session because it lasted until 9:00 p.m. with a recess of one hour or so.

156. *Tribune*, July 30, 1938. The minutes of the 453rd meeting of the Board of Regents on August 26, 1938, under the heading *College of Engineering*, reads: "The Board confirmed the following: Reinstatement, provisionally made by the President, of Mr. Antonio Albert as Assistant Professor of Civil Engineering, at a salary of ₱2,550 per annum, effective upon entrance to duty."

157. *Philippines Herald*, July 29, 1938 and the *Tribune*, July 30, 1938, are the sources for these details. They, naturally, had reporters accompanying the presidential party.

158. "Transcript of Notes Taken at the Inquiry Conducted by a Special Committee appointed by the Chairman of the Board of Regents (President Bocobo, Chairman, and Regents Gil and Sison, Members) in Connection with the Incident in the College of Engineering, Held in the Office of the President, University Hall, on Friday, July 29, 1938 at 6:40 p.m.," appended to Minutes of the Board's 452nd meeting on the same day.

The *Herald* version had Prof. Albert saying that he was hired to teach engineering, not good manners, and that this had infuriated President Quezon to the point of becoming "pale with anger."

159. A fuller discussion of the courtesy appeals is given in an earlier section of this chapter.

160. Italics added.

161. See note 159 above.

162. *Philippines Herald*, July 30, 1938.

163. Quezon to Bocobo, July 30, 1938, in the *Philippines Herald*, July 30, 1938, and the *Sunday Tribune*, July 31, 1938. The latter gives the story of Prof. Albert's going to Malacañang accompanied by his father, Don Vicente Albert, Clerk of Court of the Supreme Court.

164. Quezon to the Secretary of Public Instruction, November 18, 1937, in Minutes of the 444th Meeting of the Board of Regents, November 26, 1937, Exhibit "B"; *Philippines Herald*, December 16, 1938.

165. President Bocobo was furnished a copy of President Quezon's letter a few days after Secretary Osmeña received it and hurriedly called a meeting of the Executive Committee of the University Council, the Chairman of the President's Committee of Textbooks attending. After the latter's enumeration of the Committee's duties and the procedure for setting prices of reading materials prepared by various units of the University pursuant to a resolution of the Board of Regents on October 13, 1930, the Executive Committee adopted a number of remedial recommendations for adoption by the Board of Regents. The Minutes of the Executive Committee Meeting are given in the Minutes of the 444th Meeting of the Board of Regents, Exhibit "A"

166. Minutes of the 444th meeting, November 26, 1937. The members of the Committee were Regents Pond, Luther Bewley, Romulo and Vicente Singson Encarnacion.

167. *Philippines Herald*, December 16, 1938. *The Tribune*, December 20, 1938, quotes some of the professors as saying they had not been allowed to confront their accusers in what they termed "star chamber" proceedings.

168. *Philippines Herald*, December 2, 1938.

169. Minutes of the 458th Meeting, Board of Regents, December 1, 1938. The following discussion was based entirely on the minutes of this meeting, which were not released to the press.

170. Italics added.

171. Dr. Pedro Ylagan, Prof. Vicente Santiago, Prof. Francisco Capistrano (no longer with the College of Law by this time), and Prof. Gerardo Florendo, who was the College Secretary.

172. Minutes of the 459th Meeting, Board of Regents, December 15, 1938. The decisions at this meeting of the Board and the amended report of the Gil Committee are published in the *Philippines Herald*, December 16, 1938. I have not seen the original report of the Gil Committee, which was appended as Exhibit "F" of the Minutes of the December 1, 1938 meeting. I have used the minutes, not the newspaper version.

173. *Ibid.*

174. I discuss this briefly in a later section of this chapter.

175. This was on December 20, 1938. See the *Tribune*, December 21, 1938. President Elliott and Dean Packer were set to depart via the "Conte Biancamino" on December 25, 1938, after a "Barrio Fiesta" given in their honor by President and Mrs. Bocobo on Christmas Eve. *Sunday Tribune*, December 25, 1938.

176. This took place on December 17, wherein one of the speakers, law sophomore Mauro Calingo, was "howled down from the platform" because he had defended the Board of Regents' decision. On account of the student march to Malacañang, Executive Secretary Vargas missed the train for Tarlac where he was to have attended a reception for Agriculture Secretary Benigno Aquino, Sr. *Sunday Tribune*, December 18, 1938.

177. This is published in full by the *Philippines Herald*, December 20, 1938.

178. *Tribune*, December 21, 1938.

179. The letter, which I have not seen, is adverted to in Minutes of the 461st meeting of the Board of Regents, January 27, 1939.

180. See the issues of the *Herald* and *Tribune* for December 22, 1938.

181. Minutes of the 462nd Meeting, Board of Regents, March 10, 1938. This was an amendment to the minutes of the previous meeting, prompted by Regent Romulo's calling the attention of the Board to a *Philippine Collegian* news story (January 30, 1939) under the heading "Regents Exonerate All Professors in Book Probe."

182. December 21, 1938.

183. See Yabes, "First and Foremost," p. 175.

184. *Ibid.*, specially Chapter 8, titled "The Versatile and Innovative Sinco Regime (1953-1958)." The Sinco Presidency is treated in a later chapter of this book.

185. The text of the resolution is printed in *Survey Report*, p. 9.

186. Roxas Papers Box 47; Final Advisers' Memorandum No. 27 in *ibid.*, p. 272.

187. See John A. Hannah and Others, *A Study of the University of the Philippines* (Quezon City: University of the Philippines, 1958).

188. "Report of the Acting President . . . January 10, 1928," *loc. cit.*, p. 65. The Committee which the Board of Regents created on November 11, 1927, was to "advise the Board on educational questions and policy." Pursuant to the Committee's own recommendation (*Survey Report*, p. 20) that there be only two standing committees of the Board—the Executive Committee and the Committee on Physical Plant and Equipment—the Board of Regents would on July 12, 1939 abolish all existing committees of the Board, but retained the Committee on Educational Policy "as a special committee until its report has been acted upon by the Board." See Minutes of the 467th (July 12, 1939) and of the 472nd (November 16, 1939) meetings of the Board of Regents.

189. A copy of the final "Outline of Problems" is in *Survey Report*, pp. 97-100. For the discussions leading to its formulation, see the minutes of the 3rd and 4th meetings of the CEP held, respectively, on September 3 and September 30, 1938, in *Survey Report*, pp. 299-305.

190. The Advisers' Memoranda are printed as part one of Appendix "G" of the *Survey Report*, pp. 161-286. Memorandum No. 1 pertains to procedure, not to a substantive matter. The Final Advisers' Memorandum No. 27 contains a summary of the other memoranda.

191. One action taken in pursuance of the Committee's recommendation was the decision by the Board of Regents at its 461st meeting on January 27, 1939, even before the Board of Regents had formally accepted the Report, to send Professor Vicente Lontok, Business Director and Secretary of the Board of Regents, to the United States "on special detail to study financial administration of typical American universities, especially state Universities. . . ." The Board appropriated for the six-month trip $3,050. See the minutes of the meeting of the Board of Regents held on January 27, 1939. This was of course one of Bocobo's 16 points. See Annex A.

192. This portion of the chapter is almost a verbatim reproduction of a portion of my article on "The CAS [for College of Arts and Sciences] Administrative Structure," in *U.P. Newsletter* for May 3, 1982, p. 4. I wish to thank the editors of *U.P. Newsletter* for permission to draw freely from that piece.

193. The absorption of these two units by the College of Liberal Arts was again recommended twenty years later. See the *Hannah Report*, p. 16.

194. Minutes of the 635th meeting of the Board of Regents, June 28, 1957. Excerpt in Office of the University Secretary Files on College of Arts and Sciences, contains Dean Fonacier's Memorandum of May 2, 1957.

195. *Ibid.*

196. Minutes of the 463rd meeting of the Board of Regents, March 31, 1939.

197. Minutes of the 464th meeting of the Board of Regents, April 20, 1939.

198. Minutes of the 470th meeting of the Board of Regents, October 12, 1939.

199. *Ibid.* H.B. Reyes had until then been Assistant to the President.

200. See "Report of the Committee on Educational Policy on the Advisability of Transferring the Manila Units of the University of the Philippines to Another Site, October 27, 1938," in *Survey Report*, pp. 102-113.

201. Pond's confidential memorandum is reproduced in the Minutes of the 1st meeting of the Committee Appointed to Gather Data on a Possible New Site for the University of the Philippines, January 6, 1938. The minutes of the five meetings have been conveniently put together by V. Lontok, Board of Regents Secretary, in a thin bound volume, "Papers on the Proposed Transfer of the University of the Philippines, October 18, 1938," which is among the Roxas Papers, Box 47.

202. Minutes of the 3rd Meeting of the Pond Committee, March 14, 1938 in *loc. cit.*

203. Minutes of the 5th Meeting of the Pond Committee, March 21, 1938 in *loc. cit.*

204. Minutes of the 4th Meeting of the Pond Committee, March 15, 1938, in *loc. cit.*

205. A typescript copy is available in *loc. cit.* It is officially printed as Exhibit "A" of the "Report of the Committee on Educational Policy . . .," *Survey Report*, pp. 114-117.

206. See *loc. cit.*, pp. 126-131.

207. "Report of the Committee on Educational Policy . . .," *loc. cit.* Minutes of the Board of Regents Meeting, May 26, 1938.

208. Minutes of the 1st meeting of the Committee on Educational Policy [CEP] of the Board of Regents, July 27, 1938, in *Survey Report*, Appendix "G" (part 2), p. 287. Also in Roxas Papers.

209. Minutes of the 453rd Meeting of the Board of Regents, August 26, 1938.

210. Dean Packer arrived in Manila on September 11, 1938, but started attending the meetings of the CEP on September 30, 1938, the first meeting subsequent to his arrival. President Elliott on the other hand, did not arrive in Manila until October 9, 1938; he attended the CEP meetings for the first time on October 14, 1938.

211. Minutes of the 4th meeting of the CEP, September 30, 1938, in *loc. cit.*, pp. 304-305.

212. Minutes of the 456th meeting of the Board of Regents, October 14, 1938. The CEP met in the morning of the same day.

213. The CEP would also turn down the offer of Dr. Nicanor Jacinto to sell to the University five hundred hectares of land belonging to him in Novaliches. The Jacinto property was being offered for sale at 5¢ per sq. meter. This was the former Novaliches estate of former Executive Secretary Frank W. Carpenter which he had purchased under the Friar Lands Act of 1904. It was pronounced by the late Dr. Victor Heiser as "an ideal location for a sanitarium." Jacinto's letter, dated October 4, 1938, and transmitted to Roxas by Miguel Cuaderno is in the Roxas Papers, Box 47.

214. Minutes of the 6th Meeting of the CEP, October 21, 1938, in *loc. cit.*, pp. 310-315.

215. Minutes of the 8th Meeting of the CEP, October 28, 1938, in *loc. cit.*, 325-327. "Advisers' Memorandum No. 2: Relating to the Location of the University," is printed in *loc. cit.*, pp. 163-178.

216. Jorge B. Vargas to Manuel Roxas, October 22, 1938, in *loc. cit.*, p. 133. The Committee Report is on pp. 133-135.

217. It is printed in *loc. cit.*, 102-113, as Appendix "B".

218. Jorge Bocobo to the Board of Regents, October 28, 1938, in *loc. çit.*, 136-139, as Appendix "B-1."

219. See Minutes of the 457th (November 25, 1938), 459th (December 15, 1938), and 461st (January 27, 1939) meetings of the Board of Regents. Italics added.

220. This information was given by Regent Villanueva in answer to a query during a Board meeting on the status of Bill No. 938. Minutes of the 462nd Meeting, Board of Regents, March 10, 1939.

221. *Philippines Herald*, June 3, 1939.

222. See the four-page "U.P. 30th Anniversary Supplement" of the *Philippines Herald*, December 17, 1938.

223. *Tribune*, December 22, 1938.

224. For photos of some of the prominent personalities and events during the celebrations, see the *Herald Pictorial Magazine*, December 24, 1938, p. 7.

225. "U.P. 30th Anniversary Supplement," *loc. cit.*

226. Bocobo's annual report for academic year 1937-1938, p. 35, gives the enrolment figures from 1927 to 1938.

227. Obtained from *ibid.* and Gonzalez's first annual report (1938-1939).

228. Statistical data obtained from Bocobo's annual reports through 1938 and Gonzalez's first annual report in 1939.

229. Figures were obtained from the annual reports from 1935 to 1939.

230. Figures were obtained from the annual reports from 1934 to 1939.

231. "Report of The Acting President . . . January 10, 1928," *loc. cit.*, p. 66.

232. For Bocobo's sixteen-point program, see Annex A of this chapter.

233. *Report 1934-1935*, p. 9.

234. *Report 1936-1937*, p. 80.

235. *Report, 1937-1938*, p. 90.

236. *Report, 1934-1935*, p. 9, and *Report, 1937-1938*, p. 9.

237. *Report, 1937-1938*, p. 9, also *Report, 1936-1937*, pp. 8-9, wherein 14 topics were listed.

238. *Report, 1934-1935*, p. 9, and *Report, 1935-1936*, p. 9.

239. *Report, 1934-1935*, pp. 9-10.

240. *Report, 1936-1937*, p. 9.

241. *Report, 1934-1935*, p. 8.

242. He would emphatically announce in his inaugural address *(loc. cit.*, pp. 101-102) that the Alumni Institute would be "installed next April."

243. As printed in *Report, 1934-1935*, p. 8.

244. For these data see the reports already repeatedly cited above.

245. In 1940 the Alumni Institute was absorbed by the U.P. Summer Institute. *Twenty-Ninth Annual Report... Academic Year June 1, 1939—May 31, 1940* (Manila: University of the Philippines, 1941), p. 23.

246. *Report, 1935-1936*, p. 9.

247. *Report, 1936-1937*, p. 9.

248. *Report, 1937-1938*, pp. 9-10.

249. *Report, 1935-1936*, pp. 10-11.

250. As given in *Report, 1937-1938*, p. 12.

251. Bocobo noted in his 1935-1936 report (p. 11), that Dr. Africa "has done splendid work."

252. *Ibid.*, pp. 10-11.

253. *Report, 1937-1938*, p. 12.

254. A portion of Hon. Perfecto's letter is given in *ibid*.

255. *Twenty-Eighth Annual Report*, pp. 11-12.

256. *Report, 1936-1937*, p. 11.

257. *Twenty-Eighth Annual Report*, pp. 11-12.

258. *Ibid.*

259. *Twenty-Ninth Annual Report*, pp. 35-36.

260. See the anonymous and incompletely dated memorandum on "The Presidency of the University of the Philippines," in the Quezon Papers, Subject Matter File 1934-1941. This was prepared at Quezon's request, probably in "January 1939?" (the year followed by "?" is in handwriting.)

261. Frank B. Murphy, "Speech at the Inauguration of Dr. Jorge C. Bocobo, Manila, December 17, 1934."

BIBLIOGRAPHY — CHAPTER V

I. Manuscripts

Board of Regents, University of the Philippines. Minutes of Meetings. Office of the University Secretary Files, U.P. Diliman.

Executive Committee, University Council, University of the Philippines. Minutes of Meetings. Office of the University Registrar Files, U.P. Diliman.

Jorge C. Bocobo Papers. University Archives, U.P. Library, Diliman, Q.C.

W. Cameron Forbes Papers. Houghton Library, Harvard University, Cambridge, Mass.

Manuel L. Quezon Papers. National Library, Manila.

Manuel A. Roxas Papers. National Library, Manila.

II. Published Official Documents

Fonacier, Consuelo V. (Comp.). *The Role and Mission of the University: Inaugural Addresses of the Presidents of the University of the Philippines*. Quezon City: University of the Philippines, 1971.

Hannah, John A. and Others. *A Study of the University of the Philippines*. Quezon City: University of the Philippines, 1958.

University of the Philippines. Office of the President. *Report of Dr. Fernando Calderon as Acting President, University of the Philippines, Covering the Period from January 1, 1934, to August 31, 1934*. Manila: University of the Philippines, n.d.

________ . *Report of the President of the University of the Philippines to the Board of Regents for the Academic Year June 1, 1934–May 31, 1935*. Manila: University of the Philippines, 1936.

________. *Report of the President of the University of the Philippines... June 1, 1935-May 31, 1936*. Manila: University of the Philippines, 1937.

________. *Report of the President of the University of the Philippines... June 1, 1936-May 31, 1937*. Manila: University of the Philippines Press, 1938.

________. *Report of the President of the University of the Philippines... June 1, 1937-May 31, 1938*. Manila: University of the Philippines Press, 1939.

________. *Seventeenth Annual Report of the President of the University of the Philippines for the Academic Year 1927-1928*. Manila: Bureau of Printing, 1930.

________. *Twenty-Eighth Annual Report of the President of the University of the Philippines to the Board of Regents for the Academic Year June 1, 1938-May 31, 1939*. Manila: University of the Philippines, 1940.

________. *Twenty-Ninth Annual Report... Academic Year June 1, 1939—May 31, 1940*. Manila: University of the Philippines, 1941.

University of the Philippines, Board of Regents Committee on Educational Policy. *Report on a Survey of the University of the Philippines by the Committee on Educational Policy, Board of Regents, University of the Philippines*. Manila: University of the Philippines, 1939.

University of the Philippines. President's Committee on Courtesy. *Courtesy Appeals by the President's Committee on Courtesy, University of the Philippines*. Bulletin No. 2. Manila: University of the Philippines Press, 1936. Reissued February, 1937.

________. *Encarecimientos sobre la cortesia*. Manila: Universidad de Filipinas, 1938.

III. Books

Agoncillo, Teodoro A. and Alfonso, Oscar M. *A Short History of the Filipino People*. Quezon City: University of the Philippines, 1960.

Churchill, Bernardita Reyes. *The Philippine Independence Missions to the United States, 1919-1934*. Manila: National Historical Institute, 1983.

Cruz, Romeo V. *America's Colonial Desk and the Philippines, 1898-1934*. Quezon City: University of the Philippines, 1974.

Friend, Theodore. *Between Two Empires: The Ordeal of the Philippines, 1929-1946*. New Haven, Conn.: Yale University Press, 1965.

Kalaw, Teodoro M. *Aide-de-Camp to Freedom*. Trans. Maria Kalaw Katigbak. Manila: Friends of Kalaw Society, 1965.

Kirk, Grayson L. *Philippine Independence: Motives, Problems, and Prospects*. New York: Farrar and Rhinehart, 1936.

Olivar, Celia Bocobo. *Aristocracy of the Mind*. Abridged and Edited by Norma Occena Yabut. Quezon City: New Day Publishers, 1981.

Roxas, Felix. *The World of Felix Roxas: Anecdotes and Reminiscences of a Manila Newspaper Columnist, 1926-1936*. Translated by Angel Estrada and Vicente del Carmen. Manila: The Filipiniana Book Guild, 1970.

Salamanca, Bonifacio S. *The Filipino Reaction to American Rule, 1901-1913*. Quezon City: New Day Publishers, 1984.

Stanley, Peter W. *A Nation in the Making: The Philippines and the United States, 1899-1921*. Cambridge, Mass.: Harvard University Press, 1973.

IV. Articles

Alzona, Encarnacion. "History and National Solidarity," *The PHA Balita*, June 1980, 1, 4.

Aquino, Melchor P. "Dwight F. Davis," *Bulletin of the American Historical Collection*, II, April 1974, pp. 7-11.

Bulletin of the President's Committee on the Improvement of Teaching, Vol. I, No. 1, July, 1935.

Constantino, Josefina D. "U.P. Through the Years: Praise, Disenchantment and Hope," *The 1969 U.P. Alumni Yearbook*, pp. 14-15; 48.

Murphy, Frank B. "Speech at the Inauguration of Dr. Jorge C. Bocobo, Manila, December 17, 1934."

Panlasigui, I. "The Fourth Annual Baguio Conference, April 12-20, 1939," *Bulletin of the President's Committee for the Improvement of Teaching*, Vol. V, No. 1, August 1939, 17-28.

Peralta, Cresencio, "The Spirituo-Moral Revolution of Our Time," *Historical Bulletin*, 18:1-4 (January-December, 1974), 103-104.

Salamanca, Bonifacio S. "The CAS Administrative Structure," *U.P. Newsletter*, May 3, 1982, p. 4.

Yabes, Leopoldo Y. "Pres. Bocobo—An Appreciation," *Philippine Collegian*, August 31, 1934, p. 4.

V. Unpublished Works

Bocobo, Jorge C. "Address at the Opening Exercises of the University of the Philippines, June 8, 1936."

________. "Address at the Opening Exercises . . . June 7, 1937."

________. "Filipino Code of Ethics." (Address at the Opening Exercises for the Second Semester, University of the Philippines, October 24, 1938).

Olivar, Celia Bocobo. "Jorge C. Bocobo" (unpublished dissertation, College of Education, University of the Philippines, Diliman, Quezon City, 1975.) 2 vols.

Panlasigui, I. (Comp.). "Record of the First Faculty Conference, Baguio, May 11-16, 1936." Mimeographed.

Salamanca, Bonifacio S. "The Contributions of Filipino Historians to the Development of Philippine Nationalism." Elpidio Quirino Memorial Lecture, University of Northern Philippines (Vigan, Ilocos Sur), March 8, 1985.

"Transcript of the Meeting Re: . . . History of the College of Law, held June 25, 1983, U.P. College of Law, Diliman, Quezon City." Mimeographed.

Yabes, Leopoldo Y. "First and Foremost: A History of the College of Law, University of the Philippines." Quezon City: The Law Center, College of Law, University of the Philippines, 1982. Mimeographed.

VI. Newspapers

Malaya, June 12, 1984.

Philippine Collegian, August 17, 1934; September 28, 1934; January 28, 1935.

The Philippines Herald: August 13, 1934; August 15, 1934; October 7, 1935; July 29, 1938; July 30, 1938; December 2, 1938; December 16-23, 1938.

The Philippines Herald Pictorial Magazine, December 24, 1938.

The Sunday Tribune: July 31, 1938; December 18, 1938; December 25, 1938.

The Tribune: July 30, 1938; December 17, 1938; December 19, 1938; December 20-24, 1938.

CHAPTER V — ANNEX A

President Bocobo's Sixteen-Point Program for the University of the Philippines

1. Utmost and constant endeavor to make economy go hand in hand with high academic standards.
2. Study of present-day tendencies in university financial administration in the United States.
3. Enforcement of the stand of the Board of Regents that the name of the University should not be used or involved in partisan controversies.
4. A more earnest atmosphere of hard work, to imbue the students with qualities of character.
5. Deeper solicitude over the students' personal welfare.
6. Conservation of Filipino customs and tradition, at the same time fully appreciating the universal heritage of mankind.
7. The ethics and social obligations of each profession should be given a larger place in the curricula of the entire University.
8. Increased stress on such courses as are required by the exigencies of the times.
9. Vital articulation between the classroom and laboratory on the one hand, and the actual life of the people on the other, so that the University may give more useful and practical training.
10. Added encouragement for research, especially along lines that have a practical bearing upon the economic development of the country and the health of the people.
11. Vocational guidance.
12. Effective teaching should be considered no less important than research.
13. Study of the latest methods of university teaching to determine whether or not they are applicable to the local university.
14. Special attention to the unseen values of life rather than the physical plant in order that there may be an intellectual and spiritual quickening in the University.
15. Closer contact between the University and the alumni.
16. Self survey by the University of all the aspects of the work, in order that the institution may at all times render the best possible service.

(From Olivar, "Jorge C. Bocobo," I, 336-337, quoting from the *Philippines Herald*, August 13, 1934.)

NOTES ON CHAPTER VI — "GONZALEZ AS AN ADAMANT VISIONARY"

1. Board of Regents of the University of the Philippines, *Minutes of the 464th Meeting,* April 20, 1939, pp. 1-2.
2. Letter of B. M. Gonzalez to Edwin Copeland, May 19, 1939, Letters of B. M. Gonzalez, Volume III (1939-1940). p. 75.
3. Letter of C. F. Baker "To Whom It May Concern," March 27, 1913. Letters of B. M. Gonzalez, Vol. 1 (1912-1927). p. 4.
4. Letter of E. B. Copeland "To Whom It May Concern," April 1, 1913, *ibid.,* p. 5.
5. Letter of M. E. Caffrey, Office of the Secretary, Regents of the University of Wisconsin, to B. M. Gonzalez, October 26, 1914, *ibid.,* p. 25.
6. Leopoldo B. Uichanco, "Bienvenido Maria Gonzalez," Necrology. February 3, 1954 at the College of Liberal Arts, University of the Philippines, Quezon City.
7. Interview with Enrique T. Virata, November 26, 1954.
8. Letter of Alejandro Albert, Acting President, University of the Philippines, to B. M. Gonzalez, January 18, 1921, *op. cit.* p. 139.
9. Letter of Felipe Estella, U.P. Secretary, to B. M. Gonzalez, October 6, 1923, *ibid.,* p. 224.
10. "Gonzalez is named Dean," *Manila Daily Bulletin,* October 24, 1928, p. 1.
11. Letter of B. M. Gonzalez to President Manuel L. Quezon, July 8, 1939. Letters etc. Volume III, pp. 115-116.
12. "U.P. Head Resigns As Protest Against Bocobo Attitude," *Exposer* (Manila), July 27, 1939, p. 1.
13. Jorge C. Bocobo, "Reminiscences," *Philippine Collegian,* December 17, 1948, p. 2. (Address during the reunion of the deans of the College of Law, U.P. on December 2, 1948.)
14. *Twenty-Ninth Annual Report of the President of the University of the Philippines to the Board of Regents for the Academic Year June 1, 1939 – May 31, 1940.* Manila U.P., 1941, pp. 1-3.
15. *Ibid.*
16. *Ibid.,* pp. 4-6.
17. *Ibid.,* pp. 18-20.
18. *Philippine Collegian,* XXI (November 1939), p. 1.
19. *Op. cit.,* pp. 33-35.
20. "Gonzalez and Amorsolo," *Philippine Collegian,* XXI (February 1940), p. 12.
21. *Op. cit.,* pp. 33-35.
22. *Ibid.,* pp. 44-46.
23. Interview with Gonzalo W. Gonzalez, son of B.M. Gonzalez, February 22, 1983, at his law office.
24. "U.P. is Against Short Course," *Philippine Collegian,* XXIII (January 1941), pp. 1, 7.

25. *Philippine Collegian,* XXI (November 1939), pp. 3, 10.

26. Letter of the Honorable Jorge B. Vargas, Chairman of the Executive Commission, to Dr. Bienvenido M. Gonzalez through the Commissioner of Education, Health and Welfare, Manila, October 11, 1943.

27. B. M. Gonzalez Papers, U.P. Library, Box/Folder No. 4-5.

28. "A Century of Education in the Philippines," ed. Dalmacio Martin, *Historical Bulletin,* Philippine Historical Association, Vol. XXIV (January-December 1980), Nos. 1-4, p. 264.

29. *Thirty-Third Annual Report of the President of the University of the Philippines for the Academic Year July 1, 1945-May 31, 1946.* Manila: University of the Philippines, 1946, pp. 1-3.

30. *Ibid.*

31. *Ibid.*, p. 4.

32. *Ibid.*, p. 5.

33. *Ibid.*, p. 7.

34. *Ibid.*, pp. 12-13.

35. *Ibid.*, p. 15.

36. *Ibid.*, pp. 20-21.

37. Message of Paul V. McNutt to the student graduates during the 1946 commencement exercises, *Philippinensian* 1942-1946.

38. *Philippinensian* 1942-1946.

39. *Ibid.*, pp. 6-7.

40. Board of Regents of the University of the Philippines. *Minutes of the 506th Meeting,* September 26, 1946, p. 12.

41. *Thirty-Fourth Annual Report of the President of the University of the Philippines to the Board of Regents for the Academic Year June 1, 1946 – May 31, 1947.* Manila: University of the Philippines, 1947.

42. Board of Regents of the University of the Philippines. *Minutes of the 510th Meeting,* February 12, 1947, pp. 10-11.

43. Message of B.M. Gonzalez, "On the Rebirth of the Philippine Collegian," *Philippine Collegian,* I (September 1946), p. 3.

44. "Affirms Faith in U.P. President," *ibid.*, p. 9.

45. Editorial, *Philippine Collegian,* I (January 1947), pp. 2-3.

46. Letter of B.M. Gonzalez to Edwin Copeland, June 12, 1948, *Addresses, Messages, Articles, etc.* (7 pages, p. 3).

47. *Ibid.*, pp. 3-4.

48. "Students' Appraisal of President Gonzalez," *Philippine Collegian,* II (April 1948), pp. 4-5.

49. Editorial, *Philippine Collegian,* III (October 1948), p. 1.

50. *Philippine Collegian,* I (January 1948), p. 5.

51. *Thirty-Fifth Annual Report of the President of the University of the Philippines to the Board of Regents for the Academic Year June 1, 1947 – May 31, 1948.* Manila: University of the Philippines, 1948, pp. 59-63.

52. *Ibid.*, pp. 8-10.

53. *Ibid.*, pp. 10-11.

54. *Ibid.*, pp. 11-12.

55. *Ibid.*, pp. 1-3.

56. *Ibid.*, p. 55.

57. *Ibid.*, p. 20.

58. *Ibid.*, pp. 57-58.

59. *Thirty-Sixth Annual Report of the President of the University of the Philippines to the Board of Regents for the Academic Year June 1, 1948 – May 31, 1949.* Quezon City: University of the Philippines, 1950, pp. 5-7.

60. "*Ex*-Regent Asks Gonzalez Ouster," *Evening News,* October 21, 1948, pp. 1, 27.

61. *Collegian* Staff, "Dedication," *Philippine Collegian* III (October 1948), p. 2.

62. Editorial, "The Glorious Eve," *ibid.,* pp. 1, 4.

63. "Law Faculty Affirms Confidence in President Bienvenido Gonzalez," *Philippine Collegian,* November 30, 1948, pp. 1, 19.

64. Interview with Paterno Santos, September 30, 1954.

65. Gonzalo W. Gonzalez, "Response," *Diliman Review,* Volume II (January 1954) No. 1, pp. 105-106.

66. *Thirty-Sixth Annual Report,* pp. 12-13.

67. *Ibid.,* p. 19.

68. *Ibid.,* pp. 20-22.

69. *Ibid.*

70. *Ibid.*

71. *Ibid.,* pp. 52-54.

72. *Ibid.*

73. *Philippine Collegian,* III (April 1949), p. 1.

74. *Thirty-Seventh Annual Report of the President of the Philippines for the Academic Year June 1, 1949-May 31, 1950.* Quezon City: University of the Philippines, 1951, p. 5.

75. *Ibid.,* pp. 55-56.

76. Interview with Paterno Santos, September 30, 1954.

77. *Ibid.*

78. Enrique M. Fernando, "Bienvenido M. Gonzalez," *Philippine Collegian,* January, 1954, Outside Back Cover.

79. *Thirty-Eighth Annual Report of the President of the University of the Philippines to the Board of Regents for the Academic Year June 1, 1950-May 31, 1951.* Quezon City: University of the Philippines, 1951, p. 9.

80. *Ibid.*

81. *Ibid.,* pp. 47-48.

82. *Ibid.*

83. "Minutes of the 172nd Meeting of the University Council of the University of the Philippines held on the 3rd floor, Administration Building on Thursday, April 12, 1951 at 10:00 A.M." Minutes of the University Council, Volume VII (August 4, 1945-April 12, 1951), U.P., p. 407.

BIBLIOGRAPHY — CHAPTER VI

B.M. Gonzalez Papers, U.P. Library Box/Folder No. 4-5.

Board of Regents of the University of the Philippines, Minutes of the 464th Meeting, April 20, 1939, *506th Meeting*, September 26, 1946; and *510th Meeting*, February 12, 1947.

"Ex-Regent Asks Gonzalez Ouster," *Evening News*, October 21, 1948.

Gonzalez, Gonzalo W. "Response," *Diliman Review*, Volume II (January 1954) No. 1.

"Gonzalez is named Dean," *Manila Daily Bulletin*, October 24, 1928.

Interview with Gonzalo W. Gonzalez, Son of B.M. Gonzalez, February 22, 1983.

Interview with Paterno Santos, September 30, 1954.

Interview with Enrique T. Virata, November 26, 1954.

Letter of Alejandro Albert, Acting President, University of the Philippines to B.M. Gonzalez, January 18, 1921, Letters of B.M. Gonzalez, Volume I (1912-1927).

Letter of C.F. Baker "To Whom It May Concern," March 27, 1913, Letters of B.M. Gonzalez, Volume 1 (1912-1927).

Letter of E.B. Copeland "To Whom It May Concern," April 1, 1913. Letters of B.M. Gonzalez, Volume I (1912-1927).

Letter of M.E. Caffrey, Office of the Secretary, Regents of the University of Wisconsin, to B.M. Gonzalez, October 26, 1914, Letters of B.M. Gonzalez, Volume I (1912-1927).

Letter of Felipe Estella, U.P. Secretary, to B.M. Gonzalez, Letter of B.M. Gonzalez, Volume 1 (1912-1927).

Letter of B.M. Gonzalez to Edwin Copeland, May 19, 1939, Letters of B.M. Gonzalez, Volume III (1939-1940).

Letter of B.M. Gonzalez to Edwin Copeland, June 12, 1948. Addresses, Messages, Articles, etc. (7 pages)

Letter of B.M. Gonzalez to President Manuel L. Quezon, July 8, 1939, Letters of B.M. Gonzalez, Volume I (1912-1927).

Letter of Honorable Jorge B. Vargas, Chairman of the Executive Commission, to Dr. Bienvenido M. Gonzalez through the Commissioner of Education, Health and Welfare, Manila, October 11, 1943.

Martin, Dalmacio, ed. "A Century of Education in the Philippines," *Historical Bulletin*, Philippine Historical Association, Vol. XXIV (January-December, 1980).

"Minutes of the 172nd Meeting of the University Council of the University of the Philippines held on the 3rd floor, Administration Building on Thursday, April 12, 1951 at 10:00 A.M." Minutes of the University Council, Volume VII (August 4, 1945-April 12, 1951), University of the Philippines.

Philippine Collegian, XXI (November 1939), XXII (February 1940), XXIII (January 1941), I (September 1946), I (January 1947), III (January 1948), III (April 1948), III (October 1948), III (November 30, 1948), III (December 17, 1948), III (April 1949), and January 1954.

Philippinensian, 1942-1946.

Annual Report of the President of the University of the Philippines to the Board of Regents. Academic Year 1939-40 (29th AR), 1945-46 (33rd AR), 1946-47 (34th AR), 1947-48 (35th AR), and 1948-49 (36th AR), Manila; 1944-50 (37th AR) and 1950-51 (38th AR), Quezon City, University of the Philippines.

Uichanco, Leopoldo B. "Bienvenido Maria Gonzalez," Necrology, February 3, 1954 at the College of Liberal Arts, University of the Philippines, Quezon City.

"U.P. Head Resigns As Protest Against Bocobo Attitude," *Exposer*, Manila, July 27, 1939.

CHAPTER VI—ANNEX A

ENROLMENT FROM 1939 TO 1951*

During the first semester of the first academic year (1939-1940) of the presidency of Bienvenido M. Gonzalez, enrolment in the University was 8,109. This exceeded by 151 the enrolment for the same semester of the preceding year. It was also then the highest enrolment figure registered in the history of the University. Out of the 8,109 students, 6,999 were enrolled in the collegiate units and 1,110 in the non-collegiate units. The enrolment in the second semester decreased by 771 as the number dropped to 7,338 students. This number was 38 students less than the enrolment for the same period of the last academic year.

In 1940, the Summer Institute had an enrolment of 2,134 which was 614 more than the enrolment for the preceding year. The highest enrolment figure was, however, registered in 1928 with a total of 2,234 students.

The enrolment for the first academic year after the war (1945-1946) was 2,199 in the first semester and 3,155 in the second. Compared with the last academic year before the war (1941-1942) which had 7,567 students in the first semester and 6,659 in the second, the enrolment for the year 1945-1946 was approximately only 33 per cent. The great decrease was due to the destruction of the University campus resulting in the unavailability of the buildings to accommodate more students. In the first semester of the year, the only buildings that could render service and accommodate students were the Institute of Hygiene and the Cancer Institute buildings. More classroom space became available in the second semester as minor repairs in the University Infirmary and a pavilion of the Philippine General Hospital enabled the University to reopen its High School and the Conservatory of Music.

In the following academic year (1946-1947), partial repair of the main library and Engineering buildings resulted in more students being enrolled. There were 4,149 students in the first semester and 4,078 in the second semester. These enrolment figures show an increase of 88.68 percent for the first semester and 29.26 percent for the second semester over those for corresponding periods of the previous year.

New elements in the student population of the University were added. These were the Philippine and US army veterans enjoying educational privileges and the *pensionados* of the Philippine Government. There were 134 Filipino veterans for the second semester of the year and 35 for the summer period of 1947. The educational provisions of Republic Act No. 65 allowed these veterans to register in the University without paying any fees.

American army veterans also enrolled in the University under the US GI Bill of Rights. Their fees and expenses were to be paid in arrears to the University by the US Government. For the academic year 1946-1947, 10 US army veterans were enrolled in the first semester, 18 in the second semester and 6 in the Summer Institute. The *pensionados* of the Philippine Government who studied in the University belonged to the Bureau of Lands and the Department of Interior. There were 31 *pensionados* during the year, 22 of whom were from the Bureau of Lands while the rest were from the Department of Interior.

The Summer Institute was fully reopened by the University in 1947. There was a total of 1,602 students enrolled for the summer session. This figure was much more than the enrolment during the first two years after the war when the Summer Institute had only 92 students in 1945 and 102 in 1946.

The enrolment figures continued to increase during the ensuing academic year (1947-1948). There were 5,806 students enrolled in the first semester and 5,439 students in the second. These figures showed an increase of about 16 percent for the first semester and 34 percent for the second semester over those for similar periods of the preceding year. The further increase in enrolment was made possible when additional classroom space became available with repairs made on the north wing of the main library, a part of the old Rizal Hall, and some classrooms in Palma Hall. The Summer Institute had 1,729 students for 1948 or an increase of about 8 percent over the enrolment for summer of the previous year.

The number of Filipino veterans studying inoreased during the year. A total of 323 students registered for the schoolyear representing an increase of 185 students or 135 percent over the figure of last year. The first semester had 253 veterans enrolled, the second 280, and the summer session 43. The uncollected fees from these veterans further strained the financial situation of the University.

---

*Figures taken from the President's Annual Reports.

The number of American veterans studying, like the Filipino veterans, more than doubled. There was a total of 42 American veterans enrolled showing an increase of 23 veterans or 121 percent over the 19 American veteran students registered the previous year. Twenty-nine of these veterans enrolled in the first semester, 32 in the second, and 22 in the summer period.

There were 52 *pensionados* from the Philippine Government. Of these, 27 came from the Department of Interior, 23 from the Bureau of Lands, and 2 from the Bureau of Public Schools. Thirty-seven of them enrolled in the first semester, 42 in the second, and 6 in the summer session. The *pensionados* from the Bureau of Lands were exempted from paying tuition fees.

The progress in the rehabilitation of the physical plant of the University resulted in the steady growth of the enrolment of students. For the academic year 1948-1949 when the University transferred to its new site in Diliman, the enrolment figures reached a total which approximated that of the last academic year before the war (1941-1942) when the condition of the buildings was still good, the equipment sufficient, and the faculty greater in number. Compared with 7,567 students for the first semester and 6,659 students for the second semester of 1941-1942, there were 7,106 students for the first semester and 6,142 students for the second semester of 1948-1949. In view of the poor condition of the buildings, the inadequate equipment, and the insufficient number of faculty, the enrolment figures for the year 1948-1949 could be considered large.

There was only a slight increase in the enrolment of Philippine and American veterans studying in the University. For the academic year 1948-1949, a total of 339 Philippine veterans were enrolled while 44 US veterans were registered.

There were 84 *pensionados* from the Philippine Government who were enrolled during the year. This shows an increase of 32 from the previous year. Of the 84 *pensionados*, 72 registered in the first semester, 70 in the second, and 35 in the summer session. It should be noted that by virtue of the request of the Bureau of Forestry which detailed some of its staff members to the School of Forestry without pay, the University approved the admission of *pensionados* from the Bureau of Forestry free of tuition fees.

Only 1,594 students registered for the summer session in 1949. This represents a decrease of 135 students from the preceding year. The cause of this drop could be due to the transfer of the University to its new site.

Another increase in the enrolment of students was registered for the academic year 1949-1950. A total of 7,452 students enrolled for the first semester and 6,817 for the second semester. These figures represent an increase of 346 in the first semester and 675 in the second over the totals for the corresponding periods of the previous academic year. In contrast to the enrolment in 1941-1942, the enrolment for 1949-1950 was smaller by 115 students for the first semester but larger by 158 for the second.

There was a significant decrease in the enrolment of Philippine veterans. During the year, only 271 Philippine veterans were registered. There was, however, only a very slight decrease in the enrolment of American veterans, numbering 43 for the year.

Ninety-four *pensionados* were registered at the end of the academic year showing a further increase in their enrolment. Students enrolled in the Summer Institute registered a big increase in contrast to the previous year. There were 1,984 students enrolled or an increase of 390 students from the preceding year.

The last academic year (1950-1951) of the presidency of Gonzalez registered the highest enrolment since the last war. There were 7,792 students who were enrolled in the first semester and 7,232 in the second. These figures represent an increase of 10 percent over the enrolment of the last academic year.

NOTES ON CHAPTER VII — "TAN'S DEVOTED PRESIDENCY"

1. "Speech to the Far Eastern University Writers' Club, February 15, 1951," Vidal A. Tan Papers (hereinafter to be referred to as VAT), U.P. Archives (UPA), U.P. Library (UPL), Box 6-23, No. 471.

2. "The Role of Man in Science," Welcome Address at the opening of the Eighth Pacific Science Congress, November 18, 1953. VAT, *loc. cit.*, Box 6-23, No. 475.

3. Tan was born in Bacolor, Pampanga on April 23, 1893. He obtained his A.B. from the University of the Philippines in 1913, his M.A. and Bachelor of Civil Engineering from Cornell University in 1918, and was conferred a Ph. D. in Mathematics, *cum laude,* by the University of Chicago in 1925. He joined the faculty of the University in 1914 as an assistant instructor. Later, he became the head of the department of mathematics, Secretary of the College of Liberal Arts, later its acting Dean, Registrar of the University, faculty representative in the Board of Regents in 1930-1933; Dean of Men, first Dean of the College of Arts and Sciences, Baguio City in 1938; and finally, Dean of the College of Engineering from 1940 to 1949. In 1949, he resigned the deanship to accept the presidency of the Far Eastern University.

4. "Minutes of the Special (544th) Meeting of the Board of Regents. University of the Philippines (hereinafter to be referred to as *BOR Minutes*), March 29, 1951," UPA, pp. 108-110.

5. *Ibid.*, p. 108. Members of the Special Committee were Jose Yulo, Camilo Osias, Pio Pedrosa, Teodoro Evangelista, and Aurelio Montinola.

6. *Ibid.*, pp. 108 to 111.

7. "General Memorandum, April 21, 1951," issued by Executive Vice-President Enrique T. Virata, U.P. *VAT,* Box 6-1. Also, "Gear U.P. to policies of State, Tan advised," *Evening News,* Manila, April 24, 1951, p. 1.

8. *VAT, loc. cit.*, Box 6-2.

9. Alejandro M. Fernandez, "One Year of Pres. Tan," *The Philippine Collegian* (hereinafter to be referred to as *Collegian),* Vol. VI, No. 16, April 7, 1952, p. 2.

10. "Remarks," delivered at a dinner tendered by the BOR, Deans and Directors, on his retirement, July 18, 1956. *VAT,* Box 6-23, No. 483.

11. To date, Tan has been the only president to hold office at Palma Hall. His predecessor and his successors have held office at Quezon Hall, the administration building.

12. A.M. Fernandez, *loc. cit.* Italics his. Fernandez was Assistant Editor of the *Collegian* in 1950-1951 and Executive Editor in 1951-1952.

13. "Address to the First University Council Meeting, June 12, 1951" (hereinafter cited as "First Speech"), VAT, Box 6-23, No. 472.

14. Data taken from *Philippinensian,* 1951 and 1953.

15. "Fonacier picks dept. heads," *Collegian,* Vol. X, No. 3, September 30, 1955, p. 1.

16. *Collegian,* Vol. VI, No. 22, July 31, 1952.

17. "Dr. Panlasigui retires at 65," *Ibid.*, Vol. X, No. 24, April 18, 1956.

18. *Philippinensian,* 1951 and 1954.

19. *Ibid.*, 1951, 1953 and 1955.

20. *Ibid.*, 1951 and 1954.

21. *Ibid.*, 1951 through 1955.

22. *Ibid.*

23. "First Speech," *loc. cit.*

24. "The Role of our State University," *VAT*, Box 6-23, No. 475.

25. Vidal A. Tan, *Annual Report of the President to the Board of Regents* (hereinafter to be cited as AR), 1952-1953, UPA, p. 1.

26. *Ibid.*,1951-1952, pp. 11-12.

27. *Ibid.*, 1953-1954, p. 10.

28. *Ibid.*,1952-1953; *ibid.*, 1953-1954, pp. 9-11.

29. *Ibid.*, 1953-1954, pp. 9-11.

30. "Minutes of the 137th Meeting of the Executive Board, National Research Council of the Philippines, July 19, 1950." VAT, Box 8-4, No. 558.

31. *AR*, 1953-1954, p. 9.

32. "The Role of Man in Science," *loc. cit.*

33. *AR*, 1953-1954, p. 9.

34. *Ibid.*, p. 48.

35. "Tan leaves for UNESCO Meet," *Collegian*, Vol. X, No. 23, March 27, 1956.

36. *AR*, 1954-1955, p. 15.

37. *Ibid.*, pp. 10-21.

38. *AR* for 1951-1952, 1952-1953, 1953-1954, and 1954-1955.

39. *Ibid.*, 1954-1955; also, *BOR Minutes*, 609th Meeting, April 6, 1956, UPA.

40. "The Role of our State University," *loc. cit.*

41. "Minutes of the 182nd Meeting of the University Council, March 6, 1954", UPA, pp. 24-25.

42. *AR* for 1951-1952, 1952-1953, and 1953-1954.

43. *Ibid.*, 1952-1953.

44. "Rockefeller body gives grant to U.P.," *Collegian*, Vol. X, No. 7, October 31, 1955, p. 1.

45. *AR*, 1953-1954, p. 61.

46. *Ibid.*, pp. 34-35.

47. *Ibid.*, 1954-1955, p. 22.

48. *Ibid.*, p. 22. Also "Consultants from the University of Connecticut," *Collegian*, Vol. X, No. 2, Sept. 14, 1955, p. 1.

49. Letter of President Magsaysay quoted by President Tan in his "Address before the Manila Rotary Club, February 9, 1956," VAT, Box 6-23, No. 479.

50. *Ibid.* Also "Asian Institute Survey Team Back," *Collegian*, Vol. X, No. 1, August 31, 1955, p. 1 and "U.P. received books on Asian Studies," *ibid.*, No. 23, 1955, p. 2; *AR*, 1955-56, p. 56.

51. *BOR Minutes,* 606th Meeting, January 30, 1956, p. 19.

52. Amando M. Dalisay, "Memorandum to Secretary Nable, April 18, 1956." VAT, Box 6-11, No. 437.

53. "The Role of our State University," *loc. cit.*

54. A.M. Fernandez, *loc. cit.*

55. *AR,* 1952-1953.

56. *Ibid.*

57. *Ibid.*, 1954-1955, p. 23.

58. *Ibid.*

59. *Ibid.*, p. 24.

60. *Ibid.*

61. "Remarks. . . , July 18, 1956," *loc. cit.*

62. Figures for 1950 to 1955 are taken from the annual reports of these years. Data for 1955-1956 were culled from the BOR Minutes of the following meetings: 589th, April 23, 1955; 590th, June 17, 1955; 592nd, June 28, 1955; 594th, July 28, 1955; 595th, August 8, 1955; 596th, August 29, 1955; 598th, September 12, 1955; and 601st, October 20, 1955. UPA, UPL.

63. *AR,* 1951-1952, p. 78; 1952-1953, p. 63; 1953-1954, p. 87; 1954-1955, p. 126; 1955-1956, p. 27.

64. *Ibid.*, 1951-1952, p. 39; 1954-1955, p. 18.

65. *Ibid.*, 1953-1954, p. 47. And "UPBA starts countrywide seminars," *Collegian,* Vol. X, No. 7, November 16, 1955, p. 2. "Bus. Adm. Labor-Management Series," *ibid.*, No. 17, February 1, 1956, p. 1.

66. *AR,* 1953-1954, p. 12 and 1954-1955, p. 32.

67. *Ibid.*, 1954-1955, p. 32.

68. *Ibid.*, 1953-1954, p. 12.

69. *Ibid.*, 1954-1955, p. 32.

70. *Ibid.*, 1953-1954 and 1954-1955.

71. "Regents Approve ₱3-million GSIS Loan," *Collegian,* Vol. X, No. 5, October 31, 1955.

72. "First Speech," *loc. cit.*

73. *Ibid.*

74. I. P. Soliongco, "Seriously Speaking," *Manila Chronicle,* Year IX, No. 291, February 6, 1954, p. 4.

75. *BOR Minutes,* 552nd Meeting, December 20, 1951, p. 13. Also *AR,* 1951-1952, p. 5.

76. *AR,* 1951-1952, pp. 5-6.

77. A. M. Fernandez, *loc. cit.*

78. Celso Cabrera, "Inside Malacañang" July 5, 1953, quoted a letter purportedly from Diliman as follows: " . . . marked discrimination and rank favoritism that stink (sic) the administration".

79. *AR,* 1952-1953 and 1953-1954.

80. *Collegian,* Vol. X, No. 12, December 20, 1955, p. 13.

81. *Ibid.,* Vol. X, No. 2, September 15, 1955, p. 9.

82. Rules governing extra-curricular activities are found in Article III, Chapter 8 of the University Code, Sections 56-94.

83. "Castro Committee to wind up investigation," *Collegian,* August 20, 1954.

84. *BOR Minutes,* 581st Meeting, January 11, 1955. The Castro Committee Report and the reports of the Deans and Directors and the President of the University are appended to the minutes. UPA.

85. *Ibid.*

86. "Report of the U.P. Alumni Association Committee assigned to investigate the charges against President Vidal Tan," *Collegian,* Vol. IX, valedictory issue, July 28, 1955, p. 7.

87. "Remarks . . . July 18, 1956," *loc. cit.* Also an affidavit executed by Presentacion Perez and Nora V. Daza, on August 27, 1955, alleging that Regent Arturo Garcia had maligned Pres. Tan at the Home Economics cafeteria about the end of October, 1955. VAT, Box 7-10, No. 523.

88. "Letter of Amelita Reysio Cruz tendering her resignation," "Letter of Pres. Tan accepting her resignation, dated February 14, 1955;" and "Reply of Josefina D. Constantino to Reysio-Cruz", all printed in the *Collegian,* Vol. IX, No. 10, February 28, 1955, p. 4 and p. 8.

89. February 21, 1955. Appended to *BOR Minutes,* 589th Meeting, March 10, 1955 as Exhibit "A", UPA.

90. *"UP Head, Secretary denounced," Manila Chronicle,* Year X, No. 307, February 22, 1955, p. 4.

91. "Charges against the U.P.," *ibid.,* No. 308, Feb. 23, 1955.

92. "Tan Imposes Censorship," *ibid.,* No. 315, March 2, 1955. Also *Manila Times,* Vol. X, No. 197, March 2, 1955, p. 1.

93. *Ibid.*

94. Vol. IX, No. 19, Feb. 28, 1955.

95. The Reports of the Committee were published in full in the *Collegian,* Vol. IX, valedictory issue, July 28, 1955, on pp. 5 to 9 and 13 to 15.

96. "Memorandum of Vidal A. Tan to the Board of Regents, July 11, 1955." VAT, Box 6-21, No. 462. Also in the *Collegian, ibid.*

97. "Minority Report of the Five-Man Board of Regents Special Committee to Investigate the Charges against President Vidal A. Tan," *Collegian,* July 28, 1955, pp. 6 and 12.

98. *BOR Minutes,* 593rd Special Meeting, July 12, 1955, p. 3.

99. "Minority Report," *loc. cit.,* p. 12.

100. "Memo of Tan to BOR, July 11, 1955," *loc. cit.*

101. *Ibid.*

102. "Minority Report," *loc. cit.*

103. *Ibid.*

104. "Report of UPAA Committee," *loc. cit.,* p. 7.

105. "Letter of Francisco Arcellana, Sr. to President Vidal A. Tan, July 23, 1955," appended to *BOR Minutes,* 596th Meeting, August 29, 1955 as Exhibit "C", p. 10.

106. "Majority Report of the Five-Man Committee of the Board of Regents to Investigate the Charges against President Vidal A. Tan," *Collegian,* July 28, 1955, p. 9.

107. *Ibid.,* pp. 7 and 9.

108. "Letter of Arcellana," *loc. cit.*

109. *BOR Minutes,* 596th Meeting. . . , p. 3.

110. "Memo of Tan to BOR," *loc. cit.*

111. "Majority Report," *loc. cit.,* p. 5.

112. "UPAA Report," and "Majority Report," *loc. cit.*

113. "Minority Report," *loc. cit.,* p. 12.

114. *Ibid.*

115. "Memo of Tan to BOR," *loc. cit.,* p. 6.

116. *Ibid.,* pp. 5-6.

117. *Ibid.,* pp. 4-5.

118. "Minority Report," *loc. cit.*

119. "Majority Report," *loc. cit.*

120. "Memo of Tan to BOR", *loc. cit.*

121. *BOR Minutes* of the Special 593rd Meeting, July 12, 1955, UPA, p. 5.

122. *Ibid.,* pp. 3-4.

123. *Ibid.*

124. *Collegian,* July 28, 1955, p. 1.

125. "Minority Report," *loc. cit.,* p. 6.

126. *BOR Minutes,* 593rd Meeting, p. 6.

127. *BOR Minutes,* 593rd Meeting, pp. 6-7.

128. "Abejo Assails Board," *Collegian,* Vol. X, No. 1, August 31, 1955, p. 1.

129. "Board exonerates UP Dean of Men," *Ibid.,* No. 4, October 15, 1955, p. 1.

130. *Ibid.*

131. *BOR Minutes,* 594th Meeting, p. 17.

132. *Ibid.,* 596th Meeting, p. 2.

133. *Ibid.,* 586th Meeting, March 4, 1955, pp. 1 and 2.

134. *Ibid.,* 567th Meeting, January 14, 1954.

135. *AR,* 1954-1955, p. 31.

136. *BOR Minutes,* 586th Meeting, p. 2.

137. *Ibid.,* 593rd Meeting, p. 2.

138. Sabino Padilla, "EDITORIAL: Fr. John P. Delaney, S.J.," *Collegian,* Vol. X, No. 14, January 14, 1956, p. 1.

139. Juan M. Hagad, "Letter to the Editor, Bacolod City, August 28, 1955," *Collegian,* Vol. X, No. 2, September 15, 1955, p. 4.

140. "Letter of President Magsaysay, November 18, 1954," quoted by President Tan in his "Memorandum to BOR, September 12, 1955," VAT, Box 7-11, No. 529.

141. "Memo of Tan to BOR, September, 12, 1955."

142. "Majority Report," *loc. cit.,* p. 13.

143. *Ibid.*

144. *Ibid.*

145. Presentacion Perez, *et al.,* "Petition to the Board of Regents," *BOR Minutes,* 596th Meeting, August 29, 1955, Exhibit "A", p. 5.

146. *Ibid.,* p. 1.

147. "UP Sects' Row taken to Palace," *Manila Chronicle,* Yr. XI, No. 106, August 5, 1955, p. 1.

148. "RM stresses need for religious freedom at UP," *ibid.,* No. 107, August 6, 1955, p. 1

149. VAT, Box 7-11, No. 507.

150. *Ibid.,* No. 453.

151. "Fr. Delaney Defies Tan Ruling," *Collegian,* Vol. X, No. 1, August 31, 1955, p. 1.

152. *Ibid.*

153. "Delaney's Ouster sought by Alumni; Eight Students send charges to Regents," *Collegian,* August 29, 1955, Exhibit "B"

154. "Faulkner speaks at UP," *Collegian,* August 31, 1955.

155. "Memo of Tan to BOR, Sept. 12, 1955," *loc. cit.* Appended to it is copy of "Proposed Revision of Article III, Chapter Eight of the University Code.

156. "Regents to Re-study U.P. Code," *Collegian,* Vol. X, No. 2, September 15, 1955, p. 1.

157. Sabino J. Padilla, "Editorial," and Hagad, "Letter to Editor," *ibid.,* p. 4.

158. "To hear raps vs. Council head; Campos to refute charges," *ibid.,* No. 7, November 16, 1955, p. 1

159. *BOR Minutes,* 603rd Meeting, Nov. 25, 1955, pp. 1-2.

160. *Ibid.,* and 582nd Meeting, January 13, 1955, pp. 2-3.

161. *Ibid.*

162. "Regents Ask Tan to Stay," *Collegian,* Vol. X, No. 9, December 1, 1955, p. 1.

163. "Justice Secretary's Opinion, November 26, 1955," *ibid.,* p. 3.

164. "Tan bars Fr. Delaney from Benitez Hall," *ibid.,* No. 10, December 7, 1955, p. 1.

165. Sabino Padilla, "The President's Stand", *ibid.,* p. 4.

166. "UCCSOA Drops Charges Against the Council Head," *ibid.,* No. 11, December 14. 1955, pp. 1 and 2.

167. Padilla, "Editorial," *ibid.,* p. 4.

168. "Msgr. Santos to Bless the New Chapel," *ibid.,* No. 12, December 20, 1955, p. 1.

169. "Pay Final Tribute to Father Delaney," *ibid.,* No. 14, January 14, 1956, p. 1.

170. *"U.P. COUNCIL HEADS CHOSEN, Lagua, Castillo, Angara, win student, Senior, Junior* Posts," ibid., Vol. XI, No. 1, July 26, 1956.

171. "Rangsom Meet approves U.P. SEA Proposal," *ibid.*, Vol. X, No. 6, November 9, 1955; "Tan, University Heads discuss Bangkok Meet," *ibid.*, No. 9, Dec. 1, 1955.

172. "Last Speech, July 14, 1956," loc. cit.

173 "Agenda of the Special 611th BOR Meeting to be held June 21, 1956," Item No. VI, VAT, Box 6-27, No. 497.

174 *BOR Minutes,* 611th Meeting, June 21, 1956, p. 5.

175. *Ibid.*, 612th Meeting, June 22, 1956, pp. 1-2.

176. "Defer Action on Tan Offer Anew," *Collegian.*

177. *BOR Minutes,* 614th Meeting, July 5, 1956, pp. 1-2.

178. *Ibid.*

179. *Ibid.*

180. Padilla, "THE RETIREMENT OF THE PRESIDENT," *Collegian,* Vol. X, No. 30, July 6, 1956, p. 4.

181. "To my mind," *ibid.*, p. 4.

182. "Appendix N" of *AR,* 1955-1956, p. 131.

183. *AR,* 1955-1956, p. 13. Data have been taken from the Annual Reports of the years cited.

184. "First Speech, June 12, 1951," *loc. cit.*

185. "Speech to Deans . . . , July 18, 1956," *loc. cit.*

BIBLIOGRAPHY — CHAPTER VII

1. Primary Documents:

Annual Report of the President of the University of the Philippines to the Board of Regents, 1952, 1953, 1954, 1955, and *1956.* University Archives, University Main Library, University of the Philippines, Diliman, Quezon City.

Minutes of the Meetings of the Board of Regents of the University of the Philippines, 544th Meeting, March 20, 1951 to *614th Meeting, July 5, 1956.* University Archives, University Main Library, University of the Philippines, Diliman, Quezon City.

Minutes of the Meetings of the University Council, University of the Philippines, 1952-1955. University Archives, Main Library, University of the Philippines, Quezon City.

"Report of the U.P. Alumni Association Committee Assigned to Investigate Charges Against President Vidal A. Tan, July 1, 1955." University Archives, Main Library, University of the Philippines, Quezon City.

Vidal A. Tan Papers, Boxes 6-8, University Archives, Main Library, University of the Philippines.

II. Newspapers:

Evening News, April 24, 1951.

Manila Chronicle, Year VIII, IX, and X.

Manila Times, Vol. X.

Philippine Collegian, University of the Philippines. Vols. VI to X. University Archives, Main Library, University of the Philippines, Quezon City.

NOTES ON CHAPTER VIII "SINCO'S CLASH WITH CONSERVATISM"

1. Virata's records at the University Archives, consisting of fifteen boxes, yielded very little information on the problems that affected his administration and on how he dealt with such problems. In the meetings of the Executive Committee of the University Council and the Board of Regents, Acting President Virata generally abstained from voting on important issues.

2. U.P., Office of the President, *Annual Report, 1957-1958,* p. 147.

3. Minutes of the 623rd Meeting, Board of Regents (hereinafter cited as B.R.), (4 October 1956), p. 17.

4. Minutes of the 624th Meeting, B.R. (6 September 1956), Appendix B, p. 63.

5. Enrique T. Virata, "The State of the University," *Philippine Collegian* (18 December 1957), p. 3.

6. Cristino Jamias to Tomas Fonacier, 18 October 1957, University Files, Office of General Services 710.05. These files are hereinafter cited as OGS. See also Minutes of the 2nd meeting of the Golden Jubilee Committee, 24 July 1957, in Sinco Papers, Box 15, Folder 25, U.P. Archives.

7. Minutes of the 615th meeting, B.R. (17 July 1956), p. 2. See also Minutes of the 616th Meeting (10 August 1956), and "Candidacy to the U.P. Presidency," 1958. OGS 701-02.

8. Minutes of the 620th Meeting, B.R. (6 September 1956) and Minutes of the 621st Meeting (12 September 1956), p. 4.

9. Gumersindo Garcia, Sr. to the Chairman of the Board, 29 November 1956 in Minutes of the 625th Meeting, B.R. (29 November 1956), p. 2.

10. Garcia was apparently persuaded to abandon his plan to boycott the meetings of the Board for he faithfully attended all the meetings of the Board until this body elected Vicente G. Sinco in February 1958. See Minutes of the Board from November 29, 1956 to February 1958.

11. Editorial, *Manila Chronicle* (7 January 1957), p. 4.

12. Alfredo V. Lagmay, "The Attack on the State University," *Philippine Collegian* (5 July 1957), p. 3.

13. Editorial, *Philippine Collegian* (9 January 1957), p. 4.

14. Editorial, *Philippine Collegian* (16 January 1957), p. 4.

15. "Politics hit on indecision on Presidency," *Philippine Collegian* (23 January 1957), p. 1.

16. See, for example, Alfredo V. Lagmay and 414 faculty members of the University. An Open Resolution for the Board, 23 January 1957; Leopoldo Y. Yabes and 31 faculty members, Resolution of the Society for the Advancement of Academic Freedom, 23 January 1957 and David Wico and 37 faculty members of the Extension Division, Resolution of 24 January 1957 in Minutes of the 628th Meeting, B.R. (31 January 1957), pp. 17-21.

17. Minutes of the 628th Meeting, B.R. (31 January 1957), p. 8.

18. Minutes of the 633rd Meeting, B.R. (23 May 1957), pp. 5-8.

19. Minutes of the 634th Meeting, B.R. (1 June 1957), Appendix B, pp. 8-17.

20. Regents Consing, Gonzalez, Aldana and Tamesis voted for election while Regents Sibal, Arturo Garcia, Gumersindo Garcia, Modesto Farolan, Jose P. Laurel and Aurelio Periquet voted for postponement. As might be expected, Dr. Virata abstained from voting. Minutes of the 642nd Meeting, B.R. (3 December 1957), pp. 4-9.

21. Aries Cruz, "Voices," *Philippine Collegian* (4 December 1957), p. 4.

22. "The Regents and the Big Farce," Editorial, *Philippine Collegian* (10 December 1957), p. 8.

23. Editorial, *Philippine Collegian* (18 December 1957), p. 5.

24. "The Regents and the Big Farce," *op. cit.*

25. "The Truth of the Matter," press statement issued by the University, n.d. in U.P. Executive Committee of the University Council (hereinafter cited as Executive Committee) Minutes of the 533rd Meeting (6 April 1958), p. 7.

26. Vicente G. Sinco, "Freedom and Authority," Statement at a Press Conference, 10 April 1961.

27. Press Statement for 3 January 1958 in U.P. Executive Committee Minutes of the 527th Meeting (2 January 1958).

28. The members of the Board who elected Sinco were Manuel Lim (Secretary of Education), chairman; Regents Gonzalo W. Gonzalez, Modesto Farolan, Florencio Tamesis, Gumersindo Garcia, Arturo Garcia, Ernesto Sibal, Benigno Aldana, Aurelio Periquet, Decoroso Rosales and Manuel Enverga. Minutes of the 645th Meeting, B.R. (18 February 1958), p. 1.

29. *Ibid.*

30. *Ibid.*, p. 8. See also the *Manila Times* (18 February 1958), p. 1.

31. Sinco was born in Bais, Negros Oriental on 5 April 1894. A Bachelor of Arts (Valedictorian) graduate from the Silliman Institute in 1917, he obtained his Ll.B. and Ll.M. from the University of the Philippines in 1921 and 1925 respectively. He started teaching as a professor of economics in the National University in 1919. From 1925 to 1945, he was professor of law at the University of the Philippines. After World War II, he served the government as Commissioner of the Office of Foreign Relations (now Ministry of Foreign Affairs) from 1945 to 1946. During the same period, he was chairman of the Philippine Reparations Commission to assess Japan's accountability to the Philippines. He was also on the Philippine Committee for the revision of the Philippine-American Trade Agreement in 1953-1954. He was a member of the Philippine delegation to the United Nations Conference in San Francisco and signer of the United Nations Charter; also member of the Philippine delegation to the Japanese Peace Treaty Conference and signer of that Treaty. As a recognition of his legal expertise, he was appointed member of the presidential committee to investigate Filipino labor conditions in Guam in 1954. In the same year, he was named head of the committee which investigated Mayor Arsenio H. Lacson.

    In 1953, he rejoined the University and became Dean of the College of Law upon the retirement of Dean Jose Espiritu. Despite the pressing duties of this office, he managed quite creditably the chairmanship of the Import-Export Committee of the Central Bank as well as active membership in the Monetary Board of the Central Bank.

    He also engaged in publishing and was active in private education. From 1933 to 1953, he was president of the Community Publishers, Inc. He was president of the Foundation College of Dumaguete, Negros Oriental, which he founded in 1945. He was the author of many standard sources on law, notable among which were *Philippine Political Law, Constitutional Government of the Philippines, Administrative Law: Cases and Materials* and numerous annotations and comments on the Civil Code and the Revised Penal Code. See Sinco's personnel and appointment papers in OGS 201, Vicente G. Sinco file; U.P. Proceedings of the Inauguration of Vicente G. Sinco, 18 June 1958, pp. 5-6; Federico Mangahas, "Man of Many Parts," *Kislap-Graphic* (18 July 1958), pp. 9.12.

32. Minutes of the 656th Meeting, B.R. (10 December 1958), p. 46. The Board of Regents, cognizant of the disastrous effect upon the University of the uncertainty of the President's tenure and the frequency of changes in the position, adopted a resolution on 14 June 1961 providing for a six-year term of office for the university president without prejudice to subsequent reelection. See Minutes of the 686th Meeting, B.R. (14 June 1961), p. 32.

33. *Manila Times* (20 February 1958), p. 7.

34. Minutes of the 201st Meeting, University Council (22 March 1958), p. 3.

35. *Ibid.*

36. Vicente G. Sinco, "Some Problems of the University of the Philippines," n.d., *Sinco Papers*, Box 16, Folder 18.

37. Minutes of the 647th Meeting, B.R. (31 March 1958), pp. 5-8.

38. Minutes of the 650th Meeting, B.R. (2 June 1958), p. 31.

39. See Johnny Antillon, Emmanuel T. Santos, Epifanio San Juan and Romulo Villa, Letter to the Executive Committee, 23 January 1958 in Minutes of the 528th Meeting, E.C. (22 January 1958), Appendix C; Report of the Sub-Committee of the Executive Committee [inquiring into the motorcade to Malacañang, 17 December 1957], 7 February 1958 in Minutes of the 534th Meeting, E.C. (4 June 1958), Unnumbered Appendix (this sub-committee was headed by Prof. Jose Campos Jr., Registrar of the University); Report of the Sub-Committee of the Executive Committee, 29 March 1958 in Minutes of the 532nd Meeting, E.C. (30 March 1958), (this sub-committee was headed by Prof. Ricardo Pascual); Report of the UCCSOA Fact-Finding Committee, 17 March 1958 in *ibid.* The above documents appended to the minutes of the meetings of the Executive Committee as well as the Report of the Sub-Committee headed by Dean Crisostomo Ortigas, 24 March 1958; the UCCSOA meeting of 27 March 1958, are found in the *Philippine Collegian* (8 April 1958), pp. 4-10, under the title "The Adaza-Lagua Case."

40. Minutes of the 533rd Meeting, E.C. (6 April 1958), pp. 9-10. See also Vicente G. Sinco, "Freedom and Authority," Statement at a Press Conference, 10 April 1958 in Sinco Papers, Box 16, Folder 15 and U.P., Office of the President, *Annual Report 1957-1958,* p. 26.

41. *Philippine Collegian* (8 April 1958), p. 1.

42. Teodoro Valencia, "Over A Cup of Coffee," *Manila Times* (3, 4 and 6 April 1958), p. 4.

43. Emmanuel Pelaez, Privileged Speech, 10 April 1958 in Philippines, 4th Congress, 1st Session, *Congressional Record* (Senate), vol. 1. pp. 769-793.

44. U.P., Office of the President, *Annual Report 1957-1958,* p. 26.

45. U.P. Office of the President, *Annual Report 1958-1959,* pp. 17-18; John A. Hannah, et. al., *A Study of the University of the Philippines* (Quezon City: University of the Philippines, 1958), p. iii.

46. John A. Hannah to Vicente G. Sinco, 19 September 1958, OGS 103.01; V. G. Sinco to the Chairman, National Economic Council, 3 March 1958, OGS 103.01. See also Reports of Com mittee on Reorganization, [March 1958], Sinco Papers, Box 16, Folder 15.

47. Hannah Survey Team, Report, pp. 20-22.

48. "U.S. Survey Team Urges Pay Hike for U.P. Faculty," *Manila Chronicle* (18 April 1958), p. 3.

49. Hannah Report, p. 22.

50. 649th Meeting, B.R. (5 May 1958), p. 12. Hannah Report, p. 67. W.T. Middlebrook to Sinco, 15 July 1958, OGS 103.01.

51. V.G. Sinco to John A. Hannah, 11 July 1958, OGS 103.01.

52. See Ramon C. Portugal to the President, 18 May 1959; V.G. Sinco. Memo to all Deans and Directors, 18 May 1959; Dr. Antonio Isidro, Memo to the President, 8 July 1958 all in OGS 103.01.

53. U.P. Office of the President, *Annual Report, 1961-1962,* p. 5.

54. Minutes of the 650th Meeting, B.R. (2 June 1958), p. 1.

55. Minutes of the 672nd Meeting, B.R. (12 April 1960), p. 10.

56. This was the purpose of President Sinco's three short trips abroad during the schoolyear 1960-1961; he travelled to Great Britain in May-June 1960, to Mexico in 6-12 September, and to Japan in early December. See U.P., Office of the President, *Annual Report 1960-1961,* pp. 9-10, also Appendix X, pp. 190-196.

57. V.G. Sinco, Report to the Board of Regents [on Trip to the United States, 4 October – 21 November 1958] Mimeographed, undated in V. G. Sinco, OGS, Personnel File.

58. *Ibid.* I have not been able to locate any documents indicating any follow-up of President Sinco's representations with Secretary Dulles in behalf of an Asian Center for the University. According to Dr. Josefa Saniel, present dean of the Asian Center, in my query to her on 12 January 1984, no such follow-up was made.

59. V.G. Sinco to Lloyd Russell Williams (Assistant Agricultural Attache to the United States Embassy), 9 July 1958 in Sinco Papers, Box 13, Folder 15; Sinco to John Hannah, 19 July 1958, OGS 103.03. See Also U.P., Office of the President, *Annual Report 1959-1960.*

60. Vicente G. Sinco, "The University and Its Mission," Inaugural Speech as 9th President of the University of the Philippines. Typescript, *Sinco Papers,* Box 14, Folder 24. See also the speech reproduced in full in the *Manila Chronicle* and the *Manila Times* (19 June 1958) as well as the *Carillon* (July 1958), pp. 16-26.

61. *Ibid.*

62. *Ibid.*

63. *Ibid.*

64. *Ibid.*

65. The celebration of the University's Golden Jubilee included the Faculty-Alumni Tour of the Visayas and Mindanao, the pre-Inauguration Concert, the Inauguration of the President, Rizal Day activities, A Symposium on Economic Development, Alumni Day, A Public Lecture Series, the Inauguration of the UP Male Glee Club, the Asian Conference on Cultural Cooperation, the Presentation of the Golden Jubilee Ode, a Gala Symphony Concert, the installation of a new bronze Oblation statue and the issuance of an alumni directory.

    A delegation of sixty-two faculty members, alumni and guests toured Cebu, Maribojoc, Zamboanga, Cotabato, Dadiangas and Cebu for the purpose of getting in touch with local alumni in these places. This Golden Jubilee Tour enabled the delegation from the University to gain some insight into the role played by the alumni in community and regional development during the first 50 years of the University's existence.

    The University also sponsored during the jubilee year an international conference on "Cultural Cooperation among Asian Universities" attended by 74 delegates and observers from 23 universities of 12 Asian nations, which included university presidents, vice-chancellors, rectors, deans, professors and scholars.

    The different units of the University sponsored a series of public lectures, delivered by either members of the faculty or alumni or both. Among the topics discussed were "The University and the Government," "The University and Economic Development," "The University and Culture," and "The University and Technical Development." See U.P., Office of the President, *Annual Report, 1958-1959,* pp. 14-16.

66. V.G. Sinco, "Intellectual Imperatives – A Return to Fundamentals," Speech at the Opening Exercises of the University, 10 June 1958, *Carillon,* 8,10 (June 1958), p. 19.

67. Sinco to the Committee on General Education, 22 May 1958, OGS 401.01. The Committee, which was headed by Dean Tomas Fonacier of the College of Liberal Arts, was composed of Professors Cristino Jamias, Agustin Rodolfo and Ricardo Pascual (College of Liberal Arts), Professors Amado Castro and Severina Lui-Garces (College of Business Administration) and Professor Jose Aguilar (Extension Division).

68. Minutes of the 203rd Meeting, University Council (21 June 1958), p. 3 and Minutes of the 204th Meeting (8 November 1958), p. 6.

69. U.P. Office of the President, *Annual Report, 1959-1960,* p. 31.

70. Hannah Survey Report, p. 24.

71. Teodoro A. Agoncillo, "Philippine History and Institutions I in the General Education Program," *University College Journal,* No. 1 (First Semester, 1961), pp. 99-101.

72. S.V. Epistola, "Asian Studies in General Education," *University College Journal,* No. 7 (First Sem. 1961), p. 106.

73. *Philippine Collegian* (1 March 1961), p. 1.

74. Augusto Tenmatay (Dean, University College) to V.G. Sinco, Progress Report on Activities of the University College, 13 June 1960, OGS 143.01.

75. Cesar A. Majul to the President. Annual Report of the University College, 1961-1962, [Papers of the College of Arts and Sciences]. See also Cristino Jamias, Report of 1 June 1960, OGS 400.041. Jamias, a professor of English, was head of the Office of University Publications, an office created during the Sinco administration to publish the increasing number of research studies of the faculty.

76. V.G. Sinco, Memo to Dean Tomas Fonacier, 16 May 1960, OGS 143.01; Rules Affecting the University College, the College of Arts and Sciences and the Graduate School of Arts and Sciences, 25 November 1960, OGS 143.01 and U.P., Office of the President, *Annual Report, 1959-1960,* p. 68. President Sinco was apparently more interested in the division of the College of Liberal Arts into three or four colleges. This would entail the regrouping of 17 departments into the University College and the College of Humanities and Languages, Social and Political Sciences. In a meeting of the Academic Advisory Group, he expressed the opinion that the unwieldiness of the University College and the College of Liberal Arts and the size of the latter called for such a division. This information comes from a memorandum of Arturo M. Guerrero (Dean of Student Affairs) to Sinco, 15 March 1960, OGS 111.01. (I have not been able, however, to find the pertinent minutes of this meeting of the Academic Advisory Group.) Guerrero warned the president that the latter's proposed move for decentralization would be fraught with dangers. If the College of Liberal Arts were divided into four colleges, there would be a need for a higher official to coordinate the activities of these colleges. This official would most likely be the President. Guerrero asked: "*Would* the President have the time and effort for such direct supervision? Or better still, should the President devote time and effort for such direct supervision?" The creation of new colleges under the direct leadership of the President would merely hamper the presidential function of educational leadership in the University and the country.

77. U.P., Office of the President, *Annual Report, 1959-1960,* p. 68. See also Augusto L. Tenmatay, "General Education in the University of the Philippines," *University College Journal,* 1 (First Semester, 1961), p. 30.

78. V.G. Sinco. Circular of 9 May 1960, Enclosure to Augusto Tenmatay to V.G. Sinco, Statement and Implementation of the Objectives of the University College, 13 June 1960, OGS 143.01.

79. Minutes of the 672nd Meeting, B.R. (12 April, 1960), OGS 111.01.

80. Students enrolled in the honors course were required to earn 60 units in their major discipline and 10 units in not more than three fields while those working for a mere pass degree were required to complete 45 units in their major discipline and the remaining units in not more than five subjects outside of the major field. U.P., Office of the President, *Annual Report, 1959-1969,* p. 69.

81. U.P., Office of the President, *Annual Report, 1959-1960,* p. 69.

82. Vicente G. Sinco. Memorandum to Dean Tomas Fonacier, 16 May 1960. OGS 143.01.

83. Augusto Tenmatay to Vicente G. Sinco, 25 October 1960, OGS 143.01. I have not come across any documentation that would indicate that the Tenmatay suggestion was adopted by the University.

84. U.P., Office of the President, *Annual Report, 1959-1960,* pp. 26-34.

85. Vicente G. Sinco, "A Plan for Concentrated Guided Study," *University College Journal,* No. 1 (First Sem. 1961), pp. 9-12.

86. *Ibid.*

87. U.P., Office of the President, *Annual Report, 1959-1960,* p. 70.

88. Vicente G. Sinco, Memorandum to all Deans and Directors, 14 July 1959, OGS 400.01, Folder 3, Bundle 37.

89. Ramon Tapales (Director, Conservatory of Music) to the President, 27 July 1962. The Extension Division also experimented with the guided study plan but abandoned it after one semes-

ter. See Minutes of the 23rd meeting of the Extension Division for 1960-1961, 30 July 1960, OGS 400.031. One of the first memoranda that President Carlos P. Romulo sent to the deans and directors of the different units of the University concerned the Board of Regents' ruling calling for a return to the semestral system of instruction. See Carlos P. Romulo, Memo to all Deans and Directors, 20 July 1962, OGS 400.031.

90. Minutes of the 35th Meeting, College of Medicine, 15 August 1959, cited by Dean Benjamin Barrera, Letter to the President, 31 July 1962, OGS 400.031.

91. H. Fairfield Smith to Vicente G. Sinco, 5 April 1961 in Sinco Papers, Box 15, Folder 1.

92. I have not been able to locate any copy of the draft resolution prepared by the Tupas committee. According to Prof. Emerenciana Arcellana (Interview, 15 January 1984), very few copies of this draft were circulated among the faculty of the College of Arts and Sciences and the University College. The draft resolution, however, is quoted extensively in Vicente G. Sinco, Memorandum to the Dean, College of Arts and Sciences, Resolution on the Two-Subject Plan and the Present Academic Year, 19 April 1960, in College of Arts and Sciences, Dean's Records: Memoranda, Etc., U.P. Archives.

93. *Ibid.*

94. Emerenciana Y. Arcellana to Vicente G. Sinco, Memorandum on the President's Memorandum (19 April) on the L.A. Faculty Draft Resolution, 30 April 1960.

95. "New U.P. Scholastic Plan Bears Fruit," *Daily Mirror* (10 December 1959), p. 12.

96. U.P., Office of the President, *Annual Report, 1959-1960,* p. 71.

97. "New Grade Approved by Board of Regents," *Philippine Collegian* (22 February 1961), p. 1.

98. "Comments on the grade of '4'," *Philippine Collegian* (1 March 1961), p. 1.

99. Editorial, *Philippine Collegian* (22 February 1961), p. 4.

100. *Philippine Collegian* (13 December 1961), p. 1.

101. Josefina D. Constantino, "The Slow Death of an Institution," *Sunday Times Magazine* (4 September 1960), pp. 5-8; (11 September 1960), pp. 10-11, 22-23; (18 September 1960), pp. 28-31 and (2 October 1960), pp. 42-45.

102. *Ibid.*, (4 September 1960), p. 5.

103. *Ibid.*, (2 October 1960), p. 45.

104. Armando Bonifacio, "The University and Its Ideals," *Sunday Times Magazine* (11 September 1960), p. 18.

105. Constantino, *op. cit.* (18 September 1960), p. 28.

106. *The Manila Times* (13 October 1960), p. 18-A.

107. *Philippines Herald* (17 September 1960), p. 1.

108. *Manila Daily Bulletin* (18 October 1960), p. 1. The Paras Committee, according to an editorial of the *Daily Mirror,* was a sensible alternative to an investigation that some members of the Congress were planning to initiate. The Paras Committee investigation would discourage the intrusion of partisan politics into the University. *Daily Mirror* (19 October 1960), p. 4.

109. A committee composed of Geronima Pecson, Amparo S. Lardizabal and Vitaliano Bernardino inquired into the consequences of the term system in the College of Education; Marcelino Montemayor, Corazon Juliano Agrava, Pacita de los Reyes Philipps and Amor Melencio Herrera constituted the inquiry committee for the College of Law while Emilio Abello and Frank Co Tui composed the committee of inquiry for the University College and the College of Arts and Sciences. See Salvador San Juan, Letter to Ricardo Paras, Report on the End-to-End System, 22 May 1961, OGS 100.1.

110. *Ibid.*

111. *Ibid.*

112. *Ibid.*, Annex C.

113. *Ibid.*

114. *Philippine Collegian* (11 January 1961), p. 1.

115. On the basis of the partial Paras Committee report, the University Council voted down on 16 May 1962 the three-year-old term system. On the same day, the Board of Regents met for the sole purpose – it did not have any agenda – of rejecting the term system in favor of the re-institution of the semestral system. Minutes of the 697th Meeting, University Council (16 May 1962) and Minutes of the 697th Meeting, B.R. (16 May 1962).

116. U.P., Office of the President, *Annual Report, 1960-1961,* Appendix S.

117. Minutes of the 655th Meeting, B.R. (6 November 1958), p. 34.

118. *Philippine Collegian* (22 April 1961), pp. 1, 17.

119. *Philippine Collegian* (3 October 1961), p. 1.

120. U.P. Office of the President, *Annual Report, 1961-1962,* p. 1.

121. Documents on the Re-opening of the Baguio Branch, OGS 342.01 particularly Vicente G. Sinco, Note [on the U.P. Baguio Branch], 21 November 1961 and V.G. Sinco to the City Engineers of Baguio City, 13 May 1960.

122. U.P. Office of the President, *Annual Report, 1961-1962,* p. 2; *Philippine Collegian* (1 March 1962), p. 8.

123. U.P., Office of the President, *Annual Report, 1961-1962,* p. 5.

124. Vicente G. Sinco, Memo to all Deans, Directors and Heads of Administrative Offices, 18 April 1958, OGS 103.01.

125. Minutes of the 670th Meeting, B.R. (17 February 1960),p. 10. See also the *Philippine Collegian* (1 February 1961), p. 1.

126. *Philippine Collegian* (17 October 1961), p. 1.

127. Minutes of the 688th Meeting, B.R. (4 September 1961), Appendix B, p. 392.

128. *Philippine Collegian* (11 July 1957), pp. 1-2.

129. Teresita M. Gamboa, *et al. versus* Vicente G. Sinco and Arturo M. Guerrero, Brief enclosed in Memorandum for the Board of Regents, University of the Philippines, 21 July 1961 in Sinco Papers, Box 18, Folder 16.

130. Alfredo V. Lagmay, "The Attack on the State University," in *Academic Freedom*, a Special Issue of the *Philippine Collegian,* edited by Jose H.Y. Masakayan, *et al.* (U.P., 1957) p. 18.

131. Minutes of the 675th Meeting, B.R. (8 June 1960), p. 38.

132. Indeed, the UPSCA Chaplain, Pacifico Ortiz, S.J., said in a memorandum to President Ramon Magsaysay that the Laurel recommendations would impose a religious test for the exercise of a civil and political right and would violate the constitutional rights of students to form associations for purposes not contrary to law. Ortiz assured the President that if UPSCA's political rights were no longer attacked or denied, UPSCA itself would, "under proper and favorable circumstances, find its way clear towards avoiding direct political participation as an organization." See Pacifico Ortiz, S.J., Memorandum for President Magsaysay on the proposed change on the Code of the University of the Philippines, Sinco Papers, Box 18, Folder 15.

133. Atty. Perfecto V. Fernandez, Memo to President Sinco, 20 March 1962, Sinco Papers, Box 18, folder 15.

134. The full text of the administrative circular is in the *Philippine Collegian* (25 June 1958), p. 1.

135. Francisco Carreon (Legal Counsel to the UPSCA) to Vicente Sinco, 27 June 1958, OGS 602.01.

136. See Sabino Padilla, Memorandum to the U.P. Board of Regents, 27 November 1961, Being a Brief in Behalf of Petitioners Teresita M. Gamboa, *et al. versus* Vicente G. Sinco and Arturo M. Guerrero, Sinco papers, Box 18, Folder 10.

137. Bienvenido Tan, Court Order of 2 July 1958, OGS 602.01. See also *Manila Daily Bulletin* (23 July 1958), p. 1 and the *Philippine Collegian* (30 July 1958), p. 1.

138. *Philippine Collegian* (30 July 1958), p. 1.

139. *Philippine Collegian* (25 January 1961), p. 1.

140. *Philippine Collegian* (19 June 1961), p. 1.

141. *Ibid.*

142. Padilla, *op. cit.*

143. *Philippine Collegian* (19 July 1961), p. 7.

144. *Ibid.*

145. *Philippine Collegian* (17 October 1961), p. 7. Maria Teresa Manuel, a student of the College of Pharmacy and former member of the UPSCA hinted in her letter to Professor Barrios that the organization sought to subvert the ruling. She said that the UPSCA president, G. Abad, enjoined his members who were candidates to resign from the UPSCA – which for all intents and purposes would be a sham resignation – so that they might be allowed to run for office. Maria Teresa Manuel to Prof. Carlos Barrios (Chairman, COSECA), 21 July 1961, Sinco Papers, Box 15, Folder 23. I have not found any other letter of the same import.

146. Minutes of the 545th Meeting, E.C. (12 October 1959), p. 2. See also Arturo M. Guerrero (Dean of Student Affairs) to V.G.Sinco, 16 July 1959, OGS 602.01. The Registrar sent out 6,000 letters to parents and guardians for the purpose; 1,859 responded, out of whom 1,547 opposed fraternity or sorority membership for their children, 295 were in favor while 17 were indifferent or undecided.

147. Romulo S. Gatilao, "On the New Rule on Fraternities," *Philippine Collegian* (14 May 1959), p. 3.

148. U.P., Office of the President, *Annual Report, 1958-1959,* pp. 16-17. See also the *Philippine Collegian* (11 February 1959), p. 1 and (16 August 1961), p. 1.

149. Jose A. Velmonte. Memo to President Sinco, 3 January 1949; Felixberto Serrano (Secretary, Department of Foreign Affairs) to Vicente G. Sinco, 5 March 1959 and Sinco to Niceto Poblador, 7 January 1959, all in OGS 203.022.

150. *Philippine Collegian* (14 January 1959), p. 4.

151. *Philippine Collegian* (14 May 1959), p. 8. The editorial, to be sure, did not single out the President for overstepping his authority. It also adverted to the hostile relationship between the students and some college deans for the latter had not tried to develop friendly student relations and had reportedly asserted too much power and authority.

152. *Philippine Collegian* (8 March 1961), p. 1.

153. This article appeared in the *Philippine Social Sciences and Humanities Review,* Vol. 23 (June-December 1958), pp. 373-436.

154. *Philippinensian, 1959,* n.p.

155. *Manila Daily Bulletin* (10 May 1961), p. 9.

156. *Philippine Collegian* (14 March 1961), p. 3.

157. *Ibid.*

158. *Manila Daily Bulletin* (10 May 1961), pp 1, 9.

159. *Philippine Collegian* (14 March 1961), p. 3.

160. *Philippine Collegian* (22 March 1961), p. 1.

161. *Daily Mirror* (17 March 1961), pp. 1, 5.

162. Congress of the Philippines, *Congressional Record* (House), 13 March 1961, p. 979.

163. *Daily Mirror* (17 March 1961), pp. 1, 5.

164. Congress of the Philippines, *Congressional Record* (House), 21 March 1961, p. 1126.

165. *Ibid.*, p. 1132.

166. Teodoro M. Locsin, "The Idea of a University," *Philippines Free Press* (25 March 1961), p. 82.

167. Vicente G. Sinco, "The University Tradition Under the Constitution," Remarks made before the University Council Meeting of 13 April 1961, published in the *Diliman Review* Vol. 9 No. 1 (January 1961), pp. 17-20. See also the *Manila Daily Bulletin* (14 April 1961), p. 5 and *Manila Times* (17 April 1961), p. 6.

168. Minutes of the 684th Meeting, B.R. (10 March 1961), p. 6.

169. *Ibid.*, pp. 24-25.

170. *Philippine Collegian* (8 March 1961), p. 7.

171. *Philippine Collegian* (22 March 1961). See also Cesar A. Majul, "The Assault on the Academic Freedom of the University of the Philippines," in Leopoldo Y. Yabes, The Academic Freedom Issue of 1961 or The Ordeal of A Man of Academe, *Philippine Social Sciences and Humanities Review,* Vol. 29, 2 (June 1961), p. 197.

172. *Philippine Collegian* (29 March 1961), pp. 1, 3.

173. Locsin, *op. cit.*, p. 2 and Napoleon G. Rama, "Inside Congress: CAFA Under Siege," *Philippines Free Press* (25 March 1961), p. 10.

174. Locsin, *op. cit.*

175. Democratic Youth Forum, "The Truth Shall Make Us Free," in Yabes, *op. cit.*, pp. 165-67.

176. I.P. Soliongco, "Seriously Speaking," *Manila Chronicle* (10 March 1961), p. 4.

177. I.P. Soliongco, "Seriously Speaking," *Manila Chronicle* (12 March 1961), p. 4.

178. *Ibid.*

179. Carmen Guerrero-Nakpil, "My Humble Opinion," *Manila Chronicle* (14 March 1961). p. 4.

180. Jose Ma. Sison, "Enemies of Intellectual Freedom," *Philippine Collegian* (19 July 1961), p. 3.

181. Vicente G. Sinco to Emmanuel Pelaez (Secretary of Foreign Affairs), 24 April 1962, OGS 100.01.

182. Carlos Albert to the Board of Regents, University of the Philippines, 8 April 1961, OGS 101.04.

183. The first article appeared in the 5 March 1961 issue of the *Philippine Collegian* while the last two appeared in the 1959 *Philippinensian.* In the court hearings that followed, Alfonso Bince, business manager of the *Philippinensian,* revealed that Petronilo Bn. Daroy was the author of "The Tower of Babel and the Tower of Ivory" while Homobono Adaza was the author of "Human Dignity – The Myth and the Heresy." See *Philippine Collegian* (9 July 1961), p. 1.

184. Quoted in Yabes, *op. cit.*, p. 205.

185. Francisco Carreon, Brief Prepared in behalf of Leopoldo Y. Yabes (Criminal Case No. Q-4624), *ibid.*, p. 259.

186. Perfecto V. Fernandez, Resolution Prepared in behalf of Respondents Tomas Fonacier, *et al.*, and Carlos Albert versus Tomas Fonacier, *et al.*, 7 March 1962 in *ibid.*, pp. 207-*et seq.*

187. Sentence on Criminal Case No. Q-4624 (People of the Philippines versus L.Y. Yabes and Tomas Fonacier) in *ibid.*

188. *Manila Daily Bulletin* (14 April 1962), p. 1. See also the *Philippine Collegian* (5 January 1962), p. 1.

189. Quoted by Jose Guevara, "Point of Order," *Manila Times* (6 January 1962). p. 4.

190. *Philippine Collegian* (5 January 1962), p. 4.

191. University of the Philippines Student Union, Manifesto and Resolution of 6 January 1962, OGS 602.01. Various columnists in the *Philippine Collegian* also objected to the Macapagal "offer" to Romulo. Ferdinand Tinio, in his column "Tones and Overtones" wrote that Macapagal's "appointment" of Romulo and the latter's "acceptance" might have seemed academic but they would still amount to "transforming the Board of Regents, a legally constituted body, into a mere rubber stamp of the President." *Philippine Collegian* (17 January 1962), p. 8.

192. *Philippine Collegian* (11 January 1962), p. 1.

193. *Philippine Collegian* (17 January 1962), p. 7.

194. *Philippine Collegian* (31 January 1962). The Civil Liberties Union noted that Macapagal dispatched Constabulary Rangers to the Central Bank in the same "wanton dispatch" of presidential power even before he had assumed office. Constabulary Rangers stormed into the Central Bank Building "to throw out" Dominador Aytona, who had been appointed by outgoing President Carlos Garcia on the eve of the turnover of Malacañang Palace to Macapagal. For the development of the controversy over the so-called "midnight appointments," see the *Manila Times* and *Manila Chronicle*, January and February 1962.

195. Editorial, *Philippine Collegian* (31 January 1962), p. 8.

196. See newspaper reports for 14-16 April 1962 but particularly the *Manila Times* and *Manila Daily Bulletin.*

197. Reyes, who replaced Jorge B. Vargas in the Board, attended the meeting of the regents for the first time on 29 March 1962 when he presented the resolution of the alumni. Minutes of the 694th Meeting, B.R. (29 March 1962).

198. *Manila Times* (13 April 1962), p. 1.

199. Minutes of the 695th Meeting, B.R. (13 April 1962), p. 4.

200. Minutes of the 694th Meeting, B.R. (29 March 1962), p. 3.

201. *Ibid.*

202. Minutes of the 564th Meeting, E.C. (30 March 1962), p. 4 and Minutes of the 565th Meeting (11 April 1962), p. 3. See also the *Philippine Collegian* (14 May 1962), p. 1.

203. This remark is attributed to Vicente Barranco, a journalist. *Manila Daily Bulletin* (13 April 1962), pp. 1, 8. Macapagal denied during his commencement address that when he mentioned the name of Romulo for the University Presidency, it was with the idea of forcing Sinco out before his term expired. Press release prepared for President Diosdado Macapagal, 24 April 1962, Sinco Papers, Box 17, Folder 2. See also *Manila Daily Bulletin* (27 April 1962), p. 10.

204. *Philippine Collegian* (10 April 1962), p. 1.

205. Minutes of the 696th Meeting, B.R. (9 May 1962), pp. 4-5.

206. *Philippine Collegian* (14 April 1962), p. 16.

207. Quoted in the *Manila Daily Bulletin* (2 June 1962), p. 11.

208. *Manila Daily Bulletin* (22 June 1962), p. 3. I have not been able to locate the final report of the Paras Committee in the records of the University. The brief report in the newspaper quotes the Paras Committee to be "quite satisfied" that the charge that "Godlessness" was reigning on the campus was not borne out by facts. However, it was the "sectarianism of the over-enthusiastic type" that continued to be the source of "conflict and confusion" in the University.

BIBLIOGRAPHIC NOTE

There is no scarcity of source material for the history of the Virata and Sinco years. Except for some groups of records which are scattered and hardly classified for orderly and systematic research, the records are remarkably accessible and abundant for a serious examination of the Virata and Sinco presidencies.

The records of the University are by far the most valuable source for this chapter. Classified here as University Files, these records are preserved by the Office of General Services (OGS) in the basement of Quezon Hall. The President's Annual Reports, the records of the official functions of the University such as the minutes of the meetings of the Board of Regents, the University Council and the Council's Executive Committee as well as documents pertaining to various units of the University are an important section of the University Files. Papers on important events, problems and issues affecting the University may also be found here. Convenient accession numbers guide the researcher into these records. However, some entries are downright dead ends, leading to nothing more than empty folders.

The Office of General Services also maintains files for all faculty and non-teaching personnel of the University. These folders provide a profile of the academic community and constitute a veritable source for the history of the University.

The University Archives, a section of the University Library, duplicates the University Files' collection of the President's Annual Reports and official records mentioned above. In addition, it possesses the papers of Presidents Virata (15 boxes) and Sinco (55 boxes). The papers of Virata yield very little information on developments within the University during his interim Presidency. The Sinco papers, on the other hand, reflect a man concerned about the University and its mission. Only six or seven boxes actually contain documents related to his Presidency; the rest pertain to a rich active professional life before his appointment to the Presidency as well as to his record as a member of the 1971-1972 Constitutional Convention.

The University Archives is also a treasure house for such archival materials as student and faculty correspondence, compilations of newspaper articles on the University, programs and books on the University and other memorabilla. The Archives' collection of the *Philippinensian* and the university student newspaper, the *Philippine Collegian,* was most valuable to my research. The *Collegian* presents the whole kaleidos cope of life in the University and provides much data about the institution that are not available in the official records. The Filipiniana Section of the University Library houses copies of the metropolitan newspapers such as the *Manila Times, Manila Chronicle, Daily Mirror, Philippines Herald* and the *Manila Daily Bulletin* as well as weekly magazines like the *Kislap-Graphic* and the *Philippines Free Press.* These are full of references to the University, particularly during the period when the University was being investigated by the Committee on Anti-Filipino Activities (CAFA).

The College of Arts and Sciences, which several times occupied center stage in various events in the University during the Sinco presidency, had a document storage of sorts in a small room just off the Office of the Dean of Social Sciences and Philosophy. The papers for the Sinco years are mixed with records pertaining to both earlier and later administrations. The College, which has been split into three separate colleges, began to maintain an orderly records system only since 1978.

Prof. Emerenciana Y. Arcellana very kindly lent me a copy of her memorandum to the President dated April 30, 1960. This memorandum, which expressed faculty opposition to the term system, was not available in either the University Archives or Office of General Services.

Still, it was not possible to include all the events and the issues suggested by those who claim they were most familiar with various aspects of the Sinco administration. Not all the written sources were available and verification was not possible. The minutes of the University Council meetings illustrate this aspect. These minutes consist of mere summaries of the proceedings. I have not been able to locate faithful transcripts of the meetings. I am quite certain that I missed out on the important details or controversial aspects of some of these meetings. Dr. Pablo K. Botor suggested at the meeting of the Council on July 30, 1983 that transcripts of the Council meetings be made from which summaries might be culled for distribution if only in the interest of having a more complete record for a fair and objective history of the University.

NOTES ON CHAPTER IX — "ROMULO'S DESIGN FOR THE FILIPINO UNIVERSITY"

1. *Philippine Collegian*, January 5, 1962, p. 1.
2. *Ibid.*, p. 1.
3. *Ibid.*, p. 3.
4. *Philippine Collegian*, January 17, 1962, p. 1.
5. *Philippine Collegian*, January 24, 1962, p. 1.
6. *Philippine Collegian*, January 31, 1962, p. 1.
7. *Philippine Collegian*, May 7, 1962, p. 1.
8. *Philippine Collegian*, April 14, 1962, p. 1.
9. *Philippine Collegian*, May 7, 1962, p. 1.
10. Minutes of the 696th (Special) Meeting of the Board of Regents, University of the Philippines, May 9, 1962, p. 1. The Regents present were Alejandro R. Roces, chairman, and Benigno Aldana, Encarnacion Alzona, Gumersindo Garcia, Gonzalo Gonzalez, Maria Kalaw Katigbak, Hermenegildo R. Reyes, Jose E. Romero, Ernesto Y. Sibal, Florencio Tamesis and Salih Ututalum, members.
11. *Philippine Collegian*, May 11, 1962, p. 1.
12. Minutes of the 696th (Special) Meeting of the Board of Regents, p. 2.
13. *Philippine Collegian*, May 11, 1962, p. 1.
14. Minutes of the 697th (Special) Meeting of the Board of Regents, University of the Philippines, May 16, 1962, p. 1. The Regents present were Chairman Alejandro R. Roces and Encarnacion Alzona, Gonzalo Gonzalez, Maria Kalaw Katigbak, Hermenegildo R. Reyes, Jose Romero and Ernesto Y. Sibal. Acting President of the University Enrique T. Virata also attended.
15. *Philippine Collegian*, May 18, 1962, p. 1.
16. Minutes of the 697th Meeting of the Board of Regents, University of the Philippines, May 16, 1962, p. 1.
17. *Ibid.*
18. *Philippine Collegian*, May 18, 1962, p. 4.
19. *U.P. Today*, Vol. I, No. 1 (October 1962), p. 3. [This statement was also reprinted in the program issued on the *Inauguration of Dr. Carlos P. Romulo, Ninth President of the University of the Philippines*, Quezon City, April 7, 1963, p. 1.]
20. *Ibid.*
21. *Ibid.*
22. *Ibid.*, p. 4.
23. Minutes of the 566th Meeting of the Executive Committee of the University Council, University of the Philippines, June 4, 1962, pp. 1-3. Present were Carlos P. Romulo, presiding; Ramon C. Portugal, secretary; Enrique T. Virata, Alfredo T. Morales, Dioscoro L. Umali, Jose C. Campos, Jr., Rex D. Drilon, Florentino Herrera, Jr., Arturo M. Guerrero, Vicente Abad Santos, Pedro Abelarde, Oscar Baguio, Benjamin Barrera, Tomas S. Fonacier, Arcadio Gonzaga, Cesar A. Majul, Ricardo R. Pascual, Presentacion Perez, Jose R. Rodriquez, Enrique Ruiz, Alfredo Santos, Julita Sotejo, Gregorio Zamuco, Victor Valenzuela, Cesar Virata, Nazario Pidlaoan, Carlos P. Ramos, Ramon Tapales, and David G. Wico, members.
24. *Philippine Collegian*, June 25, 1962, p. 1.

25. *Philippine Collegian*, July 17, 1962, p. 1.
26. *U.P. Today*, October 1962, p. 10.
27. *Philippine Collegian*, August 7, 1962, p. 1.
28. *Philippine Collegian*, August 21, 1962, p. 1.
29. The address of Vice President Emmanuel Pelaez is reproduced on page 5 of the *Philippine Collegian*, August 21, 1962.
30. *Philippine Collegian*, August 21, 1962, p. 8.
31. President Romulo's address, "The Future of Filipino Literature," is given in full on page 4 of the *Philippine Collegian*, September 4, 1962.
32. Minutes of the 217th Meeting of the University Council held on September 14, 1962, Appendix H, pp. 1-15. The *Philippine Collegian* (September 18, 1962) carried a story on this meeting, p. 1.
33. The Ad Hoc Committee on Long-Range Plans had Dr. Jose D. Soberano as chairman and the following as members: Vice President Dioscoro L. Umali and Dr. Agustin Kintanar, Jr.
34. The Ad Hoc Committee on Faculty Status and Welfare had Dr. Abelardo G. Samonte as chairman and the following as members: Prof. Nemesio Ceralde, Dr. Buenaventura M. Villanueva, Dr. Raymundo A. Favila and Dr. Pascual Capiz.
35. Members of the Ad Hoc Committee on Faculty Development were Dr. Eva B. Gonzalez, Dr. Ramon C. Portugal, Dr. Jose V. Abueva and Dr. Ruben Santos Cuyugan.
36. The Ad Hoc Committee on Research had Dr. Guadalupe Fores Ganzon as chairman and the following as members: Dr. Faustino T. Orillo, Dr. Jose Encarnacion, Jr., Dr. Remigio E. Agpalo, and Dr. Adelaida Bendaña Brown.
37. Members of the Ad Hoc Committee on Central Administration were Prof. Ramon M. Garcia, Dr. Leandro A. Viloria and Prof. Felina G. Mapa.
38. Members of the Ad Hoc Committee on the Executive Committee and College Autonomy were Dr. Victor C. Valenzuela and Director Carlos P. Ramos.
39. The Ad Hoc Committee on Finance had Prof. Jose C. Campos as chairman and the following as members: Dr. Florentino Herrera, Jr. and Dean Cesar E.A. Virata.
40. The Ad Hoc Committee on Student Scholarship and Extra-Curricular Activities had Dean Arturo M. Guerrero as chairman and the following as members: Dr. Eleanor Elequin, Dr. Esperanza R. Limcaco, Dean Vicente Abad Santos and Dr. Ramon C. Portugal.
41. *University Perspectives: Reports of the President's Ad Hoc Committees*, University of the Philippines, Quezon City, 1962-1963, pp. 15-52.
42. *Ibid.*, pp. 53-88.
43. *Ibid.*, pp. 89-124.
44. *Ibid.*, pp. 125-145.
45. *Ibid.*, pp. 159-241.
46. *Ibid.*, pp. 242-266.
47. *Inauguration of Dr. Carlos P. Romulo, Ninth President of the University of the Philippines, Quezon City, April 7, 1963.* Program brochure designed by Dr. Rod Paras Perez and printed by Cacho Hermanos, Inc.
48. *Ibid.*, pp. 4-6.
49. *Gala Concert* (Program Notes issued by the Inauguration Committee, April 5, 1963).
50. *Ibid.*, "Program Notes" by Dr. Corazon Canave-Dioquino.
51. "Towards the Best University for the Filipino" by Carlos P. Romulo in *The Role and Mission of the University; Inaugural Addresses of the Presidents, University of the Philippines*, compiled by Consuelo V. Fonacier, with an introduction by Leopoldo Y. Yabes (University of the Philippines, 1971), pp. 161-167.

52. *Ibid.*, p. 162.
53. *Ibid.*, p. 168.
54. *Ibid.*, p. 171.
55. *Ibid.*
56. *Ibid.*
57. *Ibid.*, p. 172.
58. *Ibid.*, p. 174.
59. *Ibid.*
60. *Ibid.*, p. 175.
61. *Ibid.*, p. 176.
62. *Ibid.*
63. *Ibid.*, p. 178.
64. *Ibid.*, p. 179.
65. *Ibid.*, p. 180.
66. *Ibid.*, p. 181.
67. *Ibid.*

68. *Promise and Performance: A Report from the President to the Faculty*, University of the Philippines, October 16, 1964, p. 9.

69. *Ibid.*, p. 7.
70. *Ibid.*, p. 4.
71. *Ibid.*, p. 12.
72. *Ibid.*, p. 17.
73. *Ibid.*, pp. 17-18.
74. *Ibid.*, pp. 19-20.

75. *Philippine Collegian*, June 28, 1962, p. 1.
76. *Ibid.*, p. 8.
77. *Philippine Collegian*, July 9, 1962, p. 1.
78. *Philippine Collegian*, July 10, 1962, p. 1.
79. *Philippine Collegian*, August 14, 1962, p. 1.
80. *Philippine Collegian*, September 18, 1962, p. 1.
81. "The President's Report to the University Council on His Visit to the United States and Canada," Appendix M of the Agenda of the 244th Meeting of the University Council on August 1, 1964 (Mimeographed), p. 1.

82. *Ibid.*, pp. 1-2.
83. *Ibid.*, pp. 3-4.
84. *Ibid.*, p. 6.
85. *Ibid.*, p. 8.
86. *Ibid.*, pp. 9-10.
87. *Ibid.*, pp. 10-11.
88. *Ibid.*, p. 14.

89. "The Record of the Past Four Years; the Prospect for the Next Four," Address of Dr. Carlos P. Romulo before the University Council on August 18, 1966. Appendix G. of the Agenda for the 230th Meeting of the University Council (Mimeographed), p. 1.

90. *Ibid.*, p. 3.
91. *Ibid.*, pp. 4-8.
92. *Ibid.*, pp. 11-12.
93. *Ibid.*, pp. 12-13.
94. *Ibid.*, pp. 14-15.
95. *Ibid.*, p. 17.
96. *Ibid.*, pp. 19-20.
97. *Ibid.*, p. 20.

98. Minutes of the 770th Meeting of the Board of Regents, University of the Philippines, May 17, 1968 (Mimeographed), pp. 1-2.

99. *Ibid.*, Appendix A, pp. 15-19.
100. *Ibid.*, pp. 15-16.
101. *Ibid.*, p. 18.
102. *Ibid.*, pp. 18-19.
103. *Ibid.*, pp. 1-2.

104. Minutes of the 777th Meeting of the Board of Regents, University of the Philippines, December 20, 1968, p. 15.
105. *Ibid.*, p. 16.
106. *Ibid.*, p.17.
107. *Philippine Collegian*, January 9, 1969, p. 1.
108. *Philippine Collegian*, January 30, 1969, p. 1.
109. *Philippine Collegian*, July 3, 1968, p. 1.
110. *Philippine Collegian*, August 1, 1968, p. 1.

111. *Philippine Collegian*, August 7, 1968, p. 1.

112. *Philippine Collegian*, August 14, 1968, p. 1.

113. *Philippine Collegian*, August 21, 1968, p. 1.

114. *Philippine Collegian*, August 7, 1968, p. 8.

115. *Philippine Collegian*, August 21, 1968, p. 4.

116. Letter of Senator Lorenzo Tañada to President Carlos P. Romulo on August 2, 1968. *Philippine Collegian*, August 7, 1968, pp. 4-5.

BIBLIOGRAPHY — CHAPTER IX

Gala Concert, Issued by the Inauguration Committee, April 5, 1963, unnumbered pages.

Inauguration of Dr. Carlos P. Romulo, Ninth President of the University of the Philippines, Quezon City, April 7, 1963. Program brochure designed by Dr. Rod Paras Perez, printed by Cacho Hermanos, Inc., and issued by the Inauguration Committee, n.p., n.d.

Minutes of Meetings of the Board of Regents, University of the Philippines, Diliman, Quezon City, 1962-1968.

Minutes of Meetings of the Executive Committee of the University Council, University of the Philippines, Quezon City, 1962-1968.

Minutes of Meetings of the University Council, University of the Philippines, Quezon City, 1962-1968.

Philippine Collegian, Official Student Organ of the University of the Philippines, 1962-1968.

Promise and Performance: A Report from the President to the Faculty, University of the Philippines, Quezon City, October 16, 1964.

Romulo Papers, U.P. Archives, University Library, Diliman, Quezon City.

Carlos P. Romulo, "Towards the Best University for the Filipino," in *The Role and Mission of the University; Inaugural Addresses of the Presidents, University of the Philippines*, compiled by Consuelo V. Fonacier, with an Introduction by Leopoldo Y. Yabes, University of the Philippines, 1971.

University Perspectives: Reports of the President's Ad Hoc Committees, University of the Philippines, Quezon City, 1962-1963.

U.P. Today, Edited by N.V.M. Gonzalez, University of the Philippines, Quezon Hall, Diliman, Quezon City, 1962-1968.

NOTES ON CHAPTER X — "LOPEZ'S BELEAGUERED TENURE"

1. Statement of President Marcos during the oath taking at Malacañang of UP President O.D. Corpuz as quoted by S.P. Lopez in his column, "Viewpoint," *Times Journal,* October 10, 1982, p. 2.

2. S.P. Lopez's statement after his oath taking on January 23, 1969, in the *Philippine Collegian,* January 30, 1969, p. 1.

3. Letter to Mr. Arzadon (n.d.), Lopez Papers, University Archives and Records Depository (U.A.R.D.).

4. *Ibid.*

5. S.P. Lopez's statement after his oath taking on January 23, 1969.

6. S.P. Lopez, *Growth and Development Through the Years of Turmoil.* p. 3.

7. Nick Joaquin, "Diplomat at Diliman," in *Philippines Free Press,* September 6, 1969, p. 68.

8. Memorandum of the President to the Members of the Board of Regents, March 24, 1969, in *Minutes of the 780th Meeting of the Board of Regents,* March 25, 1969, Appendix B, pp. 4-5.

9. The editorship of Victor Manarang , who served from August 7, 1969 to April 10, 1970, inaugurated the "radicalization" of the *Philippine Collegian,* which went on until January 20, 1972, when a moderate, Teodoro D. Yabut, assumed the editorship. After Manarang came Ernesto M. Valencia (July 1, 1970 – Oct. 13, 1970); Antonio S. Tagamolila (December 3, 1970 – April 1, 1971); Reynaldo B. Vea (July 2 to 16, 1971) who resigned the editorship to run for the chairmanship of the University Student Council; and Eduardo T. Gonzalez (July 23, 1971 – Oct. 21, 1971).

   The examining committee that chose Victor Manarang also started the practice of keeping the members of the committee together from the giving of the examinations to the rating of the papers, until the selection of the editor-in-chief. This practice was apparently initiated to ensure that no examinee nor outside pressure could unduly influence the members of the committee in the selection of the editor. By being together throughout the period of the selection process, the decision of the members of the Committee would be above reproach since the examination papers were coded, and the envelopes containing the names of the examinees were not opened until the final selection of the editor had been made. Moreover, the sealed box containing the envelopes was kept by the Assistant Dean of Students who was called only after the judges had made their choices.

10. The Board of Regents gave due course to Sta. Maria's appeal for an investigation, but in the special meeting called to give the latter an opportunity to air his side through counsel, Sta. Maria said he would not place himself under the authority of the Board. For the Board's discussion on the Sta. Maria case, see the minutes of the 784th and the 785th meetings of the Board of Regents held July 25 and 29 respectively.

11. The declarations of those opposing and supporting the transfer of Sta. Maria are printed in full in the July 31, 1969 issue of the *Philippine Collegian.* Dean Vicente Abad Santos, who led 28 other faculty members of the College of Law in protesting the removal of Sta. Maria, subsequently resigned from the deanship of the College of Law as an aftermath of this case.

12. What could be considered as basically the first all-Pilipino issue (which included 4 poems in English dedicated to Rolando Perez, an Upsilonian killed in a fraternity rumble) came out on September 25, 1969, while the first Pilipino-English issue was inaugurated on October 2, 1969.

13. See the 8-page supplement of the January 5, 1970 issue of the *Collegian* for the full text of these and other militant articles on nationalism and the revolution.

14. The *Philippine Collegian,* January 8, 1970, p. 7.

15. *Ibid.* The latter memorandum was practically disregarded by the students. The Office of Student Affairs had to use its own resources in finding out anything about planned demonstrations, rallies and pickets.

16. Three student leaders, the editor-in-chief of the *Philippinensian '70,* the Vice-Chairman of the Student Council and the former President of the U.P. Woman's Club, when interviewed by a *Carillon* staffer after ten months of Lopez's administration, praised him for being receptive to student views and for understanding the student movement. The *Kalatas,* publication of the U.P. Student Council, in its July 26, 1969 issue was skeptical of President Lopez's concept of good administration, but the paper vented its ire on the Secretary of the University, Alejandro M. Fernandez.

17. S.P. Lopez, "The Defense of Liberty – Our Highest Duty," January 27, 1970; in the *Philippine Collegian,* January 28, 1970, p. 3.

18. S.P. Lopez, "Memorandum on the U.P. Faculty March and Demonstration at Malacañang on January 29, 1970 and the 'Confrontation' between the Faculty Delegation and President Marcos," March 10, 1970. (Mimeographed copy) pp. 1-2.

19. Other members of the committee were Dr. Ruben Santos Cuyugan, Dr. Victor Valenzuela, Dr. Francisco Nemenzo Jr., Dr. Emerenciana Y. Arcellana, Prof. Dolores Feria and Prof. Merlin M. Magallona.

20. The *Philippines Herald* reported that there were some 4,000 marchers. The *Manila Chronicle's* estimate was 1,000 participants. See Annex "C", "Memorandum on the U.P. Faculty March. . .", pp. 3 and 5.

21. *Ibid.*, p. 4.

22. *Ibid.*, p. 5.

23. Francisco Nemenzo Jr. and Dolores Feria in a press interview with the *Manila Times* on Feb. 3, 1970 charged that press reporting of the meeting with President Marcos was, with some exceptions slanted, censored or misrepresented the facts. They took to task President Marcos for assuming that 500 U.P. faculty members were either under the influence of the "subversive elements" or were tools of the Liberal Party to march to Malacañang, and for hurling veiled threats and intimidating the U.P. Faculty March.

24. Simeon G. del Rosario, "Writer Indicts S.P. Lopez" in *Weekly Nation,* April 6, 1970, pp. 5 and 42.

25. Memorandum of the Dean of Students, Abraham Felipe, to the U.P. President on the subject: "Report on the Participation of U.P. Students in Recent Demonstrations," in *Minutes of the 792nd Meeting of the Board of Regents,* February 25, 1970, Annex "C", pp. 53-57.

26. *Ibid.*

27. Ady Tempongko and Ferdie Constantino, "The Struggle in the First Quarter.1970." The *Philippine Collegian,* April 10, 1970, p. 6. See also Jose F. Lacaba, *Days of Disquiet, Nights of Rage,* pp. 11-26.

28. The Board of Student Petitions, which conducted a hearing on the petition, ruled in favor of the status quo in a decision handed down on June 11, 1970.

29. *Kalatas,* October 5, 1970, p. 1. S.P. Lopez denied that the students occupied Quezon Hall since he said that it was on his invitation that the students entered his office. See *The U.P. Report,* October 21, 1970, p. 1.

30. *Ibid.*

31. Memorandum of the President to the Board of Regents, January 26, 1971, on the subject: "The Student Blockade of the Campus on January 11 and 12, 1971," in *Minutes of the 804th Meeting of the Board of Regents,* January 28, 1971, Appendix CCC, pp. 310-323.

32. See the Report of Dean Lantican in *Ibid.,* Appendix BBB, pp. 317-319.

33. Testimony of Prof. Inocente Campos to the Committee on Inquiry on Events and Developments from February 1-9, 1971. The Committee decided not to have minutes of meetings and interviews, but as Secretary of the Committee, I took handwritten notes of all meetings and interviews.

34. *Ibid.* According to Professor Campos, he fired up in the air, specially after a student tried to grab his gun. He overheard the students saying "Patayin natin si Campos."

35. Professor Campos was later charged with homicide for the death of Pastor Mesina, but Judge Pacifico de Castro of the Quezon City Court of First Instance acquitted him on July 7, 1972, ruling that Professor Campos "acted upon an impulse of an uncontrollable fear of an equal or greater injury." See the *Philippine Collegian,* September 17, 1972, p. 1.

36. The College of Arts and Sciences played a prominent role in all these instruments of protest. The C.A.S. steps was a favorite meeting place, and a routine was perfected to disrupt classes. One group would go around the building with the use of a loudspeaker inviting students to join them. As the group swelled, they would leave the building and march around the campus to gather more supporters, ultimately ending at the C.A.S. steps where fiery speeches in Pilipino were delivered on the issues of the day.

    By the time of the suspension of the *Writ of Habeas Corpus* by President Marcos on August 23, 1971, the students were using a new technique of disrupting classes in the College: "They would close the grill gates leading to the second and higher floors of Palma Hall . . . sometimes plug keyholes of doorknobs and locks . . ." See the *Annual Report of the College of Arts and Sciences, Academic Year 1971 - 1972,* p. 24.

37. "President's Remarks on the University Under Martial Law," *U.P. Gazette,* September – October 1972, p. 132.

38. The Board of Regents, at its 826th meeting on November 27, 1972, discussed the matter of resuming student activities and agreed to ask the Dean of Students for a program of activities, emphasizing student welfare.

39. The fact that the incumbent editor-in-chief, Oscar Yabes, was a Sigma Rhoan, belonging to the moderate group, facilitated the resumption of the publication of the *Collegian.*

40. *Minutes of the 841st Meeting of the Board of Regents,* January 31, 1974, p. 34. While the Board went along with the President in the use of Student Council Funds, it did not officially recognize the existence of the CONCOMSA.

41. See the *Annual Report of the College of Arts and Sciences, Academic Year 1972-1973,* pp. 13-15 and the *Minutes of the 829th Meeting of the Board of Regents,* January 25, 1973, pp. 45-46 for the lists of those dropped from the rolls. Ester Albano of the Chemistry Department took an indefinite leave of absence effective January 3, 1973, while Francisco Nemenzo Jr. was on inactive status effective October 18, 1972.

42. Lopez, *Growth and Development,* p. 22.

43. S.P. Lopez, "Student Activism in U.P.," paper read at the Seminar on Modern Trends in University Administration, ASAIHL, held in Hongkong, December 10, 1969, reproduced in full in the *Philippine Collegian,* December 11, 1969, p. 6.

44. P.A. Zapanta, "The Mentors Speak Out," *Sunday Times Magazine,* February 22, 1970, p. 43.

45. See the *Annual Report of the School of Economics, 1971-1972,* pp. 7-8.

46. Lopez, "Student Activism in U.P.," *op. cit.*

47. S.P. Lopez, "Philippine Society in Transition," in Lopez Papers, U.A.R.D.

48. S.P. Lopez, "Statement Made Before the University Council on January 24, 1970," in *Minutes of the 241st University Council Meeting,* January 24, 1970, p. 4.

49. An examination of the participation of the four student regents shows that they performed creditably, although Ericson Baculinao at times acted haughtily and demanded such concessions as the use of a University car for the students, and the revising of University rules to allow transferees from other schools who were dropped due to their activist orientations. The first demand was disallowed by the University Auditor while the second item was referred by the Board to the University Council, which body decided that there was no need to revise any University rule because admission of these students could be considered on a case-to-case basis.

50. See the July 24 and August 7, 1969 issues of the *Philippine Collegian,* pp. 3 and 1 respectively.

51. "The President Views 'Protest' Classes," *The U.P. Report.* February 17, 1970, p. 1.

52. Letter of resignation of O.M. Alfonso dated Feb. 23, 1970, found in the files of the Office of the Dean, College of Arts and Sciences.

53. *Minutes of the 793rd Meeting of the Board of Regents,* April 7, 1970, p. 47.

54. The *Philippine Collegian,* October 21, 1971, p. 2.

55. *The U.P. Report,* April 15, 1970, p. 7.

56. Lopez, *Growth and Development*, p. 17.

57. The University Student Council through its Chairman, Fernando Barican, initiated the move to make entrance, college and University scholarships honorific. A survey made by the Office of Student Affairs did show that the majority of the recipients of these scholarships came from families belonging to the upper income bracket.

58. *Minutes of the 842nd Meeting of the Board of Regents,* February 28, 1972, Appendix "N", pp. 76-101.

59. At the 825th meeting of the Board of Regents on October 6, 1972, Regent Silva denied having a hand in the preparation of the Charter.

60. *Minutes of the 825th Meeting of the Board of Regents,* October 26, 1972, Appendix AA, pp. 201-203.

61. *Ibid.,* Appendix BB.

62. The *Philippine Collegian,* in its July 17, 1974 issue ran the column of Herminio Beltran entitled, "P.C.A.S.: Duplicating the University?".

63. Lopez, *Growth and Development*, p. 22.

64. S.P. Lopez, "The University and National Development," in *U.P. Gazette,* July 31, 1972, p. 94. Lopez defined nationalism as a "sense of belonging to, and identifying with one's people inspired by a desire to serve them unselfishly and with complete devotion. It is a belief in one's people, in their capacity to fulfill to the utmost their potentials as human beings."

65. The committee was chaired by Dr. Victor Valenzuela, with Drs. Eleanor T. Elequin and Cesar A. Majul (faculty), Theron Lacson, Judith Guthertz and Marie Magno (students).

66. "Consideration for a Review of the Curriculum in U.P.," in the *Philippine Collegian,* September 17, 1969, p. 10.

67. See the *Annual Report of the College of Arts and Sciences for Academic Year 1970-1971.*

68. *Minutes of the 243rd University Council Meeting,* June 15, 1970, p. 1.

69. The Anesthesiology Center Western Pacific was authorized by the Board of Regents to operate on December 19, 1969. Funded by the China Medical Board of New York, Inc., its mission was, among others, to offer a post-doctoral course in anesthesiology and to meet the acute need for trained anesthesiologists in the Western Pacific region. See the *Annual Report 1974, Anesthesiology Center Western Pacific.*

70. *Annual Report of the College of Arts and Sciences for Academic Year 1970-1971,* p. 1.

71. S.P. Lopez, "The Role of Universities in a Changing World," July 20, 1973, in Lopez Papers, U.A.R.D.

72. See the Minutes of the 254th – 256th meetings of the University Council held on February 2, April 24 and August 24, 1974 respectively.

73. Administrative Order No. 152, series of 1972, September 13, 1972.

74. See the Annual Reports of the Science Education Center, and the University Library, 1969-1975, for particulars on their respective contributions to the development of Philippine Culture.

75. The *Philippine Collegian,* September 17, 1971, p. 1.

76. The Council on Regional Development Studies was composed of the directors of the Asian Labor Education Center, Institute of Planning, Local Government Center, and the Institute for Small-Scale Industries. The Council aimed at providing a unified program of technical assistance to provincial universities and local governments. As of 1970, agreement had been signed with the City of Davao, Mindanao State University, and the University of San Carlos, with Iloilo City and Baguio as other proposed centers. See the *U.P. Report,* January 16, 1970, p. 1.

77. In recommending the creation of the Center for International Studies, Vice-President Alejandro M. Fernandez proposed the abolition of the Bachelor of Science in Foreign Service, with the C.I.S. offering an M.A. in International Affairs. The center was to have a small permanent staff, with "collaborating faculty" members from the various units of the University who had done or were interested in international studies. Except for some minutes showing the holding of meetings of core faculty members, no other record shows the operationalization of this center.

78. The P.E.A. became a distinct unit of the University, no longer a sub-unit of the College of Public Administration on March 3, 1973 in recognition of its growing stature in the training of executives. This contradicted the earlier impression that the program was heavily oriented toward public administration.

79. The Board of Regents at its 846th meeting changed the name of this unit from the original Institute of Planning on May 30, 1974 to involve it in economic planning.

80. S.P. Lopez, "The Faculty Welfare," *The U.P. Report,* April 5, 1970, p. 5.

81. President Lopez inherited the Agoncillo case involving an administrative charge filed by three faculty members in the Department of History against the then chairman of the Department, Teodoro A. Agoncillo for, among others curtailing their right to teach by not giving them teaching assignments for two semesters (first and second semesters, 1968-1969) even as the Board of Regents and the Dean of the College asked him to give teaching assignments to the faculty members concerned. Lopez, in consultation with the Board of Regents, ordered the investigation to proceed despite the "large shadow" cast by Prof. Agoncillo, appointing Professors Crisolito Pascual, Rodolfo Bulatao and Julita Sotejo as members of the investigating body. This body found Prof. Agoncillo guilty, among other things, of depriving the three faculty members of their right to teach and recommended the censure or reprimand of Prof. Agoncillo. The Board of Regents, however, merely noted the recommendation of the Pascual Committee on the suggestion of Regent Tomas S. Fonacier. For the President's report on the findings of the Hearing Committee on charges filed by the three professors against Prof. Agoncillo, the Hearing Committee's Report and the Comments of the Assistant for Legal Affairs, see the *Minutes of the 797th Meeting of the Board of Regents,* July 30, 1970, p. 34 and Appendix R, pp. 88-122.

82. The figures do not indicate whether some of these fellows were holdovers of the Romulo administration.

83. See the annual reports of the Offices of Admission and the Registrar from 1969 to 1974 for the complete breakdown of these fellowships.

84. A listing of research grants by units for the fiscal year 1969-1973 is found in the *Minutes of the 831st Meeting of the Board of Regents,* March 29, 1973, pp. 119-257. The report on research resulted from the displeasure of the Board of Regents, as expressed by Regent Fonacier, that money was invested on research, with no project outcome after the money was paid.

85. See the Minutes of the 804th (January 28, 1974), 813th (September 30, 1971), 835th (July 26, 1973) meetings of the Board of Regents for the President's Report on his trips to Hongkong; Bangkok and Chiengmai; and Jakarta respectively.

86. S.P. Lopez, "The U.P. System and U.P. Los Baños," September 23, 1974, in U.A.R.D.

87. *Ibid.*

88. See the supplement of the *Philippine Collegian,* January 13, 1975, for copies of resolutions prepared by the U.P. Alumni Association, the U.P. Faculty Organization, the U.P. Supervisors' Association, the ONAPUP, the CONCOMSA, and other endorsements from individuals and faculty of some colleges.

89. *U.P. Newsletter,* January 20, 1975, p. 1.

BIBLIOGRAPHY — CHAPTER X

I. Bibliographic Aid

Salvador P. Lopez, A Bio-Bibliography, The Library, University of the Philippines, Diliman, Quezon City, 1976.

II. Primary Sources

A. Documents/Reports:

Annual Report of the College of Agriculture, 1969-1974.
Annual Report of the College of Arts and Sciences, 1968-1975.
Annual Report of the School of Economics, 1969-1974.
Annual Report of the College of Medicine, 1968-1971; 1974-1975.
Annual Report of the Anesthesiology Center, Western Pacific, 1974.
Annual Report of the Natural Science Research Center, 1971-1972.
Annual Report of the Office of Admission and the Registrar, 1969-1974.
Annual Report of the Office of Student Affairs, 1969-1974.
Annual Report of the Science Education Center, 1969-1974.
Annual Report of the University Health Service, 1968-1975.
Annual Report of the University Library, 1968-1975.
Final Report of the Committee on Inquiry on the Events and Occurrences at the Diliman Campus from February 1 to 9, 1971, April 1971.
Lopez Papers, University of the Philippines Archives.
Minutes of the 778th to the 854th Meetings, Board of Regents, December 1968 to December 17, 1974.
Minutes of the University Council's 238th to the 256th Meetings, January 4, 1969 to August 24, 1974.
Position Paper Submitted by the U.P. Panel to the Joint Congressional Committee on Student Unrest, On Points Touched upon in the U.P. Faculty Declaration of Concern Dated January 28, 1970. (Mimeographed; 31pp. no authorship).
Report of the Valenzuela Faculty-Student Committee on the Review of the Curriculum, 1969.
Report of Participation of U.P. Students in Recent Demonstration (Memorandum of Dean of Students Abraham Felipe to the President, February 18, 1970).
Three-Year Development Plans of U.P., 1974-1976 (Alejandro Fernandez Committee Report), 1973.

B. President's Reports:

"Important Decisions Made Since the Last Meeting of the Board of Regents", Memorandum for the Members, Board of Regents, March 18, 1969.

Report on the Visit of President Marcos to the University of the Philippines, Memorandum for the Members, Board of Regents, March 24, 1969.

Report on the U.P. Faculty Demonstration on January 29, 1970 and Participation of Students in Recent Rallies, Memorandum to the Members, Board of Regents, February 23, 1970.

Statement before the Congressional Joint Committees to Inquire into the Causes of Student Unrest, March 2, 1970.

Additional Statement of President Lopez Submitted to the Congressional Joint Committee on Causes of Student Unrest, at its Request (March 10, 1970).

Action Taken with Respect to Student Demands Presented October 5, 1970. Memorandum to the Members, Board of Regents, October 26, 1970.

Updated Report on Measures Taken During and After the Emergency of February 1-9, 1971. Memorandum to the Members, Board of Regents, February 24, 1971.

Growth and Development Through the Years of Turmoil, 1974.

C. **President's Speeches/Remarks**

"The University as a Social Critic and Agent of Change," September 9, 1969.

"Student Activism in the University of the Philippines," December 10, 1969.

"A Year of Testing and Trial." Remarks at the 791st Meeting of the Board of Regents, January 21, 1970.

"The Defense of Liberty—Our Highest Duty," January 27, 1970.

"A Radical Proposal for Universities," April 26, 1970.

"The Faculty Welfare." Statement before the University Council, April 6, 1970.

"Greater Faculty-Student Involvement in University and National Affairs," June 3, 1970.

"Remarks at the University Council Meeting," January 29, 1972.

"Philippine Society in Transition," February 10, 1972.

"Retrospect and Prospect: Mid-Term View of the University," April 23, 1972.

"The University and National Development," June 7, 1972.

"President's Remarks on the University Under Martial Law," October 17, 1972.

"The U.P.: A University in a Developing Society," 1972.

"The Role of Universities in a Changing World," July 20, 1973.

"The U.P. Campus as a Multiversity," September 20, 1973.

"The U.P. System and U.P. Los Baños," September 23, 1974.

D. **U.P./Student Publications:**

Carillon, 1969-1974.

Kalatas (U.P. Student Council Publication), 1970.

Philippine Collegian, 1968-1975.

The U.P. Report, 1969-1970.

U.P. Gazette, 1970-1974.

U.P. Newsletter, 1972-1975.

E. **Periodicals:**

Examiner, January-February, 1971.

Philippines Free Press, September 16, 1969.

The Manila Chronicle, 1969-1974.

The Manila Times, 1969-1974.

Times Journal, October 10, 1982.

Weekly Nation, April 6, 1972.

F. **Book**

Lacaba, Jose F.., *Days of Disquiet, Nights of Rage*, Salinlahi Publishing House, Manila, 1982.

BIBLIOGRAPHIC NOTES ON THE UNIVERSITY DURING THE ADMINISTRATION OF S.P. LOPEZ

Documentary sources abound on the administration of S.P. Lopez. In fact, one is overwhelmed by the available materials that have to be pored over and examined.

A starting point is *Salvador P. Lopez, A Bio-Bibliography* which lists down his works and commemorative brochures on him. The University Archives has the Lopez papers, covering his communications, speeches and other important documents from his diplomatic years to his U.P. Presidency.

Unlike other Presidents, Lopez did not prepare a regular annual report, which made it difficult to chronicle a composite picture of the whole University in terms of statistics and other data which regularly goes in an annual report. All units of the University, however, were obliged to, and did, submit their annual reports, which are readily available, though not complete, in the University archives.

The lack of a regular presidential annual report was, however, compensated by the meticulous care in which President Lopez reported the highlights of his administration to his constituents through statements made to the University Council and the Board of Regents. For a look on his administration at mid-term, his "Remarks at the University Council Meeting, January 31, 1972," *U.P. Gazette*, Vol. III, No. 1, January 31, 1972, and "Retrospect and Prospect: Mid-Term View of the University," speech delivered at the Commencement Exercises of the U.P. Graduate School, April 23, 1972, should be read. "Selected Program Proposals," the 311-page report of the Alejandro Fernandez Committee on the Three-Year Development Plans of U.P., 1974-1976, reviews the basic policy directions of the University from 1969 to 1972, thereby evaluating the University programs during the turbulent years of activism. In September 1974, Lopez prepared a terminal report of his administration entitled, *Growth and Development Through the Years of Turmoil.*

The major policies taken by the University are reflected in Lopez's speeches, notably his inaugural speech, "The University as a Social Critic and Agent of Change" (September 9, 1969); "Greater Faculty-Student Involvement in University and National Affairs" (June 3, 1970); "The University and National Development" (June 7, 1972); "President's Remarks on the University Under Martial Law" (October 17, 1972); and "The U.P. Campus as a Multiversity," (September 20, 1973).

The voluminous minutes of the Board of Regents append important reports and documents. During the height of activism, Lopez wrote regular memoranda to the members of the Board of Regents updating them on actions taken by the University on various student protest moves. For example, lengthy reports on the barricades are found in the minutes of the 805th and 809th meetings of the Board.

The publication of the *U.P Gazette* in 1970 facilitated the inclusion in capsule form of memoranda, important decisions of the President and the Board of Regents, contracts and historical papers.

The student newspaper, the *Philippine Collegian*, provided valuable information on developments in the student front. Occasional mimeographed reports, handbills, and memoranda of the Student Council, COMSA, CONCOMSA and other University organizations are available in the files of the Office of Student Affairs, and in my private files. The University Archives kept copies of allegedly "subversive" position papers, manifestoes, and other publications during the height of activism and the martial law regime.

Finally, there are the numerous national magazines, periodicals and newspapers which carried articles on the University and/or mirrored the events of the period, 1969-1975.

CHAPTER X — ANNEX A

"WHERE ARE THEY NOW?"

The outstanding U.P. student leaders of the activist era were Fernando Barican, Ericson Baculinao, Victor Manarang, Ernesto Valencia, Antonio Tagamolila, Gary Olivar, Rey Vea, Bal Pinguel, Rafael Baylosis, Jeune and Carol Pagaduan, Sonny Coloma, all of them connected with the Student Council, the A.S. College Council or the *Philippine Collegian.* U.P. students who were KM-SDK members, and won national prominence were Jose Ma. Sison, Nilo Tayag, Mindo David, Julius Fortuna, Leoncio Co, Sixto Carlos, etc. Where are they now? Gerry Barican is now teaching part-time at the College of Law and is with the corporate planning division of Bank of P.I.; Ericson Baculinao was last heard to be in China and is on the wanted list of the military for being a top man in the C.P.P., Ernesto Valencia is finishing his Ph.D. in Economics at the U.P. School of Economics; Antonio Tagamolila was killed by the military in Panay; Gary Olivar is with the Hongkong Guaranty Co. Ltd.; Rey Vea is with the U.P. College of Engineering Faculty; Bal Pinguel is still under military detention; Rafael Baylosis is a top leader of the C.P.P. according to military information; the Pagaduan sisters are both physicians; Sonny Coloma is with the Far East Bank; Sison is still under detention; Carlos was released in November, 1983; Nilo Tayag is chairman of DAOP-PALAD, an organization of urban poor dwellers; Mindo David is head of LTD Management Consultancy Group and L. Co is Executive Assistant to the President of the Philippine Association of Service Exporters Inc. See Jarius Bondoc, "Student Leaders: The First Quarter Storm," *Observer,* 12 December 1982. Many other U.P. students quietly disappeared and have either been killed or are still fighting the Government.

NOTES ON CHAPTER XI — "CORPUZ AND SORIANO'S BIFOCAL ADMINISTRATIONS"

1. Remarks at the induction of Dr. Onofre D. Corpuz as 11th President of the University of the Philippines, Malacañang Reception Hall, January 24, 1975. In special issue of the *U.P. Gazette* (hereinafter referred to as *Gazette)*, April 13, 1975, p. 7.

2. "The Philippines Under Martial Law" (Dillingham Lecture Series, 1974). Quezon City: U.P. Press, 1974, p. 21.

3. *Gazette*, January 31, 1975 pp. 19 ff. has the text of the numerous resolutions.

4. UPFO resolution.

5. Resolution of 1,249 signatories from numerous units.

6. CONCOMSA resolution.

7. Special issue of *Gazette*, p. 13.

8. Disproving the gratuitous generalization that outstanding U.P. students were "average" at Harvard. For example, a student paper of his on "The Role of the President's Economic Adviser(s)" was published in the prestigious *Public Policy*, edited by John Kenneth Galbraith and Carl Friedrich.

9. Special issue of *Gazette*, p. 13.

10. Oscar M. Alfonso, "President 11: Day 1" in *ibid.*, pp. 15-17.

11. *Ibid.*, p. 10.

12. *Ibid.*, p. 26.

13. *Ibid.*

14. *Ibid.*

15. "President's Message," *Annual Report 1974-75*, p. 5.

16. *Gazette*, February 28, 1975, p. 28.

17. *Philippine Collegian* (hereinafter referred to as *Collegian*), February 10, 1975, p. 10.

18. *Ibid.*

19. *Gazette*, February 28, 1975, p. 34.

20. *U.P. Newsletter* (hereinafter referred to as *Newsletter*), February 24, 1975, p. 4.

21. *Ibid.* The referendum questions were the following:

    a. Do you want the present mayor-council form of government to continue?
    b. If not, do you favor the President exercising his powers to restructure the local government into an integrated system like a manager or commission form under such terms and conditions as he may decide?
    c. Do you approve of the manner President Marcos has been exercising his powers under martial law and the Constitution, including the power to issue proclamations, orders, decrees, and instructions with the force of law?
    d. Do you want the President to continue exercising the same powers?

22. *Ibid.*

23. Executive Order No. 1, April 22, 1975, *Gazette*, March-April 1975, p. 39.

24. *Annual Report, 1974-75*, p. 25.

25. *Gazette*, May 31, 1975, p. 83.

26. *Collegian*, July 30, 1975, p. 5.

27. *Ibid.*

28. *Collegian*, August 5, 1975, p. 1.

29. *Ibid.*, p. 5.

30. *Gazette*, August 31, 1975, p. 141.

31. *Collegian*, September 17, 1975, p. 1.

32. *Collegian*, August 20, 1975, p. 1.

33. *Collegian*, September 24, 1975, p. 1.

34. *Collegian*, June 24, 1976, p. 9.

35. *Gazette*, February 29, 1976, pp. 46-47.

36. *Ibid.*

37. *Newsletter*, March 1, 1976, p. 1.

38. *Ibid.*

39. *Annual Report, 1974-75*, p. 8.

40. *The U.P. System and the Future*, 1976, p. 29.

41. *Annual Report, 1974-75*, p. 7.

42. *U.P. and the Future, 1978*, p. 106.

43. *Triennial Report*, p. 12.

44. *Ibid.*, p. 31. The last two categories do not appear as such in the previous annual reports.

45. *Annual Report, 1974-75*, p. 5.

46. *Triennial Report*, p. 19.

47. *Ibid.*, p. 20.

48. "IHS: A Strategy for Health Manpower Development," *1978 Faculty Conference: Papers and Proceedings*, p. 37.

49. *Ibid.*

50. *Carillon*, January-February 1976, p. 1.

51. *Ibid.*

52. *Annual Report, 1975-76,* pp. 6, 17-18.

53. *Triennial Report,* p. 19.

54. *Ibid.,* p. 22.

55. For example, Alano and Collantes, *Factors Affecting the Scores in the U.P. College Admissions Test,* 1974.

56. *Gazette,* March 3, 1976, pp. 68-72.

57. *Ibid.*

58. *Democratization of Admissions,* Program Development Staff, 1976.

59. *Triennial Report,* p. 14.

60. *Democratization* . . . p. 19.

61. *Newsletter,* May 9, 1977, p. 1.

62. *Newsletter,* June 24, 1977, p. 1.

63. *Newsletter,* June 29, 1977, p. 1.

64. *Newsletter,* June 20, 1977, p. 4.

65. *Newsletter,* June 24, 1977, p. 5.

66. *Annual Report, 1974-75,* p. 20.

67. *Annual Report, 1975-76,* p. 21.

68. From various annual reports.

69. See for example, *Annual Report 1975-76,* p. 22.

70. *Triennial Report,* p. 34.

71. *Annual Report, 1974-75,* p. 20.

72. EVP Soriano in 1978 Research Conference,*Newsletter,* April 24, 1978, p. 5.

73. Randolf S. David, "Where Do We Go from Here? " *Newsletter,* April 24, 1978, p. 7.

74. President's Message, *Annual Report, 1974-75,* p. 6.

75. *Ibid.*

76. Quoted by President Corpuz in Memo No. 7: "Delinquent Submission of Reports of Final Grades," *Gazette,* March 31, 1977, pp. 67-68.

77. "Whithersoever the Teacher," *Perspectives,* May, 1980, p. 3.

78. Memo No. 7.

79. *Gazette,* March-April 1979, pp. 30-31.

80. *Gazette,* May-June 1979, pp. 55-57.

81. *Annual Report, 1974-75,* p. 7.

82. University Secretary Oscar M. Alfonso at May 1975 Planning Conference in Los Baños, *Carillon,* May 1975, p. 6.

83. *Ibid.*

84. *Newsletter,* May 26, 1975, p. 1.

85. *Annual Report, 1974-75,* p. 25.

86. *Ibid.*

87. "A Review of the Planning and Budget Process," *U.P. and the Future, 1978,* pp. 98-103.

    The College of Arts and Sciences had the most notable achievement in this regard. As a result of its series of workshops, the College underwent a significant reorganization under its new dean, Francisco Nemenzo, Jr. This restructured the College into three divisions, each one with a divisional assembly. The College faculty also underwent "corrective promotions" based on a mathematical formula utilized for the first time in the University.

88. *Annual Report, 1975-76,* p. 34.

89. *Ibid.,* pp. 31-32.

90. *Newsletter,* November 3, 1975, p. 1.

91. *Triennial Report,* pp. 43-44.

92. *Annual Report, 1974-75,* p. 27, and *Annual Report, 1975-76,* p. 31.

93. *Annual Report, 1974-75,* p. 27.

94. *Newsletter,* January 30, 1978, p. 7.

95. "Pipe Dream Comes True," *Newsletter,* December 5, 1977, pp. 4-5.

96. Data based on various agreements with agencies concerned.

97. "Usufruct Agreement with the Ministry of Human Settlements," *Gazette,* July-September 1980, pp. 127-128.

98. Memo No. 21: Availability of BLISS Housing Units at Bo. San Vicente, U.P Diliman Campus, August 26, 1980, *Gazette,* July-September 1980, p. 92.

99. *Newsletter,* April 21, 1975, p. 1.

100. *Annual Report, 1974-75,* p. 33.

101. *Perspectives,* July 1979, p. 1.

102. *Gazette,* July-August 1979, p. 81.

103. *Perspectives,* September 1979, p. 1.

104. *Gazette,* July-August 1979, p. 81.

105. *Triennial Report,* pp. 19-20.

106. *Perspectives,* February 1980, pp. 1,6,7.

107. *Gazette,* April-June 1980, p. 45.

108. *Collegian* issues for three months.

109. *Collegian,* July 3, 1979, p. 1.

110. *Ibid.*

111. *Collegian,* October 2, 1980, pp. 4-5.

112. "P.D. 711 puts strain on University Budget," *Collegian,* January 25, 1979, p. 1. and "Coffee Hour," *Perspectives,* May 1980, p. 3.

113. From annual reports of years concerned.

114. Dean Francisco Nemenzo, Jr. on P.B. 524, *Collegian,* July 23, 1980, p. 5.

115. *Perspectives,* August 1980, p. 8.

116. *Ibid.*, p. 1.

117. *Ibid.*, p. 8.

118. See for example, *Collegian,* July 30, 1980, p. 1.

BIBLIOGRAPHY — CHAPTER XI

Carillon, May 1975 and January-February 1976.

Lopez, Salvador, "The Philippines Under Martial Law" (Dillingham Lecture Series, 1974) Quezon City: U.P. Press, 1974.

Philippine Collegian, Februay 10, 1975, July 30, 1975, August 5, 1975, August 20, 1975, September 17, 1975, September 24, 1975, June 24, 1976, January 25, 1979, July 3, 1979, July 23, 1980, July 30, 1980, and October 2, 1980.

Program Development Staff, *Democratization of Admissions*, March 1977.

U.P. and The Future, March 1976, March 1977, and March 1978, Office of the President.

U.P. Annual Report, 1974-1975 and 1975-1976.

U.P. Triennial Report, 1977-1979.

U.P. Gazette, January 31, 1975, February 28, 1975, March-April 1975, April 13, 1975 (special issue) May 26, 1975, May 31, 1975, August 31, 1975, February 29, 1976, March 3, 1976, March 31, 1977, March-April 1979, May-June 1979, July-August 1979, April-June 1980, and July-September 1980.

U.P. Newsletter, February 24, 1975, November 3, 1975, March 1, 1976, May 9, 1977, June 24, 1977, June 20, 1977, April 24, 1978, April 21, 1975, December 5, 1977 and January 30, 1978.

U.P. Perspectives, July 1979, February 1980, May 1980, August 1980.

1978 Faculty Conference: Papers and Proceedings. Office of the University Secretary.

NOTES ON CHAPTER XII — "ANGARA'S TOUGHMINDED LEADERSHIP"

1. Juan Gatbonton, "Looking Beyond Martial Law," *The 1980 Fookien Times Philippine Yearbook*, p. 82.
2. "Choosing our President," Editorial, *Philippine Collegian*, January 21, 1981.
3. *Philippine Collegian*, January 21, 1981, p. 1.
4. *UP Perspectives*, IV, No. 2, May 15, 1981, p. 3.
5. *Ibid.*, p. 1.
6. *Ibid.*, p. 3.
7. *UP Perspectives*, IV, No. 4, June 15, 1981, p. 1.
8. *UP Perspectives*, IV, No. 5, June 30, 1981, p. 1.
9. *Ibid.*, p. 1.
10. Parliamentary Bill 524 was approved on its second reading on June 1, 1982 and was thereafter known as the "Education Act of 1982."
11. Parliamentary Bill 524, through Section 67, "vests in the Ministry of Education and Culture the power to administer, supervise and regulate the entire educational system." This was later modified into: "Pursuant to the Constitutional provision placing the educational institutions under the supervision of and subject to regulation by the state, the administration of the educational system and the supervision and regulation of educational institutions as provided for in this Act are hereby vested in the Ministry of Education and Culture, hereafter referred to as the Ministry." Section 63(4) further states: "No institution, program or course shall be operated nor shall any of the latter be required for graduation or for acquisition of professional status except upon recommendation of the Board of Higher Education for approval by the Minister."
12. Edgardo J. Angara, "State of UP Report," *UP Perspectives*, IV, No. 9, August 30, 1981, p. 1.
13. Edgardo J. Angara, "Towards an Alternative Resource Base," speech delivered on the occasion of Angara's induction into office on June 5, 1981 by President Marcos at Malacañang.
14. "Highlights of 1981," *UP Newsletter*, V, No. 9, December 21, 1981, pp. 7-8.
15. *UP Newsletter*, V, No. 7, February 15, 1982, p. 1.
16. Edgardo J. Angara, "Towards an Alternative Resource Base."
17. *1981-1982 Biennial Report of the University of the Philippines.*
18. Edgardo J. Angara, "State of UP Report," *UP Perspectives*, IV, No. 9, August 30, 1981.
19. *Ibid.*
20. Edgardo J. Angara, "Towards an Alternative Resource Base."
21. Angara made this statement before the University of the Philippines Supervisors General Assembly at the University of the Philippines in Los Baños on May 22, 1981. See *UP Perspectives*, IV, No. 4, June 15, 1981, p. 3.
22. Edgardo J. Angara, "Towards an Alternative Resource Base."
23. *UP Perspectives*, IV, No. 7, July 30, 1981, p. 2.
24. *Ibid.*
25. *UP Perspectives*, IV, No. 7, July 30, 1981, p. 3.
26. *UP Perspectives*, IV, No. 1, October 26, 1981, p. 1.
27. *Ibid.*

28. *Ibid.*

29. *UP Newsletter*, V, No. 1, October 26, 1981, p. 2.

30. The members of the CRAP were Virginia L. Aprieto (College of Fisheries), Gloria T. Aragon (Dean, College of Medicine), Irene R. Cortes (College of Law), Gloria D. Feliciano (Dean, Institute of Mass Communication), Jesus Montemayor (UPLB), Francisco Nemenzo, Jr. (Dean, College of Arts and Sciences), Paz G. Ramos (Dean, College of Education), and Ramon P. Santos (Dean, College of Music).

31. Edgardo J. Angara, "From Grove to Campus," speech delivered during the Special University Council Meeting at the University of the Philippines in Los Baños on December 5, 1981, *UP Newsletter*, V, No. 8, December 14, 1981, p. 5.

32. *UP Newsletter*, VI, No. 7, Febuary 15, 1982, p. 1.

33. *UP Newsletter*, VI, No. 4, January 1982, p. 1.

34. *UP Newsletter*, VI, No. 30, August 2, 1982, p. 2.

35. The division of the College of Arts and Sciences into three colleges was at this point only in its proposal stage.

36. A discussion of the issues may be found in *The Case of Two Philippine Studies Programs in the University of the Philippines: Problems, Issues, Alternatives and Perspectives*, a position paper based on the Seminar of the College of Arts and Sciences Faculty-Alumni-Students, Ph.D. Philippine Studies Ad Hoc Committee Submitted to Executive Vice-President Oscar M. Alfonso, Chairman of the Committee to Restudy the Philippine Studies Programs in the University.

37. *UP Newsletter*, VI, No. 4, January 25, 1982, p. 1.

38. *UP Newsletter*, VI, No. 7, December 6, 1982, p. 1.

39. *UP Newsletter*, VI, No. 4, January 25, 1982, p. 1.

40. *UP Newsletter*, VI, No. 5, February 1, 1982, p. 1.

41. *UP Newsletter*, VI, No. 7, February 15, 1982, p. 1.

42. *UP Newsletter*, VI, No. 17, May 3, 1982, p. 1.

43. *UP Newsletter*, VII, No. 1, January 9, 1984, p. 1.

44. *UP Newsletter*, V, No. 1, October 26, 1981. Magdaleno B. Albarracin (Dean, College of Business Administration), Antonio J. Gonzaga (College of Medicine), Magtanggol A. Marzan (UP in the Visayas), and Ramon L. Nasol (Institute of Agricultural Development and Administration), composed the MRC.

45. *UP Newsletter*, VII, No. 5, January 31, 1983, p. 1.

46. "Faculty Profile," *Biennial Report* 1980-1981; 1981-1982.

47. *UP Newsletter*, VII, No. 14, April 4, 1983, p. 1.

48. *Ibid.*, p. 1.

49. *UP Newsletter*, VIII, No. 1, January 9, 1984, p. 1.

50. *UP Newsletter*, VII, No. 48, November 28, 1983, p. 1.

51. *UP Newsletter*, VI, No. 44, November 8, 1982, p. 4.

52. *UP Newsletter*, VI, No. 45, November 22, 1982, p. 1.

53. *Ibid.*

54. *Ibid.*

55. *UP Newsletter*, IV, No. 4, June 15, 1981, p. 3.

56. *UP Newsletter*, VIII, No. 2, January 16, 1984, p. 1.

57. *UP Newsletter*, VIII, No. 1, January 9, 1984, p. 1.

58. *UP Perspectives*, IV, No. 7, July 30, 1981, p. 4.
59. *UP Newsletter*, V, No. 1, December 7, 1981), p. 1.
60. *UP Perspectives*, IV, No. 7, July 30, 1981, p. 1.
61. *UP Newsletter*, VII, No. 13, March 28, 1983, p. 1.
62. *UP Newsletter*, VI, No. 24, June 21, 1982, p. 1.
63. *UP Newsletter*, VI, No. 49, January 3, 1983, p. 1.
64. *UP Newsletter*, VII, No. 27, July 4, 1983, p. 1.
65. *UP Newsletter*, VII, No. 16, April 18, 1983, p. 1.
66. *UP Newsletter*, VII, No. 30, July 25, 1983, p. 1.
67. Edgardo J. Angara's speech during the Turnover Ceremonies of the Philippine Social Science Center on March 21, 1983, *UP Newsletter*, V, No. 13, March 28, 1983, p. 1.
68. *Ibid.*
69. *UP Newsletter*, VIII, No. 4, January 30, 1984, p. 1.
70. *UP Newsletter*, VIII, No. 14, April 30, 1984, p. 1.
71. *UP Newsletter*, VIII, No. 19, June 4, 1984, p. 1.
72. *Philippines Daily Express*, XIII, No. 27, June 2, 1984, p. 1.
73. *UP Newsletter*, VIII, No. 20, June 11, 1984, p. 1.
74. Order of the Quezon City Regional Trial Court, National Capital Judicial Region, Branch XCVI, Special Civil Case No. Q-41756, p. 3. Cited hereinafter as *Order*.
75. *UP Newsletter*, VIII, No. 20, June 11, 1984, p. 1.
76. *UP Newsletter*, VIII, No. 22, July 2, 1984, p. 1. See also *Order*, 9 pages.
77. *Order*, pp. 4-6.
78. *Ibid.*, p. 6.
79. Order of Judge Luis L. Victor of the Quezon City Regional Trial Court on Special Civil Case No. Q-41756, September 26, 1984.
80. This discussion on the events in the University before, during, and after the barricading of the UP Diliman campus on September 19, September 27-28, and November 15-16, 1984, is based on the author's direct personal experience and observations.
81. *UP Newsletter*, VIII, No. 1, January 9, 1984, p. 1.
82. *UP Newsletter*, V, No. 6, November 30, 1981, p. 1.
83. Vicente Arcega, "Squatters Invade UP," *Bulletin Today*, March 22, 1985, p. 7.
84. *Ibid.*
85. *Ibid.*
86. *Ibid.*
87. Letter of Oscar M. Alfonso to Benjamin Y. Encarnacion, Quezon City, February 28, 1985. The author is grateful to Dr. Alfonso for making available this important document pertaining to the squatter problem in UP.
88. Quoted in the Letter of Alfonso to Encarnacion, p. 2.
89. *Ibid.*
90. *Ibid.*, p. 3.

91. *Ibid.* See also *UP Newsletter*, IX, No. 3, February 15, 1985, p. 1; *Philippine Collegian*, 62, No. 4, February 5, 1985, p. 1.
92. *UP Newsletter*, IX, No. 3, February 15, 1985, p. 1.
93. Letter of Alfonso to Encarnacion, p. 3.
94. *Ibid.*, p. 4; *UP Newsletter*, IX, No. 3, February 15, 1985, p. 8.
95. Letter of Alfonso to Encarnacion, p. 2; *UP Newsletter*, IX, No. 3, February 15, 1985, p. 8.
96. Commencement Address at the University of the Philippines by President Ferdinand E. Marcos on May 22, 1966, *UP Perspectives*, IV, No. 1, June-July 1980, p. 1.

BIBLIOGRAPHY — CHAPTER XII

Articles

Angara, Edgardo J. "State of UP Report," *UP Perspectives*, IV, No. 9 (August 30, 1981).

__________. "From Grove to Campus," *UP Newsletter*, V, No. 8 (December 14, 1981).

Arcega, Vicente. "Squatters Invade UP," *Bulletin Today* (March 22, 1985).

"Choosing Our President," *Philippine Collegian* (January 21, 1981)

"Faculty Profile," *Biennial Report of the University of the Philippines 1980-1981, 1982-1983.*

Gatbonton, Juan. "Looking Beyond Martial Law," *The 1980 Fookien Times Philippines Yearbook.*

"Highlights of 1981," *UP Newsletter*, V, No. 9 (December 21, 1981).

Documents

Biennial Report of the University of the Philippines, 1980-1981; 1981-1982.

Letter of Oscar M. Alfonso to Benjamin Y. Encarnacion, Quezon City, February 28, 1985.

Order of Judge Luis L. Victor of the Quezon City Regional Trial Court on Special Case No. Q-41756, September 26, 1985.

Order of the Quezon City Regional Trial Court, National Capital Region, Branch XCVI, Spl. Civil Case No. Q-41756.

The Case of Two Philippine Studies Programs in the University of the Philippines: Problems, Issues, Alternatives and Perspectives.

Speeches

Angara, Edgardo J. "Towards an Alternative Resource Base," Malacañang Palace, June 5, 1981.

Commencement Address of Ferdinand E. Marcos at the University of the Philippines, Quezon City, May 22, 1966

Speech of Edgardo J. Angara before the University of the Philippines Supervisors' Association General Assembly, Los Baños, May 22, 1981.

Speech of Edgardo J. Angara during the Turnover Ceremonies of the Philippine Social Science Center, Quezon City, March 21, 1983.

Newspapers

Bulletin Today

Fookien Times

Philippine Collegian

Philippines Daily Express

UP Newsletter

UP Perspectives

CHAPTER XII — ANNEX A

Enrolment Figures for Academic Year 1983-1984

	Collegiate	*Non-Collegiate*	*Total*
U.P. in Diliman	16,235	3,372*	19,607
U.P. in Los Banos	5,685	584	6,269
U.P. in Manila	3,133	—	3,133
U.P. in the Visayas	2,023	497	2,520
U.P. Branches in:			
Cebu City	808	429	1,237
Baguio City	1,100	293	1,393
Clark Air Base, Pampanga	207	—	207
Tacloban City, Leyte	813	—	813
San Fernando, Pampanga	380	—	380
	30,384	5,175	35,559

*Non-Collegiate Enrolment in U.P. Diliman.

Nursery 301
Kindergarten 261
U.P. Integrated School:
Grades 1 to 6 1,430
Grades 7 to 10 1,380

Appendices

APPENDIX A

RECIPIENTS OF HONORARY DEGREES

DOCTOR OF HUMANE LETTERS, *honoris causa*

Jose Garcia Villa	June 26, 1973

DOCTOR OF HUMANITIES, *honoris causa*

Amado V. Hernandez	March 14, 1972
Rufino D. Tamayo	July 6, 1974
Geronimo T. Pecson	April 22, 1979

DOCTOR OF LAWS, *honoris causa*

Cayetano S. Arellano	March 29, 1911
Trinidad H. Pardo de Tavera	April 4, 1913
Newton Whiting Gilbert	April 2, 1914
Francis Burton Harrison	April 4, 1917
Leonard Wood	December 16, 1921
Victorino G. Mapa	December 16, 1921
Manuel Araullo	December 16, 1921
Florentino Torres	December 16, 1921
Manuel L. Quezon	March 16, 1929
Sergio Osmeña	March 25, 1930
Frank Murphy	March 31, 1936
David Sutherland Hibbard	March 23, 1937
Douglas MacArthur	March 29, 1938
Rafael V. Palma	December 17, 1938
Paul V. McNutt	April 4, 1939

Ramon Avanceña	October 19, 1939
Manuel A. Roxas	April 13, 1948
Elpidio Quirino	February 12, 1949
Edwin Bingham Copeland	April 26, 1949
Carlos P. Romulo	April 26, 1949
George Arthur Malcolm	April 26, 1949
Francisco Benitez (+)	April 14, 1953
Jorge C. Bocobo	April 14, 1953
Antonio G. Sison	April 14, 1953
Ronald R. Rennee	June 12, 1953
Emilio F. Aguinaldo	June 12, 1953
Ramon del Fierro Magsaysay	April 5, 1955
Bienvenido M. Gonzalez (+)	April 9, 1957
Carlos P. Garcia	April 7, 1959
Jose C. Locsin	November 15, 1959
Eulogio A. Rodriguez	April 17, 1960
Claro M. Recto	April 17, 1960
Dwight D. Eisenhower	June 16, 1960
Ricardo M. Paras	November 13, 1960
Lyndon B. Johnson	May 13, 1961
Adolfo Lopez Mateos	October 22, 1962
Bhumibol Adulyadej	July 13, 1963
Soekarno	August 2, 1963
Tunku Abdul Rahman Putra Al-Haj	August 3, 1963
Robert F. Kennedy	January 30, 1964
Henry Otley Beyer	May 4, 1964
Cesar P. Bengzon	May 4, 1964
Earl Warren	February 8, 1965
Diosdado Macapagal	May 30, 1965
Ferdinand E. Marcos	May 22, 1966
Vijaya Lakshmi Pandit	May 7, 1967
Roberto R. Concepcion	April 28, 1968
Eugenio H. Lopez	April 28, 1968
Jonas E. Salk	April 28, 1968
Quintin Paredes	June 18, 1968
Jose P. Laurel, Sr. (+)	April 20, 1969
Vicente G. Sinco	April 20, 1969
Vidal A. Tan	April 20, 1969

(+) Posthumously awarded.

Enrique T. Virata	April 20, 1969
Mohammed Hidayatullah	February 6, 1970
Jose Y. Yulo	April 11, 1970
Camilo Osias	April 11, 1970
Juan Salcedo, Jr.	April 11, 1970
U Thant	April 11, 1970
Jose A. Espiritu	October 19, 1971
Conrado F. Benitez(+)	January 4, 1972
Too Chin Palk	January 31, 1972
Jose B. Luna Reyes	April 22, 1972
Edward Gough Whitlam	February 11, 1974
Nicolae Ceausescu	April 11, 1975
Miguel Cuaderno, Sr.(+)	April 11, 1975
George R. Ariyoshi	November 9, 1975
Kurt Waldheim	February 12, 1976
Arturo R. Tanco, Jr.*	March 28, 1976
Cesar E.A. Virata	March 28, 1976
Hendrikus Johannes Witteveen	October 1, 1976
Robert S. McNamara	October 1, 1976
Francis Blanchard	December 5, 1977
Imelda R. Marcos	April 17, 1977
Amado-Mahtar M'Bow	June 7, 1977
Dioscoro L. Umali	April 15, 1978
Alfonso Calalang	April 16, 1978
Tomas S. Fonacier	April 16, 1978
Jorge B. Vargas	April 16, 1978
Lord Elwyn-Jones	April 18, 1979
Edouard Saouma	May 15, 1979
Salim Ahmed Salim	April 19, 1980
Gregorio S. Licaros	April 20, 1980
Mana Saeed Al-Otaiba	July 15, 1980
Sheik Ahmed Zaki Yamani	December 23, 1980
Lord Carrington	February 2, 1982
Siddhi Savetsila	May 25, 1983
Rafael M. Salas	August 8, 1983

(+)Posthumously awarded
* U.P. Los Baños awardee

DOCTOR OF LETTERS AND HUMANITIES, *honoris causa*

Bienvenido N. Santos	February 2, 1982

DOCTOR OF SCIENCE, *honoris causa*

Jose S. Algue	March 7, 1912
Leon Maria Guerrero	December 16, 1921
Gregorio Singian	March 21, 1936
Robert F. Chandler, Jr.*	April 17, 1972
Pedro B. Escuro	April 22, 1979
Alexander R. Todd	December 18, 1980
Francisco Nemenzo, Sr.	May 20, 1981
Abdus Salam	March 22, 1982
Geronimo Z. Velasco*	March 4, 1983
Calyampudi Radhakrishna Rao	August 3, 1983
Sir George Porter	May 8, 1985
Koji Kobayashi	September 12, 1985

MASTER OF PEDAGOGY, *honoris causa*

Librada Avelino	March 26, 1929

*U.P. Los Baños awardee

APPENDIX B

University of the Philippines
BOARD OF REGENTS

Complete Roster from 1908 to 1985

Esteban R. Abada, 1946-48; 1952
Aguedo F. Agbayani, 1967-71
Martin V. Aguilar, 1957* (Acting)
Alejandro M. Albert, 1920-21** (Acting), 1931*
Benigno S. Aldana, 1957-63
Encarnacion Alzona, 1959-66
Ruben B. Ancheta, 1982-
Edgardo J. Angara, 1981-**
Gregorio Anonas, 1932
Galicano Apacible, 1914-18
Gloria T. Aragon, 1984-

– B –

Ericson M. Baculinao, 1970-71
Fernando T. Barican, 1969-70
David P. Barrows, 1909
Murray S. Bartlett, 1911-15**
Roberto S. Benedicto, 1982-
Conrado Benitez, 1922-24
Francisco Benitez, 1946*
Helena Z. Benitez, 1972
Guy Potter W. Benton, 1921-23**
Cesar Bengzon, 1966
Vitaliano Bernardino, 1963-67
Luther B. Bewley, 1920-38
Jorge C. Bocobo, 1934-39; 1939-41***
Juan V. Borra, 1946-48
George C. Butte, 1932*

– C –

Fernando G. Calderon, 1922-25, 1934** (Acting)
Manuel T. Cases, 1950-51
Lino J. Castillejo, 1951-55
Carmen Dinglasan Consing, 1954-57
Rafael Corpus, 1913
Onofre D. Corpuz, 1968-71*; 1975-79; 1979-83***
Adrian E. Cristobal, 1982-
Frank Sinder Crone, 1913-16

– D –

Alejandro de Guzman, 1917-26
Gerardo V. de Leon, 1983-85
Sixto de los Angeles, 1914-18
Vicente del Rosario, 1920-28
Winfred T. Denison, 1913-16
Jose D. Drilon, Jr., 1972-75

– E –

Pastor M. Endencia, 1954*
Manuel S. Enverga, 1958-61
Jose Escaler, 1910-28
Eduardo R. Escobar, 1969-73

---

*Served as Chairman of the Board in the year or years indicated.
**Served as President of the University and concurrently member of the Board in the years indicated.

Edgardo B. Espiritu, 1985-
Jose A. Espiritu, 1945
Teodoro Evangelista, 1951* (Acting), 1952

– F –

Modesto Farolan, 1951-59
Arthur F. Fischer, 1922-24
Santiago Fonacier, 1922-26
Tomas S. Fonacier, 1966-81
Clifford French, 1916

– G –

Samuel Gaches, 1945
Manuel V. Gallego, 1946-48*
Arturo Garcia, 1954-61
Gumersindo Garcia, 1945-64
Clemente C. Gatmaitan, Jr. 1982-
Jose Gil, 1935-41
Newton W. Gilbert, 1909-12*
Eugene M. Gilmore, 1920-30*

Bienvenido Ma. Gonzalez, 1918-39, **1939-1943**, 1945-51****
Gonzalo Gonzalez, 1955-63
Maria Paz Mendoza Guazon, 1920-27
Leon Guerrero, 1909
Pedro Guevara, 1914-18

– H –

Jeremias Jacob Harty, 1910-16
Joseph Ralston Hayden, 1934-36
Gregorio Hernandez, 1954-57*
Florentino Herrera, Jr. 1975-83
Ludovico Hidrosollo, 1929-32
John H. Holliday, 1933*

– J –

Emil Q. Javier, 1979-85
E. Finley Johnson, 1913-18

– K –

Eva Estrada Kalaw, 1967-72
Teodoro M. Kalaw, 1922
Maria Kalaw Katigbak, 1962-64

– L –

Alejo Labrador, 1920-27
Prudencio Langcauon, 1948-50*
Jose P. Laurel, Sr. 1952-57
Jaime C. Laya, 1984-*

Mariano Leuterio, 1916
Manuel M. Lim, 1957-59
Manuel Q. Lim, Jr. 1981-85
Jose C. Locsin, 1929-31
Vicente Lontok, 1954-57

Salvador P. Lopez, 1969-74**
Conrado Ll. Lorenzo, Jr. 1984-
Pablo Lorenzo, 1916-21

– M –

Vicente Madrigal, 1933-41
Jeremias L. Manning, 1915-16
Juan L. Manuel, 1967-70, 1971-79*
Walter W. Marquardt, 1916-18
Henderson S. Martin, 1913-16

Alejandro Melchor, 1945-47
Enrique Mendiola, 1908-09
Estelito P. Mendoza, 1979-85
Aurelio Montinola, 1949-51

*Served as Chairman of the Board in the year or years indicated.
**Served as President of the University and concurrently member of the Board in the years indicated.

– O –

Manuel L. Ortega, 1971-72
Francisco Ortigas, 1920-36
Camilo Osias, 1920-27
Sergio Osmeña, 1938*

– P –

Nicanor Padilla, 1964-66
Rafael V. Palma, 1908-23, **1923-33****
Benito Pangilinan, 1949-52
Trinidad Pardo de Tavera, 1908-12

Pedro M. Pascasio, 1965*
Geronima T. Pecson, 1948-50, 1952
Pio Pedrosa, 1949-54, 1966-72

Aurelio Periquet, Sr. 1949-50, 1956-61
Horace B. Pond, 1920-41
Cecilio Putong, 1948-49, 1950-53*
Gil J. Puyat, 1964-67

– Q –

Manuel L. Quezon, 1916-18
Elpidio Quirino, 1929-35

– R –

Narciso Ramos, 1945-46
Hermenegildo R. Reyes, 1962-67
Jose S. Reyes, 1945*

Herman W. Reynolds, 1918-20
Alejandro R. Roces, 1962-65*
Dionisia A. Rola, 1982-
Jose E. Romero, 1934-35, 1959-61*, 1961-68

Carlos P. Romulo, 1932-41, 1945-48, **1962-68****, 1965-68*

Decoroso R. Rosales, 1958-61
Jose Rosales, 1908-10
Felix M. Roxas, 1916-17* (Acting)
Manuel A. Roxas, 1935-41, 1945

– S –

Orlando J. Sacay, 1972-82
Rafael M. Salas, 1966-69
Serafin Salvador, 1938-41
Abelardo G. Samonte, 1972-78
Ruben Santos-Cuyugan, 1974-79

Abraham F. Sarmiento, 1973-79
Ernesto Y. Sibal, 1954-62
Gerardo P. Sicat, 1972-82
Abel L. Silva, 1970-72
Vicente G. Sinco, 1958-62**
Vicente Singson-Encarnacion, 1938-41 1945-48
Fernando E.V. Sison, 1938-40
Emanuel V. Soriano, 1979-81**
Liceria B. Soriano, 1970-72
Alexander Sycip, 1970

– T –

Gloria M. Tabiana, 1972
Ernesto G. Tabujara, 1984-
Florencio Tamesis, 1957-64
Jaime G. Tan, 1972-73

Vidal A. Tan, 1931-33, **1951-56****
Ambrosio F. Tangco, 1962-82
Emiliano Tria Tirona, 1910

Ramon Torres, 1945
Venancio Trinidad, 1952-56
Jose Y. Tuason, 1961* (Acting)

*Served as Chairman of the Board in the year or years indicated.
**Served as President of the University and concurrently member of the Board in the years indicated.

– V –

Jorge B. Vargas, 1961-62
Ignacio B. Villamor, 1913-18**
Guillermo Z. Villanueva, 1933-41
Enrique T. Virata, 1956-58** (Acting)
Leonides S. Virata, 1970-71

– W –

Frank Russell White, 1910
Dean C. Worcester, 1910

– Y –

Charles E. Yeater, 1918*
Regino R. Ylanan, 1929-31
Manuel de Yriarte, 1912
Jose Yulo, 1946-63

– Z –

Jose F. Zamora, 1929-34
Ronaldo B. Zamora, 1972-

*Served as Chairman of the Board in the year or years indicated.
**Served as President of the University and concurrently member of the Board in the years indicated.

Editorial Note: The Board of Regents did not function during the Japanese Occupation from 1942 to mid-1945, although the University remained open and had Dr. Antonio G. Sison as President from October 14, 1943 to February 1945.

APPENDIX C

UNIVERSITY OF THE PHILIPPINES STUDENT COUNCIL
(Founded 1924)

ROSTER OF CHAIRMEN OF THE COUNCIL

1925-26 Eduardo R. Alvarado
1926-27 Juan Chuidian
1927-28 Ramon Nolasco
1928-29 Lorenzo Sumulong
1929-30 Gregorio Lantin

1930-31 Enrique J. Corpus
1931-32 Manuel Sevilla
1932-33 Wenceslao Q. Vinzons
1933-34 1. Ramon Enriquez
2. Alberto Leynes
1934-35 Avelino Pascual

1935-36 1. Potenciano Ilusorio
2. Jose B. Laurel, Jr.
1936-37 S. Angeles
1937-38 Roberto S. Benedicto
1938-39 Sotero Laurel
1939-40 Florante Roque

1940-41 Hermogenes Concepcion, Jr.
1941 Antonio Azores
1943 Quintin Gomez
1944 Troadio T. Quiazon, Jr.
1946-47 Troadio T. Quiazon, Jr.
1947-48 Delfin Villanueva
1948-49 Emilio Espinosa, Jr.
1949-50 Antonio M. Meer

1950-51 Teodoro Padilla
1951-52 Marcelo B. Fernan
1952-53 Rafael M. Salas
1953-54 Jose Palarca, Jr.
1954-55 Elias B. Lopez
1955-56 Fernando C. Campos
1956-58 Fernando A. Lagua

–– oOo ––

U.P. Student Union

1961-62 Enrique Voltaire Garcia II
1962-63 Eric O. de Guia

U.P. Student Council

1963-64 Leonardo A. Quisumbing
1964-65 Benjamin N. Muego

1965-66 Tristan A. Catindig
1966-67 Enrique Voltaire Garcia II
1967-68 Delfin Lazaro
1968-69 Antonio Pastelero
1969-70 Fernando Barican

1970-71 Ericson M. Baculinao
1971-72 Manuel L. Ortega
1972 Jaime G. Tan

––oOo––

1980-81 Maria Lourdes C. Mangahas
1981-82 Jose Fernando Alcantara
1982-83 Jessie John Gimenez
1983-84 Leandro Alejandro
1984-85 Maria Lourdes Almazan

APPENDIX D

EDITORS OF UNIVERSITY PUBLICATIONS

College Folio

Victoriano Yamzon	Oct. 1910-April 1911
Maximo Kalaw	August & October 1911
Andres Rañola	Dec. 1911-April 1912
Proceso E. Sebastian	August & October 1912
Fernando Maramag	Nov. 1912-April 1913

Varsity News

Carlos P. Romulo	1917-19
Vicente N. Villamorel	1919-20
Juan S. Reyes	1920-21
Narciso Ramos	1921-22

Philippine Collegian

1922-23	1. Jose Delgado 2. Paulino Ybañez
1923-24	Francisco Capistrano
1924-25	Rafael Dinglasan
1925-26	1. Francisco B. Icasiano 2. Cipriano D. Cid
1926-27	Celedonio P. Gloria
1927-28	Jacinto C. Borja
1928-29	1. Fortunato de Leon 2. Francisco B. Icasiano
1929-30	Teodoro Evangelista
1930-31	Emerito Ramos
1931-32	Wenceslao Q. Vinzons
1932-33	Ambrosio Padilla
1933	Arturo M. Tolentino
1934-35	Armando J. Malay
1935-36	Fred Ruiz Castro
1936-37	1. Sinai C. Hamada 2. Carlos Faustino
1937	Romeo S. Busuego
1938-39	Alexander Sycip
1939-40	Renato Constantino
1940-41	Angel G. Baking
1941-42	Delfin Garcia
1942-43	Quintin Gomez

——oOo——

1946	Troadio T. Quiazon, Jr.
1947	Juan M. Hagad
1948	Mariano V. Ampil, Jr.
1948-49	Leonardo B. Perez
1949-50	Augusto Caesar Espiritu
1950-51	Elmer A. Ordoñez
1951-52	Francisco Villanueva
1953	Ignacio Debuque, Jr.

1954 Crispulo J. Icban, Jr.

1955 Luis Q.U. Uranza, Jr.

1955-56 Sabino Padilla, Jr.

1957 Jose H.Y. Masakayan

1957-58 Homobono A. Adaza

1958-59 Caesar I. Agnir

1959 Andres G. Gatmaitan

1960 Angel Sto. Tomas

1961 1. Reynato S. Puno
2. Leonardo Quisumbing

1962 1. Luis V. Teodoro, Jr.
2. Rene J. Navarro
3. Angelito Imperio

1963 1. Angelito Imperio
2. Ronaldo Zamora

1964 1. Tristan A. Catindig
2. Salvador T. Carlota

1965 1. Salvador T. Carlota
2. Wilfredo M. Chato
3. Enrique Voltaire Garcia II

1966 1. Enrique Voltaire Garcia II
2. Ancheta K. Tan
3. Agustin V. Que

1967 1. Agustin V. Que
2. Jaime J. Yambao
3. Temario C. Rivera

1968 1. Nelson A. Navarro
2. Miriam P. Defensor

1969 1. Jose Y. Arcellana
2. Victor H. Manarang

1970 1. Victor H. Manarang
2. Ernesto S. Tagamolila

1971 1. Antonio S. Tagamolila
2. Reynaldo B. Vea
3. Eduardo T. Gonzalez

1972 1. Teodoro Yabut, Jr.
2. Oscar Yabes

--oOo--

1974 Emmanuel F. Esguerra

1975 1. Diwa C. Guinigundo
2. Abraham P. Sarmiento, Jr.

1976 1. Gerardo Anigan
2. Cosme D. Rosell

1977 1. Cosme D. Rosell
2. Alexander J. Poblador

1978 1. Alexander J. Poblador
2. Gene R. Jacinto, Jr.
3. Diwata A. Reyes

1979 1. Diwata A. Reyes
2. Ma. Lourdes C. Managahas

1980 1. Ma. Lourdes C. Mangahas
2. Roberto Z. Coloma

1981-82 Roan I. Libarios

1982-83 Napoleon J. Poblador

1983-84 Raphael Perpetuo M. Lotilla

1984 Benjamin I. Pimentel, Jr.

1985 Noel Pangilinan

PHILIPPINENSIAN

1915 Victoriano Yamzon
1916 Nemesio Mendiola
1917 Nicolas Zafra

--oOo--

1926 Pedro G. Albano

--oOo--

1930 Roque B. Ablan
1931 Fernando Leaño
1932 Jose D. Ingles
1933 Elvira Guzman
1934 Juan de Borja
1935 Rodolfo Palma
1936 Benjamin Salvosa

--oOo--

1938 Delfin L. Gonzalez
1939 Priscila G. Santos
1940 Evangeline Favis
1941 Francisco S. Santos
1942-46 Vicente Coloso

1947 Aguedo F. Agbayani
1948 Angel C. Cruz
1949 Mateo A.T. Caparas
1950 Rolando Villaraza
1951 Cesar C. Pedro
1952 Elmer A. Ordoñez
1953 Francisco D. Villanueva
1954 Maximino V. Cariño, Jr.

1955 Francisco D. Rilloraza, Jr.
1956 Santiago F. Dumlao, Jr.
1957 Benjamin C. Santos
1958 Maximo Ramos, Jr.
1959 Miguel A. Enriquez, Jr.

1960 Pacifico Agabin
1961 Magdangal B. Elma
1962 Benjamin N. Muego
1963 Ricardo H. Diño
1964 Antonio A. Hidalgo

1965 Honesto G. Nuqui
1966 Temario C. Rivera
1967 Federico M. Macaranas

--oOo--

1970 Orlando B. Vea
1971 Bienvenido M. Noriega, Jr.

Editorial Note: The University Archives has no copies of the *Philippinensian* for the years 1918, 1919, 1921 up to 1925, 1927 to 1929, 1937, 1968 and 1969 and hence the names of their respective editors can not be verified. The 1920 volume has no specified editor. The *Philippinensian* ceased publication in 1972.

APPENDIX E

PRESIDENTS OF THE U.P. ALUMNI ASSOCIATION (1913-1985)

Victor Sevilla (MD'10)	1913-1915
Victoriano Yamzon (AB'11; LLB'15)	1915-1916
Manuel Vicente M. Arguelles (MD'14)	1917-1920
Antonio E. Cuyugan (LLB'15; LLM'23)	1920-1921
Conrado Benitez (LLB'16; LLD'72)	1921-1922
Jose A. Espiritu (LLB'13; LLD'71)	1923-1925
Paulino Gullas (AB'12; LLB'16)	1925-1926
Felipe Estela (LLB'15)	1926-1929
Vicente G. Sinco (LLB'21; LLM'25; LLD'69)	1929-1930
Vidal A. Tan (AB'13; LLD'69)	1930-1931
Jorge B. Vargas (AB'11; LLB'14; LLD'78)	1931-1946
Antonio R. Quirino (ROTC'30; LLB'32)	1946-1948
Pio P. Pedrosa (AA'23; BSC'25; MA'26)	1948-1949
Hermenegildo R. Reyes (BSCE'28)	1949-1951
Ferdinand E. Marcos (ROTC'37; LLB'39; LLD'66)	1951-1952
Hermenegildo R. Reyes (BSCE'28)	1952-1954
Jose M. Aldeguer (LLB'34)	1954-1956
Hadji Ahmad Domocao Alonto (Law'38)	1956-1958
Nicanor E. Yñiguez (LLB'39)	1958-1959
Hermenegildo R. Reyes (BSCE'28)	1959-1962
Gaudencio E. Antonino (BSCE'33)	1962-1964
Gerardo M. Roxas (LLB'49)	1964-1965
Pio P. Pedrosa (AA'23; BSC'25; MA'26)	1965-1967
Eduardo R. Escobar, Sr. (ROTC'28; BSCE'28)	1967-1973
Abraham F. Sarmiento (AA'47; LLB'49)	1973-1979
Estelito P. Mendoza (AA'48; ROTC'52; LLB'52)	1979-1984
Edgardo B. Espiritu (ROTC'56; LLB'58)	1985-

NOTES ON EDITORS/CONTRIBUTORS

OSCAR M. ALFONSO : B.S.F.S. *cum laude*, UP, 1949; M.A., UP, 1955; Ph.D., Univ. of Chicago, 1966; Professor of History, Executive Vice President of the University; author of *Theodore Roosevelt and the Philippines 1897-1909*, UP Press, 1970 & Oriole Editions, 1974; former Editor, *UP Gazette;* member: Phi Kappa Phi, Pi Gamma Mu, and Phi Alpha Theta.

LESLIE E. BAUZON : A.B., Silliman Univ., 1964; M.A., Stetson Univ., 1965; Ph.D., Duke Univ., 1971; Professor of History and Dean, Coll. of Social Sciences & Philosophy, UP; former President, Int. Assn. of Historians of Asia; Pres., Phil. National Historical Society; member: Phil. Social Science Council, Pi Gamma Mu.

NAPOLEON J. CASAMBRE : A.B., UP, 1953; M.A., Cornell Univ., 1957; Ph.D., Stanford Univ., 1968: Professor of History; former Asst. Dean for Graduate Studies, Coll. of Social Sciences & Philosophy; member: Phil. Historical Assn., American Studies Assn. of the Philippines, Phil. Fulbrighters Assn., and Pi Gamma Mu.

BERNARDITA REYES CHURCHILL : A.B. *magna cum laude*, UP, 1958; M.A., Cornell Univ., 1961; Ph.D., Austrialian National Univ., 1982; Assoc. Professor and Chairman, Dept. of History, UP; author of *The Philippine Independence Missions to the United States, 1919-1934;* member: Phil. Historical Assn., American Historical Assn., The Asia Society (Washington, DC), Phil. Assn. for the Advancement of Science.

ROSARIO MENDOZA CORTES : B.S.E., *cum laude*, UP, 1951; M.A., UP, 1956; Ph.D., UP, 1979; Assoc. Professor of History; author of *Pangasinan, 1572-1800,* UP Press, 1974; Fellowship Award, Inst. of Southeast Asian Studies, Gadjah Mada Univ., Yogyakarta, Indonesia, 1982; Pres., Phil. Historical Assn; member: Phi Kappa Phi and Pi Gamma Mu.

MILAGROS C. GUERRERO : A.B., 1960 and M.A., 1965, UP; Ph.D., Univ. of Michigan, 1977; Professor of History; co-author *of History of the Filipino People*, 1969; fellowships from Rockefeller Foundation, Am. Assn. of Univ. Women, Newberry Library, Australian National Univ., Fulbright, and Levi Barbour; member: Phil. Historical Assn., Nat. Research Council, and Phil. Studies Assn.

SILVINO V. EPISTOLA : A.B., UP, 1952; M.A., 1965 and Ph.D., 1971, Harvard Univ.; Professor of History & East Asian Civilizations, Asian Center, UP; member: UP Writers' Club, Writers' Union of the Philippines.

JOSE N. ENDRIGA : A.B. *cum laude*, UP, 1958; M.A., Univ. of Wisconsin, 1969; M.P.A., Cornell Univ., 1974; Professor of Public Administration, UP; former Dean, School of Development Management, UP Visayas; prize-winning author of *Stability and Change: A History of the Civil Service in the Philippines;* former Consultant & Lecturer, UN Asian and Pacific Development Inst.; member: Phi Kappa Phi, Pi Gamma Mu and Phi Alpha Theta.

OSCAR L. EVANGELISTA : A.B., UP, 1956; M.A., Cairo Univ., 1963; M.A., Univ. of Wisconsin, 1967; Professor of History; Dean of Students, UP, 1978-1981; Ford Foundation Fellow and Visiting Lecturer, Gadjah Mada Univ., 1975; Vice Pres., Phil. Historical Assn.; member: Pi Gamma Mu, Phi Alpha Theta and American Studies Assn. of the Philippines.

RAUL R. INGLES : A.B. *cum laude*, 1952 and M.P.A., 1956, UP; CPSPA, Carleton Univ., Ottawa, Canada, 1960; Professor of Journalism, UP; former Acting Secretary of the University, Board Chairman of UP Press, and UP Writer-in-Residence; Daily Columnist, *Manila Times*, 1956-1972; author of *The Provincial Press in the Philippines*, AMIC, Singapore, 1981; Governor, Pi Gamma Mu; member, Phi Kappa Phi.

GUILLERMO R. LAZARO : Ll.B., Far Eastern Univ.; B.S.E., M.A., Univ. of the Philippines, Ph.D., Ohio State Univ.; Professor of Education; former Acting Dean, UP Coll. Clark Air Base; co-author of *World History*, Phoenix-Alemars, 1974; member: Phil. Historical Assn., Phil. Geographical Society, Phi Delta Kappa, Pi Gamma Mu, Free and Accepted Masons.

BONIFACIO S. SALAMANCA : A.B., UP, 1951; M.A., 1956 and Ph.D., 1965, Yale Univ.; Professor of History; former Dean, UP College Manila; author of *The Filipino Reaction to American Rule, 1901-1913*, Hamden, Conn., 1968 & New Day Publishers, 1984; member: Phil. Historical Assn., Am. Studies Assn. of the Phil., Pi Gamma Mu.

DONATA V. TAYLO : B.S.E., 1951 and M.A., 1955, UP; Professor and former Chairman, Dept. of History, UP; wrote "The Teaching of History—Problems and Prospects" for the *Historical Bulletin*, XXVI, 1982; member: Phil. Historical Assn., Phi Kappa Phi, Pi Gamma Mu, National Research Council, Phil. History Foundation Inc.

Index

— D —

— V —